CORPORATE SOCIAL RESPONSIBILITY

Theory and Practice with Case Studies

CORPORATE SOCIAL RESPONSIBILITY

Theory and Practice with Case Studies

Editors

RENU JATANA
Associate Professor,
Department of Banking and Business Economics,
University College of Commerce and Management Studies,
Mohan Lal Sukhadia University, Udaipur

DAVID CROWTHER
Professor,
De Montford University, UK

Foreword by

PROFESSOR B.L. CHAUDHARY
Vice-Chancellor,
Mohan Lal Sukhadia University, Udaipur (Rajasthan)

DEEP & DEEP PUBLICATIONS PVT. LTD.
F-159, Rajouri Garden, New Delhi - 110 027

CORPORATE SOCIAL RESPONSIBILITY
Theory and Practice with Case Studies

ISBN 978-81-8450-031-8

Typeset by VERONICA GRAFIC ARTS,
VP-216A, Pitampura, Maurya Enclave, Delhi-110088.

Printed in India at MAYUR ENTERPRISES,
WZ Plot No. 3, Gujjar Market, Tihar Village, New Delhi-110018.

Published by DEEP & DEEP PUBLICATIONS PVT. LTD.
F-159, Rajouri Garden, New Delhi-110027.
Phones: 25435369, 25440916

E-mails: ddpbooks@yahoo.co.in • deep98@del3.vsnl.net.in
Showroom:

2/13, Ansari Road, Daryaganj, New Delhi-110002 • Telefax: 23245122

Contents

Foreword

"Corporate Social Responsibility – Theory and Practice with Case Studies" is a topic which is considered to be highly relevant in the emerging business scenario.

By the end of 20th century, business enterprises grew to mega size, amassed wealth and had become centres of power. They influenced even the political system and governments in a big way. Their meddling in political affair and undue influence on society invited large protest from several pressure groups for being too large, too big, too powerful and being anti-social. This fierce attack compelled business executives and owners to realize that they cannot remain indifferent to society. They owe some responsibility towards society. It was felt that apart from profit, enterprises should also lean towards social causes. In Europe, steel giant Andrew Carnegie initiated the move by donating most of his wealth for education, charitable social causes. Another leading industrialist Henry Ford an auto giant, formulated health and recreation programmes for his employees. This set the momentum and business leaders started coming out of the shell of profit to move closer to social causes.

Besides that, here, I also want to emphasise about the companies who believe in corporate social responsibility in India. Although, a very big list is there: Most prominent names in Indian CSR map are Tata Sons (who operates six trusts distributing approximately Rs. 120 crores), Birla Group, Bajaj Group, etc. Lupin Human Welfare and Research Foundation (LHWRF), is an NGO run by Lupin Pharmaceuticals. LHWRF has put up 125 schools, provided drinking water facilities in 80 villages and helped 25,000 people living below the poverty line. Canara Bank's CSR projects fall mostly within the ambit of community development. Its main thrust is on giving vocational skills to unemployed computerized programmes to address the adult literacy problem in India. Sun Micro-systems has established a non-profit charitable organization to provide moral and financial support to the Gujarat earthquake victims.

Women empowerment is one of the key areas of the CSR policies of many advanced companies. Indian Tobacco Company (ITC) has a written policy on CSR, it spent Rs. 18 crores recently on various projects including those for women empowerment and education. Bharat Petroleum Corporation Limited (BPCL) believes that in womanhood are encompassed nature's best quality compassion, humanity and love; they are blessed with the capacity for a deep commitment to preserving and nourishing not only their own offspring, but the entire planet.

It is common consensus that business enterprise must make such policies, involve such technology and take such decision, which do not adversely affect society. Society expects enterprises to be more responsible. CSR is a global expectation that requires a comprehensive strategic response from business enterprises.

This book aims to provide high quality research work on all aspects of Corporate Social Responsibility including business ethics, corporate governance, accountability, globalisation, responsible marketing and social reporting. This book is inter-disciplinary in nature, and global in application and may prove an essential document for everyone with an interest in this area.

In nutshell, Corporate Social Responsibility (CSR) is the new buzzword in the modern age and, today, almost all big companies have specific guidelines on CSR. The business houses are consciously engaged in efforts to give something back to society.

This is of course deliberate and part of editors wish to show the diversity of concerns on CSR which fall within one umbrella. It is equally part of the objective of the book to show that a concern with CSR is a worldwide issue which is being addressed by scholars of many countries. The aim is to present a spectrum of approaches from a variety of scholars from different countries and from different disciplines in order to show the diversity of the debate and the diversity of the contributors.

I wish to congratulate the editors Dr. Renu Jatana and Prof. David Crowther, De Montford University, UK, with their efforts and sincere dedication, the issue of CSR has been discussed by various scholars, and compiled in the present shape. I hope, the book will be helpful for academicians, policy-makers, business houses and research scholars.

B.L. CHAUDHARY
Vice-Chancellor
Mohan Lal Sukhadia University
Udaipur (Rajasthan)

Editorial

A growing number of writers over the last quarter of a century have recognised that the activities of an organisation impact upon the external environment and have suggested that such an organisation should therefore be accountable to a wider audience than simply its shareholders. Such a suggestion probably first arose in the 1970s and a concern with a wider view of company performance is taken by some writers who evince concern with the social performance of a business, as a member of society at large. This concern was stated by Ackerman (1975) who argued that big business was recognising the need to adapt to a new social climate of community accountability, but that the orientation of business to financial results was inhibiting social responsiveness. McDonald and Puxty (1979) on the other hand maintain that companies are no longer the instruments of shareholders alone but exist within society and so therefore have responsibilities to that society, and that there is therefore a shift towards the greater accountability of companies to all participants.

Recognition of the rights of all stakeholders and the duty of a business to be accountable in this wider context therefore has been largely a relatively recent phenomenon. The economic view of accountability only to owners has only recently however been subject to debate to any considerable extent. Some owners of businesses have however always recognised a responsibility to other stakeholders and this is evident from the early days of the Industrial Revolution. Implicit in this concern with the effects of the actions of an organisation on its external environment is the recognition that it is not just the owners of the organisation who have a concern with the activities of that organisation. Additionally there are a wide variety of other stakeholders who justifiably have a concern with those activities, and are affected by those activities. Those other stakeholders have not just an interest in the activities of the firm but also a degree of influence over the shaping of those activities. This influence is so significant that it can be argued that the power and influence of these stakeholders is such that it amounts to quasi-ownership of the organisation. Indeed Gray, Owen and Maunders (1987) challenge the traditional role of accounting in reporting results and consider that, rather than an ownership approach to accountability, a stakeholder approach, recognising the wide stakeholder community, is needed.

It is readily apparent that any actions which an organisation undertakes will have an effect not just upon itself but also upon the external environment within which that organisation resides. In considering the effect of the organisation upon its external environment it must be recognised that this environment includes both the business environment in which the firm is operating, the local societal environment in which the organisation is located and the wider global environment. This effect of the organisation can take many forms, such as:

- the utilisation of natural resources as a part of its production processes,
- the effects of competition between itself and other organisations in the same market,
- the enrichment of a local community through the creation of employment opportunities,
- transformation of the landscape due to raw material extraction or waste product storage, and
- the distribution of wealth created within the firm to the owners of that firm (via dividends) and the workers of that firm (through wages) and the effect of this upon the welfare of individuals.

It can be seen therefore from these examples that an organisation can have a very significant effect upon its external environment and can actually change that environment through its activities. It can also be seen that these different effects can in some circumstances be viewed as beneficial and in other circumstances be viewed as detrimental to the environment. Indeed the same actions can be viewed as beneficial by some people and detrimental by others.

Accounting and accountability however traditionally remain focused upon the actions of the organisation and ignores the effects of the organisation upon its external environment. A growing number of writers however have recognised that the activities of an organisation impact upon the external environment and have suggested that one of the roles of accounting should be to report upon the impact of an organisation in this respect. Such a suggestion first arose in the 1970's and a concern with a wider view of company performance is taken by some writers who evince concern with the social performance of a business, as a member of society at large.

Indeed the desirability of considering the social performance of a business has not always however been accepted and has been the subject of extensive debate. Thus Hetherington (1973: 37) states

> "There is no reason to think that shareholders are willing to tolerate an amount of corporate non-profit activity which appreciably reduces either dividends or the market performance of the stock."

Conversely, writing at a similar time, Dahl (1972: 18) states

> "... every large corporation should be thought of as a social enterprise; that is an entity whose existence and decisions can be justified insofar as they serve public or social purposes."

SOCIAL RESPONSIBILITY

Social responsibility has implications not just for us as individuals but also as members of communities and society at large. Sadly this is often more apparent by its absence than by anything else. Education is one way to bring about change and this is central to the purpose of the university, and the principal reason for my involvement. Another potential way to bring about change however is through an engagement in scholarly debate, involving as many people as possible from as many different backgrounds as possible. Consequently the Social Responsibilioty Research Network (SRRNet) has been formed, comprising scholars concerned about these issues from every part of the world. As well as publishing a journal and running a website, this organisation has focused upon organising conferences in different parts of the world. The conference held in Udaipur was the third conference in the series and these papers are amongst those which were presented at this conference. They represent a diverse set of contributions – one of the features of the SRRNet activities – from people from various parts of the world who joined together for a few days to discuss issues of common importance.

We would like to place on record our gratitude to Prof. B.L. Chaudhary for the foreword note, inspiration, valuable advices and blessings. We thank all the contributors without whose cooperation this volume would not have been published. Last, but not the least we thank Shri G.S. Bhatia, Managing Director, Deep & Deep Publications Pvt. Ltd., New Delhi for his cooperation for publication of the book within stipulated time frame.

EDITORS

List of Contributors

Amita Nadkarni: Rural Management Division, St. Joseph's College of Business Administration, Bangalore, India.

Ana Maria Davila Gomez: University of Quebec, Canada.

Ananya S. Guha: Regional Director, Indira Gandhi National Open University, Shilong, India.

Anju Sondarva: Assistant Professor, Department of Commerce, Saurashtra University, Rajkot.

Anju Verma: Department of Business Economics, Guru Jambheshwar University, India.

Ashok Nagar: Asst. Professor, Department of Banking and Business Economics, Mohan Lal Sukhadia University, Udaipur, Rajasthan.

Babitha Vishwanath: Senior Research Fellow, Power Management Institute, NTPC, Noida, India.

Ben Tran: Alliant International University, USA.

Carla Pasa Gómez: UNIVATES Centro Universitário and Federal University of Santa Catarina, Brazil.

Champaben N. Jagani: J.J. Kundalia Commerce College, Rajkot.

Chandra Sekhar Gotlagunta: Department of Management Studies, JB Institute of P.G. Courses, India.

Cindy Davids: Department of Accounting and Finance, Macquarie University, Australia.

Daleen van der Nest: University of Pretoria, South Africa.

David Crowther: De Montford University, UK.

Deepti: Research Scholar, Department of Business Management, Guru Jambheshwar University, India.

D.S. Chundawat: Director, MHRM, Mohan Lal Sukhadia University, Udaipur.

Fabrice Mauleon: Ecole Superieur de Commerce et Management, Tours-Poitiers, France.

Fátima David: Instituto Politécnico da Guarda, Portugal.

Fernanda Duarte: University of Western Sydney, Australia.

Garritt Van Dyk: Independent Scholar, Sydney.

Gillian McAllister: University of Western Sydney, Australia.

Gordon Boyce: Department of Accounting and Finance, Macquarie University, Australia.

Gregório Jean V Rados: UNIVATES Centro Universitário and Federal University of Santa Catarina, Brazil.

Harsha Gohel: Assistant Professor, Department of Commerce, Saurashtra University, Rajkot.

Harshita Shrimali: Assistant Professor, Pacific College.

Helena Mitewa: School of Accounting and Finance, University of Tasmania, Australia.

Jennifer Milam: Department of Art History and Theory, The University of Sydney, Australia.

John Gray: University of Western Sydney, Australia.

Jonathan Murphy: Cambridge University, UK.

J. Solomon Prabhakar: The Hindu, Chennai, India.

Jyotsna Diwan Mehta: Assistant Professor, Subodh Institute of Management and Career Studies, Jaipur.

Kailash Sodani: Faculty of Commerce, University College of Commerce and Management Studies, Mohanlal Sukhadia University, Udaipur, Rajasthan (India).

Kaneez Fatima Sadriwala: Assistant Professor, Pacific College, Udaipur.

Kartik Dave: Assistant Professor, Birla Institute of Management Technology (BIMTECH), Greater Noida (NCR).

Kiymet Tunca Caliyurt: Trakya University, Turkey.

K. Koteswara Rao: Dean, Faculty of Commerce, Dr. B.R. Ambedkar Open University, India.

K. Uday Gowri Shankar: Research Scholar, Department of Management, Sri Venkateshwara University, Tirupathi.

Leonardo Gómez: UNIVATES Centro Universitário and Federal University of Santa Catarina, Brazil.

Mac Wright: School of Accounting and Finance, Victoria University of Technology, Australia.

Mahabir Narwal: Department of Commerce, Kurukshetra University, India.

Man Chand Khandela: Director, Subodh Institute of Management and Career Studies, Jaipur.

Mary M. McKinley: Ecole Superieur de Commerce et Management, Tours-Poitiers, France.

M.C. Garg: Department of Commerce, Ch. Devi Lal University, India.

Miriam Green: London Metropolitan University.

M. Manuneethi Cholan: Deputy Director (Inspection), Department of Company Affairs, Ministry of Finance, Government of India.

M.M. Goel: Faculty of Social Sciences, Kurukshetra University, India.

Nidhi Mathur: School of Studies in Statistics, Vikram University, India.

P.N. Sankaran: St. Joseph's College of Business Administration, Bangalore, India.

Renu Jatana: Faculty of Commerce, University College of Commerce and Management Studies, Mohan Lal Sukhadia University, Udaipur, Rajasthan, India.

R. Seminur Topal: Department of Bioengineering, Yildiz Technical University, Turkey.

Rute Abreu: Instituto Politécnico da Guarda, Portugal.

R. Varadarajan: Professor of Commerce, Directorate of Distance Education, Madurai Kamraj University, Madurai, India.

Shweta Rameja: Research Scholar, Department of Banking and Business Economics, Mohan Lal Sukhadia University, Udaipur, Rajasthan.

S.L. Jayanthi: Software Engineer, Shar Technologies Pvt. Limited, Chennai, India.

Stella Vettori: University of Pretoria, South Africa.

Sunil Mehta: Asstt. Prof., Faculty of Commerce and Management Studies, J.N.V. University, Jodhpur.

Tejinder Sharma: Department of Commerce, Kurukshetra University, India.

Ugur S. Alp: Department of Bioengineering, Yildiz Technical University, Turkey.

V. Balachandran: Reader in Corporate Secretaryship, Alagappa University, Karaikudi.

V. Balu: Reader in Commerce, D.B. Jain College, Chennai, India.

V. Chandrasekaran: Research Associate, Sr. Executive, *The Hindu*, Chennai.

Vijay Shrimali: Head, Department of Business Administration, CCMS.

V.K. Anish: Accenture, India.

Wim Vandekerchove: Ghent University, Belgium.

1

Social Responsibility: An Introduction

DAVID CROWTHER AND RENU JATANA

INTRODUCTION

A growing number of writers over the last quarter of a century have recognised that the activities of an organisation impact upon the external environment and have suggested that such an organisation should therefore be accountable to a wider audience than simply its shareholders. Such a suggestion probably first arose in the 1970s and a concern with a wider view of company performance is taken by some writers who evince concern with the social performance of a business, as a member of society at large. This concern was stated by Ackerman (1975) who argued that big business was recognising the need to adapt to a new social climate of community accountability, but that the orientation of business to financial results was inhibiting social responsiveness. McDonald and Puxty (1979) on the other hand maintain that companies are no longer the instruments of shareholders alone but exist within society and so therefore have responsibilities to that society, and that there is therefore a shift towards the greater accountability of companies to all participants.

Recognition of the rights of all stakeholders and the duty of a business to be accountable in this wider context therefore has been largely a relatively recent phenomenon.[1] The economic view of accountability only to owners has only recently however been subject to debate to any considerable extent. Some owners of businesses have however always recognised a responsibility to other stakeholders and this is evident from the early days of the Industrial Revolution. Thus, for example, in the nineteenth century Robert Owen (1816, 1991) demonstrated dissatisfaction with the assumption that only cost minimisation and the consequent profit maximisation was the only thing of concern to a business. Furthermore he put his beliefs into practice through the inclusion within his sphere of industrial operations the provision of model housing for his workers at New Lanark, Scotland. Further examples of socially responsible behaviour have continued to exist since these days. Thus there is evidence from throughout the history of modernity that the self-centred approach of accounting for organisational activity only to shareholders was not universally acceptable and was unable to satisfactorily provide a basis for human activity.

Implicit in this concern with the efforts of the actions of an organisation on its external environment is the recognition that is not just the owners of the organisation who have a concern with the activities of that organisation. Additionally, there are a wide variety of other stakeholders who justifiably have a concern with those activities, and are affected by those activities. Those other stakeholders have not just an interest in the activities of the firm but also a degree of influence over the shaping of these activities. This influence is so significant that it can be argued that the power and influence of these stakeholders is such that it amounts to quasi-ownership of the organisation. Indeed Gray, Owen and Maunders (1987) challenge the traditional role of accounting in reporting results and consider that, rather than an ownership approach to accountability, a stakeholder approach, recognising the wide stakeholder community, is needed.

It is readily apparent that any actions which an organisation undertakes will have an effect not just upon itself but also upon the external environment within which that organisation resides. In considering the effect of the organisation upon its external environment it must be recognised that this environment includes both the business environment in which the firm is operating, the local societal environment in which the organisation is located and the wider global environment. This effect of the organisation can take many forms, such as:

- the utilisation of natural resources as a part of its production processes,

- the effects of competition between itself and other organisations in the same market,
- the enrichment of a local community through the creation of employment opportunities,
- transformation of the landscape due to raw material extraction or waste product storage, and
- the distribution of wealth created within the firm to the owners of that firm (via dividends) and the workers of that firm (through wages) and the effect of this upon the welfare of individuals.

It can be seen therefore from these examples that an organisation can have a very significant effect upon its external environment and can actually change that environment through its activities. It can also be seen that these different effects can in some circumstances be viewed as beneficial and in other circumstances be viewed as detrimental to the environment. Indeed the same actions can be viewed as beneficial by some people and detrimental by others.

Accounting and accountability however traditionally remain focused upon the actions of the organisation and ignores the efforts of the organisation upon its external environment. A growing number of writers however have recognised that the activities of an organisation impact upon the external environment and have suggested that one of the roles of accounting should be to report upon the impact of an organisation in this respect. Such a suggestion first arose in the 1970's and a concern with a wider view of company performance is taken by some writers who evince concern with the social performance of a business, as a member of society at large.

Indeed the desirability of considering the social performance of a business has not always however been accepted and has been the subject of extensive debate. Thus Hetherington (1973: 37) states:

> "There is no reason to think that shareholders are willing to tolerate an amount of corporate non-profit activity which appreciably reduces either dividends or the market performance of the stock."

Conversely, writing at a similar time, Dahl (1972: 18) states:

"... every large corporation should be thought of as a social enterprise; that is an entity whose existence and decisions can be justified insofar as they serve public or social purposes."

SOCIAL RESPONSIBILITY

Social responsibility has implications not just for us as individuals but also as members of communities and society at large. Sadly this is often more apparent by its absence than by anything else. Education is one way to bring about change and this is central to the purpose of the university, and the principal reason for my involvement. Another potential way to bring about change however is through an engagement in scholarly debate, involving as many people as possible from as many different backgrounds as possible. Consequently the Social Responsibility Research Network (SRRNet) has been formed comprising scholars concerned about these issues from every part of the world. As well as publishing the journal[2] and running the website,[3] this organisation has focused upon organising conferences in different parts of the world.[4] The conference held in Udaipur was the third conference in the series and these papers are amongst those which were presented at this conference. They represent a diverse set of contributions – one of the features of the SRRNet activities – from people from various parts of the world. Who joined together for a few days to discuss issues of common importance.

NOTES AND REFERENCES

1. Mathews (1997): Traces its origins to the 1970s although arguments (see Crowther, 2002) show that such concerns can be traced back to the Industrial Revolution.
2. *Social Responsibility Journal*.
3. www.socialresponsibility.biz.
4. See www.davidacrowther.com/csrhome.html for details of past and future conference.

REFERENCES

Ackerman, R.W. (1975): *The Social Challenge to Business*; Cambridge, Ma., Harvard University Press.

Crowther, D. (2002): *A Social Critique of Corporate Reporting*, Aldershot, Ashgate.

Dahl, R.A. (1972): A Prelude to Corporate Reform, *Business and Society Review*, Spring 1972, 17-23.

Gray, R.; Owen, D. and Maunders, K. (1987): *Corporate Social Reporting: Accounting and Accountapility*; London: Prentice-Hall.

Hetherington, J.A.C. (1973): *Corporate Social Responsibility Audit: A Management Tool for Survival*, London, The Foundation for Business Responsibilities.

Mathews, M.R. (1997): "Twenty-five Years of Social and Environmental Accounting Research: Is there a Silver Jubilee to Celebrate?," *Accounting, Auditing and Accountability Journal*, Vol. 10, No. 4, pp. 481-531.

McDonald, D. and Puxty, A.G. (1979): An Inducement—Contribution Approach to Corporate Financial Reponing; *Accounting, Organisations and Society*, 4 (1/2), 53-65.

Owen, R., 1991, *A New View of Society and Other Writings*, London, Penguin.

2

Social and Ethical Responsibility: Conflicts of Interests in Professional Accounting

CINDY DAVIDS AND GORDON BOYCE

Persons who occupy positions of power or authority often find themselves in conflict of interest situations, where official duties and private interests overlap, but do not coincide. If private interests are pursued in such circumstances, this may be at the expense of the dereliction of official duties, and a failure to heed the interests of the constituency whom officials ostensibly serve.

In accountancy, conflicts of interest may be manifested in various ways. This paper focuses on conflicts of interest in relation to the accounting profession, considering problems in that arise in relation to conflicts of interest between three sets of interests: (i) various dimensions of the private interests of accounting firms and their partners and members; (ii) the private interests of the corporations for whom accountants work (and their various constituents, including managers); and (iii) a wider group of interests, including those of the society whom accountants and auditors, as professionals, profess to serve.

A fundamental clash that is brought to attention by the particular notion of conflict of interest is between narrow sectional or private interests and the wider social responsibilities of both accounting professionals and corporate players. This paper seeks to develop a clear understanding of the nature and dimensions of the problem of conflict of interest in relation to the professional practice of accountancy. The fundamental clash between wider social responsibilities and the private interest of key players in both realms, typified by conflicts of interest, is a key dimension of the current crises of ethics in business and accounting.

INTRODUCTION: THE PROBLEM OF CONFLICT OF INTEREST

The problem of conflict of interest is fundamental for the accounting profession because the discretionary element of accounting work means that there are many opportunities for accountants to neglect professional duties in the pursuit of a range of private interests. In relation to public ethics, the neglect of the public interest in the pursuit of private interests is the fundamental problematic of conflict of interest (Davids, 2005). Partly in response to contemporary ethical scandals in accounting and a decline in public confidence in professional accounting recent work has recognised the particular importance of the problem of conflict of interest. For example:

Any conflicts between the public interest and self-interest, loyalty to the entity and its governing-body, may result in ethical dilemmas and possibly lapses. A choice has to be made. The choice may have very far-reaching consequences (Dellaportas *et al.*, 2005: 13).

Despite recognition of the significance of the problem of conflict of interest in a general sense, beyond the rhetorical level the problem remains largely unaddressed. The potential clash between a range of private interests and the public interest that accountancy ostensibly aspires to serve is rarely analysed.

The concept of conflict of interest is used in this paper to examine a range of issues associated with accounting ethics. A conflict of interest arises when any person is in a situation where official duties and their private interests do not coincide. The problem of conflict of interest gives rise to significant ethical problems for persons who occupy positions in public and professional life because such positions may be (mis)used for private or personal gain (including for the benefit of family, friends, or associates). The pursuit of private interests may involve dereliction of official duty and of the interests of the constituency whom an official ostensibly serves. Conflicts of interest therefore create particular problems for both private and public sector ethics. Public perceptions of the probity of persons in official positions also present matters for particular attention. Conflicts of interest may exist whether or not the person acts on their own interests at the expense of their duties, whether or not they are aware of the conflict, or whether they perceive there to be a conflict.

Conflicts of interest may emerge in a number of professional or occupational arenas. In the political domain that a number of prominent conflict of interest concerns have emerged over the last decade, relating to government ministers and ex-ministers in Australia (Davids, 2005, 1998; Martin, 2002; Integrity Commissioner, 2002), the United Kingdom (Nolan *et al.*, 1995; Nolan 1996), and North America (Stark, 1996, 2000; Kernaghan and Langford, 1990). In the United States of America, conflict of interest concerns in political life and the public sector generally have generated a burgeoning literature on public sector ethics (see Bowles and McCanney, 1996). In the United Kingdom, the Committee on Standards in Public Life recognised that a series of well-publicised cases of misconduct by various public officials had led to conflict of interest becoming a major issue in damaging public perceptions of integrity in Britain and other Western countries. Conflicts of interest were found to contribute to an erosion of the "principles and values of public life," bringing public institution into disrepute (Nolan, 1996).

Whilst it is in the political domain that conflict of interest has often received most attention, increasing attention is being paid to problems arising from conflicts of interest in business and the accounting profession. In accounting and the corporate world more generally, conflicts of interest have been prominent in recent scandals involving Enron, WorldCom, Parmalat, OneTel, HIH, and a range of other prominent companies in Australia, the United States of America, and Europe. The problems inherent in these recent scandals bear striking similarity to a range of seemingly perennial corporate scandals — indeed, such problems have been a part of the corporate world since the corporate form itself came into being (see Sykes, 1998; 1996; Clarke *et al.*, 2003; Main, 2003; CCH Australia, 2001). Corporate and accounting scandals have combined with heightened public awareness of the problem of conflict of interest in the political realm to mean that members of the public are likely to be more sensitised to problems of conflict of interest in accounting. Thus the problem of conflict of interest raises important questions of for the legitimacy of the profession insofar as integrity and public trust that flows from it are central to that legitimacy (Mintz, 1995; Rezaee, 2004; see also Citron 2003; Preston *et al.*, 1995). Integrity and the trust may be regarded as the key values under threat from conflicts of interest across a wide array of settings (Werhane and Doering, 1992; Siemensma, 2000).

This paper analyses various dimensions of the problem of conflict of interest in relation to professional accounting. The major aims of the paper are reflected in the section which follow. First, an examination of the literature on conflict of interest is undertaken in order to clearly define the problem particularly in relation to the practice of professional accountancy. Whilst there is little specific literature relating to conflict of interest in professional accounting, the paper draws on literature from other public sector and professional domains, including medicine, the law policing business and politics. An important aim is to move beyond broad general characterisations of conflict of interest in order to develop a deeper understanding of the problem as it relates to professional accounting. The key component of conflict of interest namely conflict and interest, are examined and their various dimensions are considered.

The second major aim of the paper is to develop an outline of the various types of conflict of interest that may be manifested in professional accounting. Several types of conflict of interest are outlined and applied to the domain of professional accounting. The paper's third main section considers the public interest in relation to the problem of conflict of interest in accountancy. It is argued that the public interest is a neglected dimension of much discussion of accounting ethics and that the concept of conflict of interest provides a useful analytical frame within which to consider the public role and functions of accountancy. It is also argued that the question of how accountancy does or may serve the public interest is often not directly addressed, on the basis of an implicit assumption that in serving a range of private interests, accountancy also serves the broader public interest. However, the public interest is sidelined and effectively trivialised in this process. The paper concludes with a discussion of the implications of the problem of conflict of interest in accountancy.

DEFINING THE PROBLEM OF CONFLICT OF INTEREST

A conflict of interest involves a clash between different domains of one's life. At its most basic, a conflict of interest involves two key elements, viz. (i) private interests *versus* (ii) official or public interest (which may translate as work or professional duty). However, at least three types of interests must be distinguished when discussing the problem: (1) the personal interests of an actor; (2) the interests of the actor's organisation; and (3) the interests of society or the public (Davids, 2005; see Macklin, 1983; Rodwin, 1993: 253-255). Conflict of interest is particularly problematic in relation to occupational or professional performance within a realm of discretion, because it is the scope offered by professional (or occupational or official) discretion that provides space for decisions and actions that further private interests. A conflict of interest can emerge in relation to any part of the private interests of an employee or official and the potential of such interests to affect the discharge of work, official, or public duties and responsibilities. This includes the general duty to perform official or professional functions in a disinterested manner (Davids, 2005).

Mere differences in interests between two parties are not sufficient to constitute a conflict of interest from a professional perspective. It is the capacity of a particular interest or particular kind of interest to conflict with the discharge of occupational or professional duty that gives rise to a conflict of interest (Carson, 1994). A conflict of interest is crystallised when a professional; employee or official must make a decision between private or personal benefit or gain, or public, organisational, or collegial gain or benefit.

The key aspect of conflict of interest that has received attention in accountancy is the (potential) clash between the private interests of accountancy practitioners (or their associates) and the interests of their clients or employers. In relation to the audit function, the failure of accountants to maintain sufficient independence from client companies (or the management of such companies) provides an additional dimension of conflict of interest insofar as this situation represents a conflict of interest between what may be deemed the coincident interests of auditors and clients (or client sections), on the one hand, and the public interest on the other hand, where the public interest requires auditor independence.

In relation to officials and professionals with an ostensible commitment to the public interest, the scope of professional duties and responsibilities encompasses both clearly enunciated and specific occupational or professional roles and other factors such as the public perception of and the level of public trust in, the organisation or profession as a whole. It is arguable that professionals should be guided by a stricter standard and preparedness to question the way in which their own behaviour may appear to the public. Thus public officials and professionals may be subject to a higher ethical test than the question of whether an individual has violated a particular law, instruction or rule. Justification for this higher standard of behaviour rests with the notion of public interest, because appearances of conflict of interest may generate negative public perceptions and undermine public confidence in professional areas such as accounting and the law. The handling of conflicts of interest, requiring the application of higher standards than would otherwise prevail, is important if a professional group is to gain (or retain) public respect (Davis, 1992: 189).

THE KEY COMPONENTS: CONFLICTS AND INTERESTS

Siemensma (2000) describes conflicts of interest as "blind spots" that arise from clashes between different aspects of the lives of individuals. These problems can emerge in a range of situations. The "conflict" in conflict of interest occurs in the mind of the individual, because a conflict of interest means that capacity for judgement is impaired, and it is the impaired or undermined judgement that may flow from a conflict (rather than a role conflict *per se*) that is problematic (Davis, 1982). "Interests" that may give rise to such conflicts can include a range of financial and non-financial interests, and may be directly personal or more indirect interests.

Conflicts

Conflicts arise when personal interests (broadly interpreted) do not coincide with an obligation to serve the interests of another (Boatright, 2000; Werhane and Doering, 1992). The element of obligation to another is important because it is the potential for breach of this obligation in the pursuit of personal interests that makes a conflict of interest problematic.

Whilst the conflict in conflict of interest can be thought of as occurring in the mind of the individual, it is no mere mental construct. A conflict "is a collision between competent judgement and something that might make that judgement unable to function as the ... role requires" (Davis, 1982: 19). The conflict is relative to judgement required within a particular role such that the role requires the exercise of competent judgement, and where there is a discretionary element in the judgement to be made (Davis, 1982: 22-25).

Although the conflict in conflict of interest takes place in the mind (affecting an official or professional's capacity for judgement), it is extremely difficult to peer into the mind in order to determine whether a person actually was affected by his or her own interests, or whether his or her judgement, decision-making, and actions remained impervious to those interests (Stark, 2000). This means that the focus of attention is usually on external manifestations of possible conflicts (that is, circumstances where such situations may arise, notwithstanding the actual state of mind of the individual). A conflict is therefore regarded to be present when there is the capacity for a private interest to affect the performance of official or professional duties (see Owen, 1997: 40-42; Stark, 2000: 22).

Interests

Interests are encumbrances on an official in the performance of official duties (Stark, 2000: 9). The term "interest" is shorthand for "any influence, loyalty, or other concern capable of compromising . . ." the performance of a duty specific to a role (Davis, 1982: 18). Whether or not the capacity of an interest to affect the performance of official or professional duties is actualised, the key element of conflict of interest that distinguishes it from other forms of official wrongdoing is in the capacity to have such effects (see Owen, 1997: 41).

Traditionally the types of interests included within the concept of conflict of interest were exclusively financial or pecuniary, but more recently a wider group of interests has come to be regarded as problematic insofar as they can arguably encumber an official's judgement every bit as much as financial interests (Owen, 1997: 41-42: Stark, 2000: Ch. 10; Preston *et al.*, 2002). The concept of interests therefore includes "various associational and partisan attachments and diverse other influences, loyalties, concerns, emotions, predispositions, prejudgements, even moral beliefs and aesthetic judgements" (Stark, 2002: 4-5). Under the expanded notion of interests, even the issue of pecuniary interests has come to be regarded as problematic under the broad rubric of ideological impairment or prejudice. That is, understanding of the problem of pecuniary interests has shifted such that they themselves are regarded as problematic because they may represent an underlying encumbrance on the performance of official duties in the same manner as a broader range of non-pecuniary interests. Concomitantly, the central concern with conflicts of interest has moved towards the broad issues of integrity, public confidence, and legitimacy (see Owen, 1997).

Encumbrances on an official may be internal or external. Internal (or direct) encumbrances act from within the person, being based in personal predispositions, preferences, belief, prejudgements, pecuniary interests, and the like. A desire to enhance one's professional or personal reputation could also give rise to a conflict of interest if this desire became so significant that it influenced an individual to neglect, official duty in pursuit of an action or outcome that might enhance personal reputation (see Werhane and Doering, 1992), External (or indirect) encumbrances are imposed or initiated by others who act on the person. These include familial, friendship, business, professional, and associational relationships, where the interests of the other person may have the capacity to affect the performance of official duties (see Carson, 1994; Macklin, 1983; Boatright, 2000: 144-145).

CONFLICTS OF INTEREST AND BREACHES OF PROFESSIONAL DUTY

It is important to distinguish between problematic situations (or potentially problematic situations) and problematic actions (breaches or neglects of duty) in relation to conflict of interest. A conflict of interest breach is a neglect of professional duty that occurs when a person (in the furtherance of private interests) takes an action or decision (or fails to do so) at variance with professional duties (Davids, 2005). It is important to make a distinction between conflicts of interest and associated breaches of professional duties because although the problem of conflict of interest is recognised to originate in anterior and subjective states of mind, prevention must tackle objective circumstances that may be perceived to give rise to conflicts. Conflict of interest breaches are recognised to represent ethical lapses, but dealing with the problem requires that conflicts of interest themselves be recognised as problematic, whether or not there are subsequent and associated breaches of professional duty. Continuing to act or to decisions in a situation in which one has a conflict of interest must itself therefore be regarded as an ethical lapse whether or not the conflict actually plays out of a determinate breach of professional duty (see Davids, 2005: Ch. 3).

Conflicts of interest may be latent or actual (Davis, 1982, drawing on the American Bar Association's Code of Professional Responsibility). An actual conflict of interest is one where present actions or decisions must be taken in a situation of conflicting interests. A latent conflict of interest is where there is no such present action or decision to be taken, but such actions or decisions are within the realm of present duties, thus, the problematic private interest has not yet come into actual conflict in terms of a specific action to be taken or a decision to be made, although the particular official responsibilities of the individual are such that there is a "reasonable probability" that such a conflict will arise in the normal course of those present duties. The mere existence of a conflict of interest (latent or otherwise), with or without an attendant breach of duty, is problematic whether or not the conflict does actually produce culpable conduct.

Clarification of the distinction between conflicts of interest and wrongful conduct that flows from such conflicts is important because it is possible that dealing with conflict of interest presents a way to eliminate the potential for (and therefore the actuality of) many associated neglects of duty. This is the key justification for regulating conflicts of interest.

RECOGNISED CONFLICTS OF INTEREST IN ACCOUNTING

Conflicts of interest are pervasive in accounting because practice is replete with areas in which there is potential for an accountant to serve private interests at the expense of another whose interests the accountant is ostensibly to serve. The "other" may be a client, employer, or the public in general. The private interests served may be those of the accountant, an associate of the accountant, organisation management, or, indeed, the private interests of the client. A review of the wider literature on conflict of interest reveals a number of different manifestations of the problem which are discussed in this section as they relate to the domain of accountancy.

Outside/Secondary Employment (or Moonlighting) and Post-Employment

It goes without saying that there are a range of possible problems in relation to the performance of secondary employment in addition to the professional's principal accountancy work (whether with another employer or in private business) which may clash with the performance of professional duties. This may happen in several ways, particularly if the secondary employer (or business) is in competition with primary clients or the principal employer. Other problems arise if one's work performance is. This section draws principally on the analyses of Davids (2005), Stark (2000) and Kernaghan and Langford (1990). The discussion here is not designed to encompass all possible conflicts of interest in relation to accountancy, but rather to present a selection of affected, if client employer resources (including time and confidential information) are used in the furtherance of outside employment, or if the professional uses his or her official position to solicit private business (see Kernaghan and Langford, 1990: 147).

Post-employment involves a person, upon ceasing official employment, taking up employment with a private party with whom official dealings had been held, or whose private interests the official had the capacity to influence whilst employed in the prior position. Post-employment has been shown to be problematic in accounting when senior partners of auditing firms take corporate board positions following their retirement from audit. The key conflict of interest in such circumstances relates to the possibility that the professional has used his or her professional position to cultivate these future board membership prospects and that in so doing the professional may have favoured their interests of the client company. The essential problem here is one of independence, in that the prospect of a future seat on a company board impairs an auditor's ability to discharge his or her duty in an independent manner. This is a quintessential conflict of interest situation. Conflicts of interest may continue if a former auditor takes improper advantage of his or her previous position, such as through the use of confidential information or seeking or gaining preferential treatment from former colleagues (Kernaghan and Langford, 1990: 149-151).

The proliferation of management consulting and management advisory services, as large accountancy practices attempt to exploit all available economic opportunities provides a case in point (see Perera *et al.*, 2003; Hendrickson, 1998; Citron, 2003; Solomon and Solomon, 2004: 139-143). The key problematic that emerges is that such activity is extraneous to principal professional activities in auditing, in particular, and may thus, be regarded as a form of secondary employment. The private (economic) interests that are entailed in such activity are likely to seriously compromise the independence — in both fact and appearance — of the auditor.

Just as conflicts in conflict of interest occur in the mind, independence, too, is a state of mind. It is not possibly analytically to assess such states objectively, and thus, problems of independence are often left to the individual to decide (to relation to their own state of mind). This presents two set of associated problems. Firstly, problems associated with perspective an individual is likely to find it difficult to perceive a problem of independence from their own perspective since individuals are unable or unlikely to step outside themselves to make such judgements. This links to a second set of problems of perceptions. Even if an individual was able to make objective judgements as to their own independence, this would not necessarily translate to the perceptions or others who implicitly or explicitly rely on the independence of the professional. By focusing on conflict of interest in the manner outlined is the previous section, in the case of secondary employment and post-employment, the direct financial interests entailed give rise to clear issues of conflict insofar as they represent encumbrances on the state of mind of the auditor (evident notwithstanding the issue of appearances). The conflict is present whether or not an individual's actual independence — as a state of mind — in relation to the conduct of official duties is affected. Therefore, the conflicts of interest entailed in such relationships are problematic in and of themselves.

Political and Associational Involvement

Political involvement may have a negative impact on the impartiality, or appearance of impartiality, of a professional in the performance of official duties. This can give rise to a conflict of interest because a person may use the implicit power of their professional position to further or advance participation in political activities or political interests. This problem may particularly relate to professional accountants in situations in which active political involvement, either individually or on the part of professional bodies, is common.

In relation to individual practitioners and at the level of the profession as a whole this problem is likely to become more evident as the political visibility of the accounting profession grows and professional bodies become more active politically. Professional accounting bodies are a key player with vested interests in many political issues, including areas of legal regulation and taxation. Professional intervention in the political sphere in relation to such issues may bring its own attendant problems of conflict of interest insofar as the profession's political involvement is designed to further its own interests rather than other interests that the profession ostensibly serves. As the accounting profession seeks to further its own interests and those of its clients via political lobbying and political donations, it also furthers particular political agendas (Dwyer and Roberts, 2004; Arnold, 2005). The role of accounting is thus, a partisan one, which may be used to support particular private interests, meaning that the problem of conflict of interest in relation to the public interest commitments of the profession is likely to become more significant as such political involvements grow.

Private Gain from an Official Position

A conflict of interest is likely to be involved in situations where a professional draws on the prestige of his or her position to reap private gain (which may, for example, be in the form of board membership, fee-for-service transactions or expenses-paid trips). Even though the professional may not become beholden to the external party, and may not be in a position to advance the specific interests of the external party, the conflict of interest centres on the use of an official or professional position to gain a private benefit (Stark, 2000). The private use of the prestige of a professional position presents a conflict of interest us it may be inconsistent with the interests that the professional ostensibly serves. There may also be a subsequent influence on performance of official duty, particularly insofar as that duty involves interaction with interests relative to the original source of the private gain.

Acceptance of Benefits and Gratuities

A professional may be offered, and accept, any of a wide range of benefits from a private party, whether or not in "return" for specific acts in the performance or the professional role. The value of benefits may be nominal or significant; and benefits can range from meals, entertainment, and minor gifts, through to honorariums, paid vacations, free travel, and money. At the extreme, the acceptance of benefits may constitute bribery. In general, however, the acceptance of benefits is a less active form of conflict of interest than private gain from an official position. The benefits or rewards obtained may be relatively minor, but the key concern is that the professional may in some way become beholden to the giver (whether or not the professional is in an immediate position to advance the specific interests of the giver).

Self-dealing

Where a professional has a straightforward capacity to use their official position to affect a personal interest, self-dealing is involved. This particularly involves taking action in a professional capacity which "involves dealing with oneself in a private capacity and which confers a benefit on oneself" (Kernaghan and Langford, 1990: 142). There are many possibilities for self-dealing in accounting, for example in various aspects of the production and sale processes. If this influence is exercised in a manner that results in a private benefit—say, if goods are acquired from a vendor in which the accountant has an interest—a conflict of interest has been manifested in a breach of duty (in general, a duty to both adopt a position of neutrality with regard to such matters and, more specifically, to seek out the best or most reasonable terms that may be obtained). Self-dealing may also be regarded as having occurred if a professional seeks to acquire property that is disposed of in receivership or bankruptcy (that is, other than in the normal course of business, and under the control of the accountant). The attempt to gain such ownership may lead to the disposal of goods in a manner that is not open and transparent, and which is not the interests of the substantive ownership of the property.

Undue Influence, Preferential Treatment, and Influence Peddling

Undue influence involves an associate of professional exercising influence (or seeking to do so) over the performance of professional duties. This problem may particularly relate to accounting and auditing work where the practitioner has a personal relationship with the client. Post-employment (discussed above) may represent a specific type of undue influence. The discretionary elements within much accountancy work mean that there are potentially many instances where such influence could be applied.

Preferential treatment involves a professional acting in a way that is partial to certain individuals (or appears to be so), especially those who have a familial or other personal relationship with the professional. In contrast to undue influence, preferential treatment does not necessarily involve the associate of the professional soliciting the advantage.

Influence peddling involves the active solicitation of benefit in exchange for the exercise of influence. This takes preferential treatment a step further insofar as a professional actively seeks a private benefit in return for a professional favour.

In both undue influence and preferential treatment, the conflict of interest arises in relation to the general obligation of a professional to be fair and unbiased in the performance of duty. In relation to influence peddling, the problem is further compounded by the active solicitation of a private benefit.

Abuse of Office

Abuse of office involves professionals using their position to coerce others to provide private advantage; this coercion may be effected by advancing the interests of the other party. This type of conflict of interest is similar to influence peddling, except that a professional involved in this form of conflict of interest would seek to further the private interests of others.

Use of Official Property

The use of official property of any kind (such as stationery, computers, or office space) for unofficial activities may give rise to a conflict of interest if it impacts on the performance of professional duty. This may occur if, for example, if the use of such resources diverts them from professional purposes and they are subsequently unavailable for professional purposes, or if the desire to use professional resources for private benefit influences the way professional duties such as work allocation are performed.

Use of Confidential Information

Use of confidential information is of particular significance for accountants, who may come into the possession of great amounts of such information that may be of potential benefit to the accountant or other associates. Unofficial and unauthorised use or disclosure of such information can present obvious problems if accountants' use of such information serves the interests of a party other than one to whom the accountant owes a professional duty. This conflict of interest may be manifested in the financial world as insider trading.

The Neglected Public Interest

In accepting the obligations attached to an occupation or profession, and the attendant powers, benefits, and prestige attached to that occupation or profession, there is a correlative reduction in one's right to consider personal and outside interests not related to the official or professional role (Wueste, 1994, citing Nagel, 1978). Given explicit professional commitments (or claims) to serve society and to prioritise the public interests, a range of private interests should be regarded as secondary.

The various conflicts of interest discussed in the previous section illustrate the range of problems that may arise when practitioners of accountancy utilise the substantial discretionary element within accounting practice to serve their own interests at the cost of a neglect of the interests of others whom accountants have a duty to serve. However, the key element neglected in much of the discussion thus, far is that of the public interest. It may nevertheless be regarded that the neglect of the public in the pursuit of private interest represents the key problematic for conflict of interest in accountancy, as the notion that accounting serves the public interest provides both a key element of legitimacy underlying accountancy and a central element of the claim to professionalism (set Preston *et al.*, 1995, for example).

Where a conflict of interest is avoidable, private interest must be subsumed. These include the interests of the individual practitioner, any relevant professional body, clients, and constituent elements of clients including owner, and managers. Ostensible public interest commitments of professionals are paramount from an ethical perspective. The present social and economic dominance of corporations and the range of private interests that are attached a corporate interest make the social role of accountants in fulfilling this professional commitments to the public all the more important. The means that there is a need to look beyond what may be regarded as common affinity of accountancy with private profitability in order to seriously consider what public accountability means.

(Not) Prioritising the Public Interest

In their broad examination of ethics in accounting Dellaportas *et al.* (2005), include a chapter on conflict of interest. It will be argued in this section of the paper that their approach exemplifies a narrow conception and understanding of the nature and ramifications of the problem. A particular concern is that the public interest element is not clearly prioritised in their framework. It is often not clear whether or how the problem of conflict of interest relates to the following situations:

1. An accountant pursuing his or her personal interests at the expense of a client or employer;
2. An accountant pursuing his or her personal interests at the expense of the public; and
3. An accountant pursuing the interests of a client or employer at the expense of the public.

Of these three important dimensions of conflict of interest, only the first is clearly recognised in the types of conflict of interest outlined earlier in this paper, and in typical professional pronouncements. A conceptual confusion arise because the professional duties of accountants are elaborated in such a way that they must serve two masters clients/employers and the public, and it is never clear in this elaboration which master has priority (e.g. Dellaporta *et al.*, 2005). For example, if an accountant is engaged to assist clients to arrange their financial affairs in such a way as to legally avoid tax, but which nevertheless allows "taxpayers to avoid their taxation responsibilities" (although such responsibilities are not defined), the duties of the accountant are summarised by Dellaportas *et al.*, as follows:

> . . . a professional responsibility to ensure that client taxpayers do not pay more tax than is necessary, even though accountants have a competing ethical obligation to society to ensure that a taxpayer does not pay less than is fat (2005: 289).

The conflict of interest between the private interests of a client and the public interest is thus recognised, but it is dealt with by the accountant ensuring that it is the client that makes the decision to enter into such taxation scheme or arrangements, and that the accountant fully informs the client of possible current and future ramifications. Professional regulatory guidelines are cited in support of these points. The public interest obligation in ever taxpayer paying a fair amount of tax is recognised, as is that fact that such tax minimisation arrangements may be regarded as unethical, but conflict of interest between these public interest elements and the private interests of the client is effectively downplayed. The discussion treats conflict of interest as a problem only if it involves an accountant actively assisting a client to breach the law and / or if the accountant breaches explicit profession: regulatory guidelines in the process.

The key shortcoming here it that there is no overriding sense of the public interest being paramount, and certainly sense that the public interest should prevail over thc private interests of the client. Indeed, the opposite is the case – it is clearly the interests of the client that are paramount, within the restraints of the law: "... accountants can and should advise their clients on the benefits of such matters [legal tax avoidance arrangements]."

On this account, the problem of professional ethics does not extend into the discretionary realm of client decision. Indeed, accountants are specifically absolved of ethical responsibility in such matters, because it is said to be parliament's responsibility to deal with legal loopholes that allow for tax avoidance schemes. Here, professional accounting ethics implicitly extend no further than the requirements of the law or professional regulation, and the presentation of the problem within the framework of conflict of interest adds little to an otherwise legalistic analysis. Why this is even discussed as a conflict of interest by Dellaportas *et al.*, is unclear, since any conflict between the private interests of clients and the public interest is removed from the analysis. The discussion of conflict of interest in this context may unwillingly be a further stage in the accounting profession's complex strategy of doing "nothing" in relation to ethical concerns and responses to public crises of confidence in accounting (Fogarty *et al.*, 1991; Lee, 1995).

Implications and Conclusions

Despite an over-arching professional claim to serve the public interest, accountancy in practice seems to exist to serve a range of private interests, whether of corporations and other clients, or of the accounting profession itself. There is little evidence that the practitioners, of accountancy actually do subordinate the range of private interests that are directly served by accounting. It may be concluded that the idea of serving the public interest acts as a powerful legitimating rhetoric behind which the accounting profession principally seeks to serve its own economic interests (Preston *et al.*, 1995).

Many of the conflict of interest problems that identified in accounting including many types of conflict of interest combined in this paper revolve around clashes between various forms of private interest. For example, the interest of clients *versus* those of accountancy practitioners, or the interests of Shareholders *versus* those of management, may be central to identified problems of conflict of interest. Unless and until the accounting profession develops a concept of public interest that extends beyond a nefarious notion that the public interest is only vicariously served via a range of private interests, the "far-reaching consequences" (Dellaportas *et al.*, 2005: 13) of conflicts of interest are unlikely to be assuaged. These consequences must be seen—by accountants—as extending, beyond risks for the firm or for capital markets, which dominate conventional treatments of this problem (c.f. Dellaportas *et al.*, 2005: 16).

The post-Enron focus on corporate governance and the promulgation of various legal reforms such as—the Sarbanes—Oxley Act in the United States of America and the Corporate Law Economic Reform Program (CLERP) in Australia is essentially reactive in nature, and may be just another step in longer-term historical processes of legitimation in which the profession has engaged Broader concerns with ethics remain subdued (see Gaa and Thorne, 2004) and accounting continues to serve a range of private interests, including those of corporations and their shareholders. Dealing effectively with the problem of conflict of interest in accounting requires a transcendence of the typical ethical identity within accounting that prioritises economic over other values and equates the "good" with the maximisation of corporate profits (McPhail, 1999: 836). It is unlikely that any change to this state of affairs can come from within corporations themselves (see Bakan, 2004; Korten, 2001, 1998), but it is also difficult to imagine change from within a profession that has largely been captured both by the economic interests of clients and its own economic interest (Hendrickson, 1998).

The problem of conflict of interest at this more fundamental level must be recognised both in the broader public interest and in light of the social responsibility that attaches to any official role in a public institution (Wueste, 1994: 2 et seq.). By accepting roles in professions and public institutions, individuals who occupy such roles are obliged to serve the public interest. Service to the public is a cornerstone of professionalism, and self-regulation afforded to the profession is the flip-side of public trust and legitimacy, but these are matters that seem to have slipped from the attention of the accounting professional bodies. It is difficult to see how public confidence in the accounting profession can be (re)built unless such obligations are taken seriously.

References

Arnold, P.J. (2005): "Disciplining Domestic Regulation: The World Trade Organization and the Market for Professional Services," *Accounting Organizations and Society*, 30(4), 299-330.

Bakan, J. (2004): *The Corporation: The Pathological Pursuit of Profit and Power*, New York, Free Press.

Boatright, J. (2004): *Trade Secrets and Conflict of Interest: Ethics and the Conduct of Business*, Upper Saddle River, New Jersey, Prentice-Hall, 128-58.

Bowles, D.K. and J.M. McCartney (1996): "Conflicts of Interest," *American Criminal Law Review*, 30(3): 523.

Carson, T.L. (1994): "Conflicts of Interest," *Journal of Business Ethics*, 13(5): 387-404.

CCH Australia, Ed. (2001): *Collapse Incorporated: Tales, Safeguards and Responsibilities of Corporate Australia*, Sydney, CCH Australia.

Citron, D.B. (2003): "The UK's Framework Approach to Auditor Independence and the Commercialization of the Accounting Profession," *Accounting, Auditing and Accountability Journal*, 16(2), 244-74.

Clarke, F.L., G.W. Dean, and K.G. Oliver (2003): *Corporate Collapse: Regulatory, Accounting and Ethical Failure*, Cambridge, Cambridge University Press.

Davids, C. (1998), "Shaping Public Perceptions of Police Integrity: Conflict of Interest Scenarios in Fictional Interpretations of Policing," *Current Issues in Criminal Justice*, 9(3), 241-61.

Davids, C. (2005), Police Misconduct, Regulation, and Accountability: Conflict of Interest Complaints Against Victoria Police Officers, 1988-98, Faculty of Law, Sydney, University of New South Wales.

Davis, M. (1982): "Conflict of Interest," *Business and Professional Ethics Journal*, 1(4), 17-32.

Davis, M. (1992), "Codes of Ethics, Professions, and Conflict of Interest: A Case Study of an Emerging Profession Clinical Engineering," *Professional Ethics*, 1(1 and 2), 179-95.

Dellaportas, S.K., Gibson, R., Alagiah, M., Hutchinson, P. Leung, and D. Van Homrigh (2005): *Ethics, Governance and Accountability: A Professional Perspective*, Milton, Queensland, Wiley.

Dwyer, P.D. and R.W. Roberts (2004): "Known by the Company they Keep: A Study of Political Campaign Contributions made by the United States Public Accounting Profession," *Critical Perspectives on Accounting*, 15(6/7), 865-83.

Fogarty, T.J.; J.B. Helan, and D.L. Knutson (1991): "The Rationality of Doing "Nothing": Auditors' Responses to Legal Liability in an Institutionalized Environment," *Critical Perspectives on Accounting*, 2(3), 201-26.

Gaa, J.C. and L. Thorne (2004): "An Introduction to the Special Issue on Professionalism and Ethics in Accounting Education," *Issues in Accounting Education*, 19(1), 1-6.

Hendrickson, H. (1998): "Relevant Financial Reporting Questions not asked by the Accounting Profession," *Critical Perspective on Accounting*, 9(5), 489-505.

Integrity Commissioner (2002): Conflict of Interest in the Public Sector, Brisbane, Office of the Integrity Commissioner, Queensland Government.

Kernaghan, K. and J.W. Langford (1990): The Responsible Public Servant, Halifax, Nova Scotia, The Institute for Research on Public Policy and The Institute of Public Administration of Canada.

Korten, D. (1998): *The Post-Corporate World: Life After Capitalism*, San Fracisco, California, and West Hartford, Connecticut Current Koehler and Kumarian Press.

Korten, D. (1998): *When Corporations Rule the World*, Bloomfield, Connecticut Kumarian Press and Berrett-Koehler.

Lee, T. (1995): "The Professionalization of Accountancy: A History of Protecting the Public Interest in a Self-interested Way," *Accounting Auditing and Accountability Journal*, 8(4), 48-69.

Macklin, R. (1983): *Conflicts of Interest: Ethical Theory and Business*, T.L. Beauchamp and N.E. Bowie, Englewood Cliffs, New Jersey, Prentice-Hall, 240-46.

Main, A. (2003): *Other People's Money: The Complete Story of the Extraordinary Collapse of HIH*, Sydney, Harper Colins.

Martin, R. (2002): "The Conflict of Interest Gap," *The Australian*, March 16, 17:4.

McPhail, K. (1999): "The Threat of Ethical Accountants: An Application of Foucault's Concept of Ethics to Accounting Education and Some Thoughts on Ethically Educating for the Other," *Critical Perspectives on Accounting*, 10(6): 833-866.

Mintz, S.M. (1995), "Virtue Ethics and Accounting Education," *Issues in Accounting Education*, 10(2), 246-67.

Nolan, M. (1996): "The Values of Public Life", *The Age*, August 8, A11.

Nolan, M., C. Boulton, A. King, T. King, P. Shore Thomson of Monifieth; W. Utting,

A. Warburton, and D. Warwick (1995): Standards in Public Life: First Report of the Committee on Standards in Public Life, London, HMSO.

Owen, A. (1997): Public Sector Ethics: Some Practical Implications, Accountability and Corruption: Public Sector Ethics, G.L. Clark, E.P. Jonson, and W. Caldow, St. Leonards, NSW, Allen & Unwin, 36-52.

Perera, H.B.; A.R. Rahman, and S.F. Cahan (2003): "Globalisation and the Major Accounting Firms," *Australian Accounting Review*, 13(1): 27-37.

Preston, A.M.; D.J. Cooper; D.P. Scarbrough, and R.C. Chilton (1995): "Changes in the Code of Ethics of the U.S. Accounting Profession, 1917 and 1988: The Continual Quest for Legitimation," *Accounting, Organizations and Society*, 20(6): 507-46.

Preston, N.C. Sampford, and C. Connors (2002): *Encouraging Ethics and Challenging Corruption: Reforming Governance in Public Institutions*, Sydney, Federation Press.

Rezaee, Z. (2004): "Restoring Public Trust in the Accounting Profession by Developing Anti-fraud Education, Programs, and Auditing", *Managerial Auditing Journal*, 19(1): 134-48.

Rodwin, M.A. (1993): *Medicine, Money, and Morals*, New York, Oxford University Press.

Siemensma, F. (2000): Conflicts of Interest: The Universal Blindspot: General Principles, Conflicts of Interest: The Universal Blindspot, Melbourne, Leo Cussen Institute.

Solomon, J. and A. Solomon (2004): *Corporate Governance and Accountability*, Chichester, Wiley.

Stark, A. (1996): Public Sector Conflict of Interest at the Federal Level in Canada and the United States: Differences in Understanding and Approach, Teaching Ethics, R.M. Thomas, London, HMSO, One: Government Ethics, 121-47.

Stark, A. (2000): *Conflict of Interest in American Public Life*, Cambridge, Massachusetts, Harvard University Press.

Sykes, T. (1996): *The Bold Riders: Behind Australia's Corporate Collapses*, St. Leonards, Allen & Unwin.

Sykes, T. (1998): *Two Centuries of Panic: A History of Corporate Collapses in Australia*, St. Leonards, Allen & Unwin.

Werhane, P. and J. Doering (1992): "Conflicts of Interest and Conflicts of Commitment," *Professional Ethics*, 4(3 and 4), 47-81.

Wueste, D.E., Ed. (1994): *Professional Ethics and Social Responsibility*, Lanham, Maryland, Rowman and Littlefield.

3

The Myth of Corporate Social Responsibility

DAVID CROWTHER, RUTE ABREU AND FÁTIMA DAVID

INTRODUCTION

Corporate Social Responsibility (CSR) involved a wide range of concepts, principals, methodologies and a large diversity of empirical analysis. In recent years, the concept of CSR has gained prominence to such an extent that it seems ubiquitous, both in the popular media and among academics from a wide range of disciplines. There are probably many reasons for the attention given to this phenomenon not least of which is the corporate excesses witnessed in recent years. For many people the various examples of this kind of behaviour – ranging from Union Carbide Corporation, to Bank of Credit and Commerce International (BCCI), to Parmalat, to Enron as well as to the collapse of Arthur Andersen – will have left an indelible impression among people that all is not well with the corporate world and that there are problems[1] which need to be addressed (Crowther and Rayman-Bacchus, 2004a).

Most corporations in the world are currently trying to distance themselves from the excesses and misbehaviours which have been manifest in recent years by those corporations which have been symbolised as *rogue* corporations. Many would consider that these corporations have however behaved no differently to most others and have merely been found out. Nevertheless the distancing of the rogues from the rest has led to a tremendous resurgence of interest in behaviour which has been classified as CSR. So, corporations are busy repackaging their behaviour as CSR and redesignating their spinmasters as Directors of CSR, for there is much evidence that little has changed in corporate behaviour except for this repackaging – the power of the semiotic being far more potent in the modern world that the power of actual action, and also obviating the need for such action. Crowther and Rayman-Bacchus (2004a) have argued that the corporate excesses, which are starting to become disclosed and which are affecting large number of people have raised an awareness of the social behaviour of corporations. This is one reason why the issue of corporate social responsibility has become a much more prominent feature of the corporation landscape. There are other factors which have helped raise this issue to prominence and Topal and Crowther (2004) maintain that a concern with the effects of bio-engineering[2] and genetic modifications of nature is also an issue which is arising general concern. At a different level of analysis Crowther (2000, 2002b, 2002c) has argued that the availability of the World Wide Web has facilitated the dissemination of information and has enabled more pressure to be brought corporations by their various stakeholders. But, Wheeler and Elkington (2001: 1) talk about the end of corporate environmental report due to the fact that historically this report have not engaged stakeholders and it will appear to be

> "the development of truly interactive (cybernetic) corporate sustainability and communications delivered via the internet and other channels."

Another point of view, about the diffusion of information and its impact,[3] was presented by Unerman and Bennette (2004). They explain the difficulties in identifying all stakeholders that are affected by a corporation's activity. All these perspectives, therefore raises the question as to what exactly is CSR and how can it is manifest and to what exactly can be considered to be corporate social responsibility. According to the EU (2001b: 8; 2002: 5):

> "... CSR is a concept whereby companies integrate social and environmental concerns in their business operations and in their interaction with their stakeholders on a voluntary basis."

From these concepts we could infer that the social enterprise is not a new definition and has resonance with earlier idea such as those of Dahl (1972: 18), who stated:

"... every large corporation should be thought of as a social enterprise; that is an entity whose existence and decisions can be justified insofar as they serve public or social purposes."

Shaw (2004: 196) explains that the principal characteristics of social enterprise are:

(i) the orientation, "directly involved in producing goods and providing services to the market, making an operating surplus...."
(ii) the aim, "... explicit social aims (job creation, training or provision local services), strong social values and mission (commitment to local capacity building), accountable to their members and wider community for their social, environmental and economic impact.[4] The profits are to their stakeholders or for benefit the community."
(iii) and the ownership, "... autonomous organizations with loose governance and participation of stakeholders in the ownership structure."

All definitions – and there are many – seem to have a commonality in that they are based upon a concern with more than profitability and returns to shareholders. Indeed involving other stakeholders, and considering them in decision-making is a central platform of CSR. The broadest definition of corporate social responsibility is concerned with what is – or should be – the relationship between the global corporation, governments of countries and individual citizens. For example, the OECD has studied investment in weak governance zones.[5] More locally, the concept of CSR is concerned with the relationship between a corporation and the local community in which it resides or operates. Other case was Timberland, which logged 44,000 community service hours during the three-year period and US recognition[6] for its commitment to social responsibility (Austin *et al.*, 2004). Another concept of CSR is concerned with the relationship between a corporation and its stakeholders. In this situation, the research could be focused on employees (see Parker, 1977). The corporation develops its codes of conduct that could make some progress in improving labour rules and process, but the scope are limited and it is unclear if they can make a significant impact without the help of Governments with law-enforcement. These efforts are likely to benefit only a small segment of the target workforce.[7]

For the authors all of these definitions are pertinent and represent a dimension of the issue. A parallel debate is taking place in the arena of ethics as to other corporations should be controlled through increased regulation or whether theoretical base of citizenship has been lost and needs replacing before socially responsible behaviour will ensure. For example Fulop *et al.* (2000) state that people in Hungary often comment that ethics in the Hungarian economic life is a delusion rather than a reality.[8] However this debate is represented it seems that it is concerned with some sort of social contract between corporations and society.

THE SOCIAL CONTRACT

This social contract implies some form of altruistic behaviour – the converse of selfishness. Self-interest connotes selfishness, and since the Middle Ages has informed a number of important philosophical, political and economic propositions. Among these is Hobbes's world where unfettered self-interest is expected to lead to social devastation. A high degree of regulation is prescribed in order to avoid such a disastrous outcome, but in the process corporations sacrifice all the rights (human, labour, social, for others. Self-interest again raises its head in the utilitarian perspective as championed by Bentham, Locke and John Stuart Mill.[9] The latter for example advocated as morally right the pursuit of the greatest happiness for the greatest number. This perception, as Phillips (2001: 51-52) describes, could mean

> "... there is no longer serious market resistance to the market economy, understood as an arena in which firms compete and co-operate on the basis of free contractual arrangements. Applying market principles to the internal operations of firms is the next logical step.... "

Similarly, Adam Smith's free-market economics is predicated on competing self-interest. These influential ideas put interest of the individual above interest of the collective. Indeed, from this perspective, collective interests are best served through self-interest. At the same time this corporate self-interest has come to draw disapproval in modern times, as reflected in many of the arguments within this book. The moral value of individualism has all but vanished. Crowther and Rayman Bacchus (2004b) suggest that the pendulum swung too far towards encouraging corporate self-interest at the expense of the public interest. For example, in Portugal, there were specific changes in taxation[10] made by different governments allowing a fiscal amnesty[11] and delay of payment to football teams. Indeed the continuing conversion of public service provision to market testing by many governments suggests a strengthening belief that the two interests are not in conflict. Self-interest and altruism (promoting the welfare of others over self) need not be in conflict. There is ample evidence that encouraging corporate self-interest (and risk taking) does indeed benefit society (albeit unequally from a Marxist perspective). Some of that evidence is however contested, as in the case of Genetically Modified (GM) food (see Topal and Crowther, 2004). The European Union (EU) policies[12] intend to pursue a high level of protection of human life and health, but differences between national laws, regulations and administrative provisions concerning the assessment and authorization of GM food and feed may hinder their free movement, creating conditions of unequal and unfair competition (EU, 2003). There is also abundant evidence to the contrary; that the pursuit of corporate self-interest continues to burden society with additional costs. In the agriculture area examples could be foot and mouth disease, with higher level of costs not very well estimated till now. Nevertheless, during the last two decades most of the world's nations have set about creating anew, or refining (capitalist), economic and political institutions that encourage corporate self-interest.

STAKEHOLDER CONCERN

With the raising of CSR to prominence in society however all companies have claimed to be concerned with a variety of stakeholders and take their needs into considering in strategic decision-making. For example, the research conducted by Cooper *et al.* (2001) in UK shows that certain stakeholders are claimed to be considered by all organisations. These are shareholders, customers and employees, with suppliers and society and the environment also being considered important by the majority of companies. On the other hand, Heard and Boice (1981: 248) explain that some pressure groups increase the influence of social report:

"... organizations have been instrumental in calling attention to issues such as product quality and safety, environmental protection (...) have had a substantial impact on the development of social measurement and social reporting."

Although CSR involves a concern with the various stakeholders to a business there are several problems with this research in identifying socially responsible behaviour:

- The research shows that the concern is primarily with those stakeholders who have power to influence the organisation. Thus organisations are most concerned with shareholders, less so with customers and employees and very little with society and the environment;
- The research does not indicate the extent to which any action is taken and the extent to which this is voluntary; and
- Claiming a concern is very different to actually exhibiting that concern through actions taken (Crowther, 2004).

It therefore becomes imperative at this point to consider what is meant by any definition of CSR. There are three basic principles (Crowther, 2002a; Schaltegger *et al.*, 1996) which need to be considered sustainability,[13] accountability and transparency. In this sense, Eccles *et al.* (2001: 163) presents the words of Delfgaauw, as Shell's vice-president of sustainable development, that argues:

"... new responsibilities bring new accountabilities. Sustainability is the substance, transparency the process."

One theme which arises from any consideration of these principles is the extent to which it is possible to assess the accountability of organisations to a broader constituency by reference to an implicit or hypothetical social contract. In the process, it is attempted to show how social contract theory also helps bind the relationship between corporate social responsibility and ethical behaviour. As Shaw (2004: 196) states, one of the characteristics of social entrepreneurs is being ethical as a way to

"... ensure that public money is well used, that ideas are not corrupted by vested interests and that their full commitment is available for the project."

This raises questions about the scope and depth of commitment among corporate leaders to social responsibility, a point which is central to this paper. Assessing this commitment is made difficult[14] given what appears to be a runaway free market ideology; a belief system that seems to be elevating the corporation above the nation state, and is being transmitted through corporate global expansion and with USA led government sponsorship. This can be developed in the context of the globalising process by considering the extent to which corporate and social exploitation of Internet technology is helping both corporate bodies and consumer and citizens transform our world into a global village (McLuhan and Fiore, 1968) and then broadened to consider the broader relationship between technological innovation and social change. In examining this relationship it can be shown that technological development is underpinned by a utilitarian perspective, and at the same time technological change is unavoidably bound up with making moral choices.

While governments and consumers alike look to business to continue delivering economic and social benefits, many observers remain concerned about corporate self-interest; a self-interest, that is synonymous with those of the managers. Managerial self-interest is unavoidably driven by a combination of shareholder interests (backed up by markets for corporate control and managerial talent), and occupational rewards and career opportunity. The public interest is easily sacrificed on the altar of these managerial motivators (or constraints). So, as Jensen and Meckling (1994: 1) argue:

> "understanding human behaviour is fundamental to understanding how organizations function, whether they be profit-making firms in the private sector, non-profit enterprises or government agencies intended to serve the 'public interest.'"

Moreover, public interest is not homogeneous and therefore cannot be simply represented. Public interest has become factionalised into constituencies and stakeholder groupings, each concerned with their particular interests. Consider for example the 'not-in-my-back-yard' protests over the building of recycling plants and mobile telephone masts, yet opinion polls support the former and sales of mobile phones demand more of the latter. Parkinson (2003) explains in the continental European tradition, as Portugal, Corporations (like: Galp and Caixa Geral de Depositors)[16] are regarded as partially public bodies, with constituencies that extend beyond the shareholders to include other groups, such as employees (with retirement plans and other benefits), trade unions (with strikes and public contest) and local communities (with social and economic needs).

It has often been noted, from a global perspective, which corporate self-interest seems to be associated with an unequal distribution of economic and social benefits. However, it seems unfair to lay the responsibility for such inequality solely at the door of the corporation. National and regional politics, religious conviction and differentiated moral values all play an immeasurable role in shaping a nation's life chances. Nevertheless there is worldwide suspicion that corporate egoism is a significant (if not the most important) influence on economic and social development. For example, in an OECD (2003) study about anti-corruption management and reporting practices, the results show that corporations have different behaviour, depending on their sector of operation. Most extractive industry corporations (8 out of the 12 oil and mining companies in the sample) publish lengthy anti-corruption statements. In contrast, only one out of 13 in the sample motor vehicle company publishes any material whatsoever.

Beyond this tendency, many examples of corporations behaving altruistically, from the paternalism of nineteenth and twentieth century industrialists,[17] to modern day donations to charities and the *ad hoc* secondment of managers to community projects.[18] The perceived value of such giving is tainted by suspicions that many such acts seem self-serving. Thus, there is room to ask whether Microsoft is giving away computers out of altruism or as part of an aim to re-inforce its brand name. Many modern projects of altruism are tied to the purchase of products from the giving corporation. Other initiatives are clearly pushing at the boundaries of acceptable corporate behaviour, such as donations to political panics. These examples show that corporate altruism covers a wide range of socially acceptable behaviour, from selfless giving to self-interested giving.

Perhaps one reason for corporate self-interest being such a mixed blessing is that people are overly reliant on evaluating the consequences of corporate action, especially apparent in the fixation with the bottom line. Nothing concentrates the managerial mind like performance targets and outcomes. As Wilbur (1992) argues, self-interest encompasses not just consequences and results, but also requires freedom of choice and consistency. From this perspective the pursuit of corporate (self-interested) activity should be guided by structured alternatives and consistency, in order to ensure that the self-interest of others is not undermined by selfish action. Sensing that the citizen cannot rely on corporate altruism so, the public are demanding our governments to initiate more legislation and tighter regulation. However, even this move has shown important weaknesses. Many of the politicians and policy-makers are in the pockets of business. Self-interest is even here, and it is not acceptable to us. These arguments cast doubt on the extent to which citizens are able to arrange our economic and political institutions in order to harness self-interest to the benefit of society. The functioning of a civilised society includes putting the interests of others before self-interest. As Baron *et al.* (1992), and Mansbridge (1990) observed, altruism is part of social, political and economic life. However, the exploitative nature of capitalism sits uncomfortably with Kant's (1959) ideal of mutual respect for the interests of others, and even less with Rawls's (1971) desire to see a strong form of egalitarian liberalism. These tensions between capitalism and liberalism, and between meeting unconditional social obligations and the pursuit of economic value), drives the need for constant vigilance of corporate activity. Since, we are unlikely to abandon capitalism, nor escape from the fixation on performance measurement, managerial commitment to upholding the interests of others could straightforwardly be included in the managerial performance appraisal (Crowther and Rayman-Bacchus, 2004b).

Alongside the broad recognition that corporations are accountable to their stakeholders has come a development of the principles upon which this demonstration of accountability should be based. So, annual report and other media are used to the specific interest of some groups. As Zeghal and Ahmed (1990) present, the other media could be in detail as several narratives or quantified reports, supplements to the annual report or produced at interim dates, booklets or leaflets produced to address the social activities of the corporation advertisements or articles published detailing corporation activities and labelling of products to promote environmental and/or other concerns. Inevitably, this is predicated in accounting as a mechanism by which such action can be measured and reported. In generic terms, this has come to be called either social or environmental accounting.[19] The objective of environmental accounting is to measure the effects of the actions of the organisation upon the environment and to report upon those effects. In other words, the objective is to incorporate the effects of the activities of the firm upon externalities and to view the firm as a network which extends beyond just the internal environment to include the whole environment (see Crowther, 2000, 2002a). In this view of the organisation the accounting for the firm does not stop at the organisational boundary but extends beyond to include not just the business environment in which it operates but also the whole social environment. Environmental accounting therefore adds a new dimension to the role of accounting for an organisation because of its emphasis upon accounting for external effects of the organisation's activities. In doing so this provides a recognition, that, the organisation is an integral part of society, rather than a self-contained entity which has only an indirect relationship with society at large. This self-containment has been the traditional view taken by an organisation as far as their relationship with society at large is concerned, with interaction being only by means of resource acquisition and sales of finished products or services. Recognition of this closely intertwined relationship of mutual interdependency between the organisation and society at large, when reflected in the accounting of the organisation, can help bring about a closer, and possibly more harmonious relationship between the organisation and society. Given that the managers and workers of an organisation are also stakeholders in that society in other capacities, such as consumers, citizens and inhabitants, this reinforces the mutual interdependency.

THE DIALECTICS OF ORGANISATIONAL PERFORMANCE

According to Crowther (2002a), although organisational performance is normally presented as a dialectical performance along the two incompatible dimensions of financial performance and social performance, this is in fact a false dialectic. Although the annual reporting of organisations presents it as such, empirical evidence demonstrates that organisations actually perform equally well along both dimensions. That dialectic is a construction inherent in annual reports which is created and maintained through the semiotic of these reports, to such an extent that the perception of the dialectic as extant is generally accepted within the discourse of both corporate reporting and of accounting theory. The dialectic appears in a form which is believed so absolutely that an alternative becomes inconceivable; it has therefore assumed the mantel of a myth (Cassirer, 1946, Miller, 1992). Indeed the proponents of environmental accounting and reporting found their analysis upon the existence of this dialectic. It therefore becomes necessary to consider why, if this dialectic does not in fact exist, it is created through the semiotic of the corporate annual reporting mechanism.

If the dialectic does not exist in corporate performance itself then its creation in the annual report must be undertaken by either the authors of the script of that report or by the readers of that reporting script. Although it has been argued that the semiotic is created by the reader of the report based upon his or her understanding of the contents of that report, the implication of this is that each person produces an interpretation based upon the linguistic social and environmental experiences which underpin any understanding. Thus, each person creates an individual semiotic (Habermas, 1971)[20] from the information available to him/her but moreover seeks to create a semiotic understanding based upon the intentions of the group which holds power (Lakoff, 1975). That group is of course the authors of the script who are at the same time the managers of the organisation.[21] In the perspective of behavioural finance, as Shefrin (2001: 124) defends:

> "managers and board members need to recognize two key behavioural impediments to the process of value maximization, one internal to the firm and the other external (...). Behavioural costs sterm from psychological induced errors made by managers and employees. External obstruction stem from psychological induced errors made by analysts and investors."

For that semiotic to be created, however, in such a way that the dialectic between the internal (or traditional accounting) and the external (or social) perspectives upon corporate performance is understood to exist, it is of course necessary that sufficient signals are created within the text for the semiotic to be extracted as a general interpretation. It is in this method that the author's meaning is reinstated in the text (Gadamer, 1975). The only people with the power to achieve this are of course the author of the text. Hence, it must be concluded that the dialectic of corporate reporting is both created and maintained by the managers of the organisation. So, the corporation does not pursue justice as a fundamental aspect of its life, and if the managers and stakeholders do not devote attention to the normative question of what is just, then the perception of unfairness of each other will increase.

Corporate reporting has several purposes but one of them is the creation of certainty through its mythic role (Crowther, 2002a). This myth creation role has several aspects but one aspect is the creation of the myth of the unified whole. One of the purposes of the corporate report therefore is the creation of the myth of the unified culture of the actors on the semiotic stage—in other word the common cultural bond of identity between the authors of the script and the audience. This is achieved by the creation of a symbolic order which is an autonomous order of reality independent of the things symbolised (Jenkins: 1979). The myth itself is a symbolic form (Bradist: 1997), which assumes a life of its own. As Cassirer (1955: 5-6) states the specificity of myth lies not in its content but rather in

> "... the intensity with which it is experienced, with which it is believed—as only something endowed with objective reality can be believed."

Thus, myth has the power to present a single viewpoint as directly expressive of the existence of the organisation, which consequently exists in the form presented in the annual report. The corporate report as myth therefore provides an authoritative discourse about the organisation, and as Bakhtin (1981: 342) states:

> "... the authoritative word demands that we acknowledge it, that we make it our own; it binds us, quite independent of any power it might have to persuade us internally; we encounter it with its authority already fused into it. The authoritative word is located in the distanced zone, organically connected with a past that is felt to be hierarchically higher."

The corporate report replaces the organisation itself as the real through this power assumed from its myth creation role and the organisation becomes in the minds of both the readers and the authors (through the reflective quality of the readership) that which is presented through the corporate reponing mechanism. The concept of the corporate report can therefore be considered to have attained a life of its own through the resurrection of the myth of its origin and authenticity. It can therefore be considered to have attained hyper-reality through becoming more real than reality (Baudrillard, 1981; Mattessich, 2003).[22]

AGENCY THEORY AND CSR

Agency theory argues that managers merely act as custodians of the organisation and its operational activities[23] and places upon them the burden of managing in the best interest of the owners of that business.[24] According to agency theory all other stakeholders of the business are largely irrelevant and if they benefit from the business then this is coincidental to the activities of management in running the business to serve shareholders.[25] This focus upon shareholders alone as the intended beneficiaries of a business has been questioned considerably from many perspectives, which argue that it is either not the way in which a business is actually run or that it is a view which does not meet the needs of society in general. Conversely stakeholder theory argues that there are a whole variety of stakeholders involved in the organisation and each deserves some return for their involvement. According to stakeholder theory therefore benefit is maximised if the business is operated by its management on behalf of all stakeholders and returns are divided appropriately amongst those stakeholders, in some way which is acceptable to all. Unfortunately a mechanism for dividing returns amongst all stakeholders[26] which has universal acceptance does not exist, and stakeholder theory is significantly lacking in suggestions in this respect. Nevertheless this theory has some acceptance and is based upon the premise that operating a business in this manner achieves as one of its outcomes the maximisation of returns to shareholders, as part of the process of maximising returns to all other stakeholders. This maximisation of returns is achieved in the long-run through the optimisation of performance for the business to achieve maximal returns to all stakeholders.[27] Consequently, the role of management is to optimise the long term performance of the business in order to achieve this end and thereby reward all stakeholders, including themselves as one stakeholder community, appropriately.

These two theories can be regarded as competing explanations of the operations of a firm, which lead to different operational foci and to different implications for the measurement, and reporting of performance. It is significant however that both theories have one feature in common. This is that the management of the firm is believed to be acting on behalf of others, either shareholders or stakeholders more generally. They do so, not because they are the kind of people who behave altruistically, but because they are rewarded appropriately and much effort is therefore devoted to the creation of reward schemes, which motivate these managers to achieve the desired ends. Similarly, much literature is devoted to the consideration of the effects of reward schemes on managerial behaviour (see Briers and Hirst, 1990; Child, 1974, 1975; Coates *et al.*, 1993; Fitzerald *et al.*, 1991) and suggestion for improvements.

The simplest model of Agency Theory assumes one principle and one agent (see Crowther, 2004) and a modernist view of the world merely assumes that the addition of more principles and more agents makes for a more complex without negating any of the assumptions and opinions. In the corporate world this is problematic as the theory depends upon a relationship between the parties and a shared understanding of the context in which agreements are made. With one principle and one agent, this is not a problem, as the two parties know each other. In the corporate world, the principles are equated to the shareholders of the company. For any large corporation however those shareholders are an amorphous mass of people who are unknown to the managers of the business. Indeed, there is no requirement, of even expectation, that anyone will remain a shareholder for an extended period of time. Thus, there can be no relationship between shareholders—as principles—and managers—as agents—as the principles are merely those holding shares—as property being invested in—at a particular point of time. So, shareholders do not invest in a company and in the future of that company; rather they invest for capital growth and/or a future dividend stream and shares are just one way of doing this which can be moved into or out of at will. This problem is exacerbated, particularly in the UK, by the fact that a significant proportion of shares are actually bought and sold by fund managers of financial institutions acting on behalf of their investors. These fund managers are rewarded according to the growth (or otherwise) of the value of the fund. Thus, shares are bought and sold as commodities rather than as part ownership of a business enterprise. In another perspective of the same problem, as Scherrer and Greven (2001) explain, almost ten per cent of the total value of the commodities in the world market are produced in violation of the fundamental rights of workers. Consequently, agency theory fails as a mechanism for directing managerial behaviour (see Crowther and Ortiz Martinez, 2005).

MEASURING AND EVALUATING PERFORMANCE

The nature of the discourse regarding the measurement and evaluation of corporate performance has however broadened in recent years with the adoption of different perspectives and this has been reflected in the changing nature of corporate reporting.[28] As Mattessich (2003) argues, the transparency in present-day accounting statement presentation is much wanting and in need of improvement. The discourse therefore seems to have moved away from the concerns of shareholders in the firm and away from the economic rationale for accounting and towards a consideration of the wider stakeholder environment. At the same time, however these concerns cannot be ignored and part of the discourse has seen a return to economic values in assessing the performance of the firm. Thus, Rappaport (1986) recognises some of the problems with accounting but goes on to consider the concept of shareholder value and how this can be created and sustained. He develops a methodology of shareholder value based upon his previous work where he argues (1992) that a shareholder value approach[29] is the correct way of evaluating alternative company strategies, stating that the ultimate test of corporate plan is whether it creates value for the shareholders, and that this is the sole method of evaluating performance. The perspective of Wagner and Schaltegger (2003: 7) is that:

> "economic theory provides different perspectives on the relationship between sustainability performance and economic performance from which different predictions about the relationship can be derived."

The return to a consideration of the importance of economic value and to the theory of the firm is based upon the assumption that maximising the value of a firm to its shareholders also maximises the value of that firm to society at large. Within the discourse therefore the concept of shareholder value is frequently mentioned and there is acceptance of the need to account for shareholder value within the practitioner community. Indeed the annual reports of companies regularly expound the virtue of creating value for shareholders and it is frequently cited as a corporate objective. This objective can simply be defined as being achieved when the rate of return obtained within a business exceeds the cost of obtaining funds. So, as Unerman and Bennette (2004: 704) defend:

> "... managers fail to systematically enact the standards of behaviour resulting from more democratic stakeholder dialogue, it would then be necessary to develop enforcement mechanisms to ensure companies meet the moral responsibilities a wide range of their stakeholders (rather than just those with the greatest economic power) have, on balance, accepted that the company should fulfil."

The concept of shareholder value as an objective appears to be widely accepted within the accounting community but its use as a quantified evaluation is less often found in practice. This, it can be argued, is because the managers of a firm are preoccupied with other objectives such as growth in size, turnover, market share or accounting returns, which are more easily measured and could present a better image. The achievement of objectives such as these is also often correlated with managerial rewards but less so with increasing shareholder value (Williamson, 1963). Alleviating this would necessitate constructing a business model that shows the cause-and-effect relationships among key value drivers, and then identifying the most meaningful measures among them (Eccles *et al.*, 2001). Indeed Jensen and Meckling (1976) use agency theory to demonstrate how following managerial interests can lead to higher rewards for those managers at the expense of a reduction in the value of the company.

Govindarajan and Gupta (1985) argue that long-run criteria contribute to organisational effectiveness rather than short-term criteria, whereas Rappaport (1986, 1992) suggests that shareholder value analysis address both and maximises both. There is, nevertheless, a considerable body of evidence which suggests otherwise and that a concern with shareholder value added and returns to shareholders leads to a short-term focus and lack of regard for the longer term (e.g. Coates *et al.*, 1995). Indeed some managerial actions taken to boost short-term valuations (e.g. delayering and outsourcing) can be argued to actually reduce long-term value, particularly when the product and market development capability is externalised. In this context, as Schaltegger and Figge (2000: 7) argue:

> "the equation 'more corporate environmental protection increases the economic success and the value of the company' is wrong in this general form. Only a pollution prevention

strategy that takes the effects on the value drivers of the shareholder value into account can secure economic success and improve eco-efficiency."

ACCOUNTABILITY FOR PERFORMANCE

An organisation is of course accountable for its actions but Crowther (2002c) argues that those actions are translated into financial figures before any accountability becomes manifest. Accounting harmonization has the objective to compare different financial information made by organizations located in different parts of the world.[30] So, organisations are accountable through their financial reporting and are accountable only to those stakeholders with sufficient power to influence activity. As Walden and Schwartz (1997) explain the disclosure of environmental information in annual reports may affect the perceptions of an enterprise's earnings and cash flows. This report remains focused upon the actions of the organisation and ignores the effects of the organisation upon its external environment.[31] A growing number of writers however have recognised that the activities of an organisation impacts upon the external environment and have suggested that one of the roles of accounting should be to report upon the impact of an organisation in this respect. Such a suggestion first arose in the 1970s and a concern with a wider view of company performance is taken by some writers who evince concern with the social performance of a business, as a member of society at large. This concern was stated by Ackerman (1975) who argued that big business was recognising the need to adapt to a new social climate of community accountability but that the orientation of business to financial result was inhibiting social responsiveness. As Saravanamuthu (2004: 298) specifices, "resources are regarded as assets only if they are expected to provide future services or benefits."

Nevertheless, this must be set within a situation in which the financial performance of the business—as represented through its accounting—is paramount, and of almost religious significance. In this context Saravanamuthu (2004: 296) talks about:

> "... tangible quality to otherwise contestable notions of enterprise viability, and management responsibility to corporate stakeholders. The investing public and other interest groups rely on auditors' reports on corporate financial statements to assure

them of the plausibility of the quantified representation of reality."

For business organisations, McDonald and Puxty (1979) hand maintain that companies are no longer the instruments of shareholders alone but exist within society and so therefore have responsibilities to that society, and that there is therefore a shift towards the greater accountability of companies to all participants. Recognition of the rights of all stakeholders and the duty of a business to be accountable in this wider context therefore has been a relatively recent phenomenon and the economic view of accountability only to owners has only recently been subject to debate to any considerable extent.

Purdy (1983) however discerns two worrying trends however in the subordination of shareholders' rights to the needs of the company and its survival, and in the tendency for this to lead to short-term satisficing and risk reduction rather than to profit maximisation. This implicit assumption that profit maximisation is, or should be, the aim of a firm is a return to neo-classical economic theory and it is worth remembering that Clark (1957) pointed out that profit maximisation is a difficult concept to define, leaving room for the incorporation of good citizenship. When applied to the public sector the concept of profit maximisation is of course even more problematic and this is arguably, why the discourse has become one of cost minimisation on the assumption that cost minimisation is the equivalent of profit maximisation. Good citizenship and the provision of services have become subordinated to this drive for cost minimisation. Equally, this cost minimisation has been interpreted as in the short-term – the long-term problems with this approach can be ignored as someone else will deal with these in the future. This therefore represents part of the problem with accounting – only the present and immediate future matters and the immediate future must be better than the present. The past can be ignored in the creation of this semiotic or rewritten when necessary, to show a continuous improvement (Crowther, 2002c) without any regard to the actual experiences of people.

CONCLUSIONS

It is a central argument of this paper that CSR is a myth. It seems necessary to discuss the concept of myth and define it; in the perspective of Levi-Strauss (1963: 209) it:

> "... always refers to events alleged to have taken place long ago. But what gives the myth an operational value is that the specific pattern described is timeless, it explains the present and the past as well as the future."

And in the perspective of Sebag (1964: 143), myth provides:

> "answers to certain needs in a given society to fills certain functions."

So, the myth is founded on the arrogance of corporate managers, due to failures in Agency Theory; predicated in the ignorance of interpreters of corporate activity, dazzled by the power of the semiotic: and which legitimates corporate expropriation on an undiminished scale. All of this happens because of evolution of economic, financial and social corporate life, which happens as a universal phenomenon in time and space. Dobzhansky (1967: 409) describes it in more detail, start that it:

> "... comprises all the stages of the development of the universe: the cosmic, biological and human or cultural developments. Attempts to restrict the concept of evolution to biology are gratuitous. Life is a product of the evolution of inorganic nature, and man is a product of the evolution of life."

Thus, the authors seek to highlight how little has been said until now about the myth of CSR, and how much remains to be said. When CSR is conceptualised pragmatically as a response of businesses to society's concerns it represents an element of structural change with consequences to the firms' strategies (Decker, 2004).[32] The reality is that corporations have not changed their behaviour and the managers of these corporations are still driven by the desire to create value for shareholder above all else. In such an environment, CSR was introduced in corporate report and practices, because of law-enforcement and, especially, the public image of the corporation. The authors argue that this is based in the distancing of corporations from the communities, which they serve and in which they are physically located. This can be contrasted with the behaviour of firms which are truly located in their communities and which consequently have no need for the concept of CSR because they fully understand the obligations imposed by citizenship; for them public image does not exist.

NOTES AND REFERENCES

1. As Feeney (2005: 1) explains:
   "... is a mistake to pursue rapid reforms in weak governance zones for the benefit of foreign investors and the private sector if reforms to improve respect for civil and political rights and the overall administration of justice are not pursued with equal vigour."
2. In the words of Granat (2001: 1):
   "bioengineering is a developing speciality featuring a multi-disciplinary approach to the solution of problems in medicine and biology, based on the application of advances in science, engineering and technology. A major focus for bioengineering is to improve the quality of life of people with medical conditions that restrict independent living and integration within the community."
3. Unerman and Bennette (2004: 702) explain the interactive ways that the financial report could present. For them:
   "... it is not possible to ascertain from the web forum (i.e. it is a mechanism to ensure movement towards inter-subjective acceptance by all stakeholders of the corporate responsibilities recognised) the extent to which postings have actually affected corporate decisions."
4. An empirical study concerning the operational reporting of corporate natural assets (i.e. habitats, fauna and flora) can be seen in Jones (2003).
5. "Following the external inputs invitation, till 28 February, 2005, the concept is that:
   "... in some investment environments, public authorities are unwilling or unable to protect rights (including property rights) and to provide basic public services (e.g. social programmes, infrastructure development and prudential surveillance). These "government failures" lead to broader failures in political, economic and civic institutions that the project refers to as "weak governance" (OECD, 2005).
6. Recognition included a corporate conscience award from the council on economic priorities and public accolades from Presidents Bush and Clinton (Austin *et al.*, 2004).
7. See for example OECD (2000a, 2000b) and Scherrer and Greven (2001).
8. An Islamic perspective on business ethics can be seen in Pomezanz (2004).
9. Along with Bentham, John Stuart Mill, as an nineteenth century English philosophy developed the Utilitarianism, which was the contention that man should judge everything in life based upon its ability to promote the greatest individual happiness (Titus and Smith, 1974).

10. All changes as an opportunity to pay previously unpaid taxes and with guaranteed from penalties and court prosecution made by the Portuguese government to fight tax evasion and/or in an effort to raise additional revenue, in consequence of budget deficit.
11. In Rego *et al.* (2003: 91), an anonymous answer to the survey explains that:

    "it should not be allowed fiscal forgive. Everybody should pay taxes. It was fundamental that courts works very well. It should be publishing the name of firms that did not pay to its suppliers and others."
12. During the last years, EU develops several documents about genetically modified food and feed, because the process itself is not safety (see EU, 2001a, 2003, 2004).
13. For a empirical perspective of creating a process-based model that structures existing indicators of sustainable development see Isaksson and Garvare (2003).
14. See Crowther (2004) for any argument that there is little such commitment: Crowther and Jatana (2005) for an exploration of this in the context of managerial egotism: Andersson and Pearson (1999) for argument concerning the incivility in the workplace and growing challenge of relationship mediated by high-tech asynchronous and global interaction.
15. *Gulp* is the bigger Portuguese oil and petrochemicals corporation owned by the Portuguese State.
16. *Caisa Geral de Depositos* is the bigger traditional financial institution owned by the Portuguese State.
17. See Crowther (2002a).
18. Other such actions which are taken to be representations of corporate social responsibility.
19. Although among academics the terms social accounting and environmental accounting are deemed to denote different aspects of responsible accounting, among practitioners the terms tend to be treated as synonymous and generally called environmental accounting. This approach has been followed here.
20. Different researchers have made literature revisions that study the 'Habermas Effect,' such as Power and Laughlin (1996).
21. More specifically, it is the dominant coalition of managers.
22. See Crowther *et al.* (2001) for a consideration of the symbiotic relationship between the actors on the water company stage.
23. See for example Emmanuel *et al.* (1985).
24. Such owners are of course the legal owners of the business, that is the shareholders.
25. See the VBM discourse considered by Cooper *et al.* (2001).
26. For example, the discourse surrounding social accounting and the problems of actually measuring the benefit to be distributed.
27. See Rappaport (1986, 1992).
28. For example, Beaver (1989) states that there has been a shift from an economic view of corporate performance measurement to an informational perspective with recognition of the social implications of an organisation's activities. Similarly, Eccles (1991) states that there has been a shift from treating financial figures as the foundation of corporate performance measurement to treating them as part

of a broader range of measures, while others (see Tinker, 1985) argue for a changed basis for accounting to reflect those changes.

29. See Crowther *et al.* (1998) and Starovik *et al.* (2004) for a critique of this technique.
30. Saravanamuthu (2004: 297) comments:

    "where international standards based on British and American models emphasize profit maximization, accounting's primary purpose in China's state-owned firms, that dominated its economy, was to enable budgetary control over resources appropriated from the state (Choi and Mueller, 1984; Ng. 1991)."

31. "Indeed this is consistent with financial accounting theory, and its concern with the boundary of the organisation, and with GAAP.
32. About the impact of social responsibility on business performance see for example Zairi and Peters (2002).

References

Ackerman, R. (1975): *The Social Challenge to Business*, Cambridge, Ma., Harvard University Press.

Andersson, L. and Pearson, C. (1999): Tit for Tat? The Spiralling Effect of Incivility in the Workplace, *Academic Management Review*, 24 (3): 458-71.

Austin, J., Leonard, H. and Quinn, J. (2004), "Timberland: Commerce and Justice," *Harvard Business School*, 9-305-002. December.

Bakhtin, M. (1981): *The Dialogic Imagination*, translated by M. Holquist and C. Emerson, Austin: University of Texas Press.

Baron, L.; Blum, L.; Krebs, D.; Oliner, P.; Oliner, S. and Smolenska, M. (1992): *Embracing the other: Philosophical, Psychological, and Historical Perspectives on Altruism*, New York, New York University Press.

Baudrillard, J. (1981): *For a Critique of the Political Economy of Signs*. St. Louis, Telos.

Beaver, W. (1989): *Financial Reporting: an Accounting Revolution*, Englewood Cliffs, N.J., Prentice-Hall.

Brandist, C. (1997): Bakhtin, Cassirer and Symbolic Forms," *Radical Philosophy*, 85: 20-27.

Briers, M. and Hirst, M. (1990): "The Role of Budgetary Information in Performance Evaluation," *Accounting, Organisation and Society*, 15(4), 373-98.

Cassirer, E. (1946): *Language and Myth*, translated by S. Langer, New York, Dover Publications.

Cassirer, E. (1955): *The Philosophy of Symbolic Forms*, 2: Myth, translated by R. Manheim, New Haven, Connecticut, Yale University Press.

Child, J. (1974): "Managerial and Organisational Factors Associated with Company Performance—Part 1," *Journal of Management Studies*, 11, 73-189.

Child, J. (1975): "Managerial and Organisational Factors Associated with Company Performance—Part 2," *Journal of Management Studies*, 12, 12-27.

Clark, J. (1957): *Economic Institutions and Human Welfare*, New York, Alfred A. Knopf.

Coates, J.; Davies, M.; Davis, E.; Zafar, A. and Zwirlein, T. (1995): "Adopting Performance Measures that Count: Changing to a Shareholder Value Focus," Aston Business School Research Paper N° RP9510.

Coates, J.; Davis, E.; Longden, S.; Stacey, R. and Emmanuel, C. (1993): *Corporate Performance Evaluation in Multinationals*, London, CIMA.

Cooper, S.; Crowther, D.; Davies, M. and Davis, E. (2001): Shareholder or Stakeholder Value, London: CIMA.

Crowther, D. and Jatana, R. (2005): "Modern Epics and Corporate Well-being, in D. Crowther and R. Jatana (eds.), *Representations of Social Responsibility*, 2. Hyderabad, ICFAI University Press.

Crowther, D. and Ortiz Martinez, E. (2005): "No Principals, No Principles, No Reserves: Shell and the Failure of Agency Theory," unpublished paper.

Crowther, D. and Rayman-Bacchus, L. (2004a), "Perspectives on Corporate Social Responsibility," in D. Crowther and L. Rayman-Bacchus (eds.), *Perspectives on Corporate Social Responsibility*, Aldershot, Ashgate, 1-17.

Crowther, D. and Rayman-Bacchus, L. (2004b): The Future of Corporate Social Responsibility," in D. Crowther and L. Rayman-Bacchus (eds.), *Perspectives on Corporate Social Responsibility*, Aldershot, Ashgate, 229-49.

Crowther, D. (2000): "Social and Environmental Accounting." London, *Financial Times*, Prentice-Hall.

Crowther, D. (2002a): *A Social Critique of Corporate Reporting*. Aldershot, Ashgate.

Crowther, D. (2002b): "Psychoanalysis and Auditing," in S. Clegg (ed.), *Paradoxical New Directions in Management and Organization Theory*, Amsterdam, J. Benjamins, 227-46.

Crowther, D. (2002c): "The Psychoanalysis of On-line Reporting," in L. Holmes, M. Grieco and D. Hosking (eds.), *Organising in the Information Age*, Aldershot, Ashgate, 130-48.

Crowther, D. (2004), "Corporate Social Reporting: Genuine Action or Window Dressing?," in D. Crowther and L. Rayman-Bacchus (eds.), *Perspectives on Corporate Social Responsibility*, Aldershot, Ashgate, 140-60.

Crowther, D.; Cooper, S. and Carter, C. (2001): "Regulation—The Movie: A Semiotic Study of the Periodic Review of UK Regulated Industry," *Journal of Organizational Change Management*, 14(3), 225-38.

Crowther, D.; Davies, M. and Cooper, S. (1998): "Evaluating Corporate Performance: A Critique of Economic Value Added," *Journal of Applied Accounting Research*, 4(3), 2-34.

Dahl, R. (1912): "A Prelude to Corporate Reform," *Business and Society Review*, Spring, 17-23

Decker, O. (2004): "Corporate Social Responsibility and Structural Change in Financial Services," *Management Auditing Journal*, 19(6), 712-28.

Dobzhansky, T. (1967): "Changing Man." *Science*, 155(3761), January, 409-15.

Eccles, R. (1991), "The Performance Evaluation Manifesto," *Harvard Business Review*, 69 (1): 131-37.

Eccles, R.; Herz, R.; Keegan, E. and Phillips, D. (2001): *The Value Reporting Revolution: Moving beyond the Earnings Game*, New York, John Wiley & Sons.

Emmanuel, C.; Otley, D. and Merchant, K. (1985): *Accounting for Management Control*, London, Chapman & Hall.

European Commission (EU, 2001a): Directive n° 2001/18/EC of the European Parliament and of the Council on the deliberate release into the environment of genetically modified organisms and repealing Council Directive 90/220/EEC, *Official Journal of the European Communities*, OJ L 106, 17.4.2001, 1-38.

European Commission (EU, 2001b): *Green Paper—Promoting a European Framework for Corporate Social Responsibility*, COM (2001) 366 final, Brussels, Official Publications of the European Commission, July 18.

European Commission (EU, 2002): *Corporate Social Responsibility: A Business Contribution to Sustainable Development*, COM (2002) 347 final. Brussels, Official Publications of the European Commission, July 2.

European Commission (EU, 2003): Regulation (EC) n° 1829/2003 of the European Parliament and of the Council of 22 September 2003 on Genetically Modified Food and Feed, *Official Journal of the European Communities*, OJ L 268, 18.10.2003, 1-23.

European Commission (EU, 2004): Commission Regulation (EC) n° 65/2004 of 14 January 2004 Establishing a System for the Development and Assignment of Unique Identifiers for Genetically Modified Organisms, *Official Journal of the European Communities*, OJ L 10, 16.01.2004, 5-10.

Feeney, P. (2005): *Response from Rights and Accountability in Development (RAID)*, Paris, OECD web page.

Fitzgerald, L.; Johnston, R.; Brignall, S.; Silvestrn, R. and Voss, C. (1991): *Performance Measurement in Service Businesses*, London, CIMA.

Fulop, G.; Hisrich, R. and Szegedi, K. (2000): "Business Ethics and Social Responsibility in Transition Economies," *Journal of Management Development*, 19(1), 5-31.

Gadamer, H. (1975): *Truth and Method*, translated by G. Bardent and J. Cumming, London, Sheed & Ward.

Govindarajan, V. and Gupta, A. (1985): "Linking Control Systems to Business Unit Strategy: Impact on Performance," *Accounting, Organizations and Society*, 10(1), 51-66.

Granat, M. (2001): *Department of Bioengineering-web page*, Glasgow, University of Strathclyde.

Habermas, J. (1971): *Knowledge and Human Interests*, translated by J. Shapiro, Boston, Mass: Beacon Press.

Heard, J. and Bolce, E. (1981): "The Political Significance of Corporate Social Reporting in the United States of America," *Accounting, Organization and Society*, 6(3), 247-54.

Isaksson, R. and Garvare, R. (2003): "Measuring Sustainable Development Using Process Models," *Managerial Auditing Journal*, 18(8): 649-58.

Jenkins, A. (1979): *The Social Theory of Claude Levi-Strauss*, London, Macmillan.
Jensen, M. and Meckling, W. (1976): "Theory of the Firm: Managerial Behaviour, Agency Costs and Ownership Structure," *Journal of Financial Economics*, October, 305-60.
Jensen, M. and Meckling, W. (1994): "The Nature of Man," *Journal of Applied Corporate Finance*, 7(2), Summer, 4-19.
Jones, M. (2003): "Accounting for Biodiversity: Operationalising Environmental Accounting," *Accounting, Auditing and Accountability Journal*, 16(5): 762-89.
Kant, I. (1959): *Foundations of the Metaphysics of Morals*, translated by L. Beck, New York, The Liberal Arts Press.
Lakoff, R. (1975): *Language and Woman's Place*, Cambridge, Harper & Row.
Levi-Strauss, C. (1963): *Structural Anthropology*, New York: Basic Books.
Mansbridge, J. (1990): *Beyond Self-Interest*, Chicago, University of Chicago Press.
Mattessich, R. (2003): Accounting Representation and the Onion Model of Reality: A Comparison with Baudrillard's Orders of Simulacra and his Hyper-reality, *Accounting, Organizations and Society*, 28(5), July, 443-70.
McDonald, D. and Puxty, A. (1979): An Inducement-contribution Approach to Corporate Financial Reporting, *Accounting, Organization and Society*, 4(112), 53-65.
McLuhan, M. and Fiore, Q. (1968): *War and Peace in the Global Village*, San Francisco, Hardwired.
Miller, D. (1992): *The Reason of Metaphor*, London, Sage.
Organization for Economic Cooperation and Development (OECD, 2000a): Working Party of the Trade Committee: Codes of Corporate Conduct: An Inventory, TD/TC/WP(98)74/FINAL, Paris, OECD.
Organization for Economic Cooperation and Development (OECD, 2000b): Working Party of the Trade Committee: Codes of Corporate Conduct: An Expanded View of their Contents, Paris, OECD.
Organization for Economic Cooperation and Development (OECD, 2003): *Business Approaches to Combating Corrupt Practices*, Paris, OECD.
Organization for Economic Cooperation and Development (OECD, 2005): *Conducting Business with Integrity in Weak Governance Zones: Invitation for Public Comment*, Paris, OECD.
Pakinson, J. (2003): "Models of Company and the Employment Relationship," *British Journal of Industrial Relations*, 41(3), September, 481-509.
Parker, L. (1977): "The Accounting Responsibility towards Corporate Financial Reporting to Employees," *Accounting Education*, 17(2), 62-83.
Phillips, K. (2001): "Markets in the Firm," *Economic Affairs*, September, 48-52.
Pomezanz, F. (2004): "Ethics: Toward Globalization," *Managerial Auditing Journal*, 19(1), 8-14.
Power, M. and Laughlin, R. (1996): "Habermas, Law and Accounting," *Accounting, Organizations and Society*, 21(5), July, 441-65
Purdy, D. (1983): "The Enterprise Theory: An Extension," *Journal of Business Finance and Accounting*, 10(4), 531-41.

Rappaport, A. (1986): *Creating Shareholder Value*, New York, The Free Press.

Rappaport, A. (1992), "CFO's and Strategists: Forging a Common Framework," *Harvard Business Review*, May/Jun., 84-91.

Rawls, J. (1971): *A Theory of Justice*, Cambridge, Mass., Harvard University Press.

Rego, A.; Moreira, J. and Sarrico, C. (2003): *Gestão ética e responsabilidade social das empresas: Um estudo da situação portuguesa*. Cascais: Principia.

Saravanamuthu, K. (2004): "What is Measured Counts: Harmonized Corporate Reporting and Sustainable Economic Development, *Critical Perspectives of Accounting*, 15, 295-302.

Schaltegger, S. and Figge, F. (2000): "Environmental Shareholder Value: Economic Success with Corporate Environmental Management, *Eco-management and Auditing*, 7: 29-42.

Schaltegger, S.; Muller, K. and Hindrichsen, H. (1996): *Corporate Environmental Accounting*, Chichester, John Wiley & Sons.

Scherrer, C. and Greven, T. (2001): *Global Rules for Trade: Codes of Conduct, Social Labelling, Workers' Rights Clauses*, Munster, Verlag Westfalisches Dampfboot.

Sebag, L. (1964): *Marxisme et Structuralisme*, Paris: Payot.

Shaw, E. (2004): "Marketing in the Social Enterprise Context," *Qualitative Market Research: An International Journal*, 7(3): 194-205.

Shefrin, H. (2001): "Behavioral Corporate Finance," *Journal of Applied Corporate Finance*, 14(3), Fall, 113-24.

Starovic, D.; Cooper, S. and Davis, M. (2004): *Maximising Shareholder Value: Achieving Clarity in Decision-making*, London, The Chartered Institute of Management Accountants.

Tinker, T. (1985): *Paper Prophets: A Social Critique of Accounting*, London, Holt, Rinehart & Winston.

Titus, H. and Smith, M. (1974): *Living Issues in Philosophy*, New York, D. Van Nostrand Company.

Topal, R. and Crowther, D. (2004): "Bioengineering and Corporate Social Responsibility," in D. Crowther and L. Rayman-Bacchus (eds.), *Perspectives on Corporate Social Responsibility*, Aldershot, Ashgate, 186-201.

Unerman, J. and Bennett, M. (2004): "Increased Stakeholder Dialogue and the Internet: Towards Greater Corporate Accountability or Reinforcing Capitalist Hegemony?," *Accounting, Organizations and Society*, 29(7), October, 685-707.

Wagner, M. and Schaltegger, S. (2003): "How Does Sustainability Performance Relate to Business Competitiveness?," *Greener Management International*, 44, Winter, 5-16.

Walden, W. and Schwartz, B. (1997): "Environmental Disclosures and Public Policy Pressure," *Journal of Accounting and Public Policy*, 16, 125-54.

Wheeler, D. and Elkington, J. (2001): "The End of the Corporate Environmental Report? Or the Advent of Cybernetic Sustainability Reporting and Communication," *Business Strategy and the Environment*, 10(1), Jan./Feb., 1-14.

Wilbur, J. (1992): *The Moral Foundations of Business Practice*, Lanham, University Press of America.

Williamson, O. (1963): "A Model of Rational Managerial Behaviour," in R. Cyert and J. March (eds.), *A Behavioural Theory of the Firm*, Englewood Cliffs, NJ, Prentice-Hall.

Zairi, M. and Peters, J. (2002): "The Impact of Social Responsibility on Business Performance," *Managerial Auditing Journal*, 17(4), 174-78.

Zeghal, D. and Ahmed, S. (1990): "Comparison of Social Responsibility Information Disclosure Media used by Canadian Firms," *Accounting, Auditing and Accountability Journal*, 3(1), 38-53.

4

CSR in Indian Context: The Case Study of Ambuja Cement

KAILASH SODANI AND RENU JATANA

INTRODUCTION

Organizational identification is a cognitive connection between the society and the organization. Just as all organization have to operate within the framework of the legal framework, similarly their exists a inherent and automatic law in the environment where the organizations function which is the social responsibility towards the society. The consumer is educated, alert and intelligent. He cannot be fooled. Today corporate social responsibility has become the breath for the organizations to survive. In this paper, the author addresses the conceptual framework of corporate social responsibility and related facets of the Indian industry and decipher certain key issues pertaining to the same. The paper is encompassed by the following backdrop:

1. Introduction and Conceptualization of Corporate Social Responsibility.
2. Research and Methodology.
3. CSR in the Market—Applications: Describing the significance of Corporate Social Responsibility for Indian Corporate Organizations towards the goal of good corporate citizenship.
4. Case Study of Ambuja Cement Ltd.

1. CONCEPTUAL FRAMEWORK

Corporate Social Responsibility (CSR) is a bent or inclination on the part of the organizations to uplift the standard of living, welfare, extend a helping hand to the helpless to project a positive image in the society. In other words, the companies with the sole objective of profit earning will wiped out of the market. Today the success of a company is threefold – Financial, Environmental, Social commitment. First object is financial, that is profit, the sole reason of existence of the business. Secondly, Environmental, i.e. nature friendly. Third and most important is social commitment because the organization is operating in a society and cannot over-look this aspect.

Hopkins opines "CSR is concerned with treating the stakeholders of the firm ethically or in a socially responsible manner. Stakeholders exist both within a firm and outside. Consequently behaving socially responsibly will increase the human development of stakeholders both within and outside the corporation."

In short, Corporate Social Responsibility can be defined as a Strategy or Visionary Plan which targets the bull's eye Profit encompassing Environmental aspects along with commitment of duty towards the society.

The Market scenario is an emergence of cut-throat and a cold blooded war. The question of profit today in front of the corporate is a two-sided sword where on one hand they have to meet the cost aspects and on other hand where all standards: Quality, Price, Product benefits, Promotion are the components of the very existence. This seems to be an irony, their money has also to be used for community welfare.

Today corporate world in the society has understood that survival is possible not only by spending on the philanthropic purposes for the sake but also they will have to get involved in the society and pass the warmth of care and protection to the society. The days of focusing on gaining maximum profits and keeping satisfied are gone. To convince the society, companies have started emerging as socially responsible corporate houses in this so-called material world.

The following are the benefits reaped by the Company:

- Getting license to operate from key stake-holders not just shareholders.

- Sustainable competitiveness.
- Enhancing reputations and Brands.
- Increase Sales and consumer loyalty.
- Increase ability to attract and retain quality employees.

2. RESEARCH AND METHODOLOGY

Brief literature review on issues pertaining to CSR has been undertaken to define the significance of these issues for the corporate world and the society. A Case Study of Ambuja Cement Ltd. has been undertaken which has been developed by interaction with the CEO and employees of Ambuja Cement Ltd. and referring to their Annual Reviews.

3. CSR IN THE MARKET: APPLICATIONS

Some of the corporate houses like Reliance, HLL, ITC Limited have all undertaken to provide health services and educational services in the rural sector. It will be worthwhile considering a percentage of the profit generated to be earmarked for undertaking social responsibility functions. Of course, the corporate would also expect the encouragement of the government for availing tax exemptions for such activities. ICICI launched a social development portal, www-icicicommunities.ora. The portal comprises of a medium for online donation and resource centres on education and infant mortality prevention. Besides, a trading zone to local communities enabling them to access the global retail market is envisioned. The ATM services and phone banking services of ICICI Bank have added a feature for contribution to the Tsunami Relief Fund. This definitely shows their strategy to help the society at the right point which gives easy access to the bank account. Their phone banking and net banking services also provide a similar feature. SUN TV organizing the SUN TV Tsunami Relief Fund – this is a dual strategy. One, creating the awareness about the fund, which is the intended benefit and another, the imbibed benefit, is a different avatar of SUN TV – a socially responsible media. The Murugappa group has contributed around Rs. 2 crore to the PM and CM relief funds to help the Tsunami victims. ITC's venture of e-choupal is an effective manifestation of how corporate firms can contribute significantly to the social reform process by going rural.

4. AMBUJA CEMENT LTD.—THE NEW JINGLE—CSR: THE ROAD AHEAD

Companies need to act in socially responsible behaviour. They might cease to make a product but their relationship with the people and the natural environment will help them grow over time. Therefore, for a company to be successful, in the long run, it must contribute towards the well-being of the society and the environment.

Company Background

Gujarat Ambuja Cement was set up in 1986. In the last decade, the company has grown ten-fold. With the commencement of commercial production at its 2 mn. plant in Chandrapur, Maharashtra, Ambuja will become India's third largest cement company with a capacity of 12.5 mn. tonnes and revenue in excess of 2,500 crores. Its plants are some of the most efficient in the world with environment protection measures that are at par with the finest in the developed world.

The company's most distinctive attribute, however, is its approach to the business. Ambuja follows a unique home-grown philosophy, the authority to set their own targets, and the freedom to achieve their goals. This simple vision has created an environment where there are no limits to excellence, no limits to efficiency and has proved to be a powerful engine for the growth of the company.

CSR in Ambuja Cement Ltd.

As a part of its Corporate Social Responsibility, Ambuja Cement, a cement manufacturing company, having its plant in Bharatpura (Chattisgarh) and Sankrail (West Bengal), Ambuja Cement Foundation started out with one simple dream – to provide basic infrastructure for villagers, in one single location, Kodinar and a few surrounding villages in the state of Gujarat. When everyone in the Foundation saw the first dream turn into reality, they decided to multiply their dreams with eagerness and enthusiasm to bring about change, they have multiplied their efforts and managed to spread their activities to over 350 villages in 7 States. All this has happened with one trigger. A passion to reach out to those in the heartland of the country who deserve the best – better infrastructure, better job opportunities. Indeed a better quality of life. Also the company worked extensively on water issues and subsequently, synergy between water and land development. Today they address other allied primary issues simultaneously such as health and education to convert our efforts into an integrated rural development. What is path breaking is their unleashing of woman power. They have proved beyond doubt that woman, if provided appropriate knowledge and resources can be the fastest change agents in the country.

Profile of ACF's Programme Areas

Parameters	*Units*	*Size*
Villages covered	No.	384
Human population affected	'000	596
Livestock population	'000	288.1
Land area	'000 Ha	204.2
Cultivable land area	'000 Ha	91

Source: Ambuja Cement—Annual Review, 2004.

Company Initiatives: CSR

1. **Natural Resources Management:** Water and other natural resource management continues to remain Ambuja's core focus area. The Company has designed a Integrated Watershed Development Programme has proved to be one of the most successful models developed for water management in rural areas. To garner more support from other institutions and the government, the company has institutionalized various programmes at different levels through village level committees. These programmes address vital issues like salinity, declining water quality and biodiversity. These efforts are reaping the company not just environmental but major social and economic rewards to the communities. A staggered contour trenches have been developed and over 250 wire-crates have been constructed in the rivulets treating the drainage lines and soil erosion has been adequately treated through vegetative covers.
2. **Salinity Mitigation:** A Project called Gujarat Coastal Salinity Prevention in collaboration with Sir Ratan Tata Trust has

been devised. This involves maximizing the recharge of ground water aquifer through ground water management and rainwater harvesting, efficient water conservation and management through agriculture development by changing cropping patterns – growing horticulture crops requiring less water and use of drip irrigation and improvisations to meet the drinking water needs.

3. **Promoting Sustainable Agriculture:** The Company has put in efforts to restore soil health through organic farming and promoting the use of farm manures and are changing crop patterns. The Company teams work closely with farmers to provide round the year training in sustainable agricultural techniques. The Company makes efforts to bring expertise of agriculture universities and other institutions to train local farmers. ACF also promotes scientific techniques in animal husbandry to help improve the capacity of landless and poor farmers. These efforts include animal healthcare camps and cattle care training.
4. **Health Care:** CEO Suresh Neotia shares that while working in areas they realized that HIV/AIDS is an important issue in the community. A team was set up and HIV/AIDS awareness messages targeting the village population were spread in the programme area besides running regular mobile vans and organizing camps.

As a result, Ambuja Cement Ltd. is the most profitable cement company in India and the lowest cost producer of cement in the world.

References

Annual Review, 2004, "Ambuja Cement Foundation: Making a Concrete Difference.

Champion David, 2001, "Mastering the Value Chain", *Harvard Business Review*, June-July, pp. 109-15.

Indian Journal of Marketing, 2003, "Business to Business E-Commerce and Second Generation Reforms—Redefining Business Paradigms", Dec. 2003.

Michael Hopkins, 1998, *A Planetary Bargain: CSR Comes of Age*, Macmilian, UK.

S. Bhaskaran and Anitha Dillipan, *Global CEO*, April 2005, "CSR: The Road Ahead".

5

Social Responsibility and Marketing

VIJAY SHRIMALI AND HARSHITA SHRIMALI

Social responsibility refers to what the business does, over and above the statutory requirement for the benefit of the society. The word responsibility connotes that the business has some moral obligation to the society.

In the environment of modern economic development, the corporate sector no longer function in isolation. In modern times, the objectives of business have to be the proper utilization of resources for the benefit of others. A profit is necessary part of total picture but it is not the primary purpose. The claim of various interests will have to be balanced, not on the narrow ground of what is best for the shareholders alone but from the point of view of what is best for the community at large. The company must accept its obligation to be socially responsible and to work the larger benefit of the community.

H.S. Singhania classifies responsibility into two categories:

- The manner in which a business caries out its own business activity.
- The welfare activity that it takes upon itself as additional function.

Marketing being a social and managerial process, it must have social and environmental approach. Unfortunately very few business organization cared for it but those who cared for it they achieve success and growth in their business.

Here is the observation of some business leaders on corporate social responsibility.

According to N.R. Narayana Murthy—Corporate foremost social responsibility is to create maximum shareholders value working under the circumstances where it is fair to all its stakeholders, workers, consumers, the community, government and the environment. He points out that by living in harmony with the community and environment around us and not cheating out customers and workers, we might not gain anything in the short-run, but in the long-term it means greater profits and shareholders value.

In the opinion of Aman Mehta, CEO, HSBC says that CSR, as a concept is different to different people and in different countries.

Fundamentally CSR is balancing the conflict interest put the corporation from different stakeholders with the objectives a commercial organization in such a way that there is a minimum loss to anybody.

Bertrand Collomle, CEO, Lafarge France observes that a company can't be successful in the long-run without a happy community around and a motivated and happy workforce which would translate into greater labour productivity, lower wastage in manufacturing process and product rejection rate resulting in greater profits. According, to him, manufacturing and business practices to the developing countries and training and educating local people in new skills and knowledge.

According to The World Business Council for Sustainable Development—"Corporate Social Responsibility is the continuing commitment by business to behave ethically and contribute to economic development while improving the quality of life of the workforce and their families as well as of the local community and society at large."

CSR has been defined as "open and transparent business practices that are based upon ethical values and respect for employees, communities and the environment—(and) designed to deliver sustainable value to society at large, as well as to shareholders."—The Prince of Wales Business Leaders Forum.

Traditionally in the United States, CSR has been defined much more in terms of a philanthropic model. Companies make profits, unhindered except by fulfilling their duty to pay taxes. Then they donate a certain share of the profits to charitable causes. It is seen as tainting the act for the company to receive any benefit from the giving.

TATA GROUP

The company's philanthropic activities can be dated to as early as 1892. They have run Endowment Schemes to provide higher education for deserving Indians. Over 3,500 Tata scholarships have been awarded. J.R.D. Tata institutionalized CSR in the 1970s and decided that the group shall be mindful of its social and moral responsibilities to the consumers, employees, shareholders, society and the local community for all its major companies.

In July 2002, Tata Steel presented the first corporate sustainability report, which would serve as a benchmark and a confidence-builder for other Tata companies. It also has formed group resource under the TCCI (Tata Council for Community Initiatives) on corporate sustainability and a strategy to assist other Tata companies on corporate social responsibility. The group resource on corporate sustainability would work on developing a Tata model using technical inputs from the UNDP.

The Tatas have spent Rs. 1.5 billion on social services—the highest by any corporate house in the country during 2001-02. The thrust area was rural development, which included community health, basic education and vocational training. It also spends on basic infrastructure and disburses money through various charitable trusts and relief and reconstruction societies. Tisco had been shining example of social responsibility. Tisco appointed a social audit committee to go in to the question of whether and to what extend the company has fulfilled its social obligation.

INFOSYS

Formed in 1981 by N.R. Narayana Murthy, Infosys follows a socially responsible and sustainable path in conducting business. Even during the boom time of the 1990's when the stock prices of IT companies were skyrocketing, the company believed in sharing the wealth with the society and its employees. This practice of the company stems from the personal belief of Narayana Murthy to give back to the society more than what it gave him. It also substantiates the role and motivation of the CEO and the top management in making the company a responsible corporate citizen.

Infosys has won many awarded such as Best Employers to Work for in India, Golden Peacock Award for Excellence in Corporate Governance in the Global Category by the World Council for Corporate Governance, London and Corporate Citizenship Award by *The Economic Times*. According to a recent report, Infosys spends about Rs. 50 million on social activities.

AV BIRLA GROUP

The AV Birla group's initiatives are channelled through The Aditya Birla Centre for Community Initiatives and Rural Development spearheaded by Rajashree Birla (wife of Aditya Birla). All the Group companies are dedicated to social development. Hindalco a group company has won the FICCI-SEDF Social Responsiveness Awards 2001 instituted by FICCI Socio-Economic Development Foundation (a constructive partnership between *Busineessworld*, ICICI Communities, Partners in Change and KPMG).

The activities of the group include innovative project involving the development of rural youth and employment generation; education and training and health care projects; helping the disable people; social causes like widow remarriages; dowryless marriages; and women empowerment programmes. Also the group undertake sponsorship of the arts and Indian culture, which are need based. The Birla Academy of Art and Culture set up in 1962 in Kolkata treasures art works and exquisite exhibits and has evolved into one of India's premier institutions for art and culture.

The AV Birla group also offers scholarship to students form IITs, IIMs and BITS (Pilani) to nurture tomorrow's leader as late Aditya Vikram Birla, believed in people power and their potential to become leaders. Only the best are selected for the coveted award and are called 'The Aditya Birla Scholars'.

This concept of social marketing is latest one. It holds the organization task to determine the needs, want and interest of the target marketers and to deliver, the decided satisfaction more effectively than competitors in a way that preserves to enhances consumers satisfaction and well-being of the society. The social marketing concepts call upon marketers to balance their consideration in selling their marketing policies. Marketing strategies are formulated always in the light of requirement of social responsibilities.

SOCIAL FUNCTION OF MARKETING

Marketing management is concerned with social function, which ensure that their behaviour and action do not sacrifice the right and legitimate interest of the public.

Social function of marketing is as follows:

1. **Survival:** It is important and basic objective of any business concern. Marketing strategies are to be developed to achieve survival goals.
2. **Profitability:** It is an indicator of efficiency. Business concern resorting to profiteering, adultering, hoarding, black marketing may be restricted, penalized or put out of market by social pressure, political action, legislative interference or by economic competition. Profitability can be through of but not at the cost of social responsibility.
3. **Service:** In modern business, the marketing concepts assure those goods and services are to be provided which gives satisfaction to the consumers. The concept of service to customers and society is based on ethical views of marketing practice.
4. **Social Responsibility:** There is an immense need to formulate marketing strategies in the light of increasing social responsibilities.

Marketing manager is a link between the organization and the society. Marketing managers are involved in resolving conflict and reconciling the following responsibilities:

Responsibility to Shareholders

The responsibility of a company to its shareholder, who are the owners is indeed a primary one. The major responsibility of the organization to the shareholders is

- To safeguard the capital of the shareholders.
- To provide a reasonable dividend, the company had to strengthen and consolidate its position.

Responsibility to Employees

The success of an organisation depends to a very large extent on the morale of the employees. Employee's morale depends on the discharge of the company's responsibility to them. The major responsibility of the organisation to the workers is:

- Payment of fair wages.
- Adequate working conditions, proper training and education.
- Proper recognition, appreciation and encouragement of special skills and capabilities of the workers.

Responsibility to Consumers

The customer is the foundation of a business and keeps it is existence. Marketing manager puts the demand of consumers before the business concern and brings the company's product or service to the consumers.

The major responsibilities are:

- Improve the efficiency to increase productivity, improve quality and reduce prices.
- Innovative products to be Introduced.
- To provide after sales service.
- Provide sufficient information about product, including their adverse effects, risk and care to taken while using the product.
- The most important is to understand customer needs and to take necessary measures to satisfy these needs.

Responsibility to the Community and Society

A business has lot of responsibility to the community around its location and to society at large. Major amongst them are:

- Prevent environmental pollution and to preserve the ecological balance.
- Making possible contribution to furthering social causes like the promotion of education and population control.

The rationale of the concept of social responsibility is that industry can no longer be regarded as private arrangement for enriching shareholders. It has become a joint enterprise in which workers, management, consumers, the locality, government and trade union officials all play active role. There is a growing realization on the part of the enlightened businessmen that it is their moral duty to serve the society, as society provides necessary facilities for the establishment and operation of business concern. Businessmen enjoy wide economic and social power thus their power should be balance with social responsibility as business had the resources and capabilities to solve social problems. Marketing systems and social dependence are closely interrelated with each other. For e.g. (*Goods and services supplied by business determine standard of living in the society. If business does not supply proper goods and service at proper quality and at fair prices, society will stop or restrict the flow of inputs into business*). Therefore business must be responsive to society's needs and expectations.

CONCLUSION

Modern business is regarded as an integral component of society. The concept of responsibility requires executives to consider their acts within the framework of the social system. The social function of the marketing is survival, profitability, service and social marketing of business, ensuring law and order, moral justification, system interdependence etc.

In recent times, corporate social responsibility has gained lot of importance among companies because of its long-term benefits. Companies should be responsible to the society for their activities and owe to the environment in which they operate. But it takes more than supporting the most happening subject to get mileage.

Identifying the right cause based on inner values and common goals can bring about the best results both internally with employees and also externally with stakeholders.

Creating brand equity is the most powerful weapon in a company's armour to beat the competition. In the fiercely competitive market place of today where customer and societal expectations are changing rapidly requiring constant innovation of new ideas, products and services, strategy and social responsibility provide the shortest route to an organization's success.

A company should carefully evaluate the pros and cons for the right 'fit' and ensure a balanced view of the components of corporate social responsibility and implement the strategies in consonance with its vision, mission and values.

6

Art in the Boardroom: Questioning the Ethics of Corporate Collecting Practices

GARRITT VAN DYK, JENNIFER MILAM, CINDY DAVIDS AND GORDON BOYCE

INTRODUCTION

Historically, funding for art in the West has been dominated by the patronage of powerful social and political institutions. Today, as corporations become increasingly prominent in society, displacing the position of Church, prince and state, they also assume a greater role as patrons, sponsors and collectors, of art. Cathedrals have been symbolically replaced by skyscrapers adorned with corporate brands; palace gardens have given way to modern industrial parks; the semi-public space of Court has been superseded by public spaces built through corporate sponsorship; and the forging of national patrimony through legislated acquisition mandates are now paralleled by the establishment of corporate cultural identity through highly publicized art purchases.

This paper considers different forms of corporate interaction with the arts, including sponsorship, patronage and corporate collecting. The corporate economics of supporting the arts may alternatively involve its interpretation as a marketing expense, as a strategic device to generate a beneficial taxation position, or as an asset-building strategy. These interpretations may reflect the self-interest of the corporation, but may also be interpreted as fulfilment of society's expectation of a socially responsible corporate citizen-the corporation as benefactor, reinvesting a portion of its profits in society. The various roles of 'art in the boardroom' differ in their nature and effects, but they may all be understood as manifestations of a transformation of art patronage from an historical symbol of magnificence to a more contemporary role as an example of munificence and corporate social responsibility.

CORPORATE SPONSORSHIP

On a recent visit to the High Museum of Art in Atlanta the specter of corporate sponsorship was ever-present to the attuned eye. Starbucks, the multi-national coffee house, was the principal sponsor of an exhibition of the modern African-American artist Romare Beardon; Delta Airlines and Lincoln fund various Jazz and cinema evenings: Target and Carter's (sellers and producers of children's goods) sponsor a weekly family day. These corporations benefit from the public perception of their goodwill and an identification of their products with the 'brand' characteristics of the event they sponsor. For example, in the "Sponsor Highlight" of the High Life magazine, Starbucks is presented as a company "committed to offering the highest quality of coffee and experience by conducting its business in ways that produce social, environmental, and economic benefits in communities where it does business," a claim that is given legitimacy by its publication in the museum serial. This is not placement without consequence when we reflect on the findings of a recent survey in America in which museums topped the list of public trust in the conveyance of information.

At the High Museum, corporate logos were on every brochure, every piece of public education, every advertisement, and many walls. Although always discreetly positioned-museum officials might even say they are 'tastefully' placed-corporate identity thus assumes a new symbiotic relationship to that of the work of art, artist and museum as a destination. Financial support is important because it makes art possible, but the source and method of funding can also influence the artistic process, the final product, and public perceptions of both (specifically through its display in spaces adorned with corporate logos).

CORPORATE PATRONAGE

Corporate involvement in the arts may be difficult to separate from the wider economic and political interests of the sponsoring corporation. For example, in 1994 Philip Morris threatened to move its corporate headquarters from New York City in response to the proposed City ban on smoking in public places. This move would mean that the city would lose not only jobs and tax revenue, but also funding for the arts. Organizations that had received funding from Philip Morris were reportedly asked by the company to lobby the City Council Speaker, who had proposed the legislation, alerting him that Philip Morris would withdraw funding if the hill were passed. In its defence against charges of extortionist tactics, Philip Morris stated that a fund-raising firm trying to rally support from a number of arts institutions and organizations was responsible for the efforts, unprompted by the company. Linking public economic interests such as tax revenue and jobs with corporate interests is not new, but the increasing presence of corporate funding and the growing influence on cultural institutions to further corporate agendas raise questions about the ability of arts organizations to remain independent and true to their stated public missions.

Philip Morris is not merely a leader in funding the arts. Its corporate headquarters in New York City is also home to the Whitney Museum of American Art at Philip Morris. The corporation enjoys the cultural cachet of hosting a museum in its lobby, helping to promote general goodwill and establish its brand identity with their targeted market audience within the universe of museum-goers. In addition, the corporation enjoys a zoning concession by providing a public amenity, tax deductions related to expenses from running the museum, and a lower assessed value for the building resulting in lower real estate taxes. The corporate-museum presence, however, means that this public space is much more tightly controlled than a simple atrium.

On the other side of the alliance, the museum enjoys an additional exhibition space, allowing it to show more art to more people. Whether or not the museum can exhibit whatever it wants in this space is questionable. Both the Whitney and Philip Morris would maintain that the museum is free to make its own decisions regarding content. But what is the likelihood that art containing images negative to the company would be welcome? The relationship is symbiotic, but the two parties do not profit equally—the corporation as controlling economic entity enjoys an asymmetrical advantage. Their strategic alliance accrues both to their economic and public relations benefit, while the museum has permitted its curatorial independence to be called into question. The corporation has economic control over the space, and even if unspoken, the potential for intervention impacts viewers as part of their experience in the corporate-museum franchise.

This is exactly the situation that occurred in the early 1970s, with the Guggenheim museum's cancellation of an exhibition of Hans Haacke's work. Haacke is a contemporary artist whose work is engaged with social and political critique in visual form. The position taken by the Guggenheim was that Haacke's work was not art, but social commentary (a rather outrageous distinction for a museum that specializes in modern and contemporary art). Haacke used this as an opportunity to explore the ethically questionable professional and corporate practices of prominent members of the Guggenheim board in his show Unfinished Business at the Museum of Contemporary Art in New York.

INDIRECT CORPORATE INVOLVEMENT

There is a more complicated relationship between artists who refuse any sponsorship (private, public or corporate) of their works in their efforts to have an independent, critical voice. Haacke is one of these artists, and so is the team of Christo and Jeanne-Claude. Consider the example of Christo and Jeanne-Claude's The Gates, Central Park, New York, 1979-2005, on view in February 2005. For decades, Christo and Jeanne-Claude have eschewed corporate, public and private sponsorship of their large-scale public art installations and The Gates is no exception. The US $ 20 m installation cost was raised by the artists through the sale of preliminary drawings, sketches, collages, and photographs, as well as the sale of art objects produced in previous years. The art is conceptual—a temporary transformation of public space—imprinting a visual memory of the installation on those who viewed it. The Gates were removed after 16 days, but the memory remains. This 'art' attempts to defy ownership, because it existed in a public place and only for a short period of time. Christo and Jeanne-Claude have emphasized the need for the art to be independent of any kind of obligations.

There are, for example, no volunteers, so the artists are beholden to no one-no sponsor, no individual, no government, no cultural institution ultimately controlling the completed work. But is this utopian aim truly possible? We would argue that it is not, particularly in the mind of the 'public' viewer, who responds not only to the work of art itself, but also to references to that work of art outside of the first-hand experience of the installation.

Previously Christo and Jeanne-Claude have not licensed the marketing of their intellectual property; however in this case they allowed a licensing agreement with Nurture New York's Nature (NNYN), a not-for-profit corporation "dedicated to creating public awareness of the importance of nurturing New York's nature for the health and well-being of the City's inhabitants." Deutsche Bank, as a founding sponsor contributed $250,000 to establish NNYN and placed a full-page ad in the *New York Times* to celebrate the opening of the installation. Even though Deutsche Bank was not a sponsor of The Gates or Christo and Jeanne Claude, they linked their name with The Gates and the artists. In this way, Deutsche Bank associated itself not only with the not-for-profit it helped establish, but also with the art and the artists. Christo and Jeanne-Claude's rejection of sponsorship did not prevent Deutsche Bank from projecting its identity into the mind of viewers, transforming the visual memory of the art where it ultimately resides.

EFFECTS ON CURATORIAL INDEPENDENCE

Contemporary and avant-garde art exhibitions are lightning rods for controversy, but normally the debate centres around the content of the show, not questions of ethics or conflicts of interest. There was controversial art in Sensation: Young British Artists from the Saatchi collection exhibited at the Brooklyn Museum of Art in New York City in 1999 (notably Chris Ofili's Virgin Mary, with elephant dung), but the initial uproar over content was eclipsed by the questionable practices employed in putting on the show. Sensation exhibited contemporary works from the collection of Charles Saatchi, who was also the show's largest sponsor, and the controlling curator or both the content and the display of the collection. The Brooklyn Museum of Art did not disclose Saatchi's financial role, at his request, nor did it disclose his unusually large curatorial role. Saatchi stood to profit as his collection gained value from the exposure the exhibition brought, as did another sponsor, Christie's auction house. His overlapping roles as owner of the collection, leading financial sponsor, and curator raised serious questions about the conflicting interests of self-promotion for economic benefit and cultural benefit from the exhibition of contemporary art. The American Association of Museums was prompted by the situation to issue new ethical guidelines for museums when borrowing objects and involving sponsors. The National Gallery of Australia went a step further, and cancelled the show after reviewing information about the exhibition, which it "deemed untenable." The cancellation was a difficult public relations exercise, as the NGA was wrongly accused in the press of cancelling the show due to its controversial content.

CORPORATE COLLECTING PRACTICES

For artists whose works are bought by corporations, a degree of control over the meaning and purpose of the art is inevitably passed to the corporate entity, whatever the intentions of the original artist. More broadly, corporate collecting practices can have significant effects on the availability of works for public display and access. Corporate interaction with the arts in Australia has led to significant private collections held both by corporate entities and their executives. The existence of significant private collections remains largely unknown and unacknowledged publicly and their value is largely undocumented. The art is not publicly available as it is often hidden behind the doors of banks, law firms, stockbrokers, and a range of successful corporations. The works are on view usually only to a select few executives, employees, and valued clients.

The perceived public relations value of acquiring major works is evident when they are placed on display in the foyers of major corporate headquarters, although the significance of the art may be lost on those who pass through with other purposes in mind. Nevertheless, corporate art may serve a more instrumental purpose for example, law firms may use art to lighten the atmosphere of otherwise serious places, to place clients at ease, or as a conversation starter with a new client. Australia's Macquarie Bank—an investment bank known as the "millionaire factory"—hangs art in the public spaces of all its branches. This was a policy initiated when the bank was established, in order to signal the vitality of the new company. Corporate art collecting practices can be used to symbolise a company's commitment to indigenous or local art, to attempt to make a business appear young and dynamic, or may be used to create an ambience that generates a stimulating workplace environment.

The private collections of many corporate chief executive officers and leading stockbrokers are on view only to an even more select group of family and friends (and clients) inside their homes. There is, of course, nothing new in this, although the financing of the acquisition of multi-million dollar art collections has come into question. When the purchase and display of corporate art is principally for private gratification, at some point questions of ownership of the asset may come into play. This was the case when prominent entrepreneur Alan Bond was prosecuted in relation to the acquisition of Manet's La Promenade.

In Australia, the public relations value of corporate collecting and sponsorship has not gone unnoticed. Wesfarmers corporation, for instance, has funded a national touring exhibition of 60 pieces from its 500-strong holding, entitled Sublime: 25 Years of the Wesfarmers Collection of Australian Art. Wesfarmers started as a cooperative farming enterprise but is now a diversified industrial conglomerate which is ranked as having the second most valuable corporate collection in Australia. Other corporations and individuals sometimes lend particular pieces to galleries and museums, and some private collectors have established galleries in their own names.

Corporate collecting practices are often driven by the interests of an individual chief executive. Collections may be justified on the basis of their investment value, although such speculative investment is often officially eschewed, even though the financial value of collections may be significant. Individual executives and their private curatorial teams may be committed to corporate art collections, but following mergers and acquisitions, changes in board philosophy, or if the corporation gets into financial difficulty, corporate art collections may be disposed of. In these circumstances, the art tends to circulate around the hands of prominent private collectors. For example, following the financial collapse of Bond Corporation, the subsequent fire sale of the collection saw several major acquisitions go to prominent private and corporate collectors, although the Getty Museum in Los Angeles acquired Van Gogh's Irises. Some works may be donated to public galleries and arts institutions, thus becoming available to a wider audience (and yielding a tax benefit for the donating corporation), but most end up in private collections.

Corporate collecting practices are clearly significant in enlivening the market for major works of art, and this may have a positive effect in terms of highlighting to the wider community the value of art. However, the principal beneficiaries are a range of private interests and art markets often treat art as a commodity that can be traded in by a select few. The financial beneficiaries of art's value do not necessarily include the original artist, although a reputation effect may be positive of the artist is still living).

DISCUSSION AND CONCLUSIONS

The boundaries delineating appropriate roles for museums, sponsors, and the commercial art world have ceased to be sharply defined. In the contemporary environment, museums act like multinational corporations with branch offices, corporations house museums, and many individuals speculate in the commercial value of art. Without greater attention to these shifting roles, it is likely that commerce and culture will become indistinguishable.

Is corporate sponsorship of the arts a bad thing? Not necessarily, but it is problematic and fraught with questions of censorship, autonomy and the impact of intervention on both the artistic process and the viewing experience. Public sector funding is not available to meet the demands of cultural institutions and programs, so without other sources, the arts would suffer. Corporations must, however, be aware that their economic power demands responsibility in its application. The goodwill of the public in general, and the targeted audience of corporate marketing, can easily be negated when corporations overstep boundaries by exerting undue influence. The potential for a backlash is great—consider the negative publicity of demonstrations against globalisation directed against corporations who manipulate cultural institutions. The arts require funding and other forms of interaction with the corporate sector, but the impact on art and on the public must be considered when corporations make demands on artists and museums.

REFERENCES

"Americans Identify a Source of Information They Can Trust." American Association of Museums press release. PR contact Jason Hall. http://www.aam-us.ong/pressreleases.cfm?mode=list&id=21.

Brian Kennedy. "How much do we care about museum ethics." National Gallery of Australia. http://www.nga.gov.au/Director/Previous/Kennedy/musethics.html.

Christo and Jeanne-Claude's funding strategies have been detailed in Jutta Lehmer. "Die Kunst der Finanzierung." Berliner Zeitung. 1 July 1995 and referenced in Rectanus, *op. cit.*, 162-3.

For more information on the sponsorship practices of Philip Morris, see Sam Hunter. Art in Business: The Philip Morris Story (New York: Abrams/BCA, 1979) and Philip Morris and the Arts: 35 Year Report (New York: Philip Morris Companies. Inc., 1993).

For the most recent studies of corporate intervention in the arts, see Mark W. Rectanus, Culture Incorporated, Museums, Artists, and Corporate Sponsorships (Minneapolis and London: University of Minnesota Press. 2002) and Chin-tao Wu. Privatising Culture. Corporate An Intervention since the 1980s (New York and London: Verso. 2002).

Further critique of the Guggenheim's cancellation of the 1971 exhibition can be found in Rosalyn Deutsche. Evictions: Art and Spatial Politics (Graham Foundation/ MIT Press Series in Contemporary Architectural Discourse: Cambridge: MIT Press, 1998). For more on Haacke's engagement with corporate cultural politics, see Pierre Bourdieu and Hans Haacke. Free Exchange (Stanford: Stanford University Press, 1995) and Douglas Crimp. On the Museum's Ruins (Cambridge: MIT Press, 1993).

Hans Haacke: Unfinished Business, ed. Brian Wallis (Cambridge: MIT Press, 1987).

Hawley, *loc cit*.

High Life. High Museum of Art. Atlanta. Georgia. February/March 2005. 3.

Media coverage addressing these conflicts of interest included David Barstow. "Brooklyn Museum Recruited Donors Who Stood to Gain." *The New York Times*. 31 October 1999: Stephanie Cash. "Art under Siege in New York: 'Sensation' Battle Erupts in Brooklyn." Art in America. November 1999. 37-41: and Michael Kimmelman. "In the End, the 'Sensation' Is More in the Money," *The New York Times*, 3 November 1999.

Rushworth M. Kidder. "Building a Code of Ethics? Some Lessons from the Art World." Institute for Global Ethics. Camden. Maine. 2000. http://www.glohalethics.org/members/commentary-08-07-00.html.

See, for example, a report of the auction of the Fosters Brewing Group art collection in Sunanda Creagh. "Prized Streeton the shining light of greatest hits auction." *Sydney Morning Herald* (12 May 2005, 9).

See Janet Hawley. "Hangings in the boardroom" The Age-Good Weekend. 5 February 2005. 16-22. In some senses, corporate collections of Australian art (indigenous and non-indigenous) are used to signal a sense of national commitment that, in Australia, has also been reflected on a broader cultural level with a revival of the popularity of Australian films, books, wine, and even convict roots. Some of the public relations value of BHP Billiton's new collection of contemporary Australian art may innere in a public signal of Australianness following the merger of corporation formerly known as "Australia's BHP" with UK-based Billiton.

See Peter Fish. "Going hammer and tongs." *Sydney Morning Herald* (21 August 2004). See also Hawley, *loc cit*.

The mission statement is from Nurture New York's Nature website: http://www.nnyn.org/aboutus.html.

The New York Times. 13 February 2005, 7.

Trevor Sykes. The Bold Riders: Behind Australia's Corporate Collapses (St. Leonards: Allen & Unwin, 1996, 236).

Young British Art: The Saatchi Decade (London: Booth-Clibborn Editions, 1999).

7

Partnerships and Cause-related Marketing—Building Brands for the Future

V.K. ANISH

Cause Related Marketing (CRM) and Corporate Social Responsibility (CSR) can go a long way in building a reliable brand image and reputation. While campaigns vary in their scope and design, the nature of most such relationships carry common elements like synergy, trust and influence. This paper looks closely at some of the key factors that need scrutiny while arriving at a robust, reputed campaign from the point of view of communication, marketing and social responsibility.

A study of the mode of partnerships is called for, particularly one that enables an organization to build loyalty amongst the shareholders, develop strong local and global relationships, enter new markets, and generate positive publicity.

The source of information for this paper is first hand, primary and secondary data. The author wears two hats – one as the office-bearer of a globally recognized road safety non-government organization and the other as the communications manager of an IT corporate house on corporate social responsibility projects, thus helping him create an outline for a well defined plan and strategy.

Given the significance that companies place on their corporate culture and how they use their core values to determine CSR initiatives, it is important for development organizations and donors who want to explore partnerships with companies to understand corporate culture, the history of corporate philanthropy, and core business values. This knowledge will help frame an exploratory dialogue and set the parameters for what might be possible in a partnership.

INTRODUCTION

Corporate Social Responsibility and Cause Related Marketing are more than buzz words today. While the issue of obligation and commitment to society beyond business has risen to prominence among management circles as well as the wider public, it is still a nascent subject among stakeholders.

Companies need to be responsible and accountable to other 'stakeholders' in society such as their local communities, their employees, or non-profit organizations. The term Corporate Social Responsibility or Cause Related Marketing is generally used to express the idea that companies have obligations that extend beyond shareholders.

In recent times, corporate social responsibility has gained lot of importance among companies because of its long-term benefits. Companies should be responsible to the society for their activities and owe to the environment in which they operate. But it takes more than supporting the most happening subject to get mileage. Identifying the right cause based on inner values and common goals can bring about the best results both internally with employees and also externally with stakeholders.

Creating brand equity is the most powerful weapon in a company's armour to beat the competition. In the fiercely competitive market place of today where customer and societal expectations are changing rapidly requiring constant innovation of new ideas, products and services, strategy and social responsibility provide the shortest route to an organization's success.

A company should carefully evaluate the pros and cons for the right 'lit' and ensure a balanced view of the components of corporate social responsibility and implement the strategies in consonance with its vision, mission and values. This paper looks at a real-life case from a leading IT company which evaluated a partnership with a grass-root non-governmental agency to arrive at a successful corporate social responsibility plan. The plan led to action which linked employees and external stakeholders to the cause. It draws from an article and a paper published by the author on subject of corporate social responsibility and road safety respectively and outlines a method based on experiential learning from campaigns conducted.

CSR AND DEFINITIONS—THEORETICAL APPROACHES

Different organizations have framed different definitions—although there is considerable common ground between them. CSR is about how companies manage the business processes to produce an overall positive impact on society. Andrew Carnegie's (1835-1919) views were based on two principles—charity and stewardship. The former principle required the more fortunate members of society to provide for the least fortunate and the latter rooted itself in the Bible bestowing businesses and wealthy individuals with the right to protect wealth.

Milton Friedman mentioned that businesses should use their resources and energies in activities that increase its profits as long as they perform and carry out fair and open practices, without deception and fraud. Corporate social responsiveness is how Robert Ackerman described a corporation who became aware of social needs and reacted to it. Corporate Social Performance, a concept coined by Archie Carroll (1979) took the idea of CSR even further, resting responsibility squarely on the business and moving them away from a reactive mode to a pro-active mode of behaviour.

OTHER DEFINITIONS

According to The World Business Council for Sustainable Development—"Corporate Social Responsibility is the continuing commitment by business to behave ethically and contribute to economic development while improving the quality of life of the work force and their families as well as of the local community and society at large."

CSR has been defined as "open and transparent business practices that are based upon ethical values and respect for employees, communities and the environment—[and] designed to deliver sustainable value to society at large, as well as to shareholders."

—The Prince of Wales Business Leaders Forum

Traditionally in the United States, CSR has been defined much more in terms of a philanthropic model. Companies make profits, unhindered except by fulfilling their duty to pay taxes. Then they donate a certain share of the profits to charitable causes. It is seen as tainting the act for the company to receive any benefit from the giving. The European model is much more focused on operating the core business in a socially responsible way, complemented by investment in communities for solid business case reasons.

Personally, I feel there is an inherent need for awareness on the value CSR and CRM brings to a business and for society. When times get hard, there is the incentive to practice CSR more and better – if it is a philanthropic exercise which is peripheral to the main business, it will always be the first thing to go when push comes to shove. But as with any process based on the collective activities of communities of human beings (as companies are) there is no "one size fits all." In different countries, there will be different priorities, and values that will shape how businesses act.

LITERATURE REVIEW

Corporate Citizenship, Corporate Social Performance, Corporate Sustainable Development, Corporate Philanthropy and Corporate Community Involvement are other terms used for describing CSR. Some researchers do not buy the role of corporate social responsibility and corporate community involvement (Henderson, 2001), but some believe it is here to stay (Ernst and Young, 2002; Macken, 2002; Sadler, 2002). Greater public scrutiny, increased shareholder activism and anti-globalization social movements will ensure that CSR will continue to be an accepted part of doing business. Human Resources policy and practices are slowly being affected by CSR. (Beer *et al.* 1984; Winstanley and Woodall, 2000a;b).

The recent increased interest in CSR and Corporate Community Involvement have a few reasons. First, companies having being buffeted by external pressures from non-governmental organizations need to provide greater transparency and accountability, especially in the areas of environmental impact and human rights (Andriof and Marsden, 1998). Second, consumers have become more discerning in their purchasing and investment decisions, demanding greater choice, accountability and transparency about company activities (Logan, 1997). Third, governments' approach to social policy and the provision of social services has placed an increasing emphasis on collaboration with the corporate sector through alliances and partnerships (McClure, 2000).

From the employee perspective, employees are increasingly demanding that their work-places have sound ethical values, positive community interaction and be seen as employers of choice (Weiser and Zadek, 2000). In the 1980s, few job applicants would have raised questions about a company's social or environmental commitments. Nowadays it's a norm to have sufficient reasoning and answers to questions, thereby increasing the ability to recruit the best graduates (Cowe, 2002).

In addition to the possible recruitment imperatives noted above, it is argued that CRM and CSR are ways to increase employee motivation as well as improve employee morale and commitment to the organization.

CAUSE RELATED MARKETING—DEFINITION AND NEED

CRM refers to a commercial activity in which companies and non-profit organizations form alliances to market an image, product or service for mutual benefit. Some companies also extend their relationship with an organization or a cause beyond marketing, integrating it with other company activities, such as community involvement, employee volunteerism or corporate philanthropy.

Cause-related marketing campaigns vary in their scope and design, the types of non-profit partners, and the nature of the relationships between companies and their marketing partners. In the most common type of relationship, a company might donate a portion of each purchase made by its customers during a specific period of time to the non-profit entity. However, there are several variations on this theme and not all CRM campaigns channel money to non-profits; some engage principally in educational or awareness-building activities. (Business For Social Responsibility, 2001).

APPROACHES OF CRM—BENEFITING COMMUNITIES, SECURING BUSINESS GOALS

Cause-related marketing first became popular in the United States in the early 1990s as a marketing strategy, but more recently it has been adopted by a broad range of companies throughout the world. One reason is that companies are taking a more strategic approach to their community-involvement efforts, seeking ways of benefiting community organizations while also furthering companies' business goals. Another reason for CRM's growth is that public-opinion research has shown that effective cause programs can enhance a company's reputation and brand image and increase the credibility of its marketing effort while giving customers a convenient way to contribute to non-profit organizations through their purchasing decisions.

Originally, the principal business goal of a cause-related marketing program has been to impact a company's bottom line through increased sales. Yet research has shown that, for companies committed to corporate social responsibility, CRM programs can offer other, often unanticipated, benefits to a company as well. Long-term impacts are increased profitability or cost savings are often attributed to the observed changes resulting from effective CRM partnerships. While the value realized by cause marketing programs will differ among companies and industries, some of the potential benefits include:

Attracting and Retaining Customers

Long-term efforts help attract and build long-term relationships with customers. (Cone/Roper Executive Study, 2000). There is expectations for companies to go beyond their call of duty (Millennium Poll on CSR, 1999). Propensity of consumers to switch is far higher when they find that a company supports a social cause (Cone/Roper Cause-Related Marketing Trends Report, 1999).

Market Differentiation

CRM helps them to create an alternative and distinctive approach to brand advertising.

Outreach to Niche Markets

Partnering with non-profit organizations can help a company to connect with specific demographic or geographic markets.

Motivated and Loyal Employees

Companies can attract and retain quality employees (2000 Cone/Roper Executive Study).

Reinforced Company Mission

CRM efforts can help communicate to employees, customers, suppliers and other stakeholders a company's commitment to corporate social responsibility.

The Key Principles of Cause-Related Marketing

(Business in the Community 1998) include integrity, transparency, sincerity, mutual respect, partnership and mutual benefit.

SOME INTERNATIONAL EXAMPLES

American Express Corporation

Early pioneers of cause-related marketing, American Express has impacted issues as diverse as hunger relief and the restoration of the Statue of Liberty. In a new initiative, the company has created the Community Business program to help small business owners gain access to the credit and resources they need to start or grow their firms. In partnership with ACCION, the Association for Enterprise Opportunity, and Count-Me-In for Women's Economic Independence, American Express has committed to serving a critically under-served and under-funded segment of the small business market—micro enterprises. Central to the partnership program is the Community Business Card, a credit card offered to small business owners, which allocates 1 per cent of all card-holders spending to one of the three micro-enterprise development partners who, in turn, provides small loans and training for micro-entrepreneurs in need. Launched in April 2001, both American Express and its partners have already received significant recognition for their work from consumers and other interested parries:

ConAgra Foods

In October 1999, ConAgra Foods, the nation's second largest food company and parent company to over 80 household brands, launched Feeding Children Better, the nation's largest corporate initiative dedicated solely to ending childhood hunger. By partnering with America's Second Harvest and other leading anti-hunger organizations, the company was able to leverage its extensive food sales, advertising and distribution network in order to bring more food into the charitable food distribution. Since the inception of this program, Feeding Children Better has funded nearly 50 Kids Cafes, which are secure, after-school programs that provide balanced meals for children. In addition, fresh produce and frozen fish deliveries increased by 104 per cent and 40 per cent respectively, as a result of the program's newly created Rapid Food Distribution System, and 29 new trucks have been purchased for food banks with grants by ConAgra system, to feed hungry children, and to bring the face of childhood hunger into the spotlight Foods. In recognition of the program's impacts, ConAgra Foods was named Donor of the Year by America's Second Harvest. In addition, Feeding Children Better was named Campaign of the Year and Community Relations Campaign of the Year by the trade publication PR Week and was awarded a CIPRA (Creativity in Public Relations Award) by Inside PR for Best Corporate Philanthropy Program created in 1999.

Ford Division

Since 1995, Ford Division has been a leading partner of the Susan G. Komen Breast Cancer Foundation's Race for the Curd, events in their fight to raise awareness and the resources necessary to eradicate breast cancer. While support for the foundation is not linked to sales of Ford vehicles. Ford has donated $48 million to the Komen Foundation to date in sponsorship fees, media support and in-kind gifts. In addition, the company created Ford Force to leverage a united front of Ford dealers, employees and the general public in the fight against breast cancer. As members of Ford Force, more than 12,000 Ford employees have run or walked in Races across the country, and over 3.000 dealers have participated in local Race for the Cure® events. The impact on both the cause and consumer has been dramatic. Komen Race for the Cure® events are now the largest 5K race series in the world and they continue to grow by approximately 39 per cent each year.

SOME EXAMPLES IN INDIA

Tata Group

The company's philanthropic activities can be dated to as early as

1892. They have run Endowment Schemes to provide higher education for deserving Indians. Over 3,500 Tata scholarships have been awarded. J.R.D. Tata institutionalized CSR in the 1970s and decided that the group shall be mindful of its social and moral responsibilities to the consumers, employees, shareholders, society and the local community for all its major companies. In July 2002, Tata Steel presented the first corporate sustainability report, which would serve as a benchmark and a confidence-builder for other Tata companies. It also has formed group resource under the TCCI (Tata Council for Community Initiatives) on corporate sustainability and a strategy to assist other Tata companies on corporate social responsibility. The group resource on corporate sustainability would work on developing a Tata model using technical inputs from the UNDP. The Tatas have spent Rs. 1.5 billion on social services – the highest by any corporate house in the country during 2001-02. The thrust area was rural development, which included community health, basic education and vocational training. It also spends on basic infrastructure and disburses money through various charitable trusts and relief and reconstruction societies.

Infosys

Formed in 1981 by N.R. Narayana Murthy, Infosys follows a socially responsible and sustainable path in conducting business. Even during the boom time of the 1990's when the stock prices of IT companies were skyrocketing, the company believed in sharing the wealth with the society and its employees. This practice of the company stems from the personal belief of Narayana Murthy to give back to the society more than what it gave him. It also substantiates the role and motivation of the CEO and the top management in making the company a responsible corporate citizen. Infosys has won many awards such as Best Employers to Work for in India, Golden Peacock Award for Excellence in Corporate Governance in the Global Category by the World Council for Corporate Governance, London and Corporate Citizenship Award by *The Economic Times*. According to a recent report, Infosys spends about Rs. 50 million on social activities.

A.V. Birla Group

The A.V. Birla group's initiatives arc channelled through The Aditya

Birla Centre for Community Initiatives and Rural Development spearheaded by Rajashree Birla (wife of Aditya Birla). All the Group companies are dedicated to social development. Hindalco, a group company has won the ACCI-SEDF Social Responsiveness Awards 2001 instituted by ACCI Sodo Economic Development Foundation (a constructive partnership between *Businessworld*, ICICI Communities, Partners in Change and KPMG). The activities of the group include innovative projects involving the development of rural youth and employment generation; education and training and health care projects; helping the disable people; social causes like widow re-marriages; dowryless marriages; and women empowerment programs. Also the group undertakes sponsorship of the arts and Indian culture, which are need-based. The Birla Academy of Art and Culture set-up in 1962 in Kolkata treasures art works and exquisite exhibits and has evolved into one of India's premier institutions for art and culture. The A.V. Birla group also offers scholarships to students from IITs, IIMs and BITS (Pilani) to nurture tomorrow's leader as late Aditya Vikram Birla, believed in people power and their potential to become leaders. Only the best are selected for the coveted award and are called 'The Aditya Birla scholars.'

POSTULATING THE CRM PARTNERSHIP MODEL

While the above examples provide a list of dos and don'ts for building, controlling and managing a cause-related campaign, it does not provide an integrated framework for implementation — pre, during and post-event. The author analyses a live partnership case by Friends For Life (www.fflonline.org), road safety advocacy organization and i-flex solutions, a leading provider of technology services, on campaigns — 'Keep your head, wear a helmet' and 'Road to Safety' which delivered effective results. The author postulates the model based on Haddon's Matrix proposing a methodology for identifying, demystifying and chalking a robust campaign.

There are three main objectives of supporting cause-related marketing — brand building, contributing to society and employee volunteerism/involvement.

Brand building is a long-term view from a partnership angle but it plays a significant role in decision-making. Brand Benefits (2003/04), supported by Research International, Lightspeed Research and Dunnhumby, conducted a study which investigated the impact of Cause Related Marketing. The findings reveal the following:

- 98 per cent of consumers in the UK and the USA are now aware of at least one Cause Related Marketing program, as compared with 88 per cent in 2000.
- Per cent of consumers have participated in at least one Cause Related Marketing program, compared with 68 per cent in 2000 and 71 per cent in the USA.
- Over two-thirds of consumers (68 per cent), are still calling for more companies to be involved in Cause Related Marketing.
- 7 out of 10 consumers who had participated in a Cause Related Marketing program reporting a positive impact on their behaviour or perceptions.
- 48 per cent of consumers showed an actual change in behaviour, saying that they switched brands, increased usage or tried or enquired about new products.

Consumers have a more favourable attitude towards a Cause Related Marketing program, and are more likely to participate when there is clear affinity between the brands, the company lives and breathes the relationship, it is easy for consumers to participate in, and the program clearly communicates the company's commitment.

THE ROAD SAFETY CAUSE AND PARTICIPATION BY A CONCERNED CORPORATE HOUSE

With the rapid increase in the number of vehicles plying the roads, the issue of road safety has been neglected. Economic and social factors play a large role in the lack of adoption of effective practices for safety 'on the road.'

The World Health Organization estimates that 1,171,000 people are killed on the roads every year and 10-15,000,000 are injured or disabled every year. Over 1,61,000 of those killed and 1,500,000 of those injured or disabled are children under 15 years of age—a whopping 15 per cent of the total figure. India, too, grapples with a major road accident problem with an estimated 80,000 people killed in 1999 and at least 4,00,000 injured. The Government agencies in charge of this issue are making every effort to reduce this carnage on our roads but they cannot do it alone. They need support from the public and concerned private organizations.

Bangalore, the city in which the campaigns were initiated has a serious road accident problem with hospital records indicating at least 800 deaths and 14,000 injuries every year. The majority of victims are young adults, and the most vulnerable are pedestrians and riders or passengers of two wheelers. With planned growth of the city, action also needs to be taken now to save Bangalore from this hidden and silent epidemic that is predicted to be the world's third major killer by 2020. (http://www.blrforward.org/programmes/roads suraksha.asn).

CONTRIBUTING TO THE COMMUNITY—FRIENDS FOR LIFE AND ITS CAMPAIGNS

Promoting road safety awareness in India is the mission of Friends For Life – their way of contributing to the community. The Bangalore-based NGO, Friends for Life (www.fflonline.org), launched a public road safety awareness campaign in 2002 to promote the wearing of helmets among riders of two-wheeled motorbikes in Bangalore. Entitled "Keep Your Head, Wear Your Helmet," the advocacy campaign relied on the Internet to create awareness, increase interaction, and foster behaviour change. In addition to individual citizens, the campaign reached out to corporate managers, who were encouraged to bring the message to their employees. The purpose of this campaign is to decrease the number of motor-vehicle-related head injuries. An immediate approach is to encourage people to wear helmets; while a broader goal includes garnering the critical mass needed to influence the government to take steps to build safer roads and develop education programs for riders and drivers.

Friends for Life's stated objectives are to:

1. To ensure a high percentage of helmet usage among two-wheel motor vehicle riders.
2. To develop and improve standards of communication for safety measures.

The organizers believe that the web can be an effective medium to address public interest issues and disseminate campaigns that attempt to change behaviours and attitudes through awareness-raising. The Keep Your Head initiative is one of their first efforts in this direction.

SUMMARY OF ICT INITIATIVES

At the "Keep Your Head" site, interested citizens and communications and resource managers in corporations may access information on road safety and down load resources for initiating their own 3-month helmet safety campaigns. The Communi-Kit contains posters, stickers, logos, and wallpaper. These materials are easily downloadable in either JPG or compressed PDF formats that maintain small file sizes.

Informal surveys were conducted prior to campaign launch to assess the underlying reasons for resisting helmet use. Some of those interviewed felt that helmets were a hindrance to visibility; others thought helmets were "uncool" or "uncomfortable," while a few worried they would lose hair due to the poor ventilation. The high cost of reliable helmets, lack of awareness about choosing a good helmet, and insufficient support from the city authorities were other challenges associated with the safety campaign.

These materials highlight, among other things, the effects of head injuries. Messages like "Save your head now, or save it for posterity" (accompanied by an image of a brain in a jar) and "Helmets ruin my hair" (on a tombstone) are designed to shock people into taking responsibility for their own safety.

Detailed instructions and supporting documents are provided to facilitate independent campaign organization. The website becomes a clearing-house for easily accessible campaign materials that will facilitate and encourage wider participation. Corporations can use these tools to conduct a campaign on their company's Intranet. In addition, visitors to the site are encouraged to post-messages on the site's forum and to spread the word to friends, family, and policy-makers in their town. As part of the effort to disseminate information, booths were set-up in the premises of interested corporations and public venues. These booths were designed to encourage managers, for instance, to conduct "safety month" programs in-house. Physicians have participated by posting advocacy material in their offices and in their employee newsletters.

Other strategies included urging the Bangalore Traffic Police to post 40 signs with the campaign slogan at prominent traffic points in the city, advocacy efforts to persuade helmet manufacturers to support the campaign by manufacturing safer helmets, and hosting a three-college music concert featuring a local band. In addition, interactive sessions were held at schools, colleges, and corporations. Stickers and merchandise were distributed, and a joint exercise with the traffic police was conducted.

ROAD TO SAFETY CAMPAIGN

With the rapid change in the pace of life and in the number of vehicles plying on the roads, the issues of road safety amongst children has been neglected considerably. Statistics reveal that a large number of children have died from injury, than from cancer, asthma or other infectious diseases combined. In fact, the World Health Day on April 7, 2004, was also dedicated to Road Safety and Injury Prevention.

Even if some survive the death consequence, they are unable to escape from the strains of the accompanying physical and mental trauma. The reasons for the occurrence of such fatal accidents are lack of road safety knowledge on the part of the child, ignorance to apply traffic rules and regulations and/or carelessness on the part of cyclists and drivers.

Objectives:

- To educate children on Road Safety norms.
- To provide valuable resources to parents and teachers to encourage them to conduct road safety awareness campaigns.

i-flex Road Safety Initiative—Corporate Social Responsibility and Mission

About i-flex

i-flex solutions limited, a provider of technology solution for the financial services industry, offers its customers an end-to-end portfolio unmatched in its comprehensiveness. It provides financial institutions prepackaged products, custom solutions, consulting services and offshore development facilities. It has provided IT solutions and services to more than 390 financial institutions in over 100 countries, i-flex's flagship product, 5 FLEXCUBE, has been deployed at leading financial institutions across the world, i-flex is an SEI CMM Level 5 company, and employs more than 2000 professionals, and has established 12 global support centres across the world to support its worldwide implementations.

i-flex is headquartered in India. The country is known as a leader in the world software market in producing product and service solutions that solve technology challenges. The Indian software industry has become a worldwide brand and continues to generate huge margin profits for the nation. As per a Nasscom survey, there are currently more than 3,000 companies in India engaged in the business of software exports. The top 20 software exporters (in order of revenue) accounted for almost 60 per cent share of the software exports revenues in 2000-2001, i-flex ranks among the top 20 software exporters in the country and is among the only exporters with an exclusive product focus.

Rooting for a Cause

The website of i-flex solutions (www.iflexsolutions.com) quotes:

> "At i-flex, we believe that by creating a more inclusive business culture, we are creating a vibrant and innovative working environment where success can be forged. Corporate social responsibility plays a pivotal role in shaping corporate behaviour and actions.
>
> Our corporate vision to life is communicated through our tangible commitment to children – beyond the normal business values of price, quality and service. We'd like to raise awareness of our initiatives and activities through this section on our website.
>
> Our CSR policy document focuses on the importance of clarity, and congruence with company purpose and values.
>
> Our corporate social responsibility is aimed at children's issues like education and health.
>
> To further our initiative, i-flexers have voluntarily undertaken programs under the banner of 'i-flex for children,' with several prestigious welfare organizations.
>
> Promoting road safety awareness among children in India is the i-flex way of contributing to the community.

Building a Partnership

"A partnership is an agreement between two or more partners to work together to achieve common aims. (David Wilcox. Building Effective Partnerships, 2003).

Agreement, leadership, commitment, trust, communication and shared vision are some of the factors needed for a fruitful partnership.

The partnership life-cycle generally covers:

- **The Initiating Phase** – sparking the idea, reasons for coming together.
- **The Starting Phase** – getting to know the plans, sharing vision.
- **The Doing Phase** – starting and involving others in projects.
- **The Sustaining/Finishing Phase** – finding long-term views and re-inventing, if necessary.

There are several different types of partnerships. Large 'official' partnerships set-up by major institutions, more bottom-up partnerships initiated by non-profit organizations or groups. Even short-term alliances created around a particular project or program. Other forms of collaboration to share information and offer mutual support that may be better seen as networks. (David Wilcox, 2003).

It is difficult to provide a formal definition of partnership that suits all circumstances, but the key characteristic is that the partners aim to achieve something they could not do alone, by pooling skills and other resources. To do this they need a shared vision of their goals, and a way of working together which realizes this ambition. This may involve a long-term formal structure, or a shorter-term agreement.

This partnership developed from an initial understanding (the initiating phase) of each other's capabilities. FFL conducted an employee event around the subject of road safety for the firm (the starting phase). The appeal and impact led to building of trust and FFL taking up larger projects like the traffic signboards and child road safety posters externally (the doing phase) due to the commitment and individual activism shown by an employee. Post success of the event which involved the city's stakeholders like the Bangalore Traffic Police and road safety professionals, plans are underway to forge other campaign ideas (the sustaining phase).

While the above cycle indicates the key phases, it overlooks the employee volunteerism involving a corporate partner. The sustainability of the program would depend on how well integrated and involved can be.

Observations from the Partnership

A key point to note is the degree of involvement the campaign got from the corporate since it was driven by an employee and therefore was credible. The relationship was *experimental* in the beginning and matured over time when the corporate saw *value* in the social responsibility, employee involvement and brand building/ media coverage. Leading publications and magazines, both national and international covered the campaign (shown as news clips below).

Therefore, to draw a partnership model (Figure 7.1) which works for either party, there needs to be an element/ phase of experimental learning followed by the value creation phases which is outcome-oriented.

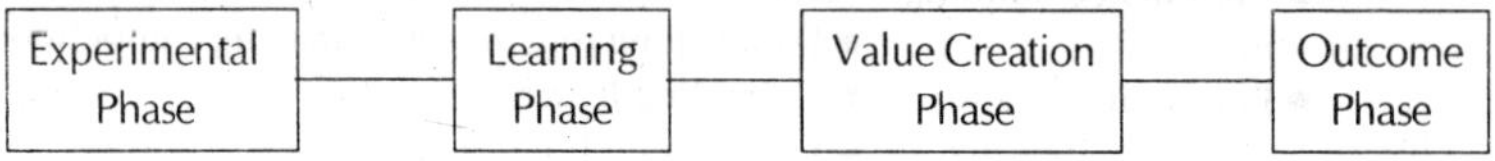

FIG. 7.1

To also understand the various factors in play during such a partnership, a matrix structure based on William Haddon Jr.'s conceptual model, the Haddon matrix can be used.

Factors

Phase	*Human Factors*	*Vehicle Factors*	*Environmental Factors*
Pre-event (crash)			
Event			
Post-Event			

Notes: Pre-event phase: all factors that determine whether the event leading to injury will take place.
Event phase: all factors that determine whether an injury will occur once the incident has been Initiated.
Post-Event phase: all factors that determine the final damage and permanent handicap stemming from injury.

FIG. 7.2

The Haddon Matrix (after Haddon, 1968)

This matrix was developed more than two decades ago applying basic principles of public health to the problem of traffic safety. Since that time, the matrix has been used as a tool to assist in developing ideas for preventing injuries of many types. As such, it provides a compelling framework for understanding the origins of injury problems and for identifying multiple counter-measures to address those problems.

However, this matrix can be adapted for other causes to arrive at measures and alternatives. As a strategic planning tool, the model can be recast in a CRM Partnering model as defined below.

Factors

Phase	*Human Factors*	*Organizational Factors*	*Environmental Factors*
Pre-event	• **Teaming** for the cause • **Confidence building** measures • **Putting metrics** for campaign tracking • **Employee involvement**	• **Identifying** and selecting—core values • **Establishing** relations • **Estimating Reach** • **Committing** time, money and effort • **Communicating** with employees	• **Media management** • **Timing** of event • **Legal issues** • **Managing** competition
Event	• **Right mix** of people to implement • **Managing and controlling** activities	• **Employee volunteerism** • Motivating and encouraging participation by rewards and recognition • **Monitoring** progress • **Updating** senior management and employees	• **Scanning for perceptions** and drawing community involvement • **Establishing** a leadership status in the cause selected
Post-Event	• **Feedback and communication** • **Creating** team for long-term engagements	• **Establishing a long-term view** on cause and company contribution • **Providing constant information flow** to employees	• **Communicating relationship maturity** with cause

CONCLUSION

The above effort showcases a broad concept in "Cause Related Marketing." A NGO or a company will be truly a responsible entity when it develops a framework of responsible action and implements it as a line function.

Though a few big Indian companies practice corporate citizenship, the extent to which it is done is unimpressive. There has been growing awareness among the academic institutions as well towards cause related marketing and corporate social responsibility as a subject to sensitize the future managers of this nation to the societal needs besides generating profits for their organizations with increased efficiency. It is easier said than done. Hopefully, this model will help identify, plan and control a comprehensive strategy for cause related marketing and build brands in the future.

References

Business in the Community—Cause Related Marketing Campaign. http://www.crm.org.uk

Business in the Community "Making Good Business Sense" report, World Business Council for Sustainable Development.
website
www.bite.orc.uk
www.icfaipress.org
www.fflonline.org

James, A.F.; Stoner, Freeman; R. Edward and Daniel R. Gilbert, *Management*, Sixth edition, 2004.

Koshy, A.V., Marketing Your Brand on a Cause Related Mission, www.marcommwise.com.

Wilcox, David, Building Effective Partnerships, 2003 (www.partnerships.org.uk) www.iflexsolutions.com

8

Ethics and Social Responsibility in the HIH Collapse: A Dialectical Approach

FERNANDA DUARTE, JOHN GRAY, AND GILLIAN MCALLISTER[1]

Greed is good. Greed is right. Greed works. Greed Cuts through, clarifies, and captures the essence of the evolutionary spirit.
'Gordon Gekko' in the film *Wall Street* (1987)

Companies have a number of legal and other obligations to non-shareholder, stakeholders such as employees, clients/customers and the community as a whole. . . .
(Principle 10, *Principles of Good Corporate Governance and Best Practice Recommendations*, Australian Stock Exchange, 2003)

In what has been dubbed as 'Australia's biggest corporate collapse' (Westfield 2003a: 241), HIH Insurance was placed into liquidation in 2001, with losses of AUS$53 billion[1] and devastating consequences, not only for the insurance industry but also for the company's employees and individual policy-holders. Disabled clients could no longer receive regular payments, retirees who had invested their superannuation or life savings in HIH shares to fund their retirement lost all their money, and thousands of holders of professional indemnity, public liability, home warranty and travel insurance policies found themselves suddenly uninsured. There were also unfortunate consequences for HIH employees, with more than 1000 of them losing their jobs as a direct result of the collapse. After a detailed Royal Commission inquiry it was revealed that HIH management and Directors had acted carelessly and extravagantly over a period of years. Justice Neville Owen, who led the HIH Inquiry in 2003, went to the nub of the issue when he said, '*Did anyone stand back and ask themselves the simple question – is this right?*' (HIHRC 2003, Vol. I, Part 1: 41).

Based on a qualitative study of the HIH collapse, this paper revisits Hegelian dialectics and theorises that potential social benefits may emanate from the clash between hegemonic business discourses and counter-hegemonic discourses mobilised from civil society. More specifically, the *thesis* of the dialectical model proposed here is that 'The business of business is profit,' and the *antithesis* is that 'The business of business is social responsibility.' It is our contention that the dynamic tension created by these opposing discourses produce a fruitful collision of ideas from which a more ethical society may emerge by way of *synthesis*.

Hegel indeed made an important point when he wrote in *Science of Logic* (1812; 1816:439) 'Everything is inherently contradictory . . . contradiction is the root of all movement and vitality; it is only in so far as something has a contradiction within it that it moves, has an urge and activity.' In other words, social processes are created from opposing forces or opposing sides. Social changes are the driving forces of important turning points in human society, where one opposite overcomes the other.

Evidence is provided that important social changes have taken place in the aftermath of the HIH collapse, when the unethical behaviour of HIH's executives was called into question. The HIH inquiry gave the notion of *social responsibility* a new impetus. Whilst this discursive shift may not take place out of altruism, it must be conceded that it has called for greater business accountability and ethical behaviour which may benefit society at large.

The paper is structured as follows:

1. the first section contextualises the analysis, placing it within the historical formation of *high modernity* (Giddens 1991);
2. the second section briefly examines the evolution of idea about corporate social responsibility in Australia;

3. the third section presents the HIH collapse case-study; and
4. the fourth section discusses positive discursive, legislative and institutional outcomes of the HIH as examples of the *synthesis* that emerges from the collision between hegemonic corporate discourses and demands for social responsibility.

CONTEXTUALISING THE ANALYSIS

The growing influence of the discourse of social responsibility in the early stages of the 21st Century cannot be understood without reference to the broad context within which it was articulated. Borrowing from Giddens (1991), we argue that this context is *high modernity*, the socio-historical formation that emerged in the last quarter of the Twentieth Century, and which has seen a considerable integration of the global economic system and strengthening of entrepreneurial capitalism. The broad contours of high modernity are shaped by the hegemonic discourse of neo-liberalism and associated practices. The core assumption of neo-liberalism that the 'market determines outcomes,' has led *inter alia* to a sustained process of deregulation and increased competition for shares of profit in the global markets. These processes increase risk-taking behaviour among entrepreneurs in response to the 'positive Utopian messages' (Fairclough and Thomas, 2004: 385) of 'golden opportunities' deployed within the meta-discourse of *globalisation* (Oswick, 2001; Fairclough and Thomas, 2004: 385).

Neo-liberal precepts have been politically identified with USA President Ronald Reagan and UK Prime Minister Margaret Thatcher in the 1980s. During the last quarter of the Twentieth Century they became institutionalised (Greenwood and Hinings, 1996; Beckert, 1999), not only in these economics but increasingly through each of the developed economies. Variations of the Chicago School of Monetarism – most clearly and influentially expressed by Milton Friedman – became the normal science of policy economics (Kuhn, 1962). The International Monetary Fund (IMF) model with its variations that became known as the Washington Collusion (so named by Joe Stiglitz whilst a Deputy President of the World Bank [Stiglitz, 2002]) evolved into Neo-liberalism, and its proponents gained control of the policy debates at the IMF, heavily influenced by the USA Treasury (see Stiglitz, 2002 for an insider's view of this). As noted by the late Bourdieu in a 1998 article in *Le Monde*, the discourse of neo-liberalism 'has today more than ever . . . the means of *making itself true* and empirically verifiable' [original italics].

Conditions of high modernity intensified globalisation processes, promoting the rapid flow of information and the interconnection of politics with the business of the market. As noted by Clegg (1989), communication flows are competitive circuits, which flow through nodes of influence. Chief of these nodes in economic significance were the IMF, the USA Academy, USA Treasury and UK Chancellery. Once these nodes were controlled by neo-liberals, their voice became the legitimate voice in society. The media was then the chief vector by which the discourse of neo-liberalism became objectified, habituated, and institutionalised (Oliver, 1991). It is instructive to buy a daily paper in one of the cities of developed nations, and compare it with its equivalent thirty years ago. The number of articles about economic matters has grown significantly and the economic sophistication assumed of the reader has multiplied even more. III the early stages of the Twenty-First Century, the global convergence on the neo-liberal model is all but complete, and Keynesiasm or Public Economics have become a thing of the past. It has become accepted knowledge that the market is the preferred solution, business and enterprise are *de facto* good, and public ownership and welfare are *de facto* bad. Gray, Clegg, and Carter (2005) trace out a history of de-regulation in Australia from about 1980 onwards showing that by about 1985 neo-liberalism had become the dominant discourse – the dominant way of understanding the roles of market, government, and community.

The neo-liberal manner of understanding the role of government in a modern economy, of re-defining public ownership, of normalising auctions of public goods and reductions in welfare was changed through contest. Previously institutionalised discourses and processes that used to take 'the social' into account were challenged by economically conservative politics. De-institutionalisation of these social discourses occurred through: delegitimisation by legislation, suasion as new ways became 'the norm,' and through abandonment so as to mimic the success of the new entrepreneurial alliances (DiMaggio and Powell, 1991).

Under conditions of neo-liberal hegemony the figure of the intrepid 'global entrepreneur' who is heroically courageous in profit making risks, has come to occupy centre stage of the meta-discourse (Beckert, 1999). This opens the door to abuses and breaches of corporate social responsibility. The dialectical model hereby proposed, nevertheless, allows a more optimistic reading of the situation; that is, as negative and devastating as they may be, corporate abuses reinforce the importance of the counter-hegemonic notion of social responsibility. The section below provides a brief overview of this concept as it emerged and evolved in Australia.

CORPORATE SOCIAL RESPONSIBILITY IN AUSTRALIA

In an article published in 1999, Carroll traces the term *social responsibility* back to the 1950s – when Howard Bowen posed the question "What responsibilities to society may businessmen reasonably be expected to assume?".[2] The notion has since developed, assuming more complex meanings, embracing ideas related to business ethics, corporate citizenship and corporate social performance.

In Australia, the term *corporate social responsibility* has evolved in a similar way, and is associated to the notion of 'triple bottom line' (Cronin, 2001: 1). The triple bottom line approach requires corporations to attend to social and environmental goals, in addition to the more traditional goals relating to financial performance.

A number of triple bottom line initiatives have emerged in Australia in recent years, including the establishment in 1998 of a Business Community Partnership at Federal Government level, aimed at achieving a 'new balance between government, business and community'.[3] The major research output of the Government's Community Business Partnership was a report entitled *Corporate Community Involvement: Establishing a Business Case* (CCPA, 2000). The Report concluded that corporate community involvement (CCI) is 'a way to maintain trust, support and legitimacy with the community, governments and employees (CCPA, 2000: 11).

Other examples of the growing importance of social responsibility in Australia include the publication of the Good Reputation Index in 2000, 2001 and 2002 by two of Australia's leading newspapers, the *Sydney Morning Herald* and *The Age*,[4] and the publication in March 2003 by the Australian Stock Exchange of its *Principles of Good Corporate Governance and Best Practice Recommendations*. In 2003, a conference entitled "Walking the third bottom line" was held in Sydney by the Corporate Citizenship Research Unit of Deakin University. This was sponsored by the *Australian Financial Review*, Australia's leading daily business newspaper.[5]

There is no doubt that the intensification of globalisation processes in the last two decades has contributed to the evolution of ideas about corporate social responsibility in Australia. As corporate social responsibility becomes broadly accepted in other jurisdictions, this is likely to have an impact on companies in Australia (Cronin, 2001: 11). However, recent corporate collapses such as that of One.Tel, Tricontinental Merchant Bank, Pyramid Group, Ansett, Bond Corporation, Qintex and HIH, have led to the emergence of social responsibility initiatives more specifically suited to the Australian context. For example, in a 2003 case following the collapse of communications company One.Tel, the New South Wales Supreme Court held that, in determining the liability of a defendant for his/her conduct as company chairperson, the Court's role was to apply a standard of care that reflected contemporary community expectations.[6] This example reveals an important institutional shift resulting from greater awareness of the importance of social responsibility, in that the Supreme Court itself was prepared to accept that corporations are accountable to a broad group of stakeholders and not just shareholders.

The clear message from debates on corporate social responsibility in Australia is that a corporation's obligations to the community can no longer be satisfied through charitable donations to causes of the directors' choosing (corporate philanthropy), but requires compliance with broad-based ethical standards as well. The case for corporate social responsibility has been strengthened in recent discussion in the Australian media surrounding the case of a building materials manufacturer. James Hardie was the principal supplier of asbestos in Australia for many decades and, as a result, is now the subject of hundreds of compensation claims by sufferers of asbestosis. The Company shift its liabilities to claimants into a subsidiary company, which—it was later discovered—had insufficient assets to fund the many claims. After a public inquiry, James Hardie has given undertakings to meet claims. The case provoked a great deal of public outrage and intense debate about the ethics of the Company's actions, leading one financial commentator to observe that 'executives and boardrooms across the country watching the debacle must surely realise how sustainability and corporate social responsibility have an equally important place in their decision-making as do myriad financial parameters by which they measure their decisions' (Chanticleer, 2004).

The role of the mass media must not be overlooked in discussion about corporate social responsibility (this point will be illustrated later). Without doubt media coverage of high profile corporate failures in Australia has significantly contributed to public awareness about the critical importance of corporate social responsibility. Increased public awareness in turn leads to the emergence of the *antithesis* to counter the dominant corollary that 'the business of business is profit'—an antithesis structured around demands for social responsibility and corporate citizenship. As will be seen below, the HIH case in particular highlights how corporate social responsibility is being pushed beyond ideas of corporate philanthropy and into areas of pro-active ethical action. Justice Owen, who led the HIH Royal Commission noted that the collapse of HIH was of such magnitude and affected so many people that it caused the public "to question the integrity of the market system itself" (Owen, 2003, HIHRC, 2003, Vol. I, Part I). As will be seen below, the event has moved the debate over corporate social responsibility in Australia to a new level, as it prompted important legislative and institutional shifts. These changes no doubt are contributing to the creation of a better Australian society, as they entail greater corporate accountability and transparency. The HIH collapse is discussed in some detail in the section below.

THE HIH COLLAPSE

The collapse of HIH Insurance was not the first corporate collapse that occurred in Australia, but it attracted a great deal of media interest and captured the imagination of the Australian public for a long period of time. As commented by Mark Westfield (2003a: 241) it was far greater in magnitude and spread than the spectacular losses from Tricontinental Merchant Bank, Pyramid Group, Ansett, Bond Corporation and Quintex.

The HIH collapse can be said to be a typical product of the aggressive form of entrepreneurial capitalism characteristic of high modernity. It is a complex web of interrelated events, with a broad narrative and a number of different story lines that emerged at different times and locations, over specific issues, as the Company's situation deteriorated. The broad narrative is structured around the actions and interactions of three key protagonists, HIH Directors Ray Williams Rodney Adler and Dominic Fodera. Specific story lines arise from different episodes in the troubled trajectory of the Company, which introduce an extensive cast of corporate personages directly and indirectly associated with it. Our research is particularly concerned with the story line that raises issues of ethics and corporate social responsibility as a result of the dishonest behaviour of HIH Directors.

The HIH saga begins in 1968, when entrepreneurs Ray Williams, from Australia, and Michael Payne, from England, incorporated MW Payne Liability Agencies Pty Ltd. to underwrite insurance business in Australia. The newly formed company operated as an agency for two Lloyd's of London syndicates, and its main business was the writing of workers' compensation. Between 1968 and 2001 the Company underwent a series of structural transformations in response to the unstable and rapidly changing economic environment of high modernity. (Appendix I shows a chronology of the structural mutations of the Company, and the key events leading up to its collapse.) The climax of the narrative occurs on 27 August 2001 when HIH Insurance was placed in liquidation, with reported losses of approximately $ 2.3 billion.

As previously mentioned, *expansion* and *risk* are pivotal notions in the aggressive type of capitalism characteristic of high modernity, shaped by the institutionalisation of the neo-liberal discourse. Like any other major capitalist enterprises of high modernity, HIH as personified by its Chief Executive Officer, Ray Williams, had an indefatigable will to growth, and a corresponding tendency to take risks in order to exploit the 'golden opportunities' of *globalisation* (Oswick, 2001; Fairclough and Thomas, 2004: 385). Indeed, as globalisation gained momentum in mid-1980s, the company began to expand into overseas markets, against the backdrop of an extremely competitive industry in which many insurance companies were facing hardship and bankruptcy. HIH managed to grow by 20 times over a period of nine years: its business increased from $ 42 million in 1990 to $ 940 million in 1999 (Brown, 2001: 54): The HIH Group included more than 240 separate companies, and at one time operated in five different continents, with companies incorporated in 16 nations including, apart from Australia, the United Kingdom, The United States, New Zealand, Hong Kong, Argentina, Malaysia, Sweden, Greece, Russia, Fiji, Papua New Guinea and the Philippines (Clarke *et al.*, 2003: 223-4). HIH's 'will to growth' and its consequent expansions overseas have been claimed by many witnesses at the Royal Commission as critical factors in the Company's collapse (Clarke *et al.*, 2003: 224). The main problem is that, in their determination to increase HIH's profits, its executives engaged in extremely risky activities without consideration for their consequences. As noted by Justice Owen, 'the way the [HIH] Group managed its entry and expansion in overseas markets was extremely imprudent and ultimately very costly. It involved bad decision-making and a lack of business judgement in circumstances of adverse insurance market conditions' (HIHRC, Vol. 1, Part 1:15).

In the broad narrative of the HIH failure there were three events of critical importance to understand why the Company ultimately collapsed: the Company's expansion into the UK market in 1993, expansion into the US market between 1994 and 1997, and the take-over of Australian company FAI Insurance in 1998. In the UK operations, HIH's business consisted initially of public liability and professional indemnity. After 1995, it shined into marine re-insurance and film financing, areas in which the underwriters had little experience or expertise. As commented by Justice Owen, 'The combination of a lack of underwriting controls and a lack of relevant experience and familiarity in those particular lines of business was a formula for financial disaster' (HIHRC, Vol. I, Part I: 16). The UK experience incurred losses of approximately $ 1.7 billion.

The US experience also proved disastrous. HIH first entered the US market in 1987, by acquiring the California-based Falcon Insurance Company. The focus of the operation was on worker's compensation business. Anticipating legislative changes that were expected to cause premium rates to fall, HIH sold the business in 1994. Following a period of negotiation, HIH re-acquired the business in 1997, but without due diligence or consideration of the current level of risk involved in that venture. A severe downturn in the California workers' compensation market led to the demise of the US operation in 2000, with losses estimated at $ 600 million.

Once more HIH entrepreneurs took unwise risks in the take-over of Australian company FAI Insurance in 1998. The take-over took place without research or due diligence investigation.[7] It was carried out on the basis of publicly available information, which, not surprisingly, did not reveal the excessive under-reserving of FAI's long-tail business. As HIH itself faced provisioning problems, the effect of the FAI shortfall was exacerbated. Justice Owen estimates that the acquisition of FAI cost HIH approximately $ 590 million.

By the year 2000 HIH faced a severe financial crisis, with anticipated losses of approximately $2.2 billion. The Company faced what is termed in business jargon a 'death spiral' – that is, a terminal situation in which the pay-outs are greater than revenue, and the only option is to chase new business to prevent collapse (Main, 2003: 9-10). This is why in 2001 HIH went into a joint venture with insurer Allianz Australia Ltd. This endeavour was designed as an emergency measure to provide cash injections in the already ailing Company through the sale of all of HIH's income earning businesses (personal lines and compulsory third part insurance products). Nevertheless, this venture came to further exacerbate the situation, as the $200 million payment that HIH hoped to receive from the Allianz deal had to be quarantined in the joint venture trust established to fund future claims. Ironically, this correct fiduciary process upon which HIH's new business partner insisted, hastened the death spiral. Indeed further cash flow problems resulted from this venture, as HIH had been deprived of its cash earning business. Of course for a properly prudential firm the loss of this cash flow would not have endangered its survival. But HIH was not prudential and ten weeks after the beginning of the joint venture with Allianz, HIH was placed in provisional liquidation. As commented in the Royal Commission report the Allianz venture was 'the harbinger of doom.'

HIH collapsed because of a sizeable deficit, which was found to have resulted primarily from *under-reserving*.[8] As explained by Justice Owen:

> In the year ending 31 December 1997 HIH made an underwriting loss of $33.8 million on net premium earned of $1233.5 million. In the 18 months to 30 June 1999 (making a pro rata adjustment to reduce it notionally to a 12-month period) the underwriting loss was $73 million against a net earned premium of $1550 million. The comparative figures for the year ending 30 June 2000 are $103.5 million and $1995, 4 million respectively. In other words, between 1997 and 1999 (notionally adjusting the latter to reduce it to a 12-month period) the underwriting loss more than doubled while the net earned premium rose by 25 per cent. If the comparison is made between 1997 and 2000 the underwriting loss increased three-fold and yet net earned premium increased by 61 per cent. (HIHRC, Vol. I, Part 1: 13)

Another factor that contributed to the collapse was excessive *re-insurance*. As conventionally understood, *re-insurance* is a practice whereby an insurer transfers part of the risk it has assumed on behalf of its policy-holders to offset the risk of future adverse developments in relation to claims. Whilst re-insurance is a legitimate mechanism to guarantee sufficient prudential reserve margins to cover future claims obligations, the abuse of this practice can raise ethical issues. This was the case of HIH, which employed a more aggressive kind of re-insurance aimed primarily at maintaining the appearance of its balance sheet; in other words, deceiving the auditors, regulators and ultimately the Australian public.

Here, the fundamental question is why did HIH Directors allow the Company to plunge into such an abysmal financial situation? The reasons are varied and complex, but for the purpose of this paper, the discussion will focus on the ethical aspects of the case—more specifically, the dishonest, illegal and possibly criminal, actions of the Directors who failed to disclose the Company's financial problems to the prudential regulators.

Evidence exists that HIH's financial situation had been in decline since 1998 (RC, Vol. 1, Part I: 13). However, it was found by the Royal Commission inquiry that HIH executive directors and corporate officers intentionally and consistently concealed the company's deteriorating financial position. As reported by Justice Owen, in 1999-2000 HIH's financial statements 'were distorted by questionable entries, heavy reliance on one-off end-of-the-year transactions, and aggressive accounting practices (HIHRC, 2003, Vol. I; Part 1:31).

A series of events and decisions increasingly moved the company towards institutionalising the new ways of corrupt accounting and trading insolvently. The culture of dishonesty that prevailed in HIH is particularly evident in the actions of the main protagonist of the HIH saga, the Company's founder and director Ray Williams. Westfield (2003b) recounts, for example, that when it was already known that HIH was in steep financial decline, Williams affirmed in a letter to insurance brokers, that HIH's position was 'rock solid.' A more serious ethical infringement is said to have taken place in June 2000 when Williams ordered his finance director Dominic Fodera to remove an actuaries' report from the board papers prepared for a directors' meeting. This financial report showed a deficiency of $100 million in the reserves of HIH America

(Westfield 2003b). As Westfield (2003b) put it, 'profit that year to June 30 was $ AUD 100 million overstated.'

Williams played a dominant role throughout HIH's history, always having the last word in most of the important decisions. His authority and influence in the company were such that no one was prepared to challenge his views in the boardroom. As commented by Justice Owen:

> No one rivalled [Ray Williams] in terms of authority or influence. Even as his business judgment faltered in the second half of the 1990s he remained unchallenged. No one else in senior management was equipped to grasp what was happening and to bring about a change of direction for the group. There was a lack of accountability among senior management and the board of directors, and there was a singular failure to assess performance in the context of deteriorating financial results (RC, 2003, Vol. I, Part 1:19).

In August 2001, the Government announced a Royal Commission Inquiry into the causes of the HIH collapse. In January 2003, Justice Owen of the Supreme Court of Western Australia handed down a voluminous 4,236 pages long report with a number of adverse findings and recommendations for criminal charges against 50 people involved with HIH and FAI (Westfield 2003a: 239-240). The RC Report found *inter alia* that the HIH had a lack of due process; placed no limits to the CEO's authority; lacked access to independent critical analysis, disregarded conflicts of interests, and was led by an incompetent and ineffective board. Ray Williams and Rodney Adler are denounced in the Report as the main culprits, followed by HIH financial director Dominic Fodera.

Charges of 'improperly used funds' were laid by the 'corporate watchdog' Australian Securities and Insurance Council (ASIC) against Williams, Adler and Fodera. In March 2002, they were found guilty by Justice Kim Santow of civil charges of breaching their directors' duties over the payment by HIH of $ 10 million into the Pacific Eagle Equities trust (controlled by Adler). Adler was disqualified from acting as director for 20 years, fined $ 900 000, and ordered to pay $ 53 million in compensation. Williams was banned from directorships for ten years, and ordered to share the cost of compensation with Adler. Fodera was ordered to pay a smaller fine of AUS $ 5080, for being aware of the deal but not disclosing it (Westfield 2003:235-6).

The HIH saga continued, when on 16 December 2004, Williams pleaded guilty to three criminal charges in the Supreme Court of New South Wales: of being careless and failing to properly exercise his powers and discharge his duties as HIH director; of authorising the issue of a document by HIH holdings (NZ) in October 1998 which contained a material omission, and of making a misleading statement in HIH's 1998-99 annual report. These charges involve a possible total jail term of 12 years and/or fines of $55,000 (Lampe *SMH*, 16/12/2004). At the time of this writing Adler stood trials in the Supreme Court of New South Wales, pleading guilty to three charges of share market manipulation and two of making false or misleading statements.

The 'rise and demise' of HIH have been symptomatic of the aggressive style of capitalism that predominates in high-modernity, premised upon the *thesis* that 'the business of business is profit' and an obvious disregard for the social contract. Not only did the event directly affect the lives of employees, shareholders and policyholders, but also indirectly, when subsequent to the HIH debacle other insurers increased premiums and refused to accept risks (Westfield, 2003a: 241). HIH was a major insurer of professional indemnity, and immediately following the announcement that HIH had gone into liquidation, the price of professional indemnity and public liability insurance rose exorbitantly, with severe impacts on Australian businesses. Doctors' surgeries, childcare centres and sports clubs were forced to close, and policies and unpaid claims of thousands of ordinary people were suddenly rendered worthless. As pointed out by Westfield (2003:241), it 'caused far more damage to the economy and the community than other corporate collapses that occurred at about the same time, such as phone and Internet company One.Tel and Australia's second largest airline, Ansett.'

CORPORATE SOCIAL RESPONSIBILITY DIALECTICS IN THE HIH COLLAPSE

The HIH case is a clear illustration of the negative impacts of the neo-liberal capitalist theses that 'the business of business is profit' and that 'greed is good.' Most importantly, it also demonstrates the usefulness of a dialectical model of analysis to understand the emergence and consolidation of the discourse of corporate social responsibility as an *antithesis* to aggressive capitalist practices that arise in high-modernity from neo-liberal ideology.

The deployment of counter-hegemonic discourses of business ethics and corporate social responsibility reflect the role of the increased *reflexivity* of high modernity, a reflexivity that leads to a constant process of examination of social practices which are reformed in the light of incoming information. This process constitutively alters the character of these practices (Giddens, 1991: 16-17), often in a positive way. In the case of HIH, it is important to take into account the pivotal role played by the mass media in fostering the reflexivity necessary to challenge the hegemonic thesis that 'the business of business is profit.' *Mainstream* newspapers played a particularly important role in keeping the public informed on a regular basis about the HIH saga, with a distinctive focus on the unethical activities of the Company's senior executives. The critical tone of the headlines compiled in Box 8.1, from Australian newspaper reports during the HIH trial is illustrative of a counter hegemonic challenge of the excesses of HIH, informed by a desire in civil society for more ethical business practices.

No doubt, there has been a positive synthesis arising specifically from the HIH inquiry, as in its aftermath there have been significant discursive, legislative and institutional shifts in Australian society. For example, there have been proposals for changes to corporate law, especially in relation to auditing and company financial reporting (ASIC, 2002). These proposals were first put forward in October 2002 in a discussion paper on corporate disclosure referred to as CLERP 9 *(Corporate Law Economic Law Reform Program Paper No. 9: Corporate Disclosure: Strengthening the financial reporting framework).* This paper dealt with financial reporting issues, in particular measures designed to strengthen the quality and independence of auditors. It also tackles the continuous disclosure regime, and some enforcement aspects of the financial reporting process, especially the role of the Companies Auditors and Liquidators Disciplinary Board. Many of these proposals came into law on 1 July 2004.

Another legislative outcome from the HIH Inquiry was the *APRA Amendment Act 2003,* which made changes to the structure of APRA as recommended by the HIH Royal Commission.

The HIH Inquiry also led to the commissioning of the *Palmer Report* by APRA in 2002. The purpose of the Report is to review APRA's role in its formative years in relation to the collapse of HIH and to advise on improvements in its regulatory and supervisory regime. As noted by APRA's chief executive Graeme Thompson:

BOX 8.1

A Selection of Headlines from Australian Newspapers during the HIH case

Headline	*Source*
'Making sense amid spivs and shonks'	Steven Matchett, *Weekend Australia*, 22/4/2003:13
'How ruthless corporate sharks did a job on an old man who was all at sea'	Peter Gosnell. *The Daily Telegraph*, 17/4/2003:29
'Litany of ineptitude revealed as cause for crash—the HIH verdict'	David Brearley, *The Australian*, 17/4/2003:5
'Ray's looking a million dollars and he doesn't have a worry in the world'	Peter Gosnell, *The Daily Telegraph*, 19/2/2003:7
'Money flowed freely as HIH hit the wall'	Brad Clifton, *The Mercury*, 15/1/2003:25
'No insurance against gross incompetence'	Anon., *The Australian*, 17/4/2003:12
'Where the bucks did not stop'	Anon., *The Advertiser*, 18/1/2003:19
H H collapse, the findings: too late for victims of greed 2003:4	Michael Owen-Brown, *The Advertiser*, 17/4/
'The arrogance behind HIH's inglorious fall'	Matthew Horan, *Sunday Telegraph*, 20/4/2003:84
'Blind led bland toward HIH management mayhem'	Stuart Wilson, *The Australian*, 23/4/2003:26
'HIH findings: a very bad business'	Anon., *The Australian*, 15/1/2003:10
'ASIC seeks to charge HIH trio'	Clive Mathieson, *The Australian*, 10/2/2003:27
'The HIH Report: 4,236 pages, 1000 adverse findings . . . Welcome to Wayne's World'	David Brearley, *Weekend Australian*, 18/1/2003:17

The *Palmer Report* confirms that the reforms and improvements APRA has implemented post-HIH are on the right track. As a result of significant legislative changes and many reforms in its policies and processes made over the past two years, APRA is today a much stronger and more effective regulator." (APRA, 2002).

CONCLUSION

This study of the HIH collapse has demonstrated the usefulness of Hegelian dialectics to understand the productive interplay between the *thesis* that the business of business is profit, the *antithesis* that corporate responsibility is essential for a healthy society, which results in a *syntheses* of positive social change.

The dialectic we have described is continually present in developed economics. Periodically, there is a jolt to the system which privileges the thesis or the antithesis. Synthesis results. But this is not to suggest permanence. We accept that some practices will be institutionalised in a manner which privileges certain groups and prevents ready change. Very clearly the behaviour of the Directors of HIH revealed that they treated their fiduciary duty to shareholders lightly. It is equally clear that Ray Williams had institutionalised organisational practices in which it was normal to manipulate accounting records so that they suited the espoused strategy of the firm, as embodied in Ray Williams. The HIH jolt has privileged the antithesis, empowered regulators, and made directors accountable. It has done this through the vicious but righteous release of the full power of the law. The law in this instance had an eloquent simple speaker in Justice Owen. He sifted through complex evidence and clarified HIH. He led by chastising the recalcitrants. He recommended criminal charges, and at the time of writing two Directors, Ray Williams and an officer of the firm have pleaded guilty. Two of these will almost certainly be gaoled. These same two have been disqualified from serving on Boards for at least twenty years and fined $ 5.3 million dollars.

So we have reported a jolt to the system and the reaction of the system. Our research data are very rich and we have only commenced their mining. In conclusion we can point to several leads for research. First, what is the context in which the antithesis is privileged? Second, does the history of corporate collapses indicate similar dialectic?

Third, how did HIH practices become institutionalized? Fourth, how can ethical corporate governance practices be insitutionalised? These questions, no doubt, provide material for thought-provoking contributions to the understanding of the impact of the discourse of corporate social responsibility in high-modernity.

NOTES AND REFERENCES

1. The amounts shown throughout this paper are in Australian dollars (valued as 0.78 of US dollar as at 12/02/2005).
2. Bowen, H.R. (1953): *Social Responsibility of the Businessman*, New York, Harper & Row, p. xi, cited in Çarroll, 1999, 270.
3. Prime Minister John Howard quoted in Cronin, 2001, 12.
4. The Index presents a ranked listing of Australia's top 100 companies assessed across six dimensions: employee relations; environmental performance; social impact; market position; financial performance; and management, ethics and governance (Cronin, Zappala *et al.* 2001, Johns, 2003).
5. See http://www.australianbenchmarking.com.au/seminars/seminar 1.html for details (accessed 20 January 2005).
6. ASIC *vs.* Rich (2003): NSWSC 85.
7. According to the RC report, 'all attempts to carry out such an investigation were rebuffed by FAI's chief executive officer, Rodney Adler.' (RC, Vol. I, Part 1, 10).
8. *Under-reserving* (or under-provisioning) occurs when claims from insured events in previous years are greater than a Company has provided for.

REFERENCES

APRA Media Releases http://www.apra.gov.au/media-releases/02 47.cfm (as at 12/2/2005).

ASIC (2002): "Future Directions: ASIC submission to the HIH Royal Commission." http://www.hihroyalcom.gov.au/Documents/Submissions/ASIC-%20Submission.pdf (as at 20/3/2005).

ASX Corporate Governance Council (2003): "Principles of Good Corporate Governance and Best Practice Recommendations," Sydney, Australian Stock Exchange Ltd., 76.

Beckert, Jens (1999): "Agency, Entrepreneurs and Institutional Change: The Role of Strategic Choice and Institutionalized Practices in Organizations,' *Organization Studies*, 20, 777-99.

Bourdieu, Pierre (1998): "The Essence of Neo-Liberalism," in *Le Monde*, http://mondediplo.com/1998/12/08bourdieu (as at 09/02/2005).

Brown, Bina (2001): 'Untangling the HIH disaster,' in *Asiamoney*, July, Vol. 12(6), pp. 54-55.

Carroll, A.B. (1999): "Corporate Social Responsibility: Evolution of a Definitional Construct," *Business and Society*, 38(3), 268-95.

Centre for Corporate Public Affairs (in conjunction with Business Council of Australia) (2000): *Corporate Community Involvement: Establishing a Business Case*, Sydney, BCA.

Chanticleer (2004): "Hardie must Change from the Top Down," *The Australian Financial Review*, 88.

Clarke, Frank; Dean, Graeme; and Oliver, Kyle (2003): "HIH—Unfettered Hubris," in *Corporate Collapse: Accounting, Regulatory and Ethical Failure*, Second Edition, Cambridge University Press, Port Melbourne.

Clegg, S.R. (1989): *Frameworks of Power*, Sage, London.

Cronin, C. (2001): "Corporate Social Responsibility in Australia: A Select Review of the Literature," The Smith Family, Sydney.

Cronin, C.; G. Zappala *et al.* (2001): "Measuring the Social Impact of Companies in Australia: The Smith Family's participation in The Good Reputation Index," The Smith Family, 2005.

DiMaggio, P.J. and W.W. Powell (1991): *The New Institutionalism in Organizational Analysis*, Chicago, University of Chicago Press.

Fairclough, Norman and Thomas, Peter (2004): "The Discourse of Globalization and the Globalization of Discourse," in David Grant, Cynthia Hardy, Cliff Oswick and Linda Putnam (Eds.), *The Sage Handbook of Organizational Discourse*, Sage Publications, London, pp. 379-96.

Giddens, A. (1991): *The Consequences of Modernity*, Polity Press, Cambridge.

Grant, David; Hardy, Cynthia; Oswick, Cliff and Putnam, Linda (Eds.), *The Sage Handbook of Organization Discourse*, Sage Publications, London.

Gray, John; Stewart Clegg and Chris Carter (2005): Forthcoming "How do Professions form Change and Organize?," in *Critical Perspectives in Accounting*, Sage, London.

Greenwood, R. and C.R. Hinings (1996): "Understanding Radical Organizational Change: Bringing Together the Old and the New Institutionalism," *Academy of Management Review*, 21, pp. 1022-55.

Hegel, G.W.F. (1912: 1916): "Contradiction," in *Science of Logic*, Vol. II, available at http://www.marxists.org/reference/archive/hegel/works/hl/hl431.htm (as at 12/02/2005).

Johns, G. (2003): "The Good Reputation Index: A Tale of Two Strategies," *IPA Backgrounder*, 15(2), 1-16.

Kuhn, T.S. (1962): *The Structure of Scientific Revolutions*, Chicago, University of Chicago.

Lampe, Ann (2004): "HIH founder faces 12 years' jail after guilty pleas," in *Sydney Morning Herald*, 16/12/2004.

Main, Andrew (2003): *Other People's Money: The Complete Story of the Extraordinary Collapse of the HIH*, Harper Collins Publishers, Sydney.

Oliver, C. (1991): "Strategic Responses to Institutional Processes," *Academy of Management Review*, 16, 145-79.

Oswick, C. (2001): 'The Globalization of Globalization: An Analysis of Managerialist Trope in Action,' in J. Biherman and A. Alkhafari (eds.), *The Business Research Yearbook*, IADB Press.

Owen, Neville (2003): 'The Failure of HIH: A Critical Assessment,' in *The HIH Royal Commission Report*, at http://www.hiroyacom.gov.au (as at 20/04/2004).

Owen, N.T.H.J. (2003): The Failure of HIH Insurance, Commonwealth of Australia, Canberra, 2004.

Sexton, J. and D. Brearley (2003): "Real Obscenity in the Fate of Victims—The HIH Verdict," *The Australian*, Canberra, 5.

Stiglitz Joe (2002): *Globalization and Its Discontents*, W.W. Norton & Company, New York.

Westfield, Mark (2003a): *HIH: The Inside Story of Australia's Biggest Corporate Collapse*, John Wiley & Sons Australia Ltd., Melbourne.

Westfield, Mark (2003b): "Why did the HIH Collapse?," in *CA Charta*, Vol. 74(3), pp. 24-29.

Zappala, G. (2003): "Corporate Citizenship and the Role of Government: the Public Policy Case," Canberra, Parliamentary Library, 2005.

APPENDIX 1

Chronology of the HIH Collapse's Key Events

Year	*Events*
1968	Ray Williams and Michael Payne establish MW Payne Underwriting Agency Pty Ltd.
1971	MW Payne Understanding Agency Pty Ltd acquired by Heath plc of the UK.
1980	Ray Williams appointed to the board of CE Heath plc.
1987	CE Heath plc establishes workers' compensation underwriting in the US.
1989	Business of CE Heath plc transferred to CE International Holdings Ltd (CE Heath).
1992	CE Heath lists on ASX resulting in 45 per cent of the issued capital owned by the public; 44 per cent by CE Heath plc and 11 per cent by CE Heath directors and staff.
1993	CE Heath commences operations in the UK.
1995	CE Heath acquires CIC Insurance Group funded by CE Heath issuing to CIC holdings, which becomes Winterthur Holdings Australia Ltd.
1996	CE Heath changes its name to HIH Winsterthur.
1998	HIH Winterthur acquires operations in New Zealand, Argentina, Thailand, the United Kingdom, the United States.
	Winterthur Swiss sells its 51 per cent shareholding in HIH Winterthur to the public.
1999	HIH Winterthur takes over FAI Insurance and becomes HIH Insurance Ltd. Rodney Adler appointed as Director.
2000	December: Ray Williams resigns as director of HIH.
2001	February: Rodney Adler resigns.
	March: HIH placed in provisional liquidation.
	July: The Australian Stock Exchange removes HIH from its official list.
	August 27: HIH is placed in liquidation.
	August 29: Letters Patent appointing the Royal Commission are signed.
2003	April: Commissioner Neville Owen's report is released.
2004	December: Ray Williams pleads guilty to three charges. Faces 12 years in jail.
2005	February: Adler pleads guilty on three charges.

Source: Adapted from Westfield, 2003b.

9

Protection of Environment by Waste Management and Waste Minimization Audit

D.S. CHUNDAWAT AND KANEEZ FATIMA SADRIWALA

The basic purpose of waste management is to minimize the overall waste in a given system. Waste here refers to all kinds of resources specially the material resources, which constitute a significant part.

Waste minimization is the method by which superflows by products to some central process are reduced to the extent feasible prior to their treatment, storage or dispatch. Any waste generated by an industry requires to handle the wastes in a scientific manner so that its impact on environment is minimum. Apart from this it should be handled as per legislative requirements. The cost of handling, storage, transportation of solid, hazardous waste is significant. Waste minimization audit enables an industry to know location and identification of sources of waste, risk, level of costs, benefits and schedules of action to be made. Waste minimization audit should be conducted on a periodical basis. Some waste is inevitable in any conversion process of input into outputs. To reduce waste, we have therefore to maximize the use of resources. Resource management and waste management are thus supportive to each other. Any activity that does not add value is a waste

Any activity that does not add value is a waste

CLASSIFICATION OF WASTE

Waste may be classified on the basis of:

1. Resources
2. Origin
3. Property
4. Recoverability

Waste Resources

1. Material Resources—Solid, Liquid, Gas
2. Energy Resources—Physical, Human, Solar
3. Time Resources
4. Capital Resources—Capacity, Equipment, Machine hours, Inventory
5. Service Resources—Communication, transport, health
6. Life or Human Resources
7. Data and Information

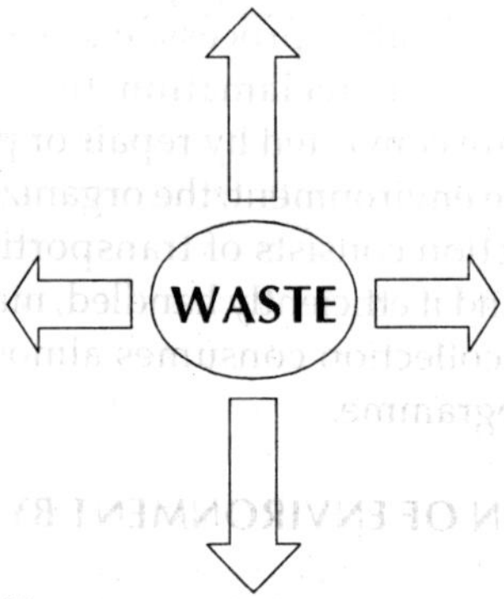

Origin

1. Industrial
2. Residential
3. Commercial
4. Office
5. Municipal
6. Construction and Demolition
7. Agriculture

Property (Type)

1. Hazardous—Plastics, solid waste, gases and fumes
2. Non-Hazardous

Recoverable

1. Direct Recycling of identical or similar product
2. Indirect recycling of products of less critical specification
3. Thermal Recycling—Generation of energy or chemical product or both

Waste is an indirect measure of productivity. If wastivity is checked, the effect, productivity will automatically improve. Thus–

Waste = Input units – Output units + Closing stock units

Net waste = Total waste – Waste recycled within the system

$$\text{Wastivity} = \frac{\text{Waste (W)}}{\text{Input (I)}}$$

$$\text{Net Wastivity} = \frac{\text{Net Waste}}{\text{Total Input}}$$

SYSTEMATIC APPROACH TO WASTE REDUCTION

1. First of all total waste in the whole system is recognised.
2. The stage at which waste is generated is identified.
3. Waste reduction is implemented at each stage by planning correcting action and eliminating the cause.

RECYCLING OF WASTES

The wastes can be recycled and reused. In **recycling** the waste is used as input to the same process/system. In **reuse**, the waste is used as input to some other process, e.g. sugarcane leagasse is reused to prepare paper. In **reclamation**, the damaged, rejected or undesired outputs are converted by repair or processing.

Waste affects the environment, the organization and the public health. Waste collection consists of transporting the waste. It is a major cost element and if efficiently handled, may reduce the overall cost of WH. Waste collection consumes almost 80 per cent of the waste reduction programme.

PROTECTION OF ENVIRONMENT BY RECYCLING

On one hand recycling may be helpful in reduction of cost, on the other hand it increases overall economic productivity. Social benefit from recycling is that it can minimize the pollution of natural surroundings. By decreasing the load of waste on land, on incineration and on water course, the quality of air, water and land sites can be improved. By reducing the use of initial mineral extraction to a declining proportion, recycling lessens the pollution which the handling of growing tonnage requires. Preference should be given to composting them rather than incineration as air pollution is associated with incineration. Composting plant can supply manure to local market and this will reduce consumption of chemical fertilizers and hence saving in the raw material and energy which goes into the manufacturing of fertilizers.

Awareness of public for anti-waste and anti-pollution should be created by the media, so that the public may accept recycled materials. Government departments and institutions should use recycled stationeries so as to set an example. Recycling reduces dependence on imports of raw material as well as finished goods. Number of small industries can be set-up for recycling materials.

WASTE MINIMIZATION AUDIT

For reducing waste, investigation and corrective measures in the following areas are required:

1. Raw Material Substitution

The quality of waste generated in plant depends on quality of Raw material and consumable chemicals used in the process. Purity of raw material/chemical should be checked. If it is possible to substitute the raw material/chemicals to produce non or less hazardous waste, then it should be done.

2. Process Design and Operation

To investigate the current process design and operation and to make changes in the following areas:

(a) New equipment that produces no waste or less waste.
(b) Modifying existing equipments to produce less quantity of waste.
(c) Altered process with different catalyst to optimize reactions.
(d) New processes to produce less waste.
(e) Modify to enhance recovery and recycling.
(f) Maximize operating efficiency.
(g) Preventive maintenance.

3. Volume Reduction

For reducing volume of waste, the following points can be considered.

(a) Prioritize the waste streams for investigation.
(b) Streams which generate largest volume of waste should be investigated first so that modification made in this stream will show greatest return.

(c) Each type of waste should be kept separate and possibilities of internal recycling should be studied.
(d) Leakages from pumps, valves, pipelines and spills from vessels, tanks should be eliminated.
(e) Ways of external recycling should be investigated as waste from one industry may be raw material from another industry.
(f) Determining the optimum balance between disposal/reuse/recycling.

4. Inventory Management

(a) Inventory of Raw Material/chemical consumables, hazardous and flammable material should be taken.
(b) Industry should purchase raw material through working out EOQ (Economic Order Quantity).
(c) Good communication (MIS) between purchase department, consuming plant and outside supplier will avoid redundant stock of raw material.
(d) Change in process or raw material will lead to unnecessary stock of raw material entailing the Company's liability for storage/disposal of material if it is of hazardous nature.

BASIC REQUIREMENTS FOR CONDUCTING WASTE AUDIT

For conducting audit basic informations required are—

1. Procedure to record all legislative regulatory requirements.
2. Inventory of activities and releases. The inventory be include:
   (a) The composition, quantity and paths of release of waste generations.
   (b) The consumption of materials, fuel and energy.
   (c) Effects of waste on environment including the workforce and workplace.
   (d) The consequences of past activities and the future consequences.
3. Procedures already established for waste management under environmental management plan.
4. To establish procedure for waste management.
   (a) Normal Operation procedures.

(b) Abnormal operation procedure that is sudden shut down of plant, incident, accident, etc., which leads to more waste than in normal plant conditions.

RECOMMENDATION OF AUDIT TEAM

After conducting the audit, the screening of the various alternatives of waste minimization is recorded. Technical and economic evaluation of the various alternatives is carried out. Analysis of the cost/payback of waste minimization are evaluated. Audit team then makes recommendations. Companies may implement all or selected options. Track and measure of progress on implementation job is made. On implementation of waste minimization job, result of such work is judged.

REFERENCES

K. Ashwatthapa, "Production and Operation Management."

Kezar Ali Shah, "Recycling of Municipal Waste," *IJEP*, Vol 14, No. 5, May 1994.

Kezar Ali Shah, "Waste Minimization Audit," *IJEP*, Vol. 15, No. 11, Nov. 1995.

Peter L. Grogan, "Taking Avoided Disposal Costs to the Bank," *Bio-Cycle*, Sep. 1989, p. 80.

P. Rosseaux, A. Navarro and P. Vermande, "Heavy Metal Distribution in Household Waste," *Bio-Cycle*, Sep. 1989, pp. 81-85.

W. Alex Cross, "Composting Reduces Solid Waste Volume," *Pollution Engineering*, July 1991, pp. 86-87, The British Library.

10

CSR in Insurance Sector

K. UDAY GOWRI SHANKAR

INTRODUCTION

The field of responsible business practice is one of the most dynamic and challenging subjects, corporate leaders face today. The need is more felt because, the world is waking up to the fact that, the worldwide problems of poverty, indebtedness, child labour, pollution and corruption are still with us. The attention has been focused upon the publicly financed international organizations. Yet many are also wondering about the role of large multinational organizations and private sector in general. Companies operating in globalised markets are increasingly required to balance the social, economic and environmental components of their business, while building shareholder value. Further it is not enough to think about their accountability to their shareholders. They must also think about their responsibility to their stakeholders, including the wider issues in the world in which they operate. Indeed, a company cannot survive, without having a clear statement of its purpose and values; followed by an understanding of the process it must follow to put these into operation. In other words, companies have to devote more and more attention to non-financial aspects to satisfy not only worldwide pressure groups, but in the end to survive at all. The extent to which corporations must consider non-financial aspects of their business or in other words their level of 'Corporate Social Responsibility' is an area of intense research today. The field of responsible business practice is one of the most dynamic and challenging subjects, corporate leaders face today. Technically CSR can be defined as "A concept whereby companies integrate social and environmental concerns in their business operations and in their interactions with their stakeholders on a voluntary basis." The definition is so simple, logical and self-evident that few would seriously disagree with it. It is noteworthy that the need for a voluntary basis is spelt out. Businesses are thus expected to feel naturally inclined rather than obliged to comply with relevant legal requirements. They are also required to be honest and accurate in reporting the financial results of their operations, respect the rights of their employees and the citizens and also to observe environmental laws and regulations. However for different industries, responsible business practice involves different issues.

AREAS OF CSR

The demands and expectations of 'Corporate Social Responsibility' impact differently on different business sectors. Some such as the manufacturing sector entail a heavy emphasis at the local level and are highly sensitized to a broad range of societal issues from human rights to health and environment. Other sectors such as financial services, often entail less physical impact at the local level, but nonetheless can have a significant influence on the development and well-being of the community in which the sector operates.

'Corporate Social Responsibility' focuses on the social, environmental and financial success of a company. The triple bottom line is with the aim to achieve social development while achieving business success. Companies now perform in non-financial areas such as human rights, business ethics, environmental policies, corporate contributions, community development, corporate governance and workplace issues. Social and environmental performances are considered side by side with financial performance. From local economic development concerns to International human rights policies, companies are being accountable for their actions and their impact. Companies are also more transparent in disclosing and communicating their policies and practices as these impact employees, communities and the environment. In the new global economy, companies that are responsive to the demands of all their stakeholders are arguably better positioned to achieve long-term financial success. 'Corporate Social Responsibility' is the point of convergence of various initiatives aimed at ensuring socio-economic development of the community which would be livelihood-oriented as a whole in a credible and sustainable manner.

Environmental risk management is not a precise science. But sophisticated financial engineering, combined with sound practical risk management, can provide solutions that work for business and an increasingly demanding society. The issue of 'Corporate Social Responsibility' is increasingly becoming the object of attention from Government, Public and Institutional investors. Until now, the way in which environmental liabilities should be reported has been rather vague. However, legislation is well on its way, which will force companies to monitor and report environmental data. From an investor's perspective, the frequency and size of claims related to environmental impairment continue to increase. There is a real need for the insurers to adapt themselves to a rapidly changing risk profile.

While 'Corporate Social Responsibility' covers many important issues like environment and relations with customers, the core of CSR is ethical behaviour. If a business is not directed by its own considered set of ethics and values, it is simply adrift. The best means of embedding ethics and values in a business is through example. Whatever example is set at the top of the organization, it will flow down through the structure. It is therefore the job of senior management of every company to ensure that, only good examples are set. Behaviour must be transparent and ambiguous.

BENEFITS OF CSR

1. Improved financial performance
2. Reduced costs
3. Enhanced brand image and reputation
4. Increased sales and customer loyalty
5. Customer satisfaction
6. Increased productivity and quality
7. Increased ability to attract and retain employees
8. Reduced regulatory oversight
9. Brand visibility, recognition and awareness
10. Increased market share
11. Favourable positioning

12. Competitive mileage
13. More engaged investors
14. Environmental sustainability

However the benefits mentioned above can be enjoyed by the corporate only if their CSR activity is measured. This need has prompted Professor Donna Wood to develop a systems model to measure the effectiveness of Corporate Social Responsibility. This is basically done through three steps. Briefly it is as follows:

1. **Principles of social responsibility** – The level of application of CSR principles is institutional and is based on a Firm's basic obligations as a business organization. Its value is that, it defines the institutional relationship between business and society and specifies, what is expected of any business.
2. **Process of social responsibility** – Corporate social responsiveness is a business's capacity to respond to social pressures. This suggests the ability of the business organization to survive through adaptation to its business environment. To do so, it must know as much as possible, about this business environment, be capable of analyzing its data and must react to the results of this analysis. However, the environment of business is not static and it is ever changing and complex. So great care should be given to successfully scan, interpret and react to the business environment.
3. **Outcomes** – The main focus of measurement is the third level of the CSR model. To know about whether, CSR has actually made a difference.

The concept and applicability of CSR will be clearer if a particular industry is taken as a case study and analyzed. In recent years business of financial services is booming and in that particularly insurance sector is growing rapidly. So this area is taken up for study.

Insurance

The history of Insurance might be traced to Babylonia, where traders were encouraged to assume the risks of the caravan trade through loans that were repaid with interest only after the goods had arrived safely. The Greeks later applied a similar system to the sea borne commerce. The Romans used burial club as a form of Life Insurance, providing funeral expenses for members and later payments to the survivors. With the growth of towns and trade in Europe, the governments of countries undertook to protect their companies on their region from loss by fire, shipwreck and earthquakes. By the middle of the 14th century A.D., as evidenced by the earliest known insurance contract, marine insurance was practically universal among the maritime nations of Europe. By the 18th century, a company from London, named Lloyd's became the first modern Insurance Company, Insurance developed rapidly in later years. Slowly other nations also gave lot of importance to the concept of insurance. When the people of different countries are putting so much trust in the insurance companies by patronizing them continuously, it becomes the responsibility of all the insurance companies in the world to live up to their expectations. Apart from giving compensation to their customers, it is increasingly becoming important for the insurance companies to focus more on their responsibility towards the society in general.

In this connection, we will look in to the CSR activities of two eminent insurance organizations from different parts of the world that are implementing the concept in tone and deed.

CSR IN INSURANCE

Aviva

Aviva is United Kingdom's largest and world's seventh largest insurer with thirty million customers and having around fifty eight thousand employees worldwide. Aviva has been ranked the top-performing insurer in the 2004 Business in the Community—Corporate Responsibility Index. This year the index had 139 participants, from which the company was ranked in fifth position overall and in top of the insurance sector. The index provides a systematic approach to managing; measuring and reporting the impacts the company has upon society and their environment. Companies were assessed in five areas: Corporate Social Responsibility strategy, Integration of CSR issues, CSR management, Performance and impact and CSR assurance. Aviva performed strongly in all the five areas. Aviva's CSR policy covers eight areas: Relations with Workforce. Customers, Suppliers and the Community. Management of the environment, Human rights, Health and safety and Adherence to standards of business conduct. The Aviva board has a clear view of the importance of CSR to the success of the business. The organization is sure of the fact that, it is vital for any business to remain alert and responsive to the changes taking place around it. Its future depends upon, how well aligned it is to the society in which it operates. The Chairman of the company is sure in his belief that, if the business has the right approach to ethics, if its driving motivation in all its dealings is to be honest and fair with all its partners, then it is earning its license to operate and it will thrive. Moreover, the organization is convinced that although CSR cover's many important issues such as relations with customers and the wider community, the environment and human rights, the core of CSR is ethical behaviour.

The company regularly reviews performances in each of these areas and publishes a report annually to report on progress. Some of the CSR activities done by Aviva are as follows:

- 98 per cent of Aviva employees are covered by the company's CSR programme.
- 86 per cent of Norwich Union Property Portfolio in the United Kingdom uses renewable sourced electricity with zero carbon dioxide emissions.
- 33 per cent reduction in paper usage worldwide achieved through increased use of electronic rather than paper-based communications.
- Around five million pounds donated to various worldwide community projects.
- Reduced supplier payment times.

Life Insurance Corporation of India

Keeping in mind the primary obligation of the corporation to its policy-holders, as enshrined in the objectives of nationalization, the funds of the corporation are deployed to the best advantage of the policy-holders as well as the community as a whole. Substantial part of the funds are invested in Central Government securities. Government guaranteed marketable securities, loans in the socially-oriented sector for approved purposes such as Power, Housing,

Water Supply, Sewage, Road Transport and Co-operative Industrial Estates. The Corporation has been promoting social welfare through socially-oriented investments. Under the Corporation's scheme of providing financial assistance for piped water supply and drainage, local bodies of 23 states in India are benefited. The Corporation also provides financial assistance to State Electricity Boards for power generation projects, by way of loans/subscriptions to their bonds. Housing is one of the basic necessities of human beings. Housing Finance therefore occupies a prime place in the Corporation's socio-purposive investments. Since inception, the Corporation has been providing finance for housing to individuals, co-operative housing societies and private undertakings under its various mortgage-housing schemes. With a view to solve the housing shortage in the country, the Corporation joined in a big way in massive efforts by providing financial assistance to state governments for social housing schemes for economically weaker sections, low income groups, middle income groups, state government employees and rural population. The Corporation has been assisting development of road transport by providing financial assistance to state road transport corporations for augmenting their fleet of buses. The scope of the socially-oriented sector was widened to accommodate infrastructure projects pertaining to ports, railways, roads and airports.

CONCLUSION

In spite of the above examples, the fact of the matter is that, the concept of 'Corporate Social Responsibility' has not penetrated too deeply in to the Insurance Sector. Apart from big companies, most of the smaller companies are still at a very nascent stage as far as their CSR is concerned. The extent to which companies must consider non-financial aspects of their business or in other words their level of 'Corporate Social Responsibility' is an area of intense research today. The need of the hour is that, those companies in the insurance industry, which has not involved itself in the area of CSR, must devote more time to understand their responsibilities towards society and should design ways and means, through which they can contribute in a positive way to the betterment of the society, which will ultimately make our planet a better place to live.

REFERENCES

Angel, Cabrena, 'Responsibility of Corporate in Building Nations,' *Business Week*, June 2004.

Charles, R. Clerk, 'Social Responsibility Ethics.'

www.csrwire.com

www.aviva.com

www.licindia.com

11

Are Non-Executive Directors Facing Insurmountable Risks?

MAC WRIGHT AND HELENA MITEWA

Since events such as the highly publicised corporate collapses of Enron Corp. in the United States and the failure of HIH Insurance in Australia occurred, "corporate governance" has become a buzz word around board rooms across the world. The prosecution of high-profile company directors led to public criticism. Crises of confidence have brought the issues of accountability into sharp focus. While board members pay lip service to the new regime, it is business as usual. For non-executive directors, relying on the briefing papers supplied by executive directors for information is becoming increasingly hazardous. Yet there are ways around this problem. This paper looks at the latest Australian regulation and best practice guidelines and proposes one possible approach that independent directors can take to overcome the weaknesses inherent in the current system. The paper will examine the strengths and weaknesses of such an approach and suggest solutions to overcome the shortcomings.

THE DIRECTOR'S DUTY TO BE INFORMED

Executive directors generally have very broad access to the operations of the organization that they are directing. As executives, they generally deal on a day-to-day basis with the problems of the organization and are, or should be, generally aware of the state of the organization and what it is doing. They should also be aware of the limitations of the organization's information systems.

Non-executive directors do not have the same day-to-day contact with the organizations they direct. They generally rely heavily on board position papers. These papers are normally prepared under the direct control of the executive directors. Thus, the information submitted to the non-executive director in board position papers is certainly not independent and may be biased. The problem for the non-executive director is to recognize when this is the case. Generally, the board position papers would not contain significant bias. However, in some organizations, very strong executive directors may introduce biased statements in order to avoid an admission to particular difficulties within the organization. Even asking for details and requisitioning information still suffers from the disadvantage that such requests and the responses thereto pass through the hands of executive directors or executive officers of the organization. Thus the responses may not be free of the influence of the senior management of the organization.

Consider, for example, what happened in the AWA case. The background to this was the establishment of a foreign exchange dealing operation by AWA Ltd., a public company with an established reputation in the electronic engineering field. The board was assured by management that adequate controls over the new dealing operation were in place and operating. This was not the case. The operation took positions in currencies which amounted to betting on the direction of movement of the currency. While the external auditors notified the dealing operation that they considered the situation unsatisfactory, and that the controls set in place should be followed, they did not inform the board of the problem.

With no warning from the auditors, management's assurances were accepted by the board. Currency fluctuations caused an enormous loss. The company sued the auditors for failing to keep the board fully informed. While Mr. Justice Phillips in the AWA case apportioned damages between the company and the auditors, he stated in his dicta that non-executive directors should be able to rely on assurances of management that organizational controls are in place and functioning.

The position in the AWA case contradicts to some extent the position taken in *Morley's case*. In *Morley's case,* Mrs. Morley was the director of a company that was managed by her son. Her son mismanaged the company and it traded while insolvent. It was held that Mrs. Morley as a director had an obligation to know what was going on in the company.

There is a real risk that directors may find that reliance on management's assurances puts them in the position of Mrs. Morley, rather than being able to rely on assurances of management as stated in Mr. Justice Phillips' earlier dicta in the *AWA case.*

This risk is further emphasized by the judgment on appeal in *Clark's case (2003).* Here, Spigelman CJ, Handley J. and Hodgson J. found that Mrs. Clark was a non-executive director of Southern Cross Interiors Pty. Ltd. They also accepted the finding of the lower court that with regard to her knowledge of the activities of Southern Cross Interiors Pty Ltd., that: *"Nothing was brought to her attention during her directorship which should have put her upon enquiry as to SCT's financial position."* Yet the judgment reinforced Mrs. Clark's duty to know what was going on in the company of which she was a director by placing her in the same position as the other (executive) director.

THE NEED FOR INDEPENDENT INFORMATION

To avoid the risk of being found in a situation such as existed in *Morley's case and Clark's case,* the non-executive director needs an independent source of information as to what is happening within their organization. One option is to exercise their general right of access to the organization as recognized in Corporations Law, and independently to seek out the records that they require from within the company. A major weakness of this approach is that it may take some time for the non-executive directors to develop sufficient understanding to efficiently find out for themselves what is happening in the organization. If they need to access internal information records, finding out where the records are may take considerable time. Furthermore, gaining an adequate understanding to be able to interpret the recorded data may take *even* more time. Uncooperative staff may also create further difficulties. While these may be surmounted, they are not helpful to the non-executive director who chooses this method of avoiding information bias. Thus, the non-executive director may face considerable limitations in obtaining unbiased information.

THE BOARD AUDIT COMMITTEE

The steady introduction of board audit committees has been regarded as a move to build stronger corporate governance. In jurisdictions such as Singapore, these Board Audit Committees are supposed to include a majority of non-executive directors and to be chaired by a non-executive director (Singapore Exchange Listing Rules). The creation of these tools or instruments of corporate governance was driven by the listing requirements of the New York Stock Exchange.

The committees generally rely on senior management for the preparation of committee position papers. This means they are still dependent on data that is under the direct influence of executive directors, and thus run exactly the same risk of bias as outlined in the above discussion. Again, independence and lack of bias in the data cannot be guaranteed. A classic example of a corporation that adopted all the recommended corporate governance procedures and yet failed to enforce proper corporate governance was that of ENRON Corporation. Simply having all the requirements in place does not mean they will be adhered to.

Audit committees often represent the first point of contact in dealings between the organization and the external auditors (Mathews *et al.*, 1993).

The role of the external auditor is defined under Australian law as to "form an opinion on the truth and fairness of the accounts" (Corporations law). Thus, the external auditors providing independent opinion to the shareholders may be considered as a potential source of information on the organization that is free from any executive management driven bias or error. However, history tells a different story.

There are a number of occurrences in recent history in Australia where the external auditors have failed to alert anyone that the organization was in severe difficulties. However, the phenomenon is not new and the more serious or unfortunate cases end up in court.

An example of a failure that resulted in litigation against the auditors (but was settled out of court) was that of the State Bank of Victoria. An earlier example was the failure of the Trustees and Executors Agency Ltd. Here, the release of the annual accounts showing a sound profit, accompanied by an unqualified audit report occurred only days before the company collapsed.

Examples of Board Failures (1)—HIH

Another topical example is HIH's failure shortly after the release of a glowing set of audited accounts (Westfield, 2003). There is little reported data that suggest that the external auditors undertook any action to warn either the non-executive directors, the shareholders, or the public of the impending crisis. HIH has even more interesting implication in that the chairman at the time was a retired senior partner in the company's auditors (Owen, 2003). This suggested that the external auditors lacked the level of independence necessary to audit effectively. This is a consideration of particular interest given that the assumptions underlying the valuation methods used to calculate the current (book) value of future assets tended to maximize the current value of the assets. At the same time, the assumptions underlying the valuation of future liabilities (the long "tails" of older insurance policies, Westfield, 2003) tended to use risk assumptions and discount rates that minimized the value of these liabilities.

Examples of Board Failures (2)—Enron

Interestingly, Enron's approach to the valuation of future cash flows was quite unreal. While concealing future loss contracts, Enron's management reward system was geared to recognize future income as earned income. Thus the moment a contract was concluded, the income flows from the contract were discounted back to a present value and this amount was recorded as present income. Executive bonuses were paid on the basis of the discounted present value of future earnings (Jensen, 2003). However, there were two difficulties. One was the fact that not all future earnings were sufficiently assured such that they could be prudently booked as present income. The other was that the discount rate used to book the future income at current values favoured the overstatement of future income. The acceptance of the assumptions made in these two areas, along with a willingness to apply GAAP on a basis that favoured the company when loss contracts were hived off, to shelf companies was created the appearance that both the auditors and non-executive directors lacked independence (Jensen, 2003). Note, however, that both these procedures were not strictly outside the guidelines of GAAP. This in effect weakened the position of those who opposed the approach that was taken. It was pushing the boundaries, but it was not actually breaking the rules. This made it difficult for the non-executive directors to reject the accounts, just as it made it difficult for the auditors to justify a report that did not accept the accounts.

GAAP, International Accounting Standards, and the AASBs are all detailed guidance notes rather than broad guidelines. Thus, anything that met a loose interpretation of the GAAP's notes would have to be accepted. A broader guideline may have given the external auditors a stronger position. That aside, the external auditors did not draw attention to the weaknesses in the accounts. Accordingly they were stigmatized as having accepted what proved to be an unacceptable set of accounts. It could be argued that neither the non-executive directors nor the auditors should not have allowed the company's management to go as far as they did, but to that extent, the failure to inform was an overall responsibility of the company's management, the non-executive board and the auditors. But some would claim that the auditors were the last line of defence, and thus their failure was the more heinous.

A counter argument is that not all companies approach their reporting responsibilities in such a cavalier fashion. For example, the Pacific Dunlop Ltd. accounts from the early 1990s to the final indignity of the abandonment of the name "Pacific Dunlop" record a litany of poor decisions with fair accuracy. Little attempt was made to gloss over the effect of the errors made by both senior management and the board on the company. The question here is: 'Should credit for this transparency be assigned to the company's board or to its external auditors?'

As an aside, considering the extent of external audit failure, the suggestion put forward some time back by the Scottish Institute of Chartered Accountants and mentioned in other parts of this discussion is not as extreme as first thought. This suggestion was that the internal audit function should actually conduct the audit, while the role of the external auditor would be to ensure that the internal audit conducts a proper and satisfactory audit (McInnes, 1993).

THE INTERNAL AUDIT AND ITS CONSTRAINTS

The major problem facing internal audit is the level of independence afforded to the internal auditor. To have any chance of being truly effective, the internal auditor must be able to stand independent of line management.

A USA-based survey in 1979 found that 80 per cent of internal auditors reported or were otherwise responsible to the chief financial officer. But only about 37 per cent of internal auditors were appointed by the board, or any committee of the board or were in situations where the board expressed any interest in their appointment (Urbancic and Cook, 1980). The later survey of the way Australian organizations managed their internal audit (Mathews *et al.*, 1993), showed that while boards continued to have only a limited involvement in the management of the internal audit function, they were slowly expanding this involvement. When questioned on this, one board member of several major Australian domestic and multinational companies stated that such a deep involvement with internal audit was considered by him to be outside the role of a normal board of directors (private interview with anonymity guaranteed).

In fact it is hard to see how the day-to-day work of a Board Audit Committee could be handled without liaison with the internal audit function of the organization. Given this, it would appear that the relationship between the internal audit and the boards of most companies will continue to expand. It would appear that the Board Audit Committees are increasing in popularity. It would also appear that these committees are increasingly willing to draw on the expertise of the internal auditor when they need to. In most cases, however, the internal auditor remains a tool of management, appointed by management, and principally reporting to management.

FURTHER DISCUSSIONS OF THE RISKS FACED BY DIRECTORS

There is little other than develop a closer relationship with a stronger internal audit that the independent directors can do. The legal obligation on company directors to be responsible for the actions of their company goes back in Australia to the prosecution of Stanley Korman in the late 1960s for permitting a company of which he was a director to act in a fraudulent manner. Korman was jailed for his role as a director of the failed Reid Murray Corporation Ltd. Korman's defence failed in part because he was also CEO and as such was expected by the courts to know what his company was doing *(Crown v. Korman)*. In a later civil case, *Morleys case,* Mrs. Morley, who was not the CEO, just an ordinary director, had executed guarantees in favour of the company in conjunction with other directors and was sued. She failed to convince a court that actions taken by the company of which she was a director were actions that she could not reasonably be expected to be aware of. Her attempt at a defence was based on the supposition that she was an elderly woman, who although a director, let others run the company. According to her, she was totally unaware of the way the company was being run and had not the capacity to understand what was going on. The court held that if she did not think herself qualified, she should not have taken a position as a director. Her defence was similar to that raised by Alan Bond in his defence of criminal charges brought against him for breaches of the corporations' law.

His defence was based on the claim that he had no idea what was going on in the company as he had contracted amnesia at the opening of the case—doctor's certificates and all. He served a three years' sentence. It should be noted that Alan Bond was effectively an executive director *(Crown* v. *Bond).* Morley's case does demonstrate, however, that non-executive directors can expect that the courts will regard their duty to know what is going on within a company as legally binding. Yet how do the non-executive directors find out the truth, other than by relying on insiders within the company. As mentioned before, personal inspection is an option, but this may not always work.

THE NON-EXECUTIVE BOARD MEMBER *V.* THE INTERNAL AUDITOR AS AN INDEPENDENT OBSERVER

There is much hearsay evidence that people put themselves on their best behaviour when facing inspections by people of far superior rank within the organization. If this is considered within a cultural perspective, it would mean that persons who were relying in information gleaned from discussion with significantly lower rank employees would be mislead as to the culture of the organization at their levels. In fact, from sampling one organization, it was found that three board members who had regular dealings with middle and lower line management had developed a consistent view of the culture of the organization. However, this view was significantly at odds, with the view of middle management. A competing value-based framework was used to identify the culture. Within this model, an organization could be predominantly hierarchical and bureaucratic, market driven, clan-based or an adhocracy. The three non-executive directors chose to view the organization more as a clan, with adhocracy tendencies. Middle management, on the other hand, consistently viewed the organization principally as a bureaucracy that was driven by the market. This gives an indication of the large extent to which a non-executive board member can become with corporate reality, even when dealing with middle management almost on a daily basis. Thus, the need to be able to rely on persons within the organization who can supply an unbiased view is imperative.

The problem is that while the internal audit's role of informing boards is expanding, boards on their part must ensure that the internal auditors have the ability to carry out the role of supplying unbiased information to the board. If the internal auditor is to inform the board audit committee without bias, then the internal auditor must feel secure and able to inform the board. Thus, if the board is to expect the internal auditor not to be biased when informing the board, the board must put adequate safeguards in place. For example, the board must expand their role, not just in the process of appointment, but also in the day-to-day management of the audit personnel so that the latter can feel confident they are working for the board.

When considering the effectiveness of internal audit, the developments at Enron Corporation are worth noting. Enron was a major player in the USA energy market in the 1990's. During this period, the company's energy buyers attempted what could be best described as the building of a "corner."

The concept of "cornering" a market is a simple one. Persons who corners a market effectively holds all the supply of that commodity. Thus, they can control the price of the commodity from a monopoly supplier position. People who wish to purchase that commodity can only obtain it from the monopoly supplier and must accept the price demanded.

Therefore a person or group who has cornered the market can charge whatever the market will hear. This leads to "monopoly" profits.

One risk run by a person building a corner, is that purchasers may look to alternate replacement materials as prices rise and availability declines. For example, in *the world of* British aircraft production during World War II, the optimal construction material, given the technology of the time, was refined high quality aluminium. This soon became very scarce but aircraft manufacturers rapidly developed substitute construction materials such as wood, which was very successfully used in a number of aircraft.

Another risk that may arise is where the material need not be considered essential in small quantities, but has a significant intrinsic value. Here at a certain price level, demand may virtually cease altogether. This situation can arise with silver. Industrial demand for silver for use in such industries as photography is relatively static, especially in view of the development of alternative technology. However, there is a large intrinsic demand for jewellery. Yet, at a certain point, many jewellery buyers may simply not enter the market as the expenditure on such items is purely discretionary.

While Enron did not face the same difficulties in trading in energy since the demand for electricity is relatively inelastic and at least in the short-term product substitution is difficult, it did face other difficulties. One was the sheer size of the USA market. The USA energy market is the biggest in the world. Another problem was that as Enron purchased more and more energy futures, the market responded by increasing prices. Enron was simply not financially strong enough to buy all the energy futures offered in the market, but their activities did force prices up, particularly in the area of energy futures where they were most active. As Enron ran out of the capacity to buy, prices started to drift down. Enron faced the traditional situation of anybody who tries to build a corner and fails. They were left with very large quantities of the commodity purchased at prices in excess of current prices. Thus any sales of the commodity were bound to crystallize a loss situation. In Enron's case, however, they had purchased futures contracts and thus did not have to face the loss immediately, not until the contracts were due. To hide the potential loss, the company arranged for what would in Australia be called "shelf companies" to accept initial responsibility for the debt. The method of concealment was developed by senior management and with advice from the external auditor's consulting arm. However, the contracts eventually fell due and the liability reverted to Enron.

At Enron, after sub-contracting their internal audit to the external auditors, a small internal audit team was re-established to work in conjunction with the externally contracted internal audit.

It was a member of the internally appointed internal audit team who eventually forced Enron management to own up to the concealment.

WHY THE INTERNAL AUDITOR?

Historically, internal auditors have been active for centuries. They and their functions are mentioned in corporate reports of the mid-nineteenth century (Irish, 1966). In fact, an audit type role undertaken by various employees (an internal audit activity) is mentioned in English documents as far back as the 11th century (Irish, 1966). It could be said that the external audit is in fact an outgrowth of the internal audit. For example, the Union Bank of Australia (a forerunner of the ANZ Bank) had no external audit until 1892 with the board of the bank expressing their confidence in the adequacy of the internal audit (ANZ Bank, Archivist). Even after the development of the external audit role, the Union Bank of Australia maintained a vigorous internal audit function with "Inspectors" and the ANZ Bank continues to have a strong Internal Audit function.

The developments which followed the Wall Street Crash of 1929 led to US corporations becoming more aware of the potential of the internal audit. Further developments following the rapid expansion of industry at the start of World War II resulted in the recognition of the importance of internal auditors to management and the development of organizational control systems. By the early 1940s, this had resulted in the foundation of a professional body for internal auditors.

The role of the internal auditor has matured since then. However, it has varied from organization to organization depending on the size of the organization and the approach taken by top management with each organization. The Corporations law is silent about the need for internal auditors. This is not surprising since the law must cover a wide range of corporate entities. Changes in top management may therefore have a significant influence on how internal audit is handled. It is often the case that changes in ownership will lead to changes in the role or even the existence of internal audit. For example, a change of ownership from British interests to American interests in one organization has resulted in the introduction of an internal audit run on a contract basis by a large multinational accounting firm. The new and remote management have a different view of the role and importance of internal audit compared to the older management (Confidential interview).

The use of contract internal auditors may have certain disadvantages when compared with the option of having an "in-house" internal audit function. The experience mentioned above reveals particular problems where the internal audit is limited to the collection and verification of particular accounting data over short, relatively widely spaced visits. The lack of continuity and changes to assigned internal audit personnel mean that the ability of the internal audit staff to both gain a thorough understanding of the organization and build up an unofficial information network is severely limited (Confidential interview).

Recently the Institute of Internal Auditors has been modifying its published position on the role of the internal auditor. This modification recognizes that besides the monitoring of the financial recording of events, the monitoring of what caused the need to record the events is also an internal audit role. Thus in looking at questions of efficient and effective use of resources, the internal auditor is going beyond the role of simply confirming the accuracy of the financial data of the organisation. The revision implicitly recognizes that every action undertaken within an organization has a financial outcome and the monitoring of these actions, and how the financial outcomes are properly recorded, is a responsibility of the internal auditor. Furthermore, the Institute is now in the process of developing a standard, which will give the internal auditor guidance in dealing with the business risk of an enterprise. This will include approach in risk recognition and management.

MANAGING RISK

Risk is not new. Businesses have faced the risk of unplanned or unforeseen events altering their operation since "time out of mind." The development of formal risk recognition and management plans is relatively new. Previously, management generally recognized the risks that an organization faced on a day-to-day routine basis and took steps to minimize and mitigate those. For example, an airline would recognize the financial danger to the organization of an aircraft crashing. Traditionally, the airline would take a two-pronged approach to control this operational risk. One prong was the training and development of high level skills in the organization's personnel, from maintenance engineers to ground handling staff to cabin crew and pilots.

This minimized risks through prevention via proper maintenance, proper ground handling procedures and proper flight operating procedures. The other prong was the training of cabin staff in rescue and life saving techniques and the maintenance of adequate insurance. These mitigated against the cost of an accident becoming financially unmanageable. Thus the airline achieved its goal of minimizing risk by minimizing the financial loss the airline would face and arranging for insurance companies to share the burden of such a loss.

In the ever changing world of business, the problem for non-executive directors is how to gauge the risks that an organization faces and to ascertain what management are doing in managing or not managing such risks.

The early part of this paper considered the pressure on non-executive directors to know about the risks. The role of the internal auditor was also examined. We now consider the possibility that the non-executive directors may be able to utilize the internal audit to discover what an organization is doing.

How do the non-executive directors remove management bias from the information they receive?

OBTAINING RELIABLE INFORMATION

This paper proposes that *the* non-executive directors take a three-step approach:

The **first step** is to establish a Board Audit Committee. This committee should be totally independent of executive directors as recommended by the Ramsay Report (Ramsay, 2001) and various other studies going back to at least the Treadway Report (1987). Without executive management present, persons reporting to the Audit Committee will feel less constrained.

The **second step** is for the Board Audit Committee to develop an intelligence network within the organization. That will ensure a flow of unbiased information. This is a more difficult task. Most large organizations already possess an alternate information network. Such networks are not subject to management control and therefore will not reflect management bias.

In organizations where management bias is extreme, often the function of the organization may depend on such an unofficial information network.

USING THE INTERNAL AUDITOR SUCCESSFULLY

One way to tap into the unofficial network is to have contact with middle management but lack of independence remains a problem here. To overcome this lack of independence, it is suggested that an interface be inserted between middle management and the Board Audit Committee Internal audit would make an ideal interface. The internal audit generally ranks equal with middle management and is free to move around the organization on missions of discovery.

Let us assume that the Board Audit Committee uses the internal audit function to access the organization's informal information network. The **next step (step 3)** is to maximize the benefits derived. However, there are two problems that may limit the benefits obtained by using the internal auditor in the manner proposed.

One is that the internal auditor may only have limited access to the required information networks. This risk is amplified if the internal auditor is a consultancy. In this situation, it is not uncommon for the internal audit personnel to change from one month to the next. Thus, the audit person has not enough time to integrate into the informal information network. This limits the efficiency of the Internal auditor in such a role, but does not totally prevent the internal auditor from undertaking the role.

The second problem revolves around the issue of independence, if the internal auditor is appointed by management, *the internal auditor's* independence from management cannot be assured. Consultants do have a slight advantage here in that they are more independent. This is often countered by the fact that they are external to the unofficial information network. But the board managing their appointment assures their independence from management. The same level of independence may be achieved if the Board Audit Committee appoints the internal auditor from within the organization.

The advantage of this approach is that the person chosen will often already be part of the unofficial information network. It must be remembered, however, that for such an approach to succeed, the internal auditor must feel secure in both the short- and long-terms.

Thus a Board Audit Committee taking this approach must manage the long-term career of such an appointment. While English (1994) recommends that the board use the internal audit function, and make certain it is highly skilled and competent, she does not go on to state that it is ESSENTIAL that the board provide the internal auditors with a secure working environment such that they are truly independent of management.

SUMMARY

The duty of non-executive directors to know about the company they are directing has become more important recently. There are many examples of non-executive directors being deeply embarrassed by their failure in this area. In particular, identifying the risks a company faces and how these are being managed is becoming a major role of the non-executive director. In the past, the non-executive director has relied on position papers supplied by the company management, however in the modern business environment, this may not be sufficient. One way of overcoming this weakness is to access the company's informal information networks. Board members being outsiders are unlikely to be able to gain such access. An alternative to the direct approach is to appoint a proxy such as an internal auditor to gain such access. If this approach is taken, then the non-executive directors will need to be able to meet with the internal auditor without management being present. Thus the use of such a device as establishment of a Board Audit Committee with no executive directors is suggested. It must be noted that such an approach will require the non-executive directors to ensure the independence of the internal auditor in both the short and long-terms.

REFERENCES

Anon, "Confidential Overview of Management of a Corporation During a Change of Ownership," unpublished, 2003.

ANZ Bank Archivist, "Notes on Auditing," ANZ Bank, 1999.

Crown, M. Korman is discussed at: http://asscts.cambridge.org/0521903351/full version/0521903351 pub.pdf.

English, L., "Making Audit Committees Work," *Australian Accountant*, April, 1994.

Jensen, R., "New Bookmarks" at www.trinity.edu/rjensen. 2002, 2003, 2004.

Mathews, C., Cooper, B.J. and Leung, P., *A Profile of Internal Audit in Australia—1992* RMIT, Melbourne, 1993.

McInnes, W.M. (Ed.), *Auditing into the 21st Century*, Research Committee of the Institute of Chartered Accountants in Scotland, Edinburgh, 1993.

National Commission on Fraudulent Reporting, "*Report*", Treadway Commission, American Institute of Certified Public Accountants, New York, October, 1987.

Ramsay, I., "*Independence of Australian Auditors,*" Department of Treasury, Canberra, 2001.

Singapore Exchange listing rules are to be found at http://info.sgx.com/

The Hon. Justice Owen Commissioner, "*The HIH Royal Commission,*" National Capital Printing, Canberra, 4 April 2003.

Urhancic, Frank R.; Cook, Timothy, "To Whom Do Internal Audit Directors Report?," in *Baylor Business Studies*, Waco, Vol. 11, No. 3, Aug./Sept./Oct. 1980.

Westfield, M., *HIH: The Inside Story of Australia's Biggest Corporate Collapse*, John Wiley & Sons, Milton, Queensland, 2003.

CASES

AWA Case: AWA Ltd. *vs.* Daniels t/a Deloitte Haskins and Sells and Others (1992): 10 ACLC 933.

Clark's case: Deputy Commissioner of Taxation *vs.* Clark (2003), NSWCA 91.

Crown *vs.* Bond.

Morleys case: Morley *vs.* Statewide Tobacco Services (1993), 1 VR 451.

12

Managing Corporate Social Responsibility: A Study of Private Banks in India

KARTIK DAVE

1. INTRODUCTION

The business of business is no longer just business. It has to consider additional aspects of running the business other than productivity and profits. Social Responsibility is the recognition of the fact that organizations have significant influence on the social system. Corporate Social Responsibility (CSR) has been defined as "companies integrating social and environmental concerns in their business operations and their interaction with stakeholders on a voluntary basis". (COM, 2001.) Corporate Social Responsibility implies that the organizations have an important social role in the different segments of the society who are directly or indirectly influenced by the company. Concepts such as "Corporate Social Responsibility" and "Corporate Citizenship" have gained momentum and prominence in the Indian corporate world.

The modern business has manifold responsibilities: (i) to itself, (ii) to its customer, (iii) stakeholders, (iv) employees, (v) community, and (vi) the nation. Growing trend of Corporate Social Responsibility reflects changing social attitude about the obligation that firms hold with respect to the societies in which they operate. CSR and the systematic adoption of stakeholder dialogue can build-up important intangible assets in the form of "Social Capital". Social capital has been defined as "Networks together with shared norms, values and understandings that facilitate cooperation within or among groups". (OCED, 2001.)

In India, industrial dynasties such as Ambanis, Tatas and Birlas, concepts of nation-building and trusteeship have been alive in their operations decades before CSR become a popular cause. The special context in which business works in modern India is the co-existence of public and private sectors. It can be said to be mixed economy. Banking sector is not exception to this.

CSR has entered the financial sector with increasing public awareness and concern about the role played by financial institutions in the global economy, on one hand, and the Socially Responsible Investing (SRI) movement, on the other. The role of banks in contributing towards sustainable development is, however, potentially enormous, because of their intermediary role in an economy. According to Jeucken (2001) sustainable banking varies between regions, countries and banks.

Though the banking sector has been slow to pick-up the challenge of sustainability, change is underway. The present paper focuses on status of CSR in overall Indian banking sector in general and private banks in particular.

2. REVIEW OF LITERATURE

In this section an attempt has been made to review relevant literature available in context of CSR practices in banking, financial and other sectors.

According to research done by a NGO called Partners in Change show that corporate involvement in development tends to be *ad hoc* and CEO-driven. This is best illustrated by the fact that only 11 per cent of the companies had a written policy. This is in spite of the fact that over 85 per cent of the companies agrees that they have a responsibility to society. Companies that work with communities do not necessarily distinguish between the privileged and the under privileged amongst them. While a few companies and business groups have taken a lead in promoting CSR in India, the role of the industry associations must be recognized as significant.

While the CII has various committees for social development activities and have even developed a voluntary social code for its members, chambers like FICCI, PHDCCI, and Bharat Chamber of Commerce and so on have set up foundations for this purpose. However, the overall approach still seems to be driven by philanthropy rather than integrating it with business as has been happening in the west.

CSR is neither a fashionable craze of the moment, nor a PR or communication tool because consumers, shareholders and pension funds particularly, wage-earners, NGO's, local authorities, etc. i.e. all those people or groups called stakeholders are sensitive to what businesses do, be it good or bad. (European Commission Green Paper on CSR, 2001.)

According to Decker (2004) when CSR is conceptualized pragmatically as a response by businesses to society's concerns it acts as an element of structural change with implications for the strategies of firms and ultimately for industry structure. Furthermore, industry specific aspects of CSR are important and governmental influences and financial regulations provide an added dimension to the impact of CSR on the financial services industry.

As an element of structural change, CSR acts as an environmental discontinuity and forces firms to realign their positions within their operating environment. A structural change paradigm is developed to examine trends which are emerging within retail banking as a result of CSR.

In the UK retail banking sector, the impact of CSR is increasingly manifest in the efforts to create a competitive advantage out of CSR strategies, the growing prominence of mutual financial institutions in government policy and collaborative efforts between a ranges of financial institutions.

Sharma and Talwar (2005) opines that with increasing competitiveness today's business scenario has become highly complex and focus is on corporate social responsibility (CSR), which has become increasingly important in the modern era.

CSR encompasses a wide variety of concerns such as ethical values in business, welfare of society, awareness, respect and protection of the natural and built environment as regular action that business can take to solve the problems being faced by the Society. CSR is an integral part of Vedic philosophy. Vedic philosophy emphasizes that those actions, which are coming from the core of heart, will provide the long lasting results.

Veda advocates for minimum accumulation, mutual cooperation and maintenance of natural harmony. Veda reiterates non-centrality of money in human life, but for corporations money is the real nerve of business systems. Vedic economic philosophy is pure and focused on "Prosperity for all". The present study attempts to critically evaluate the modern concept of CSR and enrich it with the path described by Vedic philosophy to attain the corporate excellence.

Rivoli (1996) argues on adoption of socialistic ideology which underlies the communitarian or family model, which says that societies should be thought as communities in which benefits and burdens are distributed on the model of family.

Lantos (2002) discusses morality of altruistic CSR and altruistic activities which are appropriate and commendable for private firms and individuals.

According to Genest (2005) corporate philanthropy is a reflector of corporate values; global corporate philanthropists have a history of commitment to corporate social responsibility (CSR) activities; global companies practice international philanthropy; programme delivery differs as a reflection of corporate history, values, mission, and business drivers; global corporations utilize CSR to gain and maintain their "license to operate"; and corporate cultural learning is pursued as an explicit activity; cross-cultural learning is generally perceived as an implicit outcome. CSR shares values, opportunity for integrated cultural learning.

Mayo (1997) argues that, at the very least, banks have a broad responsibility to understand the social impact of the major changes they undertake and to minimize the costs and benefits. It is doubtful that this minimum responsibility may be enough in the present climate. This is because as firms increasingly recognize CSR as a constraint for profit maximization, it becomes an element of structural change in the industry.

3. CSR INITIATIVES IN PRIVATE SECTOR BANKS

Banking in the 1960s was known as "class banking" as credit facilities was available to the wealthy. In 1969, the Government of India nationalized 14 leading banks. In 1980, six more banks were nationalized. The objective of nationalization was to ensure the flow of credit to agriculture and allied sectors. In the process, banks are saddled with huge NPAs and threat for survival because of focus on priority sector. To study the problems and suggest remedial measures committee has been formed, which is popularly known "Narasimham Committee".

The committee suggested various measures to strengthen financial system. The post liberalization era witnessed various changes including a liberal licensing policy for setting up new private sector banks and other banks.

CSR in banking is highly relevant as banks are the custodian of public money hence the social responsibility towards general public and stake holders have greater importance.

3.1 Corporate Governance

Corporate governance is essentially concerned with matters arising out of separation of ownership and control. Implementation of corporate governance in banks posits many problems especially private banks since the parties' involved well beings of the banks are many. There are depositors besides the shareholders who have an active interest in governance of the bank. Private Banks like ICICI Bank, HDFC Bank, UTI bank, IDBI Bank and foreign bank like HSBC, CITI and ABN Amro are very keen regarding their corporate governance practices.

3.2 Customer Service

The new generation banks are consolidating themselves and innovating new methods of customer delight. With the emergence of Indian global banks and techno savvy foreign banks customer service may have more technology dimension with greater sense of responsibility.

3.3 Micro Finance

Micro finance, lending tiny sums to poor people, is gaining popularity among private banks because of increasing political support for improving access to credit for rural poor. Private Banks have partnership with Micro Finance Lenders (MFLs) thus they are saving cost of opening new branches and also enjoying expertise of MFL's judgment of credit risk. ICICI, HDFC, UTI have taken a lead along with foreign players like ABN AMRO and ING Vyasa Bank. They offer micro-finance in India, to fulfil its mission of Sustainable Development. Most of the above banks believe that microfinance is a very powerful tool that can be used effectively to address poverty, empower the socially marginalized poor and strengthen the social fabric.

Especially when directed at women, the benefits of micro-finance multiply many folds. Through micro-finance, the bank believes, we can enhance human as well as financial capital for the future and leave behind a better world for our children. The micro-finance program of the bank is aimed at delivering credit to the target community, through Micro-finance Institutions (MFIs). The target community is the poor women of India, especially in the rural areas. The products offered to the MFIs are term loans of varying tenors, structured suitably to match the specific needs of the individual MFI at a commercial, competitive rate of interest.

3.4 Other initiatives

Following are the some initiatives undertaken by leading private banks in the field of CSR.

ICICI Bank seeks to perform its role in the social sector through a dedicated non profit group, the Social Initiative Group (SIG). The bank is also working in the field of NGO capacity building, modernization of Indian Financial System through research assistance, infants' health through Early Child Health Resource Centre, Primary education, volunteering of time and skill and disaster management like recent Tsunami Relief Fund.

HDFC Bank Consolidated its operations in weaker section housing, advancing and reconstruction in bad affected areas like after Gujarat Earthquake, active in NGO operations.

HSBC has focused on education and environment spending 75 per cent of its funds with Hongkong Bank Foundation. Also contributing society through Scholarships, Volunteering and research support to various NGOs like IndianNGOs.com.

Citigroup supports society through providing local employment, client profit sharing, engaging in philanthropy and volunteerism, partnering with social organizations, heritage, women welfare and urban development.

Another emerging player YES BANK is pioneer in responsible banking business approach which integrates Sustainability and Corporate Social Responsibility (CSR) within the larger philosophy of the Bank. The bank has adopted a social and economic value generation model and supporting businesses that do so. They are operating in a "Sustainability Zone" to mainstream environmental and social issues, structure bankable projects and provide innovative financial services.

At YES BANK, Responsible Banking is being championed through a model that is geared to identify and provide innovative sustainable finance and services.

This is further strengthened by a bank-wide vision to develop strong internal governance and CSR processes and an external outreach model. More importantly, this model addresses cutting edge sustainability approaches which may be defined as Second Generation Sustainability (SGS) – a key component of new age banking.

This includes Socially Responsible Investing (SRI) – awareness and social capital building through sustainable financial literacy, SRI principles and SRI funds, Asset Management – SRI approaches, Sustainable Asset Management, assets under management with high social and environmental benefit, and Specialized Banking extending banking services to classes, communities or projects not traditionally included in the banking fold, e.g. microfinance, NGO banking, etc.

ING Vyasa bank as a part of its Corporate Social Responsibility has partnered with Parikrma Humanity Foundation. Parikrma Humanity Foundation is a non-profit company aiming to unleash the potential of slum children in urban India.

Their mission is to help the poor break their cycle of poverty and live meaningfully through tools necessary to succeed in a knowledge based world. For the past two years, ING Vyasa Bank and Parikrma partnered together to promote the unique programme – "Change Your World in ½ a day", with the aim to transform the lives of hundreds of under served children in Bangalore.

4. CONCLUDING REMARK

From the above discussion it can be concluded that private banks are in process of adopting integrated approach to CSR, in the sense that policies and practices are extended beyond the organization itself. Private Banks are known for their excellent service quality in value delivery as well as processes. Banks are emphasizing on customer service not only for profit maximization but also in enhancing service standards.

Due to cut throat competition every bank is benchmarking their services and vying to position themselves in market and society. It is also found that private sector banks are more serious in implementation of the directives of regulatory authorities like RBI about customer complaints, grievance handling and service standards. Private Banks are also very much concerned by social and environmental issues.

References

Capaldi, N. (2005): "Corporate Social Responsibility and the Bottom Line", *International Journal of Social Economics*, Vol. 32, No. 5, pp. 408-23.

Commission of the European Communities (2001): Promoting a European Framework for Corporate Social Responsibility, COM (2001) 366, Brussels.

Commission of the European Communities (2002): Corporate Social Responsibility: A Business Contribution to Sustainable Development, COM (2002) 347 final, Brussels.

Conaty, P. (1997): "New Mutuality in Practice: The Example of Art", in Rossiter, J. (Ed.), *Financial Exclusion: Can Mutuality Fill the Gap?*, New Policy Institute, London.

Decker, O.S. (2004): "Corporate Social Responsibility and Structural Change in Financial Services", *Managerial Auditing Journal*, Vol. 19, No. 06, pp. 712-728.

Genest, C.M. (2005): "Cultures, Organizations and Philanthropy", *Corporate Communications*, Vol. 10, No. 4, pp. 315-27.

Jeucken, M. (2001): "Sustainable Finance and Banking—Slow Starter and Gaining Pace", *International Financial Institutions Magazine*, www.ifimagazine.com

Lantos, P.G. (2002): "The Ethicality of Altruistic Corporate Social Responsibility", *Journal of Consumer Marketing*, Vol. 19, No. 3, pp. 205-30.

Mayo, E. (1997): "Policy Responses to Financial Exclusion", in Rossiter, J. (Ed.), *Financial Exclusion: Can Mutuality Fill the Gap?*, New Policy Institute, London.

OCED (2001): "The Well-being of Nations—The Role of Human and Social Capital", Centre for Educational Research and Innovation.

Porter, M. (1985): Competitive Advantage: Creating and Sustaining Superior Performance, Macmillan Publishing, New York, NY and London.

Rivoli, P. (1996), *Ethical Aspect of Investor Behaviour*, Zondervan Publishing House, Grand Rapids, MI, pp. 255-68.

Sharma, A.K. and Talwar, B. (2002): *Insights from Practice Corporate Social Responsibility: Modern vis-a-vis Vedic approach, Measuring Business Excellence*, Emerald Group Publishing Limited, Vol. 9, No. 1, 2005, pp. 35-45.

13

Programme Aid Partners in Mozambique: A Textual Analysis*

MIRIAM GREEN

INTRODUCTION

It is proposed in this paper to analyse or 'deconstruct' a report commissioned by the 'Programme Aid Partners' in Mozambique and financially supported by the UK DFID (Department for International Development) and by the Swiss SEC A (State Secretariat for Economic Affairs). The report was published in May 2005 and was directed to the Programme Aid Partners and to the Government of Mozambique.

The purpose of this paper is two-fold. The author has, as indeed have we all, certain views or prejudices about the intentions and policies of 'developed' countries to those in the 'third' and 'fourth' worlds. Aid (and debt) are two major ways in which these intentions and policies are articulated. The report in question is possibly a way of acquiring more insight about a particular instance of recent aid policies to a 'developing' country.

POLITICAL FRAMEWORK

The author's preconceptions broadly are that developed countries

*I would like to thank Tom Burns for reading through all 56 pages of the report and commenting on it. The report, as I am sure its authors would agree, does not make for the most rivetting reading.

have, whatever altruistic motives may have existed and continue to among certain groups in these countries, ultimately acted in their own political interests and in the hegemonic interests in their societies particularly the commercial ones. This is regarded as pertaining particularly to western countries as they have had more opportunity over a longer period of time to involve themselves in the affairs of countries primarily in the 'south'.

From the end of the 'middle ages' when European technological developments and enterprise allowed explorers and later traders to treat with other countries until the present, it can be argued that European companies and countries have by various means, some fairer than others, acted to their political and commercial advantage. In the case of sub-Saharan Africa, particularly foul means used include the slave trade, in which it is estimated that some 17 million Africans were removed from their homes to become slaves mostly in North America. Colonialism in Africa, though not always as harsh—with the notorious exception of the Belgian Congo—was a further incursion into the political, economic and social lives of the indigenous communities.

Colonialism made further inroads into African social, political and economic life. The British for example, it may be judged wisely, tried to conduct their administration through existing traditional authorities, often chiefs; had respect for the traditional laws and courts, which continued to exercise judicial authority in lower level cases; and for existing economic activities. However where there was a conflict of interest there was interference in African arrangements, some of which had a drastic effect on African societies.

Economically where the new western industries needed labour, particularly in the mines, a tax was placed on African households/individuals (I think able-bodied males). This had the effect of forcing initially able-bodied males to work in western industry. Later more and more people moved to work in European businesses and household to earn cash that became increasingly enticing and status enhancing as a way of acquiring western goods. The effect of this on traditional African agriculture was in some cases devastating, as the strong young men were not there to do the heavy work required in certain seasons.

In areas with a substantial white population further inroads were made into African agriculture. Where land was wanted for farming, Africans were moved off the most fertile and accessible land. This happened most severely in South African and what was then Southern Rhodesia – which have become major issues for resolution. It also happened in present-day Zambia and Kenya. In Mozambique the position was that large tracts of land were awarded to commercial companies where plantations and mines were developed. Here too African labour was contracted 'differing little from forced labour'. After World War II there was substantial Portuguese immigration into Mozambique, giving these Europeans substantial economic benefits, as in the British settler colonies. (www.historyworld.net/wrldhis/PlainTextHistories.asp?historyid=ad29)

All these had effects on traditional social and political life. Because of the new wealth and power exhibited by European colonial society, and the contact the indigenous population had with it, the youth particularly lost some respect for their own culture. This was exacerbated by the fact that non-traditional 'chiefs' were appointed by the colonial authorities where traditional rulers were unwilling to co-operate.

However, African traditional societies were, with provisos such as the ones raised above, left largely to their own devices, albeit more impoverished with less labour, poorer land in some instances and the weakening of traditional values. They were in fact in some instances deliberately excluded from participating in the new European economy when this involved competition with European settlers. In Northern Rhodesia (present-day Zambia) for example, African farmers were prevented from selling milk from their cows, the reason given that it did not meet the hygiene standards of European farmers.

It can be argued that in this respect western policies have changed substantially. This author takes a similar view to that referred to by Held *et al.*, 1999 (cited in Fairclough and Thomas, 2004: 379), as one interpretation of the 'hyperglobalist thesis' – the one concerned with issues of oppression. It seems to this author and to other 'cynics', that western intentions and policies now are to 'colonise' substantially areas of economic activity in third world countries. Taking African countries again as example, Ghana, under Chu-e Short's leadership in what is now the DFID, had to agree to the privatisation of its water industry in order to receive aid.

This has been justified recently by Hilary Benn, current minister of the DFID, with regard to Tanzania. Presumably the privatisation would be enjoyed by British/western companies. 'Aid' too often takes the form of a grant to a western company to do some work in the recipient country. *The Guardian* of 29th August 2005 reported that hundreds of thousands of pounds earmarked for aid to Malawi was paid to American consultancies (termed 'phantom aid' by Action Aid and the World Development Movement). More than £ 700,000 of a £ 3 million budget was spent on hotels and meals for US workers. Another project funded by the DFID, according to the BBC spent some of the money on flying in US pens and notebooks instead of buying them locally.

As implied above, the author is in very good company with such interpretations of western countries' intentions and actions in the Third World. Development and globalisation theorists have explained and linked the relative wealth and well being of people in general in the advanced economies with the exploitation and underdevelopment of the third world:

> "... the historical development of the capitalist system ... [has] generated underdevelopment in the peripheral satellites whose economic surplus was expropriated, while generating economic development in the metropolitan centres which appropriate that surplus – and, further, that this process still continues." (Frank, 1971: 27.)

Stiglitz, Nobel Prize winner 2001, former chief economist at the world bank and before that chairman of President Clinton's council of economic advisors, has confirmed that there is a growing disparity between the rich and the poor; and that the numbers living on less than $ 2 a day were 2,718 billion in 1990, increasing to 2,801 billion in 1998. (n5) It is within this political framework and set of assumptions that the report will be analysed.

TEXTUAL ANALYSIS

The second purpose of this paper is to see whether textual analyses can suggest meanings possibly hidden on a superficial reading. In recent decades the meaning of a text has become highly contestable. On the one hand it has been argued that once a text is 'out in the open', it can be subject to many interpretations. There is no one fixed meaning that can be attributed to it or claimed for it. Some theorists have argued that a text is not in any way an independent work. However, it has been argued, and will be shown here, that some meanings become privileged and taken for granted and some discourses dominate over possible alternative ones. (Hardy, 2001, cited in Grant *et al.*, 2004.)

Death of the Author

At one extreme Barthes has argued that a text is dependent on many previous concepts and allusions in the literature. An author does not start with a blank slate. She works from a literary and cultural framework which has provided her with ideas and assumptions and an 'immense dictionary'. Thus the work produced is not simply that of the author's. It does not have a single 'theological' meaning but is made up of 'a tissue of quotations' from other texts and 'the innumerable centres of culture'. (Barthes, 1977: 146.) Barthes takes this further. The reader too has an immense dictionary which is brought into play when reading the text. As there must be differences for each reader in her particular cultural and other frameworks and in her dictionary there will perforce be different interpretations of the same text. Barthes finally comes down in favour of the reader as the producer and final arbiter of the text as against the author and the author's intentions. (Burke, 1998.) Somewhat uneasily he declared for 'death of the author', realising that this may be giving readers undue authority. (Barthes, 1977: 146.)

Critical Discourse Analysis

Barthes' idea of the 'death of the author' will not be attempted here, but his idea of people's 'immense' dictionaries will be used in the analysis where it can be seen to be relevant as will the other ideas mentioned above. Other ideas for textual analysis will also be applied, principally Fairclough's concepts of critical discourse analysis. Fairclough is impatient with some postmodernist discourse analysts who claim that 'language is all'. Fairclough, like Foucault and the critical theorists mentioned above, believes that context is an important part in discourse analysis and imputing language with sole ontological reality is in effect compressing epistemology with ontology and leaving the context free-floating. (Check)

Fairclough by using the notion of 'identity' as a way of analysing texts, seeks to show the power relations in the text. In management texts, for example, certain people are shown to be the 'movers and shakers' in organisations (usually senior managers), while others are not even mentioned (employees often enough). It will be instructive to see in this report who have been given powerful identities and whether and to what extent the Mozambican government has been able to have the opportunity of coming to their own conclusions about what has happened; the strengths and weaknesses and how help to Mozambique should be handled in the future.

Epoch/Power/Knowledge

Foucault also decries the idea that an author writes independent work. His concept of *epistemes* involves the claim that each epoch has different conceptions of what knowledge is and that what counts as knowledge conforms to these conceptions. He describes what individuals write as prescribed by the 'author-function' as received from the particular epoch. (Foucault, 1981: 59.)

Another important idea of his—the relationship between knowledge and power -relates to his arguments against a writer's independence. Foucault has the notion of 'rarefaction'—a reduction in what is considered permissible discourse. 'Doctrine' makes for individuals' allegiance to the same truths and rules. (Foucault, 1981: 63.) Different categories of people—the rich and the poor in sixteenth and seventeenth century Europe, for example, had their separate forms of discourse (Foucault, 1981)—a question relevant to the text to be studied here. Foucault talks of the application of rules of discourse to certain individuals and not others.

> 'There is a rarefaction . . . of the speaking subjects; none shall enter the order of discourse if he does not satisfy certain requirements . . . not all the regions of discourse are equally open and penetrable. . . .' (Foucault, 1981: 61-62.)

Later on Foucault's analyses, held also by many critical theorists including Fairclough, is the relationship on the one hand between the epistemological questions of what counts as knowledge and how it is acquired, and 'on the other the prevailing power structures of the period. Foucault wrote about more detailed forms of power exercised through discourse.

Prohibitions on discourse, he argued, was likewise a powerful force, as we do not have the right to say everything, and some are excluded from the right to say many things. Identities are wrought and strengthened through the discourse and its silences – in other words, through who is talking, and who is not. Despite the apparent respect and freedom in regard to discourse, Foucault claimed that because of fear, prohibitions, barriers, thresholds and limits were set up to remove the most dangerous aspects of the richness of discourse and to order and control it. (Foucault, 1981.)

Difference and Binary Oppositions

Derrida was interested in looking for meanings in a text that might be there in addition to those intended by the author, and ones that would not necessarily remain unchanged. One of Derrida's central concepts is that of 'difference', (the ceaseless differing from and 'deferral' of the meaning of any word or phrase to other words and phrases in the same and also in other texts) offering limitless possibilities for interpretation. (Derrida, 1976.) And the concept of 'supplementarity' is another important concept linked to the indeterminacy of meaning.

This concerns Derrida's attack on the acceptance of binary opposites in western culture starting with the great philosophical texts. Derrida claims that the way opposites are treated in western writings is that they are always posed as a positive and negative – good/bad; strong/weak; male/female; and so on. The positive is always regarded as the strong factor the driving force which determines what happens. Derrida has shown that with a 'patient and minutely philological '*explication de texte*'' (Culler, 1983: 23), this is not always the case and that sometimes it is the negative, supposedly 'weaker' factor that is in fact more powerful and driving the 'stronger', and showing a more ~overt meaning in the text. (Derrida, 1972/81.)

THE TEXT

The text is a report by 'independent consultants' about the performance of certain European countries and western institutions in their aid programme to Mozambique. The 'programme aid partners' include 14 western countries, with the EU, the World

Bank, the IMF and the 0-20 (an NGO umbrella organisation) in the background. Their 'silent voices' will be discussed later on.

What the text shows abundantly is that there are serious unequal power relationships between the partners and Mozambique. These inequalities in power and control are manifested in the content of the text, in the discursive way the text has been written, in the assumptions made and in its silences. The inequality is stated bluntly in relation to deciding on performance criteria for the Mozambican government in relation to donor expectations:

> 'it was stressed to us that capabilities and power relations between donors and government [i.e. the Mozambican government] are clearly asymmetrical in favour of donors. Thus, negotiations are not taking place on a level playing field.' (Killick *et al.*, 2005: 35.)

One way that this may have been manifested is in regard to fundamental economic policies and direction. There was very little overt resistance to the economic frameworks being installed, the authors speculated, because local officials did not expect to be able to change such policies or trust the evaluation exercise to be open to opposing ideas.

> 'Mozambique appears like many . . . aid-dependent countries, with the government apparently believing that its undoubted reliance on assistance means that it is not in a position to insist on its own priorities.' (Killick *et al.*, 2005: 50.)

One expression of dissent was in parliament, which though also powerless in relation to donor policies, and subject to pressures by the government, made overt its opposition to having to rush legislation through with regard to some of these policies. One major bone of contention was pressure for the 'large number of privatizations' put through the parliament. (Killick *et al.*, 2005: 37.)

Similarly when it came to assessing the partners' performance, the consultants declared themselves 'uneasy about the extent to which the PAPPA [programme assistance partners' performance assessment] processes are seen largely as matters for the donors, with the GoM [Government of Mozambique] somewhat passive.' (Killick *et al.*, 2005: 40.)

The above are concerns about asymmetrical power relations by the authors of the report and included are suggestions as to how these might be begun to be overcome in certain areas. The power asymmetry is not unexpected, given the comparative histories over recent centuries of these different regions. Those concerned with the welfare of countries in the underdeveloped 'south', might commend the authors for their honesty and intentions regarding the rectification of some of these problems.

POWER/KNOWLEDGE

However there is more to say with regard to the discourse of the report about inequalities of power between Mozambique and the European and American 'partners'. Ideas about knowledge, supported by many of Foucault's writings, claim that there are fashions or, to put it more seriously, conventions as to what counts as knowledge. Foucault's ideas about what counts as knowledge being related to current power structures can be used to uncover deeper manifestations of the force of dominant power structures having a more subtle influence on the authors and the way the text has been written.

Foucault's concept of the 'archaeology' of knowledge contains the idea that certain 'epistemes' are particular to certain epochs. In this modern period there has been an emphasis on rationality: dealing with observable, measurable objects that are verifiable imposed on the knowing subject and prior to all experience (Foucault, 1981). Technical values providing useful knowledge is valued over 'commentaries'. (Foucault, 1981: 55.)

Habermas makes a similar point through his notion of 'technical' reasoning which consists of an instrumental rationality and where the focus is on control to achieve required ends as against "the attainment of a possible consensus among actors in the framework of a self-understanding derived from tradition." (Habermas, 1968/71: 310.) In a balanced system both types of reasoning would operate jointly, but instead technical reasoning, aided by social science, expertise and organisational structures, is the dominant rationality. (Alvesson and Deetz, 1996: 200). Thus from the start knowledge, included in which is the representation of theory, is at risk of being pre-determined.

What is made visible as 'knowledge' is that which is made epistemologically, normatively and ethically acceptable.

Our report bears this out. It is positively boring in terms of its 'scientism'. It is based, for example, on 'aggregated responses of . . . questionnaire responses' designed around a (PAPPA) performance assessment matrix (Killick *et al.*, 2005: 4); the study of relevant background documents and interviews with 'relevant' parties. The authors however acknowledge the superficiality of their conclusions based on the interviews because of the brief time available in which to conduct them. This is manifest in the vagueness of the information obtained, despite the technical language and the existence of graphs, designed presumably to purport scientifically acceptable, measurable and verifiable information.

One instance of an attempt to deal with measurable objects, or at least to speak in that discourse concerns the various partners' contributions to Mozambican aid. This was assessed in terms of their several contributions to the range of 'aid modalities' they used – principally general budget support and project aid. Their share of aid to each modality was calculated and from this a table was produced showing the amount of different types of aid given by each country, without any details about the aid given. (Killick *et al.*, 2005: 6, Graph 1.) There follows another table in which the sectors to which aid is given are mapped, based on the reports of the various donor countries. (Killick *et al.*, 2005: 7, Graph 2.) The report then contains 'future perspectives' for the overall portfolio of aid. These future intentions contain statements as vague as 'some increase' for 6 countries, not always quantified; 'increase as a possibility' for other countries and a decrease (with no quantification) by one donor. (Killick *et al.*, 2005: 6.)

On the basis of this information and statements of the donors' future intentions, predictions are made about aid effectiveness in the future. One could argue that even in its own terms this report is deficient in detail and that the classifications therefore are not refined enough to be meaningful. However, where the information is completely lacking is to do with questions about how the aid was implemented and more importantly, its effects on the local population and their views on it.

Local views at most levels are not there. (Official views – what few there were – as suggested earlier, are not necessarily reliable as people may have felt intimidated or disempowered to disagree with any evaluation of the donors, as well as their policies.) A whole category of 'other' or 'others' knowledge which must be germane to an evaluation of the effectiveness of the aid, is entirely absent. The views of the people likely to be affected – the general urban and rural populace are outside what are considered relevant parameters for the knowledge required in this context.

Thus a report using inadequate and some might argue spurious statistics about aid, completely ignoring its effectiveness on the ground and the views of the supposed recipients of this support, is considered legitimate as an official document, as an appraisal report and as a valid basis for future action. Foucault has described what we call the division between true and false, or knowledge, as the 'will to truth'. He claimed that what has governed our will to know is a system of exclusion–'a historical, modifiable, and institutionally constraining system'. (Foucault, 1981: 54.) He argued that this knowledge is reinforced institutionally and by a range of practices to do with the production and dissemination of knowledge. It sets the parameters of that knowledge, its procedures, classification and ordering as well as the doctrines and assumptions on which that knowledge is made valid – the 'order of discourse' in which the knowledge is formed and produced. (Preface to Foucault, 1981: 48.)

Thus, according to Foucault, dominant interests and power structures determine what is not valid knowledge as much as what is. The former is consequently ignored or not written about. This has powerful ramifications. As well as setting what counts as knowledge, it also significantly determines what can be ignored or excluded. Foucault describes these parameters and prescriptions as a 'violence that we do to things, or in any case a practice that we impose on 'them'. (Preface to Foucault, 1981: 50.) He described knowledge as ritualised discourses, with excluded knowledge as 'buried significance'.

Questions Fairclough addresses are related to Foucault's ideas about what knowledge is excluded. Fairclough examines *inter alia* are the way a text has been written in terms of transparency. For instance, has it been written showing the actors and processes involved, or have they been hidden through abstraction, and consequently masking how things actually happen, who drives them, what the successes and importantly the failures are? Fairclough has called this style of abstraction 'nominalization' and emphasises that it is a way of hiding power relations in the concepts, policies and events a text is describing.

In the text in question there are countless examples of nominalisation, which serve to hide who are responsible for decisions and processes. In the summary at the beginning, for example, there are many abstract nouns employed in the text, hiding the processes and the actors involved. The authors write that they found 'clear and strong support' for increasing the share of direct budget support in total aid with regard to Mozambican perceptions (p. 1). We do not know who in Mozambique had this awareness; was it only those interviewed or were more widely held views represented and were there any reservations or conditionalities to that support? Many processes are similarly written about in the passive tense, so that the actors are obscured.

Using the same example, we are told with regard to Mozambican perceptions on direct budget support there 'was awareness of some risks . . . and the desirability, therefore, of a gradual transition' (p. 1). Again we do not know if these are the same people who supported it or whether they are different people entirely, and again one of the consequences of this type of discourse is that a sense of process including the actions of the respondents gets lost. There is very little about participants and their effects on structure and other constructs in these representations. (Fairclough and Hardy, 1997.) What also gets lost is the power dynamics: who has been influential over whom, what arguments have been won and lost and what are the consequences for the donors and for Mozambican institutions.

Fairclough also places importance on power relationships by looking at exclusions in terms of the powerful as well as the weak. In this report there seem to be two key players who are not as visible as the other players. First the World Bank. It did not figure prominently in the evaluations of donor performance and was reported as having few joint procedures either with the other partners or with the Mozambican government. (Killick *et al.*, 2005.) Yet we are told that in 2004 a late 'large up-front World Bank disbursement' rescued the level of aid, which was 'limited' for the first two thirds of the year. (Killick *et al.*, 2005: 34.) The IMF is barely mentioned. It was not one of the partner institutions but it is mentioned in the report that there was 'a large area of common interest . . . as regards macro-economic management' and that 'substantial efforts' had been made to co-ordinate its programme assistance with the partners. No details of such co-operations are given. (Killick *et al.*, 2005: 43.)

Stiglitz has written about the secrecy of the IMF in terms of its lack of accountability the for policies that would drastically affect much of the world's population. Far from being transparent, the IMF, according to Stiglitz, operated so as not only to prevent citizens from the countries affected in participating in discussions on the economic policies the IMF was demanding, but also denied them knowledge of what agreement had been made. Stiglitz claimed that this secrecy extended to withholding information from the World Bank, their partners, as well as from the US Congress (2002).

BINARY OPPOSITIONS/INFINITE MEANING

According to Derrida, the description of concepts and situations is often not as they seem. His concept of supplementarity, as mentioned earlier (p. 6), suggests that within the strong! the good! the positive there may be elements of the opposite 'other' that can influence the primary situation substantially so as to result in changes in the meaning of the situation or concept and of the terms themselves. Thus, an extreme interpretation is that 'because meaning is not fixed, all textuality is infinitely interpretable, and all texts are composed of an endless freeplay of meanings. . . .' (Wolfreys, 1998: 66.)

It might be argued, however, that in this report the situation from the point of view of Mozambique is not easily divisible into 'positives' and 'negatives' and there is very little 'freeplay of meaning'. The disempowerment of Mozambique described below seems to be outside Derrida's concept of supplementarity as there do not appear to be any strengths in this weak Mozambican position. Here a closer analysis might uncover some supplementarities, but there seems to be a situation here of almost complete weakness on the one hand, and strong, almost unmitigated power on the other, exercised in capricious and, as the report shows, self-serving ways.

What is portrayed in the report is really two negatives—both opposites in important ways, but both acting as driving forces in favour of the donors and against Mozambique. The issue in which this is apparent is to do with whether the donors should give more of their aid in direct budget support to the government of Mozambique, or whether there should be more aid through bilateral agreements. The report generally is in favour of more aid in direct budget support so as to achieve more harmonisation among the donors and greater control over them. Where donors act independently, planning is hindered because of donors not listing their contributions in full detail and predictability of disbursements though improving were 'still unsatisfactory'. (Killick *et al.*, 2005: 33.)

From the point of view of the Mozambican government, the options, as hinted above, constituted a double-edged sword. If the government were to choose more bilateral aid, it would be more subject to vagaries, capriciousness and different interpretations of common agreements by each donor country. (Killick, *et al.*, 10.) This would more seriously hinder its planning for the future than would more harmonisation, which itself has been shown to be unreliable and indeterminate. (See also Killick *et al.*, 34). Another serious disadvantage would be an increased administrative burden on the government which it could ill afford. (Killick *et al.*, 17.)

If the option in favour of more aid going through direct budgetary support was considered, it might, despite substantial continuing lack of co-ordination among the donors even when supposedly harmonised, be of more help to the Mozambican government in terms of planning and negotiation. However on the other side, there was

> 'a perceived danger of "ganging up" by donors, as greater coordination among them strengthens their already powerful bargaining capability.' (Killick *et al.*, 33.)

They could stop disbursements if they felt that Mozambique was not performing adequately, which would do nothing to mitigate the existing asymmetrical power position. One risk mentioned for the donors was that of 'fiduciary risk' – that the aid fed into the general budget would not find its way to previously agreed targets. (Killick *et al.*, 40.) This, it can be argued however, is a different order of risk from the ones facing an underdeveloped society like Mozambique depending on outside aid.

It is clear that Mozambique would be disadvantaged whichever option it were to take. The consultants' solution is one that would not change the situation substantially. They recommend that the country retains a mixed portfolio of aid modalities but under the rubric of certain principles previously agreed. (Killick *et al.*, 46-7.) In one paragraph, however, the consultants justify the situation. Having said that the power relations were 'clearly asymmetrical in favour of donors', the authors continue that:

> 'Nevertheless, [sic] there was recognition that the performance indicators for the government are related to desirable reforms, and to other activities that the government has to learn to do better.' (Killick *et al.*, 35.)

Therefore, rather than trying to find a serious solution to this disempowering situation for Mozambique the consultants justify the position by blaming the Mozambican government for its inadequacies and making it accountable to the donors rather than what, one could argue, should be the other way round. The accountability of weak nations to strong western institutions has also been highlighted by Stiglitz. He claims, with regard to the IMF, that the strength and scope of the global market system has turned the concept of accountability on its head (2002).

Third World countries, were in many cases afraid to question the IMF policies that were wreaking economic devastation and severe poverty on them, in case they would lose funding. Rather, it was they who had to be accountable to the IMF in order to acquire or keep their funding. Stiglitz cites the example of Ethiopia, which forfeited IMF funds because it would not follow its 'formula', despite the fact that Ethiopian economic policies made sense, in Stiglitz' view, for a government trying to raise the living standards of its people in a situation where there were droughts and starvation (2002).

NEO-LIBERAL FRAMEWORK

Where Derrida's deconstruction ideas might apply more readily is regard to the indeterminacy of meaning. Derrida (1992) analyses the concept of 'gift', and what it entailed in the social context of a short story by Richard Jefferies titled 'Snowed Up' (cited in Wolfreys, 1998). The concept of 'aid' can be deconstructed in a similar way, showing what these concepts mean in the context of the report—what is involved theoretically, politically and practically.

One way of deconstructing the concept of 'aid' is to examine the economic assumptions on which policy decisions about aid and the report itself were based. One reason perhaps why the consultants could not find a strong solution to overcome Mozambique's admittedly difficult position was the over-arching assumption in the report of what are permissible ideas—Foucault's concept of 'rarefaction'—the reduction in what is considered permissible discourse at any given period, and who are the permitted discoursers. (Foucault, 1981: 61-62.)

Here the only permissible discourse appears to be based on a 'neo-liberal' economic global system. The authors regard it as 'positive' that there is no serious controversy about the direction of development policy, and recommend that the government should take the lead in working out an assistance strategy with its donor partners. (Killick *et al.*, 51.) They appear to ignore earlier statements about Parliament's opposition to legislation rushing through a large number (Killick *et al.*, 40) of privatisations, particularly the cashew nut industry (Killick *et al.*, 37.)

The authors also ignore their own reservations about the reasons for Mozambican officials' lack of disagreement about the policy orientation of the partner institutions. Although they acknowledge the possibility of a truly national consensus about the economic policies instituted, they also acknowledge that this might be because the government saw no alternative. They might have interviewed officials mainly concerned with implementation rather than direction of policy. Dependence on aid in Mozambique was so high that officials may have decided in favour of 'letting it go', believing that they could not change fundamental policies in any case. (Killick *et al.*, 38.) They might also have not trusted the consultants and played it safe 'by feigning alignment with established policy frameworks'. (Killick *et al.*, 39.) Most telling from the consultants' standpoint was the admission that their brief was about implementation rather than about policy, and they therefore 'did not ask specifically about such possible conflicts' (Killick *et al.*, 38).

Thus one could begin to deconstruct the meaning of aid in this context as constituting a complete submission by Mozambique (and other developing countries in Africa) to western hegemonic institutions. That includes acceptance of the lack of consultation and of the need for any feedback from the recipients—both from government and other institutions, and from the people on the ground in urban and rural areas. It also means total acceptance of a neo-liberal economic policy in the form, for example, of privatisations. Policy, as seen above, is not even on the table for discussion. This is a different kind from the silence of Mozambican people's voices. The lack of the need to discuss policy matters is a kind of 'violence' – a violence to the consideration of alternative ideas about economic policy and their implementation; a system of exclusion of what might be equally, if not more, valid knowledge. (Foucault, 1981: 50.) All this, it can be argued, is what aid means in the context of western-African relationships.

Stiglitz would support such a 'deconstruction'. He argues that the ideology of the free market was strengthened in the 1980s under the regimes of Reagan in the US and Thatcher in the UK, not only in these countries but throughout the world. Powerful international institutions such as the IMF and World Bank imposed these ideas on third world countries, the ideology strengthened by a purge of economists at the World Bank who had as their main goal the elimination of poverty, replaced by those believing the solution for developing countries were free markets. The ideological fervour with which this was pursued militated against free discussion. Stiglitz describes how when he first dealt with the International Monetary Fund (IMF) he saw how their policies were imposed on countries without considering the effects on those societies.

> "Rarely did I see thoughtful discussion and analyses of the consequences of alternative policies. There was a single prescription. Alternative opinions were not sought. Open, frank discussion was discouraged – there was no room for it. Ideology guided policy prescriptions and countries were expected to follow the IMF guidelines without debate." (2002: xiv.)

CONCLUSION

It has been argued that the document analysed reveals the continuing, if not greater, disempowerment of a 'developing' country in sub-Saharan African at the expense of western countries and global institutions. In colonial times, traditional economies and social and political systems were subverted in colonies where white settlers were competing economically with African farmers, where African labour was needed for European industry or where traditional rulers would not accept colonial rule. Outside these imperatives, traditional systems were left alone. The end of colonial rule saw a vicious civil war between the official independence movement, Frelimo, with its socialist rhetoric and Soviet support and a US-supported counter-movement,

Renamo. This devastated the population and economy, and may be that an additional reason why help is needed so desperately in that country.

However, what this report has shown is a more encompassing 'colonisation' by the continuing ascendance of western countries and institutions and their overwhelming ability to call the tune in terms of how, when and how much aid they will distribute and in what form. More disturbing for those concerned with oppressive aspects of neo-liberal economic policies is the assumption on which all policy is based that this is the only possible way forward for the country and for the aid policies on which it is dependent.

Unlike many other texts, the discourse in this report is less equivocal than either Barthes or Derrida have argued in relation to other texts. Foucault's argument against the independence of authors in the face of epochal epistemological conventions and the subservience of knowledge to hegemonic interests seems to be incontrovertible in the case of the discourse in this report.

References

Alvesson, M. and Deetz, S. (1996): "Critical Theory and Postmodernism: Approaches of Organizational Studies", in S.R. Clegg, C. Hardy and W.R. Nord (Eds.), *Handbook of Organization Studies*, London, Sage.

Barthes, R. (1977): "The Death of the Author" in *Image Music Text*, trans. Stephen Heath, London, Harper Collins.

Burke, S. (1998): *The Death and Return of the Author: Criticism and Subjectivity in Barthes, Foucault and Derrida*, Edinburgh, Edinburgh University Press.

Derrida, J. (1972/81): *Dissemination*, trans. Barbara Johnson, London, Athlone Press.

Derrida, J. (1976): *Of Grammatology*, trans. G. Chakravorty, Spivak, Baltimore, John Hopkins University Press.

Fairclough, N. and Hardy, G. (1977): "Management Learning as Discourse" in J. Burgoyne and M. Reynolds (eds.), *Management Learning: Intergrating Perspectives in Theory and Practice*, London, Sage.

Fairclough, N. and Thomas, P. (2004): "The Discourse of Globalization and the Globalization of Discourse" in D. Grant, C. Hardy, C. Oswick and L. Putnam (eds.), *The Sage Handbook of Organizational Discourse*, London, Sage.

Foucault, M. (1981): "The Order of Discourse" in R. Young (ed.), *Untying the Text: A Post-Structuralist Reader*, London, Routledge.

Frank, A.G. (1971): *Capitalism and Underdevelopment in Latin America: Historical Studies of Chile and Brazil*, Harmondsworth, Penguin.

Grant, D.; Hardy, C.; Oswick, C. and Putnam, L. (2004): "Introduction: Organizational Discourse: Exploring the Field" in D. Grant, C. Hardy, C. Oswick and L. Putnam (eds.), *The Sage Handbook of Organizational Discourse*, London, Sage.

Habermas, J. (1968/71): *Knowledge and Human Interests*, translated by J.J. Shapiro, Boston, Beacon Press.

Killick, T.; Castel-Branco, C.N. and Gerster, R. (2005): *Perfect Partners? The Performance of Programme Aid Partners in Mozambique*, 2004, A report to the Programme Aid Partners and Government of Mozambique.

Stiglitz, J. (2002): *Globalization and its Discontents*, London, Penguin Books.

Wolfreys, J. (1998): *Deconstruction: Derrida*, New York, St. Martin's Press Inc. (www.historyworld.net/wrldhis/PlainTextHistories.asp?historyid=ad29)

14

Corporate Social Responsibility and the Neo-American Model of Company Law

STELLA VETTORI

INTRODUCTION

The inability of governments worldwide to protect individuals from economic insecurity has led to a renewed interest and public expectation that corporations have public responsibilities in furthering the interests of the public or the public good. There exists no consensus as to what the 'interests of the public' or the 'public good' entail. In this paper these terms will refer to benefits that may be made available to certain sections of the community including employees, customers, suppliers, even the community as a whole as a result of corporations' philanthropic acts.

Other factors contributing to this renewed interest in corporate social responsibility have been an increased awareness of impending ecological crises as well as changes in the structure of the economy. The political climate in the 1980's and 1990's has led to a move towards ideological preference for private sector solutions to socio-economic ills. Conservative and social democratic governments in Europe and Australasia have generated a non-interventionist trend and a move to privatisation.[1]

This renewed interest has re-opened the debate as to whether decision-making in companies or corporations should be guided purely by considerations of profit or whether companies should also consider the interests of third parties including the community at large. This question is shrouded with controversy. There is also uncertainty and controversy as to the following:

(i) What exactly does corporate social responsibility entail?
(ii) What motivates companies to spend money for the benefit of others?
(iii) On what basis, if at all, do companies owe this responsibility?
(iv) Does the law allow for such philanthropic acts by companies, and if so, to what extent?
(v) To whom and to what extent are there responsibilities owed?
(vi) Is corporate social responsibility good for business?[2]

It is the purpose of this paper to consider whether in terms of the neoclassical model of company law a corporation or company is legally entitled to consider the interests of stakeholders other than the shareholders of the company.

THE CONCEPT "CORPORATE SOCIAL RESPONSIBILITY"

Socially responsible behaviour has been described as "action that goes beyond the legal or regulatory minimum standard with the end of some perceived social good rather than the maximisation of profits."[3] The recipients of this socially responsible behaviour can be categorised into the following groups:

(i) The community within which the company operates,
(ii) Suppliers of the company,
(iii) Employees of the company,
(iv) Consumers of the company's goods or services,
(v) Society generally, and
(vi) The environment.

Parkinson distinguishes between relational responsibility and social activism.[4] Relational responsibility refers to assistance to groups such as employees, suppliers, consumers or the community who are affected by the company's business activities. Social activism on the other hand, benefits groups who fall outside the scope of the company's business activities. Parkinson explains it thus: "Social activism, in contrast, constitutes an effort by companies to address social issues that arise independently of the way the company conducts its business and thus represents an extension of corporate activity into essentially non-commercial spheres."[5] Although, as Parkinson admits, these concepts can sometimes overlap in practice, the distinction is useful since relational responsibility will usually coincide with company objectives to make profits, or at least have a neutral effect on profits, whereas social activism can result in profit sacrifice and consequently a shift in the corporate goal of profit maximization. Purely charitable donations that are not related to the company's business are difficult to reconcile with the goal of profit maximization. The constraints imposed by the law on such philanthropic acts are discussed hereunder.

It has been demonstrated by many writers on this topic,[6] including Parkinson that usually there is no real conflict between profit maximization and socially responsible behaviour on the part of companies. This being so from whatever viewpoint one departs, such philanthropic behaviour causes no controversy. Problems arise however, as will be demonstrated hereunder, when the conduct elastics with a profit maximization motive. This will be the case where the philanthropic behaviour is not a response to exterior or interior forces in the interests of profit maximization of the company, but rather it is conduct for the sake of the interests themselves. In short, the interest of outsiders, not those of the company are preferred. Therefore, Parkinson makes a further distinction:

Responsibility that requires a change in company objectives as opposed to responsibility that only constrains the pursuit of existing company objectives to maximise profits.[7] These constraints might be legally imposed such as minimum wage laws or legislation that protects the environment, or they can be self-imposed in the sense that they constitute an economically rational response to market pressure in the form of public opinion generally, or the opinion of the parties with whom the company has dealings. These self-imposed constraints usually reduce profits in the short-term in the interests of bigger long-term company profits. They are therefore not inconsistent with the goal of profit maximization.

Parkinson concludes that the content of company codes, the attitude of managers and directors and the way companies spend their money indicate that there has been no shift away from the profit goal in the corporate world.[8] The same conclusion is reached by Slaughter when she states: "Much of the debate about social responsibility can be disposed of by the simple observation that what is considered to be socially responsible behaviour is often also good for business or at least a sensible course of public relations which will improve the company's image and contribute to profitability in the long-run."[9] After having done a thorough survey of US cases Carter concludes[10]: "Corporate managements rightly believe that it is their responsibility to obtain corporate benefit from every dollar spent and courts have almost uniformly insisted on it" and the author has searched the literature and his memory without success for a purely altruistic corporation act. Those which have come to his attention could be or usually were justified on the basis that they satisfied public expectations and therefore were of value to the corporation or were otherwise of direct benefit to the corporation. Furthermore, in more than 25 years of attending meetings of a board, which was known to be quite public-spirited, the author does not recall ever having heard the term public interest or a synonym uttered. It is his distinct impression that with respect to all decisions the members of the board believed they were acting in the corporate interest." He also refers to a study undertaken by the Conference Board, an independent, non-profit business research organization, to determine the motivation for corporate giving, as well as a study undertaken by the Foundation of the South Western Graduate School of Banking of Corporate Ethical Policy Statements and concludes: "In summary it appears corporate altruism under the present system of corporate governance and under the law today, not only is not practiced, it is not permissible. Corporations make contributions and other expenditures for social benefit only when, in the business judgment of management it is in the corporate self-interest."[11]

On the other hand, the view that companies are not always motivated by self-interest and that companies can and do act altruistically for no other reason than charity has also been put forward.[12]

Although it is rarely possible to predict or accurately calculate in real money terms exactly what the long-term benefit to the company of socially responsible acts will be, it is clear that the bulk of such corporate conduct can easily be classified or interpreted to be of benefit to the company in the long run.[13]

In terms of Slaughter's definition of social responsibility quoted above, therefore, most of the so-called socially responsible conduct which companies indulge in would not be classified as socially responsible behaviour since its end is the maximization of profits as opposed to some perceived social good.

MOTIVATIONS OF COMPANIES TO SPEND MONEY FOR THE BENEFIT OF THIRD PARTIES AND THE COMMUNITY AT LARGE

1. Introduction

Motivation for these seemingly philanthropic acts is many and varied. Furthermore, it is impossible to establish with certainty what the motivation of a company is. It is usually based on a combination of factors. As shown hereunder benefits a company can possibly derive from such actions are largely dependent on whom the beneficiaries of such conduct are.

2. Benefits to the Company

Although moral responsibility might be a motivating factor for company expenditure on for example the control of pollution, or community projects, or the provision of safe and pleasant working conditions, or ensuring products and services are of an acceptable quality, or the sponsorship of art or education, and so on, it is apparent that such expenditure can also provide benefits to the company.[14] These include:

- (i) an enhanced public image,
- (ii) tax rebates, for example, where a company contributes to social welfare,
- (iii) education or the arts,
- (iv) the ability to attract and retain a productive, loyal and competent workforce,
- (v) (usually by sponsoring education, paying competitive wages and providing superior working conditions),
- (vi) companies can commercially apply the results of research they have sponsored,
- (vii) involvement in community projects such as job creation schemes can improve morale amongst employees and the community at large. This in turn will stimulate the local economy on which the company relies for survival. A social environment, which is healthy, is essential for the conduct of successful business enterprises,
- (viii) opportunities for business contacts, staff perks, an advertising medium for high profile groups as well as tax

incentives can all now from company sponsorship of the arts, and

(ix) Another long-term benefit identified by Parkinson[15] is the prevention of further government intervention. Where companies address social and environmental problems it will not be necessary for government to find their own solutions such as increased taxes, prohibitive legislation, compulsory regulations and intervention. In this way, voluntarily assumed constraints for the prevention of for example environmental damage reduce the need for government intervention.

Most authors[16] including Parkinson[17] and Slaughter[18] would agree that socially responsible behaviour is usually also good for business and will contribute to the profitability of the company in the long-run. It is often not possible to predict or gage exactly how much money particular socially responsible conduct will generate especially where the pay-off comes in the form of an enhanced public image or the conduct serves as a form of advertising. Nevertheless it seems to be generally accepted that companies will act in the public interest so long as it is also in the company's interest. Self-interest and not altruism therefore seems to be a major motivating factor for corporate social responsibility.[19]

Abuse by Directors

Since spending on charity is often up to the discretion of directors, the abuse by directors of company money in the pursuit of self-interest is commonplace. Donations to an art gallery or a favourite charity might benefit no one besides the director in that s/he will receive preferential treatment amongst those of high social profiles. Clearly such donations are inconsistent with the goal of profit maximization.

THE NEO-CLASSICAL MODEL OF COMPANY LAW

Introduction

Company law plays an important role in how well the economy works. How well the economy works, in turn, is crucial to the economic and social well being of a country's citizens. Re-election of governments operating in democratic systems is largely dependent on the overall performance of the economy, which is in turn largely determined by business. It follows therefore, that it is essential till any capitalist democratic state to retain the confidence and hence the co-operation of the business sector. Such confidence can only be achieved where a country's laws not only permit but also encourage profitability. In an increasingly globalised world economy, governments must be sensitive to the possibility of reduced investor confidence (both local and international), resulting in not only massive capital outflows, but also a failure to attract foreign investment. The *King Report on Corporate Governance for South Africa* (hereinafter "The King Report") is fully aware of this fact and states as follows:[20]

> "However, it must constantly be borne in mind that entrepreneurship and enterprise are still among the important factors that drive business: Emerging economies have been driven by entrepreneurs, who take business risks and initiatives. With successful companies, come successful economies. Without satisfactory levels of profitability in a company, not only will investors who cannot earn an acceptable return on their investment look to alternative opportunities, but it is unlikely that the other stakeholders will have an enduring interest in the company."

Government policies and legislation that are insensitive to business confidence will clearly have disastrous effects on employment and economic growth and stability. The King Commission Report continues:[21]

> "The Company remains a key component of modern society. In fact, in many respects companies have become a more immediate presence to many citizens and modern democracies than either governments or other organs of civil society. As a direct consequence, companies remain the legitimate and necessary focal point for profit-making activities in market economics. They are also increasingly a target for those discontented with business liberalisation and globalisation, an agenda that companies are perceived as driving. In the global economy are many jurisdictions to which a company can run to avoid regulation and taxes or to reduce labour costs. . . ."

Any suggestions therefore that companies should be forced by law to be more socially responsible and to allocate funds to the public good at the expense of profitability should be considered carefully in the light of the above.

The Neo-American Model

The company laws of South Africa, England and the United States of America (hereinafter USA) will be compared hereunder. All three of these countries embody what has been referred to as the neo-American model of capitalism as compared with the Rhine model found operating in parts of Western Europe and Japan.[22]

In terms of the neo-American model the starting point is that since companies are essentially the property of shareholders, shareholders have the right to insist that the company be run for their benefit.

The separation of ownership and control (i.e. shareholders own the shares of a company whereas directors control the administration and general running of the company), has led to the need for company law in these systems to intervene to protect the interests of shareholders. As such, company law places some constraints on management behaviour thus curtailing the ability of management to use company funds for philanthropic ends. These constraints come in the form of the common law *ultra vires* doctrine, the common law duty of directors to act in good faith in the best interests of the company, and the duty of directors to exercise diligence, care and skill. These will be discussed in turn hereunder.

THE *ULTRA VIRES* DOCTRINE

The objects clause in a company's memorandum of association sets out the activities for which the company has been formed. These activities, however, may be altered by special resolution in terms of both South African and English company law. In terms of the *ultra vires* doctrine a transaction beyond the scope of the objects clause is *ultra vires* and void. The justification for this doctrine, which could easily result in hardship to innocent third parties contracting with the company, was that it protected both shareholders and creditors of the company from abuse of power by directors. The English Companies Act has been amended so that the objects clause no longer limits the company's capacity in that the validity of such act or contract may no longer be questioned on the grounds of lack of capacity.[23] The company is bound by the transaction. Nevertheless, directors who enter into contracts beyond the capacity of the company in terms of its objects clause remain liable to the company for any loss that may result from entering into such *ultra vires* transaction. Where such transactions are beneficial to the company they can be ratified.[24]

Section 36 of the South African Companies Act[25] states:

> "No Act of a company shall be void by reason only of the fact that the company was without capacity or power so to act or because the directors had no authority to perform that act on behalf of the company by reason only of the said fact and except as between the company and its directors neither the company nor any other person may in any legal proceedings assert or rely upon any such lack of capacity or power or authority."

As is the case with English law, despite the validity of the *ultra vires* transaction the directors in South African law are still liable to the company. Prior to the conclusion of the *ultra vires* act, a court on application of a member/shareholder can grant an interdict preventing such action. If the act has already been concluded the director(s) responsible can be held liable for breach of their fiduciary duty.[26]

The modern trend however has been to have very broadly drafted objects clauses so that most activities will probably not be *ultra vires*.[27] Insofar as philanthropic acts that fall outside the objects clause are concerned, the law will in order to protect the interests of the company and indirectly the interests of the shareholders, hold directors responsible for such acts liable for any loss.

DUTY TO ACT IN GOOD FAITH IN THE INTERESTS OF THE COMPANY

An action, which is within the power or capacity of the company, may still constitute a breach or fiduciary duty on the part of directors. This duty to act *bona fides* is in technical terms owed to the company as a separate legal entity in terms of both English and South African law. However, usually in promoting the success of the business, the best interests of the shareholders are also served. The fact that directors owe a fiduciary duty to the company, as a separate legal entity is not incompatible with the notion that directors owe such a duty to shareholders. Despite the fact that the standard formulation of the duty of directors in running the business is expressed in terms of benefiting the company. Parkinson[28] argues that this does not mean that the directors must literally direct their efforts at benefiting a legal entity. This he concludes would be futile since an artificial entity is not incapable of expressing well-being nor is it capable of having interests. Therefore he concludes[29] that "the duty of management can accordingly be stated as a duty to promote the success of the business venture in order to benefit the members."

The law in the USA differs from South African and English law in that in many states the legislation specifically states that fiduciary duties are owed to the shareholders.[30] In USA shareholders can specifically define duties of directors for which they will be held liable for breaching and which breaches could bear the sanction of loss of office.[31]

The *King Commission Report*,[32] in stating the role of directors reiterates this common law duty of directors by stating that directors must always:

> "exercise the utmost good faith, honesty and integrity in all their dealings with or on behalf of the company"[33] and "act in the best interests of the company and never for any sectoral interest."[34]

It appears however, that in the view of the Report this duty can coexist and is quite compatible with a duty to take other stakeholder's interests into account. The report states further that directors "must act with enterprise for and on behalf of the company and always strive to increase shareowner's value, while having regard for the interests of all stakeholders relevant to the company."[35]

This statement is reminiscent of English company law. Legislation provides that: "The matters to which the directors of the company are to have regard in the performance of their functions include the interest of the company's employees in general as well as the interests of its members."[36] The Act then goes on to provide that this duty is owed "to the company and is enforceable in the same way as any other fiduciary duty owed to the company by its directors."[37] In other words it would be incumbent upon the directors themselves to enforce such duty and the employees would not be able to bring an action to prevent a breach of such duty. It seems unlikely however that the directors would bring an action against themselves!

Since, in terms of both South African and English law fiduciary duties are owed to the company, directors must enforce compliance on behalf of the company. Although shareholders can bring actions for breach of fiduciary duties, it appears that the 'employees' in the English legislation to whom the directors must have regard and "all the stakeholders relevant to the company" to which directors are to have regard in terms of the *King Commission's Report* have no means to enforce such duty (unless of course they are also shareholders).

In summary therefore, despite the mandatory language used in both the English law and the *King Commission Report,* such obligations are practically unenforceable, and merely provide directors with the discretion to have 'due regard' to the other stakeholders.

The *King Commission Report* does not spell out who all the stakeholders relevant to the company are. However stakeholders are defined as follows:[38]

"1.1 Shareowners as providers of capital.

1.2 Parties that contract with the enterprise either as providers of input to its various business processes and activities, or as purchasers of its output. This would include, for example, customers, employees, suppliers, sub-contractors and business partners.

1.3 Panics that have a non-contractual nexus with the enterprise but provide it with its licence to operate and thereby exercise an influence on its ability to achieve its objectives. This class could include, for example, civic society in general, local communities, non-governmental organisations ("NGOs") and other special interest groups whose concerns may be with issues such as market stability, social equity and the environment.

1.4 The State as policy-maker, legislator and regulator of the economy generally and specific sectors of it. The State's power, as opposed to mere influence, over the activities of companies sets it apart from other parties with a non-contractual nexus."

In summary, stakeholders can be described as those upon whose co-operation and creativity it depends for its survival and prosperity.

Whether Section 309 of the English Companies Act allows the

interests of employees to take precedence over those of shareholders is not entirely clear. The weight of opinion however is that shareholder's interests can never be subordinated to employee interests.[39] Nevertheless Parkinson argues that this section will provide directors who have favoured employee interests over shareholder's interests with a defence.[40]

The wording in the *King Commission Report* appears to subordinate the interests of all stakeholders relevant to the company to the shareholders' interests since the directors "must act with enterprise for and on behalf of the company and **always** (my emphasis) strive to increase value, **while** (my emphasis) having regard for the interests of all stakeholders."[41]

Even though USA corporate law also provides for standard from fiduciary duties. USA law differs in that many states have introduced legislation that specifically permits corporate powers that go beyond profit maximization.[42] The first such piece of legislation was promulgated in Texas as early as 1917. Many other states subsequently followed suit. Some states specify charitable, humanitarian and social goals of which contributions are permitted. Generally companies are entitled to act for mixed profit and humanitarian purposes. It should be noted that this legislation is enabling in that it permits such conduct. It is not mandatory and does not enforce or oblige companies to make any contributions or perform any other form of charitable conduct.

In all three countries, USA, England and South Africa it is very easy for directors to satisfy the standards of good faith. The duty to act in good faith is subjective. The courts will not look into the merits of directors' decisions but will look merely to their subjective intention. If their subjective intention was to pursue the interests (albeit long-term interests), of the company, they will have satisfied the duty to act in good faith. It will be difficult to prove that a director's motivation was something other than maximisation of profits, even where maximisation of profits did not result from the action. For example, donations to charity can usually be defended on the basis that they contribute to the goodwill of the company. The English and American court cases generally bear this out.[43] Some American cases however, have openly permitted and justified US corporations making charitable donations not on the basis of long-term profit maximisation, but rather on the basis of public policy arguments.[44] In contrast to these decisions the court in *Dodge* vs.

Ford[45] (hereinafter the *Dodge* case) ignored public policy arguments and implemented what has been termed the 'contract model' of corporate responsibility[46] where the corporation is exclusively responsible to shareholders who have contractual rights for profit maximisation. However Mangrum contends[47] that as far as USA is concerned, "the strict contract version articulated in Dodge had little historical support then and has since been substantially revised by common law decisions and statutory reform."

A number of English and American cases that were decided prior to the *Dodge* case permitted altruistic actions by corporations on the basis of economic and humanitarian justifications.[48] Although these decisions could be justified on the basis that the conduct complained of was conceivably beneficial to the long-term interests of the company, the language used by some of the judges indicates the pursuit of social purposes beyond profit maximisation.[49]

Mangrum[50] highlights how many of the post *Dodge* decisions in both England and USA display an even greater tolerance towards legitimate objectives besides the pursuit of profit maximisation. The conclusion arrived at is that some decisions have paid lip service to the fiction of long-term benefit to the company.[51] Mangrum states:[52] "Some courts revise the strictures of *Dodge* by considering what appears to be altruistic corporate acts as compatible with the long-term economic interest of the corporation. These cases give descriptive credence to both the contract and economic models. At some point the liberality of the interpretation of economic interest transforms the profit maximisation constraint into a legal fiction which obscures the real justification for the decision."

Carter,[53] having reviewed the US cases comes to a very different conclusion to that of Mangrum. He argues that the requirement that some kind of benefit be derived by the company, albeit indirect has remained constant. Slaughter and Parkinson[54] come to a similar conclusion concerning the English cases and suggests that the English courts insist on corporate benefit to legitimize corporate acts even though the benefit may not be immediate or calculable.

Although some decisions may have interpreted the profit maximization goal very liberally the fact remains that usually socially responsible conduct is good for business,[55] even though the extent of the benefit is often incapable of exact calculation. This is especially the case when socially responsible actions serve the purpose of public relations, advertising and the creation of general goodwill.[56]

Solomon[57] in analyzing two publicity held corporations that are noted for being socially responsible and having objectives other than profit maximization, namely, *Bell and Jerry's Homemade Inc.* and *The Body Shop International PLC,* actually demonstrates how the socially responsible conduct brought in great profits.

There are however, always exceptions to the rule, and socially responsible conduct might not always be in the best interest (albeit long-term interests) of the company. Charitable donations are the type of socially responsible conduct by companies which are the most difficult to reconcile with the profit maximisation object. This usually occurs where directors are motivated by self-interest in making donations with company funds. In the light of preceding discussion concerning the ease with which the duty to act in good faith is complied with and the liberal interpretation the courts have sometimes given to the end of profit maximisation, it might be argued that shareholders might be unable to prevent such self-interested acts by directors. In situations like this, the effect of market forces (which go beyond the scope of this article) might well step in to act as a restraint on management conduct.[58]

In short therefore, it appears that although the law is not mandatory and does not oblige companies to be socially responsible, the law usually does permit such conduct. The driving force behind such conduct is not any legal obligation but rather market forces that render such conduct good for business.[59] A rather ironic illustration of this is the *Dodge* case: Henry Ford was prevented from acting for the benefit of his employees and the community on the basis that this would not be in the best interests of the company. Ford subsequently paid out the minority shareholders (the *Dodge Brothers*) who had objected to this conduct and obtained the court order preventing it, and proceeded with his social policies that resulted in the company being more profitable than it had ever been.[60]

DUTY TO EXERCISE DILIGENCE: CARE AND SKILL

Directors in England, South Africa and USA must exercise certain standards of care and skill. In all three countries the standards of care and skill are very low. The standards of the ordinary prudent man[61] have been constantly applied in England. The similar reasonable man test is applied in South Africa. This means that the care and skill required is that which "can reasonably be expected of a person with his knowledge and experience. A director is not liable for mere errors of judgement."[62]

Historically the courts have been reluctant to second-guess business judgments. Another reason that judges were reluctant in the past to interfere with managerial discretion is that the courts felt that shareholders could control management. Clearly today, particularly with large, public companies shareholder control is not always possible. Contributing to the particularly low standard of care and skill required by the courts has been the misconception that management is not a profession requiring specific skills.[63] Clearly this is not the case. The extensive literature and qualifications available on the topic of 'management' verify this.

Imposing a higher standard of care and skill on directors however, might result in a reluctance on the part of directors to take risks. Risk-taking is, and always has been part of any successful business. Too stringent a standard therefore might hinder progress, productivity and profitability. It has been suggested[64] that courts should scrutinize decisions more closely from a procedural aspect in order to ensure that at least, the risk embarked upon was preceded by adequate research. The argument is that requiring directors to gather reasonably sufficient information before embarking on a risk will help insure that more calculated risks are taken without hampering risk-taking to too great an extent.

The *King Commission Report*[65] may require a slightly more stringent duty of care and skill expected of directors in terms of the common law. It states that directors must in line with modern trends worldwide, not only exhibit the degree of skill and care as may be reasonably expected from persons of their skill and experience (which is the traditional legal formulation), but must also:

(i) exercise both care and skill any reasonable persons would be expected to show in looking after their own affairs as well as having regard to their actual knowledge and experience;

(ii) qualify themselves on a continuous basis with a sufficient (at least a general) understanding of the company's business and the effect of the economy so as to discharge their duties properly, including where necessary relying on expert advice;[66]

(iii) "must insist that board papers and other important information regarding the company are provided to them in time for them to make informed decisions";[67]

(iv) "must ensure that procedures and systems are in place to act as checks and balances on the information being received by the board and ensure that the company prepares annual budgets and regularly updated forecasts against which the company's performance can be monitored";[68] and

(v) must be diligent in discharging their duties to the company, regularly attend all meetings and must acquire a broad knowledge of the business of the company so that they can meaningfully contribute to its direction."[69]

In line with Parkinson's suggestions[70] what was envisaged by the *King Commission Report* is an emphasis on procedural aspects with a more stringent obligation on the acquisition of knowledge and information. Nevertheless, it appears that there still would be no grounds for questioning an error of judgment provided it was preceded by the necessary accumulation of information and knowledge.

CONCLUSION

Pressure to perform competitively provides the impetus or incentive to constrain management conduct that serves personal management interests as opposed to shareholder or company interests.[71] The threat of management job losses through hostile take-overs, mergers and so forth and not company law rules may inhibit management conduct. Capital markets, product markets, markets for managerial talent all act as incentives for directors to run a company in a professional, efficient, and productive manner.[72] However, since the constraints afforded by the markets might not be complete,[73] some argue that the law should be amended to provide for a more comprehensive duty of skill and care with more stringent liability for management.[74]

Such constraints however will also not necessarily be completely effective in controlling management conduct. Secondly, more rigid legal constraints could easily result in the costs exceeding the benefits.[75] Thirdly, such legal constraints might prevent socially responsible conduct that would normally result in increased profits for the company. Fourthly, litigation and enforcement by the courts carries with it the following pitfalls:

(i) It is expensive, disruptive to the company and can result in bad publicity.
(ii) The outcome is uncertain.
(iii) Damages are payable to the company not individuals thus significantly reducing the incentive to pursue a matter via the courts.
(iv) Minority shareholders do not always have *locus standi* to enforce liability.

In conclusion, it appears that it would be difficult to successfully challenge philanthropic acts of a company for the following reasons:

(i) The revision of *ultra vires* doctrine and the trend towards open-ended and general objects clauses;
(ii) The fact that the fiduciary duties of good faith and care and skill are easily met and hence seldom violated;
(iii) The liberal interpretation of long-term interest generally accorded by the courts; and
(iv) The general refusal by the courts to interfere with management judgement and discretion.

This however, is not too disturbing in the light of the overall benefit that usually accrues to the company as a result of philanthropic conduct as well as the constraining effect on managerial discretion that market forces provide. A reliance on the effect of the market on management conduct is apparent in the King Report in its recommendations for remuneration of directors and it reads:[76]

> "Levels of remuneration should be sufficient to attract, retain and motivate executives of the quality required by the board" and "performance-related elements of remuneration should constitute a substantial portion of the total remuneration package of executives in order to align their interests with the shareowners, and should be designed to provide incentives to perform at the highest operational standards."

It appears that such reliance on market forces is not unfounded as it has been demonstrated that management controlled companies do not spend more on social expenditure than those under ownership control.[77] Ironically then, market pressure generally functions as a constraint on management conduct in that it ensures that the company is run efficiently, and at the same time, market pressure is an incentive for socially responsible conduct. This is also the view of the King Commission when it states: "Impetus for change will therefore come from market and society which will be the ultimate arbiters in corporate behaviour."[78]

It consistently refers to a company's responsibility to other stakeholders. For example, it states:[79] "Boards should recognise that companies do not act independently from the societies in which they operate. Accordingly corporate actions must be compatible with societal objectives concerning social cohesion, individual welfare and equal opportunities for all. At times however, there may well be a trade-off between short-term social costs in respect of decisions that will derive longer-term benefits for the company and thereby those having an interest in it. Nonetheless, this presents some intricate and complex challenges that require to be balanced carefully by a competent board. This does not remove the fundamental tenet in law, that the board is accountable to the company for the performance of the business, but all the same the modern inclusive approach expects a company to act responsively to and responsively towards relevant stakeholders."

It is clear therefore that in this view the pursuit of company interests is not incompatible with being socially responsible. The Report emphasizes the importance of social, ethical and environmental issues and specifically states that they can "no longer be regarded as secondary to more conventional business imperatives."[80] The conclusion is that a company's long-term survival and success is "inextricably linked to the sustainable development of the social and economic communities within which it operates"[81] and that "this inclusive approach (i.e. inclusion of other stakeholders) is the way to create sustained business success and steady, long-term growth in shareowner value"[82] since "stakeholders have a direct bearing on ongoing corporate viability and financial performance."[83]

CONCLUSION

Most socially responsible behaviour is also in the benefit of the company. Market forces have been the driving impetus to the advent and growth of corporate social responsibility. Amongst these market forces have been the inability of governments to provide adequate social security, moves towards privatisation, growing public concerns for the environment, the positive effects to the company of a good corporate image and so on. The judicial trend toward allowing companies to benefit society is merely an illustration of how the common law will adapt to suit the current socio-economic environment within which it operates.

The fact that there might be exceptional cases where the socially responsible behaviour is not in the company's best interests does not justify more stringent and constraining legislation. Aside from the fact that market forces are more effective in constraining self-interested director conduct, constraining legislation might well result in a reduction of socially responsible acts that would otherwise have been in the interests of the company and the economy as a whole.

It appears that Mervyn King, the author of the *King Report* shares my view and is quoted as saying, "The report is a set of guidelines and I would resist any attempt to have these recommendations legislated. Global market forces will sort out those companies that do not have sound corporate governance.[84]

Notes and References

1. Deery and Mitchell, "The Emergence of Individualisation and Union Exclusion as an Employment Relations Strategy" in Deery and Mitchell, *Employment Relations* (1999), 3; Parkinson, *Corporate Power and Responsibility* (1996), xiii of Preface and Harrington, "Public Sector on the Wane," *Business and Society Review*, 1992, 28.
2. Carter, "The Limit of Corporate Social Responsibility," *Merc Law Review*, 1982, Vol. 33, 519 and Butler and McChesney, "Why They Give at the Office—Shareholder Welfare and Corporate Philanthropy in the Contractual Theory of the Corporation," *Cornell Law Review*, 2001, Vol. 84, 1195.
3. Slaughter, "Corporate Social Responsibility: A New Perspective," *The Company Lawyer*, 1997, Vol. 18, 321.
4. Parkinson, *Corporate Power and Responsibility* (1996), Ch. 9.
5. *Ibid.*, 269.
6. See Carter, "The Limit of Corporate Social Responsibility," *Merc Law Review*, 1982, Vol. 33, 519 and Slaughter, *op. cit.*, 10.
7. Parkinson, *op. cit.*, 268-71.
8. Parkinson, *Corporate Power and Responsibility* (1996), Ch. 9.
9. Slaughter, "Corporate Social Responsibility: A New Perspective," *The Company Lawyer*, 1997, Vol. 18, 321.
10. *Ibid.*, 534.

11. *Op. cit.*, 537-39.
12. See Mangrum, "In Search of a Paradigm of Corporate Social Responsibility," *Creighton Law Review*, 1983, 21.
13. For discussion on how socially responsible behaviour towards the community, customers and consumers, employees and various charities are of benefit to companies see Slaughter, *op. cit.*, 322-24 and Parkinson, *op. cit.*, 281-303.
14. Parkinson, *op. cit.*, 290-301.
15. Parkinson, *op. cit.*, 299.
16. See Carter, *op. cit.*, 538-39.
17. Parkinson, *op. cit.*, chapter 9.
18. Slaughter, *op. cit.*, 321.
19. Sec Carter, *op. cit.*, where the author's thesis is that the limit of corporate social responsibility in USA is long-term self-interest.
20. *King Report on Corporate Governance for South Africa* (2002), p. 8, para. 7.
21. *Ibid.*, para. 14.
22. For a detailed description of these models see Parkinson, *Corporate Power and Responsibility* (1996), pp. ix-x of the Preface.
23. Companies Act, 1989, 5108 inserting SS 35-35B into the Companies Act of 1985.
24. S. 35(3) of the English Companies Act of 1989 specifically provides for this.
25. Companies Act 61 of 1973.
26. Cilliers et *al.*, *Entrepreneurial Law* (2000) 150.
27. Slaughter, "Corporate Social Responsibility: A New Perspective," *The Company Lawyer*, 1997, Vol. 18, 326.
28. Parkinson, *op. cit.*, 76.
29. *Ibid.*, 77.
30. Slaughter, *op. cit.*, 320.
31. Butler and McChesney, "Why They Give at the Office—Shareholder Welfare and Corporate Philanthropy in Contractual Theory of the Corporation," *Cornell Law Review*, 2001, Vol. 84, 1201.
32. *King Commission Report* (2002), 54-56.
33. *Ibid.*, par 2.2.
34. *Ibid.*, par 2.4.
35. *Ibid.*, par 2.13.
36. S. 309(1) of English Companies Act of 1985.
37. S. 309(2) of English Companies Act of 1985.
38. *King Commission Report* (2002), 97-98.
39. Parkinson, *Corporate Power and Responsibility* (1996), 84-85.
40. *Idem.*
41. *King Commission Report* (2002), 98.
42. For an overview of such legislation see Mangrum, *op. cit.*, 66-70.
43. See Slaughter, "Corporate Social Responsibility: A New Perspective," *The Company Lawyer*, 1997, Vol. 18, 316-24 for a survey of the English and US cases.
44. *Ibid.*, 320.

45. 204 Mich 459.170 N.W. 668 (1919).
46. See Mangrum, "In Search of a Paradigm of Corporate Social Responsibility," *Creighton Law Review*, 1983, 50-55, for a detailed discussion of this model and *Dodge* vs. *Ford*.
47. *Op. cit.*, 54.
48. *Ibid.*, 55-57.
49. See *Steinway* vs. *Steinway & Sons*, 17 Misc. 43 40 N.Y.S. 718, 1896; *People* vs. *Hotchkiss* 136 A.D. 150. 120 N.Y.S. 649, 1909; *Hawes* vs. *Oakland*, 104 U.S. 450, 1881; *Tounton* vs. *Royal Ins. Co.*, 71 Eng. Rep. 413 (1864).
50. Mangrum, *op. cit.*, 58-66.
51. Parkinson, *op. cit.*, 280 comes to a similar conclusion concerning US cases. See for example *AP Smith Manufacturing Co.* vs. *Barlow*, 39 ALC 2D 1179 (1953) 1187.
52. *Op. cit.*, 54.
53. Carter, "The Limit of Corporate Social Responsibility," *Merc Law Review*, 1982, Vol. 33, 533.
54. Slaughter, "Corporate Social Responsibility: A New Perspective," *The Company Lawyer*, 1987, Vol. 18, 316 and Parkinson, *Corporate Power and Responsibility* (1996), 272.
55. See Slaughter, *op. cit.*, 321-22 and Parkinson, *op. cit.*, 273-74 for discussion of *Evans* and *Brunner Mond and Co. Ltd.* (1921).
56. For a discussion of socially responsible conduct as a response to consumer opinion see Slaughter, *op. cit.*, 322-24.
57. Solomon, "On the Frontier of Capitalism: Implementation of Humanomics by Modern Publicity Held Corporations—A Critical Assessment" in Mitchell, *Progressive Corporate Law* (1996), 78.
58. Butler and McChesney, "Why They Give at the Office—Shareholder Welfare and Corporate Philanthropy in Contractual Theory of the Corporation," *Cornell Law Review*, 2001, Vol. 84, 1197-1202 argue that market fines have a much more profound effect than the law on managerial conduct.
59. Supra.
60. Mangrum, "In Search of a Paradigm of Corporate Social Responsibility," *Creighton Law Review*, 1983, 54.
61. *Overrend and Gurney* vs. *Gibb* (1872) LRS HL 480 HL.
62. Celliers *et al.*, *Entrepreneurial Law* (2000), 153.
63. For an illustration of this misconception by English courts see Parkinson *Corporate Power and Responsibility* (1996), 108.
64. *Ibid.*, 110-13.
65. *King Commission Report* (2002).
66. *Ibid.*, Ch. 4, para 2.3.
67. *Ibid.*, para 2.6.
68. *Ibid.*, para 210.
69. *Ibid.*, para 211.
70. *Supra.*

71. See Yoshiro Miwa, "Corporate Social Responsibility: Dangerous and Harmful. Though Maybe not Irrelevant," *Cornell Law Review*, Vol. 84, 1195 (1999) 1227, 1232-33.
72. For a detailed analysis of the likely effects of the various markets on management behaviour see Parkinson, *op. cit.*, 113-32 and Butler and McChesney, "Why They Give at the Office—Shareholder Welfare and Corporate Philanthropy in Contractual Theory of the Corporation," *Cornell Law Review*, 2001, Vol. 84, 1197-1202.
73. Parkinson, *op. cit.*, 33 for a discussion of the inability of the markets to prevent inefficiency as a result of the imperfection of markets.
74. *Ibid.*, 132.
75. *Idem* and Butler and McChesney, *op. cit.*, 1206.
76. *King Commission Report* (2002) 61.
77. Parkinson, *Corporate Power and Responsibility* (1996), 64.
78. *King Commission Report* (2002), para 23.
79. *King Commission Report* (2002), 48.
80. *Ibid.*, 92.
81. *Idem.*
82. *Idem.*
83. *Idem.*
84. *Sunday Times Business Times*, August 18 (2002) 14. I am not however suggesting that the market alone can curb all inappropriate, unethical and dishonest conduct on the part of directors that is usually motivated by greed. Such conduct obviously cannot be condoned and sufficient transparency and monitoring of management decisions and actions should be mandatory so that errant directors can be held personally accountable for dishonest and unethical conduct. This aspect however goes beyond the scope of the discourse contained in this paper.

15

Excellence Models for Manpower in Marketing for an Era of Continuous Change

M.M. GOEL

In the present paper an attempt is being made to diagnose the deteriorating standards in marketing of goods and services and to prescribe the essentials for the crucial manpower of marketing to become relevant for smooth management process in an era of continuous change. Change is the law of nature. Everything should change except the love for change. But the changes in India are taking place so rapidly that anything becomes obsolete after certain period of time. There was an era in which an adage, "Jack of all trades master of none" was popular. In the course of time it was replaced by "Jack of all trades but master of one" justifying specialization. Now the scenario is inclined towards "Jack of all trades and master of all" which makes a strong case for generalization of marketing education instead of specialization. As fellow teachers of marketing, it becomes our moral duty to introspect on this important observation and should come out with remedial steps to face the challenges of an era of continuous change in business environment. To my mind, Spiritual bankruptcy and the ethical crisis of marketing are the root causes of deteriorating marketing standards and are serious issues of concern for polluting relationship between marketer and customer of today. It is important to note carefully that the consumer Protection Act, 1986 have far reaching implications in relationship between seller and buyer leading to behavioural pollution. All this attract adverse comments on marketing system in general and marketers in particular and compel us to think whether marketers, are honest, humane, hard-working in providing real value products and services to the customers.

In order to change the perception of a marketer, seller and advertiser from a villain to a hero, we need sincere, dedicated and enthusiastic manpower in marketing for which I would like to justify feminisation of marketing manpower through 'SHE' model made excellent with ASK model with skills in MCA model for the sustainable human development through SIMPLE model.

S H E

- E → Existential
- H → Humanistic
- S → Spiritualistic

To survive, sustain and develop in 21st century the marketers need to be made existential through Retention, Respect and Responsibility (3R of Human Resource Management). Woman manpower is more existential because of her higher emotional quotient (EQ) including patience, motivating herself, motivating others and empathizing with others in all circumstances. Further, to make a marketer existential, I have developed 'ASK' model of existence given below:

A S K

- K → Knowledge
- S → Skills
- A → Abilities of head and heart

According to ASK model of existence a marketer must have complete, full, up to date, accurate knowledge of the good and services. Skill of writing script of advertisement is not an easy task and is an art. It is worth quoting Alexander Pope.

"True ease in writing come by Art not by chance
As s(he) moves easiest who has learnt to dance."

The skill of writing can certainly be developed through lot of reading. It needs to be noted that societies and nations can live without writing but no society can exist without reading. Further, we need the skill of operating computer in the modern era of information technology, which calls for MCA model given below:

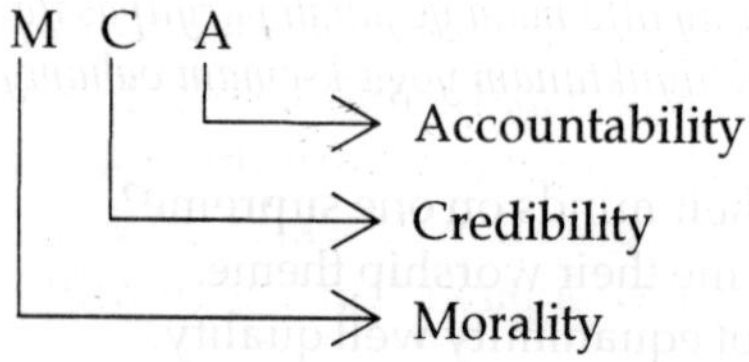

According to MCA model, a marketer needs to be self-accountable and must establish his/her credibility through ethics of morality.

The last (but not the least) attribute of ASK model of existence is the abilities of head and heart to form the positive attitude for becoming existential in the marketing profession through enthusiastic endeavour with patience, confidence and intelligence.

The second important component of the SHE model is to make a teacher Humanistic. Without being humanistic, we cannot and will not be able to perform our duties properly. Therefore, humanistic approach needs to be accepted as a panacea for understanding the duties of a marketer. For this essential attribute we need to follow completely and absolutely sloka number 15 of chapter 17 of Bhagwad Gita given below:

anudvega-karam vaykam satyam priyahitam ca yat
svadhyayabhyasanam caiva van-mayam tapa ucyate

(B.G.: 17:15)

(Words that neither hurt nor provoke,
Truthfully to benefit others are spoke.
Or in process of self study pronounced,
O Arjun, to penance of speech amount.)

Meaning thereby, meditative communion with one's own true self and uttering words that cause no agitation and that are truthful, pleasant and beneficial, are called the austerity of speech. Thus, the marketing manpower needs to be objective, dependable to know or to tell the truth by becoming humanistic.

The third and final attribute of the SHE model is spiritualistic. It needs to be noted that the period of consciousness has already started and will be the name of the game in 21st century. To ensure spirituality among the marketers we have advocated sloka number 22 of chapter 9 of Bhagwad Gita given below:

ananyas cintayanto mam ye janah paryupasate
tesam nityabhiyuktanam yoga-ksemam vahamy aham

(B.G.: 9:22)

(Who set their minds on one supreme?
And make me their worship theme.
As yogies of equanimity well qualify.
I aid them and there needs supply.)

Meaning thereby, those who always worship me with exclusive devotion, meditating on my transcendental form – to them I carry what they lack, and I preserve what they have. In fact, spiritually guided materialism needs to be understood and propagated and calls for moving from wants-based economy to needs-based economy. Spirituality is essential for the removal of stress and strain as well as the social and economic health of the society for all times to come.

Thus, I would like to emphasize that gender sensitisation can be taken care appropriately only through feminisation of marketing manpower through SHE model. Marketing can be customer friendly and socially beneficial only if undertaken in accordance with NAW approach. Here, NAW stands for Need, Affordability and Worth of the good and service. The pertinent questions before the customer are:

Does s(he) need the good or service, which has been so glamorously advertised?
Is the good or service *Affordable*?
Is the good or service *worth* its price?

I would like to take this opportunity to point out that a marketer would be popular only if it satisfy the essential need of the customer, is utilitarian. Glamour alone cannot be a substitute for the basic requirement of Need, Affordability and Worth (NAW) of the good or service.

To develop a positive attitude in the marketing team, the moral values are the essential requirement and we have to adopt and accept the normative approach to HRD in marketing manpower. It is essential to understand SIMPLE model of HRD consisting of six human development activities such as Spiritual Quotient (SQ) development, Intuition development, Mental level development, Love yourself attitude development and Emotional Quotient (EQ) development. The synergy of these six aspects of HRD is essential requirement of the desirable professionals for the Indian economy to emerge and realize its full potential.

Now, we venture to discuss the components of our model in reverse order one by one.

1. Emotional Quotient Development

Everyone wants success in life. What determines success then. A recent spate of management thoughts and practices champion the cause of EQ (Emotional Quotient) as that arm, which when added to IQ, define success. How simple is it to test, measure and take steps to increase your IQ. But we usually run into difficulties even in defining EQ, let alone getting to the bottom of it. A variety of words and phrases have been used to define the factors which govern EQ. 'The ability to get along with people and situations. A positive and pro-active attitude towards all aspects of life. The ability to command respect by building relationships.'

EQ focuses on the softer skills of building and maintaining human relationships. This aspect of life assumes a lot of importance since nowhere is a person detached from the human element. Be it the work place; the home front or the social circle, human interactions are inevitable and our success depends to a large extent on what we make of these interactions and relationships. For this shloka number 15 of ch. 17 of Bhagwad Gita quoted earlier needs to be adopted. Persons with high EQ can be great leaders; get promoted and thrive during uncertainty and change.

There are four cornerstones for emotional intelligence. Executing EQ begins with 'emotional literacy' as the first cornerstone which develops self-confidence through emotional honesty, energy, emotional feedback, initiations responsibility and connection. The second cornerstone is of 'emotional fitness' which strengthen our authenticity, believability and resilience. The third cornerstone of 'emotional depth' explores way to align our life and work with unique potential and purpose. The fourth cornerstone advances to 'emotional alchemy' through which we extend our creative instinct and capacity to resolve problems constructively.

There are three major components to improve EQ such as motivating oneself, motivating others and empathising with others; which clearly prescribe the functional areas which determine the EQ of a person. All these three components of EQ are related to the teachings of Bhagavad Gita to a greater extent. We can motivate ourselves by understanding, analysing and adopting the teachings of Bhagavad Gita in our life. We can motivate others by directing them to understand analyse and adopt Bhagavad Gita in their life. The increasing acceptance of EQ as an important contributor to SHD helps in taking momentous decision, or even decisions which are not repetitive in nature. EQ takes the participants through the process of improving their positions in life to achieve a win-win situation.

2. Love Yourself Attitude Development

In Brihdaranyak Upnishad, Yagnavalka says to his wife Maitri that "Husband loves his wife not for wife's sake but for the sake of the self and a wife loves her husband not for husband's sake but for own sake; mother loves her child not for child's sake but for own sake and a child loves his mother not for mother's sake but for own sake." It means all the activities which we are doing in our ordinary business of life are guided by self-interest, i.e. love for our ownself. It is a love of ownself that urges to take those activities where we get pleasure and discard all those activities where pain is there. So everywhere self interest or love for ownself is the guiding force.

According to Swami Ram Tirth, there are two types of selves – Little self, i.e. our body which is composed of all sense organs and the purest self, i.e. our soul.

Now in the first chapter of Bhagavad Gita when Arjuna throws away his Gandiv and wants to run away from his Dharma that is he is not ready to light for the sake of truth by arguing that there is no use of killing our own relatives, friends, gurus even for the kingdom of three lokas. Now this is the little self which is speaking in Arjuna. He is in the grip of Moha. He does not realise that his foes want dominion. This type of Moha distracts one from one's dharma (duty) and have been oppressors and have heaped inequities on the just and the innocent. Arjuna justifies his dereliction of duty with fancy rationalizations.

Bhagavad Gita teaches us self love of the highest order. So, a person is to develop himself so that he can shun love for little self and act according to the dictates of the purest self, i.e. soul. So it is the realisation of the purest self when a person loves his soul then his actions and he becomes a useful member of the society. Then he has no desire and no object to gratify himself. His karmas are automatic as the sun shines. As sun gives light to everybody irrespective of caste, creed and religion; in the same way, he works for the welfare of everybody and he observes the same purest self. In brief, a journey from little self to purest self constitutes SHD.

3. Physical Development

An old and wise saying—'A sound mind lives in a sound body' makes the justification for physical development. Having a sound body is very essential for the proper development of one's life. If our body is not working properly it is diseased. We cannot perform our duty well and will be inefficient in our work, the growth and development of one's life depends upon the development of physical powers. Physical development contributes a lot in human life and hence necessary for SHD. Physical development is possible by understanding, analysing and adopting Bhagavad Gita in our life.

For the proper maintenance, growth and development of the body, first of all, we must have knowledge about constituents of the body. In sloka 4 of 7 of B.G., Lord Krishna clearly explains the constituents of body—

> *bhumir apo nab vayuh*
> *kham mano budhir eva ca*
> *Ahankara itlyam me*
> *bhinna prakrtir astadha*
> (Earth, water, fire, air, mind,
> intelligence and ego;
> these constitute My nature eight-fold divided.)

The body which is transient changing consists of live elements fire, water, air and earth; within which live sense objects are included. They are manifestations of the physical sound, touch, form, taste and smell. If these senses are active and competent, then we will have a sound body. Air must be devoid of pollution and it is possible through yagnas as prescribed in Bhagavad Gita. Some of the bodily diseases are due to polluted water. Rainy water is considered pure containing many useful elements for the bodily development. In the past, we used to perform yagnas for am which is also the basis of our agricultural development.

To have a healthy body, we must know, what are its needs? It needs proteins, vitamins, carbohydrates, minerals and fats for its proper growth and development. It needs a balanced diet. Balanced diet is one that contains all these elements in the right proportion required for proper growth of the body. This balanced diet provides energy to our body which in turn provides us the power for our routine work. The purpose of food is to increase the duration of life purify the mind and aid bodily strength. In the past, great authorities selected those foods that best aid to health and increase life's duration; such as milk products, ghee, wheat, fruits and vegetables. In Bhagavad Gita (17: 8, 9, 10), food which is agreeable to different men according to their innate nature is of three kinds.

ayuh-saytva-balarogya
suk-priti-vivardhanah
rasyah snigdhah sthira hrdya
aharah sattvika priyah
(Foods which promotes life's duration, intelligence, vigour, health, happiness and cheerfulness are dear to 'Sattavika' type of man, such food are juicy, fatty, wholesome and pleasing to the heart.)

Katv-amla-lavanaty-usna
tiksna-Rusuksa-vidahinah
ahara rajasasyesta
duhkh-sokamaya pradah
(Foods which are bitter acid, salty, over hot, pungent, dry and burning and which cause suffering, grief and sickness are dear to the 'Rajasika' type of man.)

Yata-yamam gata rasam
puti paryusitam ca yat
ucchistam api camedhyam
bhojanam tamasa-priyam
(Food which is half cooled or half ripe, insipid, putted, polluted and stale is dear to a men of tamasika disposition).

As already stated that our body needs such a balanced diet which contains all the essential components required for bodily growth. So a diet must contain all these; such as cow milk and ghee. The cow milk contains protein (3.4 per cent), lactose (4.1 per cent), solids (13.7 per cent), fats (4.9 per cent), solids without fats (8.8 per cent), minerals (10.7 per cent).

That is why cow milk has been prescribed by Krishna in Gita as a food which promotes intelligence, vigour and bodily strength. On the other hand, the third type of food liked by tamasika has adverse effect on our body. It increases infection and diseases. Such food stuffs although very palatable to the persons but the conclusion of a systematic medical study shows that it is not and essential diet for human and is unsuitable diet. It actually has harmful effects on various parts of the body.

Lastly, regulation of diet and sleeping is recommended for healthy body. Too much eating and sleeping, both injurious for health. In B.G. (6.16) it has been clearly explained that—

> *Naty-asnatas tu-yogo' sti*
> *na caikantam anasata*
> *na cati svapna-silasya*
> *jagrato naiva cariuna*
> (There is no possibility of one's becoming yogi, if one eats too much or eats too little, sleeps too much or does not sleep enough.)

Extravagance in the matter of eating, sleeping, defending and mating, which are the demands of the body, can block advancement of physical development. We should be regulated in our eating, sleeping, mating and all other bodily activities for proper growth and development.

4. Mental Level Development

Without the mind's help, nothing can succeed. So in the process of development, the cooperation of mind is essential as a means of growth, external actions and inward attitude of mind, both are needed. Action is must if you want to test your mind. External actions reveal the quality of mind. The surface of the water is clear, but throw a stone into it and at once and rises up. Our mind is just like that.

Now the question arises – what makes our mind polluted? When we do any work, we are guided by our senses, which in turn are guided by our mind and mind ultimately is guided by our discriminating intelligence (*Vivek*). If our mind has a mixture of lust, *krodha* and illusion, it will not guide us in proper direction so these three can be treated as obstacles in the way of mental development.

The most important thing what should cultivate in his life is the need purify the mind. We have to cleanse mind of its dirt. To light a lamp, one needs not only the oil and wick, but a flame. When the lamp is lit, the dark disappears. Purity of mind is that which will dispel darkness in our life. To attain purity of mind, many prescribed. Firstly, there is *'yagna,'* and *'dana'* (sacrifice and gifts), *Jap* (prayer and penance), *dhyan* and (meditating and concentration). These means can be compared with washing soda and soap. But *Bhakti* is water. Without water, these other things are useless, but even without these, water can cleanse. If in *yagna, yoga, dhyan* and *tap*, the heart does not enter, how can purity of mind result? It is the involvement of heart that is *Bhakti*. *Bhakti* is essential for all kinds of efforts. If a trained nurse, attending on a patient, has not the *Bhavna*, the mental attitude of service, how could it be true service. In work without heart, there is neither strength nor satisfaction. Secondly, the things we practise day and night stick to us. We will have to train the mind right from childhood. Take constant care that food impressions alone come to the mind. By letting the mind go as it pleases, we will defeat ourselves. Then we will never acquire good impressions. Similarly wisdom should be gathered without wasting even a single moment. Noble thoughts should pass through our mind so that good impressions should be created. These should go on constantly. Thirdly, purity of mind can be attained by assuming erect posture. All our activities should be pure. To purify activities, its motive should be transformed. Activities should not be performed for one's individual profit, for satisfying the instinct for outward object but for the whole world. In B.G. (17: 16),

> *"Manah prasaduh saumyatvam mounam atmavinigraha*
> *bhva samsudir ity etat tapo manasam uceyate."*

Meaning thereby a calm and contented mental clarity, kindness silence, self-control and purity of character constitute the austerity of the mind.

5. Intuition for Intelligence Development

As students, how often have we heard the dismissive statement, "if you do not do well in class, you can never be successful." And while in job, how many times we have been told, "your success is not related to your performance in class." It was a very surprising statement by a senior official of the examination board which went on to say the same thing in the light of the recent furore over the Mathematics paper in an examination. Taken together, the two statements send very contradictory messages to those who are striving for success.

What determines success then; if it is not Intelligence Quotient (IQ)? By stating otherwise, are we not shifting from an old age paradigm which has permeated the very consciousness of every parent, child and educationist? A recent spate of management thoughts and practices champion the cause of EQ (Emotional Quotient) as that warm which when added to IQ define success.

Where sailing in the life-boat, we have to face many hurdles and obstacles. For 3 successful journeys, one must be aware of all hurdles and obstacles that come in the way of journey of life. Now even to have a very correct and precise picture of all these obstacles, intelligence is required. Intelligence refers to the power to analyse things in their proper perspective. The individual is the passenger in the car of the material body, and intelligence is the driver. Mind is the driving instrument and senses are the horses. The self is thus the enjoyer or sufferer in the association of the mind and senses. Intelligence is supposed to direct the mind, but the mind is so strong and obstinate that it often overcomes the intelligence sometimes, although the mind is supposed to be subservient to the intelligence. The ability not to read many looks on different subjects but understand them and apply them when necessary is intelligence.

It is *krodha* that hinders in the way of intelligence development. In (B.G. 2.63) –

Krodhad bhavati sammohah
sammohat smrti vibhramah
smrti bhramsad buddhi-naso
buddhi-nasat pranasyati

(From anger, complete delusions arises, delusion bewilderment of memory). When memory is bewildered, intelligence is lost and when intelligence is lost one falls down again into the material pool.

So, to attain sustainable development, it is very important for us to develop intelligence to understand and accept situations, people and the changes happening around us through intuition which is possible only by undertaking *bhakti*.

6. Spiritual Quotient (SQ) Development

Spiritual development is essential for the removal of stress and strain as well as social and economic health of the society. Spiritual development must be performed in order to convert human beings into human capital. Besides the development of senses and mind, there is one thing more which is most important that is spirit, soul or *atma*. We are to realise that which is the spiritual path.

The figure which we see with our eyes, we call it body or image. But even after seeing with our eyes the outer form, we still have to enter into the object and see it from with in. We have to remove the armour, the skin of the fruit and the pulp with in. Despite the rough sharp exterior of the coconut, the fruit is full of sweet juicy pulp. When look at ourselves or others, we have to distinguish the inside from outside, soul can be compared to a driver and body to a vehicle. It is the spark of life that makes the body appear. The Soul pervades the body with consciousness as a lamp fills a room with light. The lamp that gives light to the entire room may be in one corner of the room. Similarly the soul is situated in the region of our heart. The soul is not removed during heart transplantation as soul is spiritual. For example when stepney or radiator of a car is changed, nothing happens to the driver. B.G. (2: 23) Krishna tells—

nainam chindanti sastrani
nainam dahati pavakah
a chinam kledayanty opo
a sosavati marutah
(The soul can never be cut to pieces by any weapon, not burned by fire, not moistened by water, nor withered by the wind.)

Now Lord Krishna says that we are to realise our soul; once a person realises his/her soul, then his/her outlook becomes quite different from that of the worldly people and s(he) becomes the source of inspiration to all. It is the ideal state of spiritual development. So, long we do not realise the soul, we remain absorbed in ordinary activities. We know nothing beyond eating, drinking, sleeping and mating. For these, we fight, in this way, we are involved in activities relating to the body. Progress begins only later. All this time. Soul remains merely watching like a mother watching her child crawling near the well. With some care, the soul watches us. One day the soul wakes up and knowledge dawn upon it that it has been living like an animal. When the soul begins to think like this, the foundations of ethics are laid. It starts exercising the power of discrimination. Discipline takes the place of self-elegance. When the soul thus enters the domains of ethics, the soul does not merely stand aside and watch. Then it expresses approval from within saying—'well done.' In the next stage, a man through doing his duty tries to cleanse his mind and heart. When he feels tired, then the soul begins to pray—'I have come to the end of my efforts. Give me more strength.' Until a man realises that he cannot achieve success by his own efforts, however hard, he can not understand the secret of prayer. Then a man 5 own efforts to do a work prove inadequate, he should call on the supreme with a sad and yearning heart as Draupadi did. The stream of Lord's compassion and succour flows continuously. This is the third stage: The supreme now comes very close. He comes running now to help you.

Thus progressively, we should learn to experience the Lord; the Lord comes towards us for our help. After this, we have to give over to the Lord the fruit of action, and make Him the enjoyer. And in the end, we should surrender to him the right to resolve and thus fill all our life with him. This must be the ultimate goal of a person and it is the ideal stage of spiritual development. In true sense, HRD is possible through self-realization and spiritual development.

In brief, I wish to emphasise that for every ill in marketing in 21st century there are vedic pills and Bhagwad Gita is the panacea. To create work culture among marketers, there is need of converting holiday culture in to holyday culture. It is firmly believed by the author that the rate of progress in spiritualism is faster than the rate of progress in materialism, therefore, there is need of accepting spiritually guided materialism making a case for 'needonomics' and not 'greedonomics' as a solution of various problems in an era of continuous change. There is no doubt that India can provide leadership to the world on its spiritual strength only and not on the basis of any thing else. To make it happen we should adopt an evolutionary approach and should not expect miracles. Truly, Bhagvad Gita is a treatise on welfare economics and needs to be accepted as a sacro-secular epic for the entire humanity including the marketers—the most crucial manpower of marketing to face the challenges of an era of continuous change.

References

A.C. Bhaktivedanta Swami Prabhupada, *Bhagvad Gita—As It Is*, The Bhaktivedanta Book Trust, Bombay, 1983.

M.M. Goel, 'Feminisation of Media and Advertising,' *Media Newsense*, September, 2000.

M.M. Goel, *Implications of Bhagvad Gita for Sustainable Human Development*, Smarika by Gita Kendra, Kurukshetra Development Board, 1999.

M.M. Goel, 'Lessons from Bhagvad Gita for Banking Industry,' *Economic Dateline*, Volume II, No. 1, January, 2002.

16

International Impact of Celebrity Endorsement of Transfer Pricing

R. VARADARAJAN

INTRODUCTION

Transfer pricing and international taxation are two highly inter-related issues. Both will clearly affect multinational corporations management decisions regarding the size, type, location and degree of autonomy of operations in other countries. Transfer pricing decisions are heavily influenced by different taxation system and tax rates in the countries of operations. Pricing of goods and services transferred across national boundaries could be used to shift corporate income to low income-tax rate. Hence, tax authorities and government agencies the most countries pay close attention to transfer pricing practices, to ensure that these practices are not used for tax avoidance.

PURPOSE AND SCOPE OF STUDY

Transfer pricing has captured the attention of taxing authorities worldwide. New rules, documentation requirements, and tax penalties have been promulgated to compel rigorous enforcement, as well as to support and enhance the audit function. The amounts recently placed in controversy by these taxing authorities have been raised to all-time high proportions. The impact of these issues on a multinational company's financial statements, tax planning, and arrangement compensation programs has been dramatic. The drain of a company's internal resources to resolve transfer-pricing disputes can be of equal concern.

Transfer pricing affects the entire supply chain: from research and development, to manufacturing, marketing, distribution and after-sales service. All over the world, enterprises are redesigning functions, implementing new structures and re-engineering flows of goods and services to reduce costs and improve business process. Thinking about tax issues up-front can lead to optimal supply chain structure. To address these issues that arise from supply chain re-configuration, it is necessary that direction towards transfer pricing, direct and indirect tax, customs, accounting and law is essential. In view of various issues globally the study is highly purposeful and scope is also very wide with futuristic approach.

CONCEPTUAL FRAMEWORK

The transfer price is the mechanism for distributing the revenue. The transfer price is not primarily an accounting tool; rather, it is a behavioural tool that motivates managers to make the right decisions. In particular, the transfer price should be designed so that it accomplishment the following objectives:

- It should provide each segment with the relevant information required to determine the optimum trade-off between company costs and revenues.
- It should induce goal congruent decisions—that is, the system should be so designed that decisions to improve business unit profits will also improve company profits;
- It should help measure the economic performance of the individual profit; and
- The system should be simple to understand and easy to administer.

OBJECT OF TRANSFER PRICING REGULATIONS

Having adopted Article VII of the GATT, the Customs Co-operative Council, Brussels (now World Customs Organization—WCO) in the year 1949 brought out the Brussels Definition of Value or BDV for short, which was signed in December, 1950 and came into force during July, 1953. It is now agreed that an equitable standard should be adopted discounting influence thereon of special relationship existing between the negotiated parties, so that discrimination between various importers is avoided. It is therefore the current international practice to make "transaction value" the basis of customs valuation and the ascertainment of such value takes note of relationship between parties to the transaction in international trade, if such relationship taints the price and hampers the principle of "arms-length transactions."

OBJECTIVES OF THE STUDY

The main objectives of the study are:

- To examine the transfer pricing systems globally with taxation concepts.
- To find out the Indian scenario from the point of erosion of tax revenues and low tax locations.
- To find out the controlling techniques of revenue leakages and documentation system in India.
- To set parameters in between transactions for inter-company operations.

The Organization for Economic Co-operation and Development (OECD) has defined transfer prices to mean prices at which multinational enterprises transfer physical goods and intangible property or provide services to the associated enterprises. The methods and principles set forth in the OECD Report on Transfer Pricing and Multinational Enterprises generally from the basis for detailed regulations issued by various countries.

Virtually, all countries have adopted the arm's length standard for determination of transfer pricing. An arm's length standard requires an arm's length pricing on transactions.

STATEMENTS OF THE PROBLEM

Transfer Pricing has become the most contentious area of the international taxation. Due to variance in tax rates in various jurisdictions, shining profits to low tax locations benefits, corporations that operate in more than one tax jurisdiction. Tax administrators in various countries have recognized this revenue leakage and have established "Transfer Pricing Regulations" to curb it. These regulations set the parameters for determining the optimum transfer price for transactions between group companies (or related parties). Transactions between group companies or related parties are called, inter-company transactions.

Since transfer pricing is quickly developing into one of the most important and complex issues facing modern business today, a proper understanding of the concept is required by one and all. A proper transfer pricing policy will enhance operations performance, minimize the overall tax burden and reduce legal exposures. It is thus, an essential part of business planning and strategy.

REVIEW OF LITERATURE

In the 60's, mathematical programming techniques were used to solve the problem for the case of multiple selling and buying divisions, multiple products (see, for example, Hass (1968) and for situations where there are selling expenses for the intermediate goods [see, for example, Arrow (1959), Gould (1964)]. An exhaustive review of these methods can be found in Abdul-Khalik and Lusk (1974). For an extensive review of the TP problem, see Grabski (1985), who reviewed 81 papers from 1974 to 1983. Kanodia (1979) considered the same model as Hirshleifer, but he included uncertainty about the market price. He introduced a transfer pricing scheme that shares the risk between the selling and the buying divisions by randomizing the transfer prices. Furthermore, Kanodia's scheme maximizes the expected firm's profit

The literature from the 70's presents three main approaches to the TP problem: the strategic approach, the accounting approach and the behaviouristic approach.

The approach emerges when there is asymmetry of information. Equating marginal cost with marginal gross profit is impossible when central management does not know the exact cost functions of the divisions. Division managers are likely to have the information (or at least partial information) about these costs, but they do not always have an incentive to reveal it to central management. Central management seeks to interact with division managers to achieve an optimal outcome. The revelation principle (Gibbard, 1973) asserts that it is sufficient for the interaction to employ "simple" mechanisms that are direct and incentive compatible. A direct mechanism is one in which every division manager reports his type (i.e., his private information). Central management then dictates an outcome and every division manager is compensated an amount (positive or negative) that depends on the reports of all the division managers. The mechanism is incentive compatible if reporting of true information by every division manager generates a Nash equilibrium. Ronen and McKinney (1970) suggest that every division manager be compensated an amount that depends on the reports of the other managers only. The division managers (and not central management) determine their production levels. Central management chooses the compensation levels so as to induce the division managers to truthfully reveal their private information. This method achieves an optimal outcome in one Nash equilibrium, but the other equilibrium outcomes may not be optimal. Another difficulty is that the mechanism is not balanced. That is, the divisions' profits may not add up to the firm's profit.

Ronen (1992) has shown that in a model of incomplete information about the divisions' cost functions, the probability that the division managers will agree on an ex-post no optimal quantity, is relatively small. A stronger concept was introduced by Groves (1976) and Groves and Loeb (1979). The difference between th Ronen-McKinney mechanism and the Groves-Loeb mechanism is discussed in Groves and Loeb (1976), who suggested a solution that achieves optimal outcome not only via Nash equilibrium but also via dominant strategies. However, like the Ronen-McKinney mechanism it is not balanced. In the Groves-Loeb mechanism, central management dictates both the compensation level and the production quantity of every division manager, whereas in the Ronen-McKinney mechanism, production levels are determined by the division managers. Green and Laffont (1977) showed that, in general, there is no balanced mechanism that generates efficient outcomes and that is incentive compatible via dominant strategy. Harris, Kriebel and Raviv (1982) dealt with the problem of resource allocation (which is a problem similar to the TP problem), where in addition to the asymmetry of information, there are moral hazard problems. The goal is to minimize production cost. They consider one division supplying resources to n divisions, each producing a different product. The production function of each division is a linear function of both the manager's effort (which is unobservable by the planner) and of the resources that they received from the supplying division.

Furthermore, the production function depends on a specific productivity parameter which is the private information of the division manager. The utility or a division manager is his salary net of his effort cost. The mechanism of Harris, Kriebel and Raviv induces truth telling by the division managers and minimizes the production cost for each level of output. Production cost is the sum of the costs of the resources and the compensation of the division managers. This mechanism induces the managers to exert effort, which is optimal for the firm. Ronen and Balachandran (1988) assumed utility functions with risk aversion, uncertainty about the production cost and moral hazard. In their model there are two divisions and the planner is the buying division, which delegates the production decision to the selling division manager, the reason being that communication of private information from the selling to the buying division is "blocked" (that is; it is too costly). Their mechanism achieves an optimal solution.

Darrough and Stoughton (1989) study the TP problem in a two-firm model. The two firms cooperate to produce a final product, acting as a monopoly in the market for the final good. Furthermore, the production cost of each firm is linear and each firm knows only its own parameter in this cost function. The authors introduce a revelation mechanism which guarantees an ex-ante second-best optimal solution. This outcome is the same as the one that Myerson (1982) obtained in his bargaining model with asymmetric information. Amershi and Cheng (1990) considered a situation where every division has private information about its cost function, which is not necessarily linear. Furthermore, the buying division has an effort parameter which is a decision variable of its manager. In this environment, Amershi and Cheng found a mechanism that is incentive compatible via dominant strategies, efficient and balanced too (notice that there is no contradiction between their mechanism and the Green-Laffont theorem since they deal with a restricted environment). Besanko and Sibley (1991) studied the problem where the planner is the buying division and dictates the mechanism to be used. In this model, the production function of the selling division is quite general and it includes one unknown parameter, which is the private information of the selling division. In addition, the model considers a moral hazard aspect. Here too a revelation mechanism is introduced that is optimal for the buying division but is not optimal for the firm.

Brown and Weida (1991) suggested a new approach to the TP problem whereby central management decides which division (buying or selling) will be the planner. It takes the decision of who is to be the leader after comparing the expected profit obtained when the buying division is the leader to that when the selling division is the leader. The practical motivation for this approach is that central management, being well aware of the inferiority of its information, prefers to leave all the decisions to the divisions themselves through negotiation. (A few industrial surveys support this motivation. For example, see Frederick and Douglas (1979)). This mechanism is balanced, but it is not necessarily optimal for the firm.

Banker and Datar (1992) extended Harris, Kriebel and Raviv's model to a situation where the division managers are allowed to cooperate in a way that enables them to increase their profits at the expense of that of the firm. Their goal was to find a mechanism that prevents such collusion. The mechanism they found also yields an optimal solution but is not balanced. Vaysman (1992) suggests a cost-plus mechanism in a model of asymmetry of information with limited communication between the division managers and the planner. The managers in this model cannot report their private information precisely. Vaysman found that a cost-based transfer pricing mechanism where the division managers taking the operating decisions strictly dominates a centralized mechanism where the planner makes the operating decision.

In the last 15 years, a vast number of papers have been published on the TP problem in multinational organizations, Stoughton and Talmor (1989), Prusa (1990), Donnenfeld and Prusa (1992) among others. These authors use similar methods to those mentioned above, though, the multinational TP is much more complex because of legal and tax considerations.

BROAD OVERVIEW—GLOBAL PERSPECTIVE

A large share of world trade consists of transfers of goods, intangibles and services within Multinational Enterprises (MNCs). Determination of the right price (the arm's length price) for the aforesaid transactions is of extreme importance in order to arrive at the correct tax liability in each jurisdiction.

Extensive guidelines have been issued by the Organization for Economic Co-operation and Development (OECD) for determination of the arm's length price in order to avoid economic double taxation and the consequent impediment to world trade. To ensure that the tax base of a MNC is divided fairly, it is important that transfers within a group should approximate those, which would be negotiated between independent firms.

It is important to note that in a sense Transfer Pricing is directly related to the concept of Permanent Establishment (PE). An organization operating in a foreign country through a PE is taxable on the profits attributable to the PE. Transfer pricing helps compute profits of the PE.

Transfer pricing is a key international tax issue for MNCs, recognizing that there is a clear connection between double taxation and transfer pricing.

TRANSFER PRICING IN INDIA—BACKGROUND

With the increased globalization of the Indian economy, the question of transfer pricing has been increasingly haunting tax authorities in India. Following upon report submitted by Committee under the Chairmanship of Mr. Raj Narian, the Union Budget 2001-02 proposes to incorporate far reaching amendments to the Income-tax Act, 1961 ('the IT Act') in this regard.

The provisions are intended to deal with computation of income arising from international transactions between associated enterprises. These provisions are a very important step taken by the country in the field of anti-avoidance. Further, the term "Associated Enterprises" has been defined widely enough to rope within its ambit organisations which have associations of any type. The terms "transactions" and "international transactions" have also been defined very widely to include virtually dealings of every type. Given this, the proposed regulations are likely to be of significant concern to almost every Multinational Organisations operating in India or having dealings with Indian concerns.

PROPOSED REGULATIONS

The existing Section 92 is sought to be deleted and substituted by Sections 92 to 92F to provide for a framework to regulate transfer pricing.

Section 92 now seeks to provide that income arising from international transactions (between associated enterprises) would be computed having regard to the arm's length price. As such, Section 92 would now act virtually as a computation Section.

It is further provided that the allowance for any expenses or interest in respect of such a transaction would also be determined having regard to arm's length price. This provision is a potential landmine because the deductibility for expenses or interest on an arm's length price, is not prefixed by a condition that the transaction should be an international transaction. To put it differently, if there is an international transaction which gives rise to income to a resident, then the corresponding transaction for expenditure incurred by the resident in relation to such a transaction is potentially subject to an arm's length price determination even if it is between non-associated domestic parties. This appears to be clearly unintended. It is hoped that this anomaly will be set right before the Bill is converted into an Act.

TRANSFER PRICING PROVISIONS

The existing provisions of Section 92 has been proposed to be substituted to provide that any income arising from an international transaction shall be computed having regard to the arm's length price. The Section further provides that the costs or expenses allocated or apportioned between two or more associated enterprises shall be at arm's length prices. Sections 92A to 92F are being introduced to provide the necessary framework to regulate the above. The proposed new Sections 92A and 92B provide meanings of the expressions "associated enterprises" and international transaction with reference to which the income is to be computed under the new Section 92.

Enterprise

Section 92F has widely defined the term "enterprise" to mean a person who is engaged or proposes to engage whether directly or indirectly in India or abroad in any activity relating to production, storage, supply distribution, acquisition or control of articles or know-how, patents copyrights, trade-marks, licenses, franchises or any other business or commercial right, provision of services and investment activities. Arm's length price has been defined to mean a price which is applied/to be applied in a transaction between persons other than associated enterprises in uncontrolled conditions.

Methodologies

Section 92C also gives various methodologies in arriving at the arm's length pricing relation to an international transaction. It specifies that having regard to the nature or class of transaction or class of associated persons or functions performed which the CBDT may prescribe, the most appropriate method needs to be applied, namely:

(a) Comparable uncontrolled price method.
(b) Resale price method.
(c) Cost plus method.
(d) Profit split method.
(e) Transactional net margin method.
(f) Such other methods as may be prescribed.

Documentation to be delivered automatically at the outset of every audit (and) Documentation to be prepared in advance and held in readiness for examination by the tax authorities.

Some of the general documentation which are called for by the tax authorities after presentation of a transfer pricing package are as detailed below:

(a) Information on economy data.
(b) Contract and supply agreement copies.
(c) Guarantee, warranty, surety and support agreement copies.
(d) Market studies information on comparable uncontrolled companies.
(e) Product/project forecasts.
(f) Product advertisement materials/brochures.
(g) Custom audit reports.
(h) Bank credit documents.
(i) Product liability insurance documents.
(j) Customs information.
(k) Budget planning memoranda.
(l) Cost sharing arrangements and agreements.
(m) Price lists and invoices.
(n) Group accounting guidelines.
(o) Internal analysis report on deviation from budget/forecasts.

In general a transfer pricing audit requires documentation and supporting evidence to convince the tax authorities that the transaction has been arrived out on an arm's length pricing.

RESEARCH METHODOLOGY

The information for the purpose of present study has been obtained by interviewing the tax authorities, tax consultant, auditors and corporate clients. Through structured and unstructured questionnaire. The observation method has also been used wherever conditions were favourable for the same. All the respondents were forthcoming in their response to the various aspects.

FINDINGS

- "Too little too late" leads to missed opportunity and increased risk.
- MNCs require global documentation solutions.
- Still international tax issue facing MNCs for the foreseeable future.
- TP is closely linked with economic double taxation about 40 per cent of adjustments result in economic double taxation.
- Only 25 per cent consider TP on a "real time" basis.
- For 35 per cent is mainly a compliance issue.
- Long way to go in understanding and adopting this approach.
- Some MNCs still feel the threat of least safety.
- Integrated Global Documentation solutions are not in finalized.
- Despite the recognition by the tax departments for the benefits of integrated global documentation, most of them are yet to perform.
- Documentation is being required by tax authorities in more than 7 out of 10 examinations.
- Most of the MNCs prepared documentation on a country-by-country basis with limited coordination resulting in increased world-wide tax border.
- Confusion remain as to which method to use, even though higher degree of sophistication is available.
- Most of the companies face almost 2/3 chance of having a TP audit.
- Many MNCs recognize that TP is not just a tax issue.

CONCLUSION

In conclusion, the following issues need to be borne in mind while administrating the Transfer Pricing. Unlike the western world transfer pricing in India is a completely new subject which takes into account more economic factors than tax law and the Indian tax administrators may not geared to administer the same, unless a specific cell is created of trained officers. We are yet in the very early stages of computerization and these voluminous data cannot be handled manually and the need to move over quickly to an electronic audit. The tax administrators should need to implement the provisions with impartiality as this may have serious repercussions for India both on the FDI front and also on the image front.

In short, their need to be a proper check and balance approach on administration of this law and the greatest challenge is not introduction of the law but on how the same is implemented! The fact that Indian law has not introduced Advance Pricing Agreements in line with international practice could be a serious impediment from a MNCs perspective and the Government may have to rethink on this.

References

Accounting Standard Board, Institute of Chartered Accountants of India, *Accounting Standard*, August 14, 2000.

CBDT, Mr. Raj Narian Committee, 2001-02.

Companies Act, 1956 (Amended—2000).

F.D.S. Choi, C.A. Frost and G.K. Meek (1999): *International Accounting*, Prentice-Hall International Inc.

GATT Agreement, 2000.

Income Tax Act (1961) (Amended—2002).

J. Kelly and R. Lapper (1995): "Plan for Global Accounting Standards," *Financial Times*, July 12.

Union Budget, India, 2001-02.

17

CSR for SMEs: An Awareness Campaign

K. KOTESWARA RAO

Solid evidence that social and environmental responsibility supports competitiveness and sustainable development, in particular in SMEs, would be the best and most effective argument to encourage the uptake of CSR among enterprises.

Commission of the European Communities
(Com. 2002) (CSR)

INTRODUCTION

Today there is a growing perception among enterprises that sustainable business success and shareholder value can not be achieved solely maximising short-term profits but instead through market-oriented yet responsible behaviour. Companies are aware that they contribute to sustainable development is managing their operations in such as way as to enhance economic growth and increase competitiveness whilst ensuring environmental protection and promoting social responsibility, including consumer interest.

The corporate social responsibility (CSR) has found recognition among enterprises, policy-makers and other stakeholders as an important element of new and emerging forms of governance which can help them to respond to all types of global changes.

CSR: THE CONCEPT

CSR is a concept where by companies integrate social and environmental concerns in their business operations and in their interaction with their stakeholders on a voluntary basis.
The commonly agreed features of CSR are:

- CSR is behaviour by businesses over and above legal requirements, voluntarily adopted because business is to be in their long-term interest.
- CSR is intrinsically linked to the concept of sustainable development, i.e. businesses need to integrate the economic, social and environmental impact in their operations.
- CSR is not an optional 'add-on' to business core activities – but about the way in which businesses are managed.

The main function of an enterprise is to create value through producing goods and services that society demands, thereby generating profit for its owners and shareholders as well as welfare for society, particularly through an ongoing process of job creation. However, new social and market pressures are gradually leading to a change in the values and in the horizon of business activity.

CSR is not uniform to all the organisations in all times and at all places. CSR depends on the particular situation of individual enterprises and on the specific context in which they operate, be it India or elsewhere.

THE GLOBAL DIMENSION OF CSR

The global responses to the nature of CSR issues and concerns, reflecting the fact that a growing number of enterprises, including SMES, are developing their business worldwide, as they take advantage of market liberalization and trade intergradations and are sourcing from subsidiaries and suppliers in developing countries.

Global governance and the interrelation between trade, investment and sustainable development are key issues in the CSR debates, awareness of CSR issues and concerns will contribute to promote more sustainable investments, more effective development cooperation and technology transfers.

Both processes of trade and financial markets liberalisation should be matched by appropriate progress towards an effective system of global governance including its social and environmental dimensions.

Ultimately, the responses would reflect a broad consensus among businesses about the expectation that CSR will be of strategic importance to ensure the long-term business success.

CSR AND SOCIETY

The potential of CSR policies to strengthen the symbiotic relationship between enterprise and society has already been demonstrated in areas such as sustainable growth, education and social cohesion. CSR can support the creation of an atmosphere of trust within companies, which leads to a stronger commitment of employees and higher innovation performance. A similar atmosphere of trust in cooperation among other stakeholders (business partners, suppliers, and consumers) can increase the external innovation performance. Consumer confidence fostered through CSR can be a major contributor to economic growth. More specifically, through CSR practices, enterprises can play an important role in preventing and combating corruption and bribery, and in helping preventing the use of enterprise for money laundering and criminal activities financing.

CSR policies can also boost the societal benefit that enterprises create with regard to innovation. Innovative practices aiming at better jobs, safer and employee-friendly workplaces, gender mainstreaming and the innovation or technology transfer to local communities and developing countries, leading to a more equitable North-South economic and social development, are further examples of societal benefits created by innovative enterprises. Indeed, CSR may play a positive role in fostering development in third countries by helping to establish a dialogue between these countries, their public authorities, social partners and civil society and foreign companies.

The desire of enterprises to improve their risk management is a powerful factor behind CSR. Enterprises generally agree that CSR helps them in managing their risks, their intangible assets, their internal processes, and their relations with internal and external stakeholders. It has also been argued that opportunities and advantages for enterprises stemming from complying with international social and environmental conventions, norms or "soft law" instruments can outweigh costs. Although most business support the assumption of a positive impact of CSR on competitiveness, particularly in the long-term, they are however not able to quantify this effect.

CSR AND SMEs

The CSR is not confined to multinational companies. It has a better role for Small and Medium Enterprises (SMEs) the countries irrespective of their status.

The CSR concept was developed mainly by and for large multinational enterprises. In line with the Commission's "Think Small First" strategy, the CSR concept, practices and instruments should be adapted to suit the specific situation of SMEs which make up the vast majority of European enterprises. Because of their lower complexity and the strong role of the owner, SMEs often manage their societal impact in a more intuitive and informal way than large companies. In fact, many SMEs are already implementing socially and environmentally responsible practices without being familiar with the CSR concept or communicating their activities. These practices are often defined and understood as responsible entrepreneurship by SMEs.

Surveys on SMEs indicate that they already carry out socially and environmentally responsible activities for the benefit of their external stakeholders. Their community and social engagement could be characterized as being local in scope, occasional in nature, and unrelated to business strategy. The main driver would be the ethical consideration of the owner/manager, even though a significant number of SMEs also recognise business benefits such as improved relations with consumers and the local community. Furthermore, a positive correlation between SMEs strategic focus and their socially responsible activities can be established: SMEs focusing on innovation, quality and growth also score higher on current or future social engagement. Lack of awareness seems to be the most significant obstacle to social engagement, especially among the smallest SMEs, followed by resource constraints. Small business associations, support organisations and networks have an important role to play in raising awareness through the provision of information, user-friendly tools and the dissemination of good practices cases.

Since SMEs do not draw value from their engagement in the same way as a large company, it is important to assist SMEs in adopting a more strategic approach. Collecting evidence on the business case for different types of SMEs operating in diverse cultural backgrounds is key to a better understanding and increased SMEs to adopt CSR practices is likely to come from their large business customers, which in return could help SMEs cope with these challenges through the provision of training, monitoring schemes and other initiatives.

CSR: PRINCIPLES AND STRATEGIES FOR SMEs

As SMEs are more in number in any country, the CSR has a greater role. Hence, there is a need to evolve certain principles and strategies for the execution of CSR in SMEs. For this purpose, the European commissioner has come out with a number of principles and strategies in this regard.

The commission proposes to build its strategy to promote CSR on a number of principles. They are as follows:

- recognition of voluntary nature of CSR;
- need for credibility and transparency of CSR practices;
- focus on activities where community involvement adds value;
- balanced and all-encompassing approach to CSR, including economic, social and environmental issues as well as consumer interests;
- attention to the needs and characteristics of SMEs; and
- support and compatibility with existing international agreements and instruments (ILO core labour standards, OECD guidelines for multinational enterprises).

The Commission proposes to focus its strategy on the following areas:

1. Increasing knowledge about the positive impact of CSR on business and societies in Europe and abroad, in particular in developing countries;
2. Developing the exchange of experience and good practice on CSR between enterprises;
3. Promoting the development of CSR management skills;
4. Fostering CSR among SMEs;
5. Facilitating convergence and transparency of CSR practices and tools;
6. Launching a multi-stakeholder forum on CSR; and
7. Integrating CSR into community policies.

The commission is prepared to involve the candidate countries as much as possible in the implementation of this strategy. It will also promote CSR as an incentive to enhancing sustainable development and good governance in developing countries.

NEED FOR FURTHER AWARENESS

The challenges to a further awareness, dissemination and adoption of CSR practices among enterprise stem from insufficient:

- Knowledge about the relationship between CSR and business performance (the "business case");
- consensus between the various parties involved on an adequate concept taking account of the global dimension of CSR, in particular the diversity in domestic policy frameworks in the world.
- teaching and training about the role of CSR, especially in commercial and management schools;
- awareness and resources among SMEs;
- transparency, which stems from the lack of generally accepted instruments to design, manage and communicate CSR policies;
- consumers' and investors' recognition and endorsement of CSR behaviours; and
- coherence in public policies.

In order to meet the challenges, the SMEs have to develop suitable practices and tools. Further, they have to integrate the CSR in all their policies.

CSR PRACTICES AND TOOLS

CSR relates to a very wide range of company activities. This is particularly the case when an enterprise operates in several countries and has to adapt its activities to the specific situations in these countries. This diversity has helped to create an impressive richness of voluntary enterprise initiatives, which often include innovative elements, but also implies challenges, namely the lack of transparency and comparability.

Transparency is a key element of the CSR debate as it helps businesses to improve their practices and behaviour; transparency also enables businesses and third parties to measure the results achieved. CSR benchmarks against which the social and environmental performance of businesses can be measured and compared are useful to provide transparency and facilitate an effective and credible benchmarking, the interest in benchmarks has resulted in an increase of guidelines, principles and codes during the last decade. Not all of these tools are comparable in scope, intent, implementation or applicability to particular businesses, sectors or industries. They do not answer to the need for effective transparency about business social and environmental performance. As expectations for CSR become more defined, there is a need for a certain convergence of concepts, instruments, practices, which would increase transparency without stifling innovation, and would offer benefits to all parties. CSR benchmarks should build upon core values and take their starting point in internationally agreed instruments such as ILO core labour standards and OECD guidelines for multinational enterprises.

Several market-driven international multi-stakeholder initiatives are emerging, which work towards convergence and transparency in the area of CSR. Member-states have taken various initiatives to promote them, in accordance with their respective approaches to CSR. The commission wishes to do its part in facilitating convergence and transparency in the area of CSR, by facilitating the development, diffusion and acceptance of these international multi-stakeholder initiatives by enterprises and stakeholders.

Increased convergence and transparency would be desirable in the following fields:

1. Codes of Conduct.
2. Management standards.
3. Accounting, auditing and reporting.
4. Labels.
5. Socially responsible investment.

INTEGRATING CSR IN ALL POLICIES

SMEs have to commit themselves to integrate economic, social and environmental considerations as well as fundamental rights including core labour standards and gender equality into its policies and actions, with due respect to both their internal and external dimensions.

(a) Employment and Social Affairs Policy

Employment and social policy integrates the principles of CSR. Within a business CSR relates to equality employment, lifelong earning, information consultation and participation of workers, equal opportunities, integration of people with disabilities, anticipation of industrial change and restructuring. Social dialogue is seen as a powerful instrument to address employment-related issues.

(b) Enterprise Policy

The role of enterprise policy is to help to create a business environment, which supports in becoming the worlds most dynamic knowledge-driven economy, supports entrepreneurship and a sustainable economic growth. Its objective is to ensure a balance approach to sustainable development, which synergies between us economic, social and environmental dimensions.

(c) Environmental Policy

Environmental requirements have developed, over the last 25 years, to become of horizontal nature, applying to all community policies at the same time CSR includes sound and progressive environmental principles. Experience shows that undertakings, which follow sound environmental standards, are in medium and long-term, more competitive on the international market, as environmental standards promote innovation and modernization of processes and products and lead to cleaner technologies. Conversers it may also be that internationally competitive firms are better able to invest in newer, more efficient cleaner technologies.

(d) Consumer Policy

CSR has fully involved in response to consumer demands and expectations. Consumers, in their purchasing behaviour, increasingly require information and reassurance that their wider interests; such as environmental and social concerns, are being taken into account. Enterprises are increasingly sensitive to these demands both to retain existing customers and to attractive customers.

Customers and their representative organisations have therefore an important role to play in the evolution of CSR. If CSR is therefore to continue to serve its purpose strong lines of communication between enterprises and consumers need to be created.

(e) Public Procurement Policy

This policy should also be integrated with CSR policy and objectives.

(f) Public Administration Policy

Public administrations, including the SMEs association Forums need to practice CSR principles in their own management and with their stakeholders. The Association has to invite public administrations at national, regional and local level in order to examine their practices with a view to integrating social and environmental considerations.

CONCLUSION

There is a need for awareness campaign on CSR in SMEs which have been facing the challenges to further awareness, dissemination, adoption and monitoring. In this context, small business associations, support organisations and networks have an important role to play in raising awareness through the provision of information, user-friendly tools and the dissemination of good practices cases. To outweigh the challenges coming the way of creating awareness, all enterprises including SMEs have to develop the sharing of experience and good practices on CSR among business. As SMEs are more in number in any country, they should be educated and convinced through awareness campaigns on CSR resulting in to the integration of social and environmental concern in their business operations. This will lead to sustainable business development.

REFERENCES

Communication from the Commission on CSR: A business contribution to Sustainable Development (Commission of the European Communities), 02-07-02.

CSR and Finance, "Forging a Path Ahead?," *MHC*, Monthly Feature, Jan. 2004.

CSR Services, Master Classes and Executive Briefings, MHC International Limited Business Training.

Hellriegel/Jackson/Slocum, Management: A Competency-Based Approach, Thomson Asia Pvt. Ltd., Singapore, 2002.

Maurice Anglow, Corporate Governance in Banking, Multi-Client Research Studies, 2003.

18

GMO: A Hope or a Frustration

R. Seminur Topal and Ugur S. Alp

Generally from the different species to the other livings, named "transgene," obtaining by a one or more genes transferred or added, defined as Genetically Modified Organisms (GMO) or Transgenic livings. Genetic modifications described that which is not occurred with natural combination of genetic material inside the organisms. Relating to the origin of the transferred gene, there are multiple gene modification types can be discussed. Basically, three groups are being focused in this application: wide transfers, closed transfers and conversions. Food and agricultural fields of GM foods are mainly represented by soybean, maize, cotton and kanola. Recent studies shows us that transgenic crops plant area reached to the 70 million hectares. Also, in 1998, world market value of transgenic crops were 30 billion $, but presently it became to the 70 billion $ levels approximately. In agriculture, as GMO applications convert to the highly scaled products and for the recent years, trade dimensions especially modified seed products, is on going to be raised highly. GM foods are widely produced and sold out as a multiple thoughtful advantages from the side of the consumers that have been seemed. The first goal of the plant producing with GM applications are focused to create more stability of plants. The other advantages of GM crops that have been discussed by some scientists is a kind of resistance dissenting to the plant diseases from the viruses, insects and also tolerance to the herbicides. Naturally, the risks that have been described much more than advantages with this subject, get a front side on this topic. Occasionally, risks and negative themes from the sides of health, agriculture, social-economic structure, legally and ethically worths get importance in the last decade. Mainly, cotton and rice, the two dominant (primer) products of GM foods, are going to be focused on, and to be made a general conclusion from the perspective of risks in this article. These subjects get the top of the importance by the world development, after like a frustration on GM colt on and rice in India that have been seeing lots of events by witnesses. From this point of view, producers, consumers and government organizations must be more and more reasonable, sensitive and get their social responsibility.

INTRODUCTION: WHAT ARE DIFFERENCES BETWEEN GM APPLICATIONS AND GENETIC ENHANCES

Many would argue that the current use of the term "GMO" is much too narrowly constructed, in that it refers more to the process by which genes are introduced rather than to the product. For example, introduction of a truly harmful gene (such as one for a human toxin) into a crop would not result in a "GMO" provided the harmful gene had been found in that crop species. But when a gene is discovered in a micro-organism, in another plant species, or in an animal and transferred into a crop plant, the resulting crop cultivar will be designated a "GMO" no matter how benign the transferred gene turns out to be. Some have taken to referring to "GM food" or "GM crops" or "Genetically Transgenic" crops, but most of the world still knows such crops as GMOs. There is often more than one gene that can be found to produce the same effect in crops. Most transformations are made not using single genes, but rather small groups of associated genes that are included to help identify and control the action of the "target" gene. Such a group of genes is called an "event," and while two events might both cause the plant to, for example, be tolerant to the same herbicide, they may act somewhat differently in the plant. For example, there are a number of Bt events that have been developed, and they may result in formation of the Bt protein (insecticide) in different concentrations, in different plant parts, or at different times during the life of the plant. Different events for the same target gene thus represent some "genetic diversity" for the trait, and this may be useful in making the trait better adapted and less subject to development of resistance by pests (Nafziger, 2005).

TRANSFERRING THE GENE

Taking a gene from one organism and inserting it into another is essentially a process of cutting the gene which codes for the trait of interest from the foreign organism and pasting this gene into the genome of the organism that you want to alter.

Generally a transgenic crop contains one or more genes that have been inserted artificially either from an unrelated plant or from different species altogether. This makes the plants safer for the consumer and allows the farmer to save money on chemicals. In conclusion, transgenic crops are an economically safer method of producing crop products, which makes them appealing and potentially profitable. As given in the same article, for many years plant breeding entailed the selection of the finest plants to get the best crops. In those days, variation occurred through induced mutation or hybridization where two or more plants were crossed. Selection occurred through nature, using a "selection of the fillest" concept, where only the seeds best adapted to that environment succeeded. For example, farmers selected only the biggest seeds with non-shattering seed heads, assuming these to be the best. Today, scientists can not only select, but also create crops by inserting genes to make a seeds bare any trait desired. In order to make a transgenic crop, there are five main steps: extracting DNA, cloning a gene of interest, designing the gene for plant infiltration, transformation, and finally plant breeding as given in Figure 18.1a,b (Pighin, 2005) and Figure 18.2 (Hall, 2003).

What are the Advantages and Disadvantages of Transgenic Crops?

The use of transgenic crops has been an issue for many years. Many concerns have been raised and these generally fall into two categories:

1. A concern about what affect genetically modified material could have on human health. For example, transgenic crops have been suggested to cause allergies in some people, although it is uncertain whether transgenic crops are the source of this reaction. Furthermore, the antibiotic resistance genes placed in these crops has been suggested to cause resistance to antibiotics leading to super bugs that cannot

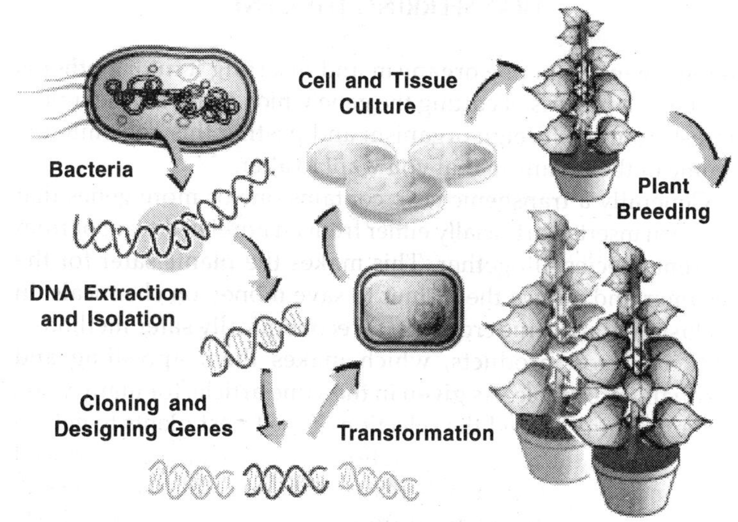

FIG. 18.1a

Overview of How Transgenic Crops are Created.

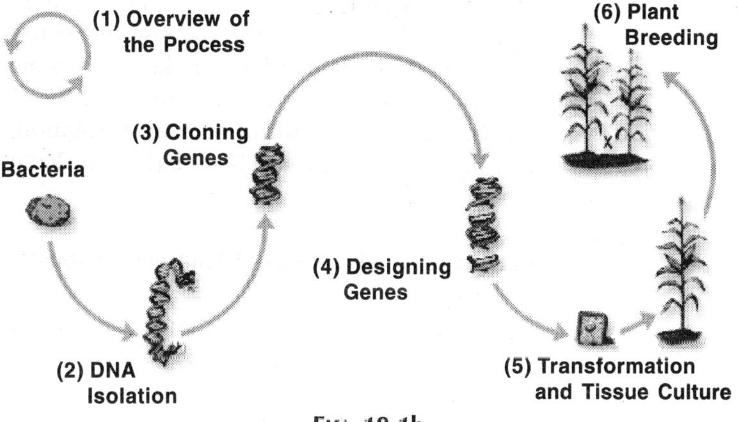

FIG. 18.1b

How to make Transgenic Plants: Animation Demo.

(http://croptechnology.unl.edu/)

be killed with antibiotic treatments (Ferber, 1999). The idea of a population being uncomfortable with ingesting DNA that originated from another source, such as a virus or bacteria, must also be considered when thinking about producing

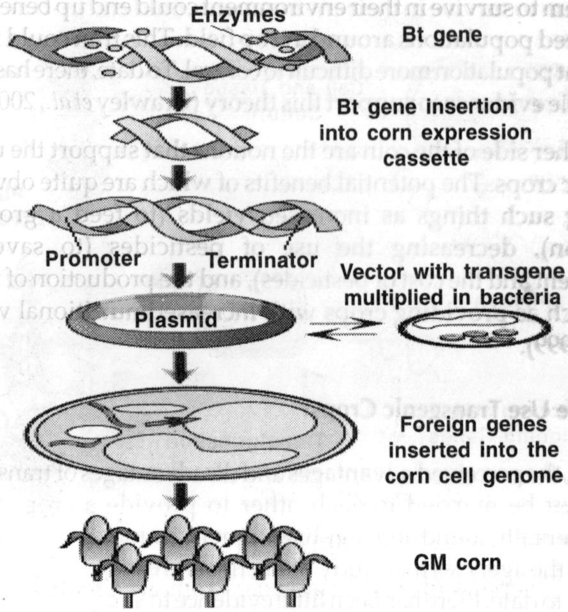

FIG. 18.2

General Schematic of GM Crop Production.

transgenic crops. However, to date, there is no evidence of the DNA from transgenic crops being any different from the DNA ingested from conventional crops.

2. A concern about whether transgenic crops cause damage to the natural environment. One example includes pollen from transgenic corn, which has been suggested to kill the Monarch butterfly larvae. It has been shown that hybrid corn expresses a bacterial toxin in its pollen, which is then dispersed over 60 meters by wind. In this range, the corn pollen is deposited on other plants near cornfields where it can be ingested by non-target organisms including the monarch butterfly. These butterflies have been found to eat less, have a slower growth rate and higher death rate. (Losey *et al.*, 1999). A second example is the hybridization of crops with nearby weeds. This could cause these weeds to attain resistance to herbicides or other things that we have been trying to avoid for many years. Genes that provide resistance to viral disease or other traits allowing

them to survive in their environment could end up benefiting weed populations around a crop field. This trait could make that population more difficult to control. To date, there has been little evidence to support this theory (Crawley *et al.*, 2001).

On other side of the coin are the notions that support the use of transgenic crops. The potential benefits of which are quite obvious, including such things as increased yields (to feed a growing population), decreasing the use of pesticides (to save the environment and the cost of pesticides), and the production of novel crops (such as providing crops with increased nutritional value) (Ferber, 1999).

Should We Use Transgenic Crops?

In the end, the perceived advantages and disadvantages of transgenic crops must be married to each other to provide a crop that is environmentally sound and non-hazardous. Producers of transgenic crops and the agencies that study their effects are aware of this point. However, to date, there has been little evidence to support either case. More research is required in this field to determine the true safety of these plants and to decide whether they are safe for both the environment and for those who consume these products over the ages. At the least, most would agree that the potential advantage of producing crops that provide the human population with more and cheaper food makes transgenic technology a useful invention (Pighin, 2005).

A gene from an insect pathogen Bacillus thuringiensis (Bt), which encodes a protein toxic to the European corn borer (ECB). As an insect pest that eats and destroys corn stems as given in Figure 18.3. Bt corn has proven effective in reducing crop damage due to ECB, yet public opposition to Bt corn has escalated amid fears of human health and environmental risks associated with the production and consumption of Bt corn. Bt corn draws its humble origins from France, where in 1938 B. thuringiensis bacteria was grown in large quantities and sprayed on corn crops to prevent ECB damage. Artificial selection of Bt strains has led to the successful targeting of many insect pests. Because no toxic effects of Bt on humans have been detected in its seventy years of use, it is now considered an acceptable pest control measure for the organic food

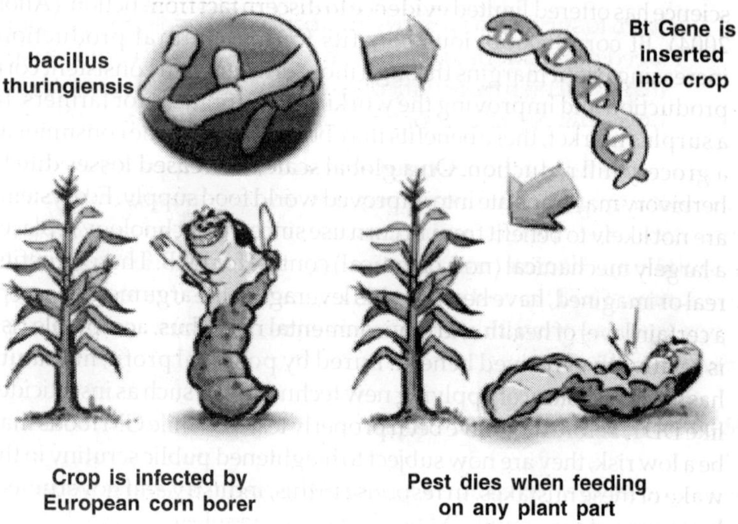

FIG. 18.3

Engineering Resistant Corn.

industry. To this day, Bt is an important part of many integrated pest management strategies. The success of the Bt spray has been limited because the bacteria cannot survive for very long on the plant's surface. The insect lives most of its larval life inside the corn stem, not on the surface: sprays are only effective when the insect is just starting its journey into the stem. A means of penetrating tissue with Bt is required to offer long-term, preventative measures against tunnelling insect (Hall, 2005).

Following the insertion of a gene from the bacteria Bacillus thuringiensis, corn becomes resistant to corn borer infection. This allows farmers to use fewer insecticides.

We currently know very little about the actual ecological risks posed by Bt corn. Past Research has largely focused on laboratory experiments. Field experiments reveal more about the true nature of relationships and provide a better assessment of risk, but are logistically more difficult to conduct. The case-specific nature of Bt corn studies has impeded the integration of knowledge and prevented the formation of broad conclusions on the safety of Bt corn. These uncertainties fuel notions of "frankenfoods" or a new spin on "agro-terrorism." While biotechnology supporters discount these fears, science has offered limited evidence to discern fact from fiction. (Anon 2004). Bt corn has obvious benefits for agricultural production, increasing profit margins through more efficient and consistent corn production and improving the working environment for farmers. In a surplus market, these benefits may be passed on to the consumer as a grocery hill reduction. On a global scale, decreased losses due to herbivory may translate into improved world food supply. Ecosystems are not likely to benefit from Bt corn use since this technology replaces a largely mechanical (non-chemical) control for ECB. These benefits, real or imagined, have been used as leverage in the argument to accept a certain level of health and environmental risk. Thus, acceptable risk is relative to perceived benefit. Lured by potential profit, humanity has a recent history of applying new technologies, such as insecticides like DDT, before they have been properly tested. While GM foods may be a low risk, they are now subject to heightened public scrutiny in the wake of these mistakes. In response to this, industry and government have agreed that some GM foods, including select Bt corn cultivars are "substantially equivalent" to the accepted, non GM foods. That is, no detectable differences exist between the GM and the non-GM foods. Public demand for assurances of GM food safety has given rise to a new concept of "substantiated equivalence," whereby human health and environmental risks are more clearly defined in long-term clinical trials and field studies (Hall, 2005).

COST-BENEFIT ANALYSIS

The guidelines are not a guide to cost (or risk)/benefit analysis of the environmental impacts of transgenic organisms, as this presupposes a valuation system for comparing effects, but they will guide the evaluation of any environmental effect, which can then be analysed in the political context of the country considering the GMO. An important approach developed by the project is the Problem Formulation and Options Assessment. Two crucial steps in risk assessment are addressed by the PFOA Model:

(1) problem identification (What is the scope of the problem, how is it defined? Problem identification frames the entire risk assessment), and
(2) the identification of potential alternative solutions to the problem.

The proposed action (the GMO) is never the only possible way to address the problem. Risk assessment depends entirely on an appropriate specification of alternatives (including taking no action and doing nothing), so that comparative risk can be assessed, and appropriate controls for risk assessment science can be defined and used.

Case-by-Case

The Bio-safety Protocol and the EU Directive on release of genetically modified organisms (GM) plants specify that risk assessment should be conducted on a case-by-case basis. Each GM plant and ecosystem must be looked at individually, because the relevant questions will differ on a case-by-case and environment-by-environment (agro-ecological region) basis. There is insufficient experience available with GM plants to allow aggregate analysis and assessment. Consequently, it is premature to propose general risk assessment guidelines, but it may be possible to develop general, robust approaches by extrapolation from detailed case studies. Hence, the project has focused on developing scientifically sound, transparent case studies to instantiate the principles of risk assessment (Anon, 2004).

Scope

The methodologies address the environmental and agricultural impacts of transgenic organisms, and do not evaluate human health impacts or ethical implications. Because most of the presently available transgenic plants produce a novel gene product used in pest control, the project has focused on these kinds of transgenic crop plants. The case studies do not aim to describe a full risk assessment for that crop and environment. They are case studies of a methodology for conducting an environmental risk assessment of that crop, and the emphasis throughout is on transparency and scientific rigor in the risk assessment methods. Invariably, however, certain sources of information are unavailable to the project, and the process has also identified certain key gaps of knowledge for each case study. Relevant organisations in each country will therefore need to conduct their own scientific risk assessments in order to inform their own Bio-safety decisions (Hilbeck and Andow, 2003).

In plantation, most likely it will not be used directly for crop production, but will be crossed with improved varieties of the crop.

This is because only a few varieties of a given crop can be efficiently transformed, and these generally do not possess all the producer and consumer qualities required of modern cultivars. The initial cross to the improved variety must be followed by several cycles of repeated crosses to the improved parent, a process known as back-crossing. The goal is to recover as much of the improved parent's genome as possible, with the addition of the transgene from the transformed parent. The next step in the process is multi-location and multi-year evaluation trials in greenhouse and field environments to test the effects of the transgene and overall performance. This phase also includes evaluation of environmental effects and food safety.

RISKS AND CONCERNS FROM THE HEALTH AND ENVIRONMENTAL SIDE

The introduction of transgenic crops and foods into the existing food production system has generated a number of questions about possible negative consequences. People with concerns about this technology have reacted in many ways, from participating in letter-writing campaigns to demonstrating in the streets to vandalizing institutions where transgenic research is being conducted.

The issues surrounding objections to transgenic crops can be broadly grouped into concerns about:

- damage to human health:
  - allergenicity,
  - horizontal transfer and antibiotic resistance,
  - eating foreign DNA,
  - cauliflower mosaic virus promoter, and
  - changed nutrient levels.
- damage to the natural environment:
  - Monarch butterfly,
  - crop-to-weed gene flow,
  - antibiotic resistance,
  - leakage of GM proteins into soil, and
  - reductions in pesticide spraying: are they real?
- disruption of current practices of farming and food production in developed countries.
  - crop-to-crop gene flow.

- disruption of traditional practices and economies in less developed countries.

These are complex issues and a thorough treatment of each one would occupy volumes. For each topic we provide a short discussion with a link to a longer discussion and outside resources (Anon, 2004).

CONCERNS ABOUT HUMAN HEALTH

Allergenicity

The possibility that we might see an increase in the number of allergic reactions to food as a result of genetic engineering has a powerful emotional appeal. Parents of a severely allergic child, already conditioned to scrutinize food labels and to watch for warning symptoms, are understandably concerned that an additional and unpredictable danger may have been introduced into the food they buy. Even people who have never experienced an allergic reaction may worry that they are being exposed to new substances for which there is little track record of safety or harm (Fig. 18.4, Anon, 2004).

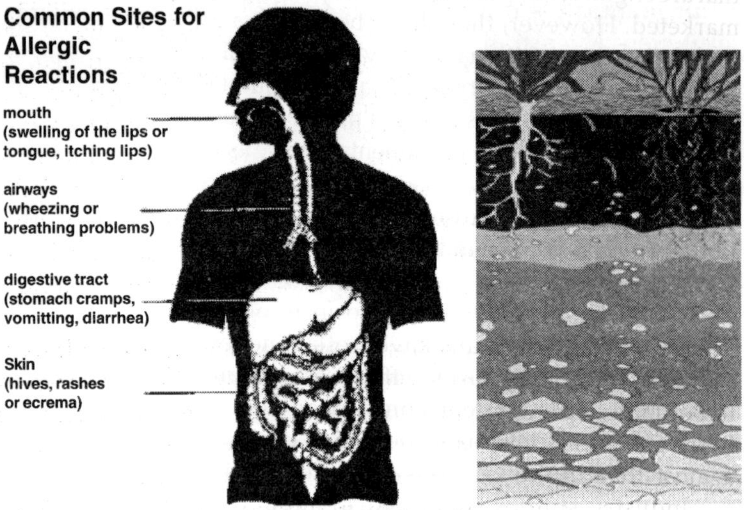

FIG. 18.4

How to make Transgenic Plants: Animation Demo.

Source: Rural Life Centre, Kenyon College, Gambier, Ohio.

The soybean, developed by Pioneer Hi-Bred, was modified by the introduction of a gene from the Brazil nut. The intention was to improve the nutritional quality of the soybean by adding the amino acid methionine, which is low in soybean and abundant in the Brazil nut. Because allergies to nuts are common, the use of a nut as the donor of the transgene raised eyebrows among regulators. The transgenic soybean was tested and people who had allergic reactions to Brazil nuts also had allergic reactions to the genetically engineered soybean. It appeared that the gene chosen to improve nutritional quality was one of the genes that trigger allergic reactions. Pioneer had intended to market the soybean only for animal feed, but the difficulty of keeping animal feed separate from human food during harvesting, transport, and storage became a consideration. Pioneer decided not to ask for approval to market the soybean.

Changed Nutrient Levels

How do genetically engineered foods compare with conventional foods in nutritional quality? This is an important issue, and one for which there will probably be much research in the future, as crops that are engineered specifically for improved nutritional quality are marketed. However, there have been only a few studies to date comparing the nutritional quality of genetically modified foods to their unmodified counterparts. The central question for GE crops that are currently available is whether plant breeders have accidentally changed the nutritional components that we associate with conventional cultivars of a crop. Because isoflavones are thought to play a role in preventing heart disease, breast cancer, and osteoporosis, the isoflavone content of RoundupReady soybeans has been investigated by several researchers.

The studies completed so far do not resolve the issue of whether RoundupReady soybeans have isoflavone levels comparable to conventional varieties, but the differences found in experiments appear to be small or moderate in comparison with natural variation in isoflavone level. Additional evidence may clarify the arguments for and against Roundup applications as a risk factor in soybean cultivation.

Industry studies submitted in support of applications for permission to sell transgenic crops indicate that the nutritional components that are commonly tested are similar in transgenic foods and conventional foods (Anon, 2004).

Concerns about Damage to the Environment

1. *Monarch Butterfly*

The suggestion that Bt corn pollen might kill Monarch butterfly larvae galvanized public interest in the effect of transgenic crops on the environment.

2. *Crop-to-Weed Gene Flow*

Hybridization of crops with nearby weeds may enable weeds to acquire traits we wish they didn't have, such as resistance to herbicides. Research results indicate that crop traits may escape from cultivation and persist for many years in wild populations. Genes that provide a competitive edge, such as resistance to viral disease, could benefit weed populations around a crop field. Many cultivated crops have sexually compatible wild relatives with which they hybridize under favourable circumstances. The likelihood that transgenes will spread can be different for each crop in each area of the world (Anon, 2004).

3. *Antibiotic-Resistance*

There is also concern that transgenic plants growing in the field will transfer their antibiotic resistance genes to soil micro-organisms, thus causing a general increase in the level of antibiotic resistance in the environment. However, many soil organisms have naturally occurring resistance as a defence against other organisms that generate antibiotics, so genes contributed occasionally by transgenic plants are unlikely to cause a change in the existing level of antibiotic resistance in the environment (Anon, 2004).

4. *Leakage of GM Proteins into Soil*

Many plants leak chemical compounds into the soil through their roots. There are concerns that transgenic plants may leak different compounds than conventional plants do, as an unintended consequence of their changed DNA. Speculation that this may be happening leads to concern about whether the communities of micro-organisms living near transgenic plants may be affected. The interaction between plants and soil micro-organisms is very complex, with the micro-organisms that live around plant roots also leaking chemical compounds into the soil. Much more research must be done before we understand the relationships that occur between micro-organisms and conventional crops. Attempts to discover whether transgenic plants are changing the soil environment, and whether they are changing it in good ways or bad ways, are hindered by our lack of basic scientific knowledge (Anon, 2004).

5. *Reductions in Pesticide Spraying: are they Real?*

One of the most appealing arguments in favour of transgenic plants is the potential for reducing the damage we do to our environment with conventional methods of farming. Pest-resistant crops such as Bt corn and Bt cotton have been promoted as a means to reduce the spraying of pesticides, while herbicide-tolerant crops such as RoundupReady soybeans are said to reduce the application of herbicides. Large reductions in chemical spraying have been claimed to result from the introduction of these transgenic varieties. Are the claims true?

Bt cotton is the only crop for which claims of reduced spraying are clear. Analysts paint a mixed picture on the results of planting RoundupReady soybeans. Bt corn and herbicide-tolerant cotton and corn have not resulted in clear reductions in the spraying of chemicals (Anon, 2004).

Concerns About Damage to Current Farming Practices

1. *Crop-to-Crop Gene Flow*

Hybridization of transgenic crops with nearby conventional crops raises concerns about separation distances to ensure purity of crops and about who must pay if unwanted genes move into a neighbour's crop. As "Identity Preservation" and segregation of GM from non-GM crops become factors in marketing products, it will be important to ensure that hybridization is not occurring in the field. If GM pollen pollinates plants in a neighbouring field, then the issue of genetic trespass may arise.

2. *Labelling Transgenic Foods*

Whether or not to require labelling of genetically engineered foods is likely to be the hot topic in food biotechnology over the next year. The European Union plans to establish a "farm to fork" tracking system that would mandate labelling for foods that contain transgenic ingredients and also for food, such as oils that do not contain transgenic DNA or protein but are derived from transgenic materials. Polls consistently show consumer support for such labelling.

Current U.S. Policy for Labelling

The Food and Drug Administration currently requires labelling of genetically engineered foods only if the food has a significantly different nutritional property, or if a new food includes an allergen that consumers would not expect to be present.

Issues in Mandatory Labelling

Although mandatory labelling of GE ingredients may appear to be a straightforward measure, there are several complex issues that would have to be resolved prior to implementation.

What specific technologies for crop variety development would require a label?

The target of most labelling efforts is food products that have been genetically engineered, that is, they contain genes artificially inserted from another organism. However, some legislative efforts have defined the term "genetically modified" more broadly to include an array of techniques that were in use by plant breeders well before the GE era (Hansen, 2001).

What Percentage of a GE Ingredient must be Present in a Food Before a Label is Required?

One per cent is a figure that is commonly proposed, but figures ranging from 0.1 to 5 per cent have also been suggested (Hansen, 2001).

Would Meat and Dairy Products Derived from Livestock Fed Transgenic Crops Require a Label?

Some labelling proposals include these products among those that would require labels, yet the biological rationale for doing so has not been demonstrated, that is, DNA or protein from inserted genes have not been found in livestock products (Auer, 2003).

What is the Economic Impact of Labelling?

The cost of labelling involves far more than the paper and ink to print the label. Accurate labelling would require an extensive identity preservation system from farmer to elevator to grain processor to food manufacturer to retailer (Maltsbarger and Kalaitzandonakes, 2000).

What is StarLink Corn?

StarLink corn is one of several kinds of Bt corn that have been genetically engineered to produce insecticide within the plant itself so that external applications of pesticides to fields can be reduced or eliminated. While other Bt corns on the market in 1999 and 2000 produced a Bt toxin called Cry 1A(b), StarLink had Cry 9C, a slightly different version of the protein. Since the majority of the corn harvest in the United States is used for animal feed and the production of fuel alcohol, this restriction did not spell the end of the line for StarLink corn as a crop. Farmers would simply have to ensure that their StarLink harvest was directed into channels that didn't lead to the human food supply. In addition, corn pollen often is blown into nearby fields where it can pollinate other varieties of corn. A low level of cross-pollination is acceptable among varieties that are approved for human consumption, but cross-pollination would be unacceptable under the zero tolerance for StarLink in human food (Anon, 2004).

StarLink Found in Grocery Stores

In September 2000 an independent laboratory confirmed that samples of taco shells submitted for testing by an anti-transgenic activist group had tested positive for the presence of StarLink DNA (http://washingtonpost.com/wpdyn/articles/A24834-2000Sep17.html). Within days, supermarkets were pulling corn products from their shelves. Aventis halted sales of StarLink seeds for the spring 2001, planting and announced it would purchase the entire 2000 harvest of StarLink corn to prevent any further use of the corn in food products. Although the StarLink acreage was not large, StarLink DNA or protein was detected in hundreds of products. Some corn varieties that were not supposed to have the StarLink gene tested positive for StarLink. Eventually StarLink DNA was detected in products made from white corn, although no white corn StarLink varieties had been produced (Kaufman, 2000). Foreign buyers quickly became nervous. Some countries already had in place prohibitions against importing transgenic food stuffs. Other countries made moves to institute such prohibitions. The StarLink episode highlighted a problem with the entire U.S. corn supply: the U.S. didn't keep conventional and transgenic loads separate. Buyers turned to South Africa, China, Argentina and Brazil for corn that was free of StarLink.

Golden Rice

Golden rice is the result of an effort to develop rice varieties that produce provitamin-A (beta-carotene) as a means of alleviating vitamin A (retinol) deficiencies in the diets of poor and disadvantaged people in developing countries. Because traditional rice varieties do not produce pro-vitamin-A, transgenic technologies were required. Through the work of two European scientists, Dr. Ingo Potrykus of the Swiss Federal Institute of Technology in Zurich and Dr. Peter Beyer of the University of Freiburg in Germany those were determined as; rice plants were developed containing two daffodil genes and one bacterial gene that carry out the four steps required for the production of beta-carotene in rice endosperm. Endosperm is the nutritive tissue surrounding the embryo of a seed and makes up the majority of the rice grain that we eat. The resulting plants appear normal except that after milling (to remove the , brown bran), their grain is a golden yellow colour due to the presence of provitamin-A (Toenniessen, 2000).

Why is Vitamin-A Important?

According to the World Health Organization (WHO), vitamin A deficiency (VAD) is the leading cause of preventable blindness in children. For children, a lack of vitamin A causes severe visual impairments and blindness and significantly increases the risk of severe illness, and even death, from common infections such as diarrhoea and measles. Pregnant mothers are also affected by VAD.

VAD in pregnant women causes night-blindness and may also be associated with higher mother-to-child HIV transmission rates as well as increased risk of maternal mortality. WHO estimates between 100 and 140 million children are vitamin A deficient. An estimated 250,000 to 500,000 children with VAD become blind every year and half of those children die within a year of losing their sight (WHO, 2002).

Who "Owns" Golden Rice?

In a highly debated move, the inventors of golden rice signed an agreement in May of 2000 through a small licensing company (Greenovation, Freiburg, Germany) with Zeneca, the crop protection and plant science business of AstraZeneca. This agreement gave Zeneca an exclusive license to charge for commercial use of the golden rice technology. In late 2000, a merger of the agrochemical division of AstraZeneca and Norvartis's agrochemical and seed business was completed to form the company Syngenta, which now holds the license for the commercial use of golden rice. Also in this agreement, Syngenta supports the humanitarian use of golden rice, as intended by the inventors, for developing countries. The agreement defines humanitarian use as individuals receiving $10,000 or less income from golden rice (Potrykus, 2001).

How Will Golden Rice Get to Those Who Need it?

In order to fulfil the inventors' goal of helping prevent vitamin A-deficiency in the poor and disadvantaged of developing countries, golden rice has to reach subsistence farmers free of charge and restrictions. Co-inventor Ingo Potrykus has outlined a strategy to get golden rice to poor farmers. As of March 2001, golden rice consisted of a series of provitamin-A producing laboratory lines whose traits must be transferred to locally adapted varieties in rice-growing countries (Potrykus, 2002).

Transgenic Crops Currently on the Market

As everybody know that; transgenic crops are easily continuous marketing since 1996. But unfortunately still we are not sure are they safely or not.

Crops, Traits and Acreage

The most important transgenic crop in terms of acreage planted is soybean, followed by corn, cotton, and canola (Fig. 18.5).

The number of acres for each crop are given in the graph below.

GM RICE IN INDIA

India is the second largest consumer of rice on the globe after China,

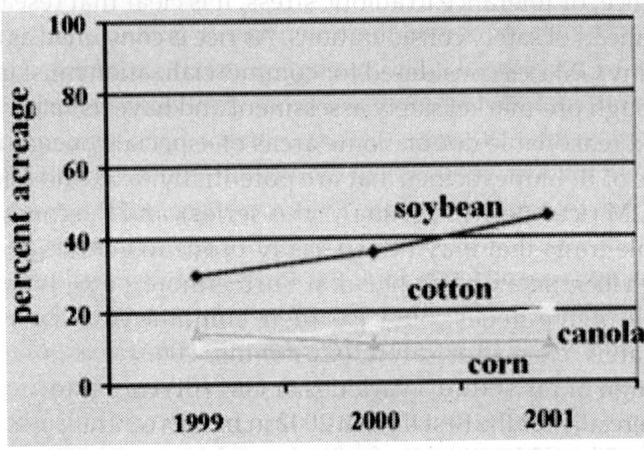

Global Area of Transgenic Crops 1962-2002 by Crop.

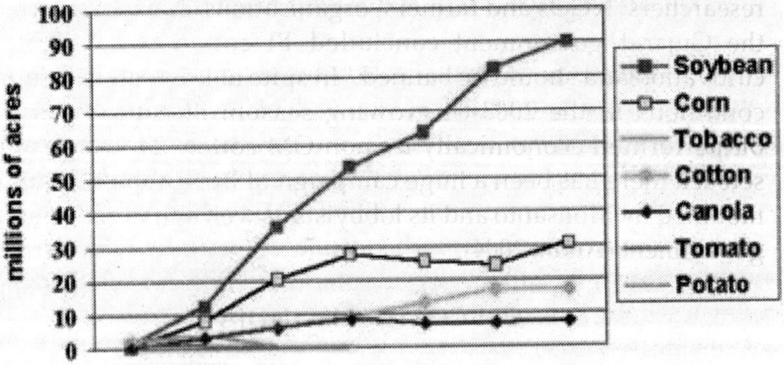

FIG. 18.5

Some of the Economical and Harvesting Perspectives.

Source: James, 2002, 2001a, 2000b, 1997.

and more than twice that of the next country, Indonesia. India produced 93 million tonnes of rice in 2001 and 2002, and the government is targeting 129 million tonnes by 2011 and 2012. India approved genetically modified (GM) cotton for food, feed and fibre in 2002 and other approvals may soon follow. A lot of technically sophisticated research on GM rice is being done in India, and we shall describe some of it here. Currently, no GM rice variety has been commercially released in India. While the GM rice being researched in India may show some promise in providing pest and disease resistance, or tolerance to abiotic stress, it is clear that research has raced ahead of safety considerations. As rice is consumed as a staple food, any GM rice considered for commercialization must undergo a thorough pre-market safety assessment and have its safety proven beyond reasonable doubt. Some areas of especial concern include the use of Bt biopesticides that are potentially toxic and allergenic (see "GM rice release in China?," this series); and the complicated, multiple traits that may be especially prone to genetic instability through illegitimate recombination. Furthermore, not only the effects of each of the genes, but also their combined effects must be adequately tested for safety (Cummins, 2003). Despite a fierce campaign of resistance 3 varieties of GM (Bt) cotton were planted commercially for the first time in 2002 in India's central and southern regions. The GM cotton performed poorly in its first year and this was reflected in the reports of state governments, academic researchers, NGOs and farmers' organisations. A panel set-up by the Gujarat government concluded Bt cotton was 'unfit for cultivation and should be banned.' In spite of less testing weather conditions in the 2003-04 growing season, Bt cotton was still outperformed economically by non-GM cotton. To counter this setback there has been a huge campaign of hype about GM crops mounted by Monsanto and its lobbyists as well as its supporters in government (Anon, 2004).

GM COTTON IN INDIA

The Introduction of Transgenic Cotton in India

Although it has the world's largest acreage of 8.9 million hectares under cotton, India is only the third largest global cotton producer, with about 2.86 million tonnes of cotton lint a year. The average productivity of cotton lint at 320 kilograms per hectare is amongst the lowest in the world. The productivity ranges from 200 kg per hectare to 600 kg for hybrid varieties. Since many of the land holdings are characterized by small-scale and resource-poor farming, a sudden and high increase in productivity using present methods is unlikely. Cotton is essentially grown in the kharif, the rainy season and treated as a perennial crop. Nearly 70 per cent of the crop is cultivated under rainfed conditions in the central and southern regions of the country: Gujarat, Maharashtra, Madhya Pradesh, Tamil Nadu, Andhra Pradesh and Karnataka. The sowing dates in Southern India differ according to the specific regions. Only in the northern regions of the country, mainly the states of Punjab, Haryana and Rajasthan, is cotton predominantly irrigated. Here, the plantings are homogenous and the emphasis is on planting high yield varieties (Ghosh, 2000).

Pests and Pesticides

In India, an estimated US $ 620 million (Rs. 28 billion) of pesticides is used in agriculture, with US $ 344 million (Rs. 16 billion) worth on cotton. Bollworm control alone takes a heavy toll, costing the farmers an annual US $ 235 million (Rs. 11 billion), and accounting for more than a third of current pesticides sales in India. If the crop fails because of weather conditions and/or pest resistance, a rising number of farmers have been known to consume the same chemicals to end their lives and escape the humiliation that comes with mounting debts. According to the official records, more than 500 cotton farmers in Andhra Pradesh, Karnataka, Maharashtra and Punjab committed suicide in 1998 (Sharma, 2001).

Bt Cotton-trials and Safety Regulations

To find possible ways of minimizing pest-linked damage to cotton and to effectively reduce the dependence on chemicals whilst keeping the environment and human health and safety in mind, the Indian government has begun experimenting with genetically modified (GM) cotton. The Department of Biotechnology (DBT) of the Ministry of Science and Technology also plans to examine whether GM cotton is environmentally safe, contributes to an increase in yield and at the same time results in a substantial reduction in chemical pesticide usage. In March 1995, the DBT had approved the import of 100 grams of cotton plantlets (by Mahyco) of the GM variety Cocker-312, a cotton variety cultivated in the USA. This variety is modified by the insertion of the Cry 1Ac gene from the bacterium Bacillus thuringiensis (Bt). Mahyco crossed the transgenic trait into elite Indian cotton varieties for six generations under controlled greenhouse conditions and then generated stable lines to breed hybrids. At least eight Indian Bt cotton hybrids containing the Cry 1Ac gene have so far been developed. DBT has subsequently given permission for their field evaluation. In November 1997, the first limited field trials on plots of 200 square meters were conducted in the provinces of Andhra Pradesh, Karnataka, Maharashtra, Tamil Nadu and Haryana. In 1998, experiments were permitted at 40 locations throughout the cotton growing areas of India, followed by an additional 11 field trials in 1999. From 1996 to 1999, Mahyco had also conducted toxicity and allergenic studies with backcrossed Indian varieties. All field trials were monitored by a Monitoring and Evaluation Committee (MEC) constituted by the DBT (Sharma, 2001).

CONCLUSION ABOUT COTTON IN INDIA

Transgenic cotton is being hastily pushed in India as a viable alternative to the chemical-intensive cotton farming systems. However, its human and environmental safety implications are being pushed into the background. Nevertheless, in a country that is considered to be a mega-diversity area with small land holdings and an increasingly large number of resource-poor farmers, the introduction of transgenic crops has to be carefully evaluated. Over the past few decades, the excessive application of pesticides on cotton has resulted in a "pesticide treadmill" whereby ever higher doses of pesticides are required to control the cotton pests because of the development of resistance and the elimination of predators. However, we should be aware that the introduction of Bt cotton can trigger off a "biological treadmill," the implications of which could be very severe for the farmers and further damage the ecological balance between pests and their natural enemies. There is sufficient evidence to show that technological alternatives do exist which promise that a switch can be made from conventional cotton production systems to more sustainable methods. But unfortunately, the focus of research priorities is not on rediscovering the mechanisms through which farmers can convert to green alternatives. In the absence of such mechanisms, more and more farmers will be forced to take the fatal route to escape the humiliation that comes with increasing indebtedness from a commercial farming system that relies solely on creating treadmills (Sharma, 2001).

REFERENCES

Anon (2004): Risks and Concerns.
http://www.colostate.edu/porograms/lifescicnces/TransgenicCrops/hotstarlink.html
http://www.colostate.edu/porograms/lifescicnces/TransgenicCrops/how.html
http://www.colostate.edu/porograms/lifescicnces/TransgenicCrops/nutrients.html
http://www.colostate.edu/porograms/lifescicnces/TransgenicCrops/risks.html

Astwood, J.D., htttp://pewagbiotech.org/buzz/display.php3?StoryID = 12

Auer, C.A. (2003): "Tracking Genes from Seed to Supermarket: Techniques and Trends," *Trends in Plant Science*, 8, 591-97.

Chaudhry, A. (2005): Genetically Modified Foods. http://www.bioteach.ubc.ca/Bioengineering/GeneticallyModifiedFoods/index.htm

Chawla, H.S. (2000): Introduction to Plant Biotechnology, Enfield, NH, USA: Science Publishers Inc. http://dra.library.ubc.ca/MARION/BAS-3290

Crawley, M.J.; Brown, S.L.; Hails, R.S.; Kohn, D.D.; Rees, M. (2001): "Transgenic Crops in Natural Habitats," *Nature*, 409, 682-3.

Cummins, J. (2003): GM Rice in India, http://www.i-sis.org.uk/GMRII.php

Ferher, D. (1999): "Risks and Benefits: GM Crops in the Cross Hairs," *Science*, 2S6, 1662-6.

Ghosh, P.K. (2000): Genetically Modified Crops in India. Silver Jubilee Lecture Series, Mumbai, India: Indian Society for Cotton Improvement, Central Institute for Research on Cotton Technology. http://www.monsantoindia.com/news/showlib1ca8.html?uid = 4947

Hall, H. (2005): A Controversy in Our Corn: Is Bt Corn Safe? http//www.bioteach.ubc.ca/Bioengineering/btcorn/index.html

Hansen, M. (2001): "Genetically Engineered Food: Make Sure It's Safe and Label It," in G.C. Nelson (ed.), *Genetically Modified Organisms in Agriculture*, Academic Press, San Diego, pp. 239-55.

Hilbeck, A. and Andow, D.A. (2003): Environmental Risk Assessment of Genetically Modified Organisms: A Case Study of Bt Maize in Kenya. http//www.gmo-guidelines.info/public/publications/books.html

James, C. (2002, 2001a, 2001b, 1997): Global Status of Commercialized Transgenic Crops, 2002, ISAAA Briefs No. 27, ASAAA, Ithaca, NY, http://www.isaaa.org/home.htm.

Kaufman, M. (2000): Gene-Modified Variety Allowed only for Animal Feed Because of Allergy Concerns. http://washingtonpost.com/wp-dyn/articles/A24834-2000Sep17.html

Kautman, M. (2001): Engineered Corn Found in White Tortilla Chips http://washingtonpost.com/wp-dyn/articles/A16045-2001Jul3.html

Losey, J.E.; Rayor, L.S.; Carter, M.E. (1999): "Transgenic Pollen Harms Monarch Larvae," *Nature*, 399(6733), 214.

Maltsbarger, R. and N. Kalaitzandonakes (2000): "Direct and Hidden Costs in Identity Preserved Supply Chains," *AgBio Forum*, Vol. 3, No. 4, www.agbioforum.org/

Nafziger, E. (2005): Genetically Modified Organisms (GMOs). http://web.aces.uiuc.edu/faq/faq.pdl?project id=28.

Pighin, J. (2005): Transgenic Crops: How Genetics is Providing New Ways to Envision Agriculture. Transgenic Crops: http://www.bioteach.ubc.ca/Biodiversity/TransgenicCrops/

Potrykus, I. (2001): "Golden Rice and Beyond," *Plant Physiology*, 125, 1157-61.

Potrykus, I. (2002): Personal Communication to Jason Sutton. http://www.colostate.edu/programs/lifesciences/TransgenicCrops.htm

Sharma, D. (2001): "The Introduction of Transgenic Cotton in India," *Biotechnology and Development Monitor*, No. 44, pp. 10-13.

Toenniessen, G.H. (2000): Vitamin A Deficiency and Golden Rice: The Role of the Rockefeller Foundation. http://www.rockfound.org/99prog/food/vitamina.html

WHO (2002): Combating Vitamin A Deficiency, World Health Organization. http://www.who.int/nut/vad.htm

http://washingtonpost.com/wp-dyn/articles/A24834-2000Sep17.html

19

Corporate Social Responsibility: Support to Education *vis-a-vis* Reservation for Backward Classes

P.N. SANKARAN AND AMITA NADKARNI

INTRODUCTION

In corporate governance and practices worldwide, there is an increasing recognition about the emerging social and environmental frontiers of intervention that lie beyond the traditional domains of pure business which satisfy only the financial interests of (quite often sleepy) shareholders/stockholders. Real concern of corporate agencies for the issues of the society at large and stakeholders[1] in particular, has transcended the charity principle[2] and the stewardship principle[3] over the years and is popularly understood as *Corporate Social Responsibility* (CSR). According to the Report of the European Multi-stakeholder Forum (EMS) on CSR 2000, it is a concept whereby companies integrate social and environmental concerns in their business operations and in their interactions with their stakeholders on a voluntary basis. The concept of CSR has outlived the variations in the corporate objectives[4] across the globe and the corporate sector is grappling with the question how to go about with the CSR conundrum, with systems and procedures that are responding to country as well as community level policies and realities in society, polity and economy. In the Indian context, fundamental economic reforms launched in 1991 shifting the productive sector to the corporate (private) sector in terms of de-licensing and disinvestment of public sector undertakings have left the state with functions mainly confined to the sphere of governance. An inevitable outcome of the liberalization policy is the declining involvement of the state in the protective sphere (programs for social justice and welfare), particularly in the support programs for employment and education of Backward Classes (BCs),[5] who constitute more than 50 per cent of the population in many states. Following the provisions in the Constitution under Articles 15(4) and 16(4),[6] the Union and State Governments have been addressing the issues of inequality and social justice through reservation in employment and (on a moderate scale) reservation in education to SC/STs and Other Backward Classes (OBCs) from time to time.[7,8]

Since economic reforms have replaced the government sector with the private sector as the key job creator, it is argued that reservation must shift to the latter. In view of the above consideration, the Common Minimum Program of UPA government and the constitution of the Group of Ministers to Examine Affirmative Action Including Reservation in Private Sector call for a national dialogue on the issue [reservation in the private sector]. Preliminary reports indicate that, despite the firm commitment to social responsibility, the corporate sector is not happy with the proposal of job reservation *per se*, though they are willing to support the *employability* of BCs through education, training and skill improvement under a suitable CSR action-framework. But we do not have:

- suitable models of CSR for the promotion of education *vis-a-vis* reservation in employment of BCs,
- well tested action-plans for improving the employability of under-privileged sections in society, and
- empirical evidence on the impact of educational intervention on job opportunities.

According to Lingane and Olsen (2004), although a number of guidelines and reporting standards have been advanced since the early 1990's, no framework has yet been articulated for quantifying the value of a company's impact on people and the environment. Though the development of a framework for CSR (in the promotion of education in lieu of reservation) is beyond the scope of the paper, the study tries to capture the related perspectives of a cross-section of corporate employers, employees and students pursuing professional education in the IT corridor of India – Bangalore city.

CSR: THEORY AND PRACTICE

CSR challenges business to be accountable for the consequences of their actions affecting the firm's stakeholders while they pursue traditional economic goals (Post *et al.*, 1996). However, being socially responsible doesn't mean that a company must abandon its primary economic mission nor does it mean that socially responsible firms cannot be as profitable as others less responsible. Social responsibility requires companies to balance the benefits to be gained against the costs of achieving those benefits. Many people believe that both business and society gain when business firms actively strive to be socially responsible. Others are doubtful[9] stating that business's competitive strength is weakened by taking on social tasks. However, it is well accepted that CSR is the offshoot of two features of the modern corporation namely the essential functions it performs for a variety of stakeholders and the immense influence it has on the lives of the stakeholders. CSR reflects cultural values and traditions and takes different forms in different societies. The concept owes its origin to the Charity Principle and the Stewardship Principle.

Over the years, the concept of CSR has acquired a wider content "whereby private companies voluntarily agree to integrate social and environmental concerns in to their business practices in strategic ways that are good for business, employment and the communities in which they operate (UNDP CSR Program in Albania 2004-06). CSR represents a key component in the UN Global Compact [2000] through which business leaders are invited to join an international initiative bringing companies together with governments, civil society and development agencies to support nine universal principles of Human rights, labour and the environment.

Though the concept of CSR is by no means a recent phenomenon, many observers agree that the globalization has spurred its growth and prominence. The notion of CSR, which now dominates thinking about corporate behaviour among a section of academics and practitioners alike is prevalent in the US and lately as Aaronson (2002) argues, Europe has taken the lead in shaping global CSR debates. Corporate philanthropy regarded as the earliest manifestation of CSR is no longer considered an adequate response to the demands for social responsibility. The term CSR includes environmental, social and human rights-based impacts and initiatives of companies (Ward and Fox, 2002) and many countries in both industrialized and the third world take the concept and practices seriously (Hopkins, 2003). The definition of CSR, therefore, is still being debated and there is no consensus among the academicians or practitioners (Mohan, 2001). According to Ward and Fox (2002) "whatever the language used, the basic idea is to understand business as part of society not somehow separate from it."

However the act of balancing the interest of stockholders with the concerns for the society has to be driven by considerations of employee's perceptions, consumer attitudes, cause-branding, rights-issues, techniques of socially reasonable pricing, social returns to investments, leadership issues, etc. It may be observed that:

- Regarding the nexus between profits and CSR, results have been mixed. If CSR improves profit it would be an example of *enlightened self interest;* the other outcome is sequential (once the company is profitable, it can afford to be socially responsible). According to David Crowther there is no inherent conflict between social responsibility and the corporate self-interest because, being socially responsible is the way to maximize shareholder value creation. In a pioneering study it has been brought out that firms which have good financial performance are also good at social responsibility thereby providing evidence that social responsibility and shareholder value creation are closely related (Crowther, D., 2002 and 2004).
- The US government provides *work opportunity tax credits* for employers who hire members of targeted groups. Then it is for the companies to decide if employing the designated percentage of target classes is worth the incentives or not.
- The experience of Parikrama Humanity Foundation, Bangalore is that corporate giving cannot be just a function but needs to be driven by leadership and be renamed as *corporate employee social responsibility*. CSR can go beyond just giving and move into the area of development of human potential (Shukla Bose, 2004).
- The concept of *socially responsible pricing* is gaining momentum. It reflects pricing decisions consistent with firm's

obligations to the society and is not necessarily maximizing the firm's economic interests. Thus drug access in developing countries, particularly for HIV/AIDS has become a major issue of CSR (Vachani Sushil and Smith, N. Craig, 2004).

- Both theory and recent research evidence suggest that a corporation's socially responsible behaviour can positively affect consumer's attitudes toward the corporation.[10] A recent study by Lichtenstein *et al.* [2004], using field survey design provides evidence that perceived CSR affects not only customer purchase behaviour through customer corporate identification but also customer donations to corporate supported non-profit organizations.
- A UK consumer survey has also indicated that the consumers count the CSR when they make purchase of products.
- It is reported that few companies approach their charitable activities with an eye toward enhancing their brands. Over the years, such cause-branding [e.g. breast cancer awareness by Avon, the cosmetic giant in USA, Con Agro Food's programme 'Feeding Children Better'] strategies have helped social causes enjoy financial awards and unprecedented support both inside and outside companies [Cone *et al.*, 2003].

It is observed that beyond the "primary" impact on the brand and company, CSR initiatives can also influence "secondary" outcomes related to both the partner organizations [e.g. non-profits[11]] and the cause or social issue at the core of the company's CSR efforts [Bhattacharya and Sen, 2004]. These secondary outcomes of CSR are something companies interested in gauging the "social return"[12] on their CSR investments need to better understand. Social Return on Investment [SROI] describes the social impact of a business or non-profit's operations in dollar terms, relative to the investment required to create that impact and exclusive of its financial return to investors. According to Lingane and Olsen, SROI differs from cost-benefit analysis. It is a practical management tool, enabling informed decision-making on a regular basis; SROI enables managers to maximize both social and financial benefits. In a pioneering study, Roger, L. Martin [2002] has designed an analytical tool called the *'virtue matrix'* which helps executives understand what generates socially responsible corporate conduct[13] and how they can use it as a framework for assessing opportunities for socially responsible behaviour.

In a recent survey of the theory and practice of CSR, Clive Crook observes that CSR is now an industry in its own right and a flourishing profession as well.... For most conventionally organized public companies, CSR is little more than a cosmetic treatment. In the light of the critical review of international experience of what is perceived as CSR and the CSR matrix proposed,[14] he concludes that business should not try to do the work of governments [public interest]. If mangers merely concentrate on discharging their responsibility to the owners of their firms, acting ethically as they do so, they will usually serve the public good in any case. The proper business of business is business. No apology required [Crook, Clive, 2005].

CSR ACTIVITY DOMAINS

The database set-up by *Socrates: The Corporate Social Ratings Monitor*, reduces the numerous, diverse CSR initiatives undertaken by over 600 companies into six broad domains:

- Community Support [e.g., support of arts and health programmes, education and housing initiatives for the economically disadvantaged, and generous/innovative giving].
- Diversity [e.g., gender, race, family, sexual orientation, and disability].
- Employee Support [e.g. concern for safety, job security, profit-sharing, union relations, and employee involvement].
- Environment [e.g., environment-friendly products, hazardous waste management, use of ozone depleting chemicals, animal testing, pollution control, and recycling].
- Non-US Operations [e.g., overseas labour practices [including sweatshops] and operations in countries with human rights violations].
- Product [e.g., safety, R&D/innovation, marketing/contracting controversies, and antitrust disputes]. [Kinder, Lydenberg, and Domini Research and Analytics, 2003].

CSR IN INDIA

India has a widely appreciated history of CSR tradition that transcends the continuum of corporate philanthropy to compliance with the laws.[15] Some families from traditional merchant 'communities pioneered indigenous industrialization in India in the 19th century and participated not only in freedom struggle but also in the nation-building process thereafter. Bombay Plan and Peoples' Plan were influenced by the Gandhian philosophy of *trutsteeship*. Public sector companies continued the CSR tradition under Five Year Plans and few Trusts were set-up by corporate houses [Mohan, *op. cit.*, 2001]. The Indian corporate sector agrees that the new found freedom under Reforms carries with it social responsibilities as well. Thus, CSR in India is closer to what UNCTAD holds associated with standards of performance that are applied to both internal and external corporate activities, redressing societal norms that are not [but may become] legally-required mandates. According to Shrivastava and Venkateswaran [2002] what constitutes socially responsible behaviour in an Indian context is that it would include all activities that a company undertakes that benefit people and communities:

- other than those whom they are contractually obliged to [this excluded employees, suppliers, customers, shareholders, etc.], and
- who are socially and/or economically disadvantaged.

Since the focus of their paper is CSR in the context of socially and economically disadvantaged groups, the coverage of the term assumes significance. According to Action Aid India [1997] the disadvantaged in India include the following groups:

1. Small and marginal farmers.
2. Home-based workers, casual and others in the unorganized, informal rural and urban areas.
3. Rural artisans depending on tribal crafts.
4. Landless labourers.
5. Tribals dependent on forests and subsistence agriculture.
6. Urban slum-dwellers.
7. Specific sections under exploitation, e.g. bonded labour.
8. Households headed by women.

Another dimension of CSR is the influence that a socially responsible company exerts on public policy in favour of the disadvantaged and the environment, while also deriving a business profit. In India the government is always consulting the business sector when formulating key economic policies. Thus, CSR in India comprises of—

- All activities aimed at communities [be they philanthropic, social investment or commercial initiatives] that benefit them in a sustainable manner.
- Basic business practices that go beyond legal compliance to benefit the disadvantaged amongst the company's stakeholders.
- Advocating for change in public policy and laws that benefit disadvantaged people [Shrivastava and Venkateswaran, *op. cit.*, 2002].

While the idea of CSR is not new to India, what is certainly new is the number and diversity of organizations engaged in facilitating this process. Thus we have—

- Specialised Organizations [like Partners-in-Change and The Business and Community Foundations—BCF].
- Other development organizations like *Donor Agencies* [Action Aid, Aga Khan Foundation, Child Care and You, Oxfam India Trust], *Organisations Promoting Philanthropy* [Centre for Advancement of Philanthropy, Indian Centre for Philanthropy], Local Initiatives.
- Other Corporate Initiatives [like CII, FICCI, ASSOCHAM] [Shrivastava and Venkateswaran, *op. cit.*, 2002].

RECENT SURVEY'S ON INDIAN CSR

In India during the past few years, different agencies have conducted surveys to capture the drivers, barriers and perceptions of CSR among companies and stakeholders. Prominent surveys include:

1. Corporate Involvement in Social Development in India by Partners-in-Change [PiC].
2. Altered Images: the 2001 State of Corporate Responsibility in India Poll by Tata Energy Research Institute [TERI].
3. Corporate Social Responsibility: Perceptions of Indian Business by Centre for Social Markets [CSM].
4. Corporate Social Responsibility Survey 2002 India presented jointly by the British Council, UNDP, CII and Price Waterhouse Coopers.

The most recent survey based on a sample of 536 companies across the country by Partners-in-Change [2004] reveal that philanthropy is the most significant driver [64 per cent] of CSR,[16] followed by image-building [42 per cent], employee morale [30 per cent] and ethics [30 per cent]. There has been a marked increase in the number of companies involving in CSR interventions; however most of the CSR activities continue to be CEO-led, except in PSUs where government policy shapes the CSR culture and practice. PiC survey 2004 also noted that older companies with greater turnover were more likely to believe in their role in CSR activities.

According to the TERI Poll that explored the perceptions and expectations of some stakeholders *vis-a-vis* workers, company executives and the general public, Indians in general expect business to play an expansive role in society with considerations for the environment, labour standards and human rights [Kumar *et al.*, 2001]. Indians continue to hold high brand equity and reputation of companies over the above CSR criteria. The CSM Survey 2002 Report claimed that the government with unclear policies, ineffective bureaucracy, poor monitoring record, complicated tax systems, and poor infrastructure was the key barrier to CSR in India [Prakash-Mani, 2002]. The CSR Survey 2002 by British Council *et al.*, revealed that many companies are still steeped in an amalgamation of transition from trusteeship/ethical model to the static model and highlighted growing recognition among companies that passive philanthropy is no longer sufficient in the realm of CSR [British Council *et al.*, 2002]. In a study commenced in 2003 by the India Committee of the Netherlands [ICN] and carried out by Consultancy and Research for Environmental Management [CREM] in the Netherlands and Partners-in-Change in India concluded that the Dutch companies operating in India practice CSR only partially in terms of internationally agreed labour and other human rights and environmental standards [CREM, 2004].

To conclude, several companies in India pursue CSR over a range of issues like health care, education, rural development, sanitation, micro credit and women empowerment, arts, heritage, culture, and conservation of wildlife and nature, etc.[17] Credit Rating Information Services of India Ltd. [CRISIL] has launched a Governance Value Creation rating in 2004 towards a more comprehensive triple bottom-line assessment. CSR, or Socially Responsible Investment [SRI] as some people would like to label it, has to be judged not only in terms of reducing pollution levels but more by their contribution to generating livelihoods and marketing services accessible to the poorest segments. In their review of contemporary CSR trends in India, Bimal Arora and Ravi Puranik [2004] observe that, although the corporate sector in India benefited immensely from liberalization and privatization processes, its transition from philanthropic mindsets to CSR has been lagging behind its impressive financial growth. Individual companies define CSR in their own limited ways and contexts. The end result being that all activities undertaken in the name of CSR are merely CEO-driven philanthropy or an extension of philanthropy practiced by trusts and foundations[18] in the form of community development work without mainstreaming CSR, in to core business processes. Hence the crucial question comes up: Does the CSR agenda really respond to the development needs, concerns and priorities of workers, communities and firms in developing countries (Arora and Puranik, *op. cit.*, 2004).

Given the socio-economic inequality that exits in India, the Constitution provides certain discriminatory clauses to safeguard the exclusive interests of Backward Classes of people and bring about social justice over a period of time. Reservation in employment and education has therefore been guaranteed to SC/STs and OBCs in the public sphere. However the benefit of constitutional protection being enjoyed by the above categories in employment and education has turned out to be less meaningful to these classes, with the transition of the Indian economy from the public domain to the burgeoning private domain. To compensate the loss to the BCs in the protective environment of the state sector employment, a reservation package is now being proposed in the private sector as well. However, despite the increasing CSR awareness, the Indian corporate sector is reported to be unhappy and uncompromising to the reservation proposal *vis-a-vis* educational support to these classes. Hence, it is hypothesised that the Indian corporate sector is sympathetic to the socio-economic issues of Backward Classes and it is willing to support their education rather than employment. The paper is an attempt to test the above hypothesis in terms of corporate and stakeholder perspectives on education of Backward Classes *vis-a-vis* reservation in the private sector.

RESERVATION FOR BACKWARD CLASSES: AN OVERVIEW

One of the most controversial and sensitive issues having a direct bearing on the questions of equality and social justice in post-independent India has been the state's power to make reservations[19] (under Articles 15[4] and 16[4], content of the expression of Backward Classes (BCs), identification of these classes, and the nature and extent of reservation for them. The problem of the BCs is one of achieving equality in a society permeated by inequality, despite the commitment of its legal order to complete equality, its legislative enactments and judicial pronouncements reiterating this commitment to implement the provisions of Articles 15[4] and 16[4], the Union Government appointed in 1953 a ten-member commission with Kaka Kalelkar as Chairman. The Commission had the mandate to determine the criteria for considering whether any sections of the people (besides SCs and STs) should be treated as socially and educationally backward classes and in accordance with such criteria, to prepare a list of such classes. The Commission listed 2399 communities as BCs and recommended reservation of at least 25 per cent jobs in Class I, 33.3 per cent in Class II and 40 per cent in Classes III and IV; and 70 per cent seats in all technical and professional institutions However, the report was not accepted by the Centre. The B.P. Mandal Commission (1979) listed 3743 communities among the Hindus alone as BCs. It estimated 52 per cent of the Indian people as BCs and recommended 27 per cent educational and employment reservation for them by the Centre and States. After a gap of one decade, the policy of job reservation for the Other Backward Classes (OBCs) was announced in August 1990, based on the report of the Mandal Commission (excluding the recommendation on educational reservation). Besides sending shock waves to pockets of forward class lobbies (with outbursts in the form of self-immolation), the decision has changed considerably regional, political and social equations (Sankaran, P.N., 1995). In fact there are also strong reservations on the impact of job reservation; "if available data are any indication, reservation has often worked against those it was intended to help: the system has been perverted in most states so that most of the privileges do not trickle down to the really needy, the lowest sections of the BCs (Radhakrishnan, P., 1999).

Though the controversy over the rationale of job reservation as a constitutional mandate was finally put to rest in November 1992 by the landmark judgment of the Supreme Court in Indra Sawhney *vs.* Union of India, 1990,[20] the likely benefit to the OBCs (as also to the SC/STs in a wider sense) from the job reservation strategy was perceived to be limited over the years, due to the shrinkage in the size of government employment and services in banking and financial sectors, following the policy of Economic Reforms, 1991. Hence it has been noted that the reservation scheme established for those seeking parity is more likely to produce poor and piecemeal results in the context of economic reforms, unless it is offered as a package with reservation in education, so that the BCs are equipped to seek employment on their own in the private sector also.

In spite of such reservations/apprehensions raised over the magnitude of the benefit of reservation in government employment (rapidly shrinking under reforms), no serious effort was made either by the government or the BC activists to equip the victims of reforms in terms of quality education responsive to the demands and standards of the private sector.[21] Similarly, the scope or rationale of extending the scheme of reservation to the burgeoning private sector was also not brought in for serious academic discussions or policy formulation. Maharashtra and Madhya Pradesh governments have, however, approved recently a package of job reservation for SC/STs in the private sector and in government contracts.[22] But the process of making Dalits full and active participants in the market economy, in sectors that generate substantial wealth is a slow and often arduous process (Mehta, 2004). Precisely because of such considerations, the Common Minimum Programme of the UPA government and the constitution of a Group of Ministers to Examine Affirmative Action Including Reservations in the Private Sector, call for a national dialogue on reservation in the private sector. The paper is framed against the above background whether to have affirmative action with reservation or without it for BCs in respect of private sector employment.

RESERVATION IN THE PRIVATE SECTOR: EMERGING PERSPECTIVES

It is observed that economic reforms have replaced the government sector with the private sector as the key job creator and that reservation must shift to the latter. Though the demand is a logical offshoot of shrinking reservation potential in the government sector, one wonders why it was not forcefully put forth or foreseen by the backward classes or industry associations during the past decade of reforms. The constitution of the Group of Ministers to examine the issue has sent shock waves to industry and business circles and they have been highly critical of the package, while accepting their social commitment to share the burden of providing quality education to the BCs. The popular apprehension of the critics centres around merit, efficiency, competition, FDI and technology that reservation might have to compromise with. The reactions of employees and job-seekers are yet to crystallize on affirmation with or without reservation. Of course, there are preliminary observations indicating that we have to think in terms of reservation at the feeder institutions rather than impose it on the private corporate sector itself. Similarly, it is held that unemployment alleviation measures are better served by building the capacity of the society rather than providing BCs jobs through reservation and that provision of *'employability'* (enabling environment) should be the focus rather than one time charity. Industry associations (RCCI and CII) need greater focus on training the workers on technical and total quality management. RCCI is trying to popularize the concept of developing entrepreneurship among the vulnerable groups through licensing, contracts and concessions in credit programs (which to some extent is already being undertaken by the Central and State level Backward Classes Development and Finance Corporations). It is reported that the CII is working on an alternative plan for job reservation in the private sector, to tap the employment generation potential for the disadvantaged sections of the society. It has kick started a programme in association with the UK-based City and Guilds Group, under which it plans to impart vocational training to one million people in the country. Narayana Moorthy has proposed that affirmative action be based on economic criteria rather than caste. But the proposal has severe limitations because, determining economic need is a tricky business and income-based preferences are not going to be necessarily advantageous.

There has also been a suggestion to follow the US model where the government provides "Work Opportunity Tax Credit" for employers who hire members of the targeted groups. The Tata Group through its Council for Community Initiatives and the ITC in terms of its social development projects propose that *Corporate Social Responsibility* should ideally converge with a *sustainable business practice* to sustain the former. A lenient view is that once reservation is accepted in principle as a valid social obligation, it should be shared by all employers—public and private. But the traditional viewpoint seems to have lost its relevance under the liberalized economic scenario. Since the private sector follows the merit norm in appointments and promotions, creation of backward employee groups in the mainstream workforce (which is inevitable under reservation) would be problematic for employers as well as the block of reserved beneficiary groups. Branding people in the competitive employment market as backward, involves identity and psychological issues with overtones of frustration and possible decline in productivity and efficiency. Hence it is advisable that we leave the industry associations to work out an amicable formula in lieu of mandatory reservation. The options suggested are:

- To adopt reservation of jobs.
- To pay a consolidated sum to the government in lieu of reservation and the funds be utilized for education and training of BC candidates to equip them for the competitive employment market.
- To trade the reservation obligations for each job with other companies willing to accommodate BC employees.

Empirical evidence on the persistence of caste discrimination in private sector against untouchables justifies the need for corrective measures (Thorat Sukhadeo, 2004). Since India has limited experience of affirmative action policies in private sector, it could draw lessons from the international experience relating to:

(a) The type of the economic sector or markets for which the policies against discrimination are developed, and
(b) The strategies used to give practical shape to the policies.

As regards the economic spheres, countries like the US, Northern Ireland, South Africa and Malaysia have developed legal and affirmative action policies for minority groups, not only for labour markets, but also for agricultural land, capital and other markets. Under the strategies, these countries have used at least three kinds of measures:

1. Equal Opportunity Laws (EOL),
2. Affirmative Action Measures, and
3. Reparation or Compensation.

Legal protection against discrimination in the form of EOL prohibit private or public employers from discrimination of workers based on group identities and provide legal safeguards to discriminated groups. Affirmative action goes a step forward and attempts to ensure a fair share to the discriminated groups in employment and other spheres based on some reasonable criterion. The instruments of reparation are specifically used in terms of compensation for the denial of property rights or injustices in the past. Given the range of economic discrimination against marginalized groups like SCs, STs and OBCs, the reservation policy for the private sector ought to cover not only employment, but also markets, agricultural land and capital, consumer goods, education, housing, government contracts, etc. (Thorat Sukhadeo, *op. cit.*, 2004). According to Mehta, while conceptually reservations and anti-discrimination policies are two beasts, in practice they metamorphose into one. In the context of the reform agenda, the government can make a commitment that any proceeds from disinvestments or gains made from restructuring the public sector will be earmarked to empower the most vulnerable groups. However in a larger perspective, we should all admit that a discussion in terms of reservation is, after all, a second best option. It would be a tragedy if modern India became a project, not for transcending caste, but perpetuating it. Unless used in a very limited sense, reservations threaten to do the latter (Mehta, *op. cit.*, 2004).

There is also the apprehension that, even if the private sector agrees to reservation or the government makes it mandatory, private sector may be able to weed out non-meritorious candidates or applicants against reserved posts, by using examinations stipulating cut-off marks, changing the composition of the workforce, converting officers, technicians and skilled workers into consultants, etc. Over and above crippling the private sector, it is feared that reservations may benefit only a microscopic minority (creamy layer) of BCs while leaving behind hundreds of millions that are systematically deprived of education and skills. Hence, it is held that to uplift them we need high quality schools, colleges and vocational establishments. Framed against the above background, the paper tries to examine the issues of CSR in reservation and education for BCs in terms of the perspectives of employers and employees in the corporate sector as also of students taking professional courses in Bangalore.

EMPLOYER, EMPLOYEE AND STUDENT PERSPECTIVES: A DISCUSSION

(a) The Methodology

The study is exclusively based on opinion collected from the survey (using the interview schedule) of a sample of respondents, identified through convenient sampling in the city of Bangalore. In order to collect the opinion of three categories of respondents, presumed to be really concerned about the issues under investigation, a structured interview schedule was developed and administered through personal interview. The three groups identified for the opinion survey are 121 employers [represented by seniors/heads in the personnel and HR departments of corporate agencies and business units], 114 employees in those establishments and 60 students pursuing professional education in management/business schools, engineering and medical colleges, institutes of technology and post-graduate science colleges. For want of an authentic list of institutions, especially of the employers' category [which is so varied and heterogeneous], the method of convenience sampling was followed and therefore the same procedure was also adopted for the selection of employees and student respondents. The broad spectrum of employers [and by implication employees attached to them] and educational institutions [for identification of students] covered by the opinion survey are associated with rubber industries, air travel, fashion design, property developers, power generation and automation, private banks, soft drinks, medical laboratories, iron castings, automobile sales and finance, dealers in popular materials, etc., apart from IT institutions, engineering and business schools. Simple statistical tools like percentage and average are used in data analysis and interpretation.

(b) Opinion Survey: A Reflection

The results of the opinion survey of employers, employees and students are analysed below. From Table 19.1, which summarizes responses of all the groups of respondents taken together, it is observed that:

- All the respondents attribute the rapid expansion of the private sector in the last decade to the opportunities opened up by economic reforms.
- Similarly, opinion is very much strong (95.38 per cent) on the need for strengthening education so as to sustain the development of BCs.

TABLE 19.1

Reservation in the Private Sector: Response on Common Issues [Employers, Employees and Students]

No.	Issues/Statements on which opinion is sought	Response (%)	
		Positive	Negative
1.	Economic reforms [Liberalisation, Privatisation and Globalisation] have led to rapid expansion of the Private Sector	100	–
2.	Economic reforms have reduced the size of the public sector	72.9	27.1
3.	Economic reforms have brought down employment in Government Sector	58.54	41.46
4.	Growth of the Pvt. Sector and fall in government employment have led to the demand for reservation in private sector	77.62	22.38
5.	Reservation in Pvt. Sector is a socially relevant issue	62.9	37.1
6.	Other Backward Classes [OBCs, Scheduled Castes, Scheduled Tribes and other socially, educationally and economically backward classes] face learning handicaps in the educational system	57.95	42.05
7.	OBCs, being low profile achievers, face handicaps in the employment market	53.28	46.72
8.	Job reservation is only a palliative	70.85	29.15
9.	For sustained development of OBCs, their education need to be strengthened	95.38	4.62

Source: Opinion Survey.

- A very high percentage of the respondents (77.62) consider that the growth of the private sector and fall in government employment have led to the demand for reservation.
- Decline in the size of the public sector is attributed by 72.90 per cent of the respondents to the spread of economic reforms.
- Opinion is also sharp on the observation that job reservation is only a palliative for improving the lot of BCs.
- However, there is some disagreement (among 46.72 per cent) on the statement that BCs, being low profile achievers, face handicaps in the employment market. Similarly, the statement that BCs face learning handicaps in the educational system is also not endorsed by 42.05 per cent of the respondents taken together. On the statement that economic reforms have brought down employment in the government sector, 41.46 per cent has expressed their disagreement.

To sum up, the response on common issues and statements suggests that with the private sector forging ahead under reforms and the size of the public sector declining, there has been a demand for reservation in the private sector. But reservation *per se* is only a palliative and sustainable development of BCs depends on making them more *employable* in the competitive environment through quality education. On the related questions of learning/employment handicaps of BCs, the opinion is divided and a minority among the respondents maintains that the above handicaps do not exist in reality.

Employer response on reservation in the private sector is presented in Table 19.2, which indicates that:

- Quality education to BCs is a better alternative to reservation as supported by about 87 per cent of the respondents; the argument is in fact an endorsement of the need for quality education reiterated by 95.38 per cent of the respondents to common issues brought out in Table 19.1.
- Educational reservation is more meaningful than job reservation as noted by 79.16 per cent of the employer respondents. From the angle of the common views covered in Table 19.1, the preference for educational reservation is a logical extension of the observation made by 70.85 per cent of the combined set of respondents that job reservation (in contrast to educational reservation) is only a palliative for the sustained development of BCs.

TABLE 19.2

Reservation in the Private Sector: Employer Response

No.	*Issues/Statements on which opinion is sought*	*Positive (%)*
1.	Do you look into the caste profile in recruitments?	19.83
2.	Has there been any caste-based discrimination in recruitment?	23.96
3.	Do you feel that OBC employees perform below average?	46.55
4.	Between marks in exams and interviews, do you think that OBC candidates perform less in the latter?	48.76
5.	Will reservation result in compromising merit?	76.85
6.	Will reservation adversely affect institutional efficiency?	71.66
7.	Do you feel that reservation will disrupt FDI and technology flow?	55.08
8.	Is quality education to OBCs a better alternative than reservation?	86.77
9.	Would you like to offer scholarships to OBC students?	78.99
10.	Would you like to support residential schools for OBCs?	64.95
11.	Is educational reservation more meaningful than job reservation?	79.16
12.	Would you mind recruiting OBCs as short-term trainees?	39.16
13.	Do you think that corporate have a social obligation to facilitate education of OBCs?	57.85
14.	Do you welcome reservation in the private sector?	41.32
15.	Would you like to recruit OBCs if the government is willing to offer some tax/duty concessions to you as an incentive?	45.83

Source: Opinion Survey.

- About 58 per cent of the corporate employers accept their social obligation to facilitate education of BCs; nearly 79 per cent of the employers are in favour of offering scholarships to BC students and majority of the employers (65 per cent) would like to support residential schools for BC students.
- While accepting corporate social responsibility towards supporting education for BCs, only 41 per cent of the employers' welcome reservation in the private sector; only 39 per cent mind recruiting BCs as short-term trainees and roughly 46 per cent would like to recruit BCs under tax/duty concession from the government as an incentive for recruitment of BCs.
- There exists a feeling among 47 per cent of the employers that BC employees perform below average in the private sector; however the dubious performance, perceived of BC employees is not reflected in recruitment practices in which the caste profile is reported to be looked into only by 20 per cent of the employer respondents and the chances of caste-based discrimination is reported only by 24 per cent of the employers.
- Majority of the reporting employers feel that reservation will compromise merit (77 per cent), adversely affect institutional efficiency (72 per cent) and disrupt the flow of FDI to the corporate sector (55 per cent).
- From the above observations it may be concluded that while accepting responsibility in the education of BCs, employers consider reservation in education as a better option for the development of BCs than private sector reservation. Only the minority welcomes the reservation proposal in the private sector; they consider training and incentive-based recruitment of BCs also less feasible, as reservation in itself is a compromise on merit, institutional efficiency and free flow of FDI.

The response of employees summarized in Table 19.3 gives the following observations:

- In full agreement with the common view and the employers' view, majority of the employee respondents (85 per cent) consider quality education to BCs a better choice than the proposal for reservation and welcome educational reservation than job reservation in the private sector; nearly 80 per cent of

TABLE 19.3

Reservation in the Private Sector: Employees' Response

No.	*Issues/Statements on which opinion is sought*	*Positive (%)*
1.	Did you get any caste leverage for your appointment	19.16
2.	Have you enjoyed the benefit of reservation in education [Admission, Fee, Scholarship, Hostel, Travel, Project]?	37.27
3.	Do you favour reservation in the Private Sector?	33.33
4.	If you welcome reservation, is it for the entry point?	38.73
5.	Do you propose it for promotions as well?	24.77
6.	Do you consider reservation a compromise on merit?	58.77
7.	Will reservation tell upon institutional efficiency?	46.49
8.	Is the performance of OBC employees below average?	39.09
9.	Are the corporates unhappy with the reservation proposal?	79.82
10.	Will reservation affect the flow of FDI and technology?	64.91
11.	Is quality education to OBCs a better alternative?	85.08
12.	Is educational reservation more meaningful than job reservation?	78.37
13.	Will the corporates accept the reservation formula?	36.36
14.	Do the corporates have an obligation to support the education of OBCs?	65.17
15.	Will reservation adversely affect the prospects of non-OBCs?	77.19

Source: Opinion Survey.

them share the view that the corporate employers are unhappy with the job reservation proposal.

- The statement that the corporate sector has an obligation to support the education of BCs is endorsed by 65 per cent of the respondents from the employee segment.
- Roughly 78 per cent of the employees hold that reservation will eat into the job prospects of qualified non-BCs in the country which may have a demoralizing effect on the healthy operation of the employment market.
- As in the case of employers in particular and the common responses analysed in Table 19.1, majority of the employees (59 per cent) maintain that reservation would be a compromise on merit and that the flow of FDI would be disrupted (65 per cent).
- Only 19 per cent of the employees had enjoyed the benefit of caste in their appointment and only 33 per cent favour reservation in the private sector. Reservation, if any, in promotions is welcomed only by 25 per cent of the reporting employees.
- About 39 per cent of the employees share the view that the performance of BC employees is below average.
- The popular view that the corporate agencies will not welcome the reservation proposal is accepted by majority of the employees (only 36 per cent of them feel that the employers will agree to the suggestion).

In conclusion, the perspective of the employees indicates that educational reservation should have precedence over employment reservation; though the corporate units also have a responsibility to share the burden of providing education to poor BC people, employees maintain that private sector may not agree to the job reservation proposal and that the scheme may affect the job prospects of non-BCs too.

The student perspective on reservation in the private sector, captured in Table 19.4 implies that:

- There is high level of student awareness about reservation in the private sector (67 per cent of them are aware of it) and more than half (53 per cent) have had the benefit of educational reservation at one point or other in their student life.
- Quality education to BCs should be high on the agenda of development and that educational reservation has to be

TABLE 19.4

Reservation in the Private Sector: Student Response

No.	*Issues/Statements on which opinion is sought*	*Positive (%)*
1.	Have you enjoyed the benefit of educational reservation [Admission, Fee, Hostel, Travel. Project, Scholarship]?	53.33
2.	Are you aware of the Government proposal for private sector reservation in employment?	67.24
3.	Do you think that OBCs have a learning handicap?	53.57
4.	Do the OBCs need reservation in employment?	43.85
5.	Do you advocate reservation in entry point?	37.73
6.	Is reservation meaningful in promotions?	32.14
7.	Will reservation affect individual efficiency?	60.34
8.	Will reservation tell upon institutional efficiency?	63.79
9.	Is reservation a compromise on merit?	58.62
10.	Will the corporates agree on reservation?	37.93
11.	Is quality education to OBCs a better alternative than reservation?	89.65
12.	Do you favour educational reservation?	80.70
13.	Do the corporate have an obligation to support the education of OBCs?	70.17
14.	If corporate agree to short-term training facility for OBCs, is it good?	82.75
15.	Will reservation affect the job prospects of non-OBCs?	82.75

Source: Opinion Survey.

accorded high priority in the scheme of reservations. Ninety per cent and 81 per cent of the reporting students who are undergoing professional education in the city-based institutions have expressed these views.

- Given the crucial role of quality education in socio-economic development of BCs and the increasing cost of education (rapidly getting privatized), 70 per cent of the students believe that the corporate sector has a social obligation to promote the education of BC students. About 83 per cent of them really welcome short-term training facility that could be offered to BC students by big corporate employers.
- Despite the fact that the reporting students will be job-seekers shortly, more than 60 per cent of them hold that reservation will tell upon institutional efficiency and that it is a compromise on merit (59 per cent). Most of them (83 per cent) believe that the job prospects of non-BCs will also be affected adversely if reservation is made mandatory for the corporate sector.
- Only 44 per cent of the reporting students admit any reservation requirement in the private sector and a lesser percentage favours reservation at entry points or in promotions.
- May be because about 50 per cent of the reporting students have enjoyed reservation in education, more or less the same percentage feels that the BC students face a learning handicap in the competitive and costly educational environment of modern India.

To sum up, the reporting students feel that the corporate units are not happy with reservation proposal and that there is a case for corporate social responsibility in supporting education of BCs, given the role of education in socio-economic advancement. Apart from education, the students look at corporate units to offer short-term training facility also to BC candidates. They also share the dominant view of other participants in the opinion survey that reservation is devoid of merit.

CONCLUDING OBSERVATIONS

The private sector in India accounts for 74 per cent of GDP and 71 per cent of total investments [ADB, 2003]. Corporate India is riding on a wave of new found confidence [Shourie, 2004]. However, analysts of economic reforms argue that the expectations from economic reforms have not had much success as decline in incomes and employment continues unabated [Chaudhuri, 2001]. With public, including government, sector jobs on the decline, we are experiencing jobless growth [Seminar, 2004]. The phenomenon of falling employment in the state sector has adversely affected BCs for whom reservation has turned out to be a lost dream, with the private sector taking over the public sector.

Faced with caste-related discrimination and deprivation of marginalized social groups like SCs, STs and OBCs, the Indian state has used reservation policy in select public spheres. Such concerns are however, confined to the government sector and the vast private sector where more than 90 per cent of SC/ST workers are employed, remain without protection against caste discrimination. While affirmative action policies in other countries have been used both for private and public sector, from the very beginning, in India the privatization process, concomitant with the withdrawal of the state from many spheres under the liberalisation regime, has further narrowed and compressed the little space that the discriminated groups had gained till now (Thorat Sukhadeo, *op. cit.*, 2004). But the government policy continues under the more populist proposal of job reservation, despite the solid recommendations of the Backward Class Commissions for employment-*cum*-educational reservation. Education has, in addition to its modernizing influence, enormous potential to promote and update the technological skills of the underprivileged people, make them suitable for the market economy and insulate them against chances of being further marginalized in a regime of efficiency and merit. In the discussions on protecting the weaker sections of the society from the tendencies of marginalisation perceived in economic reforms also, the crucial role of quality education as a vehicle for adaptation to the market economy was not adequately emphasized. The so called BC organizations also did not rise to the occasion and take up the case for compensatory education with the state machinery or the corporate sector, which would have supported their educational aspirations. By instituting a Group of Ministers to examine the question of affirmative action including reservations in the private sector, the government has started a dialogue that should have been done much earlier.

Respondents of the opinion survey share the view that economic reforms have triggered the rapid strides in private sector employment and its inevitable corollary, the decline in public sector employment. Cutting across inter-category differences among employers, employees and students, the dominant opinion is in favour of the need for strengthening education of BCs *vis-a-vis* private sector reservation in employment. Corporate social responsibility in education has fortunately come in for a good deal of appreciation. The scope of providing short-term training to BC candidates is limited, as the private employers agree only on supporting education and not anything that may get in to their internal systems and procedures, given the highly competitive environment in which they operate. Apprehensions on the existence of learning handicaps and discrimination in employment are not widely shared by the reporting respondents; however the need for quality education, as already stated, is widely endorsed. BC employees are perceived to be performing little lower than the non-BC counterparts in corporate employment; the performance indicator also necessitates qualitative empowerment of BC students in terms of better education. The fact that the private sector is unhappy with reservation is adequately brought out by the survey; what they expect is affirmative action (which they will definitely support) but not reservation. In the prevailing environment of cut-throat competition, reservation would be a compromise on merit, efficiency, flow of FDI and modern technology.

The findings of the opinion survey fit in well with the holistic view taken by the Backward Class Commissions that education is first and foremost in any strategy towards equality and social justice. Though the Commissions did not foresee economic reforms, it is worth remembering that the scheme of reservation recommended by them takes care of the dynamics of reforms and labour market liberalisation as well. Since the international experience with affirmative action goes beyond reservation in labour market and covers land, capital, housing, contracts, etc., it would be meaningful to commence a dialogue as to how a package of reforms could be introduced in the related markets also so that the development of BCs is rendered more sustainable.

In spite of the considerable track record of initiatives that are perceived as CSR, the task of crafting new models [of CSR] that are capable of addressing controversial issues like support for the education of BCs *vis-a-vis* reservation in the private sector, seems to be equally challenging for the corporate sector. The suggestion for introduction of CSR in management education [Sharma, Radha, R.,

2004] and the need for CSR experts in corporate HR departments aimed at nurturing healthy relationship between corporate agencies and communities [Cheholu, Radha Mohan, 2005] need serious consideration in the emerging context. However, the role of industry associations in the process remains paramount.

NOTES AND REFERENCES

1. In the case of a company, stakeholders comprise of customers, suppliers, and members of the society at large with whom they (companies) are related directly and indirectly in terms of human and environmental issues.
2. Also known as corporate philanthropy which began as individual philanthropy and later shifted to corporate philanthropy (building houses, churches, schools, libraries, provision of medical and legal services to the poor).
3. According to the stewardship principle, corporate managers have been placed in a position of trust. Having control over large volume of resources, they incur a responsibility to use those resources in ways that are good not just for the stakeholders alone but for the society generally. In this way they have become stewards or trustees for society.
4. Whereas societal expectations (the interest of employees and stakeholders) dominate in Continental Europe (Germany, France, Netherlands and South Asian countries), ownership rights (returning a profit to shareholders) dominate in US and UK.
5. The term 'Backward Classes' has never attained a fixed character. According to Mehta and Jaswal, "the judicial scrutiny leads us to form a view point that there cannot be one set of recognized methods to justify Backward Classes." See for a detailed treatment of the question, Mehta and Jaswal (1998). See also Government of Karnataka, 1990.
6. Article 15(4) relates to the advancement of any socially and educationally backward class of citizens or the SCs and STs. The second (Article 16(4)) is for job reservation in favour of any backward class of citizens, which in the opinion of the state, is not adequately represented in its services. The first was added by the Constitution (1st Amendment) Act, 1951, as parallel to the second, under pressure from Madras state when its communal quotas in educational institutions were quashed by the judiciary maintaining that classification based on caste, race and religion was unconstitutional.
7. See Government of India (1955): Report of the Backward Classes Commission, Delhi. Government of India Press and Government of India (1980): Report of the Backward Classes Commission, Delhi, Government of India Press.
8. The rates and criteria of reservation vary between different states and caste groups.
9. In a recent paper P.L. Kumar has discussed the innate paradoxes in the phrase CSR in terms of governance of companies, market reward for ethical companies,

lack of clarity in CSR definition. CSR as systematic denial of wrong doing, lack of compliance mechanism with regard to human rights and location of CSR on the periphery of the corporate structure. He concludes that unless these paradoxes are properly addressed, CSR cannot legitimately be branded as invention of public relations. See Kumar, P.L., 2004.

10. See also Bhattacharya and Sen (2004). For a detailed analysis of CSR impact on consumer response. According to them, "this positive link of CSR to consumer patronage is spurring companies to devote greater energies and resources to CSR initiatives" (p. 10). Hence many companies follow such practices as social audits, social reporting and the triple bottom-line. The triple bottom-line which the thought leaders on CSR want companies to monitor and report are: Do not just aim to make money: but protect the environment and fight for social justice as well. Using a variety of methodologies such as focus groups, in-depth interviews, survey and experiments, the authors support a consumer-centric conceptualization of CSR.
11. For a detailed analysis of company-non-profit collaboration, see Berger *et al.* (2004).
12. 'Social' means all of the non-investor stakeholders affected by business: individuals, employees, communities and society. These stakeholders may also be described as those affected by market externalities.
13. The 'virtue matrix' is composed of four quadrants with the bottom two quadrants making up the 'civil foundation' (CF) of the matrix and the top two, its 'frontiers.' CF that promotes socially responsible conduct and enhances shareholder value, has at its left conduct driven by 'choice' and at its right mandatory conduct 'compliance': the two are not watertight *inter se* and can shrink or expand with reference to the frontier quadrants, again having 'strategic' and 'structural' frontiers on left and right quadrants respectively. They encompass activities whose motivation tends to be intrinsic and whose value to shareholders is either clearly negative or immediately apparent. Socially responsible corporate practices in the strategic frontier may migrate to the CF depending on other companies imitating the innovator. The structural frontier houses activities that are both intrinsically motivated and clearly contrary to shareholder interests but beneficial to the society. It implies that executives' commendable concern for their shareholder value can sometimes stifle innovations in CSR. Behaviour in the upper quadrant can migrate to the civil foundation through imitation, collective action or government mandate. This migration ratchets up the CF. But it can be ratcheted down if a critical mass of companies abandons a socially responsible practice. See Roger L. Martin, 2004.
14. Varieties of CSR or the CSR Matrix

	Raises Social Welfare	Reduces Social Welfare
Raises Profits	Good Management	Pernicious CSR
Reduces Profits	Borrowed Virtue	Delusional CSR

Crook, Clive, 2005.

15. For a detailed account of CSR initiatives of companies in India, see "CSR: How Companies are Delivering the Goods," *Praxis*, December, 2004.
16. The ongoing wave of Corporate Charity (Giving) to tsunami victims has once again posed the pertinent question: What exactly is CSR? *Fortune*, January 24, 2005 reports that just two weeks after the disaster, the 'Contributions Academy,' a group that tracts Corporate Giving estimates that corporate contributions for relief totalled $ 178 million from 114 companies. That's on pace to top the previous record, the $ 682 million that the Giving USA Foundation which analyses charitable contributions estimates firm's eventually gave to 9/11 victims.
17. Latest instance of CSR in environmental conservation is that the New Delhi-based Conservation NGO—Wildlife Trust of India (WTI) received the whole-hearted support of Tata Chemicals Ltd. (TCL) and Gujarat Heavy Chemicals Ltd. (GHCL) to conserve the pride sea fish of Gujarat region—Whale Shark—which is almost on the brink of extinction. A unique corporate—NGO CSR Partnership indeed! See *Business India*, January 3-16, 2005. See for case studies of CSR, Shrivastava and Venkateswaran, *op. cit.*, 2002 and Praxis, *Business Line*, December 2004.
18. Referring to the 'Learning Guarantee Programme' (LGP), the CEO of Azim Premji Foundation, observes that LGP is not a Wipro CSR Project, but a personal initiative of its Chairman Azim Premji. See Anjali Prayag, 2004.
19. In Indian context, reservations were introduced during the last decades of the 19th century at a lime when the subcontinent could be broadly divided according to two main forms of governance—British India and the 600 Princely States, Mysore in South India, Baroda and Kolhapur in Western India took considerable interest in the awakening and advancement of the minorities and deprived sections of the society. The very first records of implementing reservation policies are from these princely states. See Bhagwan Das (2000), for a short account of the history of reservations.
20. The Supreme Court's order of 1st October 1990 stayed the related notification of 13th August 1990. A modified notification was issued on 25th September 1991. Besides the 27 per cent reservation notified earlier, the new government that came to power set apart 10 per cent seats for the economically backward among the forward communities. Though the provision for preference within the 27 per cent to the poorer sections of that BCs appeared as the saving grace, it was nullified by the provision for filling the unfilled quotas from the affluent sections of the BCs. See P. Radhakrishnan (1996). Besides 27 per cent reservation: (1) A National Commission to review the eligibility of caste groups for reservation was established through an Act in 1993, (2) A National Backward Classes Finance and Development Corporation with schemes for skill upgradation was established, and (3) Educational schemes for OBC welfare were also introduced.
21. Recently the 'Committee on India Vision 2020' has raised few relevant questions on the potential of the private sector to create jobs that can make up the fall in public sector employment and the chances of BCs getting the jobs. The experience with reforms is that elasticity of employment will be declining with respect to

growth. SC/STs may lag behind in technical skills and professional competence, which are crucial to private sector employment. They may crowd themselves more into unorganized and informal sectors especially under the marginalisation process reinforced by commodification of social services. See Saksena, H.S. (2004).

22. The Maharashtra State Public Services (Reservation for Scheduled Caste, Scheduled Tribes, Denotified Tribes, Nomadic Tribes. Special Backward Category and Other Backward Classes) Act, 2001 (Maharashtra Act No. VIII of 2004). It is however observed that the assembly elections scheduled to be held in October 2004 was the reason for the government's move to empower Dalits. See Jogdand, 2004.

REFERENCES

Aaronson, S.A. (2002): 'How the Europeans Got a Head Start on Politics to Promote Global Corporate Responsibility,' *International Journal of Corporate Sustainability: Corporate Environment Strategy*, 9(4), pp. 350-67.

Action Aid India (1997): *Country Strategy Paper 2*, Action Aid India, Bangalore, p. 73.

Arora, Bimal and Puranic, Ravi (2004): 'A Review of Corporate Social Responsibility in India,' *Development*, 47(3), 93-100.

Asian Development Bank (2003): 'Country Strategy and Program, 2003-06,' Asian Development Bank, India.

Berger, Ida E., Cunningham, Pegg H. and Drumwright Minette E. (2004): "Social Alliances: Company Non-Profit Collaboration," *California Management Review*, Vol. 47, Fall, pp. 58-89.

Bhattacharya, C.B. and Sen, Sankar (2004): "Doing Better at Doing Good: When, Why and How Consumers Respond to Corporate Social Initiatives,' *California Management Review*, Vol. 47, No. 1, Fall, pp. 9-24.

Bose, Shukla (2004): 'My Brush with CSR,' *Praxis*, Business Line, December, pp. 32-35.

British Council, UNDP, CII and Pricewaterhouse Coopers (2002): *Corporate Social Responsibility Survey 2002 India*, British Council.

Chaudhuri, S. (2001): 'Production and Employment Growth and Decline in Organised Manufacturing in India since 1991,' paper presented at the International Conference. Beyond the Washington Consensus: Governance and the Public Domain in Contrasting Economies: The Cases of India and Canada, 12-14 Feb. 2001, India.

Chebolu, Radha Mohan (2005): 'Corporate Community Relationship: The New Role of HR Manager,' *HRM Review*, January, pp. 50-56.

Cone, Carol L.; Feldman, Mark A. and Da Silva, Alison T. (2003): 'Causes and Effects,' *Harward Business Review*, July, pp. 95-101.

CREM (2004): *Corporate Social Responsibility in India: Policy and Practices of Dutch Companies*, Amsterdam, CREM.

Crook, Clive (2005): 'The Good Company: A Survey of Corporate Social Responsibility,' *The Economist*, January 22.

Crowther, David (2002): *A Social Critique of Corporate Reporting*, Aldershot, Ashgate.

Crowther, David (2004), 'Corporate Social Responsibility Increases Shareholder Value,' *ICFAI Reader*, July, pp. 21-25.

Das, Bhagwan (2000): 'Moments in a History of Reservations,' *Economic and Political Weekly*, Vol. XXXV, Nos. 43 and 44, October, pp. 3831-34.

Government of Karnataka (1990): Report of the Karnataka Third Backward Classes Commission, Bangalore, Government Press, Vol. 1.

Hopkins, M. (2003): *The Planetary Bargain: Corporate Social Responsibility Comes of Age*, London, Macmillan Press.

Jogdand, P.G. (2004): 'Reservation in Private Sector,' Legislation in Maharashtra, *Economic and Political Weekly*, July 24, pp. 3344-46.

Kinder, Lydenberg and Domini Research and Analytics (2003): Socrates: The Corporate Social Ratings Monitor.

Kumar, P.L. (2004): 'A Paradox called Corporate Social Responsibility,' *The ICFAI Journal of Corporate Governance*, July, pp. 7-14.

Kumar, R.; D.F. Murphy and V. Balsari (2001): *Altered Images: The 2001 State of Corporate Social Responsibility in India Poll*, TERI, New Delhi.

Lichtenstein, Donald R.; Drumwright, Minette, and Braig, Bridgette, M. (2004): "The Effect of CSR on Customer Donations to Corporate Supported Non-Profits," *Journal of Marketing*, Vol. 68, October 16-32.

Lingane, Alison and Olsen Sara (2004): 'Guidelines for Social Return on Investment,' *California Management Review*, Vol. 46, No. 3, Spring, pp. 116-35.

Martin, Roger L. (2002): 'The Virtue Matrix: Calculating the Return on Corporate Responsibility,' *Harward Business Review*, March, pp. 69-75.

Mehta, P.L. and Jaswal, Surender Singh (1998): 'Who are Backward Classes: A Scrutiny Through Judicial Lenses,' *IASSI Quarterly*, Vol. 17, No. 1, pp. 43-58.

Mehta, Pratap Bhanu (2004): 'Affirmation Without Reservation,' *Economic and Political Weekly*, Vol. XXXIX, No. 27, July 3, pp. 2951-54.

Mohan, A. (2001): 'Corporate Citizenship: Perspectives from India,' *Journal of Corporate Citizenship*, Sheffield, Greenleef Publishing.

Post, James E.; Frederic, William C.; Lawrence Anne T. and Weber James (1996): *Business and Society, Corporate Strategy, Public Policy, Ethics*, McGraw-Hill Inc., 8th Edn., pp. 35-56.

Prakash-Mani, K. (2002): *Corporate Social Responsibility in the Indian Context*, Sustainability, UK: Sustainability Radar.

Prayag, Anjali (2004): 'Premji's Passion: CSR: How Companies are Delivering the Goods,' *Praxis*, Business Line, Dec., p. 18.

Radhakrishnan, P. (1996): 'Mandal Commission: A Sociological Critique' in M.N. Srinivas (ed.), *Caste: Its Twentieth Century Avatar*, Delhi, Penguin Books.

________ (1999), 'Caste, Politics and the Reservation Issue,' in Barbara Harriss, White and S. Subramanian (eds.), *Illfare in India: Essays on India's Social Sector in Honour of S. Guhan*, Sage Publications, pp. 163-95.

Saksena, H.S. (2004): 'Issues Concerning Vulnerable Groups: Vision 2020' in *India Vision 2020, Report of the Committee on India Vision 2020*. Planning Commission, Government of India (Chairman S.P. Gupta), Academic Foundation, New Delhi.

Sankaran, P.N. (1995): 'Reservation for the Other Backward Classes: Scope and Issues in a Liberalised Economic Scenario,' *Review of Social Sciences*, Vol. 1, No. 2, January, pp. 56-67.

Seminar (2004): 'Development Journal from India,' No. 537, May 2004, India.

Sharma, Radha R. (2004): 'Corporate Social Responsibility in Management Education: Who is Responsible?' *IJTD Journal*, Vol. XXXIV, 3 July-Sept., pp. 129-36.

Shourie, A. (2001): 'Required: A New Form of Governance for a New Economy,' *Indian Express*, Newspaper Article Series—'Our Brave New Industry,' Part III, 04 April, 2004.

Shrivastava, Harsh and Venkateswaran Shankar (2002): *The Business of Social Responsibility: The Why, What and How of Corporate Social Responsibility in India*, Books for Change, Bangalore.

Thorat, Sukhadeo (2004): 'On Reservation Policy for Private Sector,' *Economic and Political Weekly*, June 19, p. 2560.

UNDP (2004): UNDP CSR Program in Albania, 2004-06 (www.undp.org).

Vachani, Sushil and Smith, N. Craig (2004): 'Socially Responsible Pricing: Lessons from the Pricing of AIDS Drugs in Developing Countries,' *California Management Review*, Vol. 47, No. 1, Fall, pp. 117-44.

Ward, H. and Fox, T. (2002): *Moving the Corporate Citizenship Agenda to South*, London, IIED.

20

Social Responsibility and Marketing

MAN CHAND KHANDELA

Human being is by every means a social creature. Social creature is the person who has some responsibilities and rights in the society. He affects the Society and affected by it through his actions/ reactions, innovations, general behaviour, aptitude, attitude, etc. If the man does not behave responsibly and does not think about the society as a whole, he has no right to be called a human being.

It is true that in this age of globalization where everybody is rushing towards money, material and power, social responsibility of individuals, companies, corporations and organizations, etc. is gradually becoming lesser. Every individual or organization has become, if not totally but to a greater extent self-centred and self-interest-oriented. Today, the success of any individual or organization is measured in terms of his capacity of generating funds and creating profits. His means for achieving the ends are, not at all important. That is why in the globalised world business ethics, norms, conventions and traditions have lost their sanctity, significance and relevance in general and the persons who possesses these qualities and behave according to the expectations of the society, have considerably shrinked and, in fact, they are now, in reality, not respected; rather they are treated as false or orthodox. It is really not only strangeful but also painful also that the social responsibility of business in which marketing has become very important element, we have totally lost our culture.

There was a time when every businessman was afraid of selling the commodities which were harmful for the consumer in any way. At that time industrial or business firms were not for "marketing" their products but they were for selling their products only. At that time sale of any product was to a greater extent, depending on the material, quality and behaviour of the seller. Every thing at that time was hundred per cent transparent and rate of profit was to some extent fixed. Even today our parents and grand parents tell us about the value of ethics in marketing during their time when the rate of profit was "Ek Rupaiya men Ikkani." That means they were to take 1/16 part as profit of their total sale and they were not bothered about their marketing. Now the scenario has basically changed. Every individual or organization now wants to make a place in the marketing not only through producing best goods, having least possible rate of profit, giving best services to the customer and making the things transparent before the consumers. Rather their marketing means creating market for their products for the future by theory of *Sham, Dam, Dund, Bhed.*

Marketing in this age of globalization has no ethics, norms, traditions or binding. Technically, the consumer is the king of the market but in practice he has become the slave of the MNCs and other larger corporations. Everybody knows that there is no specific content in cold drinks like Coca-Cola or Pepsi Cola. None of us present here knows or is in a position to tell exactly about the contents of these cold drinks. Even after the decision and directions of the highest court of the country, for informing the consumer about the contents contained in these products these companies are still not doing accordingly. I think none of us have forgotten about the undesired and harmful percentage of contents of pesticides and chemicals in these products which was also agreed by the highest court of the country. In my opinion, this is the height of immorality, as these companies are still insisting upon for not informing about the contents of pesticides and chemicals contained in their products and their marketing of such type of products is allowed unhindered. These companies have rather adopted a strategy of making false and aggressive advertisements in every possible media for telling the consumers that these products are free of any harmful contents. This is again the height of immorality of person who is the General Secretary of a living political party as he is advocating in favour of these companies in the court. It may be false or foul but ironically it is a great strategy of these companies for marketing by hiring a respected political leader as their Advocate.

In my opinion hiring Mr. Jethali as their Advocate was not only a matter of hiring the best Advocate for defending their case but under their marketing strategy they wanted to hire a famous political leader so that innocent and uneducated people of the country can believe their advocate's pleadings. This is only an example amongst many.

I want to give you another example of an irresponsible behaviour of MNCs and larger companies towards their marketing strategy. When I see on the television that one person living under the poverty line and earning not more than Rs. 30 or Rs. 40 in a day, is forced to buy Cadbury chocolate of Rs. 10 for his kid of 2 years only. This is a different matter that contents of chocklate are harmful for the small kids by every means but the matter of concern is that very poor fellow who is not in a position to give *Roti with Pani or Mirch,* and who has 5 or 6 family members is emotionally blackmailed through advertisements in the electronic media for buying Rs. 10 chocklate which gives nothing positive to his already weak kid. Again we can take marketing strategy of Cigarette and Gutka companies whose owners are knowing very well that these products are very harmful for the human beings and can be a cause of incurable cancer in the world. It is in my opinion in no way marketing but irresponsible and unethical behaviour of the persons who are greedy of money. They actually are not marketing their products but are spoiling the generation. It is again my painful experience that even in the classes of MBA teachers also teach the students about the same effective marketing strategy of such companies. They do not think that they have a social responsibility under marketing strategy for any product or services.

In advocating the policies of globalization it is claimed that ultimately the consumer is the beneficiary but this benefit, even if it is there, at all, is unfortunately measured only in terms of price or paisa. If the consumer is to pay less or lesser for any product partially it always does not mean that he is the beneficiary. We have to measure the benefits not only in terms of money but in terms of social, ethical and moral affects. I can again take an example of our own State where present Government headed by Mrs. Vasundhra Raje is trying its best and making all possible efforts in marketing wine, that we can call *sharab*. Can you agree with this strategy of marketing *sharab* in which *sharabis* are taught the way of taking wine, the place of wine sellers and glamour that is created by drinking any type of *sharab*. This is an example of irresponsible behaviour and attitude of the Government that *Sharab Thekedar* have started to make available pouches of *desi sharab* to the *Sharabis* in the early morning at their doors like *Doodhwalas* who comes in the morning. The most unfortunate part of this marketing strategy is that the Government is not doing anything against such type of marketing strategies and sellers. This is again the height of the immorality by the Government that Nagrik Senas of these *Sharab Thekedars* are protected by the Police force under the formal or informal instructions of the Government. Can you do such type of marketing strategy? If the answer is yes then I will say that we academicians and educators are also influenced by money only.

Why should we talk only about the irresponsible behaviour of producers or sellers who are openly for the money. But what is about the big Professors and educationists and marketing strategists, who charge lakhs of rupees for one or one series of lecturers for giving effective marketing strategy to such type of MNCs and Corporations. If we are talking about the social responsibility and marketing in this international seminar, at least we have to agree that most of us should behave in a responsible way and we should talk and teach only about the marketing strategy with social responsibility. It is not only my object to talk only about irresponsible behaviour of MNCs and corporations regarding their marketing strategy but I am more concerned with the cause of the common man. For making marketing strategy socially responsible I suggest in brief the following points:

(i) Laws, rules and regulations regarding Corporations should be strictly followed.
(ii) The claims or exposures which are made regarding the quality or efficiency of the goods and services by the authorities concerned of organizations should be made accountable by the law.
(iii) Advertisements made on the electronic media should be censored by the Committee of sensitive social workers, reformers, ethical leaders along with subject experts.
(iv) Time for publicity of electronic media should be divided by law so that the consumer can be separately informed about the positive sides of the goods and services at a time and negative points of the same products should be highlighted at different time on the same channel the same day.
(v) Personnel of the Corporate world should be given training by ethical and religious personalities regarding the system,

style and preferences of business and trade which should be taken periodically.

(vi) The person who is appearing as an Advocate or Brand Ambassador of any product should be compelled to use the same product in his real life otherwise he or she should be penalized in some way.

(vii) For avoiding the delay tactics of irresponsible Corporate for their faults and adopting fowl means of marketing their products country's laws should be changed so that the decision of the same court may be made applicable on all the persons who are having similar type of complaints in the courts.

21

Application of Corporate Social Responsibility with Reference to Coca-Cola Ltd.

HARSHA GOHEL

INTRODUCTION

We live in an age in which companies equivalent in wealth to countries call the shots and control much of the earth's resources. Because corporate intervene in so many areas of social life, they must be responsible towards society and the environment. In India as in the rest of the world there is a growing realization that corporations are, after all, created by society and must therefore serve it, not merely profit from it.

The ongoing revolution in communication technology and the effectiveness of knowledge-based economics has created a new model of business and corporate governance. A growing awareness about the need for ecological sustainability and the New Economy framework, with an unprecedented stress on communication and image merchandising, have paved the way for a new generation of business leaders concerned about the responses of the community and the sustainability of the environment.

The primary drive for ethical business and corporate social responsibility came from the USA and Europe in the '80s and '90s, from campaigns run pressure groups such as Green peace and Friends of the Earth. Consumer boycotts, direct action, shareholder action ethical shopping guides, ethical product labelling schemes, media campaigns and ethical competitors became increasingly effective in changing corporate perspectives.

The mid-'90s were the watershed years for the new consciousness in international corporate policy. India has also a good history, present and future in the area of corporate social responsibility. But the application of CSR varies from firm-to-firm and industry-to-industry. Many organizations have really added social value by their operations while for few organisations CSR is merely a window dressing. But the scenario is on improvement stage.

CONCEPT OF CORPORATE SOCIAL RESPONSIBILITY

Social responsibility implies the acceptance of a moral imperative to recognize duties and obligations arising from a company's relationship with customers, suppliers, employers, shareholders, and society at large, beyond the consideration of profit. Few years ago corporate social responsibility was viewed as fringe issue, marginal and radical.

Corporate social responsibility refers to business decision-making linked to ethical values, compliance with legal requirements, and respect for people and communities and environment. According to studies of business for social responsibility, CSR has a positive impact on business economic performance and is not harmful to shareholder's value. Some of the benefits are—improved financial performance, reduced operating cost, enhanced brand Image, reduced regulatory oversight, increased productivity increased customer loyalty, etc.

The Prince of Wales international business leaders forum defines CSR on the basis of crucial issues of corporate governance which includes, transparency, accountability, safety and education—product safety, worker health safety, local environment quality, other social development like education, health, etc., simply put, CSR means the conduct of company operations in a manner which would have positive impact on all the stakeholders and would be more than mere compliance with the law.

Objective of the Study

1. To know the concept of CSR.

2. To know the methods and practices adopted by sampled unit.
3. To investigate the application of this practice.

Research Methodology

This is a case study about Coca-Cola Ltd. So researcher has taken secondary data for this research work, which was published in various periodicals, journals and web sites. The period of the study is 2003-04. Researcher has collected the secondary data after that it was analyzed further objectively according to the various aspects of the study for one year. So the researcher would not in view to adopt any sophisticated techniques for research.

INTRODUCTION TO COCA-COLA LTD.

The US soft-drink giant, Coca-Cola, re-entered India in the 1990s after abandoning its businesses in the late 1970s in the wake of Foreign Exchange Regulation Act of 1973. The Act, meant to 'Indianize' foreign companies, made it mandatory for foreign companies to dilute their shareholdings to 40 per cent. Instead of diluting its shareholdings to the required limit prescribed by the Act, Coca-Cola opted to discontinue its operations in India.

In the new liberalized and deregulated environment of the nineties, after a 16-year absence, Coke made its re-entry into India through its 100 per cent-owned subsidiary, Hindustan Coca-Cola Holdings in 1993. However, Coke's re-entry was based upon several commitments and stipulations, which the company agreed to implement in due course. One such major commitment was that Hindustan Coca-Cola Holdings would divest 49 per cent of its shareholding in favour of resident shareholders by June 2002. The company's presence in India was cemented in November 1993 in a deal that gave Coca-Cola ownership of the nation's top soft-drink brands and bottling network.

Coca-Cola India has made significant investments to build and continually improve its business in India, including new production facilities, waste-water treatment plants, distribution systems and marketing equipment. During the past decade, the Coca-Cola system has invested more than US $ 1 billion in India. As such Coca-Cola is one of the country's top international investors. In 2003, Coca-Cola India pledged to invest a further US$ 100 million.

The Coca-Cola business system directly employs approximately 10,000 local people in India. In addition, several independent studies have documented that, by providing opportunities for local enterprises, the Coca-Cola business also generates a significant employment "multiplier effect." In India, we indirectly create employment for more than 1,25,000 people in related industries through our vast procurement, supply and distribution system.

The Coca-Cola system in India comprises 27 wholly owned Company-owned bottling operations and another 17 franchisee-owned bottling operations. A network of 29 contract packers also manufactures a range of producers for the Company.

Almost all the goods and services required to produce and market Coca-Cola in India are made locally, sometimes with the help of technology and skills from the Company. The complexity of the Indian market is reflected in the distribution fleet which includes 10-tonne trucks, open-bay three-wheelers that can navigate the narrow alleyways of Indian cities, and trademarked tricycles and pushcarts.

Products

Leading Indian brands Thums Up, Limca, Maaza, Citra and Gold Spot join the Company's international family of brands, including Coca-Cola, diet Coke, Sprite and Fanta, plus the Schweppes product range. Our Kinley water brand was launched in 2000 and, in 2001 our energy drink Shock and our first powdered concentrate, Sunfill, hit the market. Annual per capita consumption of soft drinks in India is nine 8-ounce servings.

Marketing

While broad direction and themes for our global brands are created at a global level, specific marketing programmes for our products are determined locally. In early 2003, Coca-Cola India collected Advertiser of the Year and Campaign of the Year awards for the *Thanda Matlab Coca-Cola* an-media campaign. Innovation has been the hallmark of other marketing campaigns, with the Company racking up "firsts" in the introduction of canned and PET soft drinks, vending machines and backpack dispensers for crowds of cricket supporters.

Major Area of CSR—"What is CSR in the Words of Coca-Cola Ltd.?"

While the Coca-Cola company is a global company with some of the world's most widely recognized brands, the Coca-Cola business in India, as in each country where they operate is a local business. Their beverages are produced locally, employing Indian citizens, their product range and marketing reflects Indian tastes and lifestyles and they are deeply involved in the life of the local communication in which they operate.

"There is much in our world to celebrate, refresh, strength and protect. We strive to serve the people who enjoy our brands, respect their customs and conduct our business in the ways that protect environment, it aims at refreshing the market, enriching the work place, preserving the environment and strengthening our communities. And in line with this belief we partner with the communities to focus on education, health, water, and environment conservation. A lesser known dimension of our business is contribution as a corporate citizen to various education, health and water-environment-related projects that are being implemented across country," says president and CEO Mr. Sanjiv Gupta. He further added, "At Coca-Cola we are committed to preserve, protect and enhance the environment and this simple belief guides us in everything that we do. We will continue to further improve our systems and are confident of making a significant positive impact on our environment in times to come."

Nine members independent India Advisory Board headed by Mr. Naresh Chandra, former Ambassador to US and seven-member environment Advisory Council headed by Justice B.N. Kirpal, former chief justice of India, reinforce their commitment to being a model corporate citizen.

Theme of CSR—"Water Water Everywhere"

Coca-Cola believes that rainwater harvesting has huge potential in India with an average 46 inches of rain every year. It is partnering with central ground water authority, local government, welfare associates, and communities to setup Rainwater harvesting structure all over the country. It facilitates NGO's projects and serves the principal funding agency. The following are the major projects undertaken by it:

1. Coca-Cola is supporting water-harvesting project along with Jal Bhagirathi Foundation in the Thar Desert area through revival of traditional structures with pro-active community participation.
2. Coca-Cola launched the latest rainwater-harvesting project at Kaladera and Anopora near Jaipur on the world water day, March 2004. It combines best traditional wisdom and latest technology.
3. Coca-Cola launched six more rainwater-harvesting project for the benefit of local communities in the Plachimada area of Kerala.
4. Coca-Cola received an award by Government of Delhi for implementing Rainwater harvesting projects and solid waste management.
5. Other contribution includes provision of potable water through tankers, repair and cleaning of village wells and setting up hand pumps, etc.

Coca-Cola India is supporting community-based primary education projects set-up to provide educational opportunities to marginalized children in slums and villages. To date, the projects have benefited 50 schools, thousands of students, over 500,000 villagers and over 10,000 slum-dwellers, as well as several villages near Coca-Cola bottling plants.

Coca-Cola India is partnering with NGOs as well as St. John's Ambulance Brigade (Red Cross) to provide free medical facilities and information to poor people who cannot afford to visit hospital facilities. These efforts are helping tens of thousands of under-privileged people in seven states in India, as well as several villages near Coca-Cola bottling plants.

Findings

The research has studied various articles and materials published in various journals and web sites. By objective analysis the researcher has tried to find the actual application of CSR in Coca-Cola Ltd. The findings of the study are quite negative and found a huge gap in the application of CSR practices. Theory of CSR in the words of Coca-Cola is a pink mood but. . . .

But the Worst Reality is . . .

In reality Coca-Cola and its subsidiary in India the Hindustan Coca-Cola Beverages Ltd. has abused human rights and environment. Various plant spread across India have resulted in severe hardship for the communities who live around its bottling plants. These hardships include serious problems of water shortages, polluted water-soil; loss of livelihood and income, as well as public health for which long-term consequences are yet unknown. A disproportionate number of community members who have been affected adversely are low-income group, indigenous, dalits, farmers and women.

In a country where 70 per cent of population makes a living related to agriculture, stealing of water and poisoning the water-soil, is sure a recipe of disaster. Thousands of farmers in India have been affected by Coca-Cola's practices and it is guilty of destroying the livelihood of thousands of people.

Specifically the Coca-Cola's operations have led to following problems:

1. *Water Shortages*

Coca-Cola's extraction of ground water is creating severe water shortages for at least four communities in India—in the states of Kerala, Uttar Pradesh, Maharashtra, and Rajasthan. It is indiscriminate mining of large amount of water from the common ground water resource has resulted in a significant drop in the water table, and many wells including bore wells have gone dry. Various studies including one by Central Ground Water Board in India, have confirmed the significant depletion of the water table. Communities now have to rely on other water sources, sometimes having to walk much longer to get water for basic use. Coca-Cola continues to deny that its operations play significant role in creating drought like condition in the area. However, the Kerala High Court has rules Coca-Cola's extraction from common ground water resource in Kerala to be illegal, ordering it to seek alternative sources of water for use in its facility. The state Government ordered the Coca-Cola facility in Kerala temporarily shut down until June 15, 2004 to ease the drought conditions in the area.

2. *Water Soil Pollutions*

Coca-Cola has polluted scarce water and soil around its bottling operations. It had been discharging its water waste back into the ground. Test by the Central Pollution Control Board found that the sludge from Coca-Cola's affluent treatment plant was hazardous and includes heavy metals. As such it had to discharge its water as per rules and regulations. It refuses to allow independent monitors to establish how it has changed its practices in regard to the disposal of hazardous water. Regardless, it has discharged sludge without applying necessary precautions to protect health and environment. The state of Kerala has deemed the water around the plant as unit for consumption.

3. *Toxic Waste as a Fertilizer*

Coca-Cola has also engaged in the practice of distributing the solid waste from its plant to farmer in the area as fertilizer. Tests conducted by a British Broadcasting Corporation crew on the samples of the solid waste confirmed the presence of known carcinogen, cadmium, etc. It stopped practice only where it received order from State Government. It claims that the cadmium and lead laced waste is perfectly harmless.

4. *Contaminated Drinks*

A very well respected environment group in India, the Centre for Science and Environment, conducted tests on samples of Coca-Cola's products in the Indian market in September 2003. The tests found high concentration of pesticides in the drink including DOT, Malathion, and Lindane. Some samples found traces of pesticides 30 times more than those allowed by the European union standards. Test conducted at the same time on products form the US and EU markets were found to be safe. The Government of India initiated an inquiry into the findings and a Joint Parliamentary Committee, one of the most authoritative bodies possible to set-up in India, confirmed the original findings that Coca-Cola's products in Indian market contained high level of pesticides. The JPC reports also found Coca-Cola guilty of miss-leading the public by broadcasting false advertisement claiming their products ere safe. Coca-Cola continues to sell its products in India and even introduces new products in Indian market.

5. *Impacting Agriculture and Livelihood*

The bottling plant at Kaladera manufactures Coke, Fanta, other soft drinks and Kinley water. Its extractions of water have been increasing with each passing year. Situation is worst due to this plant. Agriculture in this region depends upon the rainwater and ground water. They don't have other sources like canals, dams or rivers. The declining water table has multiple effects agriculture. The Mehdiganj plant began to discharge liquid effluent in the fields behind the plants and affected 20 acres. A small landowner owns a bigha was growing rice-wheat but now nothing is growing in his field. One prosperous farmer sold his land to Coca-Cola in which there was a profitable project of mango tree. But now it is dry up and he is in loss. In short agriculture problems further creates problems of livelihood of local people.

6. *Violations of Worker's Rights*

The Mehdiganj plant exercise negative practices against workers. Here people don't have other work than agriculture. They worked at plant for years but are denied the status of permanent workers and any of the benefit that go with it. Coca-Cola used to adopt the practice of lying off workers after 120 days, so none could claim the stipulated minimum days of continuous work to be permanent. A union was formed in 2000 and protested for their rights till today.

Suggestions: What should be done?

1. They must permanently shut down the bottling plant facilities in Mehdiganj, Kaladera, and Plachimada.
2. They must compensate the affected community members.
3. They must recharge the depicted water by using water harvesting projects. No doubt they are handling such projects still it should be at extensive level.
4. They must cleanup the contaminated water-soil.

5. They must ensure that worker laid off as a result of Coca-Cola's negligence are retrained and relocated in a more sustainable industry.
6. They must admit liability for the long-term consequences of exposure of toxic waste and pesticide-laden drinks in India.

Limitations of the Study

1. The data has covered the study of one year.
2. It is not empirical research, so issue-based analysis have been considered by the researcher.

REFERENCES

Crowther, David, 'CSR Looking beyond Shareholder,' *CFA*, December, 2004.
CSR Review, *Indian Express*, January, 2005.
www.indianresource.com
www.news.bbc.co.uk
www.myenjoyzone.com/press/news
www.Coco-Cola

22

CSR in Banking Sector

ANJU SONDARVA

INTRODUCTION

Social efficiency of business is a topic of discussion not only for academicians but for the corporate sector also. The corporate citizenship programmes are essential for to a good citizen. Good citizenship, includes many things, which are paying taxies, equability and on time providing fair benefit to employees, safe and healthy work place for the workers, environmental protection and safe return to the shareholder, etc.

Normally, the corporate sector has to play an important role as responsible citizen and they have to follow some social responsibilities. A corporate citizenship can perform wide range of services, to enhance the companies, positive impact on the society. The London benchmark group (a growing Group of UK based on international companies) whose aim to evaluate more accurate work of community innovation programme. It has consider that a company can play pivotal role in social development, for that, they were measuring the performance of the company in community development programmes; basic business practices and administrating linkages for work. This group has presented this approach, which is based as fundamentally management tool. In this context, reporting to the various interested groups is essential. The reporting is essential in terms of physical environment convening the whole product life cycle, quality management programme, etc.

The aspect of corporate citizenship is also related to the behavioural of pertness in Forward and Backward linkages of the value chain.

Company can stress environmental impact from acquisition of row material and manufacturing level, distribution and sale of product. Forward linkages include concern about misuse of the product, safe disposal, and safe environment. Backward linkages include wage, employment, working condition, etc. Another aspect is regarding social efficiency is voluntary aspect for the contribution toward community like healthy, education, community development, etc.

Corporate social responsibility and efficiency is important policy of any organization so, it can be express with basic three levels:

First, basic values policy and practices of a company, Company owned and operated business (Policy and Practices of Company) in other words, corporate level strategy for the basic values of social efficiency. Secondly, Social issues from raw material acquisition to product disposal (Operational Strategy). Last, improving the interest of stakeholder community society and environment stand (Community Development Contribution).

Sometime, there may be confusion about the social responsibility concept. Hence the questions a raised likes. Why the company should be socially responsible? In this reference, London Backward Group has narrated that company is living in the society. Its mission and brand would be created only in this sense the company should be responsible in all dealing about environment, government, employees, investors, business partner and local communities. Another aspect is, how the company can attain it? Company can manage this practiced by following ways:

- Single Issue Approach.
- Single Audience Approach.
- Ethical Audit.
- Social Audit.
- Bottom Line Audit.

Several leading Companies are moving to more productive and systemic approach regarding social efficiency. However, the basic question some time remain unanswered are:

1. How to get a grip on the nature and scale of the company's economic social and environmental impact without investing a disproportionate performance on its mainstream commercial goals.
2. How to focus attention on the address, a selected number of priority issues where improvement can be made that

protect of enhance the company's relations with the stakeholders.

3. How to internalise the process associated with assessing and managing social impact so that they become a natural part of line of management responsibilities.

In this reference researcher has attempted to understand to and to find out some common practices adopted by Indian Corporate Sector. Therefore, the researcher has selected this topic regarding Corporate Social Efficiency.

On the basis of above review on discussion researcher had evaluated the time practices and procedures adopted by various units with this consideration research would like to fined put the answer of basic three questions:

1. Would CSR practices are equally imported for various industries?
2. Are his Corporate social responsibility depends on financial position of the company?
3. If so, what is the ground reality?

Objectives of the Study

- To understand the concept of Corporate Social Efficiency and Citizenship.
- To document the Corporate Social Efficiency in various groups of the company.
- To examine the practices of Corporate Social Efficiency between and within the various groups.
- To Evaluate the overall Corporate Social Efficiency of Indian corporate sector.
- To give suggestions.

Methodology

It is an empirical study, so researcher has followed scientific approach to design the research methodology for investigation. For this study researcher has used secondary data as a source of information for the research like the Annual Reports, journals, magazines, newspapers, website, etc. For sampling researcher has been use stratified sampling technique. The researcher has taken the survey conducted by *Business Today*, November 2003 for selection of group, based on market capitalization have been consider for work. Total 10 banks have been selected for the one-year study (2003-04). List of the selected banks are:

1. State Bank of India
2. Vijaya Bank
3. Bank of Punjab
4. Corporation Bank
5. Kotak Mahindra Bank
6. Syndicate Bank
7. ICICI Bank Ltd.
8. IDBI Bank Ltd
9. United Western Bank Limited
10. South Indian Bank

For the evaluation of corporate citizenship researcher has developed Corporate Social Efficiency Index:

$$\text{Social Efficiency Index} = \frac{\text{Total Score Obtained by an Organisation}}{\text{Maximum Score Obtained by a Company}} \times 100$$

First selection of 21 items related to corporate citizenship which was disclosed with in balance sheet or any where is Annual report have been selected by the researcher. The selected items are: (1) Energy conservation, (2) Research and Development, (3) Foreign Exchange and Export-Import Statement, (4) Environment Upgradation and Improvement, (5) Industrial Safety, (6) Employment to Backward Class, (7) Employee Welfare, (8) Industrial Relations, (9) Establishment of Education Institution/Fellowship/Scholarship, (10) Development of Parks and Recreation Clubs, (11) Rural Development, (12) National Cause donations, (13) Manpower development and training, (14) HRA/Value added statement, (15) Welfare spending for weaker section of society, (16) Investor Relations, (17) Quality Assurance and Consumer Protection, (18) Vigilance Committee to prevent/Check corruption, (19) Industrial Development of nearby areas and setting-up of, (20) Social income statement and Social Balance Sheet, and (21) Other social Activities. Then each item was awarded '1' point if it is disclosed and if it is not disclosed '0' has been awarded to that particular discloser item. Total 210 points have been highest scored tor corporate citizenship.

Table 22.1 reveals the data regarding discloser of the items for the Employee Welfare. Other social Activities has 100 per cent discloser, while for industrial safety and manpower development and training receives 90 per cent discloser, Foreign Exchange and Export-Import Statement and Investor Relations have 80 per cent discloser, research and development receives 60 per cent that is the higher discloser, for the lower side environment up gradation and improvement, development of parks and recreation clubs and HRA/VAS and social income statement and balance sheet has 0 per cent (nil).

Table 22.2 indicates the data of Social Efficiency Index, in which higher index of Corporation Bank, State Bank of India, Syndicate Bank, ICICI Bank Ltd. respectively 66.67, 57.14, 57.14 and 57.14, while the lower index about Vijaya Bank—47.62, Bank of Punjab—19.05, Kotak Mahindra Bank—28.57, IDBI Bank Ltd.—28.57, UWBI—38.10, and SIB—23.81 has been found.

CONCLUSION

For the survival, the organization has to pay the social responsibility. Organizations are getting the profit from the society, and so social responsibility is not the charity but it is accountability of the enterprise.

REFERENCES

Aga, Anu R., "Capitalism with Human Face," *The Indian Express*, November 27, 2003.

Agrawal, R.S., "Corporate Social Information Discloser," *The Management Accountant*, June, 2003.

Anupama Mohan, "Corporate Citizenship in Developing Country," *Warwick Business School*, www.google.Com.

Crowther, David, "CSR Looking Beyond Shareholder," *Chartered Financial Accountant*, December, 2003.

CSR Survey-2002, India by UNDP British Council, CII, Pricewaterhouse Cooper: www.india partnershipforum.org

London Benchmarking Group Report, www. Business Corporate citizenship Co.uk.

Rao, Nageswer and Gupta, Deepak, "Social Responsibly Discloser Practices in Public Enterprises," *The Indian Journal of Commerce*, January, 2004.

TABLE 22.1

Social Efficiency Parameter

P. No.	Parameter	SBI	Vijaya	BOP	CB	KMBL	SB	ICICI	IDBI	UWBL	SIB	Total
1.	Energy conservation	0	0	0	0	0	0	0	0	1	0	1
2.	Research and Development	1	1	0	1	0	0	1	1	6		
3.	Research Exchange and Export-Import Statement	1	1	1	1	1	0	1	1	1	0	8
4.	Foreign Upgradation and Improvement	0	0	0	0	0	0	0	0	0	0	0
5.	Industrial Safety	1	1	0	1	1	1	1	1	1	1	9
6.	Employment to Backward Classes	1	1	0	0	0	1	0	0	0	0	3
7.	Employee Welfare	1	1	1	1	1	1	1	1	1	1	10
8.	Employee Relations	1	0	0	0	0	1	0	0	0	0	2
9.	Establishment of Education Institution Fellowship Scholarship	0	0	0	1	0	1	1	0	0	0	3
10.	Development of Parks and Recreation Clubs	0	0	0	0	0	0	0	0	0	0	0
11.	Rural Development	0	0	0	1	0	1	1	0	0	0	3
12.	National-Cause donations	1	0	0	1	0	0	1	0	0	0	3
13.	Manpower development and training	1	1	1	1	1	1	1	1	1	0	9
14.	HRA/Value added statement	0	0	0	0	0	0	0	0	0	0	0
15.	Welfare spending for weaker section of society	1	0	0	1	0	0	1	0	0	0	3
16.	Investor Relations	0	1	0	1	1	1	1	1	1	1	8

17.	Quality Assurance and Consumer Protection	1	1	0	1	0	1	1	0	0	0	5
18.	Vigilance Committee to prevent/Check corruption	1	1	0	1	0	1	0	0	0	0	4
19.	Industrial Development of nearby areas and setting-up of ancillaries	0	0	0	1	0	0	0	0	0	0	1
20.	Social Income statement and Social Balance sheet	0	0	0	0	0	0	0	0	0	0	0
21.	Other social Activities	1	1	1	1	1	1	1	1	1	1	10
	TOTAL	12	10	4	14	6	12	11	6	8	5	88

TABLE 22.2
Social Efficiency Index

Name of Organisation	*Social Efficiency Index*			*Trends*
	Total Parameter	*Disclosed Items*	*SE Index*	
	(1)	*(2)*	*(2/1)*	
State Bank of India	21	12	57.14	13.64
Vijaya Bank	21	10	47.62	11.36
Bank of Punjab	21	04	19.05	04.55
Corporation Bank	21	14	66.67	15.91
Kotak Mahindra Bank	21	06	28.57	06.82
Syndicate Bank	20	12	57.14	13.60
ICICI Bank Ltd.	21	11	57.14	12.50
IDBI Bank Ltd.	21	06	28.67	06.82
UWBI	21	08	38.10	09.09
SIB	21	05	23.81	05.68
Total	210	88	419.05	100.00

$$\text{Social Efficiency Index} = \frac{\text{Total Score Obtained by an organisation}}{\text{Maximum score obtained by a company}} \times 100$$

Overall Industry Index = 41.905

23

Corporate Social Responsibility in the Insurance Industry: A South African Perspective with a Specific Focus on Disability Insurance

DALEEN VAN DER NEST

1. INTRODUCTION

In many jurisdictions, it seems to be an accepted fact that the state has a responsibility to take care of those members of society who are for some reason not able to take care of themselves. In South Africa, the Constitution[1] states that the state has the responsibility to grant access to social security to all citizens. Like in many other countries, the South African social security system is divided into social insurance and social assistance. Also, the system provides through various programmes for the classical risks, namely old age, disability, health, unemployment and maternity, to name but a few.

However, in a country where the past is characterised by apartheid, stigmatisation and social exclusion, the state is currently unable to provide for the needs of those citizens who are in fact affected by these social risks.[2]

In no other area is this more evident than in disability provisioning. If the state is indeed unable to meet the need of the disabled, one may very well ask whether the current problem is mot maybe compounded because the insurance industry failed this vulnerable sector of society. A further question is whether corporate social responsibility plays a role in disability provisioning in private insurance and finally, how formal private insurance interrelates with social security in the South African society. This article provides a definition of corporate social responsibility and illustrates the dire need for reform in the private insurance sector.

2. CORPORATE SOCIAL RESPONSIBILITY

The onset of the industrial revolution catapulted the modern world out of a slow-paced rural existence into an industrial society in which a person offered his labour and skills to an employer in return for a wage. Although the employer-employee relationship is as old as the hills, it is the new face of the workplace and the change in power structures that gave a completely new dimension to labour. Much has been said about capitalism and how this system became the driving force in world economy.[3] Whether one believes Weber's theories on the protestant work ethic or whether one leans towards socialism, the fact remains that capitalism does stimulate economic growth. However, in this new capitalistic environment it also became evident that measures were needed to protect those who have been cast aside by the system. The old, the disabled, pregnant women, any person who is no longer able to render services in the great machine that it capitalism, needs protection.[4]

In this vein of contrasting the good elements of capitalism with the bad, Pieterse states:

> "[T]he notion of socio-economic rights was initially exclusively associated with the political ideology of socialism. Considered as the political alternative to the individualist and materialist focus of capitalism, socialism is principally opposed to notions of individual entitlement and rather propagates the concept of group rights, grounded in citizenship of a specific state. Unlike Western-liberal discourse, which strives for the protection of human dignity and autonomy through limiting public intervention in the private lives of citizens, socialism favours the general welfare of all citizens over individual liberties, and attempts to safeguard human dignity through facilitating social standards in which citizens may communally realise their potential."[5]

The fact remains that the industrial revolution and the rise in capitalism increased the individual's chances of becoming disabled and losing his earning capacity in the process.

Capitalism cannot exist separately from organisations geared towards profit making. So, along with the awakening from agricultural slumber, came corporations as vehicles to promote the ideals of capitalism.[6] Parkinson states that capitalism is the most effective system for the creation of wealth.[7] However, the writer warns that one should guard against unconstrained profit maximization for two reasons:

> "[f]irst, while the efficient creation of wealth may be regarded as a high social priority, we also recognise individual and collective interests and values that ought not to be sacrificed in its pursuit. Such recognition is reflected, for instance, in the enhancement by statute of the rights of employees against dismissal, which from an aggregate wealth viewpoint may be depicted as inhibiting factor mobility and hence on occasion as being wealth-reducing. Second, because of defects inherent in the operation of markets, the strict maximization of profits will in any case frequently fail to lead to the maximization of aggregate wealth."[8]

One may very well ask why corporations have such an influence on society and how society's needs in turn demand action from corporations. Cannon states that business exist primarily to produce the goods and services needed by society.[9] But:

> "[a]t the same time, business depends for its survival and long-term prosperity on society providing the resources – people, raw materials, services, infrastructure – which it needs to convert inputs into profitable goods or services. Business relies on society supplying a means of exchange – typically money – to allow it to convert the goods it produces into assets. Without a legal, judiciary and policing system business could not be certain that it was safe to enjoy the rewards of its enterprise. Trade agreements and defence are needed to ensure long-term, stable trading conditions. All these, in turn, depend on all the members of the society supporting the values and norms it endorses."

One senses that there is the ever-present conflict between the profit motive of corporations on the one hand and social responsibility on the other, where company law should ideally also facilitate the consideration of third party interests.[10] One such an interest of third parties and notably employees, is the capacity to earn a wage in a safe environment. Furthermore, damage to any individual's earning capacity that is left unattended, may in turn have a negative impact on the very workforce that has to sustain the corporation and its profit-seeking motives.

A number of questions arise, namely:

- how can the risk of loss of earning capacity be managed best;
- what public structures are in place to deal with this risk;
- what are the shortcomings of these structures; and
- how can private insurance be utilised to protect the workforce against this specific risk.

The following discussion first turns to the existing social security structures that deal with disability. Thereafter, the discussion will turn to the existing private insurance structures.

3. SOCIAL MEASURES THAT GUARDS AGAINST LOSS OF EARNING CAPACITY

3.1 Introduction

On the South African social security system in general, Olivier and Kalula comment:

> "South Africa has inherited a social security system, which is remarkably comprehensive by a middle income developing country standard. However, the system is characterized by a patchwork of fragmented institutions. There is no coherent social security approach and little synergy is reflected in the construction, establishment, functioning and purpose of, as well as in the cooperation between the schemes."[11]

The same may be said of disability provisioning. There is no core value in the current approach to disability. There is no uniform definition of the concept disability in the South African social security system,[12] with the result that disability is problematic conceptually. Several acts of parliament deal with disability to some extent. For instance, the Promotion of Equality and Prevention of Unfair Discrimination Act[13] lists disability as a prohibited ground of discrimination but fails to provide a definition of the term. Under labour law, the Employment Equity Act[14] attempts to define disabled people in the following way:

> "'[p]eople with disabilities' means people who have long-term or recurring physical or mental impairment which substantially limits their prospects of entry into, or advancement in, employment."[15]

The current Social Assistance Act[16] defines a disabled person as:

> "[a]ny person who has attained the prescribed age and is, owing to his or her physical or mental disability, unfit to obtain by virtue of any service, employment or profession the means needed to enable him or her to provide for his or her maintenance."[17]

The above definitions illustrate the different meanings that are attached to disability. One can also safely say that the definition offered by the Occupational Injuries and Diseases Act is better ignored, as this definition clearly deals with legal disability.[18]

From the definitions in the Employment Equity Act[19] and the Social Assistance Act[20] it is evident that the concepts disability and incapacity are almost interchangeable.

Because of this lack of a uniform concept of disability, it is also difficult to deal with this problem institutionally. The different social security institutions have a fragmented approach to disability and there is no core value or golden thread in the approach towards disabled people.

3.2 Institutional Framework

3.2.1 *General*

The South African social insurance system consists of retirement schemes, health insurance, workmen's compensation, unemployment insurance and the Road Accident Fund. Apart from the Road Accident Fund, all the systems are employment-based. Conceptual difficulties with the term 'disability' are carried over into the institutional sphere and the different meanings attached to disability cause social partners to approach disability in a fragmented way. The following exposition highlights the most important aspects of a number of disability schemes.

3.2.2 *Old Age and Retirement*

Against this background, it is evident that the retirement provisioning in South Africa is in place for one reason, namely to provide for those who do not work any more because of old age. It is further strictly employment-based. There is no provision in the Pension Funds Act[21] that deals with the situation where a contributor to an employment-based pension fund becomes disabled prior to retirement. Usually, such an employer will be entitled to certain benefits because of the contributions to the Fund, but these benefits will ultimately be calculated in accordance with the rules of that specific pension fund and will remain in the discretion of the trustees. Therefore, pension fund are currently not constructed as vehicles with built-in disability cover.

3.2.3 *Health Care*

There are at least three reasons why health care is of particular importance to disabled people. Firstly, a victim of a disability event needs proper treatment immediately after such an event.[22]

Although this report specifically investigated health care in the event of a car accident, the statement is equally true of any other victim of a disability event. During this period of total temporary incapacity, it is vital that accident victims receive proper health care. Depending on the severity of the situation, this is followed by either a period of temporary partial incapacity, or a period of permanent partial incapacity, or in the worst cases, a period of permanent total incapacity. Once again, proper medical treatment has an effect on the recovery process and may on the long-term result in partial or no permanent incapacity, where inadequate treatment will result in permanent total or at least serious incapacity.

Secondly, a disabled person needs more frequent medical treatment than a healthy person. This can include wheel chairs, operations, medication, diapers, physiotherapy and basically any treatment that can improve the quality of a disabled person's life.

Regular, quality medical care definitely helps a disabled person to cope with his new circumstances. Unfortunately South Africa does not have special hospitals where these people can receive special treatment and by the time such a victim receives a payout, it is often too late.[23]

A third and equally serious shortcoming is a focus on rehabilitation and the establishment of the necessary facilities in order to assist disabled people in recovering sufficiently to manage with the daily challenges that they are faced with and also to rehabilitate them sufficiently to enable them to follow a different career.

Apart from these shortcomings, the public health care system is still not as efficient as the private health care system. Although the Constitution guarantees every citizen the right to emergency medical treatment, it still happens that indigent people are dependent on public hospitals for care whereas wealthy patients with sufficient means or medical insurance have access to private hospitals.[24]

On the whole, there exist a number of serious shortcomings in the health care system that leads to more people having more serious and permanent disabilities. The public health care is hopelessly inadequate and unable to cope with this problem.

3.4 Workmen's Compensation in terms of the Compensation for Occupational Injuries and Diseases Act (hereafter, COIDA)[25]

The Workmen's Compensation system is most probably the longest-running system that deals with disability in South Africa.[26] In terms of the current legislation, where a person who falls within the definition of 'employee' in terms of COIDA becomes disabled because of an accident that occurs in the scope of his employment or such an employee contracts a disease in the scope of his employment, COIDA provides for the payment of benefits to these individuals.[27] In terms of the current legislation, where a person who falls within the definition of 'employee' in terms of COIDA becomes disabled because of an accident that occurs in the scope of his employment or such an employee contracts a disease in the scope of his employment, COIDA provides for the payment of benefits to these individuals.[28] These benefits include *inter alia* medical care, loss of earnings and loss of maintenance where an employee was killed while on duty.

Benefits in terms of this system are calculated with reference to a person's earnings.[29] The Compensation Commissioner also pays all medical costs upon the occurrence of an accident or where the employee contracted a disease. Protection against loss of income in terms of COIDA is of particular significance for this discussion. The legislation provides for compensation in those instances where an employee suffers either a temporary total disablement or a permanent total disablement. As far as compensation for permanent disablement is concerned, there is a distinction between disablement that is less than 30 per cent and disablement of more than 30 per cent.[30] In the first instance, a lump sum based on 15 times the employee's monthly earnings up to a specified maximum is paid out to the employee.[31] Where the disability is 31 per cent or more, a monthly pension is paid to the employee. The monthly pension is calculated in the same way as the lump sum.[32] In calculating benefits for loss of earning capacity, the Compensation Commissioner makes use of a so-called 'meat list.' This guideline contains a list of injuries and the corresponding percentage disability that is attached to specific injuries. This so-called 'meat-chart approach' of compensation where the loss of a limb, for example, is adjudged to constitute a certain percentage injury or disease that can be compensated, has been severely criticised.[33]

At this point in time it seems as though there is a duty on COIDA to pay the appropriate compensation where an employee meets the requirements and that there is far too little emphasis on reintegration and rehabilitation. This aspect was also illuminated by the Draft Consolidated Report of the Committee of Inquiry into a Comprehensive System of Social Security for South Africa.[34]

In summary it can be said that although the protection afforded in terms of COIDA for total disablement definitely plays a very important role, it is not above criticism. Firstly, only those in formal employment who qualify as employees enjoy coverage.[35] Secondly, little is done about the prevention of accidents and rehabilitation and integration and finally, even those employees who do receive lump sums or monthly pensions merely receive defined benefits and will most likely not be in a position to maintain the same standard of living that they did before the employment accident.[36]

3.5 Unemployment Insurance

In South Africa, unemployment insurance is regulated by the Unemployment Insurance Contributions Act[37] (UICA) and the Unemployment Insurance Act (UIA).[38] The UIA provides for the payment of unemployment benefits, while the UICA regulates the collection of contributions.[39] Although certain employees may have a claim for a specific period of time directly after a disability event, the main aim of unemployment insurance is not to assist the disabled and it is irrelevant for purposes of this discussion.

3.6 Motor Vehicle Accidents

In South Africa, motor vehicle accidents, like occupational accidents, are areas of personal injury law where the legislature intervenes. Intervention in these two areas is vital, as employment accidents and motor vehicle accidents most probably account for the majority of serious and permanent injuries. Instead of claiming damages from the wrongdoer, all claims are institute against the Road accident Fund. In turn, road users pay a fuel levy with every litre of petrol they purchase. This accident system is still based on common law principles, which includes, inter alia, that a wrongdoer must prove fault in order to be successful with a claim.

The Road Accident Fund is probably the largest non-employment scheme that deals with disability.[40] Unfortunately, this scheme is riddles with mismanagement and inefficiency. As far as disability is concerned, a victim receives a lump sum cash payment to compensate him for his disability. Unfortunately the assessment process is cumbersome, inaccurate and focused on compensation only. Rehabilitation and re-integration into the community and the job market are not amongst the objectives of this system.

Recommendations have been made on how to reform this system. The Committee of Inquiry into a Comprehensive Social Security System[41] also considered a number of difficulties relating to the RAF. It illuminated, amongst other things, the complexity of the legislation, the fact that the delictual basis of claims requires extensive investigations, the fact that the claims procedure is cumbersome, the high accident rate and medical inflation. Although the Committee refrained from making recommendations, it did remarked that two separate schemes for road accidents and employment accidents may very well lead to double compensation, victims shopping around for the best possible compensation, different definitions of quantum of damage and double administration costs.[42]

3.7 Disability Grants in terms of Social Assistance Legislation

The current Social Assistance Act[43] provides for the payment of a number of disability grants. Apart from the provisions in this particular act, there are no other provisions that deal with the payment of disability grants.

Disability grants almost serve as a last recourse for those who are unable to earn a living either because of a mental or because of a physical impairment. In most instances the recipients of disability grants did not have private insurance and furthermore failed to qualify for some payout in terms of any social insurance. Worse, even, where these recipients did indeed receive a lump sum under private insurance or social insurance, the funds were insufficient to enable the recipient to manage his disability or the funds were misappropriated. Often with lump sum payments from the Road Accident Fund, victims use their payouts to start a small business, and when such ventures fail and they lose their money, the only resort is to apply for a disability grant.[44] Hence the importance of disability grants in the social security system.

As far as disability as a contingency is concerned, the Social Assistance Act[45] provides for the payment of grants to persons older than 18 years who suffer from physical or mental disability for a period longer than 6 months. The disability must furthermore render the person in question unable to provide sufficiently for his or her own maintenance.[46] In order to qualify for a disability grant, a potential recipient must prove that she is a South African resident, that she is unable to provide for herself and that the degree of disability makes it impossible for him to earn a living.[47]

There is tension between an all-embracing welfare state where the government intervenes in key areas and individual autonomy. It all comes back to policy considerations and money. Paton states that:

> "[f]or the past year, Manuel has been warning that the rate of increase in social grant spending is unsustainable. This week's mini-budget was no different. If the contributory social assistance

funds—for unemployment, road accidents and occupational accidents—are added to the direct transfers, then cash payments to households will rise from R63, 3 bn. to R87, 6 bn. by 2007/ 2008."[48]

Paton adds that South Africa's social security net is under severe strain and the present trajectory is unsustainable.[49] According to the National Treasury, the disability grant is currently received by 1.3 million people. In the past four years the number of beneficiaries has doubled, causing spending on this particular grant to escalate to R6, 3 bn.

Principles vanish when resources become scarce. The take-up in disability grants may either be ascribed to more effective service delivery on behalf of the Department of Social Services, to failure on the side of private insurance and social insurance, to the increase of HIV/AIDS or to all these factors. Whatever the case might be, there is still widespread criticism against the current system.

4. THE ROLE OF FORMAL INSURANCE

4.1 Introduction

The question that needs to be answered is whether corporations, and specifically insurance companies, have a role to play in the area of disability provisioning. It is important to bear in mind that there is a dynamic relationship between the insurance industry in a country and the social security system. Ideally, economically active individuals should be in a position to adequately provide for themselves in terms of life insurance, health insurance, disability insurance as well as insurance cover. If that is the situation, these individuals are not destitute upon the materialisation of a risk that affects their capacity to provide for themselves and for others or any other risk that has dire financial consequences. However, in a society where long-term, structured unemployment is the rule rather than the exception and many of the working class are actually still very poor, very few can afford private insurance and rely on the state to provide for them. Also, many South Africans have been excluded from mainstream society in general and more specifically from formal insurance and access to credit that they regard insurance with suspicion.

Although there is no one solution to the problem of disability and the poverty that it causes in most instances, it is submitted that, although there is an obligation on the state to provide access to social security, much can be done by private insurance companies to educate the public on insurance and also to take notice of the dilemma of the disabled in South African society. On this point, Klinck states:

> "[T]he CASE Report recommends that the public be educated so that people may come to understand private insurance and start to save for themselves. However, tighter control is needed in the industry as the rate of surrendered and lapsed policies are currently 40-50 per cent."[50]

So far, it has been established that there is a serious need in South African society for protection against disability and consequent loss of earning capacity.

For centuries, formal insurance has offered a solution to this dilemma. In the following section, the role of insurance, and particularly disability insurance, will be discussed.

4.2 Nature of Insurance

South African insurance principles developed mostly from English insurance law. Today, the Long-term Insurance Act 52 of 1998 and the Short-term Insurance Act 53 of 1998 regulate the insurance industry.

It is accepted that an insurance contract is a contract between an insurer and an insured in terms of which the insurer undertakes, in return for the payment of a price or premium, to render to the insured a sum of money, or its equivalent, on the happening of a specified uncertain event in which the insured has some interest.[51]

In the case of disability insurance, the specified insured event is an event that impairs the functional ability of the mind or body of a person or of an unborn. In fact, the Long-term Insurance Act contains a definition of "disability policy". It states that a disability contract is a contract of insurance or reinsurance in terms of which a person, in return for a premium, undertakes to provide policy benefits upon the occurrence of a disability event.[52] A disability event in turn means an event, which impairs the functional disability of the mind or body of a person or of an unborn.[53]

Therefore, Reinecke *et al.* state:

> "[a] reference to a personal accident policy, in relation to long-term insurance, must be construed as a reference to a disability or health policy."[54]

The writers also point out that there is an overlap between the Long-term Insurance Act and the Short-term Insurance Act.[55] The latter regulates accident and health policies and these refer to contracts in terms of which a person, in return for a premium, undertakes to provide policy benefits if a disability event, a health event or a death event, occurs.[56] Therefore, a contract that insures a disability event may either be a disability policy regulated by the Long-term Insurance Act[57] or an accident and health policy regulated by the Short-term Insurance Act.[58]

Therefore, a clear legal structure exists in terms of which insurers can offer protection against disability. The question now is whether these insurers realise the importance of disability provisioning, whether they consciously market their products with the socio-economic situation in South Africa in mind and whether they should maybe be compelled to do business in a certain way. The following paragraph takes a look at the social role of insurance and the desirability of government interference in the area of disability insurance.

4.3 Social Function of Insurance

Reinecke *et al.* state:

> "[i]t has been said that insurance is a business, but that insurance is also a service to those who are in distress. It plays an important social role in that it sells safety."[59]

Although the writers use the word safety, it is submitted that insurance rather sells peace of mind in the sense that the insured can rest assured in the knowledge that he will be looked after upon the occurrence of a damage-causing event. However, the fact that a specific individual is insured, does not make his world any safer-risks may and will still occur. The fact remains that Reinecke *et al.* make a very important point, namely that insurance renders a service to those who have experienced a disaster. That should be the main aim of insurance. Unfortunately, it is also a fact that no insurance company insures people because of humaneness or feelings of solidarity with the suffering masses. Instead, it is a well-known principle that very few insurers these days do business on any other basis than to generate a profit.[60] Here, Reinecke *et al.* state:

"[t]he purpose of profit insurance, on the other hand, is to make a profit to be distributed amongst the insurer's shareholders. Most present day insurers do not qualify as mutual insurers."[61]

As far as the development of profit insurance is concerned, Reinecke *et al.* explain as follows:

"[i]nsurance for profit in the form known today eventually developed from risk clauses contained in maritime loans, *commendae* and certain contracts for purchase and sale. The central theme was the transfer of a risk in exchange for a monetary consideration. The profit motive provided an incentive for a careful calculation of both risk and premium. The first clear records of contracts that conform to modern-day insurance contracts, both in form and substance, would seem to be two documents containing contracts for the transfer of maritime risks concluded in Pisa towards the end of the fourteenth century. These contracts contained in so many words an undertaking to bear a risk in exchange for money. This undertaking was from an independent party not involved in the transaction from which the risk emanated. Independent risk-bearing for a premium had now developed in the form of marine insurance." [62]

Risk transfer against the payment of premiums is here to stay, and so is profit insurance. The problem does not lie so much with the fact that insurers are allowed to make a profit, but indeed with the fact that they generate huge profits while there are certain sectors in the insurance business, like disability insurance, where corporate social responsibility is urgently needed. For instance, Klinck states:

"[T]he CASE Report recommends that the public be educated so that people may come to understand private insurance and start to save for themselves. However, tighter control is needed in the industry as the rate of surrendered and lapsed policies are currently 40-50 per cent."[63]

Lapse rate obviously refers to the amount of policies over a specific period of time that had lapsed because of the insured's inability to keep paying the premiums. Where there is such a high lapse rate, there is clearly a problem. Insurance intermediaries sell products to uninformed consumers who cannot afford to pay the premiums. Where policies lapse because of non-payment, cover lapses and the premiums already paid cannot be reclaimed form the insurance company. Another worrying fact is that in 2002, only 1 per cent of the R174 901m premiums that were collected were for disability policies. These figures show that there is a problem in the industry. Whether it is the attitude of consumers towards this type of insurance or simply a lack of knowledge is not certain. If one looks at the lapse rate of policies on the other hand, it seems more probable that consumers can simply not afford this type of insurance.[64]

The question that remains is why the insurance industry may be expected to actively become involved in this dilemma of disability in South Africa. It is submitted that Cousy effectively summarises the situation where he states:

> "[f]inally, an old question surfaces. Insurance is a business, but insurance is also a service to those who are in distress. Insurance will never be able to deny that it has some social role to play. This remains the biggest challenge. Insurance is a noble trade: it sells safety. But nobility implies duties. As the French saying goes: *Noblesse oblige.*"[65]

All these theories only remain theories unless one suggests some practical ways to enforce them. In the next paragraph, a number of suggestions will be made as to how insurance companies can be enticed or forced to first of all realize their social responsibility and also to implement adequate consumer protection measures into place.

4.4 Accountability, Participation and Social Responsibility

Insurance companies in Europe had to significantly restructure their business with the advent of the welfare state. When governments, through public structures, actively started to protect individuals against illness, unemployment and loss of income, the focus shifted from protection of the insurer to protection of the insured.[66] Two other factors changed the face of insurance, namely social security and contractual certainty. As far as social security is concerned, the risks an individual normally incurred in his every day life are now transferred to a collective pool.[67] This is not really different from the situation in private insurance.[68] The only important factor in social insurance is that the government decides who bears a specific collective risk, where an individual has that option in private insurance.[69]

The other factor is the development in Europe in the 1970's of a need for contractual certainty. Wansink explains that the traditional approach to contract, namely that contractual parties are equal and neutral, ignores the reality that insurers are usually in a stronger position than consumers, notably because of standard-form contracts that leave very little space for negotiation.[70]

These rumblings that were heard in Europe also manifests in our current dispensation in South Africa. As was explained above, the South African social security system faces serious challenges but although it is not as sophisticated as the European systems, there is a formal system and there is a constitutional obligation on the state to develop this system. Furthermore, there is a constitutional obligation upon the state to provide access to social security to all citizens, which means that social security structures will gain prominence.[71] Secondly, it has been recognized that there is an unequal relationship between insurance companies and consumers, although there has not been a test case on this specific point. Insurance companies can therefore not conduct their business in total ignorance of the market needs and realities and if they do not realise their social responsibility towards consumers, specifically in the area of disability, it is time to find a way to force these companies to work towards a solution.

5. CONCLUSION

Disability is a real risk that lurks around every corner. In order to manage this risk, insurance companies should take cognisance of the current social security structures, it functions and its shortcomings and sell products that sells safety. Any possible steps taken by the insurance industry should ideally rest on three points, namely sustainability, accountability and transparency.

As far as sustainability is concerned, it is important to realise that insurance business is business for profit. If the profit element is taken away, no insurance company will be interested in selling disability policies. Instead, insurers should be encouraged to focus on prevention and rehabilitation and to create products that serve to top up insurance where social security systems fail to assist individuals.

Secondly, insurance companies should be more accountable. Where ordinary companies are usually accountable towards its shareholders, insurance companies have a much wider accountability. They are accountable to every single insured as well as his relatives and any other social partner who may be affected by such an insured's disability.

In the third instance, insurance companies must be transparent in the way in which they conduct their business. For instance, the insured should know whether he will only be compensated for total disability or also for temporary disability, and also what exactly testing for disability involves. Often insurance companies pronounce that even those with very serious disabilities such as quadriplegia are not disabled, as they have, for instance, not sustained brain damage. Such testing fails to take social circumstances and the availability of jobs into account. These facts are seldom communicated to bona fide consumers when they apply for disability insurance.

The above three principles do not offer as much of a solution as it offers guidelines for insurance companies to at least venture on a path towards greater corporate social responsibility. What is necessary is for insurance companies to make a real effort to make disability insurance more affordable, more user friendly and more accessible to all members of society.

It is also suggested that government should enter into a pact with insurance companies in order to approach disability in a more holistic manner. The aim should be to afford maximum protection for all members of society against disability by defining the risks, affording rehabilitative treatment and by closing the gaps that exist between public and private systems. In becoming a social partner with the state in the area of disability, insurance companies will truly fulfil their social responsibilities without forfeiting profit or losing business.

Notes and References

1. Constitution of the Republic of South Africa 108 of 1996.
2. On this point, Olivier and Kalula "Scope of Coverage" in Olivier, Smit and Kalula *Social Security: A Legal Analysis* (2003) 127 state: "[I]nitially the social security

system was constructed with the deliberate aim to serve the interests, through social insurance, of primarily white workers in formal employment and, through social assistance means-tested benefits, poor whites and (later) Coloureds and Indians." On the nature of the system, the writers further state on 137 that "[S]outh Africa has inherited a social security system, which is remarkably comprehensive by a middle income developing country standard. However, the system is characterized by a patchwork of fragmented institutions. There is no coherent social security approach and little synergy is reflected in the construction, establishment, functioning and purpose of, as well as in the cooperation between the schemes," 2.

3. See, for instance, Lessnoff *The Spirit of Capitalism and the Protestant Ethic* (1994) 2.
4. This idea stems predominantly from the beliefs of the social democrats. In this regard, see Pratt "Towards a 'New' Social Democracy" in Lavalette and Pratt *Social Policy: a Conceptual and Theoretical Introduction* (2001) 26.
5. Pieterse "Beyond the Welfare State: Globalisation of Neo-Liberal Culture and the Constitutional Protection of Social and Economic Rights in South Africa." (2003) *Stell LR* 5.
6. Parkinson 43.
7. Parkinson Corporate Power and Responsibility (1993) 41.
8. Parkinson (n 4) 42.
9. Cannon *Corporate Responsibility: A textbook on Business Ethics, Governance, Environment: Roles and Responsibilities* (1994) 33.
10. Parkinson (n 4) 43.
11. Olivier and Kalula "Scope of Coverage" in Olivier, Smit and Kalula *Social Security: a Legal Analysis* (2003 Lexisnexis Butterworths Durban) 127.
12. Grobbelaar-du Plessis (2003) *Obiter* 128.
13. Act 4 of 2000.
14. Act 55 of 1998.
15. S 1 of Act 55 of 1998.
16. Act 59 of 1992.
17. See also Grobbelaar-du Plessis (2003) *Obiter* 130.
18. Legal disability refers to the incapacity of a person to perform juristic acts. Legal disability generally depends on a person's gender, age, mental ability and solvency. In South African law, a person is usually classified as having full, limited or no capacity to perform juristic acts. See in general Barnard, Cronje and Olivier *Die Suid-Afrikaanse Persone-en Familiereg* (1986 Butterworths Durban) 44 where the writers state the following: "[O]m saam te vat, kan ons dus sê dat 'n persoon se status sy kompetensies, soos sy regs-, handelings- en verskyningsbevoegdheid bepaal. 'n Persoon se status is weer afhanklik van die toestand waarin hy verkeer of hoedaninghede wat hy besit waaraan die reg gevolge heg. Die belangrikste faktore wat 'n persoon se status bepaal, is domisilie, onwettige geboorte, ouderdom, fisiese of geestelike onvermoë, geslag, ras, verkwistende neigings en insolvensie."

19. Act 55 of 1998.
20. Act 59 of 1992.
21. Act 24 of 1956.
22. On this point, the Road Accident Commission (*Report of the Road Accident Fund Commission* (2002) vol II 813-814, hereafter, "*Report*") states: "[W]ithout exception, all submissions were in agreement with the view of the Hospital Association of South Africa that where patients are not promptly and appropriately treated 'there is a higher rate of complications'. The South African Orthopaedic Association points out that 'the cost of substandard and deferred treatment is tremendously high. These patients must be treated for complications and have to receive extended reconstructive procedures."
23. On this point, the Road Accident Fund Commission (*Report* 813) comments: "[I]n the years that it takes for the system of road accident compensation to contribute towards the costs of medical treatment required by the victims of road accidents, such treatment will already have been obtained to the extent that it was available or was made available at a price that could be borne by the road accident victim or family. Any assistance provided by the current compensation scheme is very much ex post facto and does absolutely nothing to ensure that required healthcare intervention is available at the time when it is actually needed and in the form and to the extent that it is required."
24. On the discrepancy between public and private health care, the Road accident Fund Committee (*Report* 847) states: "[c]linics are not open for twenty-four hours, and are understaffed. Ambulances are unavailable to transport patients or fail to provide any emergency care. Spinal and intensive care units have been closed. Provincial hospitals are unable to provide artificial limbs or incontinence equipment. Wheelchair budgets are non-existent or have been reduced in provincial health budgets. Provincial workshops do not provide well-fitting and ultramodern prostheses. Records are poorly managed and reasons for medical decisions are not recorded. X-rays are not always available and are sometimes incorrectly labelled. Provincial hospitals provide 'sub-standard treatment' and 'the system of provincial hospital care has collapsed in many places.'"
25. Act 130 of 1993.
26. The first system under the Workmen's Compensation Act 30 of 1941 came into effect during World War II. Although a new act, the Compensation for Occupational Injuries and Diseases Act 130 of 1993, was introduced subsequently, this new act retained the structure of the old Act.
27. Smit 474.
28. Smit 474.
29. Smit 477.
30. Smit 480-481.
31. *Ibid.* Where disablement is less than 30 per cent, the lump sum is calculated proportionally.
32. Smit 481.

33. Smit 480 fn 178. Thus Klinck "People with Disabilities" in Olivier *et al.* Social Security Law: A Legal Analysis" (2003) 326. states that:"[I]t is doubtful whether the existing legislation is sufficient in assisting government to comply with its constitutional duties vis-á-vis people living with disabilities which arose from employment or road accidents. In particular, when deciding on an appropriate response- in a social security sense- to the needs related to occupational injuries, deaths and disease, a policy decision has to be made as to the nature of the provision for such needs. . . . [T]he so-called 'meat chart approach' (fixed levels of compensation) has been criticised as creating the impression that this is compensation for loss of a limb rather than for the achievement of adequate or reasonable income replacement (social security as a (temporary) bypass until reintegration occurs."
34. *Transforming the Present- Protecting the Future* (March 2002) ch 12, par 12.6. The Committee states that: "[C]OIDA is not strong on reintegration measures. in contrast with the position elsewhere, there is no provision in COIDA, which specifically attempts to enforce reintegration measures such as compulsory rehabilitation or vocational training programmes. It is, therefore, especially in the area of reintegration measures that the system is extremely deficient. One would have to suggest that policy-makers should, as a matter of priority, consider the reintroduction of measures which would give effect to the principle of labour market integration. Rehabilitation, vocational training and, where appropriate, linking entitlement to benefits payment to participation in such programmes, should serve as minimal mechanisms to attain this goal."
35. This exclusion may probably be justified because the objective of the Act is to cover employment injuries and only employees who's employers contribute to the system may enjoy coverage. However, this does not mean that the self-employed and atypically employed should forever remain excluded from a system such as COIDA. In chapter 8 it will be shown how this matter is dealt with in the German social security system.
36. Reintegration into the workforce where possible, instead of the payment of benefits or sometimes in addition to the payment of minimum benefits will create a culture of independency and limited resources will be utilized more effectively. Any re-integration should, however, be part of a holistic system of social security. Once again, a policy decision is needed here on whether an employee should be granted benefits as a matter of right merely because he qualifies for a benefit or whether it is more important to re-integrate that employee into the workforce and to systematically rehabilitate him.
37. Act 63 of 2001.
38. Act 4 of 2002.
39. Van Kerken and Olivier "Unemployment Insurance" in Olivier *et al. Social Security: A Legal Analysis* (2003) 425.
40. In *Aetna Insurance Co v Minister of Justice* the court summarised the objective of the Road Accident Fund (RAF) 1960 3 SA 273 (A) at 285 by stating that: "[t]he

obvious evil that it is designed to remedy is that members of the public who are injured, and the dependents of those who are killed, through the negligent driving of motor vehicles may find themselves without redress against the wrongdoer. . . . To remedy that evil, the Act provides a system of compulsory insurance."

41. *Transforming the Present—Protecting the Future* (Draft Consolidated Report) (2002) Ch 11.
42. Once again, a core value is missing in the whole argument on why a victim should be compensated and how. As far as road accidents are concerned, the most urgent needs are proper emergency medical treatment, rehabilitative care and income replacement in the case of disability. Non-patrimonial loss is a 'nice to have' but not a necessity. A policy decision on this issue is needed urgently.
43. Act 59 of 1992.
44. Smit and van der Nest "The Satchwell Report: an Analysis of and Comment on the findings of the Road Accident Fund Commission" (2003) *TSAR* 677
45. Act 59 of 1992.
46. S 1 of the Social Assistance Act 59 of 1992.
47. S 3 and reg 2 of the Social Assistance Act, 1992.
48. Paton "Chains of Poverty" (2004) *Financial Mail* 20.
49. *Ibid.*
50. Klinck "People with Disabilities" in Olivier *et al. Social Security Law: A Legal Analysis* (2003) 336.
51. *Lake* v. *Reinsurance Corporation Ltd.*, 1967 3 SA 124 (W). See also Reinecke *et al. General Principles of Insurance* (2002) 3 and section 1(1) of the Long-term Insurance Act 52 of 1998.
52. Reinecke (n 56) 435.
53. *Ibid.* See also the definition in section 1(1) of the Long-term Insurance Act 52 of 1998.
54. Reinecke *et al.* (n 56) 435.
55. Act 53 of 1998.
56. *Ibid.*
57. Act 52 of 1998.
58. Act 52 of 1998.
59. Reinecke *et al.* (n 56) 3.
60. Reinecke *et al.* (n 56) 6.
61. *Ibid.* The writers explain mutual insurance as follows: "[i]n case of mutual insurance, the business of the insurer is not aimed at making any profit. If more premiums are collected than the amount required to cover all losses, the balance must be returned to the insured. If there is a shortfall of premiums, a call could be made on insured to make good the shortfall. Usually premiums are calculated ex post facto and insured are then asked to pay their contributions or 'calls'. Today, mutual insurers are companies without any share capital."
62. Reinecke *et al.* (n 56) 10.
63. Klinck "People with Disabilities" in Olivier *et al. Social Security Law: A Legal Analysis* (2003) 336. Case report's full reference.

64. *Ibid.*
65. Cousy "Structural and Legal Aspects of the European internal market for Insurance" (1994) *TSAR* 399 on 414.
66. Wansink "Verzekering, een juridisch product in een kritische buitenwereld—een impressie uit Nederland" (1999) *TSAR* 707.
67. *Ibid.*
68. *Ibid.*
69. *Ibid.*
70. *Ibid.*
71. haal grondwet aan hier.

24

Corporate Ethics: An End to the Rhetorical Interpretations of Endemic Corruption

BEN TRAN

Crime, fraud, and corruption, all nouns that pertain to the act of deception that depicts an intention "in increasing an opportunity in ones favour in an unlawful manner that are far-fetched or erroneous, of organizational interest and goals.

Crime, on the other hand, according to Shover and Hochstetler (2002) is behaviour that violates criminal status, regardless of whether or not it becomes known or responded to by criminal, civil or administrative state agencies. It is behaviour that is potentially sanctionable by agencies of criminal justice. Organizational crime is crime committed by officers, managers or employees of legitimate formal organizations in furtherance of their conception, however far-fetched or erroneous, of organizational interest and goals. (Shover and Hochstetler, 2002.)

Sutherland (1949: 9) defined crime as "... committed by a person of responsibility and high social status in the course of his occupation," and reported that his sample of 70 major American corporations had an average of 14 legal decisions against them for illegal acts, roughly 1 for every three years of their average corporate lifetime. The offences ranged from restraint of trade and false advertising to patent and trademark infringement and unfair labour practices. He also found significant levels of recidivism. The 41 companies that had been criminally convicted of offences averaged four convictions each. Sutherland's definition of crime prompted a debate and an investigation on the meaning of (white-collar) crime. (Wozniak, 2001.)

Following Sutherland's (1949) study, according to Reed and Yeager (1996), more recently, Clinard and Yeager (1980) also found high rate of lawbreaking by large US corporations. Their study of the largest industrial firms focused upon only a two-year period (1975-76), but they found that 46 per cent (222 companies) of the sample had been charged with non-minor violations of federal laws. While arguably not all of such cases involved force or fraud, the study found numerous offences that did, such as antitrust conspiracies, unsafe workplaces, unfair labour practices, and commercial bribery. Similarly, in his case of more than 1,000 of the nation's largest firms during the period 1970-80, Ross (1992: 9-10) found that 11 per cent (117 firms) either had been criminally convicted or signed consent decrees involving five types of offences: criminal antitrust violations, bribery, illegal political contributions, fraud, and/or tax evasion. Ross also described the numerous cases of procurement fraud, many committed by the nation's largest defence contradictions in the 1980s, as constituting "a corporate way of life" in the defence industry. (Ross, 1991.)

CORPORATE ETHICS: AN END TO THE RHETORICAL INTERPRETATIONS OF ENDEMIC CORRUPTION

Views from-and-of-the inside of corporations consistently suggest that routine nature of much offending and of the forces in organization and culture that occasion it. Indeed, surveys of corporate officials indicate that unethical and illegal practices are common.

For example, in a *Harvard Business Review* survey on corporate ethics, half of the sampled managers thought that their superiors frequently did not wish to know how results .were obtained so long as the desired outcomes were achieved. Moreover, "respondents frequently complained of superiors' pressure to support incorrect viewpoints, sign false documents, overlook superiors' wrongdoing, and do business with superiors' friends." (Brenner and Molander, 1977: 60.) Relatedly, Clinard's (1983) interviewees, retried middle managers, reported that unethical and illegal acts were connected to the culture established by top management. Intriguingly, these managers further suggested that the nature of the ethical climate depended in part on the professional backgrounds of corporate leaders and their mode of recruitment. Respondents saw leaders with engineering backgrounds, and those recruited from among long-standing employees, as being more likely to establish positive ethical climates than financial specialists and recruits from outside the firm, who focused more on bottom-line results. (Clinard, 1983: 136-37.)

Thus, the purpose of this paper is to analyze the endemic corruption and to put an end to its various rhetorical interpretations through two paradigms: social behavioural science and legality. The social behavioural science paradigm will be analyzed through Institutional Choice Analytic Frame and the Constructivist Approach and the legality paradigm will be analyzed through laws and codes of ethics. This paper will conclude with a recommendation of a CEO (Chief Ethics Officer).

25

Development of Social Financial Reporting in Different Geographies: European Union, Australia and Asia

KIYMET TUNCA CALIYURT

Corporate Social Financial Reporting (SFR) is to incorporate ethical considerations in financial statements. Business approaches, social, environmental and local impact and their influence on society are required to be included in financial statements. Recently investors are interesting with the social side of financial reports because labour and environmental policy and its reflection in the financial reports are important. In this paper, examples will be given from the European Union, Asia, and Australia on recent developments about SFR.

On the website of EU it says that social and environmental reporting is made by companies mainly on a voluntary basis. However, this is starting to change. Denmark introduced a law on mandatory "Green Accounts" for large companies in 1995. France followed in February 2002 with a legal act that obliges listed companies to include social and environmental evaluations in their annual reports. There is still no EU wide approach to social and environmental reporting. The Commission's Communication on Corporate Social Responsibility states that in this initial phase, reporting should remain as flexible as possible.

In Asia the National University of Singapore has Corporate Governance and Financial Reporting Centre. The most important objectives of the Centre are to:

Conduct high-quality academic research in the areas of corporate governance and financial reporting.

The Prime Minister's Community Business Partnership is a group of prominent Australians from the community and business sectors, appointed by the Prime Minister to advise and assist the Government on issues concerning community business collaboration. The Partnership aims to develop and promote a culture of corporate and individual social responsibility. The Partnership's role is advocacy, facilitation and recognition of corporate social responsibility and partnerships between business and community organisations in Australia. The Business Council of Australia (BCA) is a peak business representative body for large businesses in Australia. The BCA surveyed its membership of 100 leading corporations in an attempt to quantify the significant contribution these companies make to the community. This culminated in the recent release of the report 'The Community of Business'. The Community of Business survey found that BCA Member companies: contributed around $ 220 million and over 200,000 staff hours on social and community programmes across Australia; spent $ 290 million and 425,000 staff hours on environmental projects; employ 900,000 people including 250,000 in rural and regional areas; contribute approximately half of their annual revenues of $ 338 billion as payment to suppliers in other, mostly smaller, businesses; account for one-third of Australia's total export revenue; and paid $ 18 billion to shareholders in the form of dividends annually.

26

Social Responsibility and Corporate Business Ethics

V. BALU

1. INTRODUCTION

Today, the operations of business enterprises affect a wide spectrum. The resources they make use of are not limited to those of the proprietors and the impact of their operations is felt also by many a people who are in no way connected with the enterprise. The shareholders, the supplier of resources, the consumers, the employees, the local community and society at large are affected by the way an enterprise functions. Hence, a business enterprise has to be socially very responsive so that a social balance may be struck between the opposing interests of these groups. The declaration issued by the international seminar on Social Responsibility of business held in India. In 1965 also co-related the Gandhian concept of trusteeship with the social responsibility of business as "responsibility to customers, workers, shareholders and the community." There has been a growing acceptance of the plea that business should be socially responsible in the sense that the business enterprise, which makes use of the resources of society and depends on society for its functioning, should discharge its duties and responsibilities in enhancing the welfare of the society of which it is an integral part.

In the environment of modern economic development, the corporate sector no longer functions in isolation. The company must behave and function as a responsible member of society, like any other individual. It cannot show moral values nor can it ignore actual compulsions. The real need is for some focus of accountability on the part of the management which is not limited to shareholders alone. In modern times, the objective of business has to be the proper utilisation of resources for the benefit of others. A profit is still a necessary part of the total picture; but it is not the primary purpose. This implies that the claims of various interests will have to be balanced not on the narrow ground of what is best for the shareholders alone but from the point of view of what is best for the community at large.

2. SOCIAL RESPONSIBILITY

Bowen defines the concept as "the obligation (of managers) to pursue those policies, to make those decisions, or to follow those lines of action which are desirable in terms of the objectives and values of our society." He also says that the "Doctrine of social responsibility refers to the idea that voluntary assumption of social responsibility by business-men is, or might be, a practicable means toward ameliorating economic problems and attaining more fully the economic goals we seek."

Koontz and O'Donnell have given the definition of social responsibility thus: "The personal obligation of the people as they act in their own interests to assure that the rights and legitimate interests of others are not infringed."

According to Steiner, "Social responsibility is to understand public consensus, to recognise it, and to corporate in achieving this. Each business has responsibilities in some way commensurate with its power."

From the few definitions quoted above, it may be noted that social responsibility means fulfilling the obligations towards the society and the components of business, and improving its economic and social conditions by all possible means. In other words, the concept of social responsibility assumes that the business has not only economic and legal obligations but also certain other social responsibilities too, a businessman must besides taking care of his own interest must also take care others' interest too, viz., the community members.

3. DOCTRINE OR CONCEPT OF SOCIAL RESPONSIBILITY

The social responsibility concept is based on the premise that business has greater impact on society that can be measured by profit or loss. As a participant in society, business should contribute to the human and constructive social policies that guide society. The concept of social responsibility is merely a first step towards social effectiveness of business. It is the underlying value which gives businessmen a sound basis for social action. It is the philosophy which justifies business involvement in its social community, but philosophy by itself is incomplete. It must be followed by effective social action. In the words of one observer, "Philosophy without programme is a shadow without substance." Perhaps, one should take, therefore, less of corporate social responsibilities and more of corporate social responses. The former is too redolent of legalism and the nation of fixed obligations; the latter more open, permits voluntary and creative undertakings by business on behalf of society's larger needs.

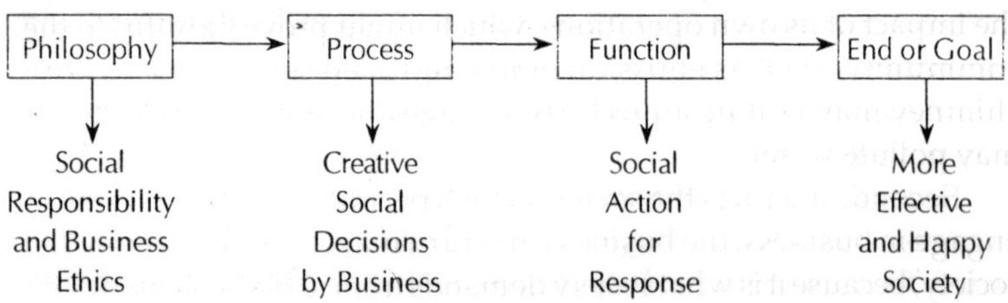

A Philosophy of Social Responsibility and Business Ethics

If business and society get stuck on the legalism of social responsibility, they will drift into inaction. The ultimate need is business response which provides progress toward the desirable end of a more effective society. The desirable end is achieved through a sequence of philosophy, process, and functions. In the area of business and society, the philosophy is social responsibility, and the process is creative decision-making by business. Creative decisions lead to the function of social action by business, which produces the desirable end of a better society. Social responsibility is only the beginning of the sequence. The fact is that business is a major social institution and as such, it is importantly involved in social values.

"The idea of social responsibility is that the decision-makers are obliged to take actions which protect and improve the welfare of society as a whole along with their own interests. It builds a better quality of life, thus harmonising organisational actions with society's wants." The idea is that the businessman acts in a manner that will accomplish social benefits along with the traditional economic gains which the firm seeks.

4. RATIONALE OF SOCIAL RESPONSIBILITY

Social responsibility recognises that each person is attached to an extended social system on which he or she is partly dependent, consequently, certain obligations or social responsibilities arise from his attachment.

General Factors

Business owes its responsibility towards society, first, as a result of the impact of its own operations, which might prove harmful to the community, such as emission of uncontrolled soot from a factory chimney may pollute air or dirty sewage and solid waste material may pollute water.

Second, since it is the society which permits men and women to engage in business, the business in return make contributions to the society, because it is what society demands from it. Elton Mayo rightly remarked that "The modern industrial society faces disintegration because of the breakdown of the social code that formerly disciplined us in effective working together." The businessman's function, according to her, is "to convert men into a modern counterpart of the tribe, clan or guild, in order to save society." Thus, the primary function of the business is "to provide the basis for social order in an industrial society."

Cultural norms are powerful determinants of behaviour, consequently, as society's norms change, the businessman's behaviour with it also changes. If society moves towards norms of social responsibility as it is now doing, then the businessman is subtly and inevitably guided by these norms. The basic objective of business, which was formerly "earning of profit for its own sake," is now undergoing a change. Now the business community has begun to recognise its stake in the well-being of its workers and community. As early as 1930, Alfred North Whitehead, in an address to the Harvard Business School, concluded that business of future must be controlled by a different type of leaders, i.e. "a socially responsible manager." In this way, "the businessman appears to be acting in a socially responsible way even though his first priority is profit." It is now a well-known fact that "profit-earning and customers' satisfaction are no longer the sole and exclusive criteria of business these days."

Business is required to share responsibility of the government to alleviate social problems. Often government's inadequacy in meeting social changes calls for other groups of society – business, voluntary agencies, institutions, charitable organisations, etc., for sharing the government's burden in terms of droughts, floods, cyclones, earthquakes, epidemics, and other unforeseen calamities. The enlightened businessman come forward to fulfil their social responsibility in helping meet the situation.

Other Factors

Changing societal values have also led to the adoption of Social Responsibility. In the past, the phrase "social responsibility of business" might have meant interest in ethics and charity. Today, it encompasses for more because the managements' personal and social values have also changed. Monsen makes the following observations in this regard: "Values for the businessman set the framework within which he can operate and do business. The boundaries of business are set by the prevailing values of society. For instance, do we allow pollution and, if so, of what kind and how much? Such questions are determined by the prevailing values in the society and become crucial for anyone trying to determine why our society allows certain acts and not others and, thus, why business makes one decision and not another."

5. CORPORATE BUSINESS ETHICS

Business is the world-wide institution touching even the most remote village in one way or another. Japanese cars, United States computers, Italian wines, British insurance, Swiss banking services, Brazilian coffee and Taiwanese transistor radios – all the result of business activities – are common throughout much of the world. Big multi-national corporations headquartered in Western Europe, North and South America, Australia, Japan, and other nations do business around the globe. The world's people have become accustomed to business and are dependent on it for many of their needs.

A growing world population that is estimated to around 6 billion by 2000 A.D. needs to be fed, clothed, housed, educated, and otherwise supported. Even in those nations, where private business plays a small role—China and the Soviet Union, for example, international trade with business firms in other nations can help feed and clothe people and equip factories with machinery.

It is difficult for those who live in the world's industrial heartland to imagine the wretched, widespread poverty and squalor found in many countries. Life is short, disease rampant, malnutrition a constant threat for many people in Africa, Asia, and parts of Latin America. The great majority of the world's peoples live much closer to the margin of existence than those in the advanced nations. These nations look to their more prosperous neighbours for help in boosting their living standards.

Business is increasingly challenged to consider ethics when it makes decisions. The need is to find a balance between economics and ethics. Society wants business to produce needed goods and services but it also expects business to conduct its economic operations in ethical ways.

All human societies have ethical systems that define what is meant by right and wrong, fairness, justice, truthfulness, and similar ideas dealing with morality and rightness. Individuals who live in those societies learn from childhood what is considered ethical and unethical. Religious institutions, parents, teachers, and others instill a sense of fairness and justice and general ethical behaviour. As a result, most persons develop a strong sense of ethics which then acts as one's conscience when faced with questions of right and wrong. In addition to individual conscience, societies spell out their ethics in laws, customs, and religious beliefs. When questions arise, these community standards are then used to sort out right from wrong and to define what is ethical or unethical.

6. THE UNETHICAL PRACTICES

Foremost among the types of unethical practices that have developed in business is that of "buying business, using baits such as bribes, grafts, the entertainment of buyers by providing call girls or presenting them expensive gifts." Corruption and unethical practices go together and exist side by side, as would be clear from the following:

"Even after an order has been passed by a higher authority, the order was not communicated to the applicant until he has paid illegal gratification to the subordinate concerned."

"Corruption is encouraged because business cannot wait and has to be kept going as an existing concern while government red-tape takes time."

"The advance of technology and science is contributing to the emergence of a mass society with a large rank and file and a small controlling elite, encouraging the growth of monopolies, the use of managerial class often amorphous and anonymous, and that of intricate institutional mechanisms." (Mamoria: *Business Ethics*).

The late American President Woodrow Wilson had laid down four important principles for the proper conduct of business viz.,

(i) "**The Rule of Publicity:** Let the people know what it is going to do. Suspicion, false conjecture, and misunderstanding arise out of secretiveness.
(ii) **The Rule of Equivalent Price:** Let the public receive goods and services fully equivalent to the money paid.
(iii) **The Rule of Conscience in Business:** To emphasise that the rules of business games must be of a higher order than those of an ordinary game, sustained by moral judgement of honourable men.
(iv) **The Rule of Spirit of Service:** To see that the things you do for the public and get money for it is the best thing of that kind that can be done."

7. GOOD ETHICS IS GOOD BUSINESS

To conclude, the most common belief is that "good ethics is good business" for it wins laurels in the long run. This has been supported by Learned, Dooley and Katz, who observed: "The businessman's reasons for supporting this saying is due to the fact that: (i) a business that behaves ethically induces others to behave ethically towards it; (ii) ethical behaviour is a form of insurance against retaliatory acts; and (iii) a good man who steadfastly tries to be ethical . . . somehow always overtakes his immoral or amoral counterpart." The last one means that "the unethical man preoccupied with deception cannot match the pure creative zeal of the honest individual whose energies are freed for maximum productivity and creativity."

REFERENCES

Mamoria & Mamoria, *Business Planning and Policy*.
P.K. Ghosh, *Business Policy and Strategic Management*.
William Glueck, *Business Policy*.

27

Agency Theory: A Cause of Failure in Corporate Governance

DAVID CROWTHER AND RENU JATANA

INTRODUCTION

A growing number of writers over the last quarter of a century have recognised that the activities of an organisation impact upon the external environment and have suggested that such an organisation should therefore be accountable to a wider audience than simply its shareholders. Such a suggestion probably first arose in the 1970s and a concern with a wider view of company performance is taken by some writers who evince concern with the social performance of a business, as a member of society at large. This concern was stated by Ackerman (1975) who argued that big business was recognising the need to adapt to a new social climate of community accountability, but that the orientation of business to financial results was inhibiting social responsiveness. McDonald and Puxty (1979) on the other hand maintain that companies are no longer the instruments of shareholders alone but exist within society and so therefore have responsibilities to that society, and that there is therefore a shift towards the greater accountability of companies to all participants.

Recognition of the rights of all stakeholders and the duty of a business to be accountable in this wider context therefore has been largely a relatively recent phenomenon.[1] The economic view of accountability only to owners has only recently however been subject to debate to any considerable extent. Implicit in this concern with the effects of the actions of an organisation on its external environment is the recognition that it is not just the owners of the organisation who have a concern with the activities of that organisation. Additionally there are a wide variety of other stakeholders who justifiably have a concern with those activities, and are affected by those activities. Those other stakeholders have not just an interest in the activities of the firm but also a degree of influence over the shaping of those activities. This influence is so significant that it can be argued that the power and influence of these stakeholders is such that it amounts to quasi-ownership of the organisation. Indeed Gray, Dwen and Maunders (1987) challenge the traditional role of accounting in reporting results and consider that, rather than an ownership approach to accountability, a stakeholder approach, recognising the wide stakeholder community, is needed.[2]

The desirability of considering the social performance of a business has not always however been accepted and has been the subject of extensive debate. Thus Hetherington (1973: 37) states:

> There is no reason to think that shareholders are willing to tolerate an amount of corporate non-profit activity which appreciably reduces either dividends or the market performance of the stock.

while Dahl (1972: 18) states:

> . . . every large corporation should be thought of as a social enterprise; that is an entity whose existence and decisions can be justified insofar as they serve public or social purposes.

One of the consequences of a concern with the actions of an organisation, and the consequences of those actions, has been an increasing concern with corporate governance. Corporate Governance is the current buzz word the world over. It has gained tremendous importance in the recent past, especially during the second half of the 1990s. Two of the main reasons for this upsurge are the economic liberalization and deregulation of industry and business and, second, demand for new corporate ethos and stricter compliance with the law of the land. One more factor that has been responsible for the sudden exposure of the corporate sector to a new paradigm for corporate governance that is in tune with the changing times in the demand for greater accountability of companies to their shareholders and customers.

Over the last several decades, industrialization and technological revolution have changed the nature of business enterprises from family owned organizations to corporate entities. The modern corporation is owned by a large body of widely dispersed shareholders and is run by managers who may not own any stake in the business; unless the board of directors is efficient and vigilant, managers may not display the necessary commitment to shareholders interests on their own. Apart from shareholder there are other stakeholders, like creditors, employees, customers, suppliers and society, whose fates are interwoven with business corporations. Corporate governance envisages a set of systems and processes which ensure that a company is managed in the best interests of all shareholders and stakeholders. In its broader sense, corporate governance is like a trusteeship. It is not simply a matter of creating checks and balances, it is about creating an outperforming organization which leads to increasing customer satisfaction and shareholder value. In the absence of effective corporate governance, the objectives of long-term shareholder value, corporate democracy, transparency in operations and reporting, and internationally acceptable standards of performance remain illusory.

REGULATING GOVERNANCE

Corporate governance has acquired a new urgency due to changing profiles of corporate ownerships, preferential allotment of shares to promoters, increasing inflow of foreign capital, and deliberate dismantling of control mechanisms that had hitherto provided protective cover to every poorly managed corporate, a consequence of economic liberalization (Fernado, 1997). Thus in India the Department of Company Affairs, Government of India, Investment/Trade Associations, companies like Hindustan Lever, Bajaj Auto, L&T, Reliance, etc., regulators like SEBI and RBI and institutes like ICAI, ICSI, etc., are dwelling upon the subject for devising rules and guidelines in order to promote healthy corporate practices in the country. The confederation of Indian Industry (CII) has prepared a comprehensive draft on corporate governance in the context of India's changing corporate environment. Similarly in the UK corporate governance is expressed in the form of a code, such as the Cadbury code, which deals exclusively with financial aspects of governance of a corporation.

Corporate Governance, in other words, can be considered as an environment of trust, ethics, moral values and confidence—as a synergic effort of all the constituents of society, that is the stakeholder, including government, general public, etc.; professional/service providers; and the corporate sector. The government through legislative measures, the professionals through their value added and independent services, and the corporate sector through their thrust to grow and flourish, may contribute to good governance level.

Every time the society faces a new problem/threat, a new legislative restriction through one or other mode tries to protect the misshapenness in future. But the same crime takes place by changing its face. Recent fallouts one after another, in spite of protective measures, are the live examples. We saw a plethora of new provision in various acts, regulations and new guidelines issued by various regulatory authorities in the last 8 to 10 years, as an effort (a) to regulate the new economic environment, (b) to introduce better systems/procedures, and (c) to allow greater transparency and accountability. The focus may be on taking precautionary measures at the initial stages rather than to adopt a wait and watch strategy. The governance code for the corporate sector has been one step in this direction. With the increase in their level of responsibility and accountability to the stakeholders, it is also felt that there is a need to develop the code for corporate governance for the professional themselves, so as to guide them to chose the right path and right direction.

A great deal of concern has been expressed all over the world about the shortcomings in the systems of corporate governance: Britain, Australia and all other English speaking countries have similar systems, but other countries do also. Germany is a good example where distance between ownership and control is much less than in the United States. Japan's system of corporate governance is in some ways in between Germany and the United States, and in other ways different from both. The international comparisons illustrate different approaches to the problem of corporate governance, the problem of ensuring that managers act in shareholders' interest. In India the corporate governance system in the public sector may be characterized as the "transient system", with the key players, viz. politicians, bureaucrats, and managers, taking a myopic view of the thing.

EFFECT OF GOOD CORPORATE GOVERNANCE

Good governance is important in every sphere of the environment whether it be the corporate environment or general society or political environment. Socially speaking, the problem of urban poverty could be checked by good governing practices. Good governance levels can improve public faith and confidence in the political environment. When the recourses are too limited to meet the minimum expectations of the people, it is the good governance level that can help to promote the welfare of the society. The way forward, to achieve the desired level in India scenario, is to promote the social thinking in a positive perspective along with the perfect monitoring mechanism of regulatory framework.

Good governance practices, entail active participation of shareholders in the direct and indirect management of a corporation through the board of directors and an arrangement of productive checks and balances among shareholders, board of directors and management of corporations. Sound corporate decision-making has emerged as the direct and positive outcome of good corporate governance system.

Corporate governance is the system by which companies are directed and controlled. Boards of Directors are responsible for the governance of their companies. The shareholders' role in governance is to appoint the directors and auditors and to satisfy themselves that an appropriate governance structure is in place. The responsibilities of the board include setting the company's aims, providing the leadership to put them into effect, supervising the management of the business and reporting to shareholders on their stewardship. The Board's actions are subject to laws, regulations and the shareholders in general meetings. Players are many in the system of corporate governance. Where the government and other regulatory agencies provide the platform through legislations and rules, on the other side the board of directors, auditors, shareholders, financial institutions, accounting professional, company secretaries and employee play their individual roles for the proper governance. However, on the wake of changes in the economy, their traditional roles need some fine tuning.

The Board of Directors has a pivotal position in the structure of corporate governance. A company in law is equal to a natural person and has a legal being of its own. Though a company is itself a person, it is an artificial legal person created by law, and can, therefore, of necessity, act only through the agency of natural persons. It is on account of the peculiar character of a company that the need for directors arises. The directors are not only agents of a company but they are also its trustees.

LIMITING LIABILITY

The developments in accounting, financial reporting and auditing were all designed to provide protection to investors in a joint stock company, with this being achieved by imposing a duty of accountability upon the managers[3] of a company. This was not however considered to be sufficient protection for potential investors in a business enterprise and further protection was introduced through the concept of limited liability. Limited liability means that the possible risk to any shareholder is a maximum of the amount paid for the shares plus any unpaid share capital (James, 1972). This limitation of liability is specified in the Memorandum of association (Smith and Keenan, 1969). The principle of limited liability was first introduced in the UK by the Limited Liability Act, 1855. According to Glautier and Underdown (1995) there was considerable opposition to the passing of this act but Parliament recognised the need to safeguard investors in companies. At the same time it recognised the potential for abuse and the requirements for stewardship and the disclosure of information to shareholders were linked to this limitation of liability, thereby safeguarding the shareholders of the company — at least in the minds of the legislators.

In legal terms a company is a person with the power to contract like any other individual[4] although the reality is that this power is vested in the managers of the company. The effect of this is that managers can enter into transactions for which they have no liability for non-fulfilment. Effectively by the introduction of this concept of limited liability risk was transferred away from the legal owners of a business and onto those with whom that business transacted. Equally the ability of managers to engage in those transactions on behalf of the business, without any necessary evidence of ownership — merely delegated responsibility — meant that most risk was thereby transferred away from the business. The potential rewards from owning a business became divorced from any commensurate risk effectively separating the risk-reward relationship upon which finance theory is based.

This of course paved the way for the attraction of many more investors, thereby enabling the growth in size of business enterprises, and this was needed for the growth of large scale businesses such as the railways during the early days of the Industrial Revolution. It can be argued that the Industrial Revolution would not have happened without this introduction of limited liability as this made those investors secure in the knowledge that they were protected from any loss greater than the sum they had invested in the enterprise. Thus for relatively small levels of risk they were able to expect potentially great rewards and thereby escape from some of the consequences of the actions of the enterprise.

CONSTRAINING MANAGERS—AGENCY THEORY

Given that managers have both the ability to commit the organisation to whatever contracts and transactions they feel appropriate and a responsibility towards the owners of the business there was a need to ensure that this responsibility took place. It is normally accepted that Agency theory provides a platform upon which this can be ensured. Agency theory suggests that the management of an organisation is undertaken on behalf of the owners of that organisation, in other words the shareholders. Consequently, the management of value created by the organisation is only pertinent insofar as that value accrues to the shareholders of the firm. Implicit within this view of the management of the firm, as espoused by Rappaport (1986) and Stewart (1991) amongst many others, is that society at large, and consequently all other stakeholders to the organisation, will also benefit as a result of managing the performance of the organisation in this manner. From this perspective therefore the concerns are focused upon how to manage performance for the shareholders and how to report upon that performance (Myners, 1998).

This view of an organisation has however been extensively challenged by many writers,[5] who argue that the way to maximise performance for society at large is to both manage on behalf of all stakeholders and to ensure that the value thereby created is not appropriated by the shareholders but is distributed to all stakeholders. Others such as Kay (1998) argue that this debate is sterile and that organisations maximise value creation not by a concern with either shareholders or stakeholders but by focusing upon the operational objectives of the firm and assuming that value creation, and equitable distribution will thereby follow.

The shareholder theory of the firm is often also referred to as agency theory as the role of the management of a firm is to act as the agents of the shareholders (the principals). The separation of ownership and control that is apparent in large modern-day (joint stock) companies, presently the most common way for a business to be organised, is another significant change since the days of Smith and Mill. It is this separation that leads to what is known as the principal-agent relationship. It is also argued that within this role it is only appropriate for managers (the agents) to use the funds at their disposal for purposes authorised by shareholders (the principals) (Hasnas, 1998; Smith and Hasnas, 1999). Further as shareholders normally invest in shares in order to maximise their own returns then managers, as their agents, are obliged to target this end. In fact this is arguing that as an owner a shareholder has the right to expect his or her property to be used to his or her own benefit. Donaldson (1982, 1989) disagrees and suggests that it can be morally acceptable to use the shareholder's money in this way if it is to further public interest. The ethical and moral acceptability of this suggestion is questionable and Smith and Hasnas (1999) point out that such an act would contravene Kant's (1804) principle. This principle states that a person should be treated as an end in his or her own right rather than as a means to an end. By using shareholders' money for the benefit of others it is argued that the shareholders are being used as a means to further others' ends. This defence of shareholder theory is as ironic as it is compelling given that the exact same principle is often cited to defend stakeholder theory.

Assumed within agency theory is a lack of goal congruence between the principal and agent and that it is costly or difficult to confirm the agent's actions (Eisenhardt, 1989). In saying this it is suggested that, left to their own devices, the agents will prefer different options to those that would be chosen by the principals. The agents would make decisions and follow courses that further their own self-interest as opposed to that of the principal. This assumption that agents behaviour will be driven by their own self-interest and nothing else has been criticised as being an overly simplistic conception of human behaviour (Williamson, 1985). It is argued that in addition to self-interested motives, altruism, irrationality, generosity, genuine concern for others . . . also characterise multi-faceted human behaviour. Sen (1987) agrees and actually states that 'to argue that anything other than maximising self-interest must be irrational seems altogether extraordinary.'

It has been argued that shareholders should have rights to determine how their property be used, as should an owner of any asset under private property rights. Etzioni (1998) suggests that this view of shareholder's property rights, which are both moral and legal, is 'widely embedded in the American political culture' and therefore needs no further introduction. Taking a step back Etzioni observes that such property rights are a social construct, as opposed to natural or inalienable rights, and as such society has the opportunity and the ability to change them if it is considered necessary. A closer consideration of what is meant by private property, as it has been socially constructed in present day Western societies, has been undertaken. Donaldson and Preston (1995) argue that the philosophy of property 'runs strongly counter to the conception that private property exclusively enshrines the interests of owners.' They specifically note the work of Pejovich (1990) as recognising that ownership does not entail unrestricted rights as they cannot be separated from human rights. Further, Honore (1961) suggests that the rights are restricted where the use would be harmful to others. Donaldson and Preston (1995) suggest that as property rights are restricted then they need to be founded on distributive justice. Interestingly Sternberg (1998) a proponent of shareholder theory, because 'it alone respects the property rights that are so essential for protecting individual liberty,' also suggests that ethical business must also be based on 'distributive justice' along with 'ordinary decency' (Sternberg, 1994, 1998). Donaldson and Preston (1995) follow Becker's (1992) suggestion that the "three main contending theories of distributive justice include Utilitarianism, Libertarianism and social contract theory." Utilitarianism and Libertarianism have already been commented upon as part of the historical roots of shareholder theory above.

Within the legal systems of the UK, the US, and most Western countries the managers of a business have a fiduciary duty to the owners of that business. This duty to shareholders is 'more general and pro-active' than the regulatory or contractual responsibilities to other groups (Marens and Wicks, 1999; Goodpaster, 1991). These more general duties have also been used as a justification of the appropriateness of shareholder theories of the firm. The purpose and meaning of fiduciary duty were considered by Marens and Wicks (1999) who suggest that in actual fact this duty does not limit managers to a very narrow shareholder approach. They argue that the purpose of the fiduciary duty was originally designed to prevent managers undertaking expenditures that benefited themselves (Berle and Means, 1933). Further Marens and Wicks (1999) suggest that fiduciary duties simply require that the fiduciary has an honest and open relationship with the shareholder and does not gain illegitimately from their office. Therefore, the tension between fiduciary responsibility and the responsibility to other stakeholder groups, the so-called stakeholder paradox (Goodpaster, 1991), is not as apparent as is often assumed. Further support for this argument is provided from the US courts. When shareholders have challenged management's actions as being too generous to other stakeholder groups then the court has 'almost always' upheld the right of management to manage. Management's justification or defence has often been on rational business performance grounds, such as efficiency or productivity, and the accuracy of such claims is difficult to prove. As such Marens and Wicks (1999) suggest that 'virtually any act that does not financially threaten the survival of the business could be construed as in the long-term best interest of shareholders.'

Thus Agency Theory argues that managers merely act as custodians of the organisation and its operational activities[6] and places upon them the burden of managing in the best interest of the owners of that business.[7] According to agency theory all other stakeholders of the business are largely irrelevant and if they benefit from the business then this is coincidental to the activities of management in running the business to serve shareholders. This focus upon shareholders alone as the intended beneficiaries of a business has been questioned considerably from many perspectives, which argue that it is either not the way in which a business is actually run or that it is a view which does not meet the needs of society in general. Conversely stakeholder theory argues that there are a whole variety of stakeholders involved in the organisation and each deserves some return for their involvement. According to stakeholder theory therefore benefit is maximised if the business is operated by its management on behalf of all stakeholders and returns are divided appropriately amongst those stakeholders, in some way which is acceptable to all. Unfortunately, a mechanism for dividing returns amongst all stakeholders which has universal acceptance does not exist, and stakeholder theory is significantly lacking in suggestions in this respect. Nevertheless this theory has some acceptance and is based upon the premise that operating a business in this manner achieves as one of its outcomes the maximisation of returns to shareholders, as part of the process of maximising returns to all other stakeholders. This maximisation of returns is achieved in the long-run through the optimisation of performance for the business to achieve maximal returns to all stakeholders.[8] Consequently the role of management is to optimise the long-term performance of the business in order to achieve this end and thereby reward all stakeholders, including themselves as one stakeholder community, appropriately.

These two theories can be regarded as competing explanations of the operations of a firm which lead to different operational foci and to different implications for the measurement and reporting of performance. It is significant however that both theories have one feature in common. This is that the management of the firm is believed to be acting on behalf of others, either shareholders or stakeholders more generally. They do so, not because they are the kind of people who behave altruistically, but because they are rewarded appropriately and much effort is therefore devoted to the creation of reward schemes which motivate these managers to achieve the desired ends. Similarly, much literature is devoted to the consideration of the effects of reward schemes on managerial behaviour (see for example Briers and Hirst, 1990, Child, 1974, 1975, Coates, Davis, Longden, Stacey and Emmanuel, 1993, Fitzgerald, Johnston, Brignall, Silvestro and Voss, 1991) and suggestion for improvements.

CRITIQUING AGENCY THEORY

The simplest model of Agency Theory assumes one principle and one agent and a modernist view of the world merely assumes that the addition of more principles and more agents makes for a more complex model without negating any of the assumptions. In the corporate world this is problematic as the theory depends upon a relationship between the parties and a shared understanding of the context in which agreements are made. With one principle and one agent this is not a problem as the two parties know each other. In the corporate world however the principles are equated to the shareholders of the company, for any large corporation however those shareholders are an amorphous mass of people who are unknown to the managers of the business. Indeed there is no requirement, or even expectation, that anyone will remain a shareholder for an extended period of time. Thus, there can be no relationship between shareholders – as principles – and managers – as agents – as the principles are merely those holding the shares – as property being invested in – at a particular point in time. So shareholders do not invest in a company and in the future of that company; rather they invest for capital growth and/or a future dividend stream and shares are just one way of doing this which can be moved into or out of at will. This problem is exacerbated, particularly in the UK, by the fact that a significant proportion of shares are actually bought and sold by fund managers of financial institutions acting on behalf of their investors. These fund managers are rewarded according to the growth (or otherwise) of the value of the fund. Thus, shares are bought and sold as commodities rather than as part ownership of a business enterprise.

Thus one of the two parties implicit within agency theory is problematic because there is in reality no principal. The agent party to the contract is normally considered to be the managers of the organisation and this too is problematic. The most senior managers of the organisation are the board of directors but their role in the principal-agent relationship is likely to be partly one and partly the other. As agents their role is to manage the organisation, and receive rewards for their ability in this respect, but they are also likely to be principals as owners of shares in the business. So there is no divide between principals and agents as far as they are concerned. This situation will almost certainly exist for other managers in the business also as managerial remuneration schemes are based, at least in part, on share option schemes. It is normally assumed that such schemes will successfully align the objects of managers with those of the owners (shareholders) but it has been argued (Crowther, 2002, 2003) that the effect is to privilege manager's objectives over those of the business itself.

One way to seek for good corporate governance in this environment is to make use of non-executive directors, with the objective of providing impartial advice and experience from elsewhere in the business world. Non-executive directors are the directors other than managing directors and functional directors. These are persons of excellence chosen from different fields with varied professional experience. The code of Best Practices of the Cadbury Committee states that the non-executive directors (NEDs) should be selected through a formal process and their nomination should be a matter for the board as a whole. They should be appointed for a specified term and reappointment should not be automatic. Thus appointment of NEDs of appropriate calibre, experience and complete independence is vital to good corporate governance. It is expected that NEDs should bring an independent judgment to bear on issues of strategy, performance and resources including key appointments and standards of conduct. In these days of growing competition and integration with global markets, the NEDs are supposed to act as the eyes and ears of the chairman. They should convey their experts' views on different matters to the chairman in order to strike a proper balance between company's mission and competitive edge with transparency and accountability. They should protect the interest of not only the shareholders but also of all the stakeholders. NED's are required to fulfil the following features:

- Non-executive directors should bring an independent judgement to bear on issues of strategy, performance resources, including key appointments, and standards of conduct.
- The majority should be independent of management and free from any business or other relationship, which could materially interfere with the exercise of their independent judgment, apart from their fees and shareholding. Their fees should reflect the time, which they commit to the company.
- Non-executive directors should be appointed for specified terms and reappointment should not be automatic.
- Non-executive directors should be selected through a formal process and both this process and their appointment should be a matter for the board as a whole.

What is generally ignored in these recommendations however is the internecine nature of non-executive appointments, these people know each other as know the directors of the organisation itself before appointment. So their impartiality is also subject to question.

A further class of director is those appointed by such organisations as financial institutions on the basis that they have a significant investment in the organisation. The role of nominee directors of financial institutions (FIs) on corporate boards is very important. The new economic environment has changed their role from mere spectators to key players. Since the FIs hold a major chunk of shares in companies, their role is significant in a way to strength the accountability. In pursuit of this objective, the FIs have prescribed a 19 point agenda for nominees in companies. The important points in this agenda are:

- Well defined and declared long-term dividend policies.
- Depreciation charging method should be examined.

- Investments in unlisted companies to be carefully examined.
- No resources raising in the form of equity or loans required for expansion and long-term working capital needs.
- Transfer of profitable divisions and hiving-off require approvals.
- The impact of merger on the equity shareholder pattern and on promoter holding to be examined.
- Loans and advances for share acquisition should be examined.

The areas in which they are expected to play an effective role include crucial areas such as investments in subsidiaries and loans, awards of contracts, merger and acquisitions, dividend and accounting policies. The list of guidelines and the areas prescribed is not static. It will keep on changing with the need but what is important to the nominee is to act in a cohesive manner with other directors on the board. For these people also there is a potential conflict of interest in their wish to serve the interests of their own company as well as the company they are a nominee director of.

CONCLUSION

One of the arguments of this paper is that there can be no relationship between the principal and the agent, which is a foundation of the validity of the theory. This problem is exacerbated in the modern world by the fact that many managers are almost as transient as the shareholders and no loyalty to the business itself is evident on the part of anyone involved. In such a situation the principal-agent contract becomes one of growth in share value for the shareholder and rewards for the manager—but all expressed in the present and without any regard for the future of the business. Thus the business can become not an entity in which the managers are expected to be concerned with stewardship but rather a cash cow to be managed for immediate benefit—shared between the managers and the owners with little regard for anyone else. It is argued here that the reliance upon agency theory as a mechanism for managing a business is one of the problems which leads to the excesses referred to at the start of this article. It is therefore argued that the foundations of corporate governance in this environment are problematic.

Notes and References

1. Mathews (1997); Traces its origins to the 1970s although arguments (see Crowther, 2002a) show that such concerns can be traced back to the Industrial Revolution.
2. The benefits of incorporating stakeholders into a model of performance measurement and accountability have however been extensively criticised. See for example Freedman and Reed (1983), Sternberg (1997, 1998) and Hutton (1997) for details of this ongoing discourse.
3. Technically this duty is imposed in law upon the directors of a company in normal circumstances. In this chapter the word manager is used synonymously with the words director to imply someone with decision-making power within the company without any necessity for partial ownership.
4. Wenlock (Baroness) *vs.* River Dee Co., 1887.
5. E.g. Herremans *et al.* (1992), Tinker (1985).
6. See for example Emmanuel, Otley and Merchant (1985).
7. Such owners are of course the legal owners of the business, that is the shareholders.
8. See for example Rappaport (1986).

References

Ackerman, R.W. (1975): *The Social Challenge to Business*; Cambridge, Ma., Harvard University Press.

Becker, L.C. (1992): "Placed for Pluralism," *Ethics*, Vol. 102, pp. 707-19.

Berle, A. and Means, G. (1933): *The Modern Corporation and Private Property*, New York, Commerce Clearing House.

Briers, M. and Hirst, M. (1990): "The Role of Budgetary Information in Performance Evaluation," *Accounting, Organizations and Society*, 15(4), 373-98.

Child, J. (1974): "Managerial and Organisational Factors Associated with Company Performance—Part 1," *Journal of Management Studies*, 11, 73-189.

Child, J. (1975): "Managerial and Organisational Factors Associated with Company Performance—Part 2," *Journal of Management Studies*, 12, 12-27.

Coates, J.B.; Davis, E.W.; Longden, S.G.; Stacey, R.J. and Emmanuel, C. (1993): *Corporate Performance Evaluation in Multinationals*, London, CIMA.

Crowther, D. (2002): A Social Critique of Corporate Reporting, Aldershot, Ashgate.

Crowther, D. (2003): "Limited Liability or Limited Responsibility?," in D. Crowther and L. Rayman Bacchus (eds.), *Perspectives on Corporate Social Responsibility*, Aldershot, Ashgate, pp. 42-58.

Dahl, R.A. (1972): "A Prelude to Corporate Reform," *Business and Society Review*, Spring, 1972, pp. 17-23.

Donaldson, T. (1982): *Corporations and Morality*, Prentice-Hall, Englewood Cliffs, NJ.

Donaldson, T. (1989): *The Ethics of International Business*, Oxford University Press, New York.

Donaldson, T. and Preston, L.E. (1995): 'The Stakeholder Theory of the Corporations: Concepts, Evidence and Implications,' *The Academy of Management Review*, Vol. 20, Issue 1.

Eisenhardt, K.M. (1989): 'Agency Theory: An Assessment and Review,' *Academy of Management Review*, 14, pp. 57-74.

Emmanuel, C.R.; Otley, D.T. and Merchant, K. (1985): *Accounting for Management Control*, London, Chapman & Hall.

Etzioni, A. (1998): 'A Communitarian Note on Stakeholder Theory,' *Business Ethics Quarterly*, October, 8(4), pp. 679-91.

Fitzgerald, L.; Johnston, R.; Brignall, S.; Silvestro, R. and Voss, C. (1991): *Performance Measurement in Service Businesses*, London, CIMA.

Freedman, R.E. and Reed, D.L. (1983): "Stockholders and Stakeholders: A New Perspective on Corporate Governance," *California Management Review*, Vol. XXV, No. 3, pp. 88-106.

Glauter, M.W.E. and Underdown, B. (1994): *Accounting Theory and Practice*, London, Pitman.

Goodpaster, K.E. (1991): 'Business Ethics and Stakeholder Analysis,' *Business Ethics Quarterly*, 1(1), pp. 53-73.

Gray, R.; Owen, D. and Maunders, K. (1987): *Corporate Social Reporting: Accounting and Accountability*, London, Prentice-Hall.

Hasnas, J. (1998): 'The Normative Theories of Business Ethics: A Guide for the Perplexed,' *Business Ethics Quarterly*, January, pp. 19-42.

Herremans, I.M.; Akathaparn, P. and McInnes, M. (1992): "An Investigation of Corporate Social Responsibility, Reputation and Economic Performance," *Accounting, Organizations and Society*, 18(7/8), 587-604.

Hetherington, J.A.C. (1973): *Corporate Social Responsibility Audit: A Management Tool for Survival*, London, The Foundation for Business Responsibilities.

Honore, A.M. (1961): 'Ownership,' in A.G. Guest (ed.), *Oxford Essays in Jurisprudence*, pp. 107-47, Oxford, Clarendon Press.

Hutton, W. (1997): *Stakeholding and Its Critics*, London, IEA Health and Welfare Unit.

James, P.S. (1972): *Introduction to English Law*, London, Butterworth.

Kant, I. (1804/1981): *Grounding for the Metaphysics of Morals*, trans. by J.W. Ellington, Hackett Publishing, Indianapolis, In.

Kay, J. (1998): "Good Business," *Prospect*, 28 (March), 25-29.

Mathews, M.R. (1997): "Twenty-five Years of Social and Environmental Accounting Research: Is there a Silver Jubilee to Celebrate?," *Accounting, Auditing and Accountability Journal*, Vol. 10, No. 4, pp. 481-531.

Marens, R. and Wicks, A. (1999): 'Getting Real: Stakeholder Theory, Managerial Practice, and the General Irrelevance of Fiduciary Duties Owed to Shareholders,' *Business Ethics Quarterly*, April, 9(2), pp. 273-93.

McDonald, D. and Puxty, A.G. (1979), "An Inducement-contribution Approach to Corporate Financial Reporting," *Accounting, Organizations and Society*, 4 (1/2), 53-65.

Myners, P. (1998): "Improving Performance Reporting to the Market," in A. Carey and J. Sancto (eds.), *Performance Measurement in the Digital Age*, pp. 27-33, London, ICAEW.

Pejovich, S. (1990): *The Economics of Property Rights: Towards a Theory of Comparative Systems*, Kluwer Academic Publishers, Dordrecht, The Netherlands.

Rappaport, A. (1986): *Creating Shareholder Value*, New York, The Free Press.

Sen, A. (1987): *On Ethics and Economics*, Blackwell, Oxford.

Smith, K. and Keenan, D.J. (1969): *Essential of Mercantile Law*, London, Pitman.

Smith, H.J. and Hasnas, J. (1999): 'Ethics and Information Systems: The Corporate Domain,' *MIS Quarterly*, March, 23(1), pp. 109-27.

Sternberg, E. (1994): *Just Business: Business Ethics in Action*, Little, Brown and Company, London.

Sternberg, E. (1997): "The Defects of Stakeholder Theory," *Corporate Governance: An International Review*, 6(3), 151-63.

Sternberg, E. (1998): *Corporate Governance: Accountability in the Marketplace*, London, IEA.

Stewart, G.B. III (1991): *The Quest for Value*, New York, Harper Collins.

Tinker, T. (1985): *Paper Prophets: A Social Critique of Accounting*, London, Holt Rinehart & Winston.

Williamson, O.E. (1985): *The Economic Institutions of Capitalism*, Free Press, New York.

28

Globalisation and Corporate Activity

CHAMPABEN N. JAGANI

In the modern context globalisation is a recent phenomenon, only about thirty years old. But, as concept and philosophy, it is as old as the globe. In non-technical words globalisation means sharing, caring, partnership, togetherness. It rests on inter-dependence, mutuality and friendliness. In a global society people sail and sink together. Tsunami earthquake is the most recent example of global concerns, there have been earthquake in different periods of history in different parts of the world but the response to Tsunami tragedy has been unique. Thirty years ago a response was unthinkable within the globe.

THE CONCEPT OF GLOBALISATION

Historically speaking globalisation is an Indian concept. A hymn in the Vedas defines it as '*Vasudhaiv Kutumbkum*' meaning that the world is one family. The old Tamil poem 'Kural' by Thiru Valluvar refers to the whole world as a village. Swami Vivekananda's Vedanta is global in its content and core. The New World Order which he visualised was based on the concept of 'Jiva is Shiva,' i.e., all human beings are equal and that a happy amalgam of the best of East and West would make the world a better place to live and contemplate. 'I want you to make European society with India's religion,' he told his American disciples.

THE INDIAN MODEL

There are several brands of globalisation and each country may choose the one which suits it most. The case for India has to be examined with reference to its constitutional commitments, its secular fabric, its age-old capacity to absorb and assimilate and its claim to lead the world spiritually. It is a country where the media is free and judiciary independent. For an average Indian globalisation has come to mean privatisation within the constitutional framework. We have already privatised telecom, electricity, cooking gas, private universities in higher education and let go private English-medium high-fee schools erroneously known as public schools. The foreign experts in India are galore from American knob-specialists to Japanese flower-arrangement experts, from timber to traffic specialists advising us the global advantages of adopting or adapting a particular global model. We are now accepting foreign aid even for primary education which was taboo thirty years ago. The Education Project in Bihar, Lok Jumbish in Rajasthan, Rajiv Gandhi Project in Madhya Pradesh are educational projects aided by foreign agencies in the field of primary education. Since education is the first step of the developmental ladder we have to see whether the poverty alleviation programme in India has really alleviated poverty or only certified it. Same about providing drinkable water to its 6.4 lakh villages, as also the nutrition and the health-care systems. We have also to see why, in spite of the best efforts of the Government, the advantages of globalisation have not reached some of the Indian villages where there is neither a village well nor a village school nor a primary health centre.

SPIRITUAL GROWTH

In the Indian context spiritual growth of the world is as important as the globalisation of economy. Here India is destined to play a significant role, in the modern times as it did and has been doing since the ancient times. 'We have, as It were, thrown a challenge to the whole world from the most ancient times,' said Swami Vivekananda. In the West they are trying to solve the problem how much a man can possess, and we are here to solve the problem on how little a man can live with. There are times in the history of man's life, nay in the history of the lives of the nations, when a sort of world-weariness becomes painfully pre-dominant. It seems such a tide of world-weariness has come upon the western world which is weary of the brutality of their commercial civilization and they are looking forward to something better. They have found out that no amount of political or social manipulation of human conditions can cure the evils of life. It is the change of the soul itself that alone will cure the evils of life. No amount of force or government or legislative correction will change the condition of a race, but it is its spiritual and ethical culture that changes wrong social tendencies. Thus, these races of the West are eager for some new thought, for some new philosophy and that can be found in Vedanta. Swamiji stood for a new world order where the God sleeping in man must be awakened. The forces of globalisation must take that into consideration the spiritual hunger of the nations.

'Living in the world,' said Swami Ramakrishna Paramhansa, 'need not be, the same thing as being worldly, live in the world but allow not worldliness to get into you. The boat should be on the water but water should not be in the boat.' We must, therefore, accept appropriate globalisation, the brand which suits the nation, the one which creates a balance between tradition and modernity.

CONCLUSION

In the modern context globalisation is a recent phenomenon, only about thirty years old. But, as concept and philosophy, it is as old as the globe. There are several brands of globaliation and each country may choose the one which suits it most. The case for India has to be examined with reference to its constitutional commitments, its secular fabric, its age-old capacity to absorb and assimilate and its claim to lead the world spiritually. In the Indian context spiritual growth of the world is as important as the globalisation of economy. Here India is destined to play a significant role. In the modern times as it did and has been doing since the ancient times. 'We have, as it were, thrown a challenge to the whole world from the most ancient times,' said Swami Vivekananda.

29

Social Responsibility for Value Addition

V. BALACHANDRAN AND J. SOLOMON PRABAKAR

INTRODUCTION

Society is an integral part of any business. Business has emerged to fulfil the requirements of the society. The requirements of society can be classified as essential and non-essential. The essential requirements of the society are vital to the very survival of society. The non-essential requirements of the society are to improve the quality of life in a society. Success of any business depends on the growth in the needs of the society, as goods and services of the business are ultimately consumed by the society. A business is an economic enterprise that depends on the fabric of moral, socio-economic, environment and cultural behaviour of the society for smooth functioning and profit or wealth maximization.

SOCIAL RESPONSIBILITY—MEANING

Social responsibility is nothing but commitment and answerability to the needs of society based on sense of subjective judgments involving varied relationships based on change in character and composition of society.

SOCIETY AND BUSINESS

Society is dependent on society for its very survival. Business being a component of the society is obligated to protect, improve welfare and enhance quality of life without compromising its interests. The purpose of any business is to acquire and keep customers and marketing activities help acquire customers and understand relationships. According to Kotler, Marketing is "a social and managerial process by which individuals and groups obtain what they need and want through creating and exchanging products and value with others." (Kotler *et al.*, 1994.)

SOCIETY AND MARKETING

Marketing has positive effects on society. It helps to identify and develop new/improved products and services. These products and services are beneficial to society and improves standard of living. Standard of living is based on quality of life. Quality of life, standard of living is dependent on higher per capita income. Higher per capita income is dependent on the level of development in the society. Development of a society is dependent on the business. Development of business is dependent on the level of development in the marketing systems.

SOCIAL RESPONSIBILITY AND ETHICS IN MARKETING

Businesses are looking for ways to add value to win loyalty. Social responsibility seeks to marry profit and purpose. It is critical to restore confidence in business by building trust. But "trust" is an extremely difficult message to communicate. The effective way for a business to be seen as trustworthy is by acting, portraying, demonstrating and practising trust. Some of the socially responsible activities that could help build trust are:

1. Nurture lasting partnerships with customers and business associates.
2. Treasure brands.
3. Respect individuals.
4. Achieve superior returns for shareholders and stakeholders.
5. Improve competitiveness and quality.
6. Conduct business ethically with uncompromising integrity.

Ignoring society's demands for responsible marketing can destroy customers' trust and even prompt government regulations. The major social responsibility issues are environmental, consumerism, diversity, and community relations. Marketers demonstrate social responsibility through programmes designed to protect and preserve the natural environment.

SOCIAL RESPONSIBILITY—A STRATEGIC MARKETING TOOL

Social responsibility underpins any successful business strategy. Social responsibility helps understand culture, traditions, organization, and physical structure of society and how it could contribute or reinforce the product. Social Responsibility helps by providing the right ambiance to reduce or eliminate problems of acceptance.

Socially-responsible marketing refers to a commercial activity where business and non-profit organizations form alliance for mutual benefit. Businesses extend relationship and integrate it with other activities like community involvement, employee volunteerism or corporate philanthropy. Socially Responsible marketing campaigns vary in scope and design based on partners and nature of relationships. Socially-responsible programmes enhance reputation, brand image and increase the credibility of the business's marketing effort. Hence, socially responsible marketing will be an effective strategic marketing tool leading to better results compared to the general marketing practices.

Components of Social Responsibility Marketing

- Public.
- Partnership.
- Policy.
- Purse Strings.

Benefits of Socially-responsible Marketing Programmes

- Attracting and Retaining Customers Enhance company or brand reputation.
- Consumers' purchase decisions.
- Demand innovation.
- Market Differentiation.
- Brand Essence.

- Lifetime Value of Customer.
- Outreach to Niche Markets.
- Motivated and Loyal Employees.
- Reinforced Mission.
- Community Support.

CONCLUSION

Socially Responsible marketing is an effective marketing strategy. Its efforts are guided by the same ethical standards as all other marketing and advertising activities. The Key Principles of Socially Responsible marketing is Integrity, Transparency, Sincerity, Mutual Respect, Partnership, and Mutual Benefit. The potential rewards of socially responsible marketing programme depend on proper planning, preparation, commitment, monitoring and follow-through. Businesses are looking at a strategic perspective to involve community-involvement, philanthropic activities, and socially responsible marketing to core business objectives by taking advantage of core competencies, and customizing focus areas based on customer needs. Socially Responsible marketing uses knowledge of customers, the value they bring to business, and the value they demand in return, to drive incremental revenues and profits. Socially Responsible marketing provides a process to uncover the needs of valuable customers met, unmet, latent to develop innovative and acceptable ways. Socially responsible marketing based on changing customer preferences, dynamic market environment can prove to be a powerful tool for value growth.

30

Globalisation Perspectives on Corporate Governance

M. MANUNEETHI CHOLAN

INTRODUCTION

Globalisations increasing importance and influence on the companies places a very large responsibility on the managements of the companies and places heavy demands on the companies' competitiveness. At the same time, the globalisation limits the possibilities, of the national governments to influence and control the frameworks which the companies must act within. This means that to a large extent it is the corporate sector itself which ensures that the companies are run efficiently and competitively and that they observe their duty to act responsibly.

The international arena has witnessed recently a significant public debate about which major principles should be employed to govern companies. The general term for these principle is corporate governance, a concept that is difficult to translate.

Initially, the corporate governance debate arose partly in response to pressure from the increasingly prevalent institutional ownership, and partly in response to financial scandals at the end of the 1980s. Thus, the report "Financial Aspects of Corporate Governance" from 1992, better known as the "Cadbury Report," was a direct reaction to the so-called BCCI bank scandals.

The Cadbury Report contained a number of specific recommendations regarding good corporate governance also called "best practice" or "code of conduct." The aim was to meet the demands of the institutional owners and to prevent new business and financial scandals.

The debate has more recently moved from primarily being driven by a wish to stimulate "Owner activism" and increase the supervision of the management, to having a broader view of the company and its relationship with its other stakeholders. In line with this, the debate about the relationship between the board and the management has also changed its focus from a narrow control and supervision perspective to a broader and more forward looking strategic perspective.

CONCEPT FRAMEWORK

The concept can be defined as: The goals according to which a company is managed, and the major principles and frameworks which regulate the interaction between the company's managerial bodies, the owners as well as other parties, who are directly influenced by the company's dispositions and business (in this context jointly referred to as the company's stakeholders). Stakeholders include employees, creditors, suppliers, customers and the local community.

OECD defines, "Corporate governance is the system by which business corporations are directed and controlled. The corporate governance structure specifies the distribution of rights and responsibilities among different participants in the corporation, such as, the board, managers, shareholders and other stakeholders and spells out the rules and procedures for making decisions on corporate affairs. By doing this, it also provides the structure through which the company objectives are set, and the means of attaining those objectives and monitoring performance."

World Bank Group defines, "Corporate governance is concerned with holding the balance between economic and social goals and between individual and communal goals. The governance framework is there to encourage the efficient use of resources and equally to require accountability for the stewardship of those resources. The aim is to align as nearly as possible the interests of individuals, corporations and society."

Peters-rapporten Holland defines, "Governance means management and power, responsibility and influence and accountability and supervision. In this respect integrity and transparency play an important part.

German Panel on Corporate Governance defines, "The purpose of Corporate Governance is to achieve a responsible, value-oriented management and control of companies. Corporate Governance Rules promote and reinforce the confidence of current and future shareholders, lenders, employees, business partners and the general public in national and international markets. The Supervisory Board, Management Board and Executive Staff of the Company identify themselves with these Rules and are contractually bound by them. They are part of the general obligation to observe other interests related to the corporate activity."

DEY-RAPPORTEN CANADA

"Corporate Governance" means the process and structure used to direct and manage the business and affairs of the corporation with the objective of enhancing shareholders' value, which includes ensuring the financial viability of the business. The process and structure define the division of power and establish mechanisms for achieving accountability among shareholders, the board of directors and management. The direction and management of the business should take into account the impact on other stakeholders such as employees, customers, suppliers and communities.

CORPORATE GOVERNANCE—A FAD OR A DAWN OF THE NEW AGE

The mantra corporate governance become a gosha in Japan, the U.S. and England, where, under the inspiration of the London Stock Exchange, Lord Cadbury outlined the basic contours of a good company from the point of view of the stock exchange. It is in this background that the Indian approach to corporate governance needs to be understood.

It would be erroneous to applaud the discovery of corporate governance as a revolutionary 'New Deal' for the investors, much less to the employees, customers, and the general community. The core of corporate governance is that companies and their board of directors, should play fair to the shareholders, be willing to share all material information about the company's progress, warts and all. The idea is "as old as the hills." Some of the core principles of corporate governance are: honesty, transparency and corporate decision-making in the best interest of the shareholders, total avoidance of any direct or indirect influencing on the part of the directors in relation to any decision of the board of directors.

The world comprises not only persons of honesty, trustworthiness, integrity and probity, but also crooks and unscrupulous characters. There are company promoters who follow no scruples and who believe the success in terms of profit is all that the community can ask for and not moral credibility on the part of the management of the company. Even the criterion of "value addition" for shareholders has become a theoretical notion because profitability is increasingly coming under pressure not only because of competition but also owing to the vulnerability of demand for many products.

In the 20th century, corporate law-makers were guided by the principle that the essence of corporate governance is the disclosure of information to the shareholders. The more voluminous the balance sheet is, the higher is the level of corporate governance obviously "padding up" the balance sheet, which is otherwise a disappointing story, with an overload of non-material information is certainly not a vindication of the honesty and competence of the directors.

OBJECTIVES OF THE STUDY

A separate and distinct study on corporate governance and shareholder enrichment are scanty, there is a need for a comprehensive study on corporate governance, corporate growth and its impact on shareholder enrichment. The present study is thus an attempt to analyze the concept of corporate governance in Indian companies, The objectives are:

1. To make it more attractive to invest in Indian listed companies and to improve access to funds by attracting foreign investments.
2. To inspire Indian companies as well as their directors and managers to tackle the strategic challenges performing from the globalisation as strengthening the competitiveness.
3. To examine and analyze the recent trends in promoting good corporate governance practices in India.
4. To evaluate the integrity as behaviour of selected performance, to measure the impact on corporate growth and relationship.

METHODOLOGY

The present study is both descriptive and analytical in nature. Important analytical tools have been used. A sample of one hundred companies whose shares are actively traded in Bombay Stock Exchange and National Stock Exchange were considered for the study. The data collected for the present study are both from primary and secondary. The data collected the way of interview techniques with directors, managers and executives of corporate secretarial departments. Data were collected from annual reports of RBI, stock exchange, Department of company affairs and the respective companies relating to the, assets, earnings, dividend and sales. The inter relationship between governance is performance is evaluated and analyzed with statistical tools.

CORPORATE GOVERNANCE AND INTEGRITY OF AUDIT FIRMS

In more recent times in India auditors have emerged as contributors to the decline in standards of corporate governance. So how do we correct this situation? We do not have confidence that the auditing profession can, through introspection and adoption of auditing standards appropriate to our companies. The result is that without our knowing it, we are making laws, which would make the auditing firms renowned for integrity, shrink in size and the volume of work. Is corporate governance meant for shareholder protection or for driving millions of small investors away from the stock markets?

When the new economic policy of deregulation and liberalization began in 1991, the general expectation was that many obsolete laws enacted during the British period would be repeated. But what are happening are new models of State interference with corporate coming, not in the name of control but for the purpose of "benevolent guardianship" of shareholders. The repeated attempts as amending the Companies Act have not made corporate investment more attractive. In fact, corporate governance is just prattle at a time when the economy is reeling under a demand-recession and when investors have reached a point where equity is "no go." If stimulating corporate investment is the national goal, what we need is a set of sensible macro-economic policies and a process of governance, which in spires confidence among investors in India and in the overseas markets including NRIs.

Corporate governance and integrity of audit firms are a matter of discussion for India Inc. too. This time it is the case of Tata Finance and its audit firm A.F. Ferguson & Company as the auditor's report on irregularities in the company was withdrawn under controversial circumstances.

Normally a report once submitted is in the nature of a final report contains fact-findings and professional conclusions. There can be situations though expectation that some new facts or additional evidence may surface after an assignment is done. In such a situation, the two parties to the assignment may have a dialogue and request for the additional facts or evidence to be examined and to validate any of these findings or opinions. "In these circumstances, it is open to the firm to withdraw the report and submit fresh findings after assessing the additional facts or evidence. This is parallel to even a statutory audit where an auditor submits the reports to the shareholders but still holds office until the conclusion of the annual general meeting where the annual accounts and the auditor's reports are adopted.

There can be circumstances where fresh evidence may come to the knowledge of the auditor before the accounts are adopted in which case the auditor will evaluate the necessity to either withdraw his earlier opinion or make supplementary observations for the consideration of the shareholders. So it is net unusual that a firm of accountants may wish to withdraw a report on the basis of additional evidence; which may be subsequently discovered. Therefore, the Company Law under Sec. 231 provides a statutory right to the auditor to attend general meeting and to be heard at such meetings.

Even by the rules of corporate governance there is an increasing trend to have independent director on the boards of listed companies. Independent directors are defined as people not having a pecuniary relationship with the company or the promoter group as may influence their decisions.

FINDINGS

Let me discuss the findings of the sample companies to deal with corporate governance issues, the answer must still be reasons and qualified.

Openness is important providing the information, which must be presumed important for the shareholders and the stakeholders to evaluate and relate to the company. It is found that above 35 per cent of the sample respondents accepted and practice and the remaining 65 per cent of them are not at it.

Transparency is regarding how company is managed for the confidence of the shareholders. Transparency is the way the directors and managers work and their basis for decisions provides the shareholders to exercise the influence. Nearly 50 per cent of the respondents positively accepted this practice.

Responsibility towards the both the shareholders and stakeholders helps ensures that the company's long-term interests are safe guard by building up and developing mutual confidence only 33 per cent of the companies attempted really for the responsibility syndrome.

Equality of treatment regarding the treatment of the shareholders in fundamental principle, which ensures that all shareholders are equals. 58 per cent of the companies never attempted to equality of treatment.

There must be room for the delivery of different business types and ownership structures, which characterize Indian companies. The operational efficiency of the committee's recommendations is only at 47 per cent in the sample companies. 53 per cent of the companies operating by their own accord.

Good corporate governance implies that the management is genuinely willing to work with the right culture, ethics and professionalism. Nearly 73 per cent of the companies are not at all bothered about the culture, ethics and professionalism.

International investors demand better information about the management's actions and the companies' long-term goals. It has declined in India from 80 per cent in 1999 to 30 per cent in 2002 due to political, industrial and economical instability.

The board should be composed of directors with the right qualifications and skills to adapt the company to future means. The board must act as a strategic player. Nearly 58 per cent of the companies' active and competent boards are questionable one.

It is observed that 100 per cent of the directors, managers, and executives accepted good corporate governance is worthwhile. The reason being is it inspires confident and stakeholders the companies' resources are used in the best possible way.

The average earning per share has declined for the past two years. The average dividend per share is minimum to 50 per cent and nil in 50 per cent of companies. The retained earning per share is declining. The market price per share has declined to 63 per cent. Average negative economic value added is observed. Total shareholders return is negative for 86 per cent majority of the companies. In general, that majority of the companies of the sample have not enriched the shareholders in all the years.

There has been a gradual increase in market price per share over the years. Average negative economic value added is observed for all the years except during the year 1996, where the average economic value added is 0.017. The fluctuations in economic value added also seem to be high for all the years.

Total shareholders' return is negative for majority of the companies during the study period.

Economic value added per share in the year 1996 was negatively correlated with other variables but a positive correlation existed between economic value added and market value added. Negative correlation is observed between economic value added and gross fixed assets per share, long-term loans per share, net fixed assets per share, net worth per share, profit after interest and tax per share, reserves and surplus per share, total funds employed per share. Hence, it may be concluded that economic value added per share was not associated with other variables.

Previous market price per share and net worth per share for the period of three years, previous economic value added per share for a period of two years, earning per share, previous earning per share, previous market value added per share and previous dividend per share for a period of one year explain the changes in market price well.

The growth rate in market value added differs widely since the coefficient of variation is very high. The distribution of market value added per share is negatively skewed since few companies may have very low growth rate.

SUGGESTIONS

Corporate governance rating is still a new concept worldwide and process is evolving. In the Indian market, a beginning has just been made with the recent announcement of the first corporate governance rating.

A recent survey, around one-fifth of the institutional investors in the sample-expressed preference towards corporate governance over financials while deciding their emerging market portfolios. Further, around two-thirds (as high as that) felt corporate governance is almost as important as the balance sheet. In fact, the respondents to the survey were ready to pay a premium of 28 per cent for governed companies in emerging markets. The survey, which covered at sample of 100 companies in six emerging markets to test the link between market valuations.

ICRA's corporate governance rating, for instance, limits its scope primarily to the interests of financial stakeholders. The basic parameters are built around the shareholding structure, governance structure and management processes, including board-level issues, inter-relationship of stakeholders, and quality of financial discipline, reporting, transparency and disclosures. Also, issues related to certain and distribution of corporate wealth are captured in the process, albeit indirectly.

The board should consist of 50 per cent executive and 50 per cent non-executive independent professionals as its Board of Directors. Individual director means a director who has no pecuniary interest in the company.

The chief executive should not be the chairman of the board. A professional non-executive chairman should head the board.

The committees should consist of at least 3 non-executive directors with at least one director having accounts and financial knowledge. The chairman of the audit committee shall be present at the Annual general meeting to answer shareholder's queries.

Key information, operating plans and budgets together with long-term plans should be disclosed in the Annual report. Quarterly and half yearly results should be provided to the shareholders.

Shareholders should be entitled to postal ballot voting. Shareholders should be provided with the bio-data of new directors and they should also be informed of any pending legal proceedings against any director.

Disclosure in the annual report about the role played by the committees, non-executive professional directors and the decision taken and the results achieved should be mandatory. Those who authenticate the accounts should authenticate this report.

Board meetings should take place in real business professional sense with all the directors, on the board are well informed of the agenda and the directors act in the larger interests of the company and every stakeholder.

CONCLUSION

To sum-up, in general, it may be concluded that majority of the companies in the sample have not, enriched the shareholders in all the years as observed from summary analysis. Economic value added, market value added and total shareholders' returns are considered major indication of shareholders' enrichment. An analysis revealed that most of the companies have generated little. It is not uniform in all the companies, hence, it may be concluded that there is poor corporate governance in India due to poor integrity, honesty, sincerity but it is only in paper.

REFERENCES

Anderson, Charles, A. and Robert H. Antony, *Corporate Governance: The Board of Directors*, John Wiley & Sons, Inc., USA, 1992.

Balasubramanian, N., *Corporate Boards and Governance*, Sterling Publishers (P) Ltd., Bangalore, 1998.

Gera, M.R., *Corporate Governance and Business Ethics*, All India Management Association, Excel Books, New Delhi, 1997.

Gopalsamy, N., *Corporate Governance—The New Paradigm*, Wheeler Publishing, 1998.

Indian Companies Act, 1956—Amended in 2000.

Raghunath, S., "Governing Corporate Governance," *Management Review*, July-Sept., Oct.-Dec., 1996.

Sundararajan, S., "Corporate Governance—Improving Accounting Practices," *Management Review*, Oct.-Dec., 1998.

The Hindu, Chennai Edition, Jan.-August, 2002.

31

SCP-Social: A Model for the Assessment of Corporate Social Performance

CARLA PASA GÓMEZ, LEONARDO GÓMEZ AND GREGÓRIO JEAN V. RADOS

The model entitled Structure, Conduct, and Performance—Social (SCP-Social) was elaborated as an alternative for the assessment of corporate social performance. The main motivation for the elaboration of this model was found in the difficulty to define when a corporation can be considered as socially responsible. That is to say, with the current models that exist to evaluate corporate social performance, the totality of corporate functions is not considered. Also, with those models it is not possible to classify the level of corporate social conduct. To overcome those gaps, the SCP-Social model takes into consideration tree main elements for the assessment of corporate social performance. First, it analyses the pressures of the market structure that have an effect over corporations, then, it examines the social conduct adopted by the corporations, and finally it determines the level of corporate social performance.

INTRODUCTION

In 1913, the difference between the 20 per cent of the richest and 20 per cent of the poorest in the world was II times. In 1960, that difference was 30 times, and it doubled in 1990. By 1997 the difference was 74 times. In practical terms, this means that 20 per cent of the world's population owes 86 per cent of the world's income (Grajew, 2001, p. 20). On the other hand, in emerging economies such as Brazil, 13.6 per cent of the population is still illiterate, 5.5 million of children are working instead of going to school, and 50 million people are working for two dollars a day. Do corporations have something to do with these facts?

In general terms, we believe, corporations have been partially responsible for the world's social and environmental degradation, and this explains why society is demanding from corporations their social and environmental commitment. Through a conscious choice of socially responsible products and services, society is getting involved in a process of corporate transformation. For instance, according to a survey conducted by Environics International, in 2002, in the United States of America, 53 per cent of the people affirmed, to prefer brands and products of corporations involved social programs, as long an they have a competitive price and quality. In the same survey, similar answers were obtained from consumers in Australia (60 per cent), Canada (50 per cent), Germany (42 per cent), United Kingdom (40 per cent), Nigeria (33 per cent), Argentina (24 per cent) and Brazil (16 per cent). Consumers perceive social responsibility as an important attribute at the time of purchase. This attitude reflects the expectations of society about corporate social performance.

In general terms, society expects and demands from corporations the practice of ethical and transparent principles. It is taken for granted that corporations comply with the social and environmental regulations; promote and develop voluntary actions on behalf of their stakeholders; contribute to sustainable development; and generate economic wealth.

From a corporate point of view, this new scenario represents an opportunity of expanding or keeping a market share, and increasing their competitive advantage, according to principles of ethical, legal, voluntary, and economic basis (Carroll, 2003). To this end, we propose the SCP-Social model, in order to expand the practice of corporate social responsibility.

THE SCP-SOCIAL MODEL

The Structure Conduct Performance – Social model (SCP-Social), is proposed to decrease the degree of uncertainty of the corporate decision making process in the areas related to social investment. The model enables corporations the visualization of corporate weaknesses in the areas of social concern, the understanding of the main causes of those weaknesses, and the establishment of goals that will improve the corporate social performance.

The SCP-Social model is composed by three dimensions that determine the corporate social performance. Thus, indicators of market structure, social conduct, as well as indicators of corporate social performance integrate these dimensions, which, at the same time, are influenced by internal and external forces, inherent to the corporate processes (Figure 31.1).

The dynamism of the SCP-Social model resides, in part; by the presence of unpredictable external forces. Since corporations depend on those external events for their operability, the SCP-Social model takes into consideration the influence of those forces in the shaping of the dimensions of market structure, social conduct, and therefore, corporate social performance. According to Abreu (2001), the external forces are basically originated by innovation in the technology front, changes of social behaviour, or by public policy. They give to the whole corporate process a dynamic and changing nature, affecting all the elements and indicators of the SCP-Social model.

Therefore, under the SCP-Social model, the corporate social performance is the result of the actions and reactions (cooperation or rivalry) of a corporation, in a competitive market, according to the standards of corporate social conduct, designed to attend the forces of the market structure, which are established by the industrial sector.

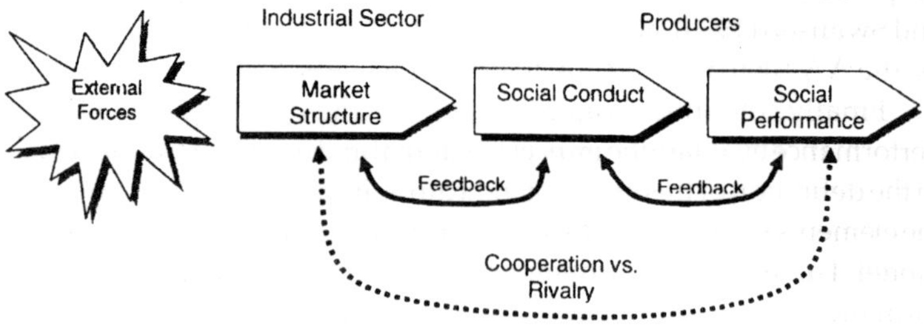

FIG. 31.1

The SCP-Social Model

THE SCP-SOCIAL FRAMEWORK

In the formulation of a framework for the SCP-Social Model, each dimension (Market Structure, Social Conduct, and Social Performance) is composed by categories of indicators, groups of elements, and specific indicators (Figure 31.2).

Since there is a lack of models that define indicators of market structure from a social point of view, the indicators for the dimension Market Structure were adapted from the economic model proposed by Scherer and Ross (1990). However, only those indicators that have a social character were taken into consideration (costumer's choice, competitiveness among suppliers, and barriers to entry). Additionally, we increased one more indicator, in order to evaluate the influence of the stake holders in the market structure (Figure 31.3).

The indicators that define the dimension of Social Conduct make reference to the behaviour adopted by corporations when they try to adapt to the pressures of the market structure or when they take voluntary actions. This behaviour reflects the forces involved in the decision making process and the internal relationships of corporations. Thus, the measurement of each element of corporate social conduct will determine the final social performance.

The indicators of Social Conduct are aimed to evaluate the social behaviour in each of the management functions. These indicators include the categories of General Management, Marketing and Communication, Management of the Supply Chain, Research and Development, Manufacturing, Environment, Finances, Human Management, Political Affairs, and Legal Affairs (Figure 31.4). They were based on the models of corporate social performance assessment, proposed by Carroll (1979), Wartick and Cochran (1985), Wood (1991) and Swanson (1995), and the norms and international standards such as, the AA 1000, BS 8800, SA 8000 and OHSAS 18001.

Finally, the indicators proposed for the dimension of Social Performance evaluate the impact to internal and external stakeholders. In the definition of this group of indicators, it was noticed that some of the elements were already included in the other two dimensions of the model. This inter-linkage demonstrates that the corporate social performance is the result of both – the corporate social conduct and the market pressure of the industry, which can be observed through the impacts of the internal and external stakeholders. Figure 31.5 shows the group of indicators proposed for the dimension of Social Performance.

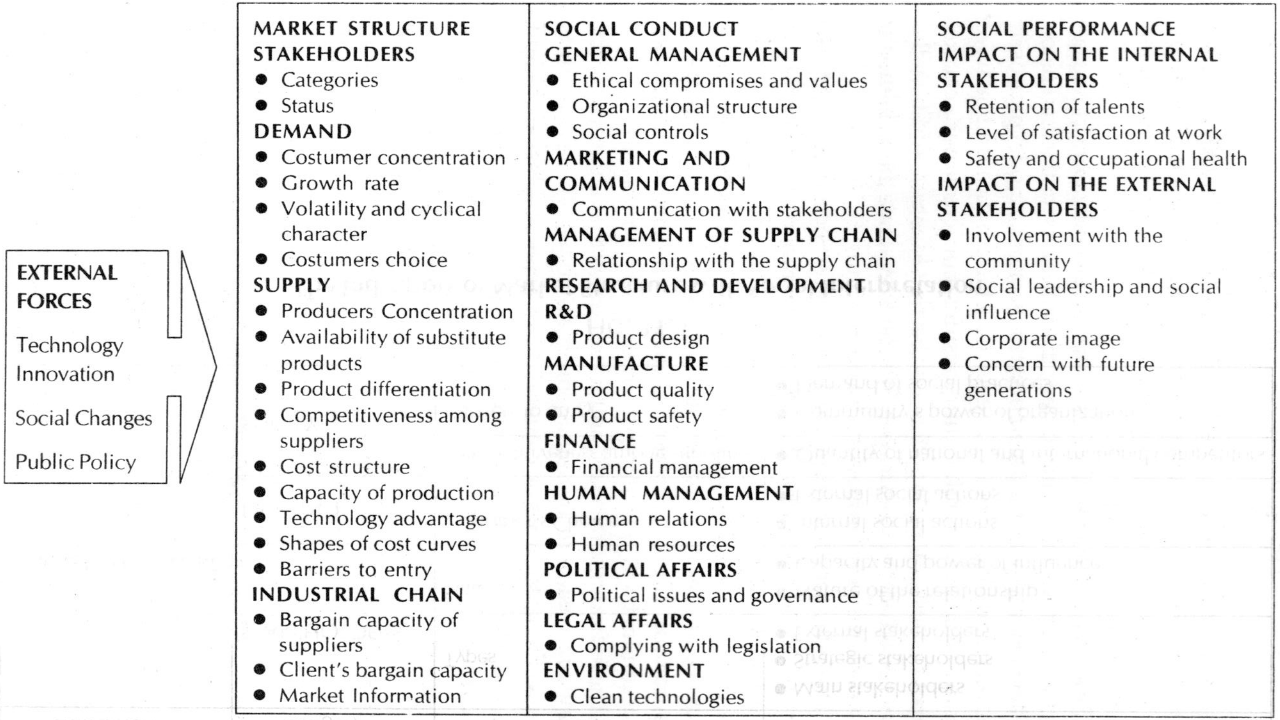

FIG. 31.2

Framework of the SCP-Social Model.

Dimension	*Category*	*Element*	*Specific indicators*
MARKET STRUCTURE	STAKEHOLDERS	Types	● Main stakeholders ● Strategic stakeholders ● External stakeholders
		Status	● Nature of the relationship ● Capacity and power of influence
	DEMAND	Customer's Choice	● Internal social actions ● External social actions
	SUPPLY	Competitiveness among suppliers	● Quantity of national and international competitors
		Barriers to entry	● Community's power of organization ● Demand of social practices

FIG. 31.3

The Indicators of Market Structure with Social Interpretation

Dimension	*Category*	*Element*	*Specific indicators*
SOCIAL CONDUCT	GENERAL MANAGEMENT	Values and ethical compromises	• Adoption of ethical values/code of conduct • Divulgation of corporate values and ethical principles
		Structure of the Organization	• Participative management • Appraisal of diversity • Elimination of discrimination
		Social Controls	• Internal and external audit • Disciplinary rules and regulations
	MARKETING AND COMMUNICATION	Communication with the stakeholders	• Communication of the potential risks of a product • Careful selection of elements and images for corporate branding and products marketing • Divulgation of corporate social results • Customers complains
	MANAGEMENT OF THE SUPPLY CHAIN	Relationship with the supply chain	• Practice of international labour legislation • Practice of human rights • Elimination of children labour
	RESEARCH AND DEVELOPMENT	Product design	• Choice of materials • Life cycle analysis
	MANUFACTURING	Quality and safety of products	• Product quality • Product safety
	ENVIRONMENT	Clean technologies	• Environmental management program, and pollution control and prevention • Environmental education

Dimension	*Category*	*Element*	*Specific indicators*
SOCIAL CONDUCT	FINANCES	Financial resources management	• Corporate governance • Social investment policy
	HUMAN MANAGEMENT	Human relations	• Relationship with labour unions • Corporate behaviour to employee's dismissal and retirement • Voluntary practices
		Human resources	• Participation of corporate revenues • Occupational health • Professional and personal education and training programmes • Social and occupational programs for employees
	POLITICAL AFFAIRS	Political affairs and governance	• Contribution with political campaigns • Anti-corruption practices • Lobbying capacity and political influence
	LEGAL AFFAIRS	Comply with regulations	• Labour legislation • Consumer legislation • Environmental legislation • Business legislation • Fiscal legislation

FIG. 31.4

Indicators of the Dimension Social Conduct of the SCP-Social Model

Dimension	*Category*	*Element*	*Specific indicators*
SOCIAL PERFORMANCE	IMPACT ON THE INTERNAL STAKEHOLDERS	Retention of talents	• Index of rotation of employees
		Level of satisfaction at work	• Work environment • Number of strikes • Evidence of commitment and involvement of employees with the corporation
		Level of safety and occupational health	• Number of occupational accidents • Number of deadly occupational accidents • Number of occupational accidents with disability • Number of occupational illnesses • Number of deadly occupational illnesses • Number of occupational illnesses with disability • Number of training hours dedicated yearly to the prevention of accidents and occupational health.
	IMPACT ON EXTERNAL STAKEHOLDERS	Involvement with the community	• Infrastructure enhancements available for the benefit of all members in the community • Improvement of the community's quality of life through education and health programs
		Social leadership and social influence	• Involvement in social programs of corporate members from all hierarchical levels • Involvement in social programs promoted by the government
		Corporate Image	• Brand rejection index • Proportion of job positions offered and supplied. • Level of costumer satisfaction

Dimension	Category	Element	Specific indicators
SOCIAL PERFORMANCE	IMPACT ON EXTERNAL STAKEHOLDERS	Concern with future generations	• Number of environmental accidents • Number of accidents related to the contamination of the soil, water or air quality. • Number of victims for product consumption • Number of victims due to product/packaging malfunction • Number of deadly accidents • Number of accidents with incapacity

FIG. 31.5

Indicators of Social Performance of the SCP-Social Model

FUNCTIONALITY OF SCP-SOCIAL MODEL

In the evaluation of corporate social responsibility, there is a gap between the existing theoretical models, and the reality of the market structure in which corporations operate. In most cases, those models indicate *what* to do in terms of actions of social responsibility, but they cannot suggest *how* to proceed.

To overcome this gap, we designed a functional tool that assists corporations in the decision-making process of social investment. The tool is composed by three matrices, which evaluate the corporate social behaviour, determine the level of social conduct, and finally define a profile of social responsibility.

In the functionality of the SCP-Social model, the first step is to identify parameters of social behaviour in the corporation. This step is carried out through the use of self-applied surveys and questionnaires, which evaluate each of the corporate management functions and their respective social indicators defined by the framework of the SCP-Social model.

The second step is to determine the level of social conduct for each of the management functions. This level is obtained from the answers of the questionnaire, which are graded according to a scale previously defined. Thus, the level of corporate social conduct can be *high*, *moderate*, or *weak*. To facilitate its visualization, the level of corporate social conduct is graphically represented with a flower (Figure 31.6), in which the petals correspond to each of the management functions, and the colours of the petals represent the respective level of social conduct.

The next step is the confrontation of the level of corporate social conduct, with the market pressure of the industry in order to obtain a corporate social profile: the lower the market pressure, and the higher the social conduct, the better the profile of social conduct (Figure 31.7). However, this profile can change over the time. Since the nature of the market structure oscillates due to external forces, the social conduct varies according to the changes in the corporate standards of social conduct along the time. For instance, a corporation with an *opportunist* social profile has a *moderate* market pressure and a *high* level of social conduct. If a sudden external change occurs in the market structure, the corporate social profile will necessarily change, even if the corporation keeps the same level of social conduct.

With the changing nature of the market structure due to

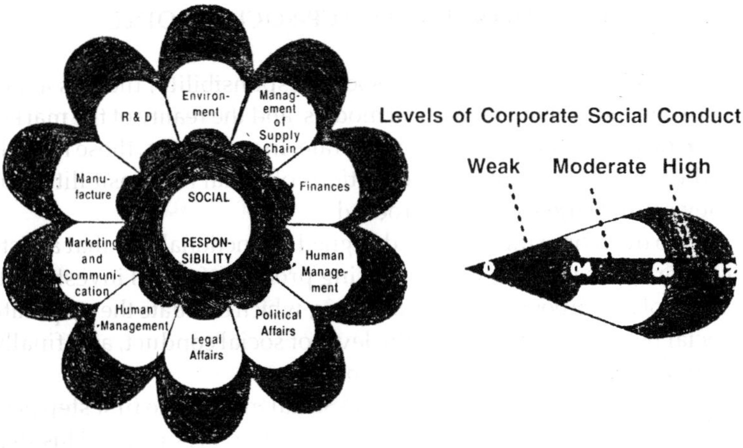

FIG. 31.6

Level of Corporate Social Conduct. The petals represent each of the corporate management functions, and the colours (red = weak, yellow = moderate, and green = high) represent the levels of social conduct

Market Pressure of the Industry	Weak	Moderate	High
Low	Indifferent	Challenging	Pioneer
Moderate	Loser	Accommodating	Opportunist
High	Defeated	Suffering	Active

Level of Social Conduct

FIG. 31.7

Social Profile of the SCP-Social Model

unpredictable external forces, the monitoring of the corporate social profile should be constant. This monitoring facilitates the decision-making process, because companies can visualize and direct their social investments, as well as their corporate social policies in a more objective and precise way.

THE APPLICATION OF SCP-SOCIAL MODEL

The effectiveness of the SCP-Social model was demonstrated through its application in two different market sectors: the Brazilian chicken industry, and Brazilian footwear industry. Both sectors have a high social impact in the Brazilian economy, since they employ a high market force and have called for attention to social issue, such as children labour abuse, product safety, and environmental degradation. The SCP-Social model was applied in both industries, according to the procedures suggested in the theoretical framework, and the following results were obtained:

On the one hand, in the chicken industry, the market pressure is *moderate* due to restricted pressure from stakeholders, such as NGOs and customers, absence of international social certifications, limited governmental influence, and a market structure dominated by oligopolist.

According to the SCP-Social model, the industries of this sector present social profiles, which oscillate between Accommodating (40 per cent), and Opportunist (60 per cent). Therefore, the companies with an *opportunist* profile have a social competitive advantage over the ones with an *accommodating* profile. These *accommodating* companies could reorient their policies of social investment through for example, benchmarking in order to visualize the areas in which they have a higher and lower social compromise, and a bett er understanding of their social performance.

In the footwear industry, on the other hand, the market pressure is considered *high*. In this industry, there is a constantly surveillance from the group of stakeholders, which continuously demand for the implementation of social and environmental practices, fare labour conditions, social and occupational programs for employees of all levels, and codes of conduct. Also, the Brazilian footwear market is huge and highly competitive. Leader companies are constantly trying to create market differentiation through the adoption of social policies, which have become standards of social behaviour for the whole sector.

Therefore, as a result of the high market pressure, the corporate social profile of the footwear industry is 80 per cent suffering and 20 per cent active (Figure 31.7). With these profiles, the social competitive advantage of this industry is limited. With the results provided by the SCP-Social tool, *suffering* companies, for example, have an immediate need of improving their social policies regarding human management and supply chain management in the short-term, otherwise they will continue receiving external pressure from stakeholders, customers, NGOs and governmental institutions. Also, these companies need to redirect their future social investments in a more objective way through the establishment of benchmarking policies between companies of the same (or different) market sectors.

CONCLUSION

The SCP-Social model provides a new perspective for the discussion between businesses and social responsibility. The model allows to evaluate the corporate social performance and helps to decrease the degree of uncertainty of the corporate decision-making process in the areas related to social investment.

With the model, companies have a wider view of their corporate social performance. It enables the visualization of weaknesses in the areas of social concern, the understanding of the main causes of those weaknesses, and the establishment of goals that will improve the corporate social performance.

With this new proposal, corporations were particularly interested in the implementation of social policies in the corporate business strategy, since the model facilitates the process of social assessment and the social strategy. The importance of the SCP-Social model resides in the fact that it facilitates the strategic decision-making process, and it establishes a dialogue between all the stakeholders and the corporation in the definition of social goals. It is expected that the consequences of this dialogue will promote an evolution and a revolution of corporate social responsibility.

REFERENCES

Abreu, M.C. Sa de, Modelo de avaliação da estratégia ambiental: Uma ferramenta para a tomada de decisão. 2001. Tese (Doutorado em Engenharia de Produção)—Programa de Pós-Graduação em Engenharia de Produção. UFSC. Florianópolis.

Buchholz, R., "A Corporate Responsibility and the Good Society: From Economics to Ecology," *Business Horizons*, Vol. 34, No. 4, pp. 19-32, 1991.

Buccholz, R.A.; Evans, W. and Wagley, R., *Management Responses to Public Issues: Concepts and Cases in Strategy Formulation*, Prentice-Hall, 1994.

Carroll, A.B., "A Three-dimensional Conceptual Model of Corporate Performance," *Academy of Management Review*, Vol. 4, No. 4, pp. 497-505, 1979.

Carroll, A.B. and Buchholtz, A.K., *Business and Society: Ethics and Stakeholder Management*, 5th edn., Ohio, Thompson Southwestern, 2003.

Corporate Social Responsibility: Global Public Opinion on the Changing Role of Companies, Environics International Ltd. Available in: <www.bsdglobal.com/issues/sr_csrm.asp>. Accessed in: January 2003.

Husted, B.W. and Alien, D.B., "Toward a Model of Corporate Social Strategy Formulation," *Academy of Management*, August 2001. Available in: <http://www.alianzas.org/busqueda.asp>. Accessed in January 2003.

McWilliams, A. and Smart, D.L., "Efficiency *vs.* Structure-Conduct-Performance: Implications for Strategy Research and Practice," *Journal of Management*, Vol. 19, No. 1, pp. 63-78, 1993.

Pasa, C.R.R.; Gómez, L.A.C. and Rados, G.J.V., Social Competitiveness: Utopia or Reality? In: 8th ERCP—European Roundtable on Cleaner Production, Cork, I.R., 2002.

Scherer, F.M. and Ross, D., *Industrial Market Structure and Economic Performance*, Boston, Houghton Mifflin Co., 1990.

Steiner, G.A. and Steiner, J.F., *Business, Government and Society: A Managerial Perspective*, 10th edn., New York, McGraw-Hill, 2003.

Swason, D.L., "Addressing a Theoretical Problem by Re-orienting the Corporate Social Performance Model," *Academy of Management Review*, Vol. 20, No. 1, pp. 43-94, 1995.

Swason, D.L., "Toward an Integrative Theory of Business and Society: A Research Strategy for Corporate Social Performance," *Academy of Management Review*, Vol. 24, No. 3, pp. 506, 521, 1999.

Swift, T. and Zadek, S., Corporate responsibility and the competitive advantage of nations. Available in: <www.copenhagencentre.org> or <www.accountability.org.uk>

Wartick, S.L. and Cochran, P.L., "The Evolution of the Corporate Social Performance Model," *Academy of Management Review*, Vol. 10, No. 4, pp. 758-69, 1985.

Wartick, S.L. and Mahon, J.F., "Toward a Substantive Definition of the Corporate Issue Construct: A Review and Synthesis of the Literature," *Business and Society*, Vol. 18, No. 4, pp. 293-311, 1994.

Wood, D.J., "Corporate Social Performance Revisited," *Academy of Management Review*, Vol. 16, No. 4, pp. 691-718, 1991.

32

Societal Perception of Corporate Social Responsibility: An Empirical Study

TEJINDER SHARMA AND MAHABIR NARWAL

The goodness of all act is not judged solely by the goodness of the results produced but by the praiseworthiness of the intention, which motivate it.
—Kant

INTRODUCTION

At the dawn of industrial revolution, the prime objective of the business firms was to earn more profit. Fostered by socio-political and technological changes, including the establishment of democracy, various sections of the society started questioning *laissez faire* approach of business. There has been a growing acceptance of the plea that business should be responsible to the society. The business enterprise, which makes use of the resources of the society and depends on it for its functioning, should contribute to enhance the welfare of the society. Business, being one of the dominant institutions of the present day market-led-economy, wields considerable influence on the resources of the society and plays an important role in the process of socio-economic and cultural modernization. Being organically linked to the wider socio-economic and cultural system, it cannot distance itself from its commitment to the society, particularly in a developing country like India.

The basic idea of corporate social responsibility is that business and society are inter-woven rather than distinct entities, therefore, society has certain expectation for appropriate business behaviour and outcomes (Wood, 1991). The concept of social responsibility was visualized during the early part of the twentieth century. Clark (1916) was among the pioneers to observe that if men are responsible for the known results of their actions, business responsibilities must include the known results of business dealings, whether or not law has recognized these. In an article published in *The Economist* in 1926, the drawbacks of limited liability of the companies were highlighted. Supporting this 70-year-old conceptualization, Broberg (1996) observed that the limited liability imparts a sense of limited responsibility on the part of the business firms. However, now there is increasing awareness that a company, which works only in order to benefit itself, might harm other groups in the society. Today, partly due to the interdependencies of many groups in our society, the social involvement of business has increased (Koontz and Weihrich, 1998). In the modern times, companies should exercise socially responsible behaviour voluntarily; otherwise they might be forced to do so. The society, in general, has definite perception on CSR, which needs to be understood. A clear understanding of the societal perception on CSR shall enable the companies to design and position their social responsibilities activities accordingly.

VIEWS ON CSR

Despite acknowledging the significance of CSR, there is a lack of consensus on the very meaning of CSR. The simplest classification of views on CSR shows the existence of atleast two viewpoints, which can be called as classical and modern.

The classical view considers social responsibility as being incompatible with a free economy (Friedman, 1962 and 1970). The proponents of this view hold that business managers have a single responsibility towards the shareholders. All their endeavours must uphold an undeterred commitment to maximizing shareholders' value. Managers, acting as the agents of the shareholders, have no mandate to embark on socially responsible projects that do not enhance the income generating ability of the firm. Further, the managers are experts in business activities and their expertise cannot be channelized to social responsibility. Pava (1996) finds Friedman's arguments as both rigorous and somewhat convincing. Numerous economists, accountants, sociologists, corporate managers and social critics, either explicitly or implicitly, accept a similar view on social responsibility. At best, the advocates of the classical view uphold that corporate goals must be based on a broad social consensus.

The advocates of the modern concept uphold that business must think beyond the shareholders' value and must not ignore its ethical and moral responsibilities. Shareholders are not the only participants of the business operations. Therefore, business must not confine its allegiance towards the shareholders only, but also should be responsible towards the stakeholders at large. Freeman's (1984) stakeholder model of social responsibility is often taken as a modern viewpoint on corporate social responsibility. This model upholds that a firm's social responsibilities consist of the sum of its obligation towards a specific set of stakeholders, i.e. the shareholders, customers, employees, suppliers and the communities in which the firm operates. Brown and Dacin (1997) considers CSR as the company's status and activities with respect (i.e. responsiveness) to its perceived societal obligations. McGee (1998) advocated a pro-active social responsiveness view, which articulates a company's long-term role in a dynamic social system. L' Etang (1995) finds CSR as an ongoing process, constantly monitoring the environment and relationship and not a fixed mission in relation to specific groups with a predetermined priority that remains static.

SOCIETAL PERCEPTION OF CSR

Besides shareholders, there exist several non-shareholder interests in a business firm. Farrar (1991) has divided these interest groups into five categories—investors, outside creditors, employees, consumers and publics. While the first three groups find their representation in the business firms in some way or another, the last two usually go unrepresented. By virtue of their representation in the firm, the first three are able to extract responsible behaviour, but the unrepresented interest groups may find it otherwise. Most of the literature on perception of CSR is either conceptual or based on the empirical research done on business managers (Quazi and O'Brien, 2000; and Singh *et al.*, 1980, etc.) or the consumers (Sen and Bhattacharya, 2001; Brown and Dacin, 1997; and Ellen, Mohr and

Webb, 2000, etc.). These studies suggest that there is a positive relationship between a company's CSR actions and its goodwill. A company's CSR record, instead of providing information about the attributes or overall quality of the products, creates a general context for consumers' evaluation. The general perception of the society towards CSR has not evolved much interest of the researchers. Literature shows that in India only a few empirical studies (Singh *et al.*, 1980; and Upadhyay 1976) have been made to assess the state of CSR. Even these studies relied on the data generated from the business managers and not the society in general. A decade prior to the economic liberalization, Singh *et al.* (1980) find that corporate actions are perceived to be predominantly profit maximizing, followed by calculative behaviour.

Research Problem

Considering the importance of CSR, its general perception in the minds of the people needs to be understood. Most of the Indian research on CSR has been done before 1991, i.e. before the economic reforms. Liberalization of economy has provided the society with a plethora of goods and services and lot of information. The present day Indian society is more aware and informed and is in the state of transition from old values to newer ones. In the changing times, the societal perception on CSR needs to be studied again. The specific research question being addressed in the paper is:

How does the informed society, in general, perceive CSR actions of business?

An understanding of the societal perception of CSR activities would help the corporates to position their CSR programmes more effectively in order to generate a favourable image in the society. Their CSR actions would reflect greater sincerity and would be better poised to achieve the societal as well as business goals.

Research Methodology

Theoretical framework was developed from the secondary data, comprising of the published literature. In line with the research problem, primary data was generated by a survey, conducted on the population of North Haryana. A structured questionnaire was used to generate primary data.

Questionnaire Design

A questionnaire was developed on the basis of the variables related to corporate social responsibility as identified from the literature. Table 32.1 shows the variables identified for the questionnaire and their literature sources:

The variables were put in the form of 20 statements and the respondents were asked to record their opinion on a 5-point Likert-type interval scale, i.e. strongly agree, agree, neutral, disagree, and strongly disagree. The questionnaire also contained questions on the demographic profile of the respondents.

A pilot survey was conducted on 30 respondents and the 3 statements were dropped as the respondents found it difficult to record their opinion on these. The language was also refined to make it more understandable. The final questionnaire contained 17 question-items relating to CSR and four relating to the demographic profile of the respondents.

Sampling

Quota sampling method was used to generate primary data, controlling the sample for sex, age, income and education. The data was taken from a sample of 187 respondents (91 females and 96 males) of Ambala, Kurukshetra, Karnal, and Jind districts of North Haryana. The sample was representative of the demographic variables such as sex, age and income as shown by low skewness of 0.024, 0.062 and 0.022 respectively. However, the sample was negatively skewed (-0.305) for education, indicating a higher proportion of highly educated respondents. This was desirable since it was felt that highly educated respondents (graduates and above) only could record their opinion on the question-items.

Data Analysis and Findings

Since the questionnaire contained 17 question-items, each related to any of the eight variables as mentioned in Table 32.1, the number of question-items was reduced by clubbing similar statements.

Eight variables, thus derived were subjected to factor analysis by using Principal Component Method with unities in diagonal (Hotelling, 1935). Following the recommendation of Kaiser (1960),

TABLE 32.1
Variables Related to CSR

Sl. No.	*Variables/Issues*	*Keyword*	*Literature Source*
1.	Social responsibility should be a planned activity and not arbitrary	Planned activity	Jones (1999)
2.	Social responsibility leads to a trade-off in profits	Trade-off	Friedman (1962)
3.	Goodwill of a firm increases by being socially responsible	Goodwill	Sen and Bhattacharya (2001), and Brown and Dacin (1997)
4.	Social responsibility is an eyewash and firms undertake it as a cover-up	Cover-up	Singh *et al.* (1980)
5.	Social obligation of business are even important than profits	SR Focus	Quazi and O'Brien (2000), and Singhapakdi *et al.* (1996)
6.	Being a part of the society, business must be responsible to it	Part of system	Koontz and Weihrich (1998)
7.	If survival is at stake then business must forget social responsibility	Ignore SR	Friedman (1962), and Singhapakdi *et al.* (1996)
8.	Even doing routine business properly is an act of social responsibility	Routine exercise	Jones (1999) and Robertson and Nicholson (1996)

the extraction of factors was stopped when Eigen value (latent roots) came to be less than 1.00. Three factors were obtained, whose Eigen value exceeded 1.00. A total variance of 53.962 (Table 32.2) is accounted for by these three factors. The extracted factors were rotated in accordance with the criterion of Kaiser's (1958) Varimax Procedure. Factor loadings greater than 0.30 are found significant at .05 level (Herman, 1960). The communalities, which give the proportion of variance for each of the original variables (denoted by h^2), are ranging from 0.229 to 0.743 (Table 32.3). One variable, i.e. routine exercise was dropped on account of low communalities.

TABLE 32.2

Eigen Value with Cumulative Percentage of Variance

Components	*Eigen value*	*Percentage of variance*	*Cumulative Percentage of variance*
1	1.771	22.143	22.143
2	1.285	16.060	38.203
3	1.610	15.759	53.962

TABLE 32.3

Rotated Component Matrix

Variables	*Components*			h^2
	1	*2*	*3*	
Planned activity	0.309	0.210	0.632	0.540
Trade-off	0.192	0.761	–0.096	0.626
Goodwill	0.621	–0.004	0.117	0.399
Cover-up	–0.383	0.715	0.072	0.663
SR Focus	0.739	0.003	–0.081	0.553
Part of system	0.694	0.027	0.285	0.564
Ignore SR	0.097	0.277	–0.811	0.743
Routine exercise	0.262	0.268	0.297	0.229

Each of the factors derived by analysis of data, represents a particular outlook of the respondents towards various issues of social responsibility and is explained in the following interpretation of the factors.

Factor I

High positive loadings have been observed on three variables—social obligation of business are even important than profits; being a part of the society, business must be responsible to it; and goodwill of a firm increases by being socially responsible.

Objective Viewpoint

Sr. No.	*Variables*	*Factor Loadings*
1.	SR Focus	0.739
2.	Part of System	0.694
3.	Goodwill	0.621

Each of these variables represents an optimistic, suave and an unbiased viewpoint, avoiding any of the extremes. Hence, this factor is labelled as *objective* viewpoint. On the basis of this factor, it can be concluded that the corporates should have an undeterred commitment towards social responsibility, imbibing it as a part of their system. This factor also shows that the society takes a positive view of the SR activities, which may help the companies in their long-term survival and competitiveness.

Factor II

In this factor also, high positive loadings are observed on the variables—social responsibility leads to a trade-off in profits; and social responsibility is eyewash and firms undertake it as a cover-up. Both these statements reflect an element of doubt in the activities of social responsibility. Respondents upholding these views look upon the expenditure on social responsibility activities as wasteful, which erode the profits of the company. They doubt the very intention

Skeptical Viewpoint

Sr. No.	*Variables*	*Factor Loadings*
1.	Trade-off	0.761
2.	Cover-up	0.715

of undertaking these activities and even believe that these do not make any substantial contribution to the society and are an eyewash.

Keeping in view the nature of these variables, this factor is labelled as *skeptical* viewpoint.

Factor III

This factor comprises of two highly loaded variables – one loaded negatively and the other loaded positively. A high negative loading is observed for the variable – if survival is at stake then business must forget social responsibility. At the same time, a high positive loading is observed for the variable – social responsibility should be a planned activity not arbitrary.

Ethical Viewpoint

Sr. No.	*Variables*	*Factor Loadings*
1.	Ignore SR	-0.811
2.	Planned activity	0.632

A high negative loading shows that the respondents have not endorsed the idea, as suggested in the variable. They seem to uphold that even in turbulent times, when the survival of a firm is at stake, it must not ignore/forget social responsibility. Even during the time of crisis, a socially responsible behaviour is expected from the business. This might be the reason that the respondents have supported the idea of social responsibility being a part of the mission of a company and an essential ingredient of their planning exercise. This viewpoint upholds a sense of morality/ethical behaviour on the part of business. Henceforth, this factor is labelled as *ethical* viewpoint

DISCUSSION

Three distinct viewpoints emerge out of the data analysis – *objective, skeptical and ethical*. Being the first factor, *objective* viewpoint has emerged as the most important one, replacing *skeptical* viewpoint, as was reported by Singh *et al.* (1980). They had conducted their research in pre-liberalization days, when business was subject to tremendous regulations. The general perception on CSR activities that the business undertakes them to avail tax exemptions and other government incentives, and the social service motive was missing. The skeptical viewpoint on CSR was most dominant in those times. However, a decade of liberalization has reduced controls and the society as well as the business is beginning to undertake SR activities voluntarily. There is a positive perception of CSR activities in the society, indicating a paradigm shift in the societal perception on CSR.

Morality and ethics still occupy an important place in the society and draws the boundaries for the business to function. It lays down normative behaviour for the firms to act, thereby supporting Pava's (1996) hypothesis. Morality and ethics guide the business activities to being more socially responsible.

CONCLUSIONS

The societal perception on CSR activities of business is changing from skeptical to objective. Liberalization of economy has reduced the regulatory framework imposed by the state, but has increased self-regulation by the business itself. Business is no longer viewed as selfish endeavour of profit maximization. Society takes a positive view of their actions and expects a responsible and ethical behaviour. The process of integration of the society and business has begun and business has to reinforce the positive momentum to strengthen the confidence in the society.

REFERENCES

Broberg, Morten P. (1996): "Corporate Social Responsibility in the European Communities—The Scandinavian Viewpoint," *Journal of Business Ethics*, Vol. 15, pp. 615-22.

Brown, Tom J. and Dacin, Peter A. (1997): "The Company and the Product: Corporate Associations and Consumer Product Responses," *Journal of Marketing*, Vol. 61, pp. 68-84.

Clark, J.M. (1916): "The Changing Bases of Economic Responsibility," *The Journal of Political Economy*, Vol. 24, No. 3, pp. 209-29.

Ellen, P.S.; L.A. Mohr and D.J. Webb (2000): "Charitable Programmes and the Retailers: Do they Mix?," *Journal of Retailing*, Vol. 76, No. 3, pp. 393-406.

Farrar, J.H.; N.E. Furey, and B.M. Hannigan (1991): Farrar's Company Law, Butterworths, London.

Freeman, R. (1984): Strategic Management: A Stakeholder Approach, Pittman, Boston.

Friedman, M. (1962): Capitalism and Freedom, University of Chicago Press, Chicago.

Friedman, M. (1970): "A Friedman Doctrine—The Social Responsibility of Business is to Increase its Profit," *The New York Times Magazine*, pp. 123-25.

Herman, H.H. (1960): "Modern Factor Analysis," University of Chicago Press, Chicago.

Hotelling, H. (1935): "Simplified Calculations of Principal Components," *Psychometrika*, Vol. 1, pp. 27-35.

Jones, Marc T. (1999): "The Institutional Determinants of Social Responsibility," *Journal of Business Ethics*, Vol. 20, pp. 163-79.

Kaiser, H.F. (1958): "The Varimax Criterion for Analytic Rotation in Factor Analysis," *Psychometrika*, Vol. 23, pp. 187-201.

Kaiser, H.F. (1960): The Comments on Communalities and the Number of Factors. Read at an informal conference on the Communality Problem in Factor Analysis, St. Louis, Washington University.

Koontz Hand H. Weihrich (1998): *Essentials of Management*, Fifth Edition, TMH Ltd., New Delhi.

L.'Etang, Jacquie (1995): "Ethical Corporate Social Responsibility: A Framework for Managers," *Journal of Business Ethics*, Vol. 14, pp. 125-32.

McGee, John (1998): "Commentary on Corporate Strategies and Environmental Regulations: An Organizing Framework," A.M. Rugman and A. Verbeke, *Strategic Management Journal*, Vol. 19, No. 4, pp. 377-87.

Pava, Moses L. (1996): The Talmudic Concept of "Beyond the Letter of the Law": Relevance to Business School Responsibilities, *Journal of Business Ethics*, Vol. 15, pp. 941-50.

Quazi, Ali M. and O'Brien, Dennis (2000): "An Empirical Test of Cross-National Model of Corporate Social Responsibility," *Journal of Business Ethics*, Vol. 25, pp. 33-51.

Robertson, Diana C., and Nicholson, Nigel (1996): "Expressions of Corporate Social Responsibility in UK Firm," *Journal of Business Ethics*, Vol. 15, pp. 1095-1106.

Sen, Sankar and Bhattacharya, C.B. (2001): "Does Doing Good Always Lead to Doing Better? Consumer Reactions to Corporate Social Responsibility," *Journal of Marketing Research*, pp. 225-43.

Singh, P.; Maggu, Ashok and Warrier, S.K. (1980): "Corporate Social Responsibility: Realities and Expectations," *Vikalpa*, Vol. 5, No. 2, pp. 117-30.

Singhapakdi, Anusom; Scott, J. Vitell; Kumar, C. Rallapalli and Kenneth, L. Kraft (1996): "The Perceived Role of Ethics and Social Responsibility: A Scale Development," *Journal of Business Ethic*, Vol. 15, pp. 1131-40.

The Economist (1926): "The Ownership of British Industrial Capital-1," *The Economist*, Vol. 103, pp. 1053-54.

Upadhyay, R.B. (1976): *Social Responsibility of Business and the Trusteeship Theory of Mahatma Gandhi*, Sterling, New Delhi.

Wood, D.J. (1991): "Corporate Social Performance Revisited," *Academy of Management Review*, Vol. 16, No. 4, pp. 691-718.

33

Enhancing Teaching and Learning: Integrated Approach to Pedagogy

ANANYA S. GUHA

INTRODUCTION

The paper is an attempt to analyse our educational system in a changed context where pedagogical approaches are innovative. Due to the impact of Distance Education the use of technological pedagogy has been instrumental, in making Education more 'vibrant' and innovative. More focus is now on the *type* of the learner, the adult learner or the working learner desiring to be trained in his/her profession. At the same time the stereotypical classroom situation needs revamping with a flexible adaptation of teaching methods. Teaching and learning heuristics is examined in such 'changed' situations. This is how we enhance teaching and learning. A lot of the change will owe to the attitudinal change of the teachers. In this way we create more classrooms, the classroom has a multiplier effect or syndrome, where we integrate the old with the new and diminish the 'value' of archaic methods of pedagogy. This 'new' thinking will also depend on the educational planners who could be intent on developing new courses suited to pragmatic needs. Open Learning has brought about a change in epistemology or in pedagogy; such 'change' should seep into the traditional classroom. Teaching and Learning then will be flexible and more learner-oriented. The paper is written keeping in mind the backdrop of the Indian Educational Scenario. The word 'our' in the first sentence alludes precisely to this. The paper also attempts simultaneously to analyse training needs as part of the broad continuum to lifelong learning: and adult and continuing education. This invests the whole concept of education with a wider connotation where work needs are matched with education or training needs. Such investiture to the 'meaning' of education extends it from school to college; to the world of work. We 'discover' an intricate connection between the world of work (profession) and the world of education (training, re-training).

NEW STRATEGIES IN EDUCATION: OPENNESS AND FLEXIBILITY

Today, educators as an extension to classroom teaching must also posit the role of facilitators in teaching and learning. A teacher is also to facilitate learning, organize not only his/her teaching mannerisms but should also be a helper in individuated learning processes. Extension of the classroom is a must whether it is organizing tutorials, holding inter-cultural programmes *or* even informally meeting students. In fact, teaching, research, and extension should be the focus of all academic activities. To facilitate learning arguably calls for innovation and experimentation. Developing good quality study texts should be a priority. Unfortunately very few academicians give importance to writing standard text books. A research paper produced by a teacher is not only a document to be mentioned in the bio-data but something which ought to be shared among students giving the wider scope to be discussed critically in the classroom. Abstruse and 'difficult' subject matters should be simplified so that students can readily grasp the underpinnings of complex theoretical abstractions, which in turn may help for future research.

Extension in teaching and learning could mean then the use of audio-visual contraptions LCD and Overhead projectors. The underlying basis of teaching is that of a sensory experience both for the teacher and the taught whereby communication processes are two-way and not simply one-way. The interactive methods of teaching can further be supplemented by using diverse formats such as group exercise, quiz, debates, seminar presentations, etc., where also switching from one format to another is experientially rewarding academically; both for teacher and student alike. In this manner too the classroom can be 'extended' to other components and formats in which peer group activity is another aspect of classroom activity, or is a miniature classroom. The much talked about student participation can be actualized by such extension-based work in the teaching/learning exercise where role play is a categorical device.

Facilitating learning in a broad and innovative sense takes the 'teaching' out of the classroom, so that the 'chalk-and-talk' theory is neatly subverted into some more fundamental processes of teaching. A student must be able to create his/her own resources of learning in addition to lecture notes and text books. This could be the use of TV, radio and audio visuals for learning; planning of study hours can be judiciously made, relating this actively to course work.

Evaluation in examinations has been simplistic where the marks or grades awarded are beyond question. Proper justification of grades awarded, strengths and weakness of an answer, supplementary references, etc., are a must which also require skilful academic handling and expertise. They are in their own right an integral part of teaching methods.

A teacher's role does not begin and end in the 'classroom.' He or she must possess the vision to organize as many 'classrooms' as possible so that teaching and learning is didactic and are discourse-based activities. A teacher is an organizer, an innovator and an academic administrator in the final reckoning.

To think of the 'disadvantaged' in educational contexts is to invest also a broad continuity to the processes of learning where educational planners and decision-makers also provide for a life long learning experience. The disadvantaged are those who want to learn and always do not get the opportunity to do so. In such situations educators must be continually pro-active in terms of planning and strategy. The term disadvantaged does not only have economic implications. The word is all embracing, encompassing all aspects of social, economic and cultural realities. But a continued effort to search let us say for education in one's life which is translated into a life long experience will benefit social reprobates, 'outcastes' and of course professionals who will be able to 'sandwich' their studies between the learning time and the working time.

Work and the job realities are so much of a prepossessing factor that even if there is the intrinsic desire to learn, extenuating circumstances of profession and work compel a person to pull out of studies. In a highly competitive ethos a common language of study is essential but bilingualism as a means of study, will be of greater help to multi-linguistic and multi-cultural societies. However, we must understand, in this context the needs also of globalization, globalization and cultural identity are complementary in a sense, they should not be necessarily viewed as a clash of ideologies, and even if there is a conflict of such values there is a need to reconcile them. The disadvantaged may not have the privilege of being educated in the language of the elites or the 'common' language. So multi-lingualism while offering courses or the indigenization of course development is a must in binary cultural situations. Course material translation from one language into different languages will drive home such essentiality in pluralistic societies. Today as we enter the twenty-first century there is a rising internationalism but at the same time there is search for specific roots. Such tension generates contradictions in societies and those who are disadvantaged for causal factors such as social, economic, inequality between sexes, etc., are caught in such a vortex of change and contradictory pulls. They must be given the chance (learner autonomy) to study courses of their own choice, in their own language and to register for such courses at any time of the year, New 'need'-based courses specially designed for say the physically and mentally challenged, drug addicts, working women, people living in geographically remote areas where economic sustenance is severely limited, should be identified on priority basis. The emphasis is also on training as part of life-long education. Inter-cultural courses in multi-ethnic situations as for example India's can help people in remote locales to be aware "of a heritage common to all humanity."

It is also the question of shared values and the inherent desire of a life-force to 'live together' which can wean away the disadvantaged from the quagmire of exploitation and the brutalization of society. Shared values will also mean:

- Opportunities to learn.
- To learn in a language of one's choice.
- Freedom of choice (of courses).
- Opportunities to be trained during work period.
- Opportunity to work and learn.
- Opportunity to be 'literate.'

Underemployment and unemployment causes the breakdown not only of family life but of society as a whole. "A hundred and twenty million people in the world are unemployed and more than one billion live in abject poverty." The marginalized and the isolated need empathetic attention so that education and distance education in particular can integrate these with the 'mainstream' of society.

Traditional knowledge and education has focused on abstractions rather than on imagination, communication and leadership skills. The challenge is: how do we promote academic excellence in such a manner so as to discover these immeasurable realities, a sense of beauty, sensitiveness to one's environment or say even the development of manual skills? Can distance education promote the aesthetic of education or inter-cultural education?

Education in the 21st century must combat all forms of exclusivism. An exclusivist educational pattern such as rejecting students because of one-time academic failure may lead to social aberrations, and the emergence of 'dropouts.' School and College dropouts are disadvantaged people but distance education methods will have to cater to such disadvantaged youth in terms of short-term and vocational modules. The rural youth for example need special attention and consideration in this regard. Devising forms of education for different minority groups both nationally and internationally needs to be given priority.

Distance education provides wide scope for renewing and refreshing our approaches to educational systems calling for absorption and gives eclecticism. It gives wide currency to change and flexibility as there is an extension of knowledge-based realities into their proper relevant and adequate applications. It is also extension-based studies and application-oriented knowledge. There must be a fine distinction between information societies and learning societies. Adapting one's self to a rapidly changing world is not only the prerogative of the educationally 'qualified' but also that of the educationally 'backward.' The inequalities too between the sexes in the sensitive field of education brings discrimination. The girl child for example in countries such as India is already destined for marriage as an axiomatic and a priority truth. Priorities are wrong, what about education for the girl child?

Basic education for everyone is one of the fundamentals if not the fundamental of teaching and learning. The jobless youth left to fend for themselves in inimical surroundings are a potential source for endangering national security.

A monolithic model of education can be developed by reducing the distinction between initial education and lifelong education. This hiatus can be bridged by Distance Education applications. The different layers of education must be perceived holistically so as to integrate them into one complex whole forgetting terminologies and description of educational heuristics. Distance Education is also a facilitator of teaching and learning not loth to retaining old practices if found suitable; in a given framework. The local circumstances of education, the indigenous needs of it are of crucial significance. In a manner of speaking all sections of the society may be 'disadvantaged' in one way or the other, or at one point of time or the other.

As we have entered the 21st century, what is discernibly evident is that the philosophy of education and its applications are undergoing sea-changes. In fact the very concepts of education are radicalized and revolutionized to introduce newer contexts, settings, into what may be described as the 'extended' classroom.

This is largely due to the fact that technological processes in education have exacerbated innovative thinking in this field. The applications of technologies here have been manifold beginning from Radio/TV broadcasts and telecasts, use of audio-video cassettes to audio video conferencing and on-line computer teaching. The 'classroom' thus has been recreated, extended and ramified to cater to the work force, service clientele and different professional groups. This again is mainly and preponderantly due to the ontologies of Distance Education methods of teaching. However, the word of caution and introspection here is that technology also has its own appropriateness depending upon the social and economic development of a place or region. We can then think of disseminating knowledge to underprivileged and disadvantaged groups of society, and also make optimum use of low cost technology such as the radio.

A 'holistic' view of education caters to vastly heterogeneous groups as well as traditional and non-traditional categories of learners. Thus, experimentation is needed in even conventional and traditional set-ups. The idea would be to gear towards non-formal and vocational courses, and towards more openness and flexibility even within an existing framework. This will lead to barriers being broken keeping in mind professional growth and definite target groups.

TOTAL LEARNING SITUATION: LEARNER AUTONOMY AND LEARNER CONTIGUITY

Learner autonomy points to the learner centric vision of education, its learner centeredness and the appropriate methods adopted to achieve it. More and more the concept of education has reached a point, where we enumerate more positively learner roles rather than teaching roles. This is the pedagogical shift that we envisage and posit emphatically in teaching-learning methods. The cultural shift that is taking place is that teaching is mediation; parallel texts and sub texts are entering the teacher learner classification. These are parallel to the methods already adopted in classroom teaching, i.e. the popular but not sacrosanct notion of the lecture method.

The cultural shift referred to above is part of the paradigmatic shift that is evolving into let us say new teaching learning systems. It is the purpose of this discussion to examine such 'newness,' to invest a philosophical basis to the concept of education. What are, who are the mediators in the teaching-learning of education? What is the relevance of target groups here? Can education be subversive, i.e. can it break the barriers of school education, higher education and university education to apprehend contiguity and wholesome features.

The mediated form of instruction by way of study texts and technology aided components makes the education experience lively, interactive and independent. Home-study for example, the opportunity to study at one's place and pace is part of the objective of continuing and adult education, where a situation is opportunistically created in which those who have missed out are given a kind of flexibility to learn to one's advantage and benefit. The learner is then not an anachronistic idiot but the creator of an ambience, a cultural situation, where the learner is: A 'Teacher' and A 'Trainee.'

Let us examine the points mentioned above non-chalantly one might think, which may be (mis)represented as a lethargic and lackadaisical view of education. For too long the concept of education in India has remained in the morass of rigid stratification: the leacher 'teaches,' the learner 'learns.' The teacher is omniscient, an intellectual glut and a powerful (but of course superior!) disseminator of information. The student-learner relationship is thus construed chiefly and pedagogically as linear and not causal. That, there may be a cause-effect relationship between the teacher and the learner is glibly overlooked. This is the cause-effect relationship to which I am looking towards a pointer; towards 'new' teaching-learning modes, the roles are reversed, the teacher is a leaner, the learner is a teacher.

The optimum use of technology aided instruction which is interactive, constantly shifting gears let us say, can achieve this. Learning is then virtual and autodidactic, classrooms are then created at homes, in trains, in buses anywhere. I am thinking of culture specifics: of the Indian situation, where the rigmarole of the educational scene has become nightmarish – learning by rote and cramming, three hours 'essay' (whatever that might mean), questions, etc. The learner is a trainee because the learner has the flexibility and the right to: 'Choose to learn' and 'Learn to choose.'

The learner may be in a position to select specific, target-oriented courses, and relates them to professionally objectivised goals ("Learning to choose"). If we are to design courses for laboratory technicians we are designing a 'professional' programme just as that of an MBA programme, or a Masters In Computer Applications programme which are very popular in this searingly competitive world, in what we try to capture as a professionally competitive ethos, such a tag also becomes a misnomer in third world countries. Leaner autonomy and academic freedom should express more independence and the freedom to choose a housewife should be in a position to pursue a programme in creative writing and a journalist in environmental studies, but who will goad them, will it not be a question of autonomy and autodidacticism, that of learning for 'disinterested' purposes? The creative will is energizing but also self-fulfilling, jobs and professions come and go but the interest to learn and the acumen for it is perennial.

We have addressed learning points of view. What then of teaching, how can 'classroom' teaching be extended into creating and multiplying a larger number of them? Let us begin with evaluation, evaluation should be continuous, both formative and summative, evaluation should be innovative, there should be lab intensive work, extended contact, etc. Tutorials should exercise maximum options such as group discussions, brainstorming sessions, quizzes, small group interactive sessions, etc. The teacher then is also a coordinator and a manager. This mediating role of teaching can then perform wide ranging functions from tutoring skills to administering and managing.

The open university experience however has wide ramifications on the Indian educational scenario especially after the establishment of the Indira Gandhi National Open University by an Act of Parliament in 1985. It radicalized teaching-learning methods and evaluation systems, it used the concept of technology with expediency and alacrity matching the print media with audio video components and updating such heuristic skills with audio/tele-conferencing. It is now in the way of marginalising conventional/classroom/face to face teaching, integrating futuristically the print and the electronic media; this is surely an attempt at upgradation of classroom systems, methods and practices. The university has proliferated into more adaptable practices of facilitating learning evolving practicably, concepts of learning facilitators, specific programme centres and work centres. This also brings us to the question of academics visualizing roles of facilitators to envision a total learning situation. The functioning of an education system in the complex form of an industry projects the 'business' environs not anarchic and profiteering, but cost effective and cost reducible. This has led to the university (IGNOU) in collaborating with partner business institutions and multimedia teaching Institutions where the state of art of technology is used for teaching courses in the active and dynamic field of management and computer sciences.

However to make this education system more mass-based, invigorating and fructuous professionally related academic programmes have also been introduced in the spheres of teacher training, higher education, food and nutrition, rural development, journalism and mass communication, health education, creative writing, etc. This spirals into an educational ethos both vertically and horizontally where a varied and complex target group with different professional backgrounds and compatibility are taken into full cognisance.

In India now the vision of higher education must be constructively understood not as compartmentalization (school education, college education, university education) but as a holistic means to achieve objectives of TLS (Total Learning Situation). To illustrate my contention the courses cited above in terms of diplomas and certificates may help to rationalize such goals. Extension studies in areas such as agriculture, horticulture, disaster management, art and craft, health and sanitation are other areas where education is mass-based, an awareness: of needs, of surroundings. Correspondence Course

Institutes, Distance Education Directorates and Open Universities must be integrated meaningfully, resourcefully and pragmatically.

The ends to teaching and learning must also be creatively envisaged as expansive, changeable and adaptable; shaped accordingly to the demands of hungry learners whose thirst for knowledge is unassuaged. Education and the attendant progress made with it is pluralistic and complementary, evolving from total literacy, total 'literate(acy)' to a total learning/ teaching situation. Indeed a sensitively tuned ambience, in line accordance with the spirit of continuing, nay; Continuous Education.

TRAINING, EDUCATION AND LIFELONG LEARNING

In multilingual societies emphasis should be given to acquisition of mother tongue literacy skills for the academic development of a child, which should be followed up by a transition to the common language; for example, English in a country like India (Delors, 1996).

Speaking about revamping the syllabus the Delors Commission Report says: "This does not call for a new subject to be added to the already crowded curricula but for existing subjects to be reorganized around a comprehensive view of the ties that bind men and women to their environment, involving both the natural and social sciences. This type of training could also be offered to everyone as lifelong education." We have to revise the 'similarities essential to life in society' to use the expression of the French Sociologist Emile Durkheim. The focus then is on a more pragmatic reinforcement of our attitudes and approaches to education. Training on the job is thus a significant component of education which will be an enabling factor to make education a lifelong reality. "It is the role of education to provide children and adults with the cultural background that will enable them, as far as possible to make sense of the changes taking place." One such area is the use of technology in education, audio and video tele-conferencing for example; the viable method of low cost technology such as the radio which is accessible to the masses. Both teacher and teacher educators should be in a position to synergize technology with education in situations that are both off campus (Distance Education) and on campus (Conventional Classroom Teaching). Power point presentations with the help of LCD projectors should be introduced in the prototypical classroom to make the educational system a visual and sensory experience.

The spoken word must be complemented with a visualization of the topics concerned, in other words, education can be more 'open' and 'flexible.' Changes are taking place in employment in parts of the world, the individual should be updated in the latest epistemology of the profession concerned; either in the work place or in a training institute. The Delors Commission report points out: "There is very clearly, a cumulative effect: the more education you have, the more education you want, as maybe observed in both developed and developing countries." Life long learning should address the desire for learning and training not only for the employed but also for those 'dropouts' who have not been able to complete their school or higher education. Again we have to dispel myths about education with a gender bias. In subsistence economies women work for longer hours and contribute more to the family income than their male relatives. "Gender bias is thus a primary cause of poverty, because in its various forms it prevents hundreds of millions of women from obtaining the education, training, health services, child care legal status needed to escape from poverty" (Jacobson 1992). In a nutshell then basic education for all is vital for the growth of the educational system breaking barriers between 'haves' and 'have nots.' Educational planners must be pro-active; we have to create opportunities not only wait for others to 'take' opportunities.

Coming back once again to the question of training, implicit in it is perhaps the teaching component, but training goes beyond teaching. It is learning for the trainee, who is also trained to train. In its best sense training is cybernetics. The trainer is a manager in a diversified situation. The following can be termed to be his/her responsibilities:

- Assessor
- Coach
- Counsellor
- Educator
- Evaluator
- Facilitator
- Friend
- Guide
- Leader
- Listener

- Manager
- Mentor
- Researcher
- Strategist
- Tactician
- Trainer

(Clements and Jones, 2004)

In a work situation a person needs to be trained and re-trained and for this he or she may be interested in studying specially designed courses or modules. Many companies in countries such as Great Britain have such courses conducted in the work place or in places outside the office or company so that the employee can alternate between work and study. Even if there is a very short-term training course of only 4-5 days meant to update professionals, the emphasis is on learning. To that extent it is pedagogy with focus on the learner, it is learner centred. The trainee is a learner. Technology today has impacted not only on education, but is transforming the work ethos in organizations. E-mail audio-video conferencing, chat sessions, etc., help in creating dialogue and interaction between company and its clients or between one company and other. Thus, there is a rapid change taking place in organizations as far as the work is concerned. To adapt to this change organisations have to train and re-train its employees by filling in the gaps in knowledge and training needs (Rao, 2004).

In the ultimate analysis it is pedagogy which drives learner autonomy, learner contiguity and *vice versa*. Yet in the changed educational contexts today, where education is also an industry, life long learning, which is both autonomy and continuity or 'contiguity'; pedagogy, the art of teaching and learning has to be viewed holistically. It is not one-dimensional but multi-dimensional, it begins with the school and ends (or 'continues' to begin) in the work situation. The teacher and the learner are close associates (in the 'middle' let us say we have the trainer) in this world of knowledge explosion. The following is a brief diagrammatic representation of my theoretical position.

Learner/Trainee

/ \

Teacher Trainer

Education in brief is to be examined critically from learner perspectives and all the paradigmatic shifts that are taking place in its total composition and entirety.

CONCLUSION: INTEGRATING DIVERSE AREAS OF KNOWLEDGE WITH THE NEW PARADIGM

The 'new vision for learning' envisages perforce the concept of learning to learn (together). The UNESCO World Conference on Higher Education (1998) posits that institutions of higher learning must play a supportive role in identifying and addressing issues that affect the well-being of communities.

What are learning organizations? The education system must constantly aim at a synthesis of 'new' methods with 'new' issues that affect community well-being (Joshi and Puspandham, K., 2000). For example, the National Council For Women's Education in 1964 recommended that sex education be imparted at the middle and secondary stages of school or collegiate education. The National Committees and Commissions have focused on a multi-dimensional approach to bring about positive directional changes in Women's Education in India. Some of the thrust areas are: developing a positive attitude towards women in curriculum, encouraging participation in vocational, technical and professional areas, promoting research centres of women's education in different Universities and setting up organizations like National Council For Women's Education. In short there must be a positive interventionist role to be played by the government (Singh, Nisha, 2000).

It is in this context that the question of extending the classroom arises. "The destiny of India is shaped in her classrooms" (Education Commission, 1996). Integrating new technologies with teaching methods posits a holistic vision of education beginning with literacy at the grassroots level to higher education; the emphasis being on continuing and lifelong education. To establish a synergy between technology and education is to autonomize it. (Ghanci, D.A., 2000). The industry university alliance is another case in point. UNESCO has designed a programme known as University Industry Science Partnership (UNISPAR) with the following objectives:

- To match university education with industry needs.
- To transfer research findings from university to industry.

- To continuously, reorient university curriculum to cater to.
- Every developmental sector.
- Prompting academics and industry to move to each other.

There must be a synergy between good academic institutes and good industries (Naik, 8.M., 2000).

In the overall framework of higher education in India there is an urgent need to design courses for those who live in semi-rural, rural and backward areas. It is pertinent to observe that about 30 per cent of the higher education institutions in the country are situated in these areas. What can Distance Education do to play 'interventionist' roles in this regard is the crux of the matter? (Vernal, Louis, 2000).

Distance Education can lead to the spread of population education, it can also be used as a powerful instrument to eradicate literacy and promote informal education. This is the holistic vision of education which I anticipate; total and composite, where teaching and learning is enhanced through an integrated systems analysis (Kalavathi, P., 1991).

REFERENCES

Delors Commission Report, UNESCO, Paris (1997).

Ghanci, D.A., *University News*, Vol. 38, No. 17, New Delhi (2000).

Joshi and Puspandham, *University News*, Vol. 38, No. 12, New Delhi (2000).

Kalavathi, P., "*Foundational Approach to Teaching Learning Process in D.E.*," Doctoral Work, Osmania University, Hyderabad (1991).

Naik, B.M., *University News*, Vol. 38, No. 17, New Delhi (2000).

Pandey, Saroj, *University News*, Vol. 38, No. 21, New Delhi (2000).

Phil Clement and John Jones, *The Diversity Training Handbook*, New Delhi (2004).

Rao, S.L., *The Telegraph*, Kolkata (6.12.2004).

Singh, Nisha, *University News*, Vol. 38, No. 7, New Delhi (2000).

Vernal, Louis, *University News*, Vol. 38, No. 19, New Delhi (2000).

34

Corporate Social Responsibility in the Banking Sector

V. Balachandran and V. Chandrasekaran

INTRODUCTION

Banking is the nerve centre of all economic activities in any country, without which the fiscal system would come to a grinding halt. The growth of this industry is phenomenal. The concept of banking developed to eliminate the disadvantages of barter system. Banks emerged because of the development of money and money market. Banks are intermediaries between supply and demand of funds of the society. Banks were started with the primary objective of accepting for the sake of lending. A closer look at these would reveal their inseparable connection with the community or society within which it operates. Hence it is imperative that banks should be socially and ethically responsible in all their activities.

Social responsibility is a concept of giving back to the society what it gets from it. Banks are no exception to this golden principle. The duty of the bank is in the nature of trust and they are custodian of public funds. Social responsibility aims at improving the quality of life. Due to their key role in the economy, banks and banking profession are obliged to be socially responsible. Bank's functions are inevitable in the development of economy. Within the objective of improving the quality of banking services, making best use of available resources and preventing unfair competition between banks, banks are expected to be socially responsible. The changing scenario in the national and international arena justifies that socially responsible organization alone would survive. The historical thought of profit maximization is no more relevant.

To-day it has become the order of the day that they not only aim at maximizing their wealth but also social wealth. Awareness of stakeholders have made banks to realign their priorities, if they to sustain and growth. Considering the need banks have to ensure effective and efficient functioning of the deposit and credit system. They have to avoid and prevent transactions and practices that could cause damage to economy, consider protecting public benefits and interests and environment as well.

Social responsible activity is divided into INTERNAL and EXTERNAL environment in which the bank functions.

INTERNAL

Customer

The need is a set of principles to assist bankers to meet the needs and expectations of customers. The banker should establish an ethical and responsible relationship. The following may be considered as important while dealing with the customer.

- The Law.
- Balancing of interests of the constituents.
- Not to damage legitimate interests of customers.
- The confidentiality.

Lending

Banking is about lending which calls for judgment and evaluation of consequences. Bankers have devised a methodology to guide their lending practices. The fundamentals are:

- Character of the borrower.
- Purpose.
- Nature of loan.
- Amount.
- Lending norms.
- Securities offered.
- Repayment arrangement/ agreement.
- Interest rate.

- Margin.
- Profitability of transaction.

Service

Banks consider service quality as a pre-requisite for offering services that meet the customer needs and expectations. As a means of continuous development of the services banks have to avail technological infrastructure and qualified human resources. No disparity in service to customers. No discrimination on nationality, religion, financial and social status and gender. NO SERVICE IS SMALL AND NO CUSTOMER IS BIG must be the motto.

Relation with Employees

Banks pay attention on hiring employees who would work with self esteem that suits to the banking society and carrying on the duty with a sense of responsibility. It is the utmost duty of the Human Relations/Public Relation department of the bank and ensures that the employees do not engage in unethical practices like:

- Mutual debt receivables, providing guarantee or opening joint account with customers.
- Not to accept any gift from any customer, not to engage them in personal gains using their position, the employees are duly recognized and receive their rights.

Relation with Institutions and Establishments

Banks behave according to the principles of integrity and transparency; provide information requested as per legislation. Complying with the statutory requirements as envisaged by the respective regulations.

Exchange of Information

Banks ensure that the information exchanged shall always be honest and complete within the framework of the legislation that prevails. To maintain the confidentiality in the whole banking sector and work to promote the common interest in the welfare of the State. Provide accurate, complete and timely information on their products and services offered. Banks should avoid unethical and surrogate advertising for promotional activities.

EXTERNAL

The external environment consists of the society in which the bank operates. The projects financed should not cause damage to the environment in any form. Banks should concentrate on project which promote Environmental Protection, Pollution Abatement, Labour Welfare, Discouraging Child Labour, Conservation of Energy, Promotion of Bio-diversity Programmes, Societal/Community Health Programmes, Rural Development, etc.

The following are practices banks can adopt to enhance the success and effectiveness of community involvement programmes:

Select a Programme

Examine the full range of programme types and structures to determine which approach(es) best fit. Factors that may help determine structure include structure and culture, internal/external communications management, and tax implications associated with making charitable contributions.

Strategic Community Involvement

Mission statement to express goals and objectives in community welfare projects. The mission statement may be general or specific. Whenever possible, the mission statement as a framework and allow local operating units autonomy in implementing projects within host countries. Incorporation of community involvement programme into business plan. Link company's community investments to its core competencies; link them to business functions where possible. Think of such initiatives strategically, harnessing all corporate assets with the aim of fulfilling key business goals. Corporate community investment can help companies expand into new markers, improve brand image, increase trust within the local community and even help companies create new products and services.

Local Advice

Seek advice on how the bank can best be of service to the community. The types of resources that could best serve their needs. In some instances, it may be appropriate to provide personnel, supplies, or facilities, while other situations may best be served through financial grants that help local communities address their own challenges. Whenever possible, seek feedback from the most diverse group possible—including representatives of both government and citizen groups—and operate with openness and honesty, keeping publicly-accessible records of meetings and projects. Involvement of local management in the decision-making process in order to design a programme that best fits local circumstances.

Monitoring projects, safeguarding resources, measuring the direct and indirect cost savings and benefits realized by both the company and the community.

Communication

Internal and external communication mechanisms to demonstrate the commitment to the communities in which the bank operates. Among the resources to consider are newsletters and magazines, annual reports, Intranet, press releases, email, video, formal meetings, conferences and video-conference calls, and advertisements in local papers. Whenever possible, partner with local government agencies and local non profit organizations to jointly issue communiques about specific projects and initiatives.

CONCLUSION

Industrial developmental programmes are essential for the growth of the economy at the same time Social Responsibility Programmes also need to the encouraged. Social responsibility programmes may not be profitable but value is added. The social welfare programmes should not be denied finance keeping the same barometer as that of a regular advance. Bank can finance participating social welfare programmes undertaken by corporate or a NGO. Banking Industry as whole should address this with open mindedness and should come out with innovative banking for promoting social welfare programmes. Reserve Bank of India with the approval of the Central Government could think of "Social Development Banks" to have better participation and narrowing the gap of societal expectation and need of society for a better tomorrow to make India Shining Bright.

35

Corporate Social Responsibility: Initiatives and Practices of IT Sector

CHANDRA SEKHAR GOTLAGUNTA, NIDHI MATHUR AND S.L. JAYANTHI

Corporate Social Responsibility (CSR) is not a new concept or philosophy to Indian Businessmen. It is a philosophy that looks at the social interest of business over the long-run as commercial with short-run self-interest. Today the drivers of business success are not the traditional drivers of quality or service or price or convenience alone but also other variables like business practices, employee treatments, community and the environment. Religion and charity have always been linked in Indian industry.

Corporations may act explicitly as responsible corporate citizens by involving in philanthropy, either for emotional reasons or business purposes. Corporate social responsibility (CSR) practiced by the companies to balance their short-term economic gains and their impact on the society. So that future generations can benefit equally.

The software industry has seen rapid growth since 1990. Many of the founders of software companies now wealthy were interested in making a mark as successful business leader in more than purely a financial or material sense. They wanted to be seen as good citizens and role models. They are mainly large organizations that are mature in their philosophy of community work and have created cells within their organizations that take care of CSR. In this context, the questions of interest are: How structured some of these wings are in some companies? How focused there about the mileage they need for every community activity? What are the past, present and future activities of their organizations.

The present paper discuss the important drivers of CSR and also examines the whole rage of issues of trends related to in selected organizations of IT sector. The study further observes that initiatives and practices of corporate social responsibility (CSR) towards development of the society.

INTRODUCTION

Social responsibility is not a new concept or philosophy to Indian businessmen. It is a philosophy that looks at the social interest of business over the long-run of compared with the short-run self-interest. However modern industrial civilization has created a new environment of challenge and struggle in which business has to view as business only. It was largely the initiative taken by late Sri Jayaprakash Narayan, Sarvodaya leader and also the active involvement of several other social activities and environmentalists which regenerated social interest among businessmen. (C. Gopal Krishna, 1992).

CORPORATE SOCIAL RESPONSIBILITY IN INDIA

The current global discourse CSR emphasizes its cultural universality and benefits (Darley and Johnson, 1993; Quazi and O'Brien, 2000). In practice, there are numerous obstacles to achieving corporate responsibility, particularly in many developing countries where the institutions, standards and appeals systems, which give some life to CSR in North America and Europe, are relatively weak. In a recently conducted study on Corporate Social Responsibility in India, it was found that public by and large, think that Indian companies are not considered socially responsible although, a few established names famous for the philanthropic model of social development programmes are mentioned frequently (CSRWORLD Survey Report, 2002 series). As far as multinational companies are concerned, they are viewed as more active in taking up CSR mainly because their efforts are more visible in the form of supply chain management and do affect a change in the scenario. In the same survey, the respondents favoured the idea of social responsibility where companies include environmental protection in their planning and strategy. Environmental responsibility featured in more than half of the replies on what CSR comprised. There was no mention of sustainable development.

The great name in social responsibility in India is that of the Tata Group. 31 per cent of the respondents included Tata group in their choice of three socially responsible companies. Next to Tata Group is Reliance Industry with 23 per cent, Ranbaxy and Infosys jointly are in the third place with 8 per cent each. The other companies mentioned are Maruti Udyog, ICICI, ST Microelectronics, ITC, Phillips, Escorts, HCL, Hero Group and so on. This finding also confirms the global trend where the CSR has been adopted through CEM practices by some of the giant firms only.

The corporations which offer their experiences in environmental management in the form of case studies and testimonials include some of the world's most widely recognized businesses: Chevron, Dow, DuPont and Proctor & Gamble (Smart, 1992 and WBCDS, 1988). Some CEOs, such as Robert Shapiro of chemicals giant Monsanto, have been become public champions of corporate environmentalism. In an interview with the *Harvard Business Review*, he argues that corporations can grow through sustainability; in other worlds, he posits that revenues may be expanded through the development of environmentally sustainable technologies and goods (Magretta, 1997). As the unprecedented number of organizations, conferences and publications by corporations illustrates, the environmental work of global business has never been so trumpeted.

PERFORMANCE OF THE IT INDUSTRY

In India the subject of sustainability is most relevant as the opportunities for corporates are quite different from those in developed countries. In developed countries, with a strong government, and some form of social security, the focus is not so much on the under-privileged, but on limiting the negative environmental impact of industrial activities. Developing countries, despite their different focus, can learn from the mistakes of their developed counterparts. For instance, developing countries may not see the full and long-term impact of smoking chimneys on the environment but only the advantages of investment and job creation in the short-term. Developing countries can strive for a more balance development when they take the learnings from the developing world.

Corporates in developing countries, and their employees, often become wealthy through the income generated from their operations. The disparity between their wealth and that of the rest of society is often evident, as in the IT industry in India. 'Digital divide' is a widely used term, though it seems to focus mostly on a narrow aspect of sustainability. If any industry should taken an interest in CSR it is IT, and it does to some extent.

The IT industry through its employment potential is a significant factor in stopping their brain drain. Companies are engaged in product development, product definition and technology and in applied or fundamental research. With the whole industry building experience and moving up to tasks requiring higher level capabilities, the need to go abroad is decreasing in many domains of engineering and science.

However, India as a country is not driving any technology and there is no leading technology in the market. The government is not driving technology innovations in many domains, or applying technology to government itself. Corporate spending on R&D and IT infrastructure is lagging behind the international mark. However, with US, European and Asian multinationals having moved their R&D activities into India, and creating opportunities to work on state-of-the-art technology, over the India will be poised to play a major role in the knowledge society. Some of the work is of 'engineering' level and often outsourced to Indian companies, the technology rich part being in captive, wholly owned offshore R&D centres. Thus, Indian engineers may not work on the edge of technology right now, but over a decade or so, knowledge and experience will build up. At a technology change opportunity, when new technology replaces the old, and old knowledge becomes irrelevant, Indian engineers will have an equal opportunity to take the lead.

PHILANTHROPY

The economic approach, as favoured by Milton Friedman, says corporates should limit themselves to what they do primarily: create wealth and give it to their shareholders. Obviously many companies have found that philanthropy helps build their branding and marketing efforts and also enhances retention of people. Tobacco companies counter the fact that their product slowly but surely kills people by supporting health activities. IT corporates are involved in philanthropy for one reason or another. Indian IT industry has a high stake in sustaining and building a healthy, cosmopolitan environment which keeps it attractive to the highly educated people it needs. Some reserve structurally a percentage of their turnover for charity, other create trusts through which they share their wealth. Employee involvement is also very popular, either as an employee initiative or as an initiative supported and stimulated by the company. As part of the community involvement efforts at Philips Software Centre in Bangalore, the Management Term has reserved a percentage of its turnover for community support which includes work among the underprivileged, working for culture and the environment. The quantitative objective is to touch at least one life per employee. The other guideline is 'start from your doorstep.' The fixed percentage of turnover, rather than profitability, provides continuity in the support, which allows for mostly continuous structural improvement programmes rather than relief.

It obviously makes sense for the industry to contribute and influence society directly other than through mere compliance with rules and regulations. Peter Drucker has argued that an order of magnitude difference of income is as much as a society finds justified. If the under privileged earn $1 a day, it sets a direction for the top. If the top wants to earn $ 100 a day it sets a target for the underprivileged. Anyway supporting a balanced development of the under privileged, in line with the development of the privileged, is crucial for the IT industry.

DRIVERS OF CORPORATE SCHOOL RESPONSIBILITY

The factors which motivate organization to be socially more responsive can be broadly categorized under two categories – internal and external. While internal factors basically emanate from the growth and profit motivation, e.g. pressure from supply chain, stake holder's awareness, etc., external factors belong to legal and mandatory regulations of the government, ethical and social dimensions of the firm looking for long-term sustainability practices. Following Exhibit 1 provides the list of CSR drivers.

Exhibit 1: CSR Drivers

CSR Driver Significance to Developing Contexts

Personal Ethics of Individual Entrepreneurs

In a number of instances it is the personal ethics of CEO or another individual that drive the CSR agenda within a company. This alone cannot secure a sustainable organizational commitment to CSR since it depends on individual engagement.

Supply chain pressures from Northern trading partners: There is a greater move to adoption by companies or voluntary codes or conduct, driven by international financing requirements and head office reputation assurance. But there is yet to be a significant drive from southern companies to adoption of voluntary codes of conduct beyond a reaction to supply chain pressures from Northern trading partners.

Laws and Regulations

Effectively enforced, law can be a significant driver to responsible behaviour. But although legal frameworks for environmental responsibility have been developed in much of the world, legal frameworks that require management of the social impact of business activities are comparatively undeveloped. In many developing countries, perceptions are strong that any kind of new regulation, standards or enforcement simply discourage foreign direct investment.

Public Relations and Reputation Assurance

Public relations considerations and reputation management are among the strongest drivers for businesses engaging in CSR. On the one hand, CSR is viewed by companies as a strategic tool for promotion of reputation and brand value. On the other hand, its potential to generate spin at the expense of real change is criticized.

Shareholder Activism and Investor Relations

There is little experience of shareholder activism in the developing world. In the North, portfolio investors such as pension funds have traditionally been largely ignorant of environmental and social issues. Investors in the North are increasingly beginning to ask questions about the environmental and social practices of the companies that they invest in. Even so, even 'responsible' investors are still too reliant on limited voluntary company reporting and questionnaires filled in by companies themselves.

Social License to Operate

The notion that business need to secure a 'social license to operate' from their stakeholders is widely touted as a significant driver for CSR. Increased time and expenditure in opening a new mine, demonstrable commitment to social advancement, and communication and cooperation with local stakeholders are amount the requirements for business operating in the developing world.

Sustaining Key Aspects of the Business

Enclave industries such as mining, tourism, plantations, and agriculture often view certain social investments as critical to the success of their business. Building clinics to treat workers, spraying to prevent malaria outbreaks, providing education and treating water are some of the social development project that businesses undertake. Companies that undertake these activities may create 'islands of development.' But history has demonstrated that in many cases these islands are fundamentally unsustainable because they rest on the continued profitability and investment of the businesses that fund them.

Co-operation in Development

There are increasing examples of co-operation, partnerships and legislation that promote opportunities for social development such as public-private partnerships, decentralization and related policies such as Economic and Social Councils in Chile. It is becoming evident that so-called 'tri-sector partnership' between businesses, NGOs and public institutions can promote more effective risk management and cost sharing whilst contributing to CSR.

Improving the business as a whole: A recognition that adoption of CSR practices has the potential to add value to business operating in the South is critical. The business imperative to manage social issues in society such as HIV and AIDS needs to be recognized.

(*Source:* Halina Ward, *IIED*, 2002)

GOVERNMENT CORPORATE RESPONSIBILITY

Indian industry has made a huge effort to invest in industry credibility abroad by going for certification to ISO standards, CMM, CMM-I and p-CMM standards. These efforts deserve to be complemented by the Government taking an active stand on significant issues. This would help protect, leverage and build more assets for the IT industry, and pro-actively encourage foreign companies to come to India. The government, on its part, must be responsible towards responsible corporates.

The drive towards modernization and excellence in corporate governance could include, for instance, a more liberal visa regime for people bringing world to India (expatriates in Bangalore need to get an AIDS test done at the Victoria Hospital, every time they have to renew their one year's grant on their resident certificate . . .); direct air connectivity to the major IT hubs; stricter administrative controls (the government's tolerance for 'bandwidths' being an issue in point) and efforts to contain political volatility; and strict software licensing regimes and zero tolerance for pirated software.

(*Source:* Bob Hoekstra, *Management Review*, 2003)

CSR INITIATIVES AND PRACTICES OF IT SECTOR

Wipro

Vision and Mission

According Mr. Vijaya Gupta Hend Corp. Comm Wipro do not have a separate vision and mission for CSR. They do not see their work as a social responsibility. They believe that if they want to have a successful business, then they must have a successful society around them. Wipro is a limited company in the private sector with a public holding. Their work in the social sector is therefore governed and funded by the company. Half the funds for Wipro looks into the voluntary work which comes from the employees, whole the other half comes from the company. Azim Premji foundation is funded almost entirely by Mr. Premji in his personal capacity.

CSR Focus Area

At present their focus area is education. They felt that education is very fundamental to develop, so they helped people to access whatever opportunities that are available. Along with their education initiatives they also have 'Wipro cares.' Wipro cares came into being three years ago. They collect funds for relief operations. For example, after the Gujarat earthquake they collected over Rs. 1 crores, sent clothes and essentials to Gujarat and also built a hospital. But later they realized that they must do something in an ongoing manner and not wait for natural calamities to start their. Voluntary activities Wipro volunteers did a quick survey around urban slums in Bangalore and Hyderabad. They identified three major issues: (1) Unemployment, (2) Hygiene, and (3) Sanitation. Now they have been started.

Initiatives in Education

Their main initiative is called "wipro applying thought in schools." It contributes improving quality of education India. It is active in 15 cities, the initiative has imparted close to 125,000 hours of training to over 2500 teachers, principals and parents from 100 schools nationally. Wipro's work prompted Business world ACCI-SEDF corporate social responsibility Award 2003 to rate Wipro as one of the top Indian corporates championing the cause of corporate social responsibility and sustainable development. Wipro has partnered with experts in education to incorporate contemporary international research and the best teaching practices across the country to each of the enrolled schools.

Wipro forum is a collection of organizations and their effort is to improve the quality of education in the country.

Partner NGOs

NGOs are also working in education, unless the work in learning methods improves Wipro shares their objective. Wipro's aim is to see that whether learning is happening in schools that already exist. Every NGOs have the same focus.

Evaluation of CSR Programmes

Evaluation process is built in each component of the Wipro applying thought in schools programme. They are still exploring effective methods to evaluate their programme. They are inviting partners to come up with ways to make evaluation possible.

Volunteers Work

Wipro volunteers identify an unemployed young person who has skills and what they require to become gainfully employed. They work to enhance their skills and monitor the entire process. They spend half a day in a week in slum teaching Maths and English to children. They want the students in slum to learn life skills.

Policies

They have policies on CSR that include sexual Harassment. HIV/ AIDS, child labour, environment, Disaster management, working with disabled. They have an integrity policy that every Wiproite signs and policy is following by every employee.

Future Plans

They identified Health is definitely an area where they hope to do a lot of work through Wipro cases.

Honeywell Technology Solutions Lab (HTSL)

Mr. Krishna Mikkileni, Managing director says that HTSL has formed a community service team which manages the company's CSR. Through the community service team they imbibe the values and the spirit of living. CSR department is as old as HTSL Company supported by the global Honey well foundation. Every year they add more initiatives to their scheme. HTSL has disbursed scholarships worth Rs. 70 lakhs during past year under a programme that involved over 1,500 students from around 120 schools. Apart from supporting education programmes with scholarships and infrastructure for local schools. They also took up societal initiatives.

Between 2003 and 2004 HTSL has supported 45 native villages of their employees by investing in projects such as bore wells.

Company employees along with doctors make weekly visits to local villages and provide health check-ups and medicines. Company helps underprivileged individuals to become self-reliant and independent with its 'start a life programme.' It sponsored auto-rickshaws, photocopying machines and the like for individuals to help them make better living.

Satyam Computers

Satyam has CSR arm called Alambana which operates in the cities and has Satyam employee volunteering work and contributing funds. This has partnership and alliances with other corporates, NGOs and the government.

Byrraju Foundation

Satyam's another CSR arm is Byrraju Foundation. Its primary focus is to develop rural areas and issues including health, potable water, environment, livelihood skills, waste disposal, recycling in areas where there is no Satyam office. They welcome any employee who thinks that his or her skills could make a difference in services that they are providing.

Focus Area

In A.P. they have adopted 140 villages. Their model includes use of technology, leveraging of best practices and also entering into partnerships with various other foundations and organisations.

Partnership with IBM

Satyam combined with IBM and are working one worldwide program for children called 'kid smart.' It is mainly to develop reading and awareness skills of young children of classes 1 to 4. They have 13 regional centres where IBM gives software programs, hardware support training program while government provides accommodation. The IBM program has been run successfully in Chennai and Bangalore rural area. Byrraju manages the program while IBM provides the computers.

Byrraju's Solutions

Byrraju's foundations made solutions for the children who don't attend schools. They basically make school a fun place to come in. They maximize pulling factors and minimize pushing factors. They influenced both parents and children. The programmes focus is to make people aware about the evils of child labour and benefits of sending children to school. The main objective of model school is easy access to high quality education for the underprivileged rural children. These model schools have large infrastructure like:

- One class room for every class.
- School furniture, separate rooms for computer lab, science lab, library staff room.
- Toilet facilities with water connection.
- Safe drinking water.
- Continuous power supply.
- Garbage disposal.
- Mid-day meals shed.
- Free plantation.
- Playground, sports equipment.
- Boundary wall.
- Stationery.

Soft infrastructures includes:

- Teaching learning materials.
- School library.
- Science lab.
- Computer lab.
- CD content for lecturers and students.
- Audio-visual equipment.
- Technology aided tools.
- Teacher training.
- 1:40 teacher ratio.
- Temporary teachers/vidya volunteers.
- Uniform.
- Sport and extra curricular activities.
- Health Program.
- Pre-school programmes.

Implementation Programme

This programme has been implemented in 119 of the 250 schools converting larger schools into model schools. Their main aim is to identify the facilities present, lacking or completely absent and to bridge the gap. Eighty thousand rupees has been allocated for each high school.

Future Plans

Planning to set-up special schools for the mentally challenged children and also for hearing, speech and visually impaired children for whom the basic infrastructure is not there. Next is to convert 233 identified schools into model school.

Tata Consultancy Services (TCS)

TCS executive Vice-President Prof. K.V. Nori and Vice-President Bhushan received the 'Asian Corporate Social Responsibility Award' (Asian CSR Award) in the support and improvement in education category.

The TATA group has designed a computer-based functional literacy model, a multimedia-based teaching method and had set-up an adult literacy programme (ALP) to help the government eradicate illiteracy. The ALP use a TCS-designed computer-based functional literacy model (CBFLM) an innovative teaching model that uses multimedia software to teach adults—spread over 1 to 1.5 hours sessions, 3 times a week, over a period of 10 to 12 weeks. This CBFLM uses animated graphics patters for visualization and audio appreciation.

According to S. Ramodorai chief executive officer TCS. No modern society can function without a literate population and no one can function well in a modern society without being literate.

Future Plans

TCS believed that developing innovative method using theories of cognition language and communication to make people literate within the next five years. Literacy increases awareness and facilities responsible action. Adult literacy empowers and will be key in moving the people and country forward. TCS committed in using computers and it to facilitate the process, monitor administration and manage logistics.

HCL Technologies Ltd.

Mr. Sujit Baksi, Executive Vice-President, Human Resources HCL said that they believe that every organization has a moral obligation towards society people in the society. HCL believed that responsible citizen of tomorrow will be brought through proper education and upbringing at the early stages of their life. This belief made HCL to dedicate the work to education of orphan, destitute and deprived children. HCL has been working with Balagurvkulam, which is in Chennai and its main objective is to upbringing orphan, destitute and deprived children, irrespective of caste, creed, religion, gender, race, etc., and provide them food, clothing, shelter, education and nurture them into responsible and respectable citizens of the world.

HCL has been making humble contributions to Mother Teresa's sisters of charity to bring joy and happiness in the deprived HCL group donated 2,000 pollution masks and six month's supply of filters for the Delhi traffic police which are presented by Sujit Baksr. He said traffic police endure a lot of hardships in the course of performing their duty and increasing pollution only adds to their problems people in the society.

HCL group collected Rs. 56,84,000 and donated it to various relief organisations including prime minister's Relief fund. Red Cross society and CRY (child relief and you) during Gujarat Earthquake.

IBM

IBM foundation and Byrraju foundation are working launched on worldwide program for children called 'kidsmart.' They launched kidsmart in 30 schools. It is mainly to develop awareness and reading skills in young children. They launched 13 regional centres. IBM is giving software programs, hardware support, training program to children while government provides accommodation. There are three components in kidsmart.

1. Technology-aided learning—not for leaving computers skills.

2. Learning corners – one is reading corner and others craft corner.
3. Training 5 teachers from each school by IBM foundation.

Byrraju foundation, IBM foundation and government are coming the program together where Byrraju manages the program while IBM provides the computers.

The IBM program has been successfully implemented in rural areas in Chennai and Bangalore.

Polaris

Polaris Software Lab Ltd. Established Ullas Trust, the corporate social responsibility (CSR) arm by employees in 1997 at Chennai. The underlying philosophy of the trust is "Give back to the society what the society gave you." 40 per cent of each scholarship is borne by Polaris employees and remaining by the company. The goal of trust is to reach out to the economically weaker section of society and encourage academic excellence among bright, young, deserving students with high academic performance. Students with good academic records are identified and awarded to 'you can do it' scholarships of Rs. 1,500.

Ullas three keys initiatives of 2003:

1. A trophy Encouraging Excellence in Education (EEE) award to recognize stellar performance of specific schools in nurturing young students. Even principals from those achieving schools were chosen for 'best principal award.'
2. Ullas encourage higher education by awarding nine brilliant students with 'Ullas Achiever's Higher Education scholarships' to pursue higher education in colleges.
3. Ullas opened bank accounts for Ulla's scholars.

Till now 7,000 students got benefited from Ullas trust. Several training programmes are conducted, and area-wise chapters (students club) receive guidance from Ulla's volunteers to participate in extra-curricular activities. Polaris is gearing up to expand to other geographies in India after initial success of Ullas trust in Chennai. Polaris spent Rs. 94 lakhs on social responsibility during 2001-02.

Sify

Sify's focus is on using the internet to build a sense of unity and nationality and a sense of community and belonging.

Alambana is a social service organization run by Sify associates. It provides support and empowers the weaker sections of society and to improve their Socio-Economic status.

Alambana Vidya provides free and quality in education to students from economically weaker families to help them find suitable jobs.

Under this scheme boys and girls between 18 and 21, who are unable to study further due to financial constraints are selected for 3 month further due to financial constraints are selected for 3 month full-time course which enables them to work as data entry operators and in retailing sector.

Sify Alambana tied up with the Tamil Nadu Corporation for Development of Women Ltd., (under Mahila Scheme) to source a bright young girl student who wants to pursue studies but are financially back.

Sify re-established its Internet backbone connectivity within hours when the earthquake hit Gujarat. Sify contributed effectively as a bridge between Gujarat people and their relations in India and abroad through e-mail and by using the search of the portal sify.com to appeal for voluntary financial assistance from users in India and Abroad. In this way, sify was able to help thousand of people who would not otherwise have been able to contract their relatives. The contributions were passed on to the Indian Red Cross Society (IRCS), New Delhi.

Sify raised Rs. 22.79 lakhs, which were about 50 per cent of the total money, raised by the Red Cross for Gujarat.

Cognizant Technology Solutions (CTS)

Mr. R. Chandrasekharan, Senior Vice-president, CTS says, "A leadership role in the Technology services sector comes with a certain responsibility and the most successful organization are the ones that give back to the community.

CTS work with academia, providing advanced developmental programmes for faculty and defines curricula and syllabi. The company also helps colleges and universities to set-up solutions labs and knowledge centres. The company has adopted various social responsibility programmes.

CTS have also earmarked sizeable SVMS to CSR.

NIIT

NIIT, provider of IT training, helps meritorious poor children become IT-literate through its Bhavishya Jyothi scholarship scheme. Over 1 lakh poor students have been covered in the last 12 years.

NIIT simplified the computer for slum children through the 'Hole-in-the wall' experiment says Sugana Mitra R&D chief a brain-child of NIITian.

The company used unmanned computer kiosks to take the internet experience to self-teaching slum children and help them navigate the 'Net' and web-enable themselves. Over 30 kiosks were placed across the country.

NIIT created a computer Assisted teaching and rehabilitation program (CATERED) for spastic and visually impaired children. They developed the 1-write package to provide interactive support to physically-handicapped persons.

NIIT has earmarked sizeable sums to CSR.

INFOSYS

The Infosys foundation established in 1996 focuses on promoting education and vocational training to less privileged members of society especially those in rural areas. Infosys has done considerable work to improve the lot of senior citizens, economically disadvantaged gifted students, the handicapped and the destitute.

Infosys foundations anchored key schemes like:

- Setting up science centres in rural areas.
- Setting up orphanages.
- Constructing hospital wards and providing medical equipments.
- A library for every school program so far 1001 libraries has been inaugurated in the name of Shalegondu Granthalaya.
- Distributing folk music cassettes and music systems to community centres.

The foundation board of trustees undertakes women's projects, healthcare, education, community development, preservation of act and culture.

Infosys foundation built a brain fever ward for the children in Bellary called the 'Infosys infant ward,' a cancer hospital in

Kanchipuram and OPD for poor patients in Amangabad. They donated ambulance and gave medical aid to patients of leprosy, heart disease, kindly failure and head injuries. They gave Air-conditioners, constructed Dharmashala – a free ward. These programmes include infrastructure development, education, research and training. They made contributions to traffic police in Bangalore. They also conducted catch them young programme, the rural reach program, train the trainer, computers and class-rooms.

They introduced computer education in village training centres through teacher training camps.

CONCLUSIONS

An important issue that emerges from the analysis is that the status and trend of corporate social responsibility in India only big Companies are sensitive to the issue of CSR. However, the companies have potential to revolutionise the structure of markets and even societies. The experts' views highlight several ways of facilitating CSR. IT companies are spending sizeable money and time are spending in the nation-building. IT sector companies are making long-term financial commitments under their CSR programmes.

NOTES AND REFERENCES

Bob Hoekstra, "CSR and the IT Industry in Bangalore: Observations of Practitioner," *Management Review*, Vol. 15, November 4-December 2003, pp. 78-81.

C. Gopala Krishna (1992): *Corporate Social Responsibility in India. A Study of Management Attitudes*, Mittal Publications, New Delhi.

CSR World Survey Report, 2002 Series.

Darley, W.K. and D.M. Johnson, "Cross National Consumerism of Consumer Attitudes towards Consumerism in Four Developing Countries," *Journal of Consumer Affairs*, No. 2, 1993, pp. 37-54.

Magretta, Joan (1997): "Growth through Global Sustainability: An Interview with Monsanto's CEO Robert B. Shapiro," *Howard Business Review*, January-February.

Peter F. Drucker (1999): *Executive Compensation and Economic Inequality Management*, Allied Publishers.

Quazi, A. and D. O'Brien, "An Empirical Test of a Cross Cultural Model of Corporate Responsibility, *The Journal of Business Ethics*, No. 25, 2000, pp. 33-51.

Ward, Halina *et al.* (2002): Corporate Citizenship in Openbion, IIED, London.

www.sustainability-index.com

www.philps.com
www.Hci.technologier.com
www.polaris.co.in
www.thehindu.co.in
www.IndianNGOs.com
www..satyam.com
www.infosys.com
www.NIIT.com
www.TCS.com
www.Sity.net
www.wipro.com
www.HTSL.com
www.IBM.com
www.Cognizant.com

36

Power Generating Sector: Softening the Impacts

BABITHA VISHWANATH

"Sustainable Development" being the 21st century's maxim, achieving it is possible by the conscious efforts of the various actors that comprise society. In this regard, companies cutting across the sectors need to make balanced efforts aiming at the triple bottom line of environmental protection, economic efficiency and social equity.

Different sectors have different levels of impact on the environment, social and economic aspects, depending on their business activities. The power-generating sector has been serving the ever-growing demand for electricity by undertaking green field projects and/or expanding. In the process, earned sufficient returns to stockholders, but other stakeholders have drawn attention to the environment and social aspects.

The Power Generating Sector, while fuelling the economic development and progress of the nation has nevertheless, left an indelible mark on the environment. The social concern was left uncared for a long time. For the past few decades however, it is thinking and caring about the environment and society at large and trying to impact positively.

The power generating companies:

- Need huge acres of land to put up their plants in place to generate electricity and transmit it across the vast length and breadth of the nation.

- Consume volumes of fuel (non-renewable) leading to the depletion of the natural resources (which had taken millennia to form); their storage also occupies large areas of land.
- Transport fuel which is risky, especially so in case of nuclear material.
- Produce greenhouse gases such as carbon dioxide, nitrous oxide, sulphur dioxide are emitted resulting in global warming.
- Produce large volumes of combustion waste/by products.

All these have a great impact on the lives of local people, the work force and the environment. In the post-globalized economy, there has been tremendous pressure on the businesses to show a greater responsibility to the social and environmental aspects. For about a quarter century, the firms are becoming cleaner, greener and extending continuous support to the society, through various initiatives. This has been possible by a paradigm shift in the business model and strategic thinking, with an aim to achieve sustainable growth.

The various initiatives undertaken by the Power Generating companies have focused on: Safety and Health (Public and Occupational), Environment, Human Rights, Ethics and Role of business entity in the society. The initiatives undertaken are environment centric, economic centric and social centric.

Economic Centric

To improve the profit, financial standing and reduction of cost: Companies are improving their top line, by meeting the ever-increasing demand for electricity by increasing the capacity through judicious capital investment policy. Cutting the costs by minimizing fuel expenses, operating expenses, and adopting latest technology, thus improving plant load factor and generation per employee and reducing the wastage. Firms are integrating (forward, backward and both), shifting laterally, trying to increase the proportion of electricity generated through renewable sources and stressing on the conservation of energy. The organization structure is being reformed to improve management quality and efficiency, trying to capitalize on their knowledge, by providing a series of services like: consultancy, training and development and R&D services.

Environment Centric

Firms initially had their own Environment Management System (EMS) in place, and later updated to meet the requirements of ISO 14000, which gives them a level playing field in the post-globalised era. As part of EMS they have a comprehensive environment policy, core environment committees which include board members, providing a blue print of the action plan and committees at unit/ plant in charge of the programmes to be implemented at various stages and would oversee day-to-day activities. Creating awareness among the workforce by imparting training, observation of environment week/ month.

Afforestation is being emphasized by planting millions of saplings around the plant thus creating green belts in the local areas. Environment Assessment and Audit is undertaken regularly, while complying the legal norms. Green procurement is being stressed, coercing suppliers to protect the environment. The alternative uses of by product (such as ash) are being explored continuously and trying to create an awareness of the same among those who can use it effectively. All these efforts are in order to reduce the impact on the environment and maintain the natural ecosystem.

Social Centric

The focus is on community and workforce. There have been initiatives to improve the standard of living of the people in the local areas by providing the basic infrastructure like roads, schools and hospitals. Companies are endeavouring to provide employment to differently challenged persons or facilitating them to find means of living.

The companies are providing a satisfactory work environment and encouraging the employees to actively participate in the community development activities. They have systems in place, which prevent accidents, promote health and raise safety standards in the work place. Companies are getting certified as OHSAS 18001.

Case Study

In the Indian scenario of Power Generation, National Thermal Power Corporation (NTPC), for nearly three decades has provided excellent support to both the industry and public in providing electricity. More than 25 per cent of the nation's electric energy is being catered by NTPC.

With a vision to be one of the world's largest and best power utilities, powering India's growth NTPC, is stressing on adding capacity in a sustainable way, focusing on Sustainable Development. Corporate Social Responsibility is integrated in the mission statement of the company and is stated as "to be a socially responsible corporate entity with thrust on environment protection, ash utilization, community development and energy conservation." In this direction, it has associated itself with the Global Compact Programme of the United Nations and has embraced the ten principles expounded by it.

The case, NTPC's Role in Indian Power Generating Sector would discuss the following:

- The impact of its activities on the environment, analyse the initiatives undertaken and the results of the same.
- The specific stakeholders demands would be enumerated and how NTPC is meeting them and how it is Planning to meet the future demands.

IMPACT ON THE ENVIRONMENT AND INITIATIVES UNDERTAKEN

As environment is a critical area in setting and running a power generating plant, NTPC has given thrust to this area in its corporate mission, by aiming at broadening its portfolio (renewable and non-renewable), protecting the environment, ash utilization, energy conservation and in adopting state-of-the-art-technologies.

While setting standards it has chalked out a set of well-defined activities that are envisaged right from the project conceptualization stage to its commissioning and operation stage, which not only comply with the statutory norms but much beyond, in order to protect and improve the environment around its projects. It has formed special groups like Environment Engineering Group (EEG), Environmental Management Group (EMG), Ash Utilization Department (AUD), SPV-A (Special Purpose Vehicle for Afforestation), Non-Conventional Energy Sources Group, etc. The Centre for Power Efficiency and Environment Protection (CENPEEP) will be an assimilating, disseminating and demonstrating technical know-how unit, which will enable to other utilities in this sector thus improving the Indian Power Sector. And has implemented Environmental Management System (EMS) as per ISO-14001, in all its projects.

In order to compensate for the vegetation cleared by it while setting up its plants, it has taken up afforestation thus bringing wasteland under the forest area. These green belts (15 million trees) around the projects act as lungs, avoid soil erosion, resulted in increased dense forest area, increase in average rainfall, decrease in wasteland, etc. It has also resulted in decrease in temperature by three degree Celsius in the Ramagundam area, which reels under high temperature during summer.

Thermal power generation produces minute particles of ash commonly known as fly ash, (consists of silica, alumina, oxides of iron, calcium, and magnesium and toxic heavy metals like lead, arsenic, cobalt, and copper) large areas of land is wasted in disposing the same, results in health hazards and endangers environment.

Fly ash management has made considerable strides over the past few years. It tries to convert the fly ash (waste) into wealth by exploring its viability to be used as a raw material in different industries as it is oxide-rich. Today, fly ash is being used in making bricks, as a part replacement of cement in mortar and concrete and in the construction of roads and embankments. NTPC has set-up two fly ash brick manufacturing plants at Badarpur and Dadri near Delhi.

Studies by TERI show that fly ash dumps can be used for commercial purpose in floriculture, a large number of farmers have accepted the use of fly ash in agricultural applications. An innovative and environmental friendly technology, known as the dry ash technology, has been developed wherein the fly ash is collected in huge mounds with a filter bed provided at the bottom of the mound, grass is planted on the slopes of the fly ash mounds and polymer layering is done to prevent the ash from being blown by the wind. Fly ash treated by this method develops certain physical properties that make it more suitable for commercial purposes.

It has been conducting Environment Impact Assessment (EIA) studies, involving various parameters affecting the environment of the areas in the vicinity of the projects, extending for a year consisting of field studies and impact assessment with regard to land use, water use, soil, hydrology, water quality, meteorology, air quality, terrestrial and aquatic ecology and noise. Based on EIA study, specific scientific studies are conducted to assess the likely impact of the pollutants on the sensitive flora and fauna in the surroundings, as also, to take preventive and mitigatory measures, wherever required. Such studies conducted from time to time around a power project have established the environment status at various post-operational stages of the project.

In general, the studies, as such, have revealed that there is no significant adverse impact on the ecology due to the project activities in any of the stations. It has set-up a Power Technology and Research Centre that will conduct research on alternative fuels, non-conventional energy resources and new technologies.

Looking at its prowess in this field, USDOE and USAID identified it as the implementing Agency for "Green House Gas Emission Prevention Project."

NTPC Fulfilling its Stakeholders' Demands

There are many stakeholders and their demands being unique, it has various initiatives specific to the set of stakeholders, let us look at some of the critical stakeholders, the impact of NTPC's activities on them and how their demands are being met.

Owners

The central government being the only owner till the accounting year 2003-04, has envisaged NTPC to play a major role in power generation to fuel the economic growth. And NTPC has lived up to the expectation of the owner and has provided 26.7 per cent electricity though with the capacity of 19 per cent. It has been playing a critical role in the power sector by taking many initiatives to make the power sector a vibrant one. It has been performing impressively year after year, for the year 2003-04 the statistics are as follows: Turnover: Rs. 25,964.2 crore, Net Profit Rs. 5,260.8 crore. During the period it has generated 149.171 billion units with a plant load factor of 84.4 per cent of coal-fired stations much above the national average of 72.7 per cent.

Employees

It has formulated an integrated HR strategy which rests on four building blocks, namely, Competence building, Commitment building,

Culture building and Systems building. All HR initiatives are undertaken within this broad framework to actualize the HR Vision of "enabling the employees to be a family of committed world class professionals making NTPC a learning organisation."

The workforce is competent and committed; the same is reflected in a continuous improvement in the number of units produced per employee, which has been 7.11 MU for the year 2003-04. In turn NTPC along with the best compensation provides the following to its employees:

- Enhancing the knowledge: Encourages employees to update their skills by taking up various courses, in this regard it has tied up with IIT, Delhi for the M.Tech. and MDI for its management programme. It also motivates, to opt for diploma courses, which would enhance the knowledge.
- The in-house training and development programmes are taken care by Power Management Institute, Noida.
- A minimum seven man days training per employee, per year and training at different levels to groom people for assuming positions of higher responsibility.
- It has in place systems for employee safety and health, welfare, well-being, social security and rewards and recognition.
- Offers hest quality of life through beautiful townships with all amenities such as educational, medical and recreational.
- It creates awareness among the employees about the latest development through circulars, in-house journal (Horizon).
- Health and Safety aspect: OHSAS 18000 certified "Best Employers in India – 2004" survey by Hewitt Associates in which NTPC bagged coveted third rank.

In a study conducted by international HR Consulting firm Mercer in association with *Business Today* magazine, National Thermal Power Corporation is the only public sector unit to feature in the top 10 list and has been ranked as the sixth best company to work for in India.

Local Populace: NTPC believes in growth with a human face, and pursues people-centred development and is a socially committed organization. It attaches great importance in discharging its overall social responsibilities to the community and the society at large where its projects are located. It is the first among the public sector units to have a comprehensives policy in place in this regard. In this regard it has various programs like:

Resettlement and Rehabilitation (R&R) Programme

The R&R cells operate at projects, Regional Headquarters and the Corporate Centre and:

- Focuses on people affected directly and/or indirectly.
- Aims at improving the overall economic status of Project Affected Persons (PAPs).
- PAPs are made partners in all the activities related to R&R.
- Provides infrastructure like primary school, dispensary, panchayat ghar, drinking water well/hand pumps, WBM roads, drainage, Sulabh Sauchalaya, etc., are provided.
- Encourages self-employment in the areas of dairy, poultry, handicraft, etc.
- Petty contracts are awarded to PAPs.

Rehabilitation Action Plan (RAP)

RAP is prepared for expansion and green field projects based on the outcomes of Socio-economic surveys (SES), conducted by independent and reputed professional institutes. RAP is finalised in consultation with the PAPs, local authorities and the State administration and:

- Encourages PAPs to be partners in implementation of the RAP.
- Vocational training in the areas of tailoring, carpet weaving, papad making, bee keeping, etc., is imparted.
- Plans are implemented in a definite time framework and specified budget.
- Each resettlement colony is provided with a primary school.
- The areas of adult education, formal and non-formal education are taken care.

Remedial Action Plan (ReAPs)

In case of 12 older projects, it has re-assessed by carrying out a 'retrofit' R&R operation to bridge the gaps wherever they had occurred and Remedial Action Plans (ReAPs) were prepared. These ReAPs were time bound with a specified budget and are completed as on date.

For effective implementation and transparency, various committees like the following were set-up: Public Information Centres (PICs) and Village Development Advisory Committees (VDACs). In addition to this, depending upon the need, various programmes are carried in association with the NGOs. The Grievance Redressal Mechanism for each project encourages PAPs to approach them if dissatisfied with the arrangements.

Society at Large

- It has framed its Community Development Policy with thrust on Decentralized Distributed Generation and Supply (DDGS), Self-reliance of physically challenged, Conservation of national monuments and, cultural heritage and assistance during the national calamities.
- National Thermal Power Corporation Foundation has been registered on 10th December, 2004, to plan and coordinate the social developmental activities.
- In the recruitment process special focus is on the marginalized section of society.
- Economic self-reliance of physically challenged people is stressed, both in the recruitment process and is planning to set-up a development centre for the physically challenged.
- Activities which would enable the unemployed youth to opt for self-employment and also strengthen the self-help groups in the villages around the project/plant.

Other Activities

- Its innovative initiatives related to Corporate Social Responsibility (CSR) are regularly posted on Global Compact Website.
- Actively participates in International and national forums.
- Enthusiastically sponsors various events/seminars.
- Member of Corporate Roundtable on Development of Strategies for Environment (CoRE) initiated by The Energy Resource Institute (TERI).
- Member of UN Global Compact.
- It has adopted the Social Code framed by India Partnership' Forum promoted by CII and UNDP.

NTPC has bagged Institute of Directors 'Golden Peacock Award' for Corporate Social Responsibility for the year 2003.

CONCLUSION

The continuous effort being made for an integrated sustainable development, encompassing the areas of economy, environment and society would ensure that the future generation would be able to meet their needs. The harmony of power sector development in tandem with societal development is demonstrated in the case study.

REFERENCES

Chad Holliday, "Sustainable Growth, The DuPont Way," *HBR*, September 2001.

Greenhouse Gas Report 2003/04, Northwest Territories Power Corporation.

Maurice Strong, Where on Earth are We Going?

Meinolf Dierkes and Ariane Berthoin Antal, "Whither Corporate Social Reporting: Is it Time to Legislate?," *California Management Review*, Volume XXVIII, Number 3, Spring, 1986.

National Thermal Power Corporation Ltd., Annual Reports, Manuals, Website.

Operating Responsibility, 2004, National Grid Corporation, UK.

Robert, B. Reich, "The New Meaning of Corporate Social Responsibility," *California Management Review*, Vol. 40, No. 2, Winter, 1998.

TEPCO, Sustainability Report, 2004.

V.K. Thota, Cemex: Eco-efficiency Program.

37

Ethics for Corporate Managers–Problems and Possibilities

JYOTSNA DIWAN MEHTA

There is real excellence in all the world which can be separated from right living. – David Starr Jordan

The issue of ethics is a perennial source of controversies. How exactly should a corporate manager think through an ethical issue? What questions should be asked? What factors should be considered? This paper attempts to define ethics and explain its dynamics. The actions and decisions of the corporate world can hugely impact society at various levels ranging from the individual to the societal level. It is imperative that managers exercise caution in ensuring that their actions and decisions are ethical. Here it is to be noted that the managers must not only identify the values, rights, etc., which could cause us to knowingly behave unethically but should also accept that in spite of being well intentioned they possess the potential for unethical behaviour caused by bias that emerges from unconscious beliefs, group favouritism, etc. An attempt is made to outline the steps that can be taken to ensure that behaviour is ethical in all its aspects. There is no easy way out. It is imperative that ethical decision-making is practised by the corporate world for the mutual benefit of all.

The complex relationship between business and society has a long history. It is a curious love-hate relationship where inter-dependency is coloured with suspicion. Yet, there can be no business without society and no organization of society without business! As the process of globalization is changing the world education and awareness is creating a need to protect the environment, and people are demanding a better quality of life, developed and developing societies are in the process of reshuffling their institutions and priorities. This has developed an understanding that businesses, to survive and grow will require to incorporate social and political concerns into their decision-making.

Business has often failed to create congruency between its economic objectives and its social responsibilities. Moreover, businessmen often find that defining ethics is as difficult as determining what is ethical and what is not! Big businesses have therefore always been criticized. Exposes of corrupt business practices have often rocked governments, indeed nations. This has resulted in various reactions ranging from public outrage to waves of government regulation! In these trying times of what is popularly known as "the ethics crisis" the line between what is blurring, so how the managers in organizations become aware of and then respond to social issues and the problems associated with ethic-based issues?

DEFINING ETHICS

Ethics broadly and simply is the study of how our decisions affect other people. It encompasses the study of people's rights and duties, the moral rules that people apply in making decisions and the nature of the relationship among people.

Business ethics are the principles, practices and philosophies that guides the business people in their day-to day business decisions. It relates to the behaviour of businessmen in business situations and is concerned with the impact of decisions of the society within and outside business organizations.

EXPLORING THE CONCEPT OF ETHICS

Ethical questions can be studied at four levels – societal, stakeholder, internal policy and personal (Fig. 37.1). At the societal level we ask questions about the basic institutions in a society. The problem of gender discrimination which causes for instance skewed representation of women bushiness organizations, the glass ceiling, syndrome, etc. How ethical is it for the organization to deny recruitment of a candidate because the candidate is a woman!

The second kind of ethical questions concerns stakeholders – suppliers, customers, shareholders, etc. There are many stakeholder issues. Lack of corporate governance as was witnessed in Reliance was an issue that came up recently.

Internal policy issues address questions about the nature of a company's relations with its employees what rights do employees have? What are the terms of the employees contract?

Personal issues ask how people should treat one another within the organization. This refers to principles of personal conduct at the workplace.

Level 4	PERSONAL	Individual conduct to be within the boundaries of ethics
Level 3	INTERNAL POLICY	Protecting the interests of Employees
Level 2	STAKEHOLDERS	(a) Shareholders (b) Suppliers (c) Consumers (d) Government (e) Competitors
Level 1	SOCIETAL	Protecting interests of: (a) Society (b) Nation (c) World community

FIG. 37.1

Issues Related to Business Standards

IDENTIFYING THE ETHICAL ELEMENTS IN ISSUES

Consciously or unconsciously, we engage in some kind of ethical reasoning while making every decision, however small. To improve ethical reasoning, it is important to understand certain accepts which can enable us to analyze the decision to be taken in a more explicit manner. Let us identify these aspects as the tools which helps to define ethics:

(i) **Values:** These are relatively permanent desires that seems to be good in itself. They help to answer the why question. Why for example are you reading this article? You might reply, it is your job, or that you want to learn about ethics or that you want to learn how to be a more ethical person.

The reason you give will reflect on the values you hold as important.

(ii) **Rights and duties:** A right is a claim that entitles a person to take a particular action whereas duties and obligations to take specific steps or obey the law. So my using a staff car I am entitled to will be an ethical decision but when I use it beyond my entitlement I will be something unethical.

(iii) **Moral Rules are the "tie breakers":** They guide us through situations where competing interests collide. Often these become internalized as values.

(iv) **Common Morality** is the body of moral rules governing ordinary ethical problems. These are the rules we live by most of the time, and include the ability to stick to your word, that is promise keeping, non-malevolence or lack of devious intent mutual aid based on principles of humanity, respect for persons and property.

These tools can help to identify whether the business decision is within the framework ethics.

Figure 37.2 shows the Parameters for determining the Ethics of a business decision.

BEYOND THE OBVIOUS

Now that we have defined ethics and laid the measures for

(i) Define the problem accurately. There should be no ambiguity. Also do not mix the solution with the problem.
(ii) Take different view points of the situation.
(iii) Look for the root cause of the problem.
(iv) Look within. Explore your intentions. Introspect.
(v) Compare intentions with desired outcome.
(vi) Identify the people whom the action or decision will impact.
(vii) Predict and analyze the long-term ramification.
(viii) Assess the potential of your action/decision to be misunderstood.
(ix) Ensure that you are transparent in your decisions/actions.
(x) Identify the conditions under which you would allow exceptions to your stand.

FIG. 37.2

Parameters for Determining the Ethics of a Business Decision.

determining the decisions we take are ethical, there comes another question to the mind. We have been working on the premise that the Manager is able to discern what is ethical and is thus able to regulate his behaviour to stay clear of the unethical. The fact is that most of us fall woefully short of our inflated self-perceptions. We are deluded by the illusions that unlike some other we are free of biases and thus will not take an unethical decision. In so far as explicit belief goes we can claim to be unbiased and fair but our decisions and actions are also prey to unconscious thoughts and feelings. Thus the most well meaning person may well be making flawed judgments that are ethically problematic and contrary to our desire to make fair decisions and morally congruent actions. For example in the case of Mahatma Gandhi Talisman that when in doubt about any action or decision just think that would you still do it if your mother knew about your action. This small check helps to ensure ethical action in most people. But what if we ourselves fail to recognize that our actions are unethical and need to be hidden! That is the issue we are now addressing. While it is easy to spot deviations where intentions are *mala fide* it is far more difficult to correct unintentional unethical decision-making. Conventional ethics training can take care of conscious actions but is unable to tackle unintentional unethical decisions. For this a new type of vigilance must be brought to bear. These unethical decisions which are unintentional can be identified as an implicit prejudice a bias which emerges from unconscious belief, bias that favours our own group, conflict of interest and a tendency to over claim credit.

It is said that to know about others is to be learned but to know about oneself is to be wise. Thus to ensure that decision-making in

(i) Rejecting the notion that conscious attitudes always represent what we think they do.
(ii) Abandon our faith in our own ability to fair.
(iii) Reveal the presence of unconscious bias through research which supplies empirical data. Data often turns out to be counter institutive.
(iv) Restructure and reshape your environment for example create an alternative environment which challenges stereotype. Therefore, altering your mind set.
(v) Broaden your outlook and consequently your decision-making prowess.

FIG. 37.3

Overcoming Unintentional Unethical Behaviour

an organization is ethical both intention and unintentional elements of decision-making will have to be weeded out. The challenge is to understand the depth and complexity of ethics and overcome the problem in all its aspects.

Figure 37.4 summarizes the process by which it is proposed that corporate actions and decisions are designed and tested to produce ethically acceptable behaviour.

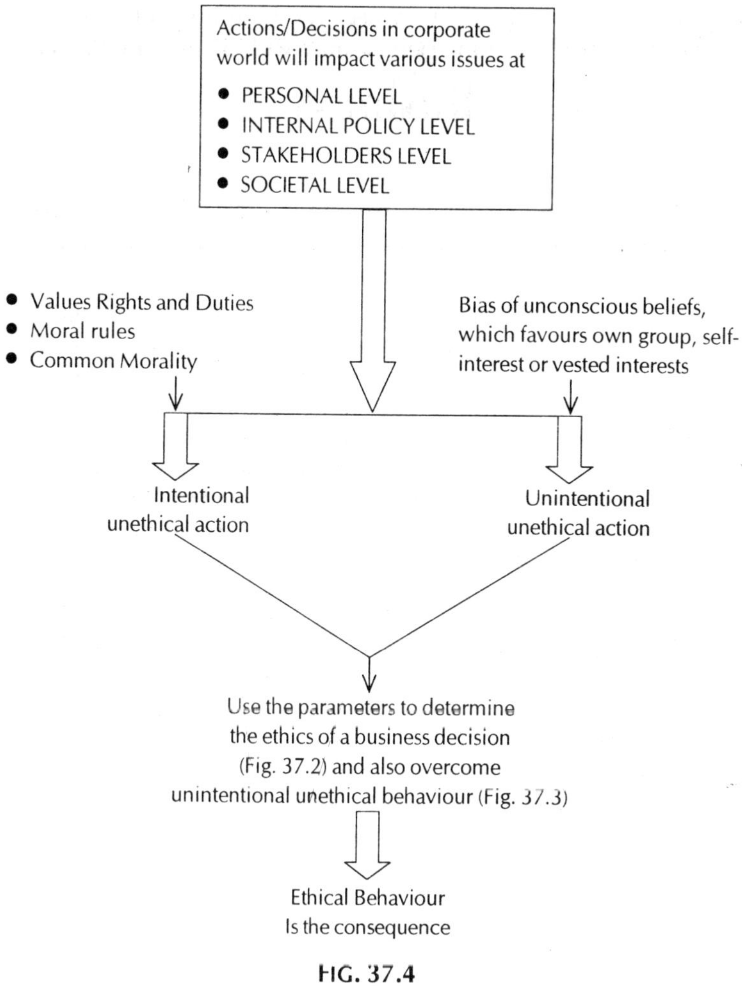

FIG. 37.4

Ensuring Ethical Behaviour at the Work Place.

38

Corporate Social Responsibility in Business

Ashok Nagar, Renu Jatana, and Shweta Rameja

As an economist Milton Friedman said—"the business of business is business". The underlying object of this argument is that the aim of business is optimum utilization of its resources and if everybody in business does that than the society is most benefited. There is one and only one social responsibility of business—to use it resources and engage in activities designed to increase its profits so long as it stays within the rules of the game, which is to say, engages in open and free competition without deception or fraud.

In the modern world, the structure and functions of business have been changing dynamically. Fierce competition, fast innovations with blinking of an eye, modern products and services, diversified business activities has changed the whole profile of business. In narrow approach, the ultimate objective of business is maximization of profit. But when seen in a wide approach, the aim of business is to help the firm in the achievement of set objective. There is consensus on this fact that the ultimate objective of the firm is to maximize welfare of the owners. How can this be maximized? For that two basis are as: (a) Profit maximization and (b) Maximization of wealth.

(a) **Profit maximization:** This objective is based on rationality as profit is indicator of economic efficiency. But sole objective of earning profit ignores social responsibility of the business. It ignores labour, consumer, public and government which are pre-requisites for corporate growth.

(b) **Wealth maximization:** The prices of shares of the company depends not only on earning capacity but also on goodwill, relations with customers, quality services and fulfilment of social responsibility. This objective watches interest of all sections of society and helps the corporate to last long in the innovative market.

A latest survey by the Tata Energy Research Institute (TERI) called 'Altered Images: The 2001 State of Corporate Responsibility in India Poll' traces back the history of CSR in India and suggests that there are four models of CSR as follows:[1]

ETHICAL MODEL

The origin of the first ethical model of corporate responsibility lie in the pioneering efforts of 19th century corporate philanthropists such as the Cadbury brothers in England and the Tata family in India. The pressure on Indian industrialists to demonstrate their commitment to social development increased during the independence movement, when Mahatma Gandhi developed the notion of 'trusteeship', whereby the owners of property would voluntarily manage their wealth on behalf of the people. Gandhi's influence prompted various Indian companies to play active roles in nation building and promoting socio-economic development during the 20th century. The history of Indian corporate philanthropy has encompassed cash or kind donations, community investment in trusts and provision of essential services such as schools, libraries, hospitals, etc. Many firms, particularly 'family-run businesses', continue to support such philanthropic initiatives.

STATIST MODEL

A second model of CSR emerged in India after independence in 1947, when India adopted the socialist and mixed economy framework, with a large public sector and state-owned companies. The boundaries between the state and society were clearly defined for the state enterprises. Elements of corporate responsibility, especially those relating to community and worker relationships, were enshrined in labour laws and management principles. This state sponsored corporate philosophy still operates in the numerous public sector companies that have survived the wave of privatization of the early 1990s.

LIBERAL MODEL

Indeed, the worldwide trend towards privatization and deregulation can be said to be underpinned by a third model of corporate responsibility—that companies are solely responsible to their owners. This approach was encapsulated by the American economist Milton Friedman, who in 1958 challenged the very notion of corporate responsibility for anything other than the economic bottom line.

Many in the corporate world and elsewhere would agree with this concept, arguing that it is sufficient for business to obey the law and generate wealth, which through taxation and private charitable choices can be directed to social ends.

STAKEHOLDER MODEL

The rise of globalisation has brought with it a growing consensus that with increasing economic rights, business also has a growing range of social obligations. Citizen campaigns against irresponsible corporate behaviour along with consumer action and increasing shareholder pressure have given rise to the stakeholder model of corporate responsibility. This view is often associated with R. Edward Freeman, whose seminal analysis of the stakeholder approach to strategic management in 1984 brought stake holding into the mainstream of management literature (Freeman, 1984). According to Freeman, 'a stakeholder in an organisation is any group or individual who can affect or is affected by the achievement of the organisation's objectives'.

Following are considered to be the social responsibility by major corporates:

1. Minimise pollution
2. International accreditation
3. Reduction of waste at source

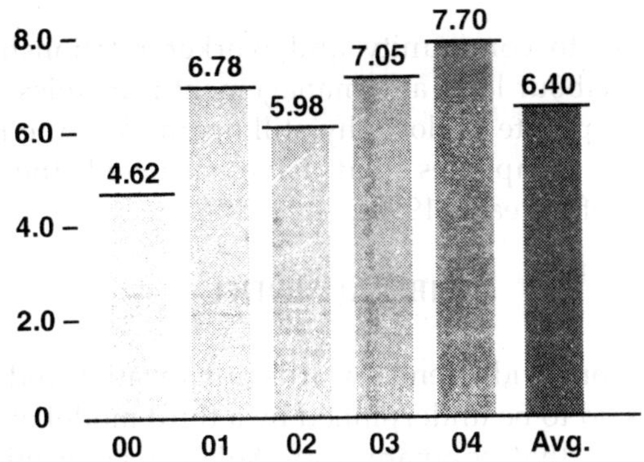

CO_2 Emissions Reductions
Reductions in percentage
Source: www.ibm.com

4. Good labour relations
5. Commitment to stakeholders
6. Quality service to customers
7. Effective abolition of child labour and forced labour etc.

IBM, one of the leading Software Company was ranked 17th in the US Environmental Protection Agency's (EPA) Top 20 Best Workplaces for Commuters (BWC) from among Fortune 500 Companies in 2005. After the earthquake in Pakistan and India the IBM Crisis Response Team was deployed in Islamabad. It is also providing servers, hosting, project management, and support for the applications involved. It also provided ThinkPads to the International Federation of Red Cross in the region, the Pakistan Red Crescent and the Indian Red Cross.[2]

Maruti Udyog Ltd., one of the leading Company in automobiles make people aware about the rights through decent advertisements on Television. Leading Corporates thus try to generate employment opportunities for mass of Indian population through their social responsibility schemes. The name of Dhiru Bhai Ambani is noteworthy in this respect.

Ethical organizations can actually have a ripple effect in the entire economy. Ethical structures discourage unhealthy behaviour and, instead, inspire superior reasoning and performance. It enhances group dynamics, improves communication greatly and lightens the burden of immorality. It increases the flow of knowledge, information and reasoning capabilities. All these are real strategic advantage. Simplistically, a business can be spoken of as a process of adding value to a product or service. This value addition is usually accomplished through people. When business concentrate on the transaction mode and try to maximize profits without worrying about the people and processes adopted to achieve the goals it will sooner or later face problems. Statistically, the more a business does something illegal or unethical, the more likely that it will be caught. A classic example is Enron. When the ethical environment is poor, organizational performance suffers because of poor group dynamics and suppressed communication, which harms openness and vital growth of business. Overall, the morale is badly affected, leaving the organization vulnerable to setbacks.

According to Mr. Anant Nadkarni, General Manager, Group Corporate Social Responsibility of the Tata Group, CSR was not the bottomline of business but the very purpose of it. Sixty-six per cent of the Tata Group's profits are spent through trusts. The Tatas spend Rs. 160 crore on community development every year and another Rs. 100 crore annually on environment management. Mr. Nadkarni said that while it was important for corporates to make profits, it should not be their sole aim. "When you discharge your social obligations by choice, it becomes an initiative and not just a responsibility," he said.

Thus the mantra for Indian business should be "Go Global in every aspect": in ambitions, in commitment to business ethics, in corporate governance, in value creation, in communication practices, in everything".-Dr. Jamshed J. Irani, Director, Tata Sons Ltd.

REFERENCES

1. *Corporate Social Responsibility* by Dr. Shankar Adawal.
2. www.ibm.com

OTHER REFERENCES

1. Sessions on Corporate Social Responsibility (US India Business Council Annual Meeting), Dr. Jamshed J. Irani, Director, Tata Sons Ltd.
2. Corporate Social Responsibility: Perceptions of Indian Business by Kate Brown.

3. *The Hindu Business Line*—Corporate Social Responsibility.
4. ITC E-Choupal Corporate Social Responsibility in Agriculture.
5. Indian Oil Corporation Ltd.—Global Compact.
6. http://ecophilo.blogspot.com
7. www.indianeconomy.org
8. www.articlecube.com
9. www.itcportal.com
10. www.cbmworld.org
11. *Ethical Business: Never out of Fashion* by M.V. Subbiah (Former Chairman/ Murugappa Group).

39

Setting Rules, Picking Winners: Multilateral Financial Institutions and the Global Managerial Order

JONATHAN MURPHY

This paper examines the process of construction of an appropriate global corporation. It demonstrates the detailed selection and rule-making process, driven by global elite interests crystallized within the institutional frameworks of the World Bank and the European Bank for Reconstruction and Development, involved in the restructuring of the global steel industry. Through an analysis of the meteoric rise of Lakshmi Mittal's Ispat Corporation to global dominance of the steel industry, the paper exposes the myth of free market globalization. It further shows that despite the multilateral financial institutions' rhetorical commitment to corporate ethical conduct and social responsibility, they either directly or indirectly countenanced breaching contracts and national laws to favour a particular company, suspension of environmental standards, non-transparent privatization of state property, and the use of tax havens in violation of OECD guidelines.

The first Multilateral Financial Institutions (MFIs) were established at the 1944 Bretton Woods Conference, with the intention of preventing the global economic instability that had helped lead to World War II, and ensuring that adequate capital was available for balanced international reconstruction and development. During the Cold War, the MFIs were overshadowed by global geopolitics, but as the Soviet Union entered its terminal crisis in the 1980's, they began designing the architecture of a new global order, built on free trade and privatized economies.

The global steel industry was an early target for the MFI privatizers. Many developing countries had established state-owned steel industries as part of a developmentalist strategy to build industrial infrastructure. In the 1970's and 1980's they were hit with falling commodity prices and high energy costs, just as neo-liberalism's simple solutions for economic problems captured the MFIs' imaginations. As developing (and later transitional) countries arrived at the Banks' doorsteps asking for bailouts, they were presented with a rigid set of 'conditionalities'; high up on the list was privatization of state-owned industries.

Since the 1950's, Mohan Lal Mittal has headed Ispat Industries, a moderately successful Indian domestic steel-maker. In 1976, Mittal's son Lakshmi left India to oversee construction of a small Greenfield Steel Plant in Indonesia for his father. For over ten years Lakshmi operated the single Indonesian plant under the umbrella of his father's company.

One of the first plants to be privatized under MFI pressure was Trinidad's Iscott, which became Lakshmi Mittal's first acquisition in 1989. Mittal separated his business from that of his father, and over the next fifteen years, purchased former state plants in Mexico, Canada, Germany, Algeria, Kazakhstan, Romania, the Czech Republic, Ireland, South Africa, and Poland, as well as several formerly private plants, to become the world's largest steel-maker. In 2004, Mittal was judged the wealthiest resident of Britain (where he relocated in the 1990's).

This paper will explore several of them. Ispat's corporate structure is complex, with both publicly-traded and privately-held wings, the latter incorporated in the Netherlands Antilles tax haven. Accusations of corrupt payments have accompanied several of the acquisitions. Nevertheless, Ispat has become a favoured client of the MFIs, receiving several hundred million dollars in loans, as well as benefiting from the Bank's 'convening power'; its ability to grant emerging companies legitimacy with vendors, particularly state actors.

This paper details the relationship between Ispat and the multilateral financial institutions as a case study in the creation of a global managerial elite that spans across the MFIs, globalizing corporations, and state actors. The case highlights the need for greater transparency in the global marketplace, and particularly in the operations of the multilateral financial institutions.

The paper is based on archival research, field research in Kazakhstan including interviews with Ispat executives, and interviews with multilateral financial institution representatives in Kazakhstan and London.

40

Whistleblowing Policies as Corporate Social Responsibility and Corporate Governance Apparatuses: Rationales and Legislation

WIM VANDEKERCKHOVE

Today, whistleblowing can be described as people blowing the whistle on organizations operating within the context of globalization of private capital oriented economy. Whistleblowing policies then are aimed at institutionalizing whistleblowing by protecting whistleblowers under specified conditions.

This paper develops rationales for whistleblowing policies within the context of Corporate Social Responsibility (CSR) and Corporate Governance (CG), and looks into a number of whistleblowing legislations to examine to what extent these legislated whistleblowing policies match the rationales.

Globalization has pushed the description of corporate activity in terms of network metaphors. In this sense, both CSR and CG mechanisms can be regarded as apparatuses of 'network governance'. In other words, CSR and CG involve mechanisms safeguarding the power balance amongst organizational stakeholders.

CSR activities represent the influence of societal norms on corporate activity and CSR communications aim at proving corporate activity abides by societal norms.

CG standards are identifying and ensuring power balance among management, boards and shareholders.

Hence, both CSR and CG entail accountability through information streams about corporate activity. In turn, whistle blowing can also be regarded as a generator of information about corporate activity.

The paper specifies how whistleblowing policies can constitute the institutionalization of whistleblowing into CSR and CG apparatuses. Rationales are developed as to how whistleblowing finds its legitimation in the contexts of respectively CSR and CG. From these rationales, criteria are identified that need to be met if a concrete whistleblowing policy is to be regarded as a CSR or CG apparatus. These criteria are formulated at the level of actor element (who can blow the whistle), subject element (about what can the whistle be blown) and recipient element (to whom can the whistle be blown).

Finally, the paper looks at a number of whistle blowing legislations covering the private sector such as the Public Interest Disclosure Act (UK), the Organizational Sentencing Guidelines (US), the Sarbanes-Oxley Act (US), the Protected Disclosure Act (South Africa) and the CLERP9 Regulations (Australia), to examine to what extent these legislated policies can be regarded as CSR and CG apparatuses.

41

Weaving Sustainable Development into Corporate Governance

FABRICE MAULEON AND MARY M. MCKINLEY

The recent scandals in large companies, such as Tyco, WorldCom, Xerox, Parmalat or Enron, lead one to think that there must be a serious weakness in the system of operation of large international firms at the level of their governance and, by extension, of the contemporary capitalist system. This alarmist report obliges one to reconsider the relations between the persons in charge of the large companies on the one hand, and the whole of their parts on the other hand: their shareholders first, but also their employees, their suppliers, their creditors and, more largely, various categories of agents or institutions affected by the decisions or activities of these large companies, i.e. the stakeholders. These "bad businesses" are not generalized; the world, extremely fortunately, is composed of many companies that function very well. There are chinks in the armour of any operating company: market deregulation, for instance, sees many companies flee to the shelter of tax havens, safe from all sanction; company directors tempted by stock options may lose sight forever of the company's true interest. Then there are auditors paid by the companies they're supposed to oversee and bankers who confuse their fiscal and advisory duties, becoming both judge and interested party. The situation is not helped by the laissez-faire attitudes of certain regulatory bodies. . . .

The beginning of the 21st century finds us thus in search of better governance of companies as there clearly is a need for corporations that would be responsible and accountable for their actions. The sustainable development concept does call for a generalized attitude of responsibility within the three pillars of financial, social and environmental reporting. However, in the search for a virtuous circle that the inception of this famous "economic triptych" represents, social and environmental improvements cannot be accomplished in the corporation without the installation of good governance. The two concepts are thus closely interdependent. The bond between the concept of corporate governance and sustainable development is doubly justified: it is, on the one hand, a fact that the most recent decisions in the principal Western governments place ethics and corporate responsibility at the heart of their reforms; at the same time, the institution of better corporate governance compels us to define the contours of a renewed contract among leaders of companies, shareholders, employees, suppliers and regulators.

This paper proposes to weave the bond between the sustainable development concept and corporate governance. The latter has just undergone a crisis that has shaken the confidence of the shareholders and investors. The economic actors are thus today in search of the principles and healthy practices to restore that lost confidence. The principles of sustainable development prove to be one of the possible solutions to stop this crisis and to erase this feeling of distrust. We will thus explore in what sense these two domains share the same preoccupations with a renewal of stronger, more trustworthy regulation of the economic market. We will then show how sustainable development and good corporate governance can be mutually nourished through their principles and practices.

42

Is it True that Social Responsibility Studies can Cause an Assimilation Problem, and Why?

R. SEMINUR TOPAL

WHAT IS CSR?

There are a variety of definitions of CSR and no overall agreement. Johnson's (2003) definition is: "CSR is concerned with treating the stakeholders of the firm ethically or in a responsible manner." 'Ethically or responsible' means treating stakeholders in a manner deemed acceptable in civilized societies. Social responsibility includes economic responsibility. Stakeholders exist both within a firm and outside. The natural environment is a stakeholder. The wider aim of social responsibility is to create ever higher standards of living, while preserving the profitability of the corporation, for people both within and outside the corporation. CSR therefore means the ethical behaviour of a business towards its constituencies or stakeholders. Nevertheless, there are a wide variety of concepts and definitions associated with the term "Corporate Social Responsibility (CSR)", but no general agreement of terms.

Managers must accept the notion of social responsibility before they work out what to do. There is no argument about the fact that, once it has been accepted, the next step is the response, or in other words that acceptance of the motivation to be socially responsible immediately leads the manager into what should be done next, that is into social responsiveness. Acceptance does not, of course, come easily and much work is going on around the world to show that corporate social responsibility makes sound economic, as well as social, ethical, political and philosophical sense. I include economic aspects in my definition of CSR simply because the study of economics is a "social" science which also encompasses financial aspects. The triple bottom line (TBL) is also implicit, since the third part of the triple is the environment, and I have always considered the environment to be one of the stakeholders of a company and the aim is to improve corporate responsibility and protect shareholders. (BFSR, 2002.)

CSR is an important factor for employee motivation and in attracting and retaining top quality employees. Corporate citizenship can provide business benefits in eight areas (Anon, 2005):

- Reputation management;
- Risk profile and risk management;
- Employee recruitment, motivation and retention;
- Investor relations and access to capital;
- Learning and innovation;
- Competitiveness and market positioning;
- Operational efficiency; and
- License to operate.

Therefore measured on the basis of the configuration of the business organization into three levels, or the *Triple-P approach to CSR:*

Principles of social responsibility;
Processes of social responsiveness;
Products (or outcomes) as they relate to the firm's societal relationships.

These can then naturally be further divided into the principles, processes and outcomes for each stakeholder group. The approach must concentrate on defining exactly what is meant by a corporation's responsibility to its stakeholders, who they are and how to measure progress through a limited number of precise key indicators. Three elements are identified as being basic to this level of the CSR model:

- *Business environment scanning* indicates the information gathering arm of the business and the transmission of the information gathered throughout the organization.
- *Stakeholder management.* A stakeholder is defined as any group or individual which can affect or is affected by the achievement of the firm's objectives, such as owners, suppliers, employees, customers, competitors, domestic and foreign governments, non-profit organizations and environmental and consumer protection groups. Stakeholder management refers to mapping the relationships of stakeholders to the firm (and among each other) whilst finding, listening and meeting their expectations that legitimate concerns should be balanced and met as a prerequisite for any measurement process.
- *Issues management.* Having identified the motivating principles of a firm and determined the identities, relationships and power of stakeholders, the researcher now turns to the main issues which concern stakeholders. (Anon, 2005.)

Corporate Social Responsibility (CSR) is an instrument of positive change taking place in organisations and businesses. It sets the framework and defines the method by which organisations and businesses must operate to be able to meet the ethical, legal, commercial and public expectations that a society has of any organisation. This means that they will need to undergo a major mind-shift and culture change to become socially, environmentally and economically responsible towards their employees, shareholders and the stakeholders involved. Corporate Social Responsibility is also an approach to be takes into account the social impact an organisation has on the community both local and global. The main aim of the concept is to bring together all sectors (public, voluntary and business) and work together to eliminate the old idea that economic and environmental issues are in conflict.

DEVELOPING PERSONAL AND SOCIAL RESPONSIBILITY

Human nature, all too often, seeks the lowest level of responsibility while seeking the highest expression of freedom and rights. When left unchecked, this often translates into disobedience, disruption, violence, truancy, early pregnancy, drug abuse and, in general, a lack of appropriate self-control and motivation in young people. Schools can play important leadership roles with students, parents and the community in teaching responsibility skills. The ideas, suggestions and model curricula set forth in Developing Personal and Social Responsibility are designed to serve as a framework on which to build successful programmes aimed at training young people to be responsible citizens. By transforming the way any business is conducted – internally and externally – companies can now maintain their success and growth and achieve sustainability. (Dunham, 1998.)

CORPORATE SOCIAL RESPONSIBILITY—A GROWING MOVEMENT ACROSS THE WORLD

To move human society to live in ways that protect the environment and its capacity to provide for the needs and aspirations of current and future generations must be the mission for all people. Corporate Social Responsibility necessitates a growing movement of concerned people across the world. Probably the feature that most starkly contrasts community building with approaches to poverty alleviation that have been typical over the past half-century is that its primary aim is not simply giving more money, services, or other material benefits to the poor. While most of its advocates recognize a continuing need for considerable outside assistance (public and private), community building's central theme is to obliterate feelings of dependency and to replace them with attitudes of self-reliance, self-confidence, and responsibility.

Biological resources are vital to humanity's economic and social development. As a result, there is a growing recognition that biological diversity is a global asset of tremendous value to present and future generations. At the same time, the threat to species and ecosystems has never been so great as it is today. Species extinction caused by human activities continues at an alarming rate. Protection of the environment and having sustainable development, and such interrelated concerns of the international system as population, conflict-resolution, governance, human-rights, trade, and women's and children's rights, are the most important phenomena in this millennium. Honour the earth provides grants to groups representing the pulse of the native environmental justice movement. Money is critically needed to strengthen the capacity of communities to protect lands, way of life and future generations. Although Small, these grants have high impact in forwarding front line environmental efforts. Working to build broad public support for communities to break the isolation and invisibility of environmental issues and create a stronger voice for the earth. (Hopkins, 2004.)

FEATURED IN LEADING PERSPECTIVES

There is increasing recognition that the current "system" for achieving good labour and environmental practices in global supply chains through private codes of conduct and monitoring, is not working. With a focus on developing nations, presents recommendations identifying ways the public sector can mobilize its resources and those of others to improve delivery on these important goals. Reputation is built around intangibles such as trust, reliability, quality, consistency, credibility, relationships and transparency, and tangibles such as investment in people, diversity and the environment. Instead of this, in order to reach final goals, CSR must discussed or established from the 3 different performance values—economic performance, environmental performance and social performance. These are also known as the triple bottom line.

Human rights abuses are linked to efforts to control two key gold mining areas in the Disability Rights Commission (DRC) and layout the responsibility which the government of the DRC and also the trans-national companies have in that process. (Anon, 2004.) There is increasing recognition that the current "*system*" for achieving good labour and environmental practices in global supply chains through private codes of conduct and monitoring, is not working. With a focus on developing nations, presented recommendations, identifying ways the public sector can mobilize its resources and those of others to improve delivery on these important goals. Considering humanity's heritage, it's no surprise that they consider a strong sense of social responsibility to be one of our most important corporate values. In fact, we can trace the roots of who we are today back to one man's commitment to improving life for the hearing impaired. We realize that with innovation and progress come responsibility. For helping to change the way the world communicates—without losing sight of our obligations to its resources and its people. Every day, engineers are working to develop new materials and processes that make many products more environmentally responsible. Every day, must be ensured that suppliers are providing consumers with energy-efficient goods and services. And also every day, for finding ways to give back to the communities where someone lives and works. To ensure that the conclusions reflect actual rather than perceived needs, from comprising 50 disabled people (BFSR, 2002), including people with a variety of impairments most affected by web accessibility problems, being:

- blindness,
- partial sight,
- dyslexia,
- *profound deafness,* including people who are Sign Language users, and hearing impairment, and
- *physical impairments* such as lack of control of arms and hands, tremor or lack of dexterity in hands and fingers.

As bringing the world closer together, all must remain committed to upholding their core values:

- A total focus on serving customers;
- A commitment to business excellence, demonstrated by a focus on results, innovation, quality, speed and the highest standard of business ethics;
- A deep respect for the contributions of each person to the team;
- A strong sense of *social responsibility.*

Working hard to create new possibilities that enhance people's lives by transforming the way the world communicates. Along the way, to help make the world a little better, must be the main target for all scientists. The science of behaviour and cultural analysis has much to offer to organizations and movements interested in social justice and human rights, who are *"acting to save the world"* (Skinner, 1987). Behaviour analysts are strongly encouraged to work with and join the following networks, and to contribute what they know in respectful ways to these efforts.

If people are to achieve "sustainability", the first steps must be to *learn to think and dialogue systemically in terms of levels of consciousness, connectedness, and processes.* All ethics and policy principles and practices are derived from or can be explained by four concepts that lie at the root of applied ethics: *shared purpose, informed choice, responsibility, learning and growth.* As a guiding principle, moreover, the first among these four equals is "shared purpose". The challenge to applied ethics is to integrate ethics and policy theory and practice to be consistent with them.

Effective managers know that success comes from assigning tasks according to individual and group abilities, and then combining those efforts to achieve a shared purpose. The same dynamic is necessary in applied ethics, but seems to have gone largely unrecognized. Ethicists analyzed the broad discipline of ethics to meet immediate needs. Now it is time to synthesize what ethicists and managers have learned from study and experience.

The complexity of organizational life demands a direct tie between ethics and policy and rejection of simple formulas or sets of universal values. However, applied ethics has responded by developing increasingly sophisticated, but separate, and narrow approaches: *business ethics, government ethics, codes of professional ethics, and environmental ethics.* Managers now need a model harmonizing these approaches: a tool to raise and treat the ethics issues they face daily. With the integration of ethical approaches, the manager approaches *ethical complexity* equipped to achieve shared goals. Without integration, a toolbox of such narrow approaches results only in bounded ethical framing, ineffective ethical choice, impotent ethical leadership, and unethical actions: in sum, *ethical chaos.* Applied ethics specialities may have lost sight of what traditional ethics was trying to accomplish: *a good life for good people over a lifetime in society with others.* Ethical integration is essential for all organizations. (Hopkins, 2004.)

Ethics and policy integration are essential for all organizations, but let us use health care—a basic human need—to flesh out a framework integrating applied ethics and social responsibility is may be especially true for health care, where there is a prevailing frustration among health care providers: *"Business and health care do not mix."* But, where health care is provided and funded by business, and received by business employees (and their families) as a significant part of compensation, this proposition is untenable. (Hopkins, 1999, 2004.) It reflects an unintegrated approach to health care ethics can take as same as "main model of systematical applications" (Fig. 42.1).

Within the *Ethics of Essential Social Responsibility* are three broad categories: *government, for-profit,* and *not-for-profit.* Each has broadly different responsibilities within society that, which are *of the essence* of its nature. Each has different stakeholders key participants. Each

Levels of Ethical Responsibility

Levels	Inputs	Participant(s)	Ethical Outcome
1. The Group	Customs and debate from other two levels	Society	Rules
2. The Individual	Customs, rules and debate from other two levels	Individual	Personal value system
3. Ethnic Definition	Customs and rules established by other levels	Singular ethical concept	Philosophy Absolute or Situational

FIG 42.1

Systematics of the Ethical Responsibility Levels

(http://highered.mcgraw-hill.com/sites/dl/free/0072415444/22499/new02002.jpg)

has different constraints on action. The essence of government is the appropriate application of its monopoly on the exercise of coercion and violence: the police, the military, and the courts. Its unique stakeholders participants are governors, the governed, and taxpayers. Bureaucracy and stability characterizes its institutions. The essence of for-profits is meeting the most urgent needs of owners and consumers of goods and services through free exchange: business and the professions. Its unique stakeholders are owners and consumers.

While the responsibilities of government and the not-for-profits seem relatively straightforward, it is helpful to think of social responsibility for business as occupying at least three distinct levels. The three levels of business social responsibility reflect the essential characteristic of business as meeting the most urgent needs of consumers and the common characteristics of members of society.

The *Ethics of Ecological Relationships,* or, *Environmental Ethics* is the domain of the relationships between species and the evolving world of which we are an integral part. It is the most fundamental of all approaches to applied ethics. It must an obligation, to believe the rest of the world to be, is, and peoples' relationship share the world as a whole. In its most fundamental and comprehensive form, it is contains each individual's worldview. *Organizational ethics* makes a difference. Ethical leadership is difficult. The bounds of responsibility for the care of a patient in a large hospital are often unclear, perhaps even, purposefully blurred. Biomedical ethics ignores the systemic, organizational issues that Chambliss calls "ethical problems" as opposed to "ethical dilemmas". It ignores the difference between these and "ethical conditions", which cannot be changed, they just are and need to be dealt with, not solved. As a result, health care providers are left vulnerable to feelings of hypocrisy and fear when situations they deal with on a *daily* basis demand a broader view for resolution than biomedical ethics permits. Taking such a narrow view results in physician decisions being constantly second-guessed by responsible others, who have different, equally limited, ethical and policy perspectives. It places physicians and nurses into situations where they feel hypocritical precisely because they do, *in fact,* make decisions based upon the limited time, energy, and, yes, money available. Again, using health care ethics as the example, on the *theoretical* level, we must put biomedical ethics into perspective and develop a truly comprehensive approach to *health care* ethics. Such an approach would take into account broader individual and social responsibilities. It would deal with the environmental aspects. It would address the toll the health care systems places on its practitioners. On the *practical* level, we need structures and systems integrating diverse ethical perspectives. (Johnson, 2003.)

The *Ethics of Ecological Relationships* must be considered as health care takes place within a context of evolving life. We influence evolution in many ways, ours and other livesfe's—and potential livefe's (next generations). These ecological relationships define us; "One way is whether we are in harmony with our world, or at war with it". Whether we contribute to the world as a place for evolution, learning, and growth, or exploit it only as a means to maintaining existence. Even more at issue are the limits on action that we recognize on our capacity to influence the course of nature—and the evolution that naturally occurs within it. The fact that we have the authority to shape our lives, that is, the power to do something, does not mean that it should be done. It is helpful to organize the SKUA point ("SKUA" means; lie the skills, knowledge, understanding and attitudes. It is necessary for shared purposes to be achieved into eight elements of ethics and policy integration (Johnson, 2003):

- **Caring:** consciousness, awareness, commitment, and/or compassion.

- **Comprehensive thinking:** critical, creative, and systemic thinking; choosing, judgement.
- **Communicating:** dialogue involving feelings and ideas.
- **Cooperating:** inquiry and action.
- **Exercising authority:** leadership, followership, participation.
- **Knowledge:** surfacing, capturing, sharing knowledge, including that which is tacit; knowing what you know, and what you don't know.
- **Pride:** self-esteem; stakeholder satisfaction and loyalty; and community sense of being.
- **Time:** time preference, time frame, time available.

Visualizing such a matrix, there is for each of the eight elements a package of training, education, and development to build and shape the SKUA required to be competent. Moreover, for ethics and policy to be integrated toward systemic thinking and dialøgue and cooperative inquiry, action, and learning, these SKUA need to be developed at all levels of society: individual, family, organizational, community, nation, and global. So we need serious, concerted efforts to integrate applied ethics and social responsibility at all levels, especially health care ethics at all levels. The Applied Ethics and Policy Integration Model demonstrated here provides a foundation for the ethics and policy leader, academic, health care provider, and others. It allows them to take a formal structural approach toward integrating biomedical, at least biomedical, nursing, and organizational ethics with its essential social responsibilities, and those of other key stakeholders in the health care system, including the environment.

Hopes for building sustainable communities—socially, culturally, and physically—most be founded on learning to think and dialogue systemically. The Applied Ethics and Policy Integration Model provides a framework bringing together the remarkable work that has been done in ethics and policy toward that end. It is founded, in turn, on the four fundamental concepts of shared purpose, informed choice, responsibility, and learning and growth.

Developed workforce comprises people across a range of ages, backgrounds, nationalities, and cultures. We know that to achieve business excellence around the world, our decisions must be based on the widest range of perspectives and contributions. Diversity also is expressed in many platform like "Employee Business Partner

Groups" that meet the needs of different ethnic and social groups. When talking about value of people, not only mean at employees, but all people, many of whom are directly or indirectly effected by the provided services. Common purpose is "Creating new possibilities to enhance people's lives by transforming the way the world communicates." The essence of ideal work is bringing *"people together – to connect"*.

From this perspective, recognizing that when employees enjoy their work and are proud of what they do, it shows in the quality of service to all customers.

Many of employees operate in a teamwork environment, creating a sense of camaraderie and interdependence to fulfil business requirements that meet the needs of customers. Also having an incredibly rich heritage of innovation and challenging problems still to solve which excites all of us to be with this strategic plan. This must be why coming to work everyday. Employees are the heart of the company/public sectors and are the key to this competitive success in a global marketplace. Their energy, intelligence and knowledge of networks is what differentiates from the other competitors. An ironclad commitment for employees has to (Hopkins, 2004):

- Promote an open and supportive work environment.
- Value diversity in all its forms.
- Encourage the candid expression of ideas.
- Allow a free exchange of points of view to make the best business decisions.
- Support each other in the pursuit of common goals.
- Help employees strive for breakthrough performance.

As a socially responsible employer, must respect their employees' interests in, and endeavour to provide a safe and supportive workplace; *fair policies and procedures regarding hiring and dismissal; equal treatment for all employees; and opportunities to contribute to the company's success through challenging work.* Employment at work remains "at will", meaning that, except as modified in contracts covering specifically identified individuals or union represented employees, the employment relationship may be terminated by the employee or employer at any time, for any reason. Company policies and procedures may be altered at any time, at the company's discretion, and are not intended to, and do not create contractual obligations. (Johnson, 2003.)

WINNING ENVIRONMENT—WINNING TEAM

One of popular strategic areas of focus over the next five years is the infusion of a *"Winning Environment – Winning Team"* philosophy within most of global business operations. This involves creating an environment where everyone (Rogerson and Gotterbarn, 2005; Anon., 2005):

- is passionate about winning.
- is accountable and empowered to make decisions to get their jobs done.
- has the right skills being applied in the right places to achieve winning results.
- is eligible to receive awesome rewards for awesome results.
- views diversify as a source of their competitive advantage.

Recommended committees to recruiting high calibre employees and providing them with the information and training needed to perform at the highest standards during their careers. Career development occurs as a result of a successful combination of training, on the job coaching and opportunities for self-development. Employees are encouraged to develop to their maximum potential. Popular foster an environment where innovation is encouraged and creativity rewarded. Individuals or teams are recognized for their efforts. Equally, employees need to have a voice, to have their views listened to and their ideas acted upon. Leaders proactively seek and listen to employees' views, as well as share information on the status of the company's attainment of business goals. This is done in a myriad of ways, including employer, local town forums and regular employee surveys. To monitor of progress towards accomplishing the most business strategy, performance criteria include both financial and non-financial measures, such as customer or students satisfaction. Also regularly conduct a global employee engagement survey to monitor their level of satisfaction with leadership and with their work environment. (Hopkins, 1999, 2004.)

WHAT IS ASSIMILATION?

Assimilation, from Latin *assimilatio* meaning *"to render similar"*, is used to describe various phenomena: The process of assimilating new ideas into a cognitive structure. In linguistics *assimilation* may also refer to the process of integrating a loanword, and if needed adapt it, into the system of the receiving language. The conversion of nutrient into the fluid or solid substance of the body, by the processes of digestion and absorption as biological function. The ability of water to purify itself of pollutants. The process whereby a minority group gradually adopts the customs and attitudes of the prevailing culture as sociological means. In economy, the absorption of a new issue by the public after all shares have been sold by the underwriting group. (Wikipedia, 2005.)

Process used by the fictional Borg race to integrate a being into the collective structure. The assimilation caused (Lee, 2003):

1: Confusion.
2: Frustration.
3: Anxiety . . .
4: Anger . . . Natively, cannot adapt to either culture. It was sort of a psychological brain-teaser.
5: Bitterness . . .

So they had feelings:

Self worthlessness.
Self-hatred.
Grief.
Anger.
Sadness.

At the end of all, these feelings created:

a. Anti-social behaviour such as child and espousal abuse.
b. Self-destruction, suicide, drugs, alcoholism, accidents (non-sensical risks) a feeling of it doesn't matter, lack of purpose and sexual promiscuity (Lee, 2003.)

In the social sciences, **assimilation** is the process of integration whereby immigrants, or other minority groups, are "absorbed" into a generally larger community. This presumes a loss of an characteristics which make the newcomers different. A region where assimilation is occurring is sometimes referred to as a "**melting pot**". Assimilation can be voluntary, which is usually the case with immigrants, or forced upon a group, as is usually the case with the receiving "host" group. Immigration, as held by some, is generally thought to be in the interest of the politically and economically powerful elites and not in the interest of the weak. This integration, or "making many into one", is one of the goals of affirmative action. Where national groups are strongly urged to assimilate, there is often much resistance in spite of the use of governmental force. (Wikipedia, 2005.) Assimilation application tiring some problem as summarized below:

Immigration

Socially pressured to adapt, the immigrant is generally the one who takes the steps to integrate the new environment he is in. Learning the language of the country or region, making new friends, new contacts, finding a job or going to school is all that is needed. The adaptation is made more difficult when the immigrant does not speak the language of his or her new home. Host, or "majority", cultures adapt by accepting newcomers as their own, and often giving them preferential treatment over themselves. Many times large scale immigration causes political unrest in societies which permit meaningful elections.

Minority Cultures

Assimilation can have negative implications for national minorities or aboriginal cultures, in that after assimilation the distinctive features of the original culture will be minimized and may disappear altogether. This is especially true in situations where the institutions of the dominant culture initiate programmes to assimilate or integrate minority cultures. The assumption of integration, the making into one society, lies behind efforts for affirmative action.

Assimilation is or has been the official language policy of many countries around the world, for better or for worse. (Lee, 2003.) It is kind of results of hegemony feelings.

HEGEMONY

Hegemony is the dominance of one group over other groups, with or without the threat of force, to the extent that, for instance, the dominant party can dictate the terms of trade to its advantage; or more broadly, that cultural perspectives become skewed to favour the dominant group. Throughout history, cultural and political power in any arena has rarely achieved a perfect balance, but hegemony results in the empowerment of certain cultural beliefs, values, and practices to the submersion and partial exclusion of others. Hegemony affects the perspective of mainstream history as written by the cultural victors for a sympathetic readership. The official history of Christianity, marginalizing its defined "heresies", provides a richly-exampled arena of cultural hegemony. (Wikipedia, 2005.)

ASSIMILATION: CAN BE A RESULT OF SOCIAL RESPONSIBILITY APPROACH AND APPLICATION

ConEstablishment types assume that "assimilation" works automatically, sort of like "osmosis", to solve any minor cultural problems created by heavy immigration. As similar as; genetic assimilation is difficult to "prove" in natural conditions. However, it can be demonstrated in the laboratory by Waddington. Waddington was one of the first developmental geneticists and a person who did not believe that genetics, embryology, and evolution were separate sciences (he called the fusion of these disciplines "diachronic biology" and worked in each area) showed that *Drosophila* had a particular reaction norm in its response to ether. Embryos exposed to ether at a particular stage developed a phenotype similar to the *bithorax* mutation, and had wing-like halters. Generation after generation was exposed to ether and the ones showing the altered metathoracic development were selectively bred each time. By twenty generations, the mated *Drosophila* produced the mutant phenotype even when ether was no longer applied. Interestingly, the *bithorax*-like phenotype had been assimilated by other genes, not *bithorax*. So assimilation, can appear as the amalgamation and modification of newly perceived information and experiences into the existing cognitive structure.

Organizational ethics applies to all organizational life, regardless of specific social purpose. The thrust of organizational ethics is to increase human authority, energy, knowledge, and trust—, and to drive out fear. It shapes the *conditions* of organizational life, the *content* of dialogue or conflict resolution, and the *context* for the ethical framing, communicating, choosing, learning, and actingons of the other circles. It is where ethical leadership may perhaps best be exercised, again at all levels. (Johnson, 2003.) Superior performance in today's world has both a moral and a financial dimension. *Organizational Integrity* provides the ethical foundation for organization design and development. It goes beyond the particular concerns of business ethics, governmental ethics, professional ethics, and environmental ethics to address how people responsibly expand their range of informed choice to achieve shared purposes. It, in turn, embodies two exciting approaches to the ethics and practices of organizations in an era of globalization. (Epic, 2003.)

There is a need to also focus on the broader impacts of the software. Software projects and programs can be significantly improved by two activities: (1) project management, which is well understood, and (2) analysis of the impact of activities on relevant stakeholders. The SoDIS (Software Development Impact Statement) process consists of four stages (Goldstone, 2003, 2004):

1. The identification of the project type together with immediate and extended stakeholders in a project.
2. The identification of the tasks in a particular phase of a software development project.
3. The association of every task with every stakeholder using structured questions to determine the possibility of specific project risks generated by that particular association.
4. Completing the analysis by stating the concern and the severity of the risk to the project and the stakeholder, and recording a possible risk mitigation or risk avoidance strategy.

Mostly work gives man nobility, and turns him into an animal. "Attention to organizational ethics surfaces the nobility of enterprise and employee alike to achieve a genuine sense of community. Forth a systems approach to organizational design and development. Holistic, it considers the mind, body, and spirit of those involved or affected by the organization. Interdisciplinary, it brings together insights from anthropology, psychology, sociology, political economics, sociobiology, literature, management theory and practice, science and technology, and, of course, philosophy to help leaders find and assert the balances needed to achieve organizational purposes and serve human need." (Epic, 2003.)

So finally can say that; social responsibility cannot cause an assimilation application in civilized organisations and countries. Otherwise it brings only negative results for the managements and worker. Also it brings undevelopmental negativeness and erosion on countrial image. All people must have to learn the rules of sharing earth. For helping to make a better world, we must share all cultures, ideas, successes, and feelings as a stakeholder.

> "If you want to build a ship, then don't drum up men to gather wood, give orders, and divide the work. Rather, teach them to yearn for the far and endless sea."
>
> — Antoine de Saint-Exupery

> There is no simple universal formula for solving ethical problems. We have to choose from our codes of conduct whichever rules are appropriate to the case in hand; the outcome of those choices makes us who we are.
>
> — Sir Adrian Cadbury

References

Anon, 2004: The Web Access and Inclusion for Disabled People. A formal investigation conducted by the Disability Rights Commission, London: TSO. Printed in the United Kingdom for The Stationery Office. ISBN 0 11 703287 5 © Disability Rights Commission 2004. hllp://www.drc-gb.org/publicationsandreports/2.pdf. http://www.w3.org/TR/WCAG10

Anon, 2005: Social Responsibility Profit. Levels of Moral Development. Cyber College Internet Campus. *In-Class Writing Assignment.* http://cybercollege.com/moral.htm

Anon, 2005: A Collaborative Framework for Guiding Post-MFA Actions. MFA Forum. March 2005. www.accountability.org.uk/research/default.asp?pageid = 180

BFSR, 2002: Behaviour Analysis Webring site owned by Behaviourists for Social Responsibility. http://www.bfsr.org/hr.html. http://www.bfsr.org/meta.html. http://www.bfsr.org/index.html. http://www.abainternational.org/

EPIC, 2003: Essential Aspects of Corporate Responsibility Programmes, Ethics and Policy Integration Centre. http://www.epic-online.net/introduction.html

Dunham, R.B., 1998: Introduction to Organizational Behaviour. http-instruction_bus_wise_edu-obdemo-lectures-intro_web-img017_jpg

Goldstone, R.L., 2004: Believing is seeing. American Psychological Society Observer, 17, 23-26. http://www.psychologicalscience.org/observer/getArticle.cfm?id = 1595

Goldstone, R.L., 2003: "Learning to Perceive while Perceiving to Learn" in R. Kimchi, M. Behrmann and C. Olson (Eds.) *Perceptual Organization in Vision: Behavioural and Neural Perspectives*, Mahwah, New Jersey, Lawrence Erlbaum Associates (pp. 233-278).

Hopkins, M., 2004: Corporate Social Responsibility: An Issues Paper, Working Paper No. 27. Policy Integration Department, World Commission on the Social Dimension of Globalization International Labour Office, Geneva (May 2004).

Hopkins, M., 1999: *The Planetary Bargain: Corporate Social Responsibility comes of Age*, Basingstoke, Macmillan, 13, *Ethical Performance*, March 2002.

Johnson, K.W., 2003: "Integrating Applied Ethics and Social Responsibility", *Ethical Complexity or Ethical Chaos? A Prescription for Integrating Applied Ethics.* (An earlier version of this article first appear in the newsletter: *Ethical Management*). http://www.epic.online.net/integration_social_responsibility.htm; http://www.Ethics-Policy.net/quest_5.html

Lee, J., 2003: Interactions between Perception and Concepts (conceived by Rob Goldstone: Assimilation and Contrast. Problems? Comments?) Created October 18, 1995. Modified August 20, 2003.
http://cognitrn.psych.indiana.edu/rgoldsto/projects/assimilation.html

Rogerson, S. and Gotterbarn, D., 2005: Ethical Risk Management (originally published as ETHIcol in the) IMIS Journal, Volume 15, No. 3 (May 2005). Centre for Computing and Social Responsibility, Faculty of Computing Sciences and Engineering De Montford University.

Skinner, B.P., 1987: "Whatever Happened to Psychology as the Science of Behaviour?", *American Psychologist*, 42, 780-786.

Wikipedia, 2005: From Wikipedia, The Free Encyclopedia. http://en.wikipedia.org/wiki/Assimilation

43

Is Lying the Best Way of Telling the Truth?

DAVID CROWTHER AND ANA MARIA DAVILA GOMEZ

Train Information

Timeline: 08:50
09:05 to London – expected on time

Timeline: 08:55
09:05 to London – expected at 09:08

Timeline: 09:00
09:05 to London – expected at 09:10

Timeline: 09:03
09:05 to London – expected at 09:20

Timeline: 09:12
09:05 to London – expected at 09:42

Timeline: 09:25
09:05 to London – cancelled

Anyone who has ever tried to catch a train[1] will be familiar with this scenario whereby information is given in a piecemeal and constantly changing manner. Naturally every additional piece of information provides those concerned with a constantly worsening situation. Equally it is scarcely credible that the situation can deteriorate like this in such a short space of time and so the conclusion must be drawn that information dissemination is being managed and the reason why this might be so is worthy of investigation.

This manner of providing information in a managed way is not of course unique to issues concerning transport: it is equally apparent in the way in which news is disseminated by the media or by the government.[2] Of particular interest for the purposes of this paper is the way in which such a devise is used by a business to provide information[3] to all stakeholders but particularly to its shareholders.[4] Significantly it is a device which is only used to disseminate bad news and is perhaps epitomised by the way in which profits warnings are handled – partial truths gradually releasing information until the whole truth become revealed.

Of course no-one likes to tell bad news and there is an inevitable tendency for such news to be modified as it is passed around an organisation. Indeed it has been demonstrated (Sridhar, 1994) that the information received by senior managers, for example, is distorted by their subordinates, because of their concern for their own reputations.[5] Equally there is a tendency to be optimistic about the future – the actuality might not be as bad as the current prognosis and so the bad news can be tempered because something might turn up to alleviate the situation. But the way in which bad news is reported is not simply explained by this timistic tendency of attribution theory. The evidence abounds that even when the actuality will not be less bad the current expectations because the actuality is known then there is still a tendency to report bad news in a serious of steps, each presenting the situation as worse than the preceding step. So bad news is being manipulated in its dissemination and it might be thought that people are not comfortable with received had news and that this is the reason. It is certainly ue that people are no keener to receive bad news than they are to tell it but the evidence suggests that people can cope with bad news in a satisfactory manner and what they and difficult is dealing with uncertainty and with incomplete information. This would suggest that the best way of reporting bad news therefore is to give as detailed and complete information as possible rather then progressive instalments. So the fact that this is not happening suggests that there must be an alternative reason for this, which we intend to explore in this paper. It is our argument here that the way news is announced in this partial manner is not for the benefit of shareholders, customers or other stakeholders and so it must be for the benefit of managers. There are several reasons which we will explore which together comprise an explanation.

MITIGATING ANXIETY

In his psychoanalytic theory Freud (1984) argues that the real motivation for any act undertaken by a person may be disguised and not apparent even to the person who performs that act. Thus for Freud the underlying basis for identity, and therefore for an explanation of individual behaviour, was based in the unconscious. He argued that an individual's identity was based upon past experience which was largely unconscious and that behaviour was largely dependant upon an attempt to resolve the conflicts and motivations inherent in the unconscious (Freud, 1975). Being a part of a group is like a form of family and a person's earliest experiences of a group are in family life. Consequently being part of a group provides a similar setting for the manifestation of anxiety and makes the boundary between self and other become less clear. This in turn arouses anxiety concerning how to manage compromise, maintain one's integrity and how to remain independent and not feel persecuted. For Hinshelwood (1989) the cementing of an individual to a group is described as projective identification. He describes the group as an affective network in which difficult feeling states are passed from one person to another and shows through his example of a small therapy group how the idea of scapegoating can occur. As he states (1989: 81), 'the person in addition to his conscious role is also unconsciously elected to a position that distorts his own identity'. Jaques (1955) argues that the primary force for people in their defence against anxiety is the cohesion of belonging to a group but that at the same time organisations are used by people as a defence mechanism against their own anxieties. Menzies Lyth (2000) develops this emphasis upon the unconscious anxiety which organisational procedures generates, using a case study of student nurses to show how feeling states, experiences and emotions are moved around by members of a social organisation so that an individual loses part of him/herself in that organisation, which thereby becomes a projective system.

These insights show that it is possible for roles within an organisation to become imbued with psychical content and that this can have the effect of modifying or even disabling the performance of the primary task of the group as depicted by Crowther (2002a). This work is based upon managers dealing with their anxieties in a way which affected the financial performance of an organisation while the work of Roberts (1994) is more concerned with authority and delegated responsibility within an organisation. Her work is situated within a critique of new managerialism (see Witz and Savage, 1994; Crowther and Greene, 2004) which is argued to represent a wholesale change programme for an organisation, and she claims that the ethos of equality within an organisation can only be adhered to in this situation at a great personal cost. In an ideal organisation, according to Roberts, there is a belief in the idea of a downward deferral of responsibility and in the idea of equality of individuals which are operating at an unconscious level. She argues that these are deleterious to the ability of the organisation to perform its functions efficiently. She uses examples to show how those in organisations based in the helping professions are particularly likely to use the work environment to project their own needs and to being filled up with powerful projections from their clients, leading to an inability to set limits to the task at hand. In extreme cases this can result in paranoid behaviour through the dominance of feelings of guilt (Klein, 1932) or in psychosis (Lawrence, 1995).

According to Roberts (1994) managers are in a particularly problematic position in being distanced from their workers and therefore prone to receive the negative projections of their staff. The manager is the person who is on the boundary of the group and must look at what is happening both within the group and outside it, and must maintain a sense of being in contact with external reality on behalf of the group. The further argues that the cultural and economic climate which characterises public and voluntary sector organisations has changed since the 1980s and that the ensuing continual reorganisation of organisational structures and procedures has left staff feeling that their own organisation is too fragile to attack. As a consequence the destructive and critical impulses that people manifest are turned inwards by those staff resulting in more intra-personal conflict. At the same time managers are under pressure from the external environment and are therefore more likely to identify with the anxieties of their staff. Thus they tend to project outwards that they are the 'boss' of the organisation and this external projection relieves them of the responsibility of being so. The consequence is a blurring of the boundary between managers and their staff and this reinforces the debilitating sense for all staff that the boundary between the organisation and external influences in weakened, with a consequent increase in anxiety and a self-reinforcing negative spiral.

This can however be contrasted with the arguments of others. Thus for example Marcuse (1956) argues that rather than the foundations of civilisation being built upon the subjugation of human instincts in the assuagement of guilt it is instead built upon the way in which power is distributed and the consequent suppression of labour. Similarly Habermas (1971) argues that Freudian psychoanalysis is based upon the voluntary self-deception of individuals as part of their anxiety reducing mechanisms; moreover he argues that corporate organisations are also involved in this deception. While this has consequences for an individual it also naturally has implications for the organisation as well and Sievers (1994) has described this as leading to organisational psychotic behaviour. As far as individual managers are concerned the implication of these arguments is that managers are motivated by unconscious conflicts and desires which they seek to reconcile through acting out these conflicts as part of their desire for individuation. One way in which they can act out these desires which differs from other people is through their role within the organisation. This is because they have, through their positions within organisations, power to affect the behaviour of others which is not available to the average person. This power is what makes possible the psychotic behaviour described by Sievers (1994). Furthermore these arguments imply that all individuals are anxious and insecure and seck to reduce anxiety and increase security through their actions. Thus the drive to reduce anxiety is manifest in the desire to seek confirmation of worth from others in order to increase self-esteem. Managers of large organisations are in a particularly powerful position to achieve this end through their actions as they are in a position to influence a large number of people. Employees of the organisation can he directly influenced by such managers but greater self-esteem can he gained from the respect of peers rather than subordinates. This is an extension of the conspicuous consumption thesis (Veblen, 1899) whereby the consumption of the respect of others gives one status in proportion to the importance of others because of the ascribed cultural capital (Bourdieu, 1984) thereby acquired.

One part of that anxiety reduction is concerned with being in control and able to affect events by making decisions – or at least of creating the impression that this is so. For managers this is an integral part of their position in the organisation. Normally with the sort of bad news with which we are concerned in the paper however the events concerned have already occurred and events cannot be changed whatever decisions are made. So all that can be affected is the way in which the announcement of the bad news is made. It is fortuitous therefore than in choosing to release bad news slowly those managers can also create an aura of being in control and of working hard to mitigate the effects of that bad news, although it might be considered that this aura is only created for themselves – but self-delusion is an integral part of anxiety reduction.

STAKEHOLDER CONCERN

Although all companies purport to recognise the importance of various stakeholders to their management of performance this is often only at the level of strategy, and it is often not carried forward into operational practice. This is despite the claims made by the senior managers of a company (see Cooper *et al.*, 2001), which raises a dichotomous question about operational activities within a company. Is a concern with stakeholders merely rhetorical or is there a problem within a company in translating this concern into operational practice? All companies claim to recognise the customers are an important stakeholder (Crowther, 2003) but for many they seems unable to deliver satisfactory service to these customers. It is suggested here that customer satisfaction is sacrificed to the drive to create shareholder value. Moreover it is argued that this value is created not through the operational activities of the business but rather through the externalisation of costs, which are passed on to customers. Examples of such practice are evidenced elsewhere (e.g. Crowther, 2002b) and it seems that companies adopt a philosophy that any individual customer does not matter. It has been argued however (Crowther, 2000, 2002b) that the advent of the internet has effected a change in the power relations that exist between companies and their customers. Indeed one of the features of the freedom of access to the Internet has been a proliferation of websites dedicated to protest about particular companies and their activities. These sites have been labelled as rogue sites (Chipchase, 1999) and in many ways tend to be parodies of the official company site about which they are protesting.

An organisation is of course accountable for its actions but Crowther (2002c) argues that those actions are translated into financial figures before any accountability becomes manifest. So organisations are accountable through their financial reporting and are accountable only to those stakeholders with sufficient power to influence activity. This reporting remains focused upon the actions of the organisation and ignores the effects of the organisation upon its external environment.[6] A growing number of writers however have recognised that the activities of an organisation impact upon the external environment and have suggested that one of the roles of accounting should be to report upon the impact of an organisation in this respect. Such a suggestion first arose in the 1970s and a concern with a wider view of company performance is taken by some writers who evince concern with the social performance of a business, as a member of society at large. This concern was stated by Ackerman (1975) who argued that big business was recognising the need to adapt to a new social climate of community accountability but that the orientation of business to financial results was inhibiting social responsiveness. McDonald and Puxty (1979) on the other hand maintain that companies are no longer the instruments of shareholders alone but exist within society and so therefore have responsibilities to that society, and that there is therefore a shift towards the greater accountability of companies to all participants. Nevertheless this must he set within a situation in which the financial performance of the business—as represented through its accounting—is paramount, and of almost religious significance.

ACCOUNTING AS RELIGION: THE ROLE OF LEGITIMATION

> "A religion is a unified system of beliefs and practices relative to sacred things, that is to say, things set apart and forbidden—beliefs and practices which unite into one single moral community called a church, all those who adhere to them."
>
> (Durkheim, 1975: 123.)

O'Dea (1966) suggests that there are three fundamental characteristics of human existence: that we live in conditions of uncertainty and scarcity and that there is limited control over these conditions. These conditions are equally true for individuals and organisations operating in modern society. For individuals one way to cope with this situation is to turn to religion as this provides a context for these circumstances and, further elucidates rules that should be followed. According to O'Dea (1966), Weber shows that by providing answers to these problems religion regulates and affects the choices and decisions made in daily life. For Durkheim (1975) therefore, certain beliefs and, possibly more importantly for daily life, practices, become sacred. By believing and following these practices an individual will find salvation and Wilson (1982) suggests that the explicit function of religion is to "offer men the prospect of salvation" where salvation is "triumph over death". In the same way we can see the role of management is, as a minimum, to ensure the survival, or triumph over liquidation, of the modern corporations that they run. Management attempts to do this under conditions of uncertainty, scarcity and limited control just as individuals do. Therefore in order to be able to cope, or to manage, beliefs and practices are required. In modern corporations the belief is that capitalism is the appropriate state of society. Once this is accepted then practices are required that enable the organisation to survive. One such, extremely influential, practice is that of reporting financial information. By gaining a good understanding of the scriptures of financial reporting and by following the practices detailed therein then the organisation should find salvation. This, metaphor, however, can be taken further as we consider in more detail how such information is reported.

Firstly, we return to the concept that we live in conditions of uncertainty and consider how accounting fulfils a religious function in organisations by providing an answer to the problems surrounding uncertainty. Accounting knowledge is conventionally deemed to provide certainty and one of the functions of accounting is to quantify and reduce uncertainty in the business environment. (Emmanuel and Gee, 1982). Accounting achieves this through the way in which data is structured, filtered, aggregated etc. (Birnbeg, Turopolec and Young, 1983). As such, accounting provides a grand narrative explanation (Lyotard, 1984) of organisational existence and of the understanding of organisational performance. (Gray, 1995). This is, however, based upon the assumed certainty of understanding of the causal relationships between actions and outcomes. (Cooper, Crowther and Carter, 2000). Emmanuel *et al.* (1990) suggest that the typical assumptions made within accounting are that there is a predictable and stable external environment, that individuals' behaviour is predictable and mechanistic, and that accounting data used as input is accurate. Given these assumptions it is implicitly possible to accurately predict the future. Emmanuel *et al.* (1990) continue that most frequently historical data are the inputs and given this accounting, as used in this manner, fails significantly to recognise the argument of Popper (1957) regarding the poverty of historicism. Despite this accounting numbers, specifically in terms of budgets and for decision making, are given much weight, as they appear to reduce uncertainty.

Against the argument that decisions are made based upon incomplete and simplified information is the argument that decisions are made by managers based upon their feel for the situation, and that accounting data is then used to justify the decisions already made. (Brunsson, 1993.) In this guise therefore accounting acts as a decision legitimation mechanism rather than a technology for decision evaluation, and in this context the use of simplified, aggregated information is either unimportant or preferable. Thus Hopper, Storey and Willmott (1987) have postulated that both accounting and decision making are social constructs, thereby implying that meaning is in the interpretation placed upon the data and the decisions made therefrom. Indeed Hopwood (1974) has stated that accounting data is subject to different interpretations according to the needs of the receiver of the data. Accounting therefore can be seen to have a legitimation role for decisions being made but it is also deterministic in nature and subject to the interpretation of the users of the information. This view does not correspond to the reduction of uncertainty considered above, but is rather more concerned with control and power and it is to these that we now turn.

The functionalist school has recognised that religion also sustains social cohesion and provides a basis for social control. These roles of social control and social cohesion religion have also been defined as the "opium of the people" (Marx and Engels, 1955, p. 42), whereby religion provides a "narcotic effect ... which diminishes the revolutionary potential of subordinate groups." (Turner, 1983, p. 85.) In a similar way accounting data is presented to other stakeholders (e.g. employees) as certainty and the decisions made therefrom are consequently logical and rational. As a result there can be no argument or uprising to take place, as the facts are plain for all to see. In order for this to be possible it is important that the other stakeholders do not have as good an understanding of the information as the management. In religion it is also the case that it is the priesthood that has the greater knowledge and understanding of the scriptures and they can therefore instruct the followers in how to behave. The claim to expertise is through understanding, but this is only possible if you have knowledge of the language. Therefore in past times the words of religion were written in languages foreign to the main body of society. It was indeed difficult for an illiterate person of the Middle Ages to challenge a priest who has read scriptures in Latin. We now consider the accounting as a language.

Belkaoui's (1978) argues that accounting is not just the language of business but is actually a language in its own right, satisfying the grammatical and lexical characteristics of a language. The acceptance of accounting as a language explains some of the interpretative difficulties with accounting data, which are common problems for any language particularly as dialects develop, but these difficulties can also be explained by the way in which accounting is used in practice. Briers and Hirst (1990) state that information can be used in a variety of ways, and in assessing the use made of accounting information two main ways are suggested for the manner in which it is used by senior managers: defining the dominant coalition and institutionalising decisions. In a similar vein it has been argued that religion functions to legitimise the purposes and procedures of society itself (Wilson, 1982) and to legitimise the power of the dominant class. (Turner, 1983.)

Accounting defines the dominant coalition as it is a language, and therefore knowledge of the language and acceptance of the precepts upon which it is based can be used to give or withhold power within the organisation. Decisions are made in an organisation by those with the information necessary to make the decisions (or at least by those who perceive themselves to be in possession of that information) and the power necessary to enforce that decision. Thus Finkelstein (1992) argues that strategic choice in an organisation is dependent upon the power of the top management team. Accounting information provides a mechanism for giving power to that team, or enabling the team to take power, as it provides a source of expert and referent power. This power is however not just obtained from access to the data but also partly from understanding the framework within which the data is being interpreted. Thus the acceptance of the managerial frame of reference for decision making is a crucial sign of the acceptance of a person within the dominant coalition of managers with the power to make decisions. Accounting data can therefore be used as a means of signalling inclusion or exclusion of parties to that decision.

The existence of the dominant coalition within an organisation is dependant upon the power of that coalition and the use of, and interpretation of, information is one source of power. Horkheimer and Adorno (1944: 110) argue that a social hierarchy is dependant ultimately upon force, stating

> "Though it may seek a legalistic covering, the social hierarchy is ultimately dependent on force. Mastery over nature is reproduced within humanity."

The use of that power therefore in determining the decisions made is a source of tension in an organisation and Horkheimer and Adorno (1944: 132) further argue that there is a tendency for stakeholders who have needs which conflict with those of the dominant coalition will have a tendency towards acceptance of the dominant view. This, they argue, is because any articulation of those differences will lead towards coincidence; any irreconcilable needs will fail to be articulated. They state:

> "Anyone who resists can only survive by fitting in. Once his particular brand of deviation from the norm has been noted by the industry, he belongs to it as does the land-reformer to capitalism. Realistic dissidence is the trademark of anyone who has a new idea in business. In the public voice of modern society accusations are seldom audible: if they are, the perceptive can already detect signs that the dissident will soon be reconciled. The more measurable the gap between chorus and leaders, the more certainly there is room at the top for everybody who demonstrates his superiority by well planned originality."

Just as this power is used to institutionalise dissident voices within the organisation so too is accounting information used as a means of institutionalising the decisions made by the dominant coalition. Thus Scapens (1994) argues that accounting, as used in practice, provides the members of an organisation with an institutional basis for making decisions within an organisational setting. Institutionalism therefore can be described as a pattern of behaviour which is regularly used and drawn upon by the members of a community (in this case the organisation) as a means of determining, or at least informing, current behaviour. Hamilton (1932: 84) states that these patterns

> "imply a way of thought or action of some prevalence and permanence, which is embedded in the habits of a group or the customs of a people. . . . Institutions fix the confines of and impose forms upon the activities of human beings."

All religions are based upon the following of prescribed rituals, which are necessary to please the gods so that they will listen to the people in supplication. Moreover all religions have a priesthood who alone have the power to mediate between the gods and the people and to interpret what the gods are saying. We have sought to show how accounting gives power to the dominant coalition of management, and in so doing elevates them to the level of the priesthood of the organisation, thereby giving them the power (and legitimacy) to interpret what the gods of capitalism are saying. And the use of this information – giving or withholding as decide by the manager – is one of the essential rituals of organisational behaviour.

For an individual, ritual is an essential part of personality integration – a process of becoming whole. (Perls, 1975.) Rituals therefore are steps along the way to completion of the whole – the rites of passage (Beit-Hallahmi and Argyle 1997) which mark the way to that wholeness. So too for organisations are rituals steps to be completed along the way to wholeness. In the case of the organisation however the integration needed is that of the various people involved in the organisation into a unified whole, based upon the rituals of organisational religion. This religion, of necessity, becomes institutionalised into the organisation and its culture and forms part of the way in which the organisation conducts itself both internally and in relating to its external environment. This institutionalisation of religion becomes part of the culture of the organisation and socialises the individual who assimilates the cultural givens of the organisation. (Dollimore, 1984.) As Bocock (1974: 174) states:

> "Ritual action can have two sorts of consequences for the society in which it takes place: either it can provide a process whereby

people become more attached to the basic way of life and values of the society, or to the major sub-groups within it of which the participants in ritual are a part, or ritual can lead to people making new demands on the way of life in their society, and a desire to see change both in action and in the values the society pursues."

It is naturally not in the interests of the managers of the organisation, who use accounting to constitute themselves as the priesthood of the organisation, to allow the ritual actions of the organisation to lead to demands for changes other then those which they ordain. It therefore becomes imperative that the ritual role or corporate activity becomes subsumed within the organisational religion.

One of the purposes of such ritual behaviour is to remove speciality from the discourse of organisational activity and to focus attention upon the temporal dimension. Thus organisational existence is legitimated in this manner as a temporal sequence proceeding from one rite of organisational existence to the next in a smooth flow of routinised ritual activity. The use of accounting information in such a ritual way serves the purpose of an organisational religion. The rituals serve to distance this priesthood from its acolytes. At the same time they signal that the knowledge of the priesthood enables them to make the best decisions on behalf of the other stakeholders, who merely worship from afar and accept the received wisdom of the priesthood.

MOTIVATING MANAGERS

Kaplan (1984) argues that it is apparent that profit is being used as a means of motivating managers and evaluating short-term performance, and therefore there is a need for new measures of performance. This point is reiterated by Govindarajan and Gupta (1985) who maintain that long run criteria contribute to organisational effectiveness rather than short-term criteria. The discourse surrounding the application of accounting techniques in practice is extensive and continuous but while this discourse continues it serves to create a level of distraction which obscures the way in which accounting itself has been subverted to serve the needs of managers. There is an inevitable encouragement in the prolonging of this discourse concerning the practical application of accounting techniques from organisations. This encouragement comes both from the accounting profession itself, in the mistaken belief (Crowther and Carter, 1998) that technical expertise enhances the status of the profession, and from managers, in the belief that this transfers attention from the subversion of accounting.

For business organisations, McDonald and Puxty (1979) had maintained that companies are no longer the instruments of shareholders alone but exist within society and so therefore have responsibilities to that society, and that there is therefore a shift towards the greater accountability of companies to all participants. Recognition of the rights of all stakeholders and the duty of a business to be accountable in this wider context therefore has been a relatively recent phenomenon and the economic view of accountability only to owners has only recently been subject to debate to any considerable extent.

Purdy (1983) however discerns two worrying trends however in the subordination of shareholders' rights to the needs of the company and its survival, and in the tendency for this to lead to short term satisficing and risk reduction rather than to profit maximisation. This implicit assumption that profit maximisation is, or should be, the aim of a firm is a return to neo-classical economic theory and it is worth remembering that Clark (1957) pointed out that profit maximisation is a difficult concept to define, leaving room for the incorporation of good citizenship. When applied to the public sector the concept of profit maximisation is of course even more problematic and this is arguably why the discourse has become one of cost minimisation on the assumption that cost minimisation is the equivalent of profit maximisation. Good citizenship and the provision of services have become subordinated to this drive for cost minimisation. Equally this cost minimisation has been interpreted as in the short term – the long-term problems with this approach can be ignored as someone else will deal with these in the future. This therefore represents part of the problem with accounting – only the present and immediate future matters and the immediate future must be better than the present. The past can be ignored in the creation of this semiotic, or rewritten when necessary, to show a continuous improvement (Crowther, 2002c) without any regard to the actual experiences of people.

The evaluation of performance is however partly concerned

with the measurement of performance and partly with the reporting of that performance, and with the greater importance being given to social accountability the changing reporting needs of an organisation are also being recognised. Thus Birnbeg (1980) states that accounting is attempting to supply various diverse groups, with different needs for information, and that there is a need for several distinct types of accounting to perform such a function. Similarly Gray (1992) considers the limitations of the traditional economic base for accounting and questions some of its premises such as: the desirability of growth; the existence of rational economic man; the exclusion of altruism; and the ignoring of the way in which wealth is distributed. He argues that there is a need for a new paradigm with the environment being considered as part of the firm rather than as an externality and with sustainability and the use of primary resources being given increased weighting. Rubenstein (1992) goes further and argues that there is a need for a new social contract between a business and the stakeholders to which it is accountable, and for a business mission which recognises that some things go beyond accounting.

Monks and Minow (1991) consider that power is an essential component of accountability and that corporations are externalising machines suited to self-preservation. They therefore argue that when faced with conflicting pressures a company will act in the interests of self-preservation with lower risk but less benefit being chosen. They also argue that the power of businesses is increasingly being consolidated into the hands of the executives rather than owners and that social accountability is not a feature of such organisations. Different perspectives therefore exist concerning the extent of disclosure of performance data, the need for reporting and the framework in which such reporting takes place. These differing perspectives however all evaluate practice from a particular viewpoint rather than from the multiple perspective stance of addressing the needs of multiple groups of stakeholders. There is recognition that these different groups require different information and that this poses a problem for accounting and for reporting, but little consideration has been given to an analysis of this problem and ways of its resolution. The various suggestions noted regarding different methods of accounting all seek to satisfy one viewpoint and perceived need at the expense of others. Organisations attempting this task of meeting differing requirements need to consider first their own position in the community and the values upon which they are founded. This was recognised by Selznick (1957: 136) who stated:

> "Truly accepted values must infuse the organisation at many levels, affecting the perspective and attitudes of personnel, the relative importance of staff activities, the distribution of authority, relations with outside groups, and many other matters. Thus if a large corporation asserts the wish to change its role in the community from a narrow emphasis on profit-making to a large social responsibility (even though the ultimate goal remains some combination of survival and profit-making ability), it must explore the implications of such a change for decision making in a wide variety of organisational activities."

The ethical implications of a firm's behaviour were considered by McCoy (1985: 87) who considers ethics to be at the core of business behaviour, stating:

> "Dealing with values requires continual monitoring of the surrounding environment, weighing alternative courses of action, balancing and (when possible) integrating conflicting responsibilities, selling priorities among competing goals, and establishing criteria for defining and evaluating performance. Along with these goes learning ways to bring this ethical reflection directly and fully into the processes by which policy is made, implemented, and evaluated. Increasingly, skills in dealing with values as integral components of performance and policy-making are being recognised as central for effective management in a society and a world undergoing rapid change."

The way in which a business performs in terms of its ethical behaviour, and identified place in society as a whole, is determined by its relationship with its stakeholder community. It is also to some extent determined by, as well as to some extent determining, the culture of the organisation. Kotter and Heskett (1992) consider corporate culture and show how this can lead to good business performance but also to bad business performance and a lack of ability to change to match changing environmental conditions. They consider that effective leadership is crucial to success. Success, like good performance, is always of course a subjective construct depending upon the perspective of the evaluator.

CREATING PERFORMANCE

One of the interesting things about bad news as far as a company is concerned (see Crowther 2002c) is that the announcement of such bad news has little relationship with share price. Any such announcement can always be coupled with optimism for the future – as this optimistic future is really all that matters. Thus it is possible that the promise of a better future can continue to be made year by year without regard to the fact that the same promise made in the previous year has not been met and the improvements forecasted have not materialised. A focus upon the future as the dominant pole of this pair of binary opposites is needed to enable this to happen and this focus both obviates the need to deliver promised performance, as the outlook is always forward, and seeks to negate any possible criticism for past failures. Action has always been taken by the management team (who are always committed and capable) which will deliver benefits in the future. One way to create the desired symbolic image of the better future however is by means of repetition in a temporal series (Deleuze, 1994) and so the repetition of the message helps create the desired image of improvement in the future without any need to actualise that improvement through achievement. Mere repetition of the message year by year is sufficient to create the image desired amongst the readers of the diachronically unfolding script. As the locus of attention is always forward then the past failures no longer matter – only the promise of the improved future matters. As Hollier (1995) observes, the act of repetition creates a break in discourse and thereby removes temporality from the act of continuous improvement; mere repetition suffices instead to create the image.

One thing that does affect share price however is a series of announcements of bad news, which would suggest that the gradual partial release of bad news is not the best way of managing the situation. So the current practice of disseminating unfavourable information in instalments is bad for shareholders as it is for other stakeholders and seems to be only of benefit for managers themselves. Given that these managers have an obligation concerning the stewardship of the property of others then this would suggest another possibility – full and frank disclosure.

Upon the promise of progress, which leads management practice towards looking for financial growth for enterprises, something within the organization must be done in order to generate the desired performance. Hence, increasingly, one of the most suitable ways of constructing functional liberal organizations, accompanied with the achievement of financial objectives, is the implementation of procedures, techniques and motivational tools towards productivity. For us, in this dominant approach, the organization is seen as a machine, in which, people are only one element of the apparatus. Consequently, people, including managers, are conceived as resources, tools or means, where thoughts, feelings and emotions cannot be different from those of the organizational machine. Thus, people's motivation is aligned with process performance (techniques and re-engineering methods).

Following Amado *et al.* (1990), and utilising our practical experience as managers and consultants in organizations, we identify that the previous approach answers the concept of "organizational development" (OD – with techniques such as BPR, TQM, CRM, ERP, among others),[7] which promises organizations, managers and people to feel part of the new era, the transformation, the ultra-successful company. Here, people's development is conceived as something that will procure in retribution, organizational development. Managers ask for people's implication on OD projects, selling the idea that the success of those projects will signify the achievement of personal success. Here, people's motivations, conditioned and fabricated, need a conductive approach: Organizational Behaviour (OB).

The postulate that lies behind the preceding is the concept of value-chain added to clients, explained by positivistic management thinkers (e.g. Drucker, 1999; Porter, 1980). The implementation of this concept will procure in response a growing profitability. Nonetheless, those approaches do not refer the need to make a deeper analysis about the connection with the social and collective components of the organization. When people are just conceived as another resource to be arranged in the chain value, meanings, questionings, senses and concern for social consequences of actions, have little space. In a sense, not necessarily productivity techniques are not valuable, but the way in which they are introduced and installed by managers (or owners) is what does not allow a consideration of people in their broader scope as subjects with meanings and concerns. Again, the difference is therefore represented by those who articulate the power inside organizations, while deciding how, why and for whom to use these techniques.

With the latter, people, and managers, are demanded by those with more power, to invest enormous quantities of energy and emotion in order to conduct successful results out of OD projects. This is sold as a positive stress to people, upon which, making part of something new (OD novelty) adds value to individuals. However, and paradoxically, despite this great confidence on OD results, we already know that these OD techniques are not necessarily as effective as it is claimed.[8]

In spite of undoubted evidence, experience and history, companies still argue and rationalise why they must continue on the same path and the same way of assuring productivity and performance: OD and OB techniques. The reality of OD and OB failure is disguised and justified through misrepresentations in financial reports. The "why" of incompetence is constructed without questioning the nature of the techniques. Instead of thinking about other ways of seeking productivity and performance, OD and OB are increasingly developed in order to avoid committing the same errors in the future, and the causes of actual errors (needed to be justified) are explained in other factors. Among these new factors, there is a special interest in communication and leadership techniques that may procure a more aligned relationship and assertiveness between managers, employees and the market, instead of questioning the non-inclusion of social and human responsibility from the beginning of any action. For the previous, only few researchers have begun to treat at least one part of our demanded criteria: the organizational cultural environment (e.g. Orlikowski, 2001; Murray and Willmott, 2001).

On the other hand, as Crowther (2002c) highlights, an organization is conceived, in a majority of cases, as an entity separated from its environment (ecological and social), except for the fact of having a permeable and selective boundary that enables it to exchange goods or services. Here, the managerial techniques for the planning of organizational action are unable to integrate the whole. Strategic planning formulas offer the SWOT tool as a panacea for environmental analysis (strengths, weaknesses, opportunities and threats).[9] In fact, the latter is sustained and validated increasingly with the management teaching and practical adoption of the Porter's (1980) "4 market forces" model[10] as the constrainers or enablers of organizational growth and internal development, for which, in the present time, a 5 year planning is justified. Nevertheless, this approach does not demand a social concern connection, or a sustainable future responsibility. Inside this perspective, there is little place for stakeholders, employees or power relationships inside and outside the organizational daily cultural life.

This reality of creating performance from these largely accepted managerial techniques, accounting as well as OD, enables us to questioning the way in which lying in organizations might have become a standard.

HIDING THE TRUTH OR BEING RESPONSIBLE?

With the previous reflections, we see that one way of lying is promising organizational success regardless of social responsibility being necessary from an ethical point of view. For instance, when there is a need for an organization to obtain governmental support and agreement when installing new factories in other places than those of the holding, there is a need to construct social promises, given that the dominant theories do not include social concern. In this construction, there is speculation about the future, where results planning is not necessarily reliable, except for a few items that fit governmental expectance of social development. And this does not only happen when multinationals go to developing countries (in order to have less expensive labour market), but also when they go to developed countries for installing factories in small communities, whose development is assured by a foreign investment.[11] As the future cannot be assured, promises are made, and when the future arrives as a present time is bought to delay the bad news because historically and socially, people, listeners and government have granted patience while hoping for alternative good news. While delaying, internal analyses are made in order to justify the gap between promises and results, because most of the time there is no place to implant alternatives or solutions. When the battle is conceded as lost within the organization as a premeditated answer because business in the local region is no longer profitable, the action is conscious and non-ethical. This shows how many times the lying is intentional. In spite of this fact, as a truth, the task to repair the actual damage that the organization is causing is assumed by managers as a governmental duty, given that the appropriate taxes have been paid and the original arrangement has been respected.

As we see, there is little space to conceive the organization as a part of the whole picture, where organizational activities transform at the same time the community; a reality of being embedded (more than only exchange) that includes the consideration of consequences that we claim as characteristic of responsibility and accountability (e.g. Crowther and Rayman-Bacchus, 2004; Davila-Gomez, 2005). Hereby, one of the principal lies of management practice and theory stands behind the way in which we conceive an organization. The mostly accepted picture of organization origins, and functioning, is a partial truth, because one part of their entire dimension is not shown. Lying is not only hiding the truth, but also showing it partially. That is why, the few new organizational tendencies that conceive organizations in a wider spectrum (e.g. Crowther, 2002c) are not necessarily yet worldwide accepted in the praxis. Information is power; its control and manipulation, transforming it or hiding it, show it as well.

As a reflection of the described dominance, financial equations and reports rarely include measures of concepts such as community satisfaction, social contribution to environmental damage or employees' contribution of individual development. Nonetheless, Crowther (2002c) has already demonstrated that there might not be incompatibility in reporting together financial and environmental performance. Despite that, until now, these criteria are mostly qualitatively measured in order to answer the internal questioning of a researcher, or a few managers and owners, or because they comprise part of an internal unit's performance such as a marketing department that needs to know a specificity of the client's behaviour. However, when needed, these values are rarely related in financial reports that will go public. Normally, accounting reports are based upon the conception of cost and investments and their transformation into profits, where, in order to evaluate organizational performance, goods and services are classified while attributing them as units of time and money following the operative value chain flow of activities. Therefore, the referred criteria we claim as necessary that need qualitative consideration, hardly fit into the accounting items of the reports.

On the contrary, there are few indications of negative consequences of this superhero manager image (Aktouf, 1988) sold by OD philosophy such as alienation, false identities, growth of economic benefits for a company without a need for employee or community contribution (other than taxes). Equally, within this supremacy, when management theories talk about human capital as organizational assets (e.g. Davenport and Prusak, 1997), or knowledge (e.g. Takeushi and Nonaka, 2004; Senge 1990), there is not yet a reciprocal financial item that enables this to be translated, measured and reflected into accounting reports. Individuals' time, effort, creativity and psychological investment in organizational activities are not contrasted with the repercussion in their families or their human development, or with the contribution to the social-collective development. Other examples of this lack of inclusion touching the social and environmental responsibility and concern are the rate of environmental energy consumption made by an organization *vs.* the external energy available in nature (the resource naturally available on the spot or the ecological consequences to the planet). Those kinds of evaluations are made only by a few scientific and socially concerned individuals,[12] or in some rare cases in management studies (e.g. Crowther and Hosking, 2005b; Topal and Crowther, 2004; Peters, 2004; Crowther, 2002c; Boiral, 1998[13]), or, paradoxically denounced by some philosophers since ancient times (e.g. Socrates – in Plato, 399-384 B.C., whose teachings have not yet been well apprehended). Largely, corporate social reports are more concerned with tangible and financial items that have been traditionally measured, some of which have been enhanced mostly because of the need to accomplish a governmental prerogative, but not necessarily because it answers an internal feeling of otherness in those who are in power.

The great danger with those situations is that even if they have already been revealed and exposed in public domains to the entire world; yet in few and not enormous spaces, we continue to lead our organizations, and mostly measure their performance socially, with a lack of the criteria we explored before. In this sense, we continue to lie to ourselves. We already know the needs, the things to be changed, and there is enough information supporting complaints and realities, yet the changes are merely isolated. This supremacy of ruling with norms (accounting reports or OD techniques) that do not fit the real "reality", with the aggravation of knowing the truth and lying to ourselves, supports the hypothesis of individualistic interest upon collective repercussion. Sometimes, managers act lying in order to achieve what the external accepted success has been sold to them as true. Hence, managers include among their ontological individual principles the belief that the dominant currents of management theory are complete and procure total performance, and that managers' will and judgment have to be always aligned with the owners expectancies, regardless of those of the other organizational actors—clients, stakeholders, employees and also themselves. Here, the authoritarian parental figure, that is not questionable as we discussed before while talking about psychic phantoms, is reproduced, as well as the hierarchical approach of professor-student for which there is little space to question the nature and profound sense of the organizational theory taught.

Hereby, as the cited techniques do not require in their theoretical corpus the need to include our concerns, managers feel freer to act without being questioned in their acting. They, in a sense, are using the socially and academically accepted ways of procuring productivity, and therefore, enhancing performance. Consequently, when the government demands reports about the social responsibility of the organization, given that the link, the connection, between performance technique and its consequences to people and the collective have not been established, there is need to create performance in financial data.

As well as accounting, OD techniques became another sort of religion, a managerial belief of invincible tools for achieving organizational success, which, as we already have discussed, is only a partial success given that many aspects have been left out. However, this partiality of the success does not frequently concern managers, or shareholders, as their interpretation of people in organization is rarely holistic; instead, it is merely mechanical. These assumptions, nowadays accepted truths, are in fact often lies about the real representation of reality.

The latter enables us to question our permissiveness and our ethics, while continuing with lies.

LYING WHILE ACCEPTING AGREEMENTS: THE TRUE AND THE FALSE SELF

Following Winnicott (1965) and Klein and Riviere (1964), we identify that while lying, a person might be doing it in a conscious or in an unconscious way. For Winnitcott, the "false self" is the one who motivates a person to do things without not always knowing that he is behaving against what he knows he wants, or what he still does not know he wants. This may be conscious or unconscious. Thus, it is extremely worrying how lying behaviours become reproducible inside groups (organizations, and also communities). Lying evolves then as a behaviour that procures success for someone against the development of others. Furthermore, and according to Dewey (1963), we identify that lying, as any other behaviour, may be learned by example, given that as individuals, our cognitive development is not only a growth of theoretical concepts, but an experience of observations and daily interactions with multiple individuals: members of the family—from whom for example we learn how to talk, and how to walk; school, academia, social groups and organizational daily life. Inside these simultaneous and permanent spaces of continuous learning, we identify at the same time the values and the behaviours that people privilege.

For instance, if an individual in an organization sees that lies and distortion of information and responsibility towards shareholders or stakeholders, is a way to climb up the organization's hierarchy, and that at the same time this will procure him more salary and consequently the possibility to increase the material goods that provide a better quality of life for his family, the employee will be very tempted to reproduce this behaviour, because of some psychic dilemma of will. By the same token, an employee is confronted with telling the truth about the causes of not performing as expected, probably risking his job—and having family repercussions on the quality of life of his family—or lying to conserve his job, and probably risking the reproduction in his children of this unwished behaviour.

Moreover, if a manager is in a position to earn more salary while lying, the dilemmas are aggravated with the phantoms of "parental pleasure" identification that was described before, following Freud (1975b), where the new parent is the shareholder. For instance, saving the interest of the owner, managers may lie on the report as an agreement between him and the shareholder. In this case, the manager will be congratulated for being loyal, paradoxically truthful to the organization even though the mutual agreement produces lies to the public and the government. This lie provides psychological relief to the manager, because the parent considers the son as someone identified with the organizational philosophy and culture, respecting its will. The manager deserves confidence and congratulations from the organization. Otherwise, if the manager lies on the report trying to hide the truth to the shareholders in order to disguise a personal incompetence implementing the performance techniques, the lying behaviour may represent a weapon that enables him to be protected against his phantom parent's (the shareholder) recrimination and disapproval.

With the latter we see that different expectancies appear as conscious to a manager when he knows that he is lying, but at the same time this might be unconscious in the sense of "why" is he lying. Even then, there are also some socially agreed behaviours of the collective unconscious referred to by Jung (see Crowther, 2003b) while exploring the psychoanalysis of management behaviour. Hereby, inside Winnicott's (1965) exploration of the false and the true self regarding expectancies, those of parents and society, there are also the ones auto-imposed that sometimes answer those of others; on other occasions they are part of the individual's psyche development as a consequence of their own life experience. Here, the great challenge is that even if others in part determine us, we remain the deciders of our actions. Being honest with ourselves, and identifying that many times we lie in a conscious way because there might be an unconscious "why", may procure managers some liberation of phantoms in order to confront, in an ethical and honest way, shareholders and society.

Furthermore, on occasion, some people feel guilty while lying (Klein and Riviere, 1964); they know that telling the truth from the beginning, and therefore not being necessary to mitigate anxiety to clients, will not procure individual (or organizational—owner, manager) satisfaction. Then, in extreme cases, even knowing that it is inevitable to tell the truth, a delaying process buys time to managers to construct reasons and justify the causes of the failure. Hereby, many times, the causes are attributed to failures inside the components of the artefacts that procure productivity (the referred OD techniques) and enable performance. In doing so, as those techniques do not include our concerns of social, human and ecological components, the analysis of justification is partial and does not explore the real roots. Hence, the finality (of a positivistic paradigm) that lies behind results is not questioned. In this sense, we convince ourselves of continuing with the agreed lie: actual productive techniques and methods are OK, thus we will continue to introduce "x" or "y" component to them and we continue to disregard the crucial human, social and ecological factors.

Therefore, when having to announce bad news, and already knowing that the anxiety of the public and the clients is constantly growing, the time bought for constructing justifications is dedicated to rationality and manipulation of information and events. There is nobody to blame; everything is attributed to failures on the components of a faceless machine (the organization). This dynamic contains also the need to present in the end, some time later, to the public, reasons for the failure that cannot be contested. Here, more than lying while delaying the news (the truth), there is also the phenomenon of giving false hope to customers, where new alternatives or solutions will never take place. Managers and some employees only know this already inevitable reality. Hence, new lies are constructed in order to not jeopardize nor destabilize the customer's confidence on the organization. Clients and stakeholders are manipulated in their control of nervousness. While delaying the truth, the distraction, the "update news", lies also.

While acting, individuals follow patterns that had served them well in the past, either by protecting them or by enabling them to being more successful in terms of social expectancy. People may reproduce lying because they have observed its results in others. Hereby, additional to the unconscious phantoms drivers of the false self, there is also in this dynamic of lying, behaviour reproduction, the feeling of fear. There is a fear to invent, to create or to propose a new alternative of behaviour, because the possible future result is unknown. In the fear of the unknown resides also the conformity of already knowing how to deal with the consequences of lying to our shareholders or stakeholders (our phantom parents) or lying to ourselves and agreeing with others in order to avoid being punished or expelled from an affiliation group. Even though many experiences of the past might not be positive, we already know how to deal with them. Having followed for many years our false self, the fear to confront powerful others, and also ourselves, our real true self, is a real challenge. In doing so, we might be liberated from our phantoms, but at the same time, we begin to decide with concern for ourselves and others; and in this new space, many things are about to be developed in our personality in order to follow our true self. The future implies to be open, to develop new behaviours, new attitudes and new qualities of being truthful; sometimes this implies to be open to the unknown. From this perspective, if we fail while acting, if the results do not meet the expectations with the initial promises, we may explore proposed solutions and be open to becoming accountable for their execution. What is not ethical is to hide the truth and not to offer alternative reliable and truthful solutions when these are known.

TELLING THE TRUTH: CHALLENGES AND DEMANDS

As we have shown, even inside a dilemma of "false self' where the unconscious "why" might still be hidden, the conscious may nevertheless know that a lie is being constructed or deployed. There exist therefore in many cases unethical conscious actions while reporting and evaluating the organizational activity. Moreover, reports allow availability of information, but behind a report (false, or true) there is a whole operation (organizational action) that lies behind.

There is not only need for more transparent reports, but also for modifications of the actions that are being reported. Many lies in reports are a conscious way to hide the real reality of damages that an organization might be committing against individuals, the collective and the ecosystem, for which there is no intention from the organization (or the manager) to repair the damage. We need to lie because we know that by informing the truth, some governmental instances or protest groups will force us to change the things we are doing in an irresponsible way. Thus, we learn how to transform and justify the reality, the truth, because even if we have an unconscious motivating past that seeks for complacency in those with power (phantom parents or groups), many times we know however that we are lying and that human and collective consequences are not taken into account. The point here, and perhaps the limits to elucidate and to claim, is that in non-ethical conscious decisions there is an ontological principal of considering oneself as more valuable than other individuals. In this sense, the fields of moral and ethics (as claimed by Socrates—in Plato, 399-384 B.C., or Rousseau, 1712-1778) demand to be truthful and consequent with actions, because senses of justice and equality are imperative (see Davila Gomez 2005).

In elucidating between the unconscious sources of lying, and the conscious decision-making of lying, there is the space for internal questioning on each human being, and the social reflection that accompanies it. As we showed before, learning and the developing of qualities, more than a theoretical issue, are practical experiences. Families, schools and organizations are the environments where individuals redefine, or fortify constantly, their apprehensions and the things they consider as correct, even if lying is taken as a way to obtain individual success or protection against punishment or the deprivation of groups of affiliation. Thus, people with power inside those environments are called to be more ethical and truthful when relying and interacting with others, in order to generate by example a change of attitude in others. We may obtain different results from what we promise, but we must offer reliable alternatives and solutions to others. The life of others is as important as it is ours. Managers control not only organizational power, but also many people's faith.

For the latter, we take what Winnicott (1965) stated about the development of "concern" as an internal feeling in individuals since the first stages of their development. Following his ideas, for the case of managers, we, as guides, as other managers or management schools, should provide an adequate environment that enables the development of awareness, consciousness and accountability in managers. In other words, in managerial actions, it is imperative to be concerned for others. Thus, attitudes of honesty and integrity, only demonstrable through practical actions, and observable and judged by others, will be the competences needed for managers. This requires, at the same time, willingness and the wish to confront those who own more power, in order to present new alternatives, to configure more new truthful reports, to rearrange internal and external actions seeking to be more socially responsible and not needing to lie. Hereby, given, the power invested in managers, and the impact that their behaviour generates in their employees, lying to obtain success will be apprehended by others upon the leaning by example dynamic as a mean for achieving success. Thus, there is a need to show that questioning about the sources of false self, individual or social, may procure conscience liberation, proposition of alternatives as a concern for others that will suffer the consequences of our actions, and finally, living the truth. There is, in this sense, a need to explore the unknown, to propose, with the truth, other alternatives and solutions, while the concern for others accompanies the rational productivity organizational logic.

Finally, inexorable, demanding to managers, and to organizations, to become truthful, generates at the same time a continuous questioning of natures that lie behind the approaches sold as true in order to increasing performance. Following Crowther (2002c), upon a pluralistic approach, we consider that there is a need to complete managerial theoretical contents with human and social components on the financial equations. It is imperative to have more thoughtful managerial conscious actions. Our conscience tell us when we are lying, ethics helps us to being responsible.

Notes and References

1. Anyone waiting in an airport to catch a plane will probably have had a similar experience except that the amount of information disseminated is much less and much less frequent.
2. See for example Crowther and Hosking (2005) concerning the treatment of news concerning the recent outbreak of foot and mouth disease in the UK.
3. Or should it be misinformation?
4. Consider for example the case of Shell and its oil reserves (see Crowther and Ortiz-Martinez, 2005) in which during January 2004 a small item of news was issued concerning the reclassification of reserves along with a statement that "There is no material effect on financial statements for any year up to and including 2003." Within 3 months of this minor announcement the after tax income of the corporation for the preceding 4 years had been recalculated and reduced by almost $ 450 million and the Chairman. Sir Philip Watts, had resigned. This recalculation involved 4 separate announcements, each of which increased the reported effect of the recalculation. Further announcements have been made subsequently and it is still uncertain as to whether the whole effect had yet been revealed.
5. This can be explained in terms of attribution theory, whereby a person has a tendency to exaggerate favourable results and attribute them to his/her individual efforts and abilities but minimise unfavourable results and attribute them to external factors.
6. Indeed this is consistent with financial accounting theory, and its concern with the boundary of the organisation, and with GAAP.
7. These abbreviations stand among the most cited ways of increasing productivity now-a-days, where BPR indicates Business Processes Reengineering, TQM indicates Total Quality Management, CRM indicates Customer Relationship Management, and ERP indicates Enterprise Resource Planning (this one is the latest sophisticated version of its predecessors: MRP2 and MRP—Materials Requirements Planning and Manufacturing Resource Planning). Moreover, the ERP concept may been seen as a related procedure that enables the other productivity techniques (e.g. BPR, TQM, CRP, among others) to integrate and synchronize the flux of materials, procedures and resources, which demands an enormous amount of information to be aligned through a transversal flux of in-progress-products (or services) among various departments as the organization. The premise here is that ERP may be also highly sophisticated while introducing, in parallel, integrated information systems in order to accelerate information disposal and decision-making inside the verticality and the transversality of organizations. For a broader description of the managerial development of those techniques, see Clark (2003), Childe *et al.* (1994), Deming (1982).

8. Bernier and Roy (2003) show what the Garnet group (Harris and Pelan 2000) established the fact that 50 per cent of information systems projects do not achieve the expected objectives. By the same token, Bernier *et al.* (2003) comment on the results of a study conducted by the Harvard Business School (Austin and Nolan, 1999) in which almost 65 per cent of managers fear that ERP systems will damage their business operation because of the problems associated with their implementation.
9. See Thompson (1967) or more recently Hafsi *et al.* (2000) for operational details about this technique.
10. Suppliers, clients, competitors and substitution products.
11. As an example, see the case of General Motors (GM) when they established a factory in the Quebec province in the locality of Boisbriand (Canada) in the 1970's. for whose approval the government demanded new jobs and offered certain tax exemptions. GM promised the creation of the new jobs and signed the agreements as economical retribution for the community, 30 years later, when initial agreements were accomplished, and new "business horizons" were estimated as better for the GM holding (upon a strategic approach), the Quebec factory was closed and 1100 employees were fired (having previously been reduced from 4300 employees in 1979 to 1100 by the end of 2002) without a real possibility for them to regain another equitable job or salary in the immediate region. Here, community damage was the consequence of pure business philosophy, leaving no space for governmental applicable measures, given that GM met the basics of the agreement. For details about this case, see Le Devoir (2002). Radio Canada (2002).
12. As an example, see Suzuki (2005) to identify a Canadian effort to preserve the planet, which is conducted by a convinced, respected and loved man among the community.
13. Boiral explores in a petrochemical factory in Montreal, the possibility of directors and employees working together in order to diminish environmental pollution as a proactive action by opposition to the reactive and reconstructive traditional way of proceeding.

References

Ackerman, R.W. (1975): *The Social Challenge to Business*, Cambridge, Ma: Harvard University Press.

Aktouf, O. (1988): "Culture organisationnelle et táche du gestionnaire de projet", *Cahiers de recherche CETAI* (Centre d'études en administration internationale—HEC Montréal), Canada.

Amado, G. *et al.*, (1990): "Changement organisationnel et réalités culturelles", dans Chanlat. J-F (dir). *L'indvidu dans l'organisation—les dimensions oubliées,* Les Presses de l'Université Laval, Québec, pp. 629-662.

Beit-Hallahmi, B. and Argyle, M., *The Psychology of Religious Behaviour, Belief and Experience* (London: Routledge, 1997).

Belkaoui, A., "Linguistic Relativity in Accounting", *Accounting, Organisations* and *Society*, Vol. 3, No. 2, 1978, pp. 97-104.

Bernier and Roy (2003): "L'évolution des rôles dans la gestion des projets de technologies de l'information: le cas des progiciels de gestion intégrée," *Gestion,* volume 28, numéro 2, été 2003. HEC Montréal, pp. 48-57.

Bernier *et al.* (2003): "Transformer l'organisation par la mise en œuvre d'un ERP: une appropriation à trois niveaux," *Gestion,* volume 27, numero 4, hiver 2003. HEC Montréal, pp. 24-33.

Birnbeg, J.G. (1980): The Role of Accounting in Financial Disclosure: *Accounting, Organisations* and *Society*, 5(1), 71-80.

Birnbeg, J.G., Turopolec, L. and Young, S.M., "The Organizational Context of Accounting", *Accounting, Organisations and Society*, Vol. 8, No. 2/3, 1983, pp. 111-129.

Boiral, O. (1998): "Vers une gestion préventive des questions environnementales", *Gérer et Comprendre,* mars, pp. 27-37. Éd ESKAS, Paris.

Bourdieu, P. (1984): *Distinction: A Social Critique of the Judgement of Taste,* trans. R. Nice, London: Routledge & Kegan Paul.

Briers, M. and Hirst, M., "The Role of Budgetary Information in Performance Evaluation", *Accounting, Organisations and Society*, Vol. 15, No. 4, 1990, pp. 373-398.

Brunsson, N., "Ideas and Actions: Justification and Hypocracy as Alternative s to Control", *Accounting, Organisations and Society*, Vol. 18, No. 6, 1993, pp. 489-506.

Childe, S.J. *et al.* (1994): "Frameworks for Understanding Business Process Re-engineering," *International Journal of Operations and Production Management,* Vol. 14, No. 12, pp. 22-34.

Chipchase, J. (1999): Rogue websites: *Internet Works,* 25, 78-83.

Clark (2003): "Organizational Process Technologies and Hybrid Networks" in Clark, Peter (eds.), *Organizational Innovations*, Sage Publications, London, pp. 145-163.

Cooper, S.; Crowther, D.; Davies, M. and Davis, E.W. (2001): Shareholder or Stakeholder Value: London: CIMA.

Cooper, S.; Crowther, D. and Carter, C. (2000): "Challenging the Predictive Ability of Accounting Techniques in Modelling Organizational Futures", *Management Decision*, Vol. 19, No. 2, pp. 137-146.

Crowther, D. (2000): "Corporate Reporting, Stakeholders and the Internet: Mapping the New Corporate Landscape", *Urban Studies*, 37(10), 1837-1848.

Crowther, D. (2002a): "The Psychoanalysis of On-line Reporting" in L. Holmes, M. Grieco and D. Hosking (eds.), *Organising in an Information Age*, Aldershot: Ashgate, pp. 130-148.

Crowther, D. (2002b): No Accounting for Fashion: The Flawed Quest for Shareholder Value; Escola Superior de Tecnologia e Gestao da Guarda Working Paper No. 02/02.

Crowther, D. (2002c): A Social Critique of Corporate Reporting: Aldershot Ashgate.

Crowther, D. (2003): "How Important is Customer Satisfaction for Long-term Shareholder Value?" *Accountancy Business and the Public Interest*, Vol. 2 (e-journal).

Crowther, D. (2003b): Modern Epics and Corporate Well-being, paper presented at SCOS Conference, Cambridge, July.

Crowther, D. and Carter, C. (1998): *Copernican Metonymy and Management Accounting*; Aston Working Paper Series RP9901.

Crowther, D. and Greene, A-M. (2004): "Deconstructing the Employee: A Critique of the Gendered American Dream" in D.E. Hodgson and C. Carter (eds.), *Management Knowledge and the New Employee*, Aldershot, Ashgate, pp. 21-29.

Crowther, D. and Hosking, D.M. (2005): Accounting in Babel? Constructing Social Accounting as a Multi-logical Performance: Critical Perspectives on Accounting, Vol. 16, pp. 535-550.

Crowther, D. and Hosking, D.M. (2005b): Accounting for Sacred: Towards an Inclusion of Ethics in Social Accounting, Accounting Forum (Forthcoming).

Crowther, D. and Ortiz-Martinez, E. (2005): "No Principal, No Principles, No Reserves: Shell and the Failure of Agency Theory", unpublished paper.

Crowther, D. and Rayman-Bacchus, L. (2004): "The Future of Corporate Social Responsibility", in Crowther, D. and Rayman-Bacchus, L. (eds.), *Perspectives on Corporate Social Responsibility*, pp. 229-249. Ashgate eds. Great Britain.

Davenport, T. and Prussak (1997): *Working Knowledge*, Harvard Business School Press, Boston.

Davila-Gomez, A.M. (2005): "Beyond Business Ethics: Managers' Ethical Challenges Concerning Community and Employees", in Crowther, D. and Jatana, R. (eds.), *Representations of Social Responsibility*, pp. 74-104, ICFAI University Press, Hyderabad.

Deleuze, G. (1994): *Difference and Repetition*, trans. P. Patton, New York, Columbia University Press.

Deming, W.E. (1982): *Quality, Productivity and Competitive Position*, Cambridge, MA: Massachusetts Institute of Technology, Centre for Advanced Engineering Study.

Dewey, J. (1963): *Experience and Education*, Kappa Delta Pi Ed., United States.

Dollimore, J., *Radical Tragedy* (Chicago: University of Chicago Press, 1984).

Drucker, P.F. (1999): *Management Challenges for the 21st Century*, New York: Harper Business.

Durkheim, E., *Durkheim on Religion* in W.S.F. Pickering (ed.), London: Routledge & Kegan, 1975.

Emmanuel, C. and Gee, K.P., "Transfer Pricing: A Fair and Neutral Process", *Accounting and Business Research*, Autumn, 1982, pp. 273-8.

Emmanuel, C.; Otley, D. and Merchant, K., *Accounting for Management Control* (2nd edn.), London: Chapman and Hall, 1990.

Finkelstein, S., "Power in Top Management Teams: Dimensions, Measurement and Validation", *Academy of Management Journal*, Vol. 35, No. 3, 1992, pp. 505-538.

Freud, S. (1984): *On Metapsychology*, trans. A. Richards, Harmondsworth: Penguin.

Freud, S. (1975): *The Psychopathology of Everyday Life*, trans. A. Tyson, Harmondsworth: Pelican.

Freud, S. (1975b): *Cinq leçons sur la psychoanalyse*, Petite bibliothèque Payot, Paris.

Govindarajan, V. and Gupta, A.K. (1985): Linking Control Systems to Business Unit Strategy: Impact on Performance: *Accounting, Organizations and Society*, 10(l), 51-66.

Gray, R. (1992): "Accounting and Environmentalism: An Exploration of the Challenge of Gently Accounting for Accountability, Transparency and Sustainability", *Accounting, Organizations and Society*, 17(5), 399-425.

Gray, J., *Enlightenment's Wake*, London: Routledge, 1995.

Habermas, J. (1971): *Knowledge and Human Interests*, trans. J.J. Shapiro, Boston, Mass, Beacon Press.

Hafsi, T. *et al.* (2000): *La stratégie des organisations: une synthèse*, 2nd éd., Les éditions transcontinental inc. Montréal.

Hamilton, W., "Institution" in E. Seligman and A. Johnson (eds.), *Encyclopedia of the Social Sciences*, 1932, pp. 84-89.

Hinchelwood, R.D. (1989): "Social Possession of Identity" in B. Richards (ed.), *Crisis of the Self: Further Essays on Psychoanalysis and Politics*, London: Free Association Books, pp. 75-83.

Hollier, D. (1995), "From Beyond Hegel to Nietzsche's Absence" in L.A. Boldt-Irons, *On Battaille*, pp. 61-78, Albany: SUNY.

Hopper, T.; Storey, J. and Willmott, H., "Accounting for Accounting: Towards the Development of a Dialectic View", *Accounting, Organisations and Society*, Vol. 12, No. 5, 1987, pp. 437-456.

Hopwood, A., *Accounting and Human Behaviour*, London: Accountancy Age, 1974.

Horkheimer, M. and Adorno, T.W. (1944): *Dialectic of Enlightenment*, J. Cumming (trans.), New York: Herder & Herder, 1972.

Jaques, E. (1955): "Social Systems as a Defence against Persecutory and Depressive Anxiety" in M. Klein, P. Heimann and R. Money-Kryle (eds.), *New Directions in Psychoanalysis*, London: Tavistock.

Kaplan, R.S. (1984): "The Evolution of Management accounting", *The Accounting Review*, LIX(3), 390-418.

Klein, M. and Riviere, J. (1964): *Love, Hate and Reparation*, The Norton Library, New York.

Klein, M. (1932): *The Psychoanalysis of Children*, London: Hogarth.

Kotter, J.P. and Heskett, J.L. (1992): *Corporate Culture and Performance*, New York: The Free Press.

Lawrence, W.G. (1995): "The Seductiveness of Totalitarian States of Mind", *Journal of Health Care Chaplaincy*, October, 11-22.

Le Devoir (2002): *GM doit s'engager ou rembourser*, Website: http://www.ledevoir.com/2002/08/30/8222.html, consulted in February 2005.

Lyotard, J.F., *The Postmodern Condition*, trans. Bennington, G. and Massumi, B., Minneapolis: University of Minneapolis Press, 1984.

Marcuse, H. (1956): *Eros and Civilisation*, London: Routledge & Kegan Paul.

Marx, K. and Engels, *On Religion*, Moscow, 1955.

McCoy, C.S. (1985): *Management of Values: The Ethical Difference in Corporate Policy and Performance*, Marshfield, Mass: Pitman.

McDonald, D. and Puxty, A.G. (1979): "An Inducement—Contribution Approach to Corporate Financial Reporting", *Accounting, Organizations and Society*, 4(1/2), 53-65.

Menzies, Lyth I. (2000): "Social Systems as a Defence against Anxiety" in P. du Gay, J. Evans and P. Redman (eds.), *Identity: A Reader*, London: Sage.

Monks, R.A.G. and Minow, N. (1991): *Power and Accountability*, Glasgow: Harper Collins.

Murray and Willmott (2001): "Putting Information Technology in its Place: Towards Flexible Integration in the Network Age" in Bloomfield et coll (eds.), *Information Technology and Organizations—Strategies, Networks, and Integration*, pp. 160-180, Oxford University Press, Great Britain.

O'Dea, T.F., *The Sociology of Religion*, NJ: Prentice-Hall, 1966.

Orlikowski, W. (2001): "Improvising Organizational Transformation Over Time—A Situated Change Perspective" in Yates, Jo Anne and Maahen, John Von (eds.), *Information Technology and Organizational Transformation—History, Rhetoric and Practice*, pp. 223-274, Sage Publications, London.

Perls, F.S., "Theory and Technique of Personality Integration" in J.O. Stevens (ed.), *Gestalt Is*, Moab, Utah, Real People Press, 1975.

Peters, J. (2004): "Social Responsibility is Free—How Good Capitalism can Co-exist with Corporate Social Responsibility" in Crowther, D. and Rayman-Bacchus, L. (eds.), *Perspectives on Corporate Social Responsibility*, pp. 205-216, Ashgate eds. Great Britain.

Plato (399-384 B.C.): *Complete Works,* Ed. by Cooper, J.M. and Hutchison, D., S. Tacket Publishing Company, Indianapolis, 1997.

Popper, K., *The Poverty of Historicism*, London: Routledge, 1957.

Porter, M.E. (1980): *Competitive Strategy*, New York, Free Press.

Purdy, D.E. (1983): "The Enterprise Theory: An Extension", *Journal of Business Finance and Accounting*, 10(4), 531-541.

Radio Canada (2002): "L'obligation morale de GM", dans *La Tribune du Québec*, Website: http://radio-canada.ca/radio/latribune/29082002/1218.shtml, consulted in February 2005.

Roberts, V.Z. (1994): "Is Authority a Dirty Word? Some Dilemmas in Idealistic Organisations", *Journal of Social Work Practice*, Vol. 8, No. 2, pp. 185-192.

Rousseau, J-J. (1712-1778): "Discourse on the Origin and Foundations of Inequality Among Men" in Rousseau, J.J., *The First and Second Discourses*, Ed. by Masters, R.D., Translated by Master, R. and Masters, J., 1964, St. Martin's Press, New York.

Rubenstein, D.B. (1992): "Bridging the Gap between Green Accounting and Black Ink", *Accounting Organizations and Society*, 17(5), 501-508.

Scapens, R.W., "Never Mind the Gap: Towards an Institutional Perspective of Management Accounting Practices", *Management Accounting Research*, 5(3/4), 1994, 97-104.

Selznick, N. (1957): *Leadership in Administration: A Sociological Interpretation*, Evanston, Ill: Row, Peterson.

Senge, P.M. (1990): *The Fifth Discipline: The Art and Practice of the Learning Organization*, New York: Toronto, Doubleday/Currency.

Sievers, B. (1994): *Work Death and Life Itself: Essays on Management and Organization*, Berlin; de Gruyter.

Sridhar, S.S. (1994): "Managerial Reputation and Internal Reporting", *The Accounting Review*, 69(2), 343-363.

Suzuki, D. (2005): *David Suzuki Foundation*, website: http://www.davidsuzuki.org/Climate Change/, consulted in February 2005.

Takeushi, H. and Nonaka, I. (2004): *Hitotsubashi on Knowledge Management*, John Wiley & Sons, USA.

Thompson, J.D. (1967): *Organizations in Action*, New York: McGraw-Hill, USA.

Topal, S.E. and Crowther, D. (2004): "Bioengineering and Corporate Social Responsibility" in Crowther, D. and Rayman-Bacchus, L. (eds.), *Perspectives on Corporate Social Responsibility*, pp. 229-249, Ashgate eds. Great Britain.

Turner, B.S., *Religion and Social Theory*, London: Heinemann Educational Books, 1983.

Veblen, T. (1899): *The Theory of the Leisure Classes*, New York: New American Library.

Wilson, B., *Religion in Sociological Perspective*, Oxford: Oxford University Press, 1982.

Winnicott, D.W. (1965): *The Maturational Process and the Facilitating Environment*, The Hogarth Press, London.

Witz, A. and Savage, M. (1994): *Gender and Bureaucracy*, Oxford: Basil Blackwell.

44

Auditing and Academic Quality in India and the UK

ANANYA S. GUHA AND DAVID CROWTHER

INTRODUCTION

To ensure delivery services in academic institutions some form of evaluation is required and in academe one of the principle forms of evaluation is self-evaluation. In India generally speaking there is hardly any monitoring or evaluation of the teachers, which can be contrasted with the UK where such monitoring is, if anything, excessive. So this paper considers how we 'measure' the performance of teachers. Additionally of course there is in academic institutions a financial and administrative auditing system and so a further consideration is to what extent such auditing ensures quality services.

Quality assurance is the catchword today in academic institutions. But auditing is primarily interpreted as to ensure that records are maintained properly, that there are no financial 'irregularities'; all contribute to the dimension of quality. But administrative or financial lacuna does not necessarily imply financial misappropriation. Registers, financial books of account, service records, receipts of money must be scrupulously maintained auditors point out. The records must reveal that everything is on order, but records can, also be manipulated. The 'Mr. Clean' image has to be maintained and this is exemplified if everything in the form of registers, files, money receipt, cash books are maintained systematically and 'cleanly'

Auditors will point out a hundred deficiencies: bills were sent but there is no record of receipt. The stock verification of goods purchased show that there was no stock entry. The 'eye' is immediately on malpractice and corruption. The telephone registers are not maintained. If an outstation call is made by the Head of Office to one of his colleagues, in the evening outside of office hours this is questioned.

But, what if teachers are not taking classes regularly? What if the syllabus is not completed? What if there is student unrest in campuses (not a new phenomena in India) who will be held responsible? Who will then 'audit' the academic resources? Both students and teachers suffer alike in such conditions. True; administrative and financial receipts/deposits must be correctly measured as a part of checks and balance especially when people are vulnerable to corrupt practices, because of disparities in economics. Corruption sadly enough in such situations becomes the order of the day.

MEASURING PERFORMANCE

Various attempts have been made to measure academic performance in a quantitative way, on the assumptions that such quantification gives added rigour and therefore added reliability and meaningfulness to such measurement. This is of course nonsense but has been prevalent within the discourse for a considerable period of time. For example, Churchman (1967) states that in order to evaluate performance it is necessary to measure performance and that measurement needs the following components: language to express results; specification of objects to which the results will apply; standardisation for transferability between organisations or over time; and accuracy and control to permit evaluation. Thus the use of performance indicators has long been accepted as a mechanism for measuring operational performance. As such, these indicators provide a means of 'attention directing' for managers towards salient features in operational procedures as well as providing a measure of performance. They also serve the purpose of providing the user with information regarding the level of service provision to be expected (Burns, 1992) and providing the basis for a dialogue between customers and the organisation itself. Such indicators therefore simulate a market orientation for the organisation (Adnum, 1993) although they suffer from the problem of simplifying the factors which constitute performance for the organisation concerned and exclude key constituents of such performance, such as quality of service delivery, through a concentration upon the measurable component such organisational performance. These performance indicators also, however, serve the purpose of directing the attention of management towards salient features of operational performance and, at the same time, a mechanism for controlling such operational performance, in much the same manner as budgetary control reporting does. Implicit within the use of such performance indicators is the assumption that setting objectives at a strategic level through the use of performance indicators can be translated into operationalisation at any level within the organisation and that managing in this way will effect the cultural transformation desired to achieve this market orientation. It is equally assumed that regular reporting upon the achievement of such indicators will in itself improve the performance of the organisation (Wholey, 1993a). In a study of the use of such indicators in the Dutch Department of Defence, Mol (1996) suggests that such indicators satisfy the criteria of relevance and coherence when incorporated into a systems of responsibility accounting but in doing so the use of such indicators is transferred into the domain of accounting, thereby reducing, by implication, the importance of non-accounting measures of performance. This problem is recognised by Clarke (1995) who argues that managers in such an environment need relevant non-financial measures of performance incorporated into the organisation's formal reporting system, which are directly linked to the strategy of the organisation.

Bowerman (1995) consider the role of the Audit Commission (UK) in overseeing the audit of performance indicators as well as the audit of financial performance and concludes that the objectives of performance reporting in the public sector appear to be moving in the reverse direction from such objectives in the private sector. This seems to accord with the objectives of New Public Management and the use of such indicators has been widely regarded as one clement within a 'shopping basket' of 'New Public Management' reforms (Pollitt, 1995). Like other elements of this broad package however, which can appear ambivalent in their interpretation, the choice of indicators in specific applications is open to debate, as indeed is the role which they play in the management of public services. Thus Pollitt (1990) saw the rise of Neo-Taylorism and classic scientific management in the limited application of such performance indicators in the UK public sector, while Hoggett (1996) has identified such indicators as one of three control strategies imposed on public and quasi-public organisations. He argued that while there has been an operational decentralisation in such organisations there has also been a reassertion of a number of fundamentally bureaucratic mechanisms of control with these indicators producing a new form of surveillance which has become more remote and less visible in a pattern of 'centralised decentralisation.'

Performance indicators act as surrogate measures for the market measures prevalent in commercial organisations and attempt to mimic customer satisfaction, as expressed through sales in a commercial organisation. Such measures often surfer from the deficiencies of all surrogate measures in failing to measure the key components of organisational success, many of which are qualitative in nature rather than quantitative, as performance indicators must inevitably be. A survey of performance indicators suggested by 57 professional associations involved in UK local government management (Ammons, 1994) suggests that such associations are heavily involved in promoting the use of such indicators as standards of performance but that the majority of standards prescribed by such organisations focus only indirectly upon the various purposes of local government operations. As such the usefulness of the indicators suggested and implemented must inevitably be questioned in the context of providing tools to managers in seeking to manage and improve performance in the organisation. Implanting such a set or performance indicators upon a quasi-market organisation, such as a university, whose rationale for existence is to provide a particular range of services to those in need, purports to provide a mechanism for controlling the provision or those services and a means to evaluate the efficiency in providing these services, at least insofar as the use or surrogate measures can provide such a measure of efficiency. In fact, such a set of indicators can be dysfunctional for the organisation concerned.

Such indicators therefore significantly fail to provide measures of effectiveness in service provision, as such measures of effectiveness tend not to be representable in terms of quantitative metrics. Indeed a concentration upon meeting targets in terms of performance indicators can actually be deleterious to achieving the actual objectives or the organisation in terms of service delivery, through a concentration upon transaction cost minimisation.

Indeed in a study of the Scottish local government experience of developing and using performance indicators Midwinter (1994) makes the point that bureaucratic models of control have unsuccessful track records, the performance indicators currently in use are inadequate, and that the political and conceptual constraints on rationality in such an environment make the use of such indicators an inappropriately prescriptive model of control. His arguments can be applied equally to any university.

Throughout the world, but especially in the UK, the USA and Australia, programs are under way to introduce better public management and more highly valued public service through the stimulation of improved performance of government bodies (Wholey, 1993b). Such programs are based upon a focus upon the results of the body concerned with a delegation of authority being exchanged for accountability for the results achieved. A key component of such programs is a focus upon performance indicators as a mechanism for strategy selection and operational control. Meekings (1995) however reports that although the potential for improvement through the use of performance measures is vast, it nevertheless remains largely unrealised. He argues that this is due to poor implementation and a lack of linking of the indicators from top level strategy formulation to lower level operationalisation. Smith (1995a) on the other hand agrees that outcome measurement is in its infancy in the public services and that such performance indicators are being developed without any clear idea about the nature of the type and standard of performance which they are being used to indicate but argues that the role of such indicators should be to inform political debate concerning the role of public services rather than as a means of operational control. He argues that, without any clear consensus as to how performance in the public sector should be interpreted, any evaluation therefore must inevitably be dependant upon the objectives and perspective of the person, or body, undertaking the analysis of performance. Smith also argues (1995b) that schemes of performance indicators have been implemented in the public sector on the assumption that they will yield benefits in terms of efficiency and equity but suggests that factors involved in their operationalisation, including potential costs of operationalisation, are such that they tend to have dysfunctional consequences. It is further argued that performance indicators as currently applied in this environment actually embed current cultural norms into the operational performance of the organisation, leading towards defensive behaviour, and that the selection of appropriate indicators is essential to facilitate the desired cultural transformation.

Likierman (1993) argues that performance indicators are valuable managerial tools if used properly but can result in wasted managerial time and distorted actions if not so used. Ammons (1994) argues that their value is both to managers of the organisation and to citizens in fostering more extensive debate prior to strategic planning, rather than in facilitating operational control. Taylor and Convey (1993) on the other hand argue that the use of performance indicators can facilitate an improvement in performance through enabling organisational learning to lead to improved operational control. They concur however that in order to do so there must be a clear link between operational indicators of performance and the objectives of the organisation as a representation of the critical success factors of the organisation. For a university therefore the question which needs to be addressed is concerned with the purpose of that university and the purpose of education.

TRANSFERABLE SKILLS

One of the things which employers are stated to want from graduates – apart from subject knowledge – is a set of skills which are useful in their subsequent employment. These skills will be acquired partly through the studying of any particular course and partly through working with others as part of the degree program. According to Bloom (1956) a course should, in ascending order, equip a student to:

- recall and recognise specified information.
- comprehend and digest the information.
- apply what they have learned.
- analyse the subject, with an understanding of the component parts and their interrelationships.
- synthesise the subject taking an overview.
- evaluate their knowledge, understanding and competence critically.

Transferable or generic skills are not specific to a particular subject, course or job. Rather they, as the name suggests, can be applied to every job. They include communication, analytical, interpersonal, quantitative, problem-solving, decision-making and learning skills, as well as computer literacy. Increasingly in the current environment importance is becoming attached to the teaching of transferable skills. This is evidenced in the UK by the Enterprise in Higher Education Initiative of the Department of Employment which commenced in 1987 with the aim of helping Higher Education Institutions to equip students for the "world of work," through the development of transferable skills which will be required in their future working lives. Further evidence of the importance of transferable skills is provided by the Accounting Education Change Commission's (AECC) Position Statement Number I (1990), which outlined the committees' views on the objectives of education for accountants. The AECC stated that an accounting degree programme should prepare students to become professional accountants, not to be professional accountants. The AECC also developed a taxonomy of objectives consisting of three components: skills, knowledge and professional orientation. Greater emphasis on communication, intellectual and interpersonal skills was advocated, along with an appreciation of ethical issues. Indeed, with regard to the knowledge requirement, subject specific knowledge was seen as only one important aspect along with general knowledge, and organisational and business knowledge. Additionally, it was considered that the focus of teaching should be on developing analytical and conceptual thinking, rather than on knowledge transfer. Such an approach can be likened to focusing on the higher objectives in Bloom's taxonomy.

It is clear, therefore, that there is a growing recognition of the importance of what students can do, as well as what they know. This has been accompanied by a shift away from the traditional teaching culture of higher education, to that of a learning culture, in which students are encouraged to take responsibility for their own learning. It is argued that the use of group work, such as case studies, has a significant role to play in promoting the development of transferable skills within this more student-centred learning environment.

Many authors have advocated the use of such group activity in education. For example, Argyns (1980) describes the following benefits:

- hearing others views,
- confronting differences,
- making decisions,
- becoming aware of the complexity of reality, and
- realising that there are rarely right or wrong answers since cases are incomplete, as are real-life situations.

Although Argyris' work relates to the use of cases in business education, Libby's work (1991) provides specific evidence that this kind of exercise is of value in developing transferable skills. Libby lists the following advantages:

- Affective benefits to students:
  - student motivation,
  - student interest in material, and
  - development of confidence.
- Skill development of students:
  - oral communication skills,
  - written communication skills, and
  - group interaction skills.
- Cognitive benefits to students:
  - development of problem-solving skills,
  - development of judgment skills,
  - development of ability to solve problems addressing multiple issues,
  - development of the ability to deal with ambiguity,
  - development of an understanding of the real world, and
  - comprehension of the material by students.

Again, most of these benefits relate to the development of transferable skills but they can also be likened to the social capital which Bourdieu (1984) refers to. Significantly of course it requires students to work together rather than to absorb knowledge in isolation and therefore runs contrary to the market forces in higher education.

A CRITIQUE OF TEACHING AND LEARNING

Teaching strategies adopted within the higher education area are based upon the learning theories which are predominant at any particular point in time. In a review of the existing theories of learning

Burgoyne and Stuart (1977) identified eight schools of thought and the teaching strategies appropriate to each school. The basis of all teaching however can be considered within the context of Bloom's (1956) taxonomy of the six aims of teaching and Kolb's (1984) analysis of the four stages in the learning cycle. More recent work has concentrated upon the preferred learning styles of students and the elements essential to the teaching process to facilitate learning. Thus Gibbs (1992) states that for effective learning the material being studied needs to provide motivation to the student and incorporate material requiring activity from the learner and interaction with others, within the context of a well structured knowledge base. Houldsworth (1994) however has argued that students have responsibility for their own learning but that the learning experience must meet both the experiential and cognitive needs of the student in order for effective learning to take place. She contrasts this with the enjoyability derived from the novelty factor of the use of the internet as a learning vehicle and argues that this novelty factor does not in itself provide a vehicle for learning.

Learning theory therefore is concerned with addressing the differences in the way people learn and with meeting their needs within the teaching strategy adopted, in order to maximise the educational value of that teaching. This learning theory is grounded in cognitive psychology and Kahney (1993) considers the problem solving aspect of learning and identifies that novices and experts differ in the way in which they structure problems to be solved and in the strategies adopted for solving those problems. This suggests that different teaching/learning strategies are needed for novices and experts. This therefore implies that the teaching of managers, who can be regarded as experts because of their possession of a more sophisticated knowledge base, needs to be different from that of undergraduates, who can be regarded as novices in the subject being taught. Rumelhart and Norman (1983) however consider the way in which knowledge is represented in memory and suggest that schemes are created which enable new knowledge to be fitted into meaningful contexts within the existing knowledge framework. Cognitive psychology however is concerned with the acquisition of knowledge and does not separate the knowledge itself from the process by which it is acquired.

The different needs of different groups of students is recognised by Grupe and Connolly (1995) who argue for the different needs of adult learners, and by Filipczak (1995) who argues, within an organisational learning context, that training must match the preferred learning style of the people involved in that learning process in order for that training to be effective. All modern learning theory, and the teaching strategies developed from that theory, is founded in the student centred learning paradigm initiated by Rogers (1951: 389) who states:

> "We cannot teach another person directly: we can only facilitate his learning."

Rogers also considers that learning takes place best in the context of a relevant situation and occurs most readily within the context of problem solving. He states (1961: 286):

> "Significant learning occurs more readily in relation to situations perceived as problems."

He bases his arguments about effective teaching upon his experience as a therapist, and relates learning to his experiences specifically when he states (1961: 288):

> "In therapy the resources for learning one's self lie within. There is very little data which the therapist can supply which will be of help since the data to be dealt with exist within the person. In education this is not true. There are many resources of knowledge, of techniques, of theory, which constitute raw material for use. It seems to me that what I have said about therapy suggests that these materials, these resources, be made available to the students, not forced upon them. Here a wide range of ingenuity and sensitivity is an asset."

The advent of computers into education as an integral part of the teaching process can be considered to match ideally the student centred paradigm of learning initiated by Rogers. This is particularly true of the development of e-learning which has been considered to be a means of putting learning entirely in the hands of the student and giving him/her complete responsibility for his/her learning. Indeed this facility has been used as a justification for the seizing upon the technology as the vehicle to use for the enhancement of the education process. At the same time this technology aids the achievement of the educationalist agenda of improving efficiency in the teaching process.

There is currently unquestioning acceptance of the existence of a place for internet-based training within the educational process and the discourse has centred around, not its validity within the process, but rather the way in which it can best satisfy teaching objectives. Thus, the discourse is concerned with its use in teaching and an anonymous paper in Personnel Journal (1995) considers the variety of ways in which computers can assist training, while Bottoms (1994) extends this unquestioning acceptance into the area of multimedia. Ward (1994) considers that e-learning is of benefit both to educators and to students but the discourse remains centred in the domain of the educators rather than that of the learners. The agenda of the discourse moreover is set by the educators rather than by those undergoing education, although the language of the discourse is intended to imply that the opposite is in fact the case. Thus Marx considers the advantages of the use of such technology and claims that its use is more effective than classroom teaching without basing this claim upon any empirical evidence. She warns however that it is not a universal panacea and its use needs to be planned for maximal effectiveness, stating (1995: 58):

> "Experts, therefore, caution that businesses shouldn't mistake a textbook transplanted to a computer and hyped up with fancy graphics and sound as interactive multimedia training. Indeed a key behind the technology is liberating learning from the linear tyranny of a textbook where one chapter moves in lock-step with the next."

The acceptance of e-learning as an educational vehicle is assumed also by Trainor (1992) who argues that its use has emphasised the quality of learning although he too recognises that it is not a universal panacea. King (1994) also recognises this limitation and states that the cognitive strategies involved in the learning process must be recognised and addressed in order to ensure that it is effective in the education process. The discourse therefore recognises that care should be taken in the way in which technology is used in education but is unquestioning in its acceptance of the place of, and benefits ensuing from using, computers as a method of delivery. Thus Laurillard, Swift and Darby (1993) consider the ways in which computers are used in education; Ball (1995) considers how the technology has been used and how it should be used in education; and Lilley (1995) extols specifically the potential benefit to be derived from the use of CDroms. Williams and Nicholson however inject a critical note into the discourse by claiming that it has not always been used to maximal advantage in an attempt to foster a student centred approach to learning. They distinguish between value for money as an aim and the values within the educational process which it is claimed that computer-based training meets, stating (1994: 3):

> "The nature of 'efficiency' gains through technology should be examined to see from whose perspective and in what context they are efficient. The effect on student learning should also be considered. The aims of tertiary education (to produce graduates who not only have a good knowledge of their subject but who have developed enquiring minds and the ability to manage their own future learning) should always be borne in mind."

The benefits to higher education institutions from e-learning are obvious – more students at a reduced marginal cost. The benefits to students are less obvious, consisting primarily of a badge to show graduation from a particular university but without necessarily acquiring the skills (as opposed to knowledge of the subject material) expected from such a graduate. Thus, the cultural capital and transferable skills which give value to a university education are likely to largely absent and the concomitant future prospects are therefore also likely to be missing. The value of such education is therefore likely to be somewhat more questionable that a traditional qualification. Universities recognise of course that a graduate from a course who does not have the expected skills is likely to devaluate the course itself and thereby undermine the brand which they so jealously guard. It order to protect against this possibility therefore universities will brand different degrees in different ways – just as they brand degrees obtained from a franchise operation differently – thereby practicing deception upon the students who pay for the course without an awareness of the difference in standing of the degree, while at the same time protecting their income stream and the performance measures upon which the remuneration of senior-managers is dependant.

REFLEXIVITY

Reflexivity is concerned with self-awareness, particularly regarding possible errors brought about by unconscious assumptions

(Crowther and Green, 2004). In the context of teaching therefore it is concerned with a consideration of how one's own teaching might be improved. Given the problems with bench-marking and the setting of performance indicators outlined above then the importance of reflexivity assumes prominence. Of course this reflexivity is aided by some external reference points and the most common is feedback.

Two techniques are in common use in the UK to obtain this feedback. The first is to ask students by means of questionnaires. Post-modernists are particularly critical of this techniques, which some have argued tells one more about the person who has determined what questions to ask, than about the subject being researched. Those with intentions of being helpful will answer the questions as best they understand them and to the best of their knowledge about what is being asked. This does not guarantee that they were the most pertinent questions for the study in hand, nor that everyone would understand the questions in the same way. Then there are those who would answer not according to their knowledge, but perhaps according to what they thought the researcher wanted to hear or for some political agenda of their own.

The other techniques in common use is that of peer review, where one lecturer observed another and provides some feedback designed to enable improvement. Although not without risk this techniques works because it is predicated upon the assumption that all academics are looking to improve in their teaching. Consequently the peer review process is not related in any way to the reward structure of the university and is run entirely by academics for their own (and students' of course) benefit.

SOCIAL RESPONSIBILITY AND HIGHER EDUCATION

The marketisation of higher education is premised in the myth of the free market as being beneficial to all (Crowther, 2002b). It is widely accepted – almost unquestioningly – that free markets will lead to greater growth and that we will all benefit from this growth. In opposition to the myth of the market is the concept of social responsibility which stems from stakeholder theory (Freeman, 1984). The acceptance of a stakeholder approach to organisations and the existence of multiple perspectives upon the objectives of an organisation inevitably imply a rejection of a monistic view of those organisations (Crowther, 2002a). Thus there can be no one single view of the objectives of the organisation and consequently no one single evaluation of the performance of that organisation. It is therefore inevitable within this paradigm that if monism is rejected as a view of organisations then this implies that the economic rationality view of organisations and their behaviour must also be rejected. For a university however the objectives of equipping students for their future life and thereby benefiting society must not be forgotten in the drive for marketisation. Growth in student numbers and/or turnover are not objectives in their own right for a university. Indeed this sort of objective, and concomitant performance measure, are not wholly subscribed to in the untrammelled free market of the commercial organisation (see Cooper, Crowther, Davies and Davis, 2001: Crowther, 2002c) and so certainly cannot be justified for a university with claims to providing tertiary education (Maskell and Robinson, 2001).

The central argument of this paper is that by treating higher education as a commodity which can best be managed by the operations of the market, and rewarding the decision makers accordingly, the objectives of such education have been betrayed and lost within a drive for growth – on the unquestioned assumption that more equates to better. Thus, the socially responsible ethos of higher education has been subordinated to the forces of marketisation and both society and the participants in such education are the poorer for it.

ACADEMIC AUDITING: TOWARDS A 'DEFINITION'

Measuring performance of teachers in higher education is to assess accountability in the processes of the educational system which keep it 'running' as it were. Accountability in our opinion will mean not only the engagement of the teacher in the classroom and whether the academics have completed teaching courses; but also their 'performance' in terms of pedagogical innovation, research and extension work, improvisation, student support, etc. The 'environment,' the ethos of teachers is not only the classroom but beyond; where they impart counselling to students, and in this manner *extend* the classroom. The classroom has a multiplier effect or syndrome, a teacher should be in a position to, through innovation and change create more 'classrooms'. Pedagogy can awaken senses of creativity, the pleasure principle of learning and learning to learn; it depends a great deal on the teacher to enkindle this in the student.

Performance is not only *a priori* but also how teachers can introduce into the classroom, the elements of surprise, change and innovation. In, India teachers do not go beyond stereotypes: the lecture method, the 'chalk and talk' method and dictating notes. This does not make teaching a two-way communication, in which the student also has an audience. The use of technology, the radio, the television and the computer, that is a technology mix; can take teaching and learning beyond the complacency of the classroom. Teachers should make the learning process as autonomous and autodidactic as possible. Measurability of performance can be examined when students are independent learners and teachers are props in the *scheme* of things. The teacher then is a facilitator, this is also not to insinuate that there should be no lectures in the classrooms, but more and more students should have a *right* to learning, not only by the manner of what is thrust or imposed upon them. The three principles here (Crowther and Rayman Bacchus, 2004) in what we will term 'environmental academic auditing' are:

- Sustainability,
- Accountability, and
- Transparency.

Teaching methods should have sustenance, an accountability not only to students but also to the institution; it should be transparent in its use of a combination and transparency of methods. Such a typology of teaching will ensure a situation where the teacher is also a learner, desires change and considers improvisation a viable teaching ontology. Such practices will be 'good' practices where the environment is relaxed, flexible, and where students can learn at their own pace. In India the emphasis willingly or unwillingly right from school education is on cramming and learning by rote, also the teacher-student ratio is one too many. This is a serious impediment to effective and independent learning. Further there should be course relevance; that, there should be a match between studying, and needs of the society. Education should be need-based and application-oriented, like training for research even from the college level onwards. Writing short dissertations can play a role in shaping young minds to be future researchers.

We raise the issue of accountability of teachers since simply and routinely taking a class owes no responsibility either to the institution or to the taught. There is no correspondence between taking classes and accountability or, 'measuring' performance. Again, teachers must be entrusted with more managerial functions like conducting examinations, preparing reports on behalf of the institution or suggesting/ designing new courses. Today, education in a country like India too; is assuming the characteristics and proportions of an industry especially with the popularity of Distance Education: buying and selling course ware at the same time attempting to make Education more cost effective/ cost efficient. Suddenly as it were we are awakening in India to evaluate education in terms of costing, financing and self-financing. The University Grant Commission, the apex body of higher education in India exercising financial and regulatory control over colleges and universities is structuring colleges and universities to generate their own revenue and not be only dependent on government largesse. This is a challenge for the academic institutions to be more autonomous, and also be in a position to award their own degrees.

However, Privatisation of Higher Education in India has been controversial. The main reason for this is that private institutions which do not get any government fund charge exorbitantly. What has gained currency is the capitation fees taken by them which is not tuition fees. The tuition fees is in addition to what is called the 'capitation' fees which is in effect a 'contribution' by the wards or parents of the student. Such people are wealthy and can afford both the 'capitation' fees as well as the normal fees to be paid. This brings in its wake the question of affordability: the poorer students that is, the students who are economically backward, are not able to get access to such institutions. Thus such institutions border on becoming educational shops, and in some cases as for example the Manipal Institute; the University Grant Commission has intervened to check the fees that are charged to students. Capitation fees are highly prevalent in South India and they exist not only in general colleges but also in specialised disciplines such as engineering and medical college. Despite a number of injunctions both from the High Courts and the Supreme Court of India testifying to the pecuniary motives and class bias of such privatisation of education these institutions continue to thrive Real assessment in terms of quality say of the faculty, the student-teacher ratio, the results of the students, etc., have not been assessed and these institutions exist in a limbo, with the public not sure of their true academic merit. They are, in that sense a 'necessary evil.' The fees of the government funded or owned colleges are at least ten times less than the privately owned institutions. Privatisation of higher education in India which began in the 80s continue till this day, but Information Technology in the form of IT and Computer courses has captured the capitalist market in a welfare state. This means that to be trained in IT, students transcend class barriers to pay and get admitted in short-term courses, with the conviction that this will fetch them something at least in the job market. But the institutions running these courses are computer firms, strictly speaking not academic institutions; and their courses are duly accredited.

The other paradigm of auditing is the more *definitive* one: that is financial auditing, assessing if there are 'irregularities' house-keeping, accounting for money received and spent, keeping records of assets, perishable and imperishable goods, maintaining records of library books, accession registers, stock registers, cash book, money receipt and payments, etc. Spending we are told, has to be in strict accordance with the delegation of powers vested with the Head of the institution. Financial bungling both deliberate and inadvertent can be detected such cases. Again the dividing line between the two is tenuous depending also on how Auditors interpret such 'tenuous-ness.' Such situations can be very uncomfortable to say the least for the authorities of higher education institutions concerned. Form the auditor's point of view an academic institution is an office or an office department. Our contention is: auditing in an academic institution should be holistic whereby the style and functioning of an institution is measured *critically* by both administrative and academic yardsticks. The policy-makers of the country as far as higher education is concerned should measure performance and 'quality control' (the buzz word today) administratively and academically, and not in a piecemeal manner as is normally done: one wing looking at financial maintenance, the other an apex body of higher education or its corollary the NAAC in India (National Accreditation Assessment Council), which visits college all over the country, grades them and suggests ways and means for improvement like for example suggesting extension course, faculty improvement, etc. Such an apex body views the academic relevance or sustainability of an institution. The former is a financial/auditors organization, the Audit and Accounts Office. Government of India for example; and the latter a government controlled academic monitoring agency. The two are not compatible nor are meant to be. Herein lies the problem, the two are operating in separate directions; hence assessment is piecemeal. But we 'critique' the 'concept' of auditing as homogeneous, two sides of the same coin; and not heterogeneous. This in the ultimate analysis is 'Academic Auditing' which must perforce be an indicator of performance at both administrative and academic levels.

With the advent of this notion of thinking that academic enterprise is also economic activity and revenue generation, maximization/ minimization of profits; then Education is construed as an industry. Herein the question of ethics and ethical practices come in as they do in the case of the corporate and business sectors; the relationship between the employer and the employee, who are the stake holders, etc. If education too, becomes 'organization centric' (Crowther and Rayman Bacchus, 2004) then will quality suffer and will we have educational 'shops' rather than good institutions, good teachers and researches, adopting a collective goodwill towards its beneficiaries/ stakeholders? If educational institutions are seen as collaborators and not as distinct identities then we are sharing cultural and academic resources. If not we are sharing money and concentrating on profit-making skills; liberalizing education. Of course an argument is that both quality and profit making can co-exist. If we are to form a complete system of Education as the Gaia hypothesis posits about Corporations (Crowther and Rayman Bacchus, 2004) then education is collaborative, partnership-oriented in the best sense of the term, a system of inter-dependence, give and take. This is in contrast to the practice of classical liberalization.

Educational institutions even in underdeveloped countries such as India, are assuming the structure of Corporations; because of economic intransigencies, the attendant job market, information technology, distance education, training needs *et al*. Education is growing fast into an industry in India, the 'market' is competitive, it is becoming increasingly privatized: and so its concomitant determinants are: market economics, market realities and job needs. The generally held notion that government owned educational institutions are better than the privately owned ones is now seriously challenged. Those driven by market economics and job needs are willing to pay any amount to get admission into professional institutions. The fundamental economies of demand and supply underlies educational ethics today. Thus the dialectics between private and government owned or funded educational institutions, and the competition existing between them has to be taken into critical account and scrutiny.

Hence the need for academic assurance, quality and auditing.

CONCLUSIONS

Academic auditing is a composite whole: consisting not only of financial status but also of the 'quality' of the academic services rendered. After all the measurability of an academic institution is in its totality: how it functions both academically and administratively. Our argument here is that the qualitative measures of the 'bench-marking brigade' do not adequately address the needs of academic quality. In particular they ignore the simple fact that the greatest guarantee of quality in teaching is the pride which an academic takes in his/her work. Although accountability is essential there are differences in expectations which need to be considered, particularly when that accountability is tinged with (real or perceived) monitoring and control. In this respect the experiences in our respective countries differ.

REFERENCES

Accounting Education Change Commission, Objectives of Education for Accountants (Position Statement Number 1), AECC (1990).

Adnum, D. (1993): "Using Performance Indicators for Effective Public Sector Management," *Management Accounting* (UK), Vol. 71, No. 1, pp. 48-52.

Ammons, D.N. (1994): "The Role of Professional Associations in Establishing and Promoting Performance Standards for Local Government," *Public Productivity and Management Review*, Vol. 17, No. 3, pp. 281-91.

Anon (1995): "Training: Computer-based Training Works," *Personnel Journal*, Jan. 1995, pp. 15-16.

Argyris, C., "Some Limitations of the Case Method: Experiences in a Management Development Programme," *Academy of Management Review*, 5(2), (1980).

Ball, C. (1995): "IT: An Impending Revolution," *Business of Education*, No. 7, p. 7.

Bloom, B.S. (ed.), (1956): *Taxonomy of Educational Objectives: Cognitive Domain*, London, Longmans.

Bottoms, D.T. (1994): "Multimedia Delivers the Message," *Industry Week*, Vol. 243, No. 7, pp. 70-72.

Bourdieu, P. (1994): *Distinction: A Social Critique of the Judgement of Taste*, London, Routledge & Kegan Paul.

Bowerman, M. (1995): "Auditing Performance Indicators: The Role of the Audit Commission in the Citizen's Charter Initiative," *Financial Accountability and Management*, Vol. 11, No. 2, pp. 171-83.

Burgoyne, J., and Stuart, R. (1977): "Implicit Learning Theories as Determinants of the Effect of Management Development Programmes," *Personnel Review*, Vol. 6, No. 2, pp. 5-14.

Burns, T. (1992): "Researching Customer Service in the Public Sector," *Journal of the Market Research Society*, Vol. 34, No. 1, pp. 53-60.

Churchman, C.W. (1967): "Why Measure" in C.W. Chuchman and P. Ratoosh (eds.), *Measurement: Definition and Theories*, London, Wiley, pp. 83-94.

Clarke, P. (1995): "Non-financial Measures of Performance in Management," *Accountancy Ireland*, Vol. 27, No. 2, pp. 22-23.

Cooper, S.; Crowther D.; Davies, M. and Davis, E.W. (2001): Shareholder or Stakeholder Value, London, CIMA.

Crowther, D. (2002a): A Social Critique of Corporate Reporting: Aldershot: Ashgate.

Crowther, D. (2002b): The Importance of Corporate Social Responsibility: Escola Superior de Tecnologia e Gestao da Guarda Working Paper No. 05/02.

Crowther, D. (2002c): Creating Shareholder Value, London, Spiro.

Crowther, D. and Green, M. (2004): Organisation Theory, London, CIPD.

Crowther, D. and Rayman Bacchus, L. (2004): "The Future of Corporate Social Responsibility," in D. Crowther and L. Rayman Bacchus (eds.), *Perspectives on Corporate Social Responsibility*, Aldershot, Ashgate, pp. 229-49.

Filipezak, B. (1995): "Different Strokes: Learning Styles in the Classroom," *Training*, Vol. 32, No. 3, pp. 43-48.

Freeman, R.E. (1984): Strategic Management: A Stakeholder Approach, Boston, Ma., Pitman.

Gibbs, G. (1992): Improving the Quality of Student Learning, Bristol, Technical and Educational Services.

Grupe, F.H. and Connolly, F.W. (1995): "Grownups are Different: Computer Training for Adult Learners," *Journal of Systems Management*, Vol. 46, No. 1, pp. 58-64.

Hoggett, P. (1996): "New Modes of Control in the Public Services," *Public Administration*, Vol. 74, Spring, pp. 9-32.

Houldsworth, E. (1994): Multimedia in Management Education—Theoretical Framework and Methodological Choices, Henley Management College Working Paper No. HWP9420.

Kahney, H. (1993): Problem Solving, Buckingham, Open University Press.

King, T. (1994): Authoring for Distance Learning, The CTISS File No. 17, pp. 30-32.

Kolb, D.A. (1984): Experiential Learning—Experience as the Source of Learning and Development, NJ, Englewood Cliffs.

Laurillard, D.; Swift, B. and Darby, J. (1993): Academics' Use of Courseware Materials: A Survey; *Association for Learning Technology Journal*, Vol. 1, No. 1, pp. 4-12.

Libby, P.A.: Barriers to Using Cases in Accounting Education: Issues in Accounting Education, Vol. No. 2 (1991).

Likierman, A. (1993): "Performance Indicators: 20 Early Lessons from Managerial Use," *Public Money and Management*, Vol. 13, No. 4, pp. 15-22.

Lilley, P. (1995): "Taking Advantage of CD-R," *Management Accounting* (UK), July/Aug. 1995, p. 20.

Marx, W. (1995): "The New High Tech Training," *Management Review* (US), Vol. 84, No. 2, pp. 57-60.

Maskell, D. and Robinson, I. (2001): *The New Idea of a University*, London, Haven Books.

Meekings, A. (1995): "Unlocking the Potential of Performance Measurement: A Practical Implementation Guide," *Public Money and Management*, Vol. 15, No. 4, pp. 5-12.

Midwinter, A. (1994): Developing Performance Indicators for Local Government: The Scottish Experience," *Public Money and Management*, Vol. 14, No. 2, pp. 37-43.

Pollitt, C. (1995): "Justification by Works or by Faith? Evaluating the New Public Management," *Evaluation*, Vol. 1(2), pp. 133-54.

Rogers, C.R. (1951): *Client Centred Therapy*, London, Constable & Co.

Rogers, C.R. (1961): *On Becoming a Person*," London, Constable & Co.

Rumelhart, D.E. and Norman, D.A. (1983): "Representation in Memory," in Atkinson, R.C.; Herrnstein, R.J.; Lindsey, G. and Luce, R.D. (eds.): *Handbook of Experimental Psychology*, London, Wiley & Sons.

Smith, P. (1995a): "Performance Indicators and Outcome in the Public Sector," *Public Money and Management*, Vol. 15, No. 4, pp. 13-16.

Smith, P. (1995b): "On the Unintended Consequences of Publishing Performance Data in the Public Sector," *International Journal of Public Administration*, Vol. 18, No. 2/3, pp. 277-310.

Taylor, L. and Convey, S. (1993): "Making Performance Measures Meaningful to the Performers," *Canadian Manager*, Vol. 18, No. 3, pp. 22-24.

Tilak, Jandhgala B.G, "Privatisation of Higher Education in India: The Capitation Fee Colleges," *Higher Education in India—In Search of Quality*, Association of India Universities (New Delhi, 1995).

Trainor, R. (1992): Computers, Arts-based Teaching and Rising Student Numbers, *The CTISS*, File No. 13, pp. 3-0.

Ward, M. (1994): "Hypermedia Learning," *Information Today*, Vol. II, No. 8, pp. 15-16.

Wholey, J. (1993a): "Goal Selling, Performance Measurement and Regular Reporting," *Public Manager*, Vol. 21, No. 4, pp. 18-19.

Wholey, J. (1993b): "Evaluation and Performance," *Australian Accountant*, Vol. 63, No. 11, pp. 28-33.

Williams, B.C. and Nicholson, A.H.S. (1994): "Values and Value for Money in Courseware Design," *Account*, Vol. 6, No. 1, pp. 2-3.

45

Economic Development and Insurance: Diagnosis and Prognosis

M.C. GARG, MS. DEEPTI AND ANJU VERMA

Insurance has become an increasingly important part of the financial sector over the past thirty years. Insurance has contributed greatly to the development of the economy through mobilizing savings. Saving from the household sector constitute major proportion 93.7 per cent of the total savings. In so far as Indian economy is concerned maximum share of total household savings comprises of financial assets. Within the category of financial savings, insurance fund is one of the major constituents contributing 13.8 per cent of total financial savings in year 2001-02. Further share of life insurance funds and non-life insurance funds in the Gross Domestic Product (GDP) is continuously increasing. In year 2001-02 life Insurance premium and non-life Insurance premium stands at 1.8 per cent and 0.47 per cent of GDP respectively. Life insurance and non-lite insurance density has also shown satisfactory growth. But when compared with global standards both life and non-life insurance is still at lower ebb. Even amongst the developing economics and other East Asian countries, the Indian Insurance Industry lagged far behind. It is observed that non-life insurance cover is not concentrated in only urban areas and among well off individuals/groups, but is equally spread in rural areas and also provide social security to economically weaker/backward people.

INTRODUCTION

Global environment is undergoing unremitting transformation. There is befogging of business and emergence of new economic models. Law of increasing returns is replacing the law of diminishing returns. In fact, everything has a life cycle – the universe, the planet the civilization, the economies, the companies and the products. The hunting and gathering nomadic economy drove the life on the earth for hundreds and thousands of years. The agricultural economy's dominance sustained for about ten thousand years. The industrial economy was dwarfed by the service sector. Today what rules the various economics is service economy. The service sector has come of age in India and contributes 55 per cent of our Gross Domestic Product (GDP). Financial sector is an important ingredient of service sector and insurance forms one of the pillar of this sub-sector. Insurance is today both a service and industry in its own right.

With this background, the objective of the present paper is to highlight the contribution of the insurance to the Indian economy. The present paper is divided into four sections. The linkage between Gross Domestic Saving (GDS) and insurance is explored in section A. This section is further divided into two sections, sub-section A.1 evaluates the growth of domestic savings and contribution of three sectors (i.e. Household, Private corporate and Public sector). Sub-section A.2 discusses the role of insurance in financial saving of household sector. Section B deals with the insurance penetration and insurance density. Sub-section B.1 links between composition of GDP and life Insurance penetration and sub-section B.2 reads the non-life insurance penetration in India. Sec. B.3 examines the per-capita growth (Insurance density) of insurance. Section C highlights the performance of general insurance and life insurance in India. Section D concludes the paper.

INSURANCE SAVING AS INSTRUMENT OF ECONOMIC GROWTH

The act of saving involves refraining from the present consumption and thereby placing a proportion of income for being consumed at a later date. Economies with high rate of saving had also the high rate of growth of Gross National Product. Sources of generation of savings could be both internal and external. Internal saving flow from three sectors namely household sector, private corporate sector and public Sector. The saving from the household sector constitute the major proportion of the total savings in the country as can be gauged from Table 45.1.

TABLE 45.1

Composition of Gross Domestic Saving at Current Price

(Rs. in crore)

Year	*Household sector*	*Private corporate sector*	*Public sector*
1970-71	4634	672	1343
	(69.69)	(10.1)	(20.1)
1980-81	19868	2339	4929
	(73.2)	(8.6)	(18.1)
1990-91	109887	15164	6279
	(83.6)	(11.5)	(4.7)
1998-99	327074	65026	–17169
	(87.2)	(17.3)	(–4.5)
1999-00	402360	84329	–20049
	(86.2)	(18.1)	(–4.2)
2000-01	453641	86142	–48022
	(92.2)	(17.5)	(–9.7)
2001-02	515565	92060	–57662
	(93.7)	(16.7)	(–10.48)

Source: Reserve Bank of India: Handbook of Statistics on Indian Economy and Indian Economic Survey.

Note: Figure in parentheses refer the percentage of component to Gross Domestic Saving.

Table 45.1 highlight the growth of domestic savings and contribution made by the different sector over a period of time. The contribution of household sector has throughout been more than private and public sector. In the year 2001-02, household sector contributes more than 93 per cent of total saving, whereas private corporate sector contributes just 16 per cent and public sector is embarking negative contribution. Trend shows that over the last three decades household sector depicted continuously increasing trends, on the other hand public sector contribution is on decline continuously.

The household saving comprises of two components viz. physical and financial. In so far as Indian economy is concerned, the percentage share of financial savings in household savings has fluctuated between 18 per cent to 60 per cent over last thirty years (Table 45.2).

TABLE 45.2
Composition of Household Saving in India

Year	*Percentage of Physical Asset to Total Saving*	*Percentage of Financial Asset to Total Saving*
1970-71	61.30	38.70
1980-81	48.94	51.06
1990-91	50.37	49.63
1998-99	40.60	59.40
1999-00	45.34	54.66
2000-01	47.70	52.30
2001-02	46.32	53.68

Source: Reserve Bank of India: Handbook of Statistics on Indian Economy, Indian Economic Survey.

FINANCIAL SAVINGS AND INSURANCE

Within the category of financial savings, insurance fund is one of the major constituents. In India, the percentage of insurance funds in domestic savings is relatively at lower ebb in comparison to developed economies.

An insurance contract provides risk coverage to the insured. In case of life insurance, since the contract periods covers a long time so premium payments have two components. One component goes towards buying risk coverage and other goes towards saving. This saving component of life insurance put the insurer in direct competition with other financial institutions and saving instruments such as bank deposits, equities and mutual funds. Since an increasing proportion of life insurance business involves pensions and annuities (insurance against 'old age') buying life insurance has elements of an investment decision. The bundling together of risk coverage and saving is peculiar to life insurance, especially in developing economies for implications of bundling savings and insurance contracts. A bank depositor can reclaim savings any time on 'demand.'

In case of life insurance, the insured can reclaim the savings embodied in premium payments amount to cancelling or renegotiating the insurance contract and hence penalty. There is thus a lock-in-effect involved in signing insurance contracts. The savings component and the typically long-term nature of the contract, make life insurance an important instrument of mobilizing long-term funds.

Table 45.3 indicates the share of Life Insurance Funds in total financial savings in India. In year 2001-02 Life Insurance Funds contributed 13.8 per cent of total financial savings which is huge amount, whereas maximum contribution still comes from bank deposits contributing nearly 37 per cent of total financial savings. But trend indicates that over last 30 years contribution of life insurance fund towards financial savings is continuously increasing. This contribution was 10 per cent in year 1970-71, then it decreased to 6 per cent in early eighties and then again started increasing in early nineties and since then trend showed continuous accretion.

LINKAGE BETWEEN COMPOSITION OF GDP AND LIFE INSURANCE PENETRATION

This sub-section deals to make a link between composition of GDP and life insurance penetration shown by Table 45.4. Table 45.4 reflects the share of Life Insurance Fund in the Gross Domestic Product (GDP) in India. Life Insurance Fund stands at 0.4 per cent to GDP in year 1970-71, there after increased to 0.5 per cent in mid seventies and were stationary at 0.6 per cent in early eighties and exhibit high growth in early nineties and were contributing 1 per cent in year 1990-91. Thereafter trends showed continuous increase and gradually increase to 1.6 per cent in 2000-01 and stands at 1.8 per cent in 2001-02.

But when compared with global standards, Life Insurance as a percentage of GDP is still at its lower level. In India, the share of life insurance premium as a percentage of GDP, i.e. insurance penetration has increased steadily from 0.4 per cent in 1970-71 to 1.8 per cent in 2001-02 (Table 45.4). However, this is much lower as compared to that of the industrialized countries. In year 2001-02 life insurance penetration in USA is 4.40 per cent, 2.97 per cent in Canada, 8.85 per cent in Japan, U.K. shows highest penetration 10.73 per cent, India 2.15 per cent. (Table 45.5)

TABLE 45.3

Composition of Financial Saving in India

Year	*1970-71*	*1980-81*	*1990-91*	*1998-99*	*1999-00*	*2000-01*	*2001-02*
Currency	17.2	13.8	10.5	10.2	87	6.8	9.3
Banking Deposit	36.6	47.2	31.6	37.1	34.6	36.6	36.7
Non-Banking Deposit	3.2	3.2	2.2	3.7	3.6	4.7	3
Life Insurance Fund	10	7.8	9.4	11	12	13.1	13.8
Provident Plus Pension Fund	24	18	18.8	21.6	22.5	21.2	17.4
Claim on Government	5	6.1	13.3	13.1	12.1	15.10	17.4
Shares and Debentures	3.3	3.5	8.4	2.3	6.3	2.7	3
Units of UTI	0.7	0.3	5.8	0.8	0.1	–0.36	–0.62

Source: Various issues of IRDA Annual Reports and Annual Reports of Life Insurance Corporation of India.

TABLE 45.4

Composition of Saving in India (As percentage of GDP at Current Market Prices)

Year	*1970-71*	*1980-81*	*1990-91*	*1998-99*	*1999-00*	*2000-01*	*2001-02*
Currency	0.8	1.1	1.1	1.2	1.1	0.8	1.2
Banking Deposit	1.6	3.8	3.3	4.5	4.2	4.5	4.8
Non-Banking Deposit	0.1	0.3	0.2	0.4	0.4	0.6	0.4
Life Insurance Fund	0.4	0.6	1	1.3	1.5	1.6	1.8
Provident Plus Pension Fund	1	1.5	1.9	2.6	2.8	2.6	2.3
Claim on Government	0.2	0.5	1.4	1.6	1.5	1.8	2.3
Shares and Debentures	0.1	0.3	0.9	0.3	0.8	0.3	0.4
Units of UTI	0.03	0.02	0.6	0.1	0.01	−0.04	−0.18

Source: Various issues of IRDA Annual Reports and Annual Reports of Life Insurance Corporation of India.

TABLE 45.5

Insurance Penetration: Premium in Percentage of GDP in 2001

Country	*Total Business*	*Non-Life Insurance*	*Life Insurance*
U.S.	8.97	4.57	4.40
Canada	6.42	3.45	2.97
Brazil	2.14	1.78	0.36
Mexico	1.81	0.95	0.86
United Kingdom	14.18	3.45	10.73
Germany	6.59	3.60	3
France	8.58	2.85	5.73
Russia	3.06	1.51	1.55
Japan	11.07	2.21	8.85
South Korea	12.07	3.38	8.69
India	2.71	0.56	2.15
Malaysia	5.18	1.80	3.38
Indonesia	1.13	0.60	0.53
South Africa	17.97	2.78	15.19
Kenya	2.70	1.87	0.82
Nigeria	0.71	0.56	0.14
Australia	9.15	3.44	5.70

Source: Swiss Re, Sigma No. 6/2002.

NON-LIFE INSURANCE PENETRATION

This section of the paper deals with non-life insurance. There are very few events against the happening of which insurance is now-a-days unable to provide protection. In the growing complexities of the modern economic and social system, man has ever been continuously planning to counteract the financial consequence of unfavourable event. The hand mind that is ready and forth with responds to his call is insurance. It reduces the extent and the number of risks and uncertainties. General Insurance has therefore, become an important facet of a country's economy. It plays significant role in many ways to boost the economy in general and trade, commerce and industry in particular. In other words, the development of general insurance industry has to go hand-in-hand with the general economic development of a country.

From Table 45.6 it has been established that the years for which the percentage of agriculture in GDP is higher, insurance penetration

TABLE 45.6

Non-Life Insurance Penetration in India at Factor Cost

Year	Non-Life Premium	GDP	As per cent of GDP			Insurance as per cent of GDP
			Agriculture	Industry	Services	
1970-71	23.5	42222	46	15.6	38.4	0.05
1980-81	322.7	130176	39	19.6	41.4	0.25
1990-91	1909.26	510954	31.26	22	46.7	0.37
1998-99	672.5	1590148	27.83	20.7	51.8	0.42
1999-00	7732.29	1761932	26.22	19.88	54	0.44
2000-01	8847.85	1917724	24.95	20.57	54.5	0.46
2001-02	10920.94	2094013	24.25	19.87	55.2	0.47

Source: Various issues of IRDA Annual Reports, Annual Reports of Life Insurance Corporation of India and Bombay Stock Exchange Manuals.

is lower for those corresponding years. In the 1970-71 percentage of agriculture in GDP was 46 per cent while service sector was contributing 38.4 per cent toward GDP. Further a visible trend is that as the economy has progressed contribution of agriculture sector toward GDP is on decline while of service sector is on increase. In the year 2001-02 agriculture sector is contributing 24.25 per cent in GDP of country while service sector contribution has increased to 55 per cent.

Table 45.7 highlights that in India, the share of gross and net premium for non-life insurance as a percentage of GDP, i.e. non-life insurance penetration has increased from 0.3 per cent and 0.2 per cent respectively in 1974-75 to 0.5 per cent and 0.4 per cent respectively in 2001-02. This is despite the growth of the gross direct premium by 54 times corresponding the above time period. However, this is much lower in comparison with world standards. Non-life insurance penetration is as high as 4.57 per cent and 3.60 per cent in USA and Germany respectively in year 2001-02. Even amongst the developing economies and other East Asian countries, the Indian Insurance Industry lagged far behind in this area. For instance, it was 338 per cent for South Korea, 2.21 per cent for Japan, 1.80 per cent for Malaysia, 1.87 per cent for Kenya and 0.60 per cent for Indonesia. This reveals the vast scope for non-life insurance growth in India.

TABLE 45.7

Penetration and Insurance Density of General Insurance in India

Year	Gross Premium Rs. Crore	Insurance penetration	Net Premium Rs. Crore	Insurance penetration	Gross Premium per capita	Net Premium Per capita
1974-75	220	0.28	180.6	0.23	3.7	3
1980-81	469.4	0.32	385.1	0.27	6.9	5.7
1990-91	2796	0.49	2419.0	0.42	33.3	28.8
1998-99	8759	0.50	7732.3	0.44	89.10	78.6
1999-00	9522	0.49	8847.8	0.45	96.1	88.4
2000-01	9799.8	0.46	9318.3	0.44	96.2	91.4
2001-02	11917.6	0.51	10920.9	0.47	114.9	105.3

NON-LIFE INSURANCE DENSITY

Insurance Density has been defined as per capita expenditure on insurance premium. Table 45.7 indicates that the per capita net premium has increased from Rs. 3.7 in 1974 to Rs. 114.9 in 2001. It is a satisfactory growth but the amount per person is still very nominal. The insurance density has a direct correlation to per capita GDP income of the country. The low per capita GDP translates itself into low insurance density in the country. But what surprise is that the insurance density in India is lower even compared to several developing economies where per capita income is even lower than India. In year 2001 for non-life side, it was 4.1 per cent for Indonesia, 6.6 for Kenya. (Table 45.8).

When compared with developed countries Japan as 77 times high non-life insurance density as compared to India. The low insurance density and penetration are also partly due to lack of awareness on the part of general masses regarding the benefits flowing from insurance in improving their standard of flowing and welfare. In terms of Insurance premium per capita, India is at the bottom of the league among to relevant Asian countries. This statistic's proves that India is currently under insured by world standards.

PERFORMANCE OF GENERAL AND LIFE INSURANCE IN INDIA

General Insurance

The Table 45.9 reflects that with the growth of national income, the

TABLE 45.8

Insurance Density: Premium Per Capita in USD in 2001

Country	*Total Business*	*Non-Life per Capita Insurance*	*Life Insurance per Capita*
U.S.	3266	1664.1	1602
Canada	1460	784.6	676
Brazil	64	53.2	10.8
Mexico	112.6	59.4	53.2
United Kingdom	3393.8	826	2568
Germany	1484.2	819.9	674.3
France	1898.8	630.6	1268.2
Russia	65.8	32.6	332
Japan	3507.5	701.1	2806.4
South Korea	1060.1	296.7	763.4
India	11.5	9.1	2.4
Malaysia	198.3	68.7	129.5
Indonesia	7.7	4.1	3.6
South Africa	446.3	69.1	377.2
Kenya	9.4	6.6	2.9
Nigeria	2.3	1.8	0.5
Australia	1668.3	1040.3	628.0

Source: Swiss Re. Sigma No. 6/2002.

general insurance business has shot up to a new height. While the national income has grown-up by 1577 per cent during 1980-81 to 2001-02 and the general insurance business has grown-up by 2836 per cent during the same period. It is also evident from the table that the index number for general insurance has shown an increasing trend like the index number of industrial production. What is remarkable that the growth in the industrial production has lagged behind that of the growth in general insurance business. Thus by all measures general insurance contribution to growth of trade and commerce is tremendous.

Life Insurance Density

Business in force has increased from Rs. 25267 crore in 1980-81 to Rs. 720597 crore in 2001, by 29 per cent. But, it is not a matter complacence as the real success is revealed only after analysing the

TABLE 45.9

Performance of General Insurance of India

Index Base 1980-81 (100)

Year	*National Income*	*Non-Life Premium*	*Industrial Production*
1980	100	100	100
1981	116	127	122
1990	381	628	439
1995	797	1321	963
1998	1197	2008	1294
1999	1323	2298	1649
2000	1440	2420	1698
2001	1577	2836	1848

Source: Annual Reports of General Insurance Corporation of India, Economics Survey, 2002-03.

success with economic indicator. The per capita premium income has increased from Rs. 14.21 in 1980-81 to Rs. 336 in 2001. Life insurance capacity has also Increased from 0.82 per cent to 2 per cent during the period although it has been at very low ebb. (Table 45.10)

The General Insurance Industry was directed to provide need-based and low-cost general insurance covers to the rural population keeping in mind their premium paying capacity and to develop and introduce insurance with social security benefits. The introduction of various rural insurance covers made the industry secure an amount of Rs. 92239.63 lakh as premium in rural sector (Table 45.11). Further 6.4 per cent of total premium of general insurance come from rural sector in the year 2002-03. During the same year the total amount of lives covered under various social security scheme is 36950582 as can be gauged from the table.

CONCLUSION

The above analysis reveals that insurance sector play a very vital role in the process of economic development of the country. The sector seems to be catalyst for economic development. The process of capital formation is stimulated by the insurance services. Insurance services lead to efficient and productive allocation of

TABLE 45.10

Life Insurance Business-in-Force, Premium Income and Economic Indicator

Year	Business in force (Rs. in crore)	Premium income	National income	Per capita business in force	Life insurance carrying capacity	Per capita premium	Life insurance capacity
1980-81	25267	964.8	118233	372.12	21.4	14.21	0.82
1990-91	118651	5600.8	450145	1414.2	26.3	66.7	0.80
1995-96	359471	14181.7	941861	3873.6	38.1	152.8	1.50
1996-97	408103	16351.4	1093961	4314.03	37.30	172.8	1.49
2000-01	720597	34207.8	1702454	42.32	42.32	335.69	2.00

Notes: 1. Life Insurance Carrying Capacity = Business in Force/National Income × 100.
2. Life Insurance Carrying Capacity = Premium Income/National Income × 100.

TABLE 45.11

Rural/Social Sector Performance—2002-03 (Non-life Insurers)

Insurer	*Total Gross Premium (Rs. in Lakh)*	*Number of Policies*	*Policies in Rural Areas*	*Gross Premium in Rural Area (Rs. in Lakh)*	*Per cent of rural sector business*	*No. of lives concerned in Social sector*
Private Sector	134637.75	1677758	144356	5264.63	3.9	886363
Public Sector	1296467.12	39720131	6328911	86975.00	6.7	36064219
Total	1431104.87	41398489	6328911	92239.63	6.4	36950582

Source: IRDA Annual Reports.

capital resources, prevent the losses to the firms by encouraging loss preventive measure, facilitate growth of trade of insurance both in terms of penetration and countries. But a country like India with its vast resources is still lacking in the development of both general insurance and life Insurance. The per capita insurance premium is microscopically small.

REFERENCES

Agarwal, Raj, "Insurance Funds, Savings and Economic Growth In India," *Management and Accounting Research*, July-December 2001, pp. 20-34.

Bajpai, G.N., "Role of Life Insurance in Building up a Nation's Economy," *The Insurance Times*, May 1992.

Government of India: Economic Survey, 2001-02, 2002-03.

IRDA's Annual Report Various issues.

Kulkarni, G. Kishore, "Comparison of Saving and Investment Behaviour in India," *Dhyanajyoti*, Vol. 15, No. 2, Dec. 1998.

Life Insurance Corporation Annual Report Various issues.

Malhotra Committee Report (The Report of the Committee on Reforms in the Insurance Sector) a precursor to IRDA.

Nishanth, P.V. and Mitra, Anindita, "Structure of World Insurance," *Yojana*, July 2002, pp. 10-12, 22-24.

Samarth, R.D., "Economic Environment, Economic Policy and Non-life Insurance Business," International Insurance Conference, 1999.

Singh, Satpal, "A Decade of General Insurance Industry in India," *The Insurance Times*, July 1988.

Srivastava, D.C. and Srivastava, Shashank, *Indian Insurance Industry Transition and Prospects*, New Century Publication, 2001.

Subramanyan, S., "Role of the Life Insurance in Economic Development," *The Insurance Times*, June 1992.

Thampy, Ashok and Sitharamue, S., "Life Insurance Potential in India: An Economic Approach," *The Journal of Business Perspective*, July-Dec. 2002, pp. 12-26.

46

Towards an Improved Corporate Governance

SUNIL MEHTA

As rational human being we expect good governance in every facet of our life, in the economy, in polity, in our social and cultural life. Every stakeholder in every kind of enterprise expects good governance. There are several reasons for our insistence on good governance, we naturally expect leader's to lead, to provide appropriate direction, to achieve the goal set for the organization in their care. We look for transparency and disclosure of relevant facts and figures. We expect leaders to remain accountable for their action and in action. Stakeholder in any enterprise rightfully expects their interest to be protected.

Economic liberalization, de-regulation of industry and business and increasing integration of the Indian economy with rest of the world has paved the way for corporate governance. The need to conform to internationally accept standard corporate governance has become essential, as stakeholders in the Indian industry are no longer confined to this country alone. Also there have been same important changes in the evolution of the Indian corporate System. Many family owned enterprises have moved from private limited companies to closely held public limited companies and further on to widely held limited companies. The recognition of the need for a code of corporate governance has also moved in line with this trend.

BACKGROUND

In the late 1980's in the UK the corporate sector was beset with a number of problems. These involved creative accounting, spectacular business failures, the limited role of auditors, and the weak link between executive compensation and company performance etc. Under these circumstances that the Cadbury Committee was setup by the financial reporting council, London Stock Exchange and the accountancy profession to address particularly the financial aspects of Corporate Governance.

The Cadbury Committee followed by the Green Bury Committee in the U.K. has more or less set the tone for Corporate Governance in the Anglo-Saxon world. The Hampel committee took the concept further and included the ideas of growth and shareholder prosperity within its ambit.

DEFINITION AND CONTENTS

Corporate Governance is not a term which can be defined easily. The earliest definition of Corporate Governance stated that 'the purpose of Corporate Governance is to conduct the business in accordance with owner or shareholders' desire, which generally will be making as much money as possible, while confirming to the basic rule of the society embodied in laws and local customs' (Milton Friedman). It stresses on the economic concept of the shareholder capitalism. Over a period of time the definition of corporate governance has been widened to encompass the interest of not only the shareholder but also other stakeholder e.g. customers, employees, suppliers, dealers, government, society etc.

In the modern view the Cadbury Report defines it as the system by which companies are directed and controlled. The Cadbury report has focused on accountability and the Hempel report has focused on enterprise and initiative as well as on accountability. According to Kumar Mangalam Birla Committee the basic objective of corporate governance is "the enhancement of the long term share holder value while at the same time protecting the interest of other stakeholder.

The Corporate Governance has two key elements. The first is to the enhancement of the corporate performance via supervision and monitoring of management performance and second, ensuring the accountability of management to shareholders and other stakeholders. Corporate Governance is the system by which corporate entities are directed and controlled. It is also a manifestation of the personal beliefs and values of its Chief Executive which go to configure the organizational values and culture and influence the thoughts, beliefs and action of its employees leading to sustained delivery of quality service and value to every constituent of the company. Corporate Governance is about the sprit in which one does business and about creditability and accountability as shareholders want to the assured of a board's independence and its willingness to act in their best interests.

CORPORATE GOVERNANCE IN INDIA

The recurring financial crises and the scams that rocked the nation in the recent past calls for a sharper focus on corporate governance. The only way we can protect our interest and also those of the public at large is to build "Firewall" by putting in place of practices of good Corporate Governance.

The concept of Corporate Governance receives statutory recognition with the insertion of Section 292A in the Companies Act, 1956 with an amendment made to it through the Companies (Amendment) Act, 2000. The Institute of Chartered Accountant of India has issued six accounting standards which are mandatory in nature SEBI based on Kumar Mangalam Birla report directed all the stock exchanges to amend the listing agreement between them and entities whose securities are listed with them.

EFFECTIVE AND SOUND CORPORATE GOVERNANCE SYSTEM

Effective Corporate Governance System implies real participation of shareholder and co-ordination of different viewpoints of different stakeholder. For effective corporate governance the prerequisite condition are education, technical skills, core competency and effective communication and MIS and all effective corporate governance system are required to enhance the value of the enterprise and protect the right of the stakeholders. An effective and sound corporate governance system meets the following objectives of the firm:

1. Optimal utilization of resources for enhancing the value of the firm.

2. Ethical behaviour of the firm to protection of the right of all stakeholders.

IMPACT OF EFFECTIVE AND SOUND CORPORATE GOVERNANCE SYSTEM

- An effective and sound corporate governance provide stability and growth to the enterprise.
- A good governance ensures the enhanced business prosperity and greater accountability.
- An effective and sound governance practices will help reinforce the confidence of investors across the border, may reduce the cost of capital and ultimately induce more stable capital flow.
- An effective and sound governance promotes stability and long-term sustenance of stakeholders' relationship.
- Potential stakeholders aspire to enter into relationship with enterprises whose governance credentials are exemplary.

TOWARDS AN IMPROVED CORPORATE GOVERNANCE

- The art of improved governance lies in establishing an appropriate relationship between institutions who are shareholders and the management.
- Each country should adopt its own corporate governance principles that are appropriate for that market.
- The rules of corporate governance as are understood in the international arena can not be easily imported because these rules are first and foremost rooted in the culture of the people.
- These principles should be developed by the market participants themselves, through co-operative action and consensus, giving due consideration to the reality of the global market place.
- The companies must broad base the composition of their Boards through induction of independent directors and adopt a code for corporate governance practices.
- Independent directors must be compensated appropriately for their personal commitment and involvement in providing direction to the management team.

- Further, independent directors should be members of all key committees to bring more transparency in the operations.
- Government has an important responsibility for shaping an effective regulatory framework that prov 'de for sufficient flexibility to allow market to function effectively.
- The essence of good corporate governance is to achieve the right balance between stakeholders and management interest.
- It is to ensure that corporate governance principles for the institution that are supported by it are strictly followed.
- Good Governance requires that the decision maker think beyond his or her own interests of all the stakeholders.
- Good corporate governance musk begin by asking, whose interest is the 'method and system' of governance required to promote.
- The governance of Business Corporation must fulfil the requirement of trusteeship on behalf of all stakeholders and not only owner's interest.
- Good governance depends on the cooperation and involvement of a large number of citizens and organizations.

CONCLUSIONS

Corporate Governance under the new paradigm imposes may responsibilities on professionals. The essence of good corporate governance lies in achieving a balance between autonomy for management which is necessary for enterprise and growth and accountability to the organization's various stakeholders. Issues of corporate governance that appear compelling today may recede tomorrow. These should be reviewed on an ongoing basis by companies, institutions and shareholders in order to assess their responsiveness to the prevailing corporate governance climate to ensure that they remain truly beneficial for all.

Index